NEWS DICTIONARY 1974

1974 NEWS DICTIONARY

an encyclopedic summary of contemporary history

Editor: JUDITH TROTSKY

Staff: Foreign Affairs—HAL KOSUT, MYRNA LEBOV, CHRISTOPHER HUNT, MAURIE SOMMER

National Affairs—JOSEPH FICKES, MARY ELIZABETH CLIFFORD, GERRY SATTERWHITE, STEPHEN ORLOFSKY, RUSSELL KAHN

Facts on File, Inc.

119 West 57th Street, New York, N.Y. 10019

NEWS DICTIONARY 1974

Library of Congress
Catalogue Card Number: 65-17649
ISBN 0-87196-099-0 (cloth-bound)
ISBM 0-87196-100-8 (paperback)

Using the News Dictionary

You will find the 1974 NEWS DICTIONARY as easy to use as the WEBSTER'S that stands beside it on the shelf. The editors of FACTS ON FILE—who themselves spend much of their time buried in reference books—designed the NEWS DICTIONARY to overcome the shortcomings of the typical yearbook: a complicated index, nine-month coverage, and an eclectic choice of material. Here you will find a self-index, complete coverage from January 1 through December 31, and the details of *every* significant news development of 1974.

The principle of the NEWS DICTIONARY is the alphabet. To find the story and facts of an event, the researcher simply looks up—as he would in a dictionary—the subject, the country concerned, or the name of a key person or organization involved in the event; if the story is not found in the first place he looks, an explicit cross-reference will direct him to the proper location without further effort or guesswork. Thus, developments in the trial of John Mitchell and Maurice Stans for violations of campaign financing law are found under WATERGATE AFFAIR, but the researcher also would be referred to the proper location from cross-references under the names of Mitchell and Stans and other headings.

A useful feature of the NEWS DICTIONARY is the system of numbered paragraphs to make the work of the researcher less time-consuming. Whenever there are more than a few paragraphs under any heading, numerals in the margin number the paragraphs consecutively. The cross-references refer the researcher—by number—to the specific paragraph(s) in which the desired information is recorded. For example, a researcher seeking material involving capital punishment will find the reference "*See* CRIME [6, 39-40]." This refers him to paragraphs 6, 39 and 40 of the CRIME entry.

AARON, HENRY—*See* BASEBALL

ABORTION—Panel hears abortion debate. The Senate Judiciary Constitutional Amendments Subcommittee held hearings March 6-7 on two proposed constitutional amendments aimed at rescinding the 1973 Supreme Court decision upholding a woman's right to decide whether or not to have an abortion. An amendment offered by Sen. Jesse Helms (R, N.C.) would guarantee, without exception, the right to life at the instant of conception. The other amendment, offered by Sen. James Buckley (R-Conservative, N.Y.), would allow abortion only when a reasonable medical certainty existed that the mother's life would be endangered by the continuation of the pregnancy. Testifying before the subcommittee March 6, Buckley expressed a desire to restore the "traditional understanding" of the 14th Amendment, which he construed as the right to life. "It matters not, under my amendment," he said, "whether one is come to full term in a mother's womb."

Appearing in opposition to the amendment was Rep. Bella Abzug (D, N.Y.), who warned March 6 that the amendments "would impose a particular religious or moral ethic upon a nation that at its inception . . . rejected any dogma or creed as mandatory for all." Colgate University Professor Barbara McNeal testified March 7: "Should a male dominated [Catholic] religious hierarchy determine the moral posture and legal status of the opposite sex when the woman in question is caught up in a dilemma no man can fully understand?"

Boston MD indicted in fetus death. A Boston physician was indicted on manslaughter charges April 12 in connection with the death of a legally aborted fetus. The indictment accused Dr. Kenneth Edelin, chief resident for obstetrics and gynecology at Boston City Hospital, of causing the death of a 24-week-old fetus. Called a "viable baby boy" by the prosecutor, the fetus had been removed during a therapeutic abortion performed at the mother's request.

Ford favors abortion amendment. A White House spokesman indicated Sept. 5 that President Ford continued to favor passage of a constitutional amendment permitting states to decide whether or not to allow abortions.

See also FRANCE [7, 11]; HUNGARY; POPULATION; RELIGION [16]; ROCKEFELLER, NELSON [24]

ABPLANALP, ROBERT H.—*See* WATERGATE AFFAIR [12]
ABRAMS, GEN. CREIGHTON—*See* APPOINTMENTS & RESIGNATIONS; OBITUARIES

ABU DHABI—Under an agreement signed in Abu Dhabi Sept. 3, the Persian Gulf emirate received a 60% share, up from 25%, of the Abu Dhabi Petroleum Co., retroactive to January. The remaining 40% was divided by the six Western oil companies that owned Abu Dhabi Petroleum. They were British Petroleum Co., Royal Dutch-Shell Group, Compagnie Francaise des Petroles, Exxon Corp., Mobil Oil Corp. and Partex. The accord provided for Abu Dhabi to pay the firms $40 million for its additional share of the producing operations and to sell its share of crude oil to the firms for $11.90 a barrel.

See also ETHIOPIA [15]; MIDDLE EAST [34]; MONETARY DEVELOPMENTS [5]; OIL [5, 15]

ACADEMY AWARDS—*See* MOTION PICTURES
ADVERTISING—*See* CONSUMER AFFAIRS [9-10]; CRIME [7]
AEGEAN SEA—*See* TERRITORIAL WATERS
AEROSOL SPRAYS—*See* ENVIRONMENT & POLLUTION [17]

AFGHANISTAN—A military tribunal sentenced one person to death and 11 to jail terms of up to 15 years for attempting to overthrow the government of President Mohammad Daud, Kabul radio reported Aug. 20. It was the second reported attempted coup since Daud seized power in July 1973.

See also PAKISTAN

AFRICA—OAU solidarity weakened. The 11th annual meeting of heads of state of the Organization of African Unity (OAU) was held June 12-16 in Mogadishu, Somalia. It was preceded by the 23rd meeting, June 6-11, of the members' foreign ministers. Both meetings revealed growing uneasiness over Arab attempts to exert more influence on the continent. Anti-Arab sentiment emerged on economic, political and religious grounds. Most serious confrontation was over the price of oil. On June 19 a Kenyan official suggested African countries reconsider their severance of relations with Israel in face of "the Arabs' uncompromising attitude toward Africa on oil." The issue was joined at the foreign ministers' meeting June 8 when an OAU committee reported Arab oil-producing states had refused to lower prices to African nations. The Arabs maintained prices were fixed by the Organization of Petroleum Exporting Countries (OPEC) and were therefore not negotiable. The ministers voted June 9 to accept "in principle" an Arab offer to set up a $200 million fund for soft loans to African states at about 1% interest. At the Mogadishu meeting, Mahmoud Riad, secretary general of the Arab League, defended the offer against critics who called for larger sums of money and better loan facilities. Riad said Arab economic offers to poor African nations were "far higher" than the estimated annual increase they faced in the cost of petroleum. However, increased oil prices were said to be costing black African countries more than $1 billion, the *New York Times* had reported June 9. An OAU report stated 33 of the organizations' 42 members had been hard hit by the crisis. Not affected were Algeria, Egypt, Libya, Morocco, Sudan, Tunisia, Zaire, Nigeria and Gabon.

The break into pro-Arab and black African camps was underscored by the 20-ballot, 15-hour meeting on June 16 needed to elect a successor to OAU Secretary General Nzo Ekanghaki who had announced his resignation June 1, effective Aug. 31. (Ekanghaki cited "personal reasons," but he had been severely criticized for signing an agreement on Jan. 9 with the London and Rhodesia Mining and Land Co. [Lonrho] which was to serve as OAU's oil consultant. Lonrho's other activities included dealings with South Africa, Mozambique and

Rhodesia. The contract was reported canceled March 15.) A compromise between disputing factions at the OAU meeting resulted in election of William Eteki Mboumoua of Cameroon. As head of state of the host country, Somali President Maj. Gen. Mohamed Siad Barre became chairman for the year.

Religious differences erupted as a result of a March 23 speech in Benghazi by Libyan leader Col. Muammer el-Quaddafi who had called for a "holy war" to expel Christianity from the African continent because it had been a "tool of colonialism." (There were reportedly 100 million Christians in Africa, compared with 140 million Moslems.) Bernard Yago, archbishop of Abidjan, the Ivory Coast, charged that "a Moslem is a person least qualified to give lessons in liberalism and tolerance to the Christian churches in black Africa."

Among other developments at the OAU conference: Gen. Barre called for multi-national African military force as "the only answer" to what he called "the inevitable confrontation with South Africa." A resolution was passed on June 16 calling for intensification of sanctions against white minority governments of southern Africa. A committee was directed to continue efforts to ease the dispute between Ethiopia and Somalia over control of the Ogaden Desert in eastern Ethiopia. The OAU declared itself ready to assume diplomatic relations with Portugal if Lisbon recognized the state of Guinea-Bissau which was admitted as OAU's 42nd member at the conference.

OCAM seeks reorientation. The Afro-Mauritian Common Organization (OCAM), formerly the Africa-Malagasy-Mauritius Common Organization held summit and ministerial meetings in Bangui, Central African Republic Aug. 6-12. (The ministerial conference was held Aug. 6-9 and heads of state and government conferred Aug. 10-12.) The group's ten members, reduced from the 16 of its founding in 1965, were: Central African Republic, Dahomey, Gabon, Ivory Coast, Mauritius, Niger, Rwanda, Senegal, Togo and Upper Volta. OCAM was faced with threats of more membership withdrawals at the Bangui meeting. Presidents Omar Bongo of Gabon and Gnassingbe Eyadema of Togo warned Aug. 9 that their respective countries would quit the organization unless it reorganized into a stronger and more viable unit. In the group's final communique, reported Aug. 13, it was stated that OCAM would no longer function in the political sphere but would "adapt to present realities . . . by consolidating solidarity, economic, cultural and social cooperation among its member states."

Mali-Upper Volta border dispute. The presidents of Mali, Upper Volta, Togo and Niger agreed Dec. 27 to establish a mediation commission to help settle the 13-year border dispute between Mali and Upper Volta. Togo would head the commission. The dispute involved a 100-mile segment of the Mali-Upper Volta border which, according to the French magazine *Jeune Afrique* Oct. 26, was believed to be the site of manganese, titanium and limestone deposits, as well as oil and natural gas. Following frontier battles in November and December 14 and 16, Mali and Upper Volta exchanged charges of illegal incursions and mounted strident radio campaigns against each other.

See also specific African countries; Civil Rights [19]; European Economic Community [16]; Famine & Food; Oil [18-21]

AGED PERSONS—*See* Civil Rights [14]; Medicine & Health [6, 17]
AGENCY FOR INTERNATIONAL DEVELOPMENT (AID)—*See* Famine & Food; Foreign Aid; Nicaragua

AGNEW, SPIRO THEODORE—Secret Service guards removed. The Treasury Department Feb. 17 announced the removal of Secret Service protection from former Vice President Spiro Agnew who had continued to receive it on order of then-President Nixon since Agnew's resignation in October, 1973. The General Accounting Office (GAO), which was responsible for payment, had reported on Jan. 29 that no statutory authority existed for the President's action.

Disbarment in Maryland. The Maryland Court of Appeals May 2 barred Agnew from the practice of law in Maryland, the only state in which the former vice president was a member of the bar. The ruling came in an action by the Maryland State Bar Association seeking disbarment. It followed a unanimous recommendation Jan. 14 by a special three-judge court appointed by the Court of Appeals that Agnew should be disbarred. In its May 2 ruling, the Court of Appeals held unanimously that "automatic disbarment" resulted from conviction on a charge involving moral turpitude in the absence of "compelling reason to the contrary." It added that the charge of income tax evasion to which Agnew had pleaded no contest after resigning as vice president in 1973 was "infested with fraud, deceit and dishonesty."

See also CRIME [9-10]

AGRICULTURE—Crop estimates and reports. The nation's Midwest grain belt experienced a severe drought during July that was followed by heavy damaging rains in early August, conditions that were expected to have an adverse effect on meat supplies and consumer food prices over the next year. Consequences of the smaller grain harvests were not limited to U.S. consumers. The U.S. ordinarily exported two-thirds of its wheat crop, a fifth of its corn and half of its soybean production. Smaller supplies of grain available for export were coinciding with periods of bad weather in food exporting nations, increases in fertilizer costs, and rising demand for foodstuffs. As a result, the pressure on the U.S. as the world's major food exporting nation was intense.

Higher than anticipated food prices could be expected during 1975 the Agriculture Department said in November. (An early frost in the Midwest had caused widespread damage to the corn and soybean crops. Corn and soybeans were among the chief ingredients in livestock feed. Because crop supplies would be reduced, animal production was expected to decline through 1976, officials said.) The Agriculture Department Nov. 8 reduced its estimates of the disappointing corn crop, predicting a harvest of 4.62 billion bushels, down 18% from the previous year. The sorghum crop was expected to be the smallest in 10 years, totaling 609 million bushels, down 35% from the 1973 level. Soybean production was projected at 1.2 million bushels, smaller than the 1973 crop by 323 million bushels. Total feed grain production was expected to total 165 million tons, 20% below the previous year's level. (1 million tons equaled 38 million bushels.) The sugar beet crop was expected to fall 9% short of 1973 production. A 2% drop in sugar cane harvests also was forecast.

Farm, food prices. Faced with a continuing food price spiral and evidence that the gap between farm and retail food costs was widening, the Administration announced several actions in an effort to reduce the price spread. In a Washington speech Oct. 31, Treasury Secretary William Simon said he was "greatly concerned" that "farm prices have declined 9%, while consumer prices for food have gone up 6%. The spread between the farm price and the retail price of food is expected to increase 21% between 1973 and 1974. This jump is three times larger than anything we have ever experienced before." In another attack on possible food industry misconduct, Thomas Kauper, head of the Justice Department's antitrust division, said Oct. 31 in Chicago that Congress would be asked to increase the maximum penalty for price fixing and other antitrust violations from one year in jail to five years. Agriculture Secretary Earl Butz, who had steadfastly defended agricultural interests despite rising food costs to the consumer, said Oct. 31 that there were "valid reasons" for the widening farm-retail margins. The solution to rising food prices, Butz said, could be found in raising productivity at the farm level and in the food processing and distribution chain.

A senior Agriculture Department official, economist Don Paarlberg, disagreed with Butz's view that price increases were valid. According to Paarlberg, farmers had received 7% less in September than they had been paid the previous year, but retail prices had risen 11% over the same 12-month period. Food prices had risen 15% during 1974, Paarlberg said, but he attributed 80% of the increase to the widening farm-retail spread.

The Council on Wage and Price Stability held a public hearing Nov. 13 in Washington to discuss supermarket markups of items already on the shelf. At the meeting, consumer and industry groups agreed that a ban on repricing would result in little actual savings for customers, but all the participants at the hearing recognized that the practice angered consumers. Clarence Adamy, president of the National Association of Food Chains, declared Nov. 12 that profits in the supermarket business were "basically a dry hole" and unrelated to inflationary food prices. Referring to Agriculture Department data showing that 80% of the 15% rise in food prices in the past year was caused by the widening farm-retail price spread, Adamy said the margin had increased because of soaring business costs, and not rising profits.

Yet third quarter earnings reports issued by some of the nation's major food processors indicated that other middlemen were reaping large gains. According to the *New York Times* Dec. 2, these firms' earnings had increased an average 7% annually in recent years, but for the third quarter of 1974, their profits were sharply higher. Earnings were up at Borden Co. by 22%; Campbell Soup Co., 15%; General Mills, 11%; H. J. Heinz, 19%; Kraftco Corp., 22%; Ralston Purina Co., 14%; and Kellogg Co., 10%. (Percentage changes were over a one-year period.) The *Times* noted, however, that the processors' increased profitability chiefly reflected dollar gains; profit margins on sales were not necessarily up. Borden's profit margin on sales had been 2.8% in 1973 third quarter, 2.7% in 1974; Kraftco's margin also had declined, from 2.7% in 1973 to 2.6% in 1974. Pillsbury's margin increased from 1.6% to 2.5% and Oscar Meyer reported a margin gain from 2.2% in 1973 to 4% in 1974.

Prices received by farmers for raw agriculture products for the 30-day period ending Dec. 15 declined 3%, the Agriculture Department announced Dec. 31. It was the first monthly drop in farm prices in three months and brought prices to a level 4% below that set in the previous year. Prices paid by farmers to meet expenses during the 30-day period rose .5% to a level 16% higher than that set in mid-December 1973. The costs of farm produced foods needed to feed a theoretical household of 3.2 persons for a year rose $19 in November, Agriculture Department officials announced Dec. 24. At an annual rate, the November market basket cost $1,798. The record increase was entirely due to a $31 rise in the middleman's share of the food dollar. The farmer's share fell by $12 during the same period.

Cattlemen face price squeeze. President Nixon July 26 signed a bill providing $2 billion in government-backed emergency loans to livestock producers. The bill set a $2 billion ceiling on the credit extended to cattlemen and other livestock producers, set the maximum loan to any borrower at $250,000, and set loans for three years—renewable for an additional two. The loan program would run for one year, but could be extended another six months at the request of the secretary of agriculture. Interest levels would be at normal market rates. Opponents of the bill, which was aimed primarily at benefiting the depressed cattle industry, labeled the measure a "great beefdoggle" that would provide little relief to consumers. Proponents argued that without federal credit, livestock producers would be forced out of business, thereby reducing the nation's available meat supplies and generating higher prices. Cattle prices had slumped to $40-$42 per hundredweight from the year's record high of $50.50 per hundredweight, set in January. Chaotic supply conditions were resulting from the immediate oversupply of animals ready for slaughter: in protest against the low prices, cattle feeders were withholding fattened livestock from market and choosing to sell their grain rather than use it to feed young animals. The Texas Cattle Feeders Association had reported April 3 that the nation's cattle feeders had lost nearly $900 in the previous six months.

Members of the National Farmers Organization (NFO) in central Wisconsin Oct. 15 slaughtered more than 650 calves and buried them in trenches to protest high feed costs and low prices received for farm products. Although President Ford criticized the action as "shocking and wasteful" in remarks made Oct. 16 during a campaign trip to South Dakota, and despite a loud outcry from the public, the killings continued. In other protests, cattle producers in Washington, Minnesota and New York slaughtered calves rather than pay escalating feed costs. An estimated 100 South Dakota cattle producers carried their protest about low beef prices, high production costs and federal farm policies to Agriculture Secetary Butz Dec. 12 when a herd of 45 cattle was driven to the Agriculture Department headquarters in Washington. The caravan had left Bison, S.D. Dec. 6 in an effort to publicize the plight of ranchers with a "cross country beef-in."

See also ANTITRUST ACTIONS [9]; BUDGET; BUTZ, EARL L.; CAMPAIGN FINANCING [17]; CANADA [28-29, 35-36]; CONSUMER AFFAIRS [4, 7]; ECONOMY, U.S. [2-3, 17]; FAMINE & FOOD; LABOR [4, 6]; MEDICINE & HEALTH [20]; MEXICO [18]; NIXON, RICHARD M.; SUGAR, SYRIA; TARIFFS & TRADE; UNION OF SOVIET SOCIALIST REPUBLICS [14, 35-36]

AGRICULTURE, DEPARTMENT OF—*See* MEDICINE & HEALTH [26]; PRIVACY [6]; VENEZUELA

AIR POLLUTION—*See* ENVIRONMENT & POLLUTION [1-7]

ALABAMA—*See* CIVIL RIGHTS [9]; LABOR [13]; POLITICS [2]; WEATHER

ALASKA—*See* ARCHEOLOGY; CANADA [23]; ENERGY CRISIS [35]

ALBANIA—The Albanian Ministry of Foreign Affairs delivered a note to the Italian embassy in Tirana May 21 to "energetically protest" the bombing of the Albanian embassy in Rome that day. One bomb had caused extensive damage, but no injuries to personnel, and three other bombs were discovered unexploded.

Authoritative sources in Yugoslavia said Sept. 10 that Albanian Defense Minister Beqir Balluku had been stripped of all government and Communist party posts and might have been executed in a purge of pro-Soviet elements from the Albanian armed forces. Balluku, who had been a close associate of Communist Party First Secretary Enver Hoxha, was also a Politburo member and a deputy prime minister. It was believed that Balluku, who had not been reported at any official functions in Tirana since July 10, had aroused the wrath of Hoxha for delivering a speech some months before in which he said that the U.S. and the U.S.S.R. did not represent equal threats to Albania; official Albanian policy considered both powers equally dangerous. Premier Mehmet Shehu announced a new Cabinet Oct. 29 in which he assumed the post of defense minister previously held by Balluku.

See also COMMUNISM, INTERNATIONAL

ALBERT, REP. CARL—*See* BUDGET; CONGRESS; ELECTIONS [1]

ALCOHOLISM—*See* CONGRESS; MEDICINE & HEALTH [16]; MILLS, REP. WILBUR D.

ALGERIA—Oil, gas developments. Sonatrach, the Algerian national oil company, signed two contracts with the Compagnie Francaise des Petroles Feb. 5 to increase cooperative oil exploration ventures in Algeria. The first agreement gave Sonatrach a 51% interest in offshore drilling and the second almost doubled the total extent of Saharan exploration to about 75,000 square miles.

A consortium of six Belgian, French, West German, Austrian and American firms signed a contract Sept. 2 with Sonatrach for construction of a natural gas liquefaction complex to process gas, produced at Hassi R'mel, in Arzew about 300 miles to the northwest. The gas output from the project—which would be the world's largest—would be mainly for the European market.

Emigration to France banned. Foreign Minister Abdelaziz Bouteflika said Jan. 10 that Algeria would continue its ban on emigration to France until it was satisfied that the security of 750,000 Algerians in France could be guaranteed. The ban was imposed Sept. 19, 1973 following a series of racial attacks.

Final nationalization. The *Wall Street Journal* reported Dec. 19 that Algiers had announced the nationalization of the last important privately-owned companies operating in Algeria. Among the 22 firms, most of them French, was the Algerian subsidiary of Citroen S.A.

Desert containment project launched. The "Green Wall," a project aimed at halting the advance of the Sahara Desert and at arresting the impact of the western African drought, was begun Aug. 14. A major undertaking within Algeria's "agrarian revolution," the 20-year project would establish a eucalyptus and pine forest stretching about 875 miles across Algeria from the Tunisian to the Moroccan borders. The 12-mile wide wall, to be situated between the cities of Djelfa and Laghouat, would cover 7.5 million acres.

U.S.-Algerian ties resumed. Algeria resumed diplomatic relations with the U.S., according to an announcement made simultaneously in Washington and Algiers Nov. 12. Diplomatic ties between the two countries had been severed during the 1967 Middle East war.

See also AFRICA; APPOINTMENTS & RESIGNATIONS; FAMINE & FOOD; MIDDLE EAST [7, 24]; MOROCCO; OIL [5-6, 11-12, 18-19]; PORTUGAL [21]; SPANISH SAHARA; TARIFFS & TRADE; UNITED NATIONS [2, 5-6, 10]; VIETNAM, PEOPLE'S REPUBLIC OF

ALLENDE GOSSENS, SALVADOR—*See* CENTRAL INTELLIGENCE AGENCY; CHILE [1, 13, 20, 23, 26-27]

ALPERT, JANE L.—*See* RADICALS

ALUMINUM & BAUXITE—The seven nations that produce 63% of the world's bauxite met in Conakry, Guinea, March 1-9, and agreed to set up an international organization for coordinating and formulating policy on the mineral ore used in the manufacture of aluminum. Known as the International Bauxite Association, the group included Australia, Guinea, Guyana, Jamaica, Sierra Leone, Surinam and Yugoslavia. Although there had been speculation that the countries would attempt to apply embargo tactics in the manner of the Arab oil-producing nations, the association implicitly acknowledged that bauxite was not so vital a resource as petroleum and that the countries lacked the leverage to exact concessions from the bauxite importers. The association's final accord, released March 9, called on the bauxite producers to develop domestic aluminum-producing industries; urged member nations to "secure the maximum national ownership of their natural resources"; and stated that the group would seek to "secure fair and reasonable profits for member countries in the processing and marketing of bauxite, bearing in mind the interests of the consumer nations."

The Association met in Georgetown, Guyana Nov. 4-8 and agreed to establish a committee to study a possible minimum price for bauxite exports. A second working group was set up to examine the mechanics of bauxite taxation to insure a fair and reasonable return for producing nations, whose bauxite industries were largely controlled by foreign corporations. Ghana, Haiti and the Dominican Republic were admitted as new members Nov. 7, and Greece, India and Trinidad and Tobago were granted observer status in the association.

See also AUTOMOBILES [3]; GUYANA; JAMAICA

AMBASSADORS—*See* APPOINTMENTS & RESIGNATIONS; CAMPAIGN FINANCING [12-14]

AMERICAN BAR ASSOCIATION—*See* JUDICIARY; PRESS

AMERICAN FEDERATION OF LABOR—CONGRESS OF INDUSTRIAL ORGANIZATIONS—*See* ECONOMY, U.S. [10, 13, 17]; LABOR; POLITICS [8]

AMERICANS FOR DEMOCRATIC ACTION (ADA)—*See* PRIVACY [10]; ROCKEFELLER, NELSON [25]

AMERICAN TELEPHONE & TELEGRAPH CORP. (AT&T)—*See* ANTITRUST ACTIONS [7]; CIVIL RIGHTS [15]; PRESS

AMERICA'S CUP—*See* BOATING

AMNESTY & CLEMENCY—Ford favors leniency for war resisters. President Ford told an audience of veterans in Chicago Aug. 19 that he favored "leniency for Vietnam war draft evaders and deserters and wanted them "to work their way back" into the American system. While he continued to oppose "unconditional blanket amnesty," Ford said, he rejected "revenge" for the estimated 50,000 war resisters. (The Pentagon listed 28,661 deserters at large, and 20,500 draft evaders.) The President stated his position before the national convention of the Veterans of Foreign Wars (VFW). Sen. Edward M. Kennedy (D, Mass.) addressed the VFW convention Aug. 21, the day after the group unanimously adopted a resolution declaring its "total opposition to both general and selective amnesty for draft dodgers and military deserters." Kennedy urged the convention to reconsider its position, which he said was "in error" and "narrow." It was, Kennedy said, a rebuff to a bid from a commander in chief to back "a proposal that had mercy and leniency built into it."

Clemency board established. President Ford signed a proclamation Sept. 16 offering clemency to Vietnam War era draft evaders and military deserters. They were given an opportunity to earn re-entry into the U.S. by swearing an oath of allegiance and then performing up to 24 months of alternate public service. For those already convicted of draft evasion or desertion, Ford established a nine-member clemency board to review their cases. The most immediate effect of the proclamation was an order from Attorney General William B. Saxbe Sept. 17 releasing from prison on 30-day furloughs 83 men serving jail terms for violating Selective Service laws. Similarly, James R. Schlesinger, secretary of defense, announced that the approximately 660 men currently imprisoned for desertion convictions would be freed as soon as they applied to the clemency board.

The clemency program, a White House fact sheet said, applied only to draft evaders and military deserters whose offenses occurred during the period between the Gulf of Tonkin Resolution (Aug. 4, 1964) and the withdrawal of U.S. forces from Vietnam (March 28, 1973). Unconvicted draft evaders would report to the U.S. attorney in whose district their offenses had been committed. The evaders would acknowledge their allegiance by agreeing to perform alternate public service, the duration of which would be a maximum of 24 months, although this might be reduced by mitigating factors. The director of the Selective Service

System would have the responsibility of finding alternate service jobs, but participants would not be precluded from finding their own jobs so long as the pay would bring a standard of living comparable to that enjoyed by those entering military service, and the jobs were otherwise acceptable. Following completion of the alternate service, the U.S. attorney would move to dismiss any outstanding indictment, or in cases where no indictment had been handed up, agree not to press charges. Failure by a returning draft evader to satisfactorily complete the alternate service would free the U.S. attorney to resume prosecution. Aliens who fled the U.S. to avoid the draft would not be eligible to participate. "Unconvicted military absentees" (deserters) would be required to execute a "reaffirmation of allegiance" and pledge to perform alternate civilian service. They would be given undesirable discharges. Although their discharges would not be coded in any manner, the recipients would be ineligible for any benefits normally provided by the Veterans Administration (VA). The length of alternate civilian service, not to exceed 24 months, would be prescribed by the parent service on a case-by-case basis. Completion of the alternate service would result in the substitution of a new type of discharge—a clemency discharge—for the undesirable discharge. However, the clemency discharge would not bestow VA benefits. Evaders and deserters would have until Jan. 31, 1975 to take advantage of the clemency offer. Those who were in exile would also have a period of 15 days after their re-entry into the U.S. during which to report to appropriate authorities.

The first priority of the clemency board, the White House said, would be cases of men currently confined. In recommending clemency for any individual, the board could tie its action to performance of satisfactory alternate service. It could also substitute clemency discharges for other discharges previously awarded. Former Sen. Charles E. Goodell, 48, a friend and political adviser to the President, was named by Ford to chair the clemency board.

Congress voiced general support for the President's offer of conditional clemency, Sept. 16, but veterans groups, as well as draft evaders and deserters themselves, voiced disapproval. Mike Mansfield (D, Mont.) Senate majority leader, remarked that although the plan was not amnesty, it was "opening a door and facing up to a problem which should not be avoided any longer." Rep. Bella Abzug (D, N.Y.) characterized the offer as "punitive," not "clemency."

Clemency response termed disappointing. Officials involved in the implementation of the program indicated that response to the offer had been disappointing. Defense Department figures, as of Nov. 22, showed that only 1,470 of an eligible 12,500 deserters had applied for clemency. Of the 6,200 men sought for draft evasion, the Justice Department said, 103 had come forward to sign clemency agreements. The Clemency Review Board said that only 623 had applied to have their discharges upgraded.

See also CALLEY, WILLIAM L.; DEFENSE [9]

AMNESTY INTERNATIONAL—*See* CHILE [2]; URUGUAY
ANDEAN GROUP—*See* ARGENTINA [18]; VENEZUELA
ANDERSON, JACK—*See* DEFENSE [2-3]; PRESS; SOUTH AFRICA [13]

ANGOLA—Junta installed. Rear Adm. Antonio Rosa Coutinho, a member of the Lisbon military junta, arrived in Luanda July 24 to head the military council appointed July 23 to take over the Angolan government. Col. Silvino Silverio Marques, the territory's governor, had been recalled to Lisbon a week earlier. (Marques, known for his rightist views, had been sworn in June 11.) The military council was placed in control following a week of racial violence in

Luanda that erupted when black workers called a strike July 15. Subsequent demonstrations that continued through July 23 resulted in at least 43 dead and 160 injured. Coutinho called on the three Angolan liberation movements July 26 to join in a coalition government and not jeopardize plans for a referendum to be held in March 1975.

Dissension among Angola rebel groups. The three main independence movements in Angola, the Popular Movement for the Liberation of Angola (MPLA), the National Front for the Liberation of Angola (FNLA) and the National Union for the Total Independence of Angola (UNITA), were competing for leadership and power in the evolving chain of events since the April 25 coup in Lisbon. Although Portuguese Foreign Minister Mario Soares had said May 22 that he would negotiate with all three groups, each sought to establish itself as the sole legitimate agent of the Angolan liberation movement. According to a July 29 report, however, the MPLA and the FNLA had agreed to join their forces in a "common front," a move that would facilitate efforts toward the territory's independence from Portugal.

According to a report Aug. 20, the FNLA was the only one of the three major independence movements continuing to engage in warfare; it announced Aug. 13 that it was launching a new offensive in the North. The MPLA and UNITA had reportedly agreed to unofficial cease-fires. Despite earlier reports suggesting progress, the three movements remained unable to agree on a united front to negotiate with Lisbon. An Aug. 10 announcement from Lisbon setting a two-year "blueprint" for Angola's independence was rejected by the FNLA Aug. 11 as an attempt to cause "secession and chaos" in the territory. The MPLA followed suit Aug. 16.

2-year referendum plan scrapped. Secretary of State for Foreign Affairs Fernando Falcoa said Oct. 7 that Lisbon's proposal for a referendum in Angola in two years had been abandoned following the resignation Sept. 30 of Portuguese Provisional President Antonio de Spinola. Angola's provisional government had been sworn in Sept. 12.

Cabinda clash spurs military action. Portuguese troops assumed control of Cabinda Nov. 2 following two days of separationist violence in the oil-rich Angolan exclave. Fighting had erupted between supporters of the Front for the Independence of Cabinda (FLEC) and members of the MPLA faction headed by Agostinho Neto which demanded that Cabinda remain a part of Angola. A Portuguese army spokesman, Cmdr. Martins da Silva, had said Oct. 9 that Lisbon would not permit Angola to be partitioned as the Cabinda separatists demanded.

Violence in Luanda. As many as 100 persons, most of them black, were killed and about 200 were wounded in rioting and shooting that took place in Luanda and its surrounding slums Nov. 5-10, Portuguese officials in Angola said Nov. 12. According to a *New York Times* report Nov. 12, much of the violence was believed to have been sparked by a faction of the MPLA. Jorge Correia Jesuino, secretary of state for social communication in the Angolan government, said Nov. 12 the plan for an interim coalition government that would include the liberation movements had been put aside for the present. He said the Portuguese negotiators had decided instead to establish a guerrilla commission to serve in an advisory capacity to Lisbon and the present Angolan administration. Liberation group representatives had arrived in Luanda in early November for coalition-formation talks, it was reported Nov. 11. MPLA had earlier refused to participate in the proposed coalition unless it was allotted 60%-70% of the coalition government's posts. The dissenting faction was headed by Agostinho Neto. A second MPLA faction, headed by the organization's military commander, Daniel Chipenda, and the FNLA had warned the Angolan government Nov. 8 that they would resume hostilities if Portugal recognized the Neto MPLA faction. Neto announced Dec. 15 that Chipenda and his faction had been expelled from the MPLA.

Progress toward independence. Rear Adm. Coutinho announced Nov. 29 the dissolution of Angola's military council and said he had been named by Lisbon to serve as high commissioner in the territory. The change was said to indicate progress toward independence. Portuguese officials had held a number of meetings with representatives of Angola's liberation movements in Tunis Nov. 7 and Algiers Nov. 19. A cooperation agreement between the FNLA and the UNITA was signed in Kinshasa, Zaire, the FNLA's headquarters, Nov. 25, according to the French newspaper *Le Monde* Nov. 27. UNITA signed a similar agreement with Agostinho Neto of the MPLA Dec. 19, the *London Times* reported Dec. 20.

See also PORTUGAL

ANGUILLA—*See* WEST INDIES ASSOCIATED STATES
ANTHROPOLOGY—*See* ARCHEOLOGY; BRAZIL [9]
ANTISEMITISM—*See* ARGENTINA [14]; DEFENSE [15]; SAXBE, WILLIAM B.

ANTITRUST ACTIONS—Decisions on ITT-Hartford case. International Telephone & Telegraph Corp. (ITT) announced March 6 that the Internal Revenue Service (IRS) had revoked its 1969 ruling that had enabled ITT to acquire the Hartford Fire Insurance Co. in what had been the largest corporate merger in history. (The Connecticut Supreme Court had, on Feb. 26, rejected an appeal by consumer advocate Ralph Nader, who had challenged the merger, on the grounds that Nader lacked sufficient personal interest to justify his suit.) The 1969 ruling had been integral to ITT's take-over plans. Under it, 17,000 Hartford shareholders, whose approval was required, were allowed by the government to exchange their stock for ITT stock without immediately paying capital gains taxes. With retroactive revocation of that favorable tax ruling, the former Hartford shareholders could be liable for up to $50 million in back taxes, according to the *Wall Street Journal.* ITT, which declared it would seek a court review of the IRS action, said March 7 that the shareholders would be reimbursed if a court refused to sustain their tax-free status. Observers believed the IRS action could threaten the actual merger of ITT and Hartford, which was allowed to stand in July 1971 when the Justice Department accepted a consent decree by which ITT could retain Hartford if it divested itself of several other companies, including Avis, Inc., within its conglomerate structure.

[2] In compliance with the terms of the 1971 Justice Department ruling, ITT announced March 12 that American Express Co., the credit card and travelers' services firm, had agreed in principle to a merger of Avis and an American Express subsidiary. (ITT owned 52% of the Avis stock.) The Avis merger was subject to approval by the Justice Department, the boards of Avis and American Express and a two-thirds vote by owners of Avis common stock, which was 48% publicly-held. ITT failed to meet the Sept. 24 deadline for divesting itself of its interests in Avis Inc. and Levitt & Sons Inc., a construction development subsidiary, prompting the government to take action to force the conglomerate to fulfill the terms of the divestiture order contained in a 1971 settlement of three antitrust suits. The Justice Department filed separate petitions with federal district court in Hartford, Conn. asking that the court appoint trustees to implement the Avis and Levitt divestiture orders. Under terms of the 1971 consent decree, ITT was given the option of either divesting itself of the Hartford Fire Insurance Co. or of three other subsidiaries—Avis, Levitt and the Hamilton Life Insurance Co. ITT chose to retain control of the

Hartford, but had only completed the divestiture of Hamilton within the required period. ITT had already sold 48% interest in the car rental firm in two previous public offerings, but it retained 52% ownership. The proposed American Express Co. take-over of Avis was called off in April. American Express officials refused comment on the cancellation. An ITT spokesman said the merger effort collapsed because ITT was uncertain whether the Justice Department would give its approval of the Avis sale to a company deeply involved in the travel industry. These same antitrust considerations caused another possible purchaser of Avis, UAL, Inc., the parent company of United Air Lines, to withdraw from talks with ITT.

[3] The Federal Trade Commission (FTC) filed a complaint Dec. 10 against ITT Continental Baking Co., the maker of Wonder Bread. The baking unit was accused of trying to monopolize the wholesale bread baking industry. ITT was also charged with joining in "most or all" of the anticompetitive practices alleged against ITT Continental.

[4] **IBM settles dispute; others pending.** The International Business Machines Corp. (IBM) announced July 28 that it had agreed to pay Ampex Corp. $13 million to settle a dispute involving allegations against IBM of patent infringement and antitrust violations. Under the agreement, Ampex was to drop charges that IBM had infringed on tape and disc patents and violated antitrust laws in marketing peripheral and memory equipment used in computers. The companies also agreed to an exchange of existing and future patent licenses covering their data-processing interests. Several other suits against IBM had been filed in various courts, based on a 1973 Tulsa federal district court decision in a case involving Telex Corp. (The Telex decision had been appealed by both parties and was awaiting a ruling.) In the Telex case, Judge A. Sherman Christensen had ruled against IBM, finding "intent to obtain or maintain a monopoly in the market." Among other suits against IBM was a consolidated action filed by Memorex Corp., ILC Peripheral Leasing Corp., Transamerica Computor Co., California Computer Products Inc., Marshall Industries Inc., Hudson General Corp., and Century Data Systems Inc. The companies, all involved in manufacture or leasing of peripheral computer equipment, were seeking about $3.6 billion in treble damages in San Francisco federal district court.

[5] The Justice Department filed a pretrial brief Nov. 6 renewing its efforts to restructure the alleged monopoly held by IBM in the computer industry. The brief, filed with U.S. District Court in New York, provided the most comprehensive outline of the government's case since the antitrust charges were brought against IBM in January 1969. According to the government, IBM sold 73% of the computers used in the U.S. and had established such dominance in the field that other computer makers, even large firms such as General Electric and RCA Corp., either operated at a loss and quit the field or were forced to provide more services and equipment than a new entrant in the computer business could afford.

[6] **FTC settles Xerox case.** The FTC, which had filed a complaint in January 1973 against the Xerox Corp., charging it with monopolizing the office copier business, settled its complaint Nov. 15. The FTC unanimously adopted a consent agreement that required Xerox to license competitors to use its more than 1,700 patents. Xerox also agreed to share its manufacturing expertise on a royalty free basis with all of its domestic competitors, except IBM, to enable them to develop products using the patents. Wall Street analysts termed the consent agreement a victory for Xerox because the firm had developed so many other skills—in manufacturing, sales and promotion—that access to patents and technology guaranteed its competitors by the consent agreement would not prove sufficient to break Xerox's grip on the office copier market.

[7] **Biggest antitrust suit filed.** The Justice Department filed a civil antitrust suit Nov. 20 against American Telephone & Telegraph Corp. (AT&T), the world's largest privately owned corporation. AT&T and two other defendants—Western Electric Co. Inc., AT&T's wholly owned subsidiary which manufactured telecommunications equipment for the Bell System, and Bell Telephone Laboratories Inc., the nation's largest industrial laboratory and owned equally by AT&T and Western Electric—were accused of combining and conspiring to monopolize telecommunications service and equipment in the U.S., in violation of the Sherman Act. The suit, which was filed with U.S. District Court in Washington, asked the divestiture of Western Electric by AT&T and the division of Western Electric into two or more competing firms, if necessary, to assure competition in the manufacturing and sale of telecommunications equipment. The government also sought to promote competition with its request that "some or all" of AT&T's Long Lines Department, which handled long distance calls, be separated from "some or all" of the 23 local Bell Telephone Operating Cos., which together with the three defendant firms made up the Bell System. The local Bell companies were named co-conspirators in the antitrust suit.

[8] **Steel price-fixing.** The FTC announced July 11 that it had filed suit against U.S. Steel Corp., the nations largest producer, and Lukens Steel Co. for allegedly violating a 1951 FTC order prohibiting price-fixing. The suit, which sought an injunction against further violations and assessment of maximum civil penalties, charged the companies had engaged in a "common course of action" to fix prices of alloy steel, used primarily in Navy ships.

[9] **A&P guilty on meat prices.** A federal court jury in San Francisco July 25 found the Great Atlantic & Pacific Tea Co. (the A&P supermarket chain) guilty of conspiring to fix wholesale and retail beef prices. The jury awarded actual damages of $10.9 million to six livestock producers, and the damages were automatically trebled under antitrust law. The verdict came in a suit filed in 1968, in which the plaintiffs accused A&P of conspiring with other major food chains to set high, noncompetitive retail prices and low wholesale prices paid to packers.

[10] **New York clothiers plead not guilty.** Three major New York retail stores and two executives pleaded not guilty Nov. 11 to federal charges that they had conspired to fix the price of women's clothing in the New York City area. Named as defendants were Saks & Co., which operated Saks Fifth Avenue, a subsidiary of Gimbel Brothers Inc.; Bergdorf Goodman Inc., a unit of Carter Hawley Hale Stores Inc.; Genesco Inc., which operated Bonwit Teller; Barrie Sommerfield, a vice president of Saks; and Leonard Hankin, executive vice president of Bergdorf Goodman.

[11] **Justice Department studies 10 industries.** Attorney General William B. Saxbe disclosed Dec. 6 that 10 major U.S. industries were being studied by the Justice Department's antitrust division for possible price fixing and monopoly violations of federal laws. The concentrated industries cited by Saxbe were automobiles, steel, primary metals, tobacco, coal, chemicals, beef, earth-moving equipment, newsprint and other paper products, and heavy electrical equipment. Saxbe said the Justice Department was also examining state regulated professional groups, such as "doctors, dentists, accountants, pharmacists, engineers, funeral directors and veterinarians," for possible price fixing violations. Saxbe had warned Dec. 3 that the Justice Department was conducting antitrust investigations of illegal price fixing in beef, sugar, and egg products.

[12] **Antitrust penalty bill cleared.** A bill increasing penalties for antitrust violations was passed by the Senate Dec. 9 and House Dec. 11 and signed by President Ford Dec. 23. The new law made criminal violation of the antitrust

laws, such as price fixing, a felony, subject to a maximum prison term of three years. Maximum fines would be $100,000 for individuals and $1 million for corporations. (Both fines had previously been $50,000.) Requirements were set for public disclosure of the details of proposed negotiated settlements of antitrust suits.

See also AGRICULTURE; BOOKS; CAMPAIGN FINANCING [7-10]; ECONOMY, U.S. [12, 17]; ENERGY CRISIS [10]; SUGAR; TELEVISION & RADIO

APPOINTMENTS & RESIGNATIONS

Nixon Administration

Executive branch. Kenneth W. Clawson, a White House aide, Jan. 30 appointed White House director of communications, replacing Herbert G. Klein. Clawson announced his resignation Aug. 16, effective Nov. 7. George P. Shultz, the last member of President Nixon's original Cabinet, announced his resignation as secretary of the Treasury March 14, effective in May. He was replaced by William E. Simon, named by the President April 17. The White House announced Feb. 15 that Dean Burch would leave his post as chairman of the Federal Communications Commission (FCC) to become counselor to the President with Cabinet rank. Burch was retained in that position by President Ford, but resigned in a Dec. 2 announcement to join a Washington law firm. Joseph J. Sisco, the State Department's Middle East expert was confirmed by the Senate Feb. 8 as undersecretary of state for political affairs, the department's third ranking post. The White House announced the appointment Jan. 5 of W. J. Usery Jr. as a special asistant to the President for labor relations. Usery also retained his post as director of the Federal Mediation and Conciliation Service.

Departments and Agencies. Romana Acosta Banuelos, the highest ranking person of Hispanic descent in the Administration, resigned Feb. 21 as Treasurer of the U.S. She was replaced by Francine I. Neff, Republican national committeewoman, who was nominated May 29, confirmed June 17. Wiliam J. Casey, undersecretary of state for economic affairs, was confirmed March 5 as president of the U.S. Export-Import Bank, succeeding Henry Kearns. Irving M. Pollack was confirmed Feb. 8 as securities and exchange commissioner, succeeding Hugh F. Owens. Carla A. Hills, a Los Angeles attorney, became the first female assistant attorney general (civil division) since the 1920s on her confirmation March 7. Dr. Virginia Y. Trotter, vice chancellor for academic affairs at the University of Nebraska, was appointed by the President April 18 as assistant secretary for education, the top post in the education division of the Health, Education and Welfare Department. Donald E. Santarelli resigned as administrator of the Law Enforcement Assistance Administration following publication of his statements calling for Nixon's resignation. Santarelli's resignation was accepted by the President June 4. Richard W. Velde was named to succeed him July 31 and was confirmed Aug. 22. John C. Sawhill, deputy administrator, Federal Energy Office, (FEO) was named administrator of the Federal Energy Administration (FEA) which replaced the FEO. Sawhill, who replaced William E. Simon, resigned in an administrative shakeup of the FEA, it was announced Oct. 29. Peter M. Flanigan, White House aide since 1969, resigned as executive director of the Council on International Economic Policy, which oversees foreign trade, it was reported June 25. Flanigan, who was later nominated by President Ford as ambassador to Spain, ran into difficulties due to allegations of Watergate-related improprieties. His name was withdrawn Nov. 16. William O. Doub, resigned as commissioner of the Atomic Energy Commission, it was reported Aug. 3. Nicholas W. Craw, resigned as director of the Peace Corps effective Aug. 31.

Military. Adm. James L. Holloway 3rd, vice chief of naval operations, named chief of naval operations succeeding Elmo R. Zumwalt: nominated April 1, confirmed May 31. Gen. David C. Jones, commander in chief of U.S. air forces in Europe, named Air Force chief of staff succeeding Gen. George S. Brown: nominated May 15, confirmed June 5.

Ambassadors. Major ambassadorial appointments were: William J. Jorden, Panama, confirmed Feb. 8; Thomas W. McElhiney, Ethiopia, confirmed Feb. 8; G. McMurtrie Godley, Lebanon, Feb. 8; Davis E. Boster, Bangla Desh, Feb. 27; David L. Osborn, Burma, Feb. 27; Thomas R. Pickering, Jordan, Feb. 27; Hermann F. Eilts, Egypt, March 13; John Gunther Dean, Cambodia, March 13; Leonard Unger, Nationalist China, March 13; L. Douglas Heck, Niger, March 20; Leonard K. Firestone, Belgium, April 25; Robert Strausz-Hupe, Sweden, April 25; Michael Sterner, United Arab Emirates, May 22; Joseph W. Twinam, Bahrain, May 22; Deane R. Hinton, Zaire, June 12; Robert P. Paganelli, Qatar, June 12; William D. Wolle, Oman, June 12; James D. Hodgson, Japan, June 19.

Ford Administration

Executive branch. J. F. terHorst was named press secretary, it was announced Aug. 9. He resigned in protest related to Nixon pardon, Sept. 8 and was replaced Sept. 20 by Ron Nessen, former news correspondent for the National Broadcasting Co. The White House announced retention of Anne Armstrong as counselor to the President Sept. 4. Armstrong, the highest-ranking woman in the Ford Administration, resigned Nov. 28 "because of unforeseen and pressing family responsibilities." White House counsel Philip W. Buchen was promoted to Cabinet rank Sept. 12. Donald Rumsfeld, ambassador to the North Atlantic Treaty Organization and a member of President Ford's transition team, was named Sept. 24 to be an assistant to the President with Cabinet rank in charge of administration and coordination. He succeeded Alexander M. Haig, Jr. J. Fred Buzhardt, legal aide to former President Nixon and a major figure in the Watergate defense, resigned as White House legal counsel Oct. 5. Leonard Garment resigned from the White House staff Dec. 6 to join a New York law firm. Max L. Friedersdorf, special assistant to President Ford, was named to head the White House legislative liason staff, it was reported Dec. 7. Dixy Lee Ray, chairman of the Atomic Energy Commission, was named assistant secretary of state for oceans and international, environmental and scientific matters Dec. 4, and confirmed Dec. 13. Attorney General William B. Saxbe resigned Dec. 13, was nominated the same day to be ambassador to India and was confirmed Dec. 19. The resignation of Claude S. Brinegar as transportation secretary was announced Dec. 18, effective Feb. 1, 1975.

Departments and agencies. Lee Richardson resigned as head of the Office of Consumer Affairs of the Federal Energy Administration (FEA) Aug. 8, charging that the office had no influence over policy decisions and that the plight of the consumer was largely ignored by the FEA. Clay T. Whitehead resigned as director of the White House Office of Telecommunications Policy, a post he held since its creation in 1970, it was reported Sept. 13. Robert C. Gresham was named commissioner, Interstate Commerce Commission June 3 and confirmed Sept. 19. Richard L. Roudebush, former representative from Indiana, deputy administrator of Veterans Affairs (V.A.), was named V.A. administrator succeeding Donald E. Johnson Aug. 20 and confirmed Oct. 1. Henry E. Petersen resigned as assistant attorney general Nov. 4, ending a 27-year career with the Justice Department. Although his role during the Watergate inquiry between President

Nixon and the Justice Department had been criticized by many as having helped Nixon formulate a cover-up, Petersen said he had no regrets over how he covered the investigation. Roy L. Ash announced his resignation Dec. 17 as director of the Office of Management and Budget. The resignation would become effective in early 1975.

Military. Fred C. Weyand, 58, vice chief of staff of the Army, was named Army chief of staff succeeding Creighton Abrams (who died Sept. 4), Sept. 26 and confirmed Oct. 3. Gen. Alexander M. Haig, was named supreme commander, North Atlantic Treaty Organization, Sept. 16.

Ambassadors. Major ambassadorial appointments and resignations were: Richard W. Murphy, Syria, confirmed Aug. 7; Richard L. Sneider, Republic of Korea, Aug. 21; Jack B. Kubisch, Greece, Aug. 21; Kenneth Rush, France, Sept. 12; John Sherman Cooper, German Democratic Republic, Sept. 12; Shirley Temple Black, Ghana, Sept. 12; David K. E. Bruce, head of the U.S. liaison office in Peking, China, named permanent U.S. representative to NATO; Walter H. Annenberg, Great Britain, resigned Nov. 19; Frank C. Carlucci, Portugal, Dec. 2; Richard B. Parker, Algeria, Dec. 3; Daniel P. Moynihan, resigned, India, replaced Dec. 19 by William B. Saxbe; Thomas J. Scotes, Yemen Arab Republic, Dec. 19.

See also AVIATION [9]; BUDGET; ECONOMY, U.S. [3]; ENERGY CRISIS [30-31, 39]; FORD, GERALD R.; GREECE [11]

ARAB LEAGUE—*See* AFRICA; EUROPEAN ECONOMIC COMMUNITY [7]; MIDDLE EAST [22, 33]

ARAFAT, YASIR—*See* LIBYA; MIDDLE EAST [24, 27, 34, 42]

ARCHEOLOGY—More proof for Bering connection theory. Two finds in separate expeditions, one on the Soviet Union's Pacific coast and another on the Aleutian chain off Alaska, gave added proof to the theory that a land bridge once existed at the present site of the Bering Strait which now separates the Soviet Union from the U.S. by 50 miles of water. The Soviet press agency Tass reported April 6 that an expedition located in the Kamchatka peninsula in the U.S.S.R. had discovered objects, such as beads and belts, that had previously been found only on American territory. A joint Soviet-U.S. expedition, working for two months on Anongula Island off Alaska, announced Aug. 22 the discovery of 9,000-year-old artifacts, adding further proof to the theory that North America's original inhabitants came from Siberia. The relics included tool blades that matched implements previously discovered in Siberia.

Fossil find in Baja California. A team of U.S. and Mexican scientists reported Oct. 8 that it had discovered what appeared to be one of the largest unexplored deposits of marine and terrestrial fossils in North America. The deposits, some of which reportedly date back 60 million years, included human artifacts that may have been over 50,000 years old, and would be one of the earliest pieces of evidence of man's presence in North America.

Earliest human fossils found. Human fossils believed to be over 3 million years old, older by previous finds by as much as a million years, were discovered Oct. 17 and 18 by an international team of scientists. The find, discovered in the Afars region of northeastern Ethiopia near the Awash River, was called an "unparalleled" break-through in the search for man's evolutionary cycle, the team spokesman said. The archaeologists said the small size of the teeth of the fossils led them to hypothesize that man "was walking, eating meat, and probably using tools to kill animals" 3-4 million years ago. "It also means there was some kind of social communication," they said.

See also SHIPS & SHIPPING; UNITED NATIONS [16]

ARGENTINA—Peron dies, wife assumes presidency. President Juan Domingo Peron died of a heart attack July 1. He was 78. The presidency was assumed by Peron's widow, Maria Estela (Isabel) Martinez de Peron, who became the first woman chief of state in the Americas. Peron was first reported ill June 18, when he failed to go to his office because of a "grippe condition." Executive powers were assumed by his wife on June 29 when doctors ordered "absolute rest" for the president. Mrs. Peron had been vice president. Peron had assumed the presidency of Argentina for the third time in October 1973, following the resignation of President Hector Campora and Peron's election by a wide margin. Peron had returned to Argentina the preceding June, ending an 18-year forced exile. He had previously been elected president in 1946 and 1951, and had been overthrown and exiled by the armed forces in 1955. Since his return to office, Peron and his advisers had slowed inflation, opened diplomatic and trade relations with many Communist countries, and checked military influence in politics. However, they had been unable to heal the deep rifts within Peron's large, heterogeneous Justicialista movement, or to control violence by feuding Peronists and by the left-wing People's Revolutionary Army. In recent months, political violence had been accompanied by a resurgence of economic problems, which challenged Peron's policies and led him to threaten to resign.

[2] **Peron rites held.** Hundreds of thousands of citizens lined the streets of Buenos Aires July 2 to watch Peron's body be transported to the Metropolitan Cathedral for a requiem mass and then to Congress to lie in state for two days before it was returned to the presidential palace for burial. The service was attended by Mrs. Peron, government and labor leaders, and foreign dignitaries including Uruguayan President Juan Maria Bordaberry. Heads of state throughout the continent expressed sorrow at Peron's death, including the government of Cuba and the right-wing Brazilian regime, which both declared three days of mourning July 2. Virtually all Argentine sectors, including the armed forces and the opposition political parties, expressed sorrow at Peron's death and support for Mrs. Peron's presidency July 2-4. Only one newspaper, *La Prensa*, an old foe of Peron, attacked the late president in its editorial July 2. (In retaliation, the Peronist Newspaper Vendors Union "broke relations" with *La Prensa*—implying it would cut off the paper's distribution—and Peronists attacked the newspaper's offices in Cordoba and Rosario July 6.). The Montoneros organization, the acknowledged leader of the Peronist left wing, expressed support for Mrs. Peron July 2 but warned that "the political vacuum left by Gen. Peron's absence may be filled by adventurists and unscrupulous persons who already are making plans to take power." The Montoneros apparently referred to Social Welfare Minister Jose Lopez Rega, a close adviser of both Peron and his widow whom they considered reactionary.

[3] **Political factions at war.** Peron's death left the future of the government in a state of great uncertainty, with growing economic problems and deep political divisions held in abeyance only temporarily by the mourning period. By August dissensions had greatly increased with the Montoneros increasingly critical of alleged rightist influence over Mrs. Peron. This conflict grew through the rest of the year, with assassinations and open warfare between left and right reaching such a peak that Mrs. Peron placed the nation under a state of seige Nov. 6, suspending constitutional guarantees and empowering security forces to search and detain without warrant and to hold prisoners without charges.

[4] The increasingly serious economic problem also caused political divisions when, on July 8, Mrs. Peron modified her husband's "social pact" by declaring a general wage bonus. The pact, imposing wage and price controls, had been signed in 1973 by Peronist labor and management groups. (The inflation rate,

which the pact had reduced from 80% to 12% according to government figures, reportedly tripled in May, and price-controlled foodstuffs such as eggs, milk and sugar were reported scarce.) The labor movement, already divided in its attitude toward the pact, was left in further disarray by the July 14 death of Adelino Romero, head of the General Labor Confederation (CGT). An increase in power by more conservative CGT elements followed.

[5] Argentina's poltical strife focused on the competition for control between various factions: (1) the leftist, Marxist-oriented People's Revolutionary Army (ERP), a guerrilla group whose targets were mostly national and foreign business interests and the army; (2) the right-wing Peronists, whose main strength was in the more conservative labor unions and in politicians such as Lopez Rega; and (3) the left-wing Peronists, themselves splintered into various independent organizations such as the Peronist Youth (JP), the Montoneros guerrillas, the Peronist University Youth (JUP) and the Peronist Working Youth (JTP). The illness and death of Peron was followed by an increasingly violent struggle between these factions, and the gradual ascension to open power of Lopez Rega's conservatives who eventually took power in five moderate or left-wing controlled provinces: Cordoba, March 12; Mendoza, July 12; Catamarca, July 18; Santa Cruz, Oct. 7; Salta, Nov. 22. Rightists were accused of the formation of and participation in a new terrorist organization, the Argentine Anticommunist Alliance (AAA), whose harassment and assassinations of leftists and those suspected of leftist sympathies caused many of its announced targets to flee the country. (Two Uruguyans who claimed to have been kidnapped and tortured by the AAA in September asserted in Stockholm Nov. 4 that the AAA was composed of Argentine and Uruguayan police and that it was "directed by the government." (Leftists charged that a government anti-terrorism bill, passed Sept. 28, was designed to fight leftist guerrillas, although the government said it would also be used against rightist assassins. Arrests of hundreds of extremists in November-December reportedly included no members of the AAA.)

[6] **Police change.** Alberto Villar, a police commander denounced by the Peronist left for alleged close links to the 1973 military government, had been appointed federal police chief May 10. He replaced Miguel A. Iniguez, who had resigned April 10, citing "health reasons." Villar, appointed temporarily in April and then confirmed permanently the following month, was assassinated along with his wife Nov. 1. The Montoneros took credit for the murders; they had frequently accused Villar and his deputy, Luis Margaride (also appointed May 10) of encouraging the torture and murder of political prisoners. Villar was the first high government official assassinated since the Peronists returned to power in May 1973. The assassination of Villar and of former Peronist union official Carlos Ligusti Nov. 6 were precipitating factors leading to the imposition of the state of siege. (The London newsletter *Latin America* claimed Nov. 29 that Villar, Eduardo Ottalagano, rector of Buenos Aires University, and Carlos Frattini, an official in the Education Ministry, had organized the AAA.)

[7] **Kidnappings and assassinations.** Fear of abduction or murder has caused more than 500 U.S. business executives to leave Argentina by the early months of the year. Esso Argentina, an Exxon Corp. affiliate, announced March 13 a record ransom payment of $14.2 million for its refinery manager, Victor Samuelson, who had been kidnapped by ERP in December 1973. Samuelson was not released, however, until April 21. On June 4 the ERP's official publication, *Red Star,* said the guerrillas would spend $7 million of the ransom money to help finance "armed struggle in Chile, Argentina, Bolivia and Uruguay." On April 12 ERP wounded and briefly kidnapped Alfred A. Laun III, director of the U.S. Information Service in Cordoba province. Laun, the first U.S. diplomat kid-

napped in Argentina, was released the same day, evidently because the guerrillas feared he would die of his wounds. The ERP claimed Laun had been involved in "counterrevolutionary activities," with ties to the CIA, allegations denied by the U.S. Embassy in Buenos Aires. On April 21, however, the Argentine Chamber of Deputies called for an investigation of Laun's activities, saying a high-powered transmitter had been found in the American's home.

[8] Other kidnappings included: Douglas Roberts, administrative director of Pepsi-Cola S.A. Jan. 4, released Feb. 2; Charles Hayes, engineer for A. G. McKee construction company, December 1973, released Jan. 31 on payment of a reported $1 million ransom; Henry Anderson, Danish executive of the Bank of London and South America, seized in late 1973, released Feb. 19. Also abducted were Antonio Valloccia, an executive of Swift and Company, and Peugeot factory director Yves Boisset who was released in March after payment of a reported $4 million. The ERP denied responsibility, however, for kidnapping Boisset.

[9] By Nov. 6, when the state of seige was declared, at least 138 persons had died as a result of political violence, among them retired Gen. Carlos Prats Gonzalez, the former Chilean army commander, and his wife who were killed Sept. 30 when a bomb exploded in or under their car as they drove to their Buenos Aires home. Prats had a reputation as a leftist because he had served in the Cabinet of the late Chilean President Salvador Allende and had taken refuge in Argentina following Chile's 1973 military coup. Also assassinated was former Interior Minister Arturo Mor Roig, who had served under the military government that preceded Peron's. Although the ERP was accused of the July 15 killing, they denied responsibility. Intra-Peronist violence was responsible for, among others, the July 31 death of Rudolfo Ortega Pena, a leading left-wing Peronist congressman and lawyer who had defended imprisoned guerrillas under the military government. Ortega Pena was the first congressman to be killed in recent years.

[10] **Cabinet shuffle.** Mrs. Peron shuffled her Cabinet Aug. 13 in what was widely interpreted as a shift toward more conservative policies. Mrs. Peron accepted the resignations of Interior Minister Benito Llambi, Defense Minister Angel Robledo and Education Minister Jorge Taiana, replacing them with men who had served in the second administration of her late husband, President Juan Peron, in the 1950s. Alberto Rocamora, a former president of the Chamber of Deputies, was named interior minister; Oscar Ivanissevich, a former education minister, reassumed that post; and Adolfo Savino was appointed defense minister. Rocamora and Savino were close associates of Social Welfare Minister Lopez Rega, the most conservative member of the Cabinet and the official closest to Mrs. Peron, according to *Latin America* Aug. 23. The replacement of Taiana as education minister was denounced by left-wing students at Buenos Aires University, some 800 of whom occupied six faculties and the rector's office Aug. 14. The rector's office was cleared peacefully later in the day.

[11] **Violence resumes.** Although violence diminished temporarily following Peron's death, it resumed again in August, reaching epidemic proportions. (Terrorist attacks had claimed one victim every 19 hours since Aug. 1, according to the *New York Times* Sept. 18.) Montoneros leader Mario Firmenich said at a clandestine press conference Sept. 6 that his movement had begun a "people's war" against the government, which, he claimed, had been "captured by imperialists and oligarchs" since Peron's death. The AAA also stepped up violence against leftists Sept. 19-30. A report in *El Nacional* of Caracas Sept. 28 said the AAA had a "black list" of 49 persons to be assassinated, most of them left-wing Peronists. Other assassinations were committed by the ERP and the Montoneros. The two

organizations agreed to coordinate operations in the future despite their serious ideological differences, the newsletter *Latin America* reported Sept. 27.

[12] In an attempt to gather support amid the increasing violence, Mrs. Peron held a rally in Buenos Aires Sept. 20. Only 30,000-50,000 persons attended even though the General Labor Confederation called an eight-hour nationwide strike to enable workers to see the president. The crowd chanted slogans against the Montoneros as Mrs. Peron denounced "those who only know how to kill, . . . those who obstruct the road to liberation and national pacification."

[13] Montoneros leader Roberto Quieto said Oct. 4 that the Montoneros were prepared to negotiate a truce with the government if it would grant emergency wage increases, end its intervention in the trade unions, restore freedom of political expression, repeal repressive security legislation, stop the AAA assassination campaign and fire Villar and Margaride. The ERP offered a truce of its own Oct. 6, asking the government in return to free all political prisoners, repeal the new anti-subversion act and restore the ERP to legality. The government did not respond and violence resumed Oct. 7 with the assassination of army Maj. Jaime Gimeno. Police announced the same day that 138 persons had been arrested in raids against subversives. Meanwhile, concern was expressed over the new anti-terrorism law, which Mrs. Peron signed Sept. 30. The Association of Argentine Newspaper Enterprises, the nation's leading press group, charged the law "affects freedom of the press," the Mexican newspaper *Excelsior* reported Oct. 3. The law set prison terms of two to six years for persons who possessed, published or reported "facts, communiques or photographs related to terrorist actions."

[14] Despite the imposition of the state of seige Nov. 6 and the arrest of at least 100 alleged extremists in the 10 days following the announcement, terrorist activities continued and accelerated during the last two months of the year. Mrs. Peron sent a bill to Congress Dec. 6 asking for power to call up the armed forces to fight subversion and to set up a centralized national security program under her office. Among recent bombings, leftists were held responsible for explosions at a branch of First National City Bank of New York and two General Motors Corp. showrooms in Buenos Aires Nov. 25, and rightists were accused of firebombing a movie set in the capital Nov. 17. The movie was about Jewish gauchos in 19th century Argentina. Anti-Semitic slogans had been shouted at a recent Buenos Aires rally by rightists demanding the return to Argentina of the remains of Juan Manuel de Rosas, the 19th century Argentine dictator who died and was buried in England.

Economic Developments

[15] **Foreign firms to be 'Argentinized.'** Mrs. Peron announced at a rally attended by 80,000 persons in Buenos Aires Oct. 17 that three major foreign electronics companies would be "Argentinized." She did not elaborate on the term. The firms were Standard Electric Argentina Co., a subsidiary of International Telephone and Telegraph Corp. of the U.S.; Siemens S.A., a subsidiary of the West German concern Siemens A.G.; and the Italo-Argentine Electricity Co., controlled by Swiss capital. The government Aug. 23 had ordered the nationalization of oil marketing, but postponed expropriating the foreign oil refineries. Gasoline service stations were ordered nationalized Aug. 28. Until these measures were taken, the state oil firm YPF had marketed about 50% of Argentina's oil. The nation was virtually self-sufficient in petroleum.

[16] **Economy minister quits.** Jose Gelbard, who had directed the Argentine economy since the Peronists returned to power in May 1973, resigned as economy minister Oct. 21. His departure was seen by many as signaling the end

of the Social Pact. Gelbard was replaced by former Central Bank President Alfredo Gomez Morales, who had repeatedly criticized his policy. Gomez Morales, a right-wing Peronist, was backed by Lopez Rega, the conservative social welfare minister and private secretary to Mrs. Peron.

[17] **Drought cuts grain yield.** A persistent drought in the major grain producing areas threatened the nation's agricultural production and its ability to help relieve the world's acute food shortage, the *New York Times* reported Dec. 15. Leading farmers' organizations said the drought had already cut the grain crop in southern Buenos Aires Province and La Pampa Province by one-third and the yield in Entre Rios Province by half. The three provinces produced more than half of Argentina's wheat, corn and sorghum.

[18] **Foreign trade.** A 135-member Argentine mission arrived in Moscow May 5 and departed for Poland, Czechoslovakia and Hungary May 8. Agreements were reached with the Eastern-bloc nations for the sale of Argentine foodstuffs, chemicals and wines and extensions of credit by Poland for the purchase of technical equipment and machinery. The Argentine subsidiary of General Motors Corp. agreed to sell 6,000 taxis to Cuba for about $30 million, it was reported June 26. An Argentine economic mission in Moscow Sept. 20 signed an agreement under which Argentina would sell 90,000 tons of meat to the Soviet Union over the next three years. Argentina would enter the six-nation Andean Group by the end of 1974, according to a statement Oct. 10 by Leopoldo Tettamanti, Argentine secretary for international economic relations. Argentine meat exports to Europe in January-September were 48.9% behind those of the same period in 1973, earning 37.9% less in foreign exchange, it was reported Nov. 8. Prices for beef on the bone reportedly had dropped from $1,300 a ton to $900 a ton during the period.

See also AUTO RACING; BOLIVIA; BRAZIL [10]; CHILE [7, 18]; CUBA; EUROPEAN ECONOMIC COMMUNITY [10]; FAMINE & FOOD; LATIN AMERICA; MEXICO [21]; SUGAR; WEATHER

ARIZONA—*See* ELECTIONS [1, 7]; WOMEN'S RIGHTS

ARKANSAS—*See* ELECTIONS [3, 10]; MILLS, REP. WILBUR D.; WEATHER

ARMAMENTS, INTERNATIONAL—*See* CHILE [28]; JORDAN; OIL [3]; PAKISTAN; SAUDI ARABIA; SOMALIA

ART—An enraged man sprayed the words "Kill Lies All" on the "Guernica," Picasso's 1937 anti-fascist work, hanging in the Museum of Modern Art in New York. The vandal was seized immediately after the Feb. 28 incident. The lettering was removed within an hour, leaving no damage.

In an attempt to still reports that purchase of a vase for $1 million in 1972 was illegal, the Metropolitan Museum of Art released a statement March 5, documenting its owner as Dikran Sarrafian from whom they bought it. The Italian government had implied the vase was stolen. The new report presented evidence the vase was in Sarrafian's possession long before the alleged robbery took place.

Joseph Hirshhorn donated his private art collection, worth over $1 million, to the new Hirshhorn Museum and Sculpture Garden in Washington, it was reported Aug. 12.

See also IRELAND, REPUBLIC OF; OBITUARIES [SIQUERIOS]; UNION OF SOVIET SOCIALIST REPUBLICS [24]

ARTS & LETTERS—*See* ART; BOOKS; MOTION PICTURES; MUSIC; NOBEL PRIZES; THEATER; UNITED NATIONS [19]

ASSAD, HAFEZ AL—*See* MIDDLE EAST [5, 6, 8, 38, 41]; SYRIA

ASSASSINATIONS—*See* ARGENTINA [7-9]; CRIME [19]; GERMANY, WEST [8]; KOREA, REPUBLIC OF [1-5]; PAKISTAN; SPAIN [1-3, 11]; URUGUAY

ASTRONOMY—*See* NOBEL PRIZES; SPACE

ATOMIC ENERGY

Atomic Testing

[1] **India explodes first A-device.** India May 18 became the sixth nation to explode a nuclear device, with an underground explosion of a 10-15 kiloton device in the Great Indian Desert in Rajasthan State. In announcing the test, the Indian government said the nuclear program was designed for "peaceful uses," such as mining and earth-moving, and reiterated the nation's "strong opposition to military uses of nuclear devices." According to the Indian Atomic Energy Commission, the test involved use of an implosion device and the "plutonium required for the explosion was produced in India." (The U.S. and Canada, which had long aided India in peaceful nuclear energy projects, had forbidden India from using the plutonium produced by its reactors for any purpose other than fueling the reactors themselves. Initial domestic reaction to the explosion seemed to be favorable, except for opposition from the Gandhi Peace Foundation, one of whose charter members had been the late Prime Minister Jawaharlal Nehru, father of the current prime minister. Many other nations, however, expressed concern over the test, as did the 25-nation disarmament conference in Geneva.

[2] On May 22 Canada suspended its nuclear aid to India because of India's detonation of the nuclear device. Canadian External Affairs Minister Mitchell W. Sharp said, "What concerns us about this matter is that the Indians, notwithstanding their great economic difficulties, should have devoted tens or hundreds of millions of dollars to the creation of a nuclear device for a nuclear explosion." The aid suspension would affect all shipments of nuclear equipment and material to India as well as technological information. Food and agricultural aid would continue.

[3] Prime Minister Indira Gandhi said May 25 "allegations and apprehensions" that India was developing nuclear weapons were unfounded. In response to criticism that India was too poor a nation to spend resources on nuclear development, she said the same objection had been made "when we established our steel mills and machine-building plants." Such things were necessary, she said, because it was "only through the acquisition of higher technology" that poverty could be overcome. Gandhi was reported to have sent a letter to Pakistani Prime Minister Zulfikar Ali Bhutto May 22, reiterating that India's explosion did not pose any threat to Pakistan's security. Bhutto told his nation's National Assembly June 7 that Pakistan would develop its nuclear program in response to India's explosion. He added that Pakistan's program would be restricted to peaceful purposes.

[4] The U.S. suspended delivery of enriched uranium fuel to India until New Delhi pledged not to use the atomic fuel in any nuclear explosion, officials of the U.S. Atomic Energy Commission (AEC) disclosed Sept. 7. Shipment was halted on an Indian order of enriched uranium for its atomic power plant near Bombay, built with U.S. assistance. Under a 1963 accord, the U.S. had promised to provide fuel for the reactor over 30 years. A spokesman for the AEC said Sept. 16 that India had agreed to give the specific assurances sought by the U.S.

[5] **French and Chinese hold tests.** France and China conducted nuclear explosion tests in the atmosphere June 17. The French blast, announced by Australia and New Zealand but not confirmed or denied by the French government, was conducted over Mururoa atoll in the South Pacific. China's explosion was announced by the U.S. AEC and later confirmed by China's official Hsinhua news agency. The test, according to the AEC, was conducted at the Lop Nor test

site in Sinkiang Province. The Australian, Indonesian and Japanese governments protested to both France and China over their tests, it was reported June 19. Australian longshoremen, who boycotted French ships in 1973 because of the tests, voted to resume the boycott this year but decided against protesting the Chinese blast. New Zealand had already protested the explosion.

[6] The International Court of Justice at The Hague decided by a 9-6 vote to drop the case brought by Australia and New Zealand calling for a halt to France's atmospheric nuclear tests in the South Pacific, it was announced Dec. 20. In the majority decision, President Manfred Lachs ruled that since France had committed itself to switch to underground testing, a case no longer existed, that "the claims of Australia and New Zealand no longer have any object." France, which rejected the court's competence, boycotted the sessions.

[7] France concluded its latest series of atmospheric nuclear tests over Mururoa atoll Sept. 15. Confirming earlier pledges by President Valery Giscard d'Estaing, Defense Minister Jacques Soufflet said Oct. 11 that France was "ready to carry out underground tests from now on." Following the beginning of the series in June, nuclear tests were conducted July 7, 17, 26, 29, Aug. 15, 25 and Sept. 15, bringing to 60 the number of atmospheric tests France had conducted since 1960, 43 of them in the South Pacific. The eight tests in the latest series were all reported by either New Zealand or Australia without confirmation from the French government. According to informed sources quoted in *Le Monde* Aug. 15, France had made major progress in developing a multiple nuclear warheads missile in the latest South Pacific tests. A five-kiloton trigger device for MIRV (multiple independently targetable re-entry vehicle) warheads was tested June 16 and a 150-ton MIRV warhead July 7, the latter successfully using the miniaturization necessary to produce the cluster of warheads used for a MIRV, *Le Monde* said.

[8] **U.S., U.S.S.R. conduct tests.** Both the U.S. and the Soviet Union conducted underground nuclear tests during July-October. AEC staged three nuclear tests, with a yield range of 20-200 kilotons, at its Nevada test site July 10, Aug. 30 and Sept. 26. A test with a yield range of less than 20 kilotons was conducted Aug. 14. The Soviet tests, announced by the AEC and observatories in Sweden and Norway, were conducted July 10 (measuring 5.2 on the Richter scale, indicating a test of more than 200 kilotons), Aug. 14, 19 (with a yield of 1-3 megatons), 29, Sept. 13 and Oct. 16. None was confirmed by the Soviet government. The tests were staged in eastern Kazakhstan and northwestern Siberia.

International Actions

[9] **Atomic Energy Act amendment.** A bill amending the Atomic Energy Act was passed by the Senate July 11 and House Aug. 1 and signed by President Ford Aug. 17. The major change permitted the AEC to increase the amount of nuclear material it distributed to groups of nations for peaceful purposes. The amount could be increased above statutory ceilings if both houses of Congress did not disapprove the increase within 60 days. The provision retained Congressional control over such distribution. The AEC had sought elimination of the requirement for statutory approval of the distribution levels. The bill also permitted export of small amounts of nuclear material for peaceful purposes to countries not having a nuclear-cooperation pact with the U.S.

[10] **Curbs set for nuclear sales.** In an attempt to prevent nuclear weapons proliferation, major exporters of nuclear materials, except for France and China, had compiled a list of equipment they would supply to other nations only under assurances it would not be diverted for explosive use, the *New York Times* reported Sept. 24. The decision was set forth in governmental letters to the Inter-

national Atomic Energy Agency in Vienna (IAEA). Among the supplier countries agreeing to the new curbs were the U.S., Great Britain and the Soviet Union.

[11] **U.S. conditions nuclear aid.** U.S. negotiations with Egypt and Israel on providing atomic assistance had slowed as the result of a new American proposal requiring both countries to agree to place all future nuclear facilities under international inspection as a condition for receiving U.S. power plants, the State Department disclosed Oct. 1. Egypt favored the proposed controls, while Israel expressed reservations. The U.S. had previously required inspection by the IAEA only over the atomic reactors and fuels the U.S. supplied to a foreign country. In the case of Egypt and Israel, the U.S. was proposing a broader agreement requiring international inspection of all atomic power plants and fissionable material the two countries might receive in the future from any nation to prevent the plutonium produced as a by-product from being diverted into the manufacture of atomic weapons. U.S. officials regarded the international control issue as the principal reason for Israel's delay in responding to the proposal. Israel was wary of such controls since it would open up to inspection its Dimona reactor, which was capable of producing enough plutonium for a few atomic bombs a year. It had only reluctantly agreed to token inspections of the Dimona facilities by U.S. officials.

[12] **Nuclear cooperation pacts.** Legislation allowing Congress to take a stand on international agreements entered into by the U.S. for cooperation in nuclear technology for peaceful purposes was approved by both houses of Congress Oct. 10 and by President Ford Oct. 26. The measure arose from Congressional concern over the Nixon Administration's decision in June to sell nuclear reactors and fuel to Egypt and Israel for peaceful purposes.

U.S. Regulatory Developments

[13] **Nuclear theft threat seen.** A report prepared for the AEC and released April 26 stated that the worldwide increase in terrorist activities and the proliferation of nuclear power plants had heightened the possibility that nuclear raw materials could be stolen in quantities sufficient for the production of homemade atomic weapons. The *New York Times* reported May 2 that the AEC had begun ordering utilities to hire armed guards for their plants, despite objections from some companies that security should be a government function, and that the weapons used by private guards might pose new dangers.

[14] **Power plant 'events' reported.** The AEC reported May 28 that 861 "abnormal events" had occurred at the U.S.' 42 nuclear power plants during 1973. None of the incidents resulted directly in health hazards, the agency said, but 371 were potentially hazardous. The report said the incidents included loss of power supply, failures of electronic monitoring equipment and cooling system leaks. Each of the 42 plants recorded at least one "event."

[15] **Reactor hazards found slight.** According to a study released by the AEC Aug. 20, the risks from nuclear power plant accidents were smaller than from other man-made or natural disasters. The study concluded that, given the 100 conventional water-cooled plants expected to be in operation by 1980 (51 were currently operating), the chance of an accident involving 10 or more fatalities was one in 2,500 a year; an accident involving 1,000 or more deaths carried a risk of one in one million a year.

[16] **Few penalties for violations reported.** Reporting on a study of AEC records, the *New York Times* said Aug. 25 that the commission had imposed penalties on only a small fraction of nuclear installations at which violations had been found, despite the fact that many of the violations could have created

significant radiation hazards. According to records for the year ended June 30, the AEC found 3,333 violations in 1,288 of the 3,047 installations inspected. The commission imposed punishment in eight cases: license revocations involving two companies and civil penalties totaling $37,000 against six others.

[17] **AEC orders inspection shutdown.** Electric utilities operating 21 water-cooled nuclear reactors were under AEC orders to close down the facilities for a special inspection of cooling systems, it was reported Sept. 22. The inspection was ordered after cracks were discovered in pipes of three reactors within 10 days. According to the AEC, leakage of radioactive water had occurred in only one case, and there was no release of radioactivity into the environment. The AEC also said the reactor's overall cooling system was not impaired. The affected reactors produced about 45% of U.S. nuclear-produced power.

[18] **New energy agency established.** A bill establishing a new Energy Research and Development Administration was approved by the House Oct. 9, Senate Oct. 10 and signed by President Ford Oct. 11. The new agency, which would consolidate federal energy research, replaced the AEC, which was abolished under the legislation. The AEC's licensing and regulation activities would be handled by a new Nuclear Regulatory Commission which was required to make public disclosure of any safety-related "abnormal occurrences" at nuclear plants within 15 days. Manufacturers and nuclear facility officials were required to report equipment or operating defects threatening public safety. A maximum penalty of $5,000 was set for each individual violation. The nuclear weapons development aspect of the AEC operation was tentatively put under the aegis of the new agency, which, along with the Defense Department, would prepare recommendations for the future disposition of the responsibility.

[19] **AEC denies safety data suppressed.** AEC Chairman Dixy Lee Ray denied Nov. 15 that the AEC had suppressed data on the safety of nuclear power plants. She conceded that "while there may be some validity for such accusations in the past, the situation has changed today."

[20] **AEC safety report criticized.** The AEC report on the safety of nuclear reactors made public in August was criticized in a document released Nov. 23 by the Union of Concerned Scientists (UCS) and the Sierra Club, a conservationist group, as speculatvie and unreliable. The UCS and Sierra statement said the AEC study prepared by Dr. Norman C. Rasmussen contained a number of flaws. The safety analysis used by Rasmussen to estimate the probability of an accident, they said, had been developed and then abandoned by the aerospace industry and the federal government because it had been found to drastically underestimate existing hazards. The AEC report was also criticized for the low number of projected casualties based in part on the successful evacuation of persons living near an atomic plant. A major accident at a nuclear plant could kill or seriously injure 126,800 people, 16 times the casualties estimated by the AEC report, the scientists said.

See also Appointments & Resignations; Australia [22]; Aviation [12]; Disarmament; Energy Crisis [26-27]; Environment & Pollution [17]; Finland; France [6, 19]; India; Iran; Israel; Japan [12]; Middle East [38]; Obituaries [Bush, Condon, Gold, Strauss]; Oil [19]; Sweden

ATTICA PRISON—*See* Radicals; Rockefeller, Nelson [7, 23-24]

AUSTRALIA

Government & Politics

[1] **Parliament dissolved, elections set.** The Senate and House of Representatives were dissolved April 11 and Prime Minister Gough Whitlam announced that general elections would be held May 18. His Labor Party had been voted

into power Dec. 2, 1972. Whitlam had reached the decision April 10 after accusing the Senate opposition of "unparalleled obstruction of legislation people elected us to implement." He charged the opposition with blockage of House-approved bills. The Senate action that had led directly to Whitlam's decision to dissolve Parliament was its threat to vote against appropriation bills to provide funds for the government's operation. The bills were finally approved by the Senate April 10 after Whitlam had requested and received approval by Governor General Sir Paul Hasluck to hold an election on the constitutional grounds that the balloting could be called in the case of prolonged disagreement between the Senate and House. The Senate opposition had opposed the House bills as a means of forcing the election issue. Under the Australian system, an election for the Senate was scheduled later in 1974, one for the House of Representatives was due in 1975. The double dissolution meant all congressmen again had to run for their seats. In addition to the national elections, several state contests had been scheduled.

[2] Whitlam announced April 29 that in the next three years his governing Labor Party would seek lower housing repayments for young people, free hospital care and a review of the tax structure. He also pledged child care facilities for all children by 1980 and additional funds for nursing homes and state transport. The Liberal-Country Party's (LCP) position of foreign policy, outlined by Andrew Peacock April 23, called for the country's return to close ties with the U.S. as an equal partner. The party, Peacock said, also favored greater U.S. involvement in the Indian Ocean, improved relations with China and establishment of ties with North Vietnam. Sen. Francis P. McManus, leader of the Democratic Labor Party, opened his party's campaign April 28 with a statement supporting heavier defense spending and greater reliance on Australia's ties with the U.S., Britain and Southeast Asian nations, particularly Indonesia.

[3] **Election results.** The Labor Party retained its 67 seats in the House in the May 18 election. The Liberal-Country Party coalition collected 60 seats; it had previously held 58. In the Senate, Labor and the Liberal-Country coalition each won 29 seats. Previously, Labor had held 26 of the 60 Senate seats; the Liberals, 20 and the Country Party, 5. The Democratic Labor Party, which had four senators previously, failed to win any in the election. The Liberal Movement and the Independent Party each won one seat, giving them tie-breaking power.

[4] **Joint sitting of Parliament.** In the absence of a majority in the Senate, Prime Minister Whitlam had the governor general invoke a little-known section of the Constitution that provided for a joint Parliamentary session in order to insure passage of bills held up previously. The sitting opened Aug. 6. The six bills, which had been passed by the House but repeatedly rejected by the Senate, included a change in the Electoral Act, the Petroleum and Minerals Authority bill, to provide for oil and gas exploration, and a universal health insurance scheme. The Electoral Act, which restricted the size of constituencies, and the petroleum bill were both passed by the joint session.

[5] **Western Australia State elections.** The Labor Party had lost the Western Australia State elections March 30 to a coalition of the Liberal Party and the National Alliance. The latter, the result of a merger between the Country Party and the Democratic Labor Party on Jan. 9, was opposed to federal encroachment on states' rights. Sir Charles Court was sworn in as premier April 8, replacing Labor Party Premier John Tonkin. The formation of an organization advocating the secession of Western Australia State from Australia was reported by the *New York Times* July 15. The movement reportedly reflected the growing opposition in Western Australia and other states toward moves by Whitlam's government to enlarge its power at the expense of the states. Court said that al-

though he did not favor withdrawal, he believed that any federal government that ignored the secessionist feeling in his state did so "at its own peril." Court and Johannes Bjelke-Petersen of Queensland agreed after a two-day meeting Sept. 8 to cooperate with other states in blocking central government moves to "stifle private enterprise" and take control of certain state rights.

[6] **Coalition re-elected in Queensland.** Queensland's National Party-Liberal Party coalition was returned to office with an increased state parliamentary majority in elections Dec 7. The National Party, formerly the Country Party, won 40 seats, an increase of 14, while the Liberals captured 29 for a gain of eight. The Labor Party suffered a loss of 22 seats, winning only 11.

[7] **Election campaign fund curbs.** A government bill submitted to the House of Representatives Dec. 6 would set a limit on spending by political parties and candidates during elections and would require them to make public the source of their campaign funds. Campaign expenditure limits would be based on the size of the electorate.

Economic Development

[8] **Minimum wage law revised.** Women workers were successful in 1974 in their fight to have Australia's minimum wage laws revised. The Arbitration Commission announced May 2 that women would be given an equal minimum wage with men, with their salaries being increased in three stages by the end of June 1975. The action was the result of efforts by the National Council of Women, the Union of Australian Women and the Women's Electoral Lobby. Final determination came as part of a package raising the minimum wage by $A8 a week, increasing average weekly earnings to almost $69. Workers in higher income brackets were granted an additional $A2.50 a week plus 2%, giving a worker earning $A150 an extra $A5.50. The new pay scale was effective May 23. Weekly minimum wages were increased again under a ruling released by the Arbitration Commission Dec. 18. The rate for men was set at $A76.10, a boost of $A8, while women's wages were increased by $A7.20 to $A68.40.

[9] **Anti-inflation program.** Treasurer Frank Crean presented a broad anti-inflation program to Parliament on July 23. Included were immigration provisions, increased postal and telecommunications charges, higher taxes and deferment of plans to liberalize entitlement for old age pensions and for government-sponsored pre-school child care. Earlier, on June 7, Prime Minister Whitlam had disclosed sharp reductions in federal expenditures and layoffs of federal civil servants. He had also prohibited additional aid for the states. State premiers accused Whitlam of unfairly placing the inflation-fighting burden upon the states. In an Aug. 13 meeting, however, the country's six state premiers agreed to cooperate with the federal government by offering to join it in action to control prices and wages. Inflation had risen by 5.4% in the third quarter of 1974, the Federal Bureau of Statistics reported Oct. 21, raising the total inflationary increase in consumer prices over the past 12 months to 16.3%. It was the highest quarterly price rise since 1951.

[10] **Federal budget submitted.** The government's 1974-75 budget was submitted to Parliament Sept. 17 by Crean. Expenditures were expected to increase by $A3.980 billion to a total of $A16.274 billion, while income was expected to rise by $A3.702 billion to $A15.704 billion. The budget provided for a large increase in economic assistance to less developed countries, a greater outlay for education and Aboriginal Affairs and income tax reductions for individuals earning up to $A10,500.

[11] **Whitlam announces tax cuts.** Whitlam announced Nov. 12 that his government would reduce taxes on personal and business income as part of a

major effort to stimulate the lagging economy and reverse rising unemployment. The new measures, which would supplement the previously announced budget, were the direct result of government concern over the October jobless figures, which had risen to 189,000.

[12] **Trade deficit.** The country incurred a trade deficit of $A678 million during the 1973-74 fiscal year, the highest in 22 years, it was reported July 31. The figure was attributed by the Bureau of Statistics largely to rises in imports and freight rates. It was the country's first trade deficit since 1966-67. Australia had a $A981 million surplus during the previous fiscal year. Australia devalued its dollar Sept. 25 by 12%. The new rate was one Australian dollar to 1.3090 U.S. dollars, compared with the previous rate of one Australian dollar to 1.4872 U.S. dollars.

Other Domestic Developments

[13] **Queen Elizabeth visits.** Britain's Queen Elizabeth II toured Papua New Guinea Feb. 22-26 and arrived in Australia Feb. 27 for her fifth visit to that country. Her visit was interrupted a day later when she returned to Britain for the elections. The queen, opening the new session of the federal Parliament in Canberra Feb. 28, said the government would assume constitutional responsibilities for aborigines and Torres Straight Islanders. She pledged that discriminatory State legislation against aborigines would be abolished.

[14] **Aboriginal affairs.** Charles Perkins, an assistant secretary of the Department of Aboriginal Affairs was suspended Feb. 26 after accusing the Liberal and Country Parties of Western Australia of being "the biggest racist parties in the world." He was reinstated March 4 following an inquiry. The government announced Sept. 20 that it planned to take over seven million acres of Aboriginal reserves in Queensland State and hand them over to the Aboriginal communities.

[15] **Union lifts Sinatra ban.** American singer Frank Sinatra cancelled a tour of Australia July 10 after labor unions had imposed a boycott on him following a dispute with the press. The controversy began soon after Sinatra's arrival in Melbourne July 9 when he and members of his bodyguard allegedly assaulted television cameramen. At a concert that evening Sinatra told an audience that the male members of the Australian press were "bums and parasites" and the women journalists were "hookers and broads." Angered by his remarks, the unions threatened to wreck the remainder of Sinatra's tour unless he apologized. Sinatra then decided to cut short his tour and return to the U.S., but transport workers in Melbourne refused to service his jet. The ban was lifted and Sinatra resumed the tour after he settled the feud at a meeting in Sydney July 11 with Robert Hawke, president of the Australian Council of Trade Unions.

[16] **Commonwealth migration rules set.** Whitlam announced Aug. 1 that beginning Jan. 1, 1975 citizens of the Commonwealth countries of Britain, Ireland, Canada and Fiji wishing to migrate to or visit Australia would be subject to the same visa requirements as other migrants or travelers to the country. Heretofore, residents of those countries required no visas. Whitlam said the decision would remove a long-standing discriminatory practice from Australia's immigration policy. Labor Minister Clyde Cameron announced Oct. 2 a temporary suspension of immigration to Australia to ease the country's unemployment problem. Migrants whose applications were approved would be permitted to enter, but in general no new applications would be accepted.

[17] **Cyclone devastates Darwin.** Cyclone "Tracy" with force winds measuring as high as 160 m.p.h. struck Darwin Dec. 25, killing 50 persons and destroying 90% of the city. A massive evacuation was immediately effected and by Dec. 31 half the city's 45,000 residents were transferred and the emergency was declared at an end.

U.S. Relations

[18] **U.S. base protests.** The U.S. communications base at North West Cape was the target of violent demonstrations May 16 and 20. About 200 persons were marching on the facility to protest the base May 16 when police ordered them to stop in Perth, more than 1,000 miles south, on the grounds that the demonstration was unauthorized. The police then clashed with the demonstrators and arrested 15. Thirty-four of 200 demonstrators were arrested outside the North West Cape base May 20 after a scuffle with police that erupted when the demonstrators set fire to a U.S. flag. An agreement revising the 1963 military base accord had been signed in Canberra March 21 by Prime Minister Whitlam and U.S. Ambassador Marshall Green. The amendments were agreed upon during a January visit to Washington by Australian Defense Minister Lance Barnard. The U.S. was to retain exclusive rights only to the base communications building. The accord also limited Australia's financial responsibility for its own participation. On April 3, during a House of Representatives debate, Whitlam said he was opposed to the continuance of foreign installations. Whitlam's statement was in reply to Liberal Party leader Billy M. Snedden's demand that the prime minister reject a Soviet proposal to build a jointly-manned scientific station in Australia. If the Soviet project had any military significance, it was likely the government would reject it, Whitlam said. On April 10 the government disclosed that it had turned down the Soviet proposal, but no further explanation was provided.

[19] **Whitlam defends U.S. envoy.** Prime Minister Whitlam July 2 defended Ambassador Green against criticism leveled at him the previous week by Sen. William W. Brown. Brown was reported as having said that Green was in Australia "to protect American financial interests and the maintenance of its military installations" in the country. Asserting that Green was "the top United States hatchet man," Brown linked him with coups and other acts of violence in some of the other countries in which he had served. Whitlam challenged Brown to provide information to support his charges. "I don't believe there is such information," he said.

Relations with Other Nations

[20] **North Korean ties established.** Australia and North Korea signed an agreement July 31 establishing diplomatic relations between the two countries. The accord was signed in the Australian embassy in Jakarta, Indonesia. A statement issued by the South Korean Foreign Ministry expressed regret over Australia's action. Australia also moved to establish diplomatic relations on the ambassadorial level with Sudan and Saudi Arabia, recognized Guinea-Bissau and signed its first trade agreement with East Germany during 1974.

[21] **Shah visits.** Shah Mohammed Riza Pahlevi of Iran visited Australia Sept. 20-27, holding talks with Whitlam and other government officials. Whitlam said the shah signed a $A100 million trade agreement Sept. 25. At a Parliamentary luncheon in Canberra Sept. 25, Whitlam and the shah called on the U.S. and the Soviet Union to recognize the Indian Ocean as a zone of peace.

[22] **Japanese premier visits.** Japanese Premier Kakuei Tanaka visited Australia Oct. 31-Nov. 6 to discuss a wide range of economic matters, including the possibility of securing long-term access to uranium, iron ore and other vital raw materials. Following two days of talks between Tanaka and Whitlam, a communique issued Nov. 2 said both nations planned to build a joint uranium-processing plant in the Northern Territory at a cost of $1.3 billion-$2.6 billion, with Japan providing the financing, Australia the uranium, and a third country the technology. Japan was to receive an immediate supply of 9,000 metric tons of Australian uranium, and possibly larger supplies after 1976, and both nations

would begin joint research into the production of oil from coal, the communique said.

[23] **Whitlam foreign tours.** Prime Minister Whitlam returned to Australia Oct. 13 following a tour of the South Pacific, the U.S. and Canada that had started Sept. 27. During the tour, he addressed the United Nations General Assembly and met with President Ford and Prime Minister Pierre Elliott Trudeau. Whitlam left Australia Dec. 14 on a tour of Europe but cut short his trip and returned from London Dec. 27 to give personal attention to the problems arising from the cyclone that struck Darwin. Whitlam resumed his trip Dec. 30 and landed in Crete Dec. 31, preparatory to a visit to mainland Greece.

See also ALUMINUM & BAUXITE; ATOMIC ENERGY [5-7]; BOATING; DEFENSE [14]; EUROPEAN ECONOMIC COMMUNITY [10, 18]; FAMINE & FOOD; MONETARY DEVELOPMENTS [4]; PAPUA NEW GUINEA; TARIFFS & TRADE; TENNIS; UNITED NATIONS [6, 15]; VIETNAM, PEOPLE'S REPUBLIC OF

AUSTRIA—Rudolf Kirschlaeger, 59, foreign minister since 1970, was sworn in as president July 8 following election on June 23. Kirschlaeger, who did not currently belong to a political party, was the ruling Socialist Party candidate as a result of political pressure exerted by Chancellor Bruno Kreisky. The new president filled the vacancy left by the death of Socialist Franz Jonas who succumbed to cancer at age 74 on April 23. Kirschlaeger was opposed by People's Party candidate Alois Lugger, burgomaster of Innsbruck, who trailed by 154,471 votes out of 4,630,831 votes cast. The election campaign had been unexpectedly heated. Both candidates were disclosed to have been members of authoritarian right-wing groups before Hitler's 1938 take over of Austria.

See also ALGERIA; AUTO RACING; BANKS & BANKING; COMMUNISM, INTERNATIONAL; CYPRUS [20]; EUROPEAN SECURITY; ITALY [7]; MEXICO [19]; MIDDLE EAST [11]; MONETARY DEVELOPMENTS [4, 15]; UNITED NATIONS [15]; YUGOSLAVIA [11]

AUTOMOBILES—Price rises in industry. Prices on 1974 and 1975 model cars and trucks were raised by General Motors Corp. (GM), American Motors Corp. (AMC), Ford and Chrysler. Spokesmen from the various companies cited increased costs of raw materials, transportation, wage and employe benefits, and pollution devices. GM had increased the cost of 1974 cars over $500. Another $416 was added to the cost of 1975 models, the company announced Aug. 21. GM had originally projected 1975 price increase of approximately $500 but this was lowered in response to an Aug. 12 rebuke by President Ford who, expressing disappointment, stated he hoped "the General Motors action will not be viewed as a signal by other auto companies or other industries." GM had instituted six price rises in 1974. Reduction on 1975 models affected cars only, according to company spokesmen. New truck prices were actually raised again, with a $624, or 10.9% increase earmarked for 1975 models. It was reported Aug. 27 that the bulk of the car price increases would be attached to the small car market. GM announced Dec. 9 that the base price of 1975 model cars was being reduced by $13, less than .3% of the average cost of a GM car, because the government no longer required that an ignition interlock system be installed on new cars.

[2] On Aug. 10, Ford Motor Co. President Lee A. Iacocca said Ford's planned $418, or 8%, increase was "low" and that an additional price hike was planned. Ford's 8% across-the-board increase meant that 1975 cars would cost an estimated $407 more than previous year's models, which had seen six increases through the year. Ford quietly raised prices on its 1975 model cars and trucks another 2%, or about $75 a unit, the *Wall Street Journal* reported Nov. 20. The announcement

of the price increase, confirmed by Ford officials Nov. 20, was made in a private letter to car dealers. In a public announcement Nov. 21, Ford reduced the base price of its lowest priced small car by an average $150 or 5.1%. It was the first price cut made by any U.S. carmaker since the fall of 1973.

[3] Chrysler had instituted nine price hikes on its 1974 models, increasing the cost well over $500 during the year. Chrysler announced Sept. 11 an average price increase of more than 8.5% on 1975 model cars. The $415 price hike represented a $350 increase in the base sticker price, a $50 increase for higher optional costs and optional equipment now included as standard items; and a $15 rise in shipping charges. Chrysler also eliminated several cheaper big car models and affixed large price increases to its more popular small car models, while raising the price of big car models by smaller amounts. AMC announced Oct. 7 that it was increasing the price of its 1975 model cars an average $414—about 10% above average 1974 prices. The increase included the tentative 7.7% price hike announced in September. AMC's percentage increase was larger than those announced by the major automotive makers, but its dollar range was comparable to their price increases. Volkswagen of America Inc., the largest importer of cars to the U.S., announced Dec. 5 that it was raising prices of 1975 model cars $270-$450, 7.9%-10.3%. The largest percentage increase was attached to the firm's low-priced, high volume small car. A *New York Times* report on June 20 cited a wide range of raw material price increases that had contributed to auto price hikes at the retail level: copper, up 34% since the start of the model year; glass, 11%; plastic, 21%; lead, 30%; steel, 18%; aluminum, 42%; iron, 17%; rubber, 16%; zinc, 70%. (The cost breakdown was based on production costs at Ford Motor Co.)

[4] **Production decline and layoffs.** Big cars with low gasoline mileage were the principal casualties of production cutbacks and sales drops during the early part of 1974 as customers exhibited a sudden and marked preference for the more economical small cars. Industry leaders admitted that changes in the nation's car buying habits had forced manufacturers to undertake what Ford President Iacocca called the "greatest industrial conversion in history, at least in peacetime."

[5] GM announced Jan. 24 plans to close 14 of the company's 22 assembly plants for several weeks, an action which idled 75,000 workers. Another three shutdowns were slated on March 5. Further GM cuts through the year included an Oct. 17 white collar work force reduction of 10,000. GM, hardest hit by a drop in sales, had placed 30,000 workers on indefinite layoff by Nov. 8. Plans for additional GM closings were disclosed Nov. 29 after it was decided that production in January would be reduced to 337,500 cars. That figure represented a 5.5% gain over the previous year, when GM made deep cuts in production because of the oil embargo. The newest move would close some plants entirely, temporarily idling 41,000 workers and cause 64,000 employees to be laid off indefinitely. Further layoffs were announced Dec. 18: 41,000 temporary furloughs and another 18,000 indefinites for the first quarter of 1975. With the latest announcement, the total number of GM workers on indefinite layoff would total 91,000, 25% of GM's hourly work force. (GM's third quarter net earnings, announced Oct. 25, had fallen from a record $266.6 million in the third quarter of 1973 to $16.7 million in the same period of 1974. It was GM's second lowest income level since World War II. Sales declined 9% to $6.93 billion.)

[6] By Feb. 15 the number of Ford workers on temporary or indefinite furloughs was more than 19,000. Ford had also reduced its white collar work force by Oct. 17 to 63,000, a cut of 2,000 jobs. By Nov. 7 the total number of Ford workers on indefinite furlough was 8,400. Several weeks later, on Nov. 27, Ford

officials disclosed additional layoffs, bringing to 15,500 the number of employees laid off for an indefinite period. A total of 21,400 were on temporary leave. Ford announced Dec. 19 that auto production during the first quarter of 1975 would be cut back 35% from the depressed level of 1974's first quarter. Truck production would be slashed 34%, increasing to 27,000 the number of Ford employees on indefinite leave. (Ford had announced Oct. 30 that its quarterly earnings dropped 50% to $47.4 million. Sales were up 21% compared with 1973, to $6.02 billion.)

[7] Chrysler closings in February and March caused 10,000 workers to lose their jobs temporarily. Another significant layoff occurred during the three weeks between November and Christmas when the company put 4,000 workers on temporary leave. Chrysler had also cut back 2,400 white collar jobs between October 1973 and October 1974. Seventeen thousand Chrysler workers were put on indefinite leave by Nov. 8, another 8,400 were added Nov. 19. Production in the fourth quarter was slashed 41% from the original schedule and 53% from the comparable period of 1973. Another 22,000 white collar workers were temporarily laid off during December, bringing the total number of Chrysler employees without work to more than 80,000. (On Oct. 22 Chrysler had reported an $8 million third quarter loss. Faced with an 86-day supply of unsold cars and drastic production cutbacks, the company said Dec. 24 that it would no longer pay cost-of-living benefits to 18,000 of its 39,000 white collar workers; and would suspend a stock purchase plan for such employees for five months. The action affected nonunion and lower-level staff: unionized white-collar workers and upper-level management personnel had never received the cost-of-living benefits.) Although initially reporting a rise in sales, due to its small car production, by November AMC had experienced a 50% drop, compared to 35% for the Big 3 auto makers. AMC announced Dec. 16 that production cutbacks involving 13,000 workers would be made at three of its small car assembly plants, including one in Canada. The facilities would be shut for one week in January because of a 112-day backlog of unsold cars.

[8] By Dec. 18 142,000 auto industry workers were on permanent layoff and another 76,000 were temporarily without work. The slump also affected related industries. Other firms scheduling heavy layoffs included General Electric Co., Motorola Inc., Uniroyal Inc., Goodyear Tire and Rubber and Libby-Owens-Ford Co. Industry officials said Dec. 8 that inventory supplies of unsold cars were large enough to last 86 days if all assembly plants in the nation were shut down. It was reported Dec. 13 that the industry planned its smallest production level since 1961 during the first quarter of 1975. Planned output of 1.6 million units was off 11% from the previous year's depressed level and 40% below the record first quarter production of 1973. Auto industry officials met with President Ford at the White House Dec. 11 to ask that he extend special aid to the financially distressed industry. Ford President Iacocca proposed that the Administration freeze federal emission and safety requirements for five years and cut taxes in order to stimulate car sales. Industry leaders also sought a "one shot" 20% investment tax credit, removal of the federal excise tax on heavy trucks and a general easing of the nation's money supply to make financing of car purchases easier. United Auto Workers President Leonard Woodcock, who also attended the meeting, backed the industry's position and said he would support a "pause" in federal auto standards.

[9] **Auto makers' breakup urged.** In four days of public hearings Feb. 26-March 1, the Senate Antitrust Subcommittee heard testimony from a wide range of witnesses about the Big 3 auto makers' "shared monopoly," which witnesses said accounted for the ascendency of the automobile and the decline of other

forms of ground transportation throughout the country. Witnesses, including San Francisco Mayor Joseph Alioto, former Attorney General Ramsey Clark and Donald E. Weeden, chairman of the Wall Street stock and bond firm Weeden & Co., supported moves leading to the breakup of GM, Ford and Chrysler Corp.

[10] **GM delays rotary car.** GM announced Sept. 24 that the planned introduction of a rotary-engine automobile had been postponed indefinitely because the engine currently could not meet antipollution standards without significant loss in fuel economy. The announcement came a few days after GM had said it would begin marketing the new rotary-engine "Monza," a sport model in the subcompact class, by late in the 1975 model year.

[11] **Seatbelt lock made optional.** A bill making optional the seatbelt ignition interlock system for automobiles was signed into law by President Ford Oct. 27. The requirement that seatbelts be fastened before 1974 and 1975 model cars could be started had met with widespread public resistance. The bill, passed by voice votes of the Senate Oct. 10 and House Oct. 15, also authorized federal safety standards for school buses. The secretary of transportation was to promulgate the standards within 15 months. The bill added a number of other amendments to the National Traffic and Motor Vehicle Safety Act, which it extended for two years with authorizations of $55 million for fiscal 1975 and $60 million for fiscal 1976.

[12] **Meeting on increased auto efficiency.** Auto industry officials met at the White House Oct. 29 with Administration officials to discuss President Ford's call for a 40% increase in fuel economy by 1980. After the meeting, Transportation Secretary Brinegar said industry officials had agreed to cooperate with the voluntary program to upgrade auto efficiency. According to a White House table, which combined results for large and small cars, gasoline efficiency would have to be upgraded to 19.6 miles per gallon for 1980 model cars, compared with the 1974 model car average of 14 miles per gallon.

See also CANADA [33]; CONSUMER AFFAIRS [10-11]; ECONOMY, U.S. [8, 10]; ENERGY CRISIS [4]; ENVIRONMENT & POLLUTION [1, 3, 6]; INSURANCE; LABOR [9]; LATIN AMERICA; STOCK MARKET

AUTO RACING—Pete Revson, 35, considered the top U.S. road-racing driver, was killed March 22 in Johannesburg during a practice run for the South African Grand Prix. Revson won the 1973 British and Canadian Formula One Grand Prix and placed second in the 1971 Indianapolis 500. South African Grand Prix, run on March 30, was won by Carlos Reutemann of Argentina.

Other results: Argentine Grand Prix, Jan. 13, Buenos Aires, won by Dennis Hulme of New Zealand (Brazilian Emerson Fittipaldi charged his car had been sabotaged). Brazilian Grand Prix, Jan. 27, Sao Paulo, won by Fittipaldi. Daytona (Fla.) 500, Feb. 17, won for fifth time by Richard Petty in shortened 450-mile race for $36,000 purse. East African Safari, April 15, top score in 3,470-mile race posted by Joginder Singh of Kenya. Fiftieth Grand Prix of Spain, April 28, Madrid, won by Australian Niki Lauda. Belgium Grand Prix, May 12, Nivelle, won by Fittipaldi. Grand Prix of Monaco, May 26, won by Ronnie Peterson of Sweden. Indianapolis (Ind.) 500, May 26, won by Johnny Rutherford who collected $245,031 purse (New fuel quality limitations, the result of 1973 fatalities, kept Rutherford's average speed at 158.589 mph in his McLaren-Offenhauser car.) Swedish Grand Prix, June 9, Anderstorp, won by Jody Scheckter. Le Mans, France, June 16, won by Henri Pescarolo and Gerard Larrouse driving a Matra-Simca. French Grand Prix, July 7, Dijon, won by Peterson. British Grand Prix, July 20, Brands Hatch, won by Scheckter. German Grand Prix, Aug. 4, Neurburgring, won easily by Clay Regazzoni of Switzerland. Austrian Grand Prix,

Aug. 18, Zeltweb, won by Reutemann. Italian Grand Prix, Sept. 8, Monza, won by Peterson. Canadian Grand Prix, Sept. 22, Mosport, Ontario, won by Fittipaldi.

Fittipaldi beat out Regazzoni for the world Formula One driving championship Oct. 6 in the final event of the 15-race Formula One competition, the U.S. Grand Prix at Watkins Glen, N.Y. Both men had been tied with a total of 52 driving points, but Fittipaldi finished fourth in the last race, earning three points, while Regazzoni's 11th position earned him no additional score. The race, won by Reutemann, was marred by the death of Austrian Helmuth Koinigg, who died when his car smashed through two fences and under a stationary guard rail.

AVALANCHES—*See* MOUNTAIN CLIMBING

AVIATION

Fares & Routes

[1] **U.S. carriers face cost squeeze.** The airline industry in 1974 was financially threatened by the rising cost of scarce jet fuel. According to the Civil Aeronautics Board (CAB) Feb. 20, the average cost of a gallon of jet fuel for domestic airlines climbed 20.5% from December 1973 to January 1974. The cost was 47% higher than for the year ending June 30, 1973. In testimony before Congress March 4, airline executives warned that the industry's fuel bill could double in 1974 to $2.4 billion. The $1.2 billion increase would be six times the industry's profits in 1973, they said.

[2] Pan American World Airways appealed to the CAB Aug. 23, seeking an emergency $10 million a month federal subsidy, retroactive to April 3, to "stave off the imminent financial crisis" facing the airline because of rising fuel costs and declining passenger loads. The airline contended that its global network, which included 90,000 route miles providing service to 17 cities in the U.S. and more than 100 cities in 77 other countries, was a "national asset" vital to commerce and defense. The Ford Administration and the CAB refused Pan AM's request. Transportation Secretary Claude S. Brinegar, who announced the White House decision Sept. 18, said, "President Ford has concluded that it is not now fair to the nation's taxpayers to ask them to support our U.S. international flag air carriers with direct cash subsidy payments." Instead, Brinegar said, the Administration supported an alternative seven-point program aimed at providing long-term aid to the financially distressed airline. Measures included efforts to persuade more Americans to use U.S. airlines on overseas flights; "corrective actions" taken against governments that "discriminate" against U.S. carriers with higher airport landing and other fees; in order to reduce excess seating capacity available on many routes, efforts would be made to seek inter-airline agreements reducing competitive flight and "prompt action" was promised against foreign airlines whose flight capacity to the U.S. "exceeds their rights provided by their bilateral agrements"; U.S. flag airlines would be encouraged to consolidate and restructure overseas routes and explore mergers (Pan Am proposed major changes in transatlantic operations in papers filed Sept. 10 with the CAB); action would be accelerated on proposed increases in international mail rates; increased efforts would be made to raise international passenger fares to levels "more in line with costs"; efforts would be intensified to "eliminate or at least reduce" the practice of some high volume travel agents of obtaining kickbacks from airlines, and the licensing of travel agents would be studied. At the same time, the CAB also rejected Trans World Airlines' request for both an emergency and permanent subsidy, which were needed, according to the airline, to meet rising fuel costs. Pan Am and TWA agreed Oct. 16 on a scheduling

realignment plan to swap route authorities and suspend mutually competing service in an effort to overcome financial problems caused by rising fuel costs and declining passenger loads. The five-year plan was expected to increase revenues for each carrier by $25 million a year.

[3] Details of the Administration's plan to aid Pan Am were released Oct. 2 by the Transportation Department, which claimed that its proposals would reduce the airline's operating losses by $149 million by the end of 1975. Success of the program, according to government officials, depended on the willingness of Pan Am's bank creditors to continue to make loans to the carrier. In another action related to Pan Am's financial crisis, the CAB issued guidelines Oct. 21 to establish a floor for charter airline fares on transatlantic routes. The effect of the move, which would not take effect until 1975, was to raise transatlantic rates and reduce some of the competition posed to regularly scheduled airlines by the cheaper charter fares. The guidelines would raise charter fares by up to 35% over current levels, and by 70% over the previous year's level. The action was coupled with the CAB's approval of another fare increase for scheduled transatlantic flights, effective Nov. 1. The increase, the sixth in 1974, was in addition to rates which had raised North Atlantic fares 35% over the rates at the end of 1973. The increases ranged from 3.6% to 19%, with the cheapest fare rising 18% from current levels (up 60% from the price of an off season ticket a year earlier). Higher fuel costs justified the increase, the CAB said. The CAB voted unanimously to increase fares between the U.S. and Central and South America by 3%-5%, according to reports Sept. 3. The Justice Department filed a petition with the CAB Nov. 11, formally asking the agency to reconsider its guidelines setting minimum air fares for transatlantic charter flights. According to the government, this action constituted rate setting, which the CAB was not authorized to perform.

[4] Pan Am announced Nov. 25 that for the first 10 months of 1974 the airline's total deficit was $45.2 million, compared with a $5.5 million loss reported for the comparable period of 1973. A 97% rise in fuel costs over the past 12 months accounted for much of the increase, officials said. Officials had disclosed Oct. 30 that a new credit agreement had been concluded with 36 lending banks, allowing Pan Am to borrow $30 million immediately and draw up to $125 million for working capital by March 1975. The CAB Nov. 16 had rejected the Pan Am-TWA route swapping proposal because it was too vague and too sweeping. The airlines were ordered to redraft the plan. A revised plan was filed with the CAB Dec. 17. (Pilots for Pan Am announced Dec. 22 that they had agreed to an 11% "discount" on their wages for 1975, enabling the airline to save up to $10 million during the year.)

[5] A bill to provide relief for U.S. airlines operating internationally was passed by the Senate Dec. 17 and House Dec. 18. The bill directed the CAB to set the rate for carrying mail abroad to reflect cost increases to the airlines and to give the carriers a "reasonable" rate of return. Under another provision, the government was required to act to reduce discriminatory practices and user charges by foreign countries against U.S. airlines. If negotiations failed, the government was authorized to exact retaliatory charges on foreign airlines with the funds passed along to the U.S. lines. Government employes were required to use the U.S. airlines when abroad whenever possible.

[6] U.S. Secretary of State Henry Kissinger and Netherlands Foreign Minister Max van der Stoel had agreed Dec. 11 that their countries would resume deadlocked talks on U.S. demands for a reduction in the number of flights to America by KLM Royal Dutch Airlines. Negotiations between the U.S. and Netherlands had collapsed Nov. 15. Dutch sources said the U.S. had demanded a reduction in

KLM transatlantic flights from about 25 to 8 a week, an action the Dutch maintained was designed to aid the deficit-ridden Pan Am on the U.S.-Amsterdam flights. The U.S. maintained that about 60% of the passengers flying KLM's trans-Atlantic routes began or ended their trips outside the Netherlands in violation of a Dutch-U.S. air treaty.

[7] **Domestic air fares rise.** The CAB March 22 authorized a temporary 4% increase in domestic air fares, effective April 16 through Oct. 31, citing a "precipitous" rise in the price of jet fuel. The CAB also indicated that airlines could raise fares an additional 2% at the same time if they wished. (On March 29 the CAB also approved a 7% increase for most Western Hemisphere flights. A similar increase had been imposed on March 14 for most transpacific passenger and cargo flights. Cargo rate increases for North Atlantic routes were approved April 4. The increases of 7.5%-8% would bring an expected $5 million in additional revenues.)

[8] The CAB Oct. 31 approved a new 4% increase in the price of domestic air fares and made permanent a 6% fare increase granted earlier on an interim basis. The fare increases were expected to raise airlines' revenues $300 million-$400 million annually. Domestic airfares had increased approximately 25% in the past 12 months. The CAB also approved an amended agreement submitted by the International Air Transport Association (IATA) calling for a 6%-11% fare increase on transatlantic flights.

[9] **Ford drops Timm as CAB chairman.** President Ford said Dec. 20 that he would not reappoint Robert D. Timm as chairman of CAB and named CAB Commissioner Richard O'Melia as acting chairman. Timm had been criticized for his close contacts with the airlines and related industries which the CAB regulated.

Air Safety & Crashes

[10] **346 die in worst air crash.** In the worst catastrophe in civil aviation history, a Turkish jumbo jet crashed shortly after takeoff March 3 near Paris' Orly airport, killing all 345 persons aboard. Initial reports indicating the tail had blown off while the DC-10 was in flight sparked speculation that sabotage was the cause. But findings of an international team of experts March 10 explained that depressurization, due to what appeared to be an improperly locked rear cabin door, would have caused the tail rupture and was the likeliest cause of the crash. The plane had stopped in Paris on a scheduled flight from Istanbul to London. On April 3 the Federal Aviation Administration (FAA) reported that failure to implement safety recommendations caused the crash. The findings were announced to the Senate Aviation Subcommittee. A mandatory safety directive concerning the plane was recalled by the FAA in 1972 which then issued a voluntary "service bulletin." On March 27 McDonnell Douglas Corp., U.S. manufacturer of the plane, admitted the Turkish aircraft had left the factory without a critical cargo-door change, although records showed the change had been made. FAA Administrator Alexander Butterfield told the subcommittee that all future design changes "to correct an unsafe condition" would be dealt with by compulsory "air-worthiness directives." The findings were followed by the filing of numerous law suits against McDonnell Douglas, the FAA, Turkish Airlines and General Dynamics, a DC-10 sub contractor.

[11] **Virginia crash sparks debate.** A TWA 727 jet en route from Indianapolis and Columbis, Ohio to Washington's Dulles Airport crashed in the Blue Ridge mountains of Virginia Dec. 1 while preparing to land, killing all 92 persons on board. The crash was the worst U.S. aviation disaster of 1974. According to reports, the plane had dropped to an altitude of 1,700 feet, 50 feet short of Mt. Weather into which it crashed; it should have been at an altitude of 3,400 feet. The crash stimulated a debate between pilots and air traffic controllers over their

respective areas of responsibility for controlling flight altitudes during landing approaches. National Transportation Safety Board officials said Dec. 8 that the pilot apparently made an initial descent too low for that area. The report was immediately assailed by the Air Line Pilots Association as implicitly blaming the pilots for the crash. It laid the blame on the air controllers for giving faulty landing instructions. The crash, along with that of a Northwest Orient Airlines jet 30 miles north of New York Dec. 1 which killed its crew of three, brought the number of persons killed on flights of U.S. airlines in 1974 to 461, more than twice the figure of any of the five previous years, and the second largest total in history. [In 1960, 499 persons were killed.]

[12] **Shipment of hazardous material.** The House passed and sent to the President Dec. 19 a bill to restrict shipment of hazardous materials on passenger aircraft. The transportation secretary would have increased authority to set safety regulations. The bill would prohibit shipment by passenger aircraft of any hazardous or radioactive materials except short-lived isotopes used for research or medical purposes.

[13] **FAA changes instituted.** Following a House subcommittee report Dec. 28 charging the agency with "sluggishness which at times approached an attitude of indifference to public safety" and an "oversolicitous attitude on the part of some within the agency concerning the economic well-being of the aircraft industry," the FAA Dec. 30 named a panel to review all charges and report back by Jan. 17, 1975 on action to correct deficiencies.

[14] **Other major 1974 crashes.** Among the other fatal air crashes during the year were the following: A Turkish jet crashed on takeoff from Izmir's military airport Jan. 26, killing 63 of the 73 persons aboard. A Pan American World Airways jet crashed on a landing approach at Pago Pago, Samoa Jan. 31, killing 92 of the 101 persons aboard. A Pan Am 707 crashed in a mountainous area of Bali, Indonesia, April 27, killing all 107 aboard. The same day a Soviet Ilyushin 18 crashed shortly after takeoff from Leningrad airport, reportedly killing at least 108 persons. A TWA flight from Tel Aviv to New York crashed in the Ionian sea off Greece Sept. 8, killing all 108 persons aboard. (Investigators suspected that the plane may have been sabotaged, but withheld a conclusive verdict on the cause of the crash; an obscure Palestinian terrorist group claimed responsibility for sabotaging the airliner.) An Eastern Airlines DC-9 crashed Sept. 11 while attempting to land in Charlotte, N.C., killing 71 of the 82 persons aboard. All 191 persons were killed Dec. 4 when a Dutch DC-8 chartered jet, carrying Indonesian Moslems to Mecca, crashed on a hillside 60 miles from Sri Lanka's capital of Colombo, which the airliner was approaching for a landing. All 77 persons aboard a Venezuelan airliner were killed Dec. 22 when the plane exploded in midair shortly after taking off from the airport at Maturin. There was speculation that the plane may have been sabotaged.

Other Developments

[15] **SST testing resumed.** The Soviet Union announced May 5 it had resumed test flights of the TU-144 supersonic jetliner, a model of which had crashed at the Paris air show in June 1973. The aircraft now being tested bore a number of modifications, including a redesigned rear engine arrangement. The supersonic Anglo-French Concorde set down in Miami June 14 following a flight from Boston in an unprecedented 80 minutes, less than half the flight time of conventional jets. (The Concorde had made a record 3 hour, 9 minute flight from Paris to Boston June 13, reaching a speed of 1,550 m.p.h.)

[16] **U.S. plane breaks Atlantic record.** A U.S. Air Force SR-71 reconnaissance plane flew from New York to London in one hour 55 minutes and 42 seconds, cutting nearly three hours off the previous 3,490-mile Atlantic crossing record, it

was reported Sept. 1. The plane reached speeds of around 2,000 m.p.h. but its average speed was 1,817 m.p.h., due to refueling over the Atlantic.

See also BALLOONING; CAMPAIGN FINANCING [17]; CANADA [37]; CHILE [28]; CRIME [18]; DEFENSE [11-12]; ENERGY CRISIS [5]; FRANCE [9]; GREAT BRITAIN [11, 18]; IRAN; JAPAN [14]; JORDAN; LIBYA; MIDDLE EAST [28-29, 34, 39]; MOROCCO; OBITUARIES [deSEVERSKY, LINDBERGH, SPAATZ]; PORTUGAL [12]; TRANSPORTATION; UNION OF SOVIET SOCIALIST REPUBLICS [22]; VIETNAM, REPUBLIC OF [41]

AWARDS—*See* BASEBALL; BOOKS; MOTION PICTURES; MUSIC; NOBEL PRIZES; PULITZER PRIZES; TELEVISION & RADIO; THEATER

B

BAHAMAS—A reorganization of the Cabinet was reported Jan. 4, following the resignation of Development Minister Carlton Francis in an apparent dispute with Deputy Prime Minister Arthur Hanna over government policy toward casino gambling. (Hanna had announced in November 1973 that the government would assume full control over local casino gambling when privately held licenses expired in 1976 and 1977.) In the Cabinet shift, Prime Minister Lynden O. Pindling replaced Francis with Alfred Maycock and transferred the Development Ministry's planning unit to his own portfolio as minister of economic affairs. George A. Smith replaced Darrell Rolle as transport minister. Rolle became home affairs minister, with added responsibility (previously held by Pindling) for immigration, police and internal security, and nationality and citizenship.

See also CUBA; HAITI; VESCO, ROBERT L.

BAHRAIN—*See* APPOINTMENTS & RESIGNATIONS; OIL [5]
BALLET—*See* UNION OF SOVIET SOCIALIST REPUBLICS [21, 28]

BALLOONING—The U.S. Department of Defense gave up its air search March 6 for balloonist Thomas L. Gatch, believed to be lost in the South Atlantic. Gatch, who set out from Harrisburg, Pa. Feb. 17 in an effort to become the first balloonist to cross the Atlantic alone, was last sighted Feb. 21 about 900 miles south of the Azores. Robert C. Berger, a Philadelphian attempting to make the first transatlantic crossing in a helium balloon, was killed Aug. 6 when his plastic balloon burst, plunging the gondola in which he was riding into Barnegat Bay, N.J. He had lifted off an hour earlier from Lakehurst (N.J.) Naval Air Station.

BANANAS—*See* HONDURAS; LATIN AMERICA

BANGLA DESH—Indian Prime Minister Indira Gandhi and Bangla Desh Prime Minister Sheik Mujibur Rahman announced May 16 that they had resolved the outstanding bilateral issues "that had eluded solution for a whole generation." The joint declaration followed five days of talks in New Delhi. One of the major settlements made at the talks involved the dam India was building on the Ganges River to keep the port of Calcutta deep enough for year-round operation. The dam was interrupting the flow of some water into Bangla Desh. India also agreed to provide Bangla Desh with a $50 million credit; to build several plants there, including cement and fertilizer factories; and establishment of a joint commission dealing with jute.

Speaker of Parliament Muhammadullah was elected president Jan. 24 and was sworn in Jan. 27. Muhammadullah had been acting president since the December, 1973 resignation of Abu Sayeed Chowdhury.

Prime Minister Mujibur carried out a major revision of the Cabinet July 8, after accepting the resignations of six ministers and three state ministers July 7. The portfolios of the resigned ministers were redistributed among the remaining Cabinet members. Mujibur assumed additional portfolios, including Cabinet affairs, information and broadcasting, and aviation.

Muhammadullah declared a state of emergency and suspended the Constitution Dec. 28 to curb an increase of political violence in the country. At least six Parliament members and 3,000 followers of the Awami League Party had been killed in the last year, apparently for political motives, according to government officials.

See also APPOINTMENTS & RESIGNATIONS; FAMINE & FOOD; INDIA; PAKISTAN; UNITED NATIONS [2]; WEATHER

BANKS & BANKING—Credit policy and interest rates. Federal Reserve Board Chairman Arthur F. Burns reaffirmed, in an April 22 news conference, the board's firm monetary policy against inflation despite soaring interest rates and their impact on the housing industry. Burns emphasized his concern about an excessive expansion of the money supply. "We're having a veritable explosion of business loans," he said. "We aren't going to get inflation under control if that continues." Preliminary figures released by the Federal Reserve Bank of New York April 4 had indicated that commercial and industrial loans made by 12 major New York banks in the previous week had expanded by $736 million, or just under another record set in June 1970. Reserve figures for the week ending June 19 showed that commercial and industrial loans made by the leading New York banks rose $719 million. For the week ending June 26, there was a $551 million increase. That figure nearly doubled the following week when loans increased $1.1 billion. It was the fourth consecutive weekly advance for the period ending July 3, bringing the total of loans outstanding to a level $6 billion above that set 12 months earlier.

The Federal Reserve attempted to dampen the demand for business loans through a policy of limiting expansion of the nation's money supply. As a result, prime interest rates climbed during the first half of the year. The 8.75% rate of March 15 was followed by 9%, March 20. By April 8, the rate had reached 10%; by May 3, 11%; by July 3, 12%. Continued heavy demand for bank loans by corporations and high interest rates on the short-term money market accounted for the upward pressure on the prime. Increasing prime rates were reflected in consumer loan rates. Four major banks in New York announced June 4 and June 14 that they had increased lending rates for consumer installment loans ranging from 1-1.6%. The increases were the first made by New York banks on unsecured personal loans in nearly five years.

The credit markets were in such a slump that the concept of disintermediation could be said to apply, according to the *Wall Street Journal* June 26. Disintermediation occurred when depositors withdrew funds from savings and loan institutions or banks in order to obtain higher interest rates on the short-term money market, disrupting the normal circulation of money by depriving the market of money to lend as mortgages and other forms of loans. The lending operations of savings and loan institutions were especially hampered by this process. Analysts also believed that other institutions, such as the long-term bond and equity markets, were now being disintermediated, the *Journal* reported.

The prime interest rate charged by banks on loans to major corporate borrowers registered its first significant decline since March when Morgan Guaranty Trust Co., the nation's fifth largest bank, lowered its base lending rate a quarter point to 11.75% Sept. 25. The move toward lower rates did not spread quickly, however. The nation's two largest banks, Bank of America and First National City, which announced cutbacks to 11.75% Oct. 4, waited until the Federal Reserve had reported Oct. 3 that most money market interest rates were continuing to decline. Although the demand for business loans rose sharply by $496 million in the week ending Oct. 2 (after showing moderation in recent months from the peak borrowing record set during the first half of 1974), the Federal Reserve also reported a strong slowdown in the growth of the nation's money supply. The money supply (total demand deposits plus cash in public hands) expanded at an annual rate of 1.3% in the quarter ending Sept. 25, compared with a 6% growth rate posted during the first half of 1974. (Growth slowed to 1% at an annual rate in the three months ending Oct. 2.) First National City announced Oct. 11 that its prime had been cut to 11.5%. A slackening of corporate loan demand in the week ending Oct. 9, when borrowing rose by only $64 million, also contributed to the reduction in the prime rate and optimism that the nation's tight money situation was easing. Drain on deposits from savings banks also slowed. First National City continued to lead the banking industry in lowering its prime rate during November. Citibank officials announced Nov. 15 that its minimum interest rate would be set at 10.25% and on Nov. 22, announced a further reduction to 10%—its lowest rate since mid-April. Citibank had initiated the rate reduction for eight consecutive weeks. Few other major banks followed suit, but the 10.5% prime rate was adopted throughout the industry by Nov. 22.

As the threat of recession grew, the Federal Reserve signaled its intention to further ease its tight money policy by announcing Dec. 6 that the discount rate charged on loans to member banks in two regions had been reduced from 8% to 7.75%. A reduction in the discount rate was expected to apply soon to the Federal Reserve's 10 other regions. The action was taken hours after the government announced a sharp increase in the nation's unemployment rate to 6.5%. Bank reserve requirements were altered Nov. 18. The new reserve requirement was raised from 5% to 6% on all deposits maturing in less than six months and reduced to 3% on large deposits that matured in six months or more. It was expected that $760 million in idle reserves would be freed for use as a result of the latest changes.

Eximbank to end fixed loan rate. The U.S. Export-Import Bank announced July 8 that its fixed interest rate policy was being abandoned and replaced with a system of flexible rates ranging from 7%-8.5%. The new policy was the result of tight money conditions and Congressional criticism stemming from the fact that the rate was considerably below the prime interest rate available to major U.S. businesses. Legislators accused the Eximbank of subsidizing foreign borrowers in their purchase of U.S. goods and services. Eximbank Chairman William J. Casey said the bank would also seek to limit its participation in export transactions in an effort to make the bank's resources go further.

West German bank closed. Bankhaus I. D. Herstatt of Cologne, one of West Germany's largest private banks, was officially ordered liquidated June 26 because of heavy foreign exchange trading losses. Herstatt was the first bank to collapse because of the current instability in foreign exchange trading. The West German Banking Federation said Herstatt's small depositors with accounts up to DM 20,000 (about $8,000) would get all their money back and bigger depositors would eventually be reimbursed for about 75%. Non-German banks were caught in uncompleted foreign exchange transactions in which the banks transferred West German marks to Herstatt but did not receive their payment in dollars before the bank was ordered liquidated. Among these were the Morgan Guaranty Trust Co. of New York, and the First National Bank Zurich, a subsidiary of the Seattle First National Bank. The Bundesbank (central bank), which together with West Germany's supervisory bureau for banking ordered the closure, said Herstatt had gone heavily into debt on the foreign exchange trading, which "appeared incorrectly in the bank's books." The Cologne public prosecutor announced June 27 it was investigating possible fraud. (Estimated losses of the bank were put at $200 million as of July 1.) The Chase Manhattan Bank, international clearing agent for Herstatt, asked a U.S. federal court in New York July 15 to decide how it should allocate $156 million it held in Herstatt's account. Chase said claims against Herstatt's account could total up to $1 billion. First National City Bank (Citibank) announced Aug. 6 that it and other institutions had petitioned the U.S. federal court in New York to declare Herstatt bankrupt under U.S. laws. Citibank said the petition was aimed at protecting the interests of Herstatt's creditors and assuring equitable distribution of Herstatt's assets in the U.S. The Allgemeine Wirtschaftsbank of Vienna closed as a result of excessive withdrawals of deposits since the collapse of the Herstatt, it was reported Sept. 4. At the end of 1973, Allgemeine Wirtschaftsbank had assets of about $50 million.

A majority of Herstatt's creditors, at a mass meeting in Cologne Dec. 17, approved a settlement of their claims against the bank; as a result, Hans Gerling, a major shareholder of the Herstatt bank, would not undertake bankruptcy proceedings. The settlement plan, agreed upon Nov. 12, called for creation of a special compensation fund totaling DM325 million (about $133 million), of which Gerling would contribute DM210 million and German banking associations the rest. The fund would be combined with Herstatt's assets of DM984 million for settlement of claims by the 15,000 still unsatisfied creditors, with domestic banks to receive 45% reimbursement, foreign banks and local authorities 55% and nonbank creditors 65%.

Swiss bank closed, Israeli scandal. The International Credit Bank of Geneva announced Oct. 9 it had closed, pending a Swiss court ruling on its request for a payments moratorium, because certain bank clients had withdrawn large holdings after "unfounded" press reports of liquidity difficulties. The bank's majority shareholder, Hungarian-born Swiss financier Tibor Rosenbaum, was a major figure in an Israeli financial scandal in which an investment company, of which Rosenbaum was a large shareholder, had placed unauthorized deposits in an international company owned by him and registered in Liechtenstein.

Franklin declared insolvent. Franklin National Bank of New York was declared insolvent Oct. 8 by James Smith, comptroller of the currency, who named the Federal Deposit Insurance Corp. (FDIC) receiver to arrange a take-over of Franklin's assets and liabilities. The FDIC had accepted secret bids that morning from four major New York banks. After the close of banking hours, when Franklin's insolvency was declared, the FDIC named European-American Bank & Trust Co. as the winner in the take-over bidding. European-American was a federally insured bank, chartered in New York State and owned by six of Europe's largest banks—Amsterdam-Rotterdam Bank N.V., the Netherland's largest bank; Creditanstalt Bankverein, Austria's largest; Deutsche Bank A.G., West Germany's largest; Midland Bank Ltd., a major London clearing bank; Societe Generale de Banque S.A., Belgium's largest bank; and Societe Generale, one of the largest banks in France. European-American, which prior to the take-over had only three New York offices and deposits of $480 million, paid $125 million for Franklin and promised to assume its $1.7 billion in liabilities. Under arrangements made with the FDIC, all of Franklin's deposits were fully protected and automatically transferred to European-American, which also pledged to operate all of Franklin's 104 branch offices. European-American, which had been the 190th largest bank in terms of deposits, advanced to 48th rank after the take-over. Franklin, which had ranked 20th among the 14,000 federally insured banks, was the largest bank ever to fail in U.S. history. Prior to the take-over, the Federal Reserve announced that it had assumed responsibility for Franklin's $800 million portfolio of foreign exchange commitments. According to a government spokesman Sept. 26, the move was intended to restore confidence in the foreign exchange market, which had been badly shaken by Franklin's huge losses in currency trading and the recent collapse of a major West German bank. The Securities and Exchange Commission (SEC) filed fraud charges Oct. 17 against Franklin New York Corp., the former holding company of the Franklin National Bank, and nine of the firm's former officers, directors and employes. The civil suit, filed with U.S. District Court in New York after a five-month investigation, sought an injunction against further alleged violations of federal securities laws. The SEC complaint followed Franklin New York's filing of bankruptcy proceedings Oct. 16. The firm's chief asset had been the bank.

Bank Secrecy Act upheld. The Supreme Court April 1 upheld the 1970 Bank Secrecy Act, which gave the government broad access to bank customer records. Justice William H. Rehnquist, writing for the 6-3 majority, cited "the heavy utilization of our domestic banking system by the minions of organized crime." Justices William O. Douglas, William J. Brennan Jr. and Thurgood Marshall all wrote dissenting opinions. Douglas warned that a government agent could invade an individual's private life merely by scrutinizing the checks he wrote. Marshall conceded that law enforcement officials would be aided by the "dragnet requirements" of the act, but added, "Those who wrote our Constitution, however, recognized more important values." Under regulations established by the Treasury Department, banks were required to record all customer checks and microfilm those over $100, keep records of depositor's identities and all loans over $5,000 except mortgages, and report domestic deposits or withdrawals larger than $10,000 and foreign financial transactions exceeding $5,000. The regulation of foreign transactions was aimed at preventing leakage of untaxed money to secret Swiss bank accounts.

See also ECONOMY, U.S. [3, 5, 13, 15]; GREAT BRITAIN [27]; ITALY [8]; MONETARY DEVELOPMENTS [12, 22, 24-26]; OIL [31-32]; PAKISTAN; SWITZERLAND; TAXES; UNION OF SOVIET SOCIALIST REPUBLICS [7]

BARBADOS—*See* SUGAR

BARKER, BERNARD—*See* CAMPAIGN FINANCING [17]; WATERGATE AFFAIR [78, 80, 83, 86]

BASEBALL—A's win 3rd World Series. The Oakland A's became the first team in 21 years to win the World Series three years in a row Oct. 17, defeating the Los Angeles Dodgers 4-1 in the best-of-seven game championship. The Dodgers had entered the first all-California series as favorites against the A's, whose winning percentage had slumped in the final month of the season. (According to published reports, the A's were also beset by internal dissension.) But Oakland's poise and pitching vexed the Dodgers' hitting attack, limiting it to 11 runs-batted-in for the five games. Indicative of Oakland's expert pitching was the selection of Oakland relief pitcher Rollie Fingers as most valuable player. Fingers was credited with saves in games four and five, as well as a victory in the first game. Alvin Dark managed Oakland and Walter Alston piloted the Dodgers. (Los Angeles had defeated Pittsburgh in the National League pennant playoffs. Oakland had defeated Baltimore to win the American League pennant.)

NL wins All-Star game. The National League (NL) won the 45th All-Star game July 23, overpowering the American League (AL) 7-2 before 50,706 fans at Three Rivers Stadium in Pittsburgh. The AL had won only one of the last 13 games.

Aaron breaks Ruth's record. Henry Aaron, 40, broke Babe Ruth's record for career home runs April 8 when he hit a pitch thrown by Los Angeles Dodger pitcher Al Downing over the left field fence of Atlanta Stadium. The home run was his 715th. Aaron ended the season with a total of 733. The Atlanta Braves star had tied the record April 4 in Cincinnati on a pitch thrown by Jack Billingham of the Reds. The blast came during Aaron's first appearance at bat in the 1974 season. Ruth, who died in 1948, played 22 seasons, got into 2,503 games and was at bat 8,399 times. Aaron broke the record in his 21st season, on his 11,295th time at bat and in his 2,967th game. Aaron was traded by the Braves to the AL Milwaukee Brewers Nov. 2. Aaron subsequently signed a two-year contract with the Brewers.

Brock breaks stolen base record. By stealing second base against the Philadelphia Phillies Sept. 10, Lou Brock 35, broke the major league record of 104 stolen bases in one season, set by Maury Wills of the Los Angeles Dodgers in 1962. The St. Louis Cardinal outfielder finished the year with 118 thefts.

Cleveland names black manager. Frank Robinson, 39, was named major league baseball's first black manager by the Cleveland Indians Oct. 3. Robinson, the only player to win the most valuable player award in both major leagues (1961 and 1966), was given a one-year contract as a player-manager with a salary of $175,000. Through 19 seasons, Robinson had a career batting average of .295, with 574 home runs, 2,900 hits and 1,778 runs batted in. He replaced manager Ken Aspromonte, who was fired by the Indians Sept. 27.

Hunter ruled a free agent. Jim (Catfish) Hunter, winner of the AL's 1974 Cy Young award, was declared a free agent Dec. 16 by a three-member arbitration panel. Hunter had sought binding arbitration in a dispute with Charles O. Finley, owner of the Oakland A's, who, Hunter claimed, had not lived up to the terms of his contract. Under the terms of Hunter's 1974 contract, Finley had agreed to pay his pitcher $100,000: $50,000 was to be paid to Hunter as straight salary and the remaining $50,000 was to be put into a tax-deferrable plan of Hunter's choice. By the end of the season, Finley apparently had yet to pay any money into the tax-deferred plan. Hunter argued that his contract had been broken. Finley denied violating the contract, calling the situation merely a difference of interpretation. He offered a lump sum payment of $50,000. AL President Lee MacPhail agreed with Finley that no free agent question was involved. Hunter subsequently invoked his right to binding arbitration contained in the Baseball Players' Association's contract with the major league owners. The result was a 2-1 ruling ordering Oakland to pay Hunter $50,000 and 6% interest, figured since Aug. 1, on the amount until it was paid. The panel also upheld Hunter's claim that he was now a free agent. The panel's impartial arbitrator, Peter Seitz, and Marvin J. Miller, head of the players' association, voted for Hunter. John J. Gaherin, attorney for the baseball owners, cast his ballot against Hunter. Hunter signed a five-year pact with the New York Yankees Dec. 31. The contract's total value, including salary, deferred compensation and legal fees, was reported at $3.75 million.

Six named to Hall of Fame. Mickey Mantle and Whitey Ford, former New

York Yankee stars, were elected to the Baseball Hall of Fame, it was announced Jan. 16. Mantle was only the seventh player to be elected in his first year of eligibility (five years after retirement as an active player). Ford, a pitcher, compiled the highest win-loss percentage (.690) in modern major league history. Named to the Hall of Fame by the Negro Baseball Selection Committee Feb. 13 was James (Cool Papa) Bell, a renowned base stealer and hitter, whose 26-year career was spent in the Negro Leagues during the 1920s, '30s, and '40s. Jim Bottomley, Sam Thompson and Jocko Conlon were elected to the Hall of Fame by the Veterans Committee, it was announced Jan. 28.

Garvey, Burroughs named MVPs. Steve Garvey, first baseman for the Los Angeles Dodgers, was named the NL's most valuable player (MVP) by the Baseball Writers Association of America Nov. 12. Garvey batted .312 for the season, hit 21 home runs and batted in 111 runs. Jeff Burroughs, a Texas Ranger outfielder, was named the AL MVP by the baseball writers Nov. 21. In 1974, Burroughs averaged .301, hit 25 home runs and batted in 118 runs.

Little League bars foreigners. Little League Baseball Inc. said Nov. 11 that future Little League world series would be open only to teams from the continental U.S. The announcement meant that teams from Taiwan and Japan, which had won seven of the last eight championships, would be excluded. Reasons for the ban, a Little League spokesman said, were travel costs for foreign teams and nationalistic approaches taken abroad. Taiwan's recent domination of the championship—open to boys aged 8 to 12—had resulted in an investigation of the island's baseball program, but no violations of Little League rules were found.

See also CAMPAIGN FINANCING [23]; OBITUARIES [DEAN, HOOPER, TOPPING, WEBB]; WOMEN'S RIGHTS

BASKETBALL—Celtics win NBA title. The Boston Celtics won their 12th National Basketball Association (NBA) championship in 18 years May 12, defeating the Milwaukee Bucks 102-87. Victorious in the finals, four games to three, the Celtics beat the Bucks three times on their home court, the Milwaukee Arena, an unusual accomplishment in a sport in which the host team generally had an advantage. Boston had reached the finals by eliminating Buffalo in the quarterfinals and New York in the semifinal playoffs. Milwaukee defeated Chicago in the semifinals and Los Angeles in the quarterfinals.

Kareem Abdul-Jabbar, center for the Bucks, had been named the NBA's most valuable player March 20. The game-dominating play of Jabbar enabled the Bucks to reach the NBA playoff finals despite injuries to key players.

Nets take ABA title. The New York Nets defeated the Utah Stars 111-100 May 10 to give them a 4-1 victory in the best of seven American Basketball Association (ABA) championship finals. In gaining the finals, the Nets had eliminated their semifinal opponent, the Kentucky Colonels, in four straight games, and their quarterfinal rivals, the Virginia Squires, four games to one. Utah had reached the finals by defeating Indiana in the semifinals and San Diego in the quarterfinals. Net forward Julius Erving was named most valuable player in the finals. Erving, who had led the ABA in scoring with a 27.3 points a game average, was selected the league's most valuable player in voting announced April 8.

North Carolina State dethrones UCLA. North Carolina State University defeated Marquette University 76-64 March 24 in Greensboro, N.C. to win the National Collegiate Athletic Association (NCAA) championship. In a critical semifinal match in Los Angeles March 23, North Carolina had defeated UCLA 80-77. It was the first time in eight years that UCLA had failed to win the NCAA title.

(UCLA's consecutive winning streak had been ended at 88 games when Notre Dame defeated the Bruins 71-70 on Jan. 19.)

ABA franchises change. Mike Storen resigned as ABA commissioner July 17, after purchasing the financially troubled Memphis franchise from the ABA, which had redeemed the team from owner Charles O. Finley for an undisclosed price June 20. Replacing Storen as commissioner was Tedd Munchak, who had sold his own ABA franchise, the Carolina Cougars, to a group of New York City businessmen. They in turn transferred the franchise to St. Louis and renamed the team the Spirits. The Memphis Tams had been provisionally sold to Stax Records, Inc. of Memphis, but the deal fell through.

Schoolboy signs pro pact. Moses Malone, 19, the Petersburg, Va. high school basketball superstar who was offered more than 300 college scholarships, signed a seven-year professional contract to play with the Utah Stars of the ABA Aug. 29. The signing of Malone by the Stars, who reportedly gave him a package with a potential value of $3 million, ended a battle between the ABA team and the University of Maryland, which had hoped that Malone would make good on a previously signed but nonbinding letter of intent to attend Maryland. (Although Malone chose to bypass college for professional sports, the Stars included a $120,000 scholarship fund in his contract. He would receive $30,000 for each year of college he attended in the off season.)

Black deputy NBA commissioner. Simon Gourdine, an attorney, became the highest ranking black administrator in professional sports Nov. 7, when the NBA board of governors named him deputy commissioner. Gourdine, 34, previously had been vice president of administration for the NBA.

See also OBITUARIES [ALLEN]

BAUXITE—*See* ALUMINUM; GUYANA; JAMAICA

BELGIUM—Government crisis. The year-old government of Premier Edmond Leburton resigned Jan. 19 following an economic crisis precipitated by the failure of a projected pact with Iran to build a $200 million oil refinery near Liege. A new government was not formed until April 25, 96 days later. Leburton's government had been composed of a coalition of the Christian Social Party, Socialists and Liberals. Christian Social Party members and the Liberals had thought the refinery uneconomical. The project had nevertheless been approved Jan. 16, on condition that the National Iranian Oil Co. (NIOC) give new guarantees on the price and supply of oil for the refinery. Iran, however, replied that Belgium had failed to meet a Jan. 15 deadline for a final decision and cancelled the project Jan. 18.

Following resignation of the government, King Baudouin asked Leo Tindemans, leader of the Flemish wing of the Christian Social Party, to form a new government. The party's French wing opposed Tindemans, however, because of his plan for formation of regional economic councils. Tindemans' failure to form a new government led the King to dissolve Parliament on Jan. 29 and call for new elections. Major issues in the campaign were economic policy and federalism, a movement which demanded reform of the state structure to give more independence to the three language units of Belgium: French-speaking Wallonia, Dutch-speaking Flanders and bilingual Brussels. The Christian Social Party took a moderate stand on both the economic and federalism issues.

The Christian Social Party remained the country's strongest, after the March 10 elections, winning 32.3% of the vote for a total of 72 Chamber of Representatives seats, an increase of five since the November 1971 elections. The election results divided the Chamber as follows (1971 results in parentheses):

Liberals 30 (31); Socialists 58 (60); French-speaking Democratic Front-Walloon Union (FDF-RW) and dissident Brussels liberals 25 (27); Flemish-speaking Volksunie 22 (21); and Communists 4 (5). Senate results were: Christian Social 37 (34); Liberals 16 (15); Socialists 29 (30); FDF-RW 13 (14); Volksunie 10 (12); and Communists 1 (1).

Following the elections, and another failure to form a coalition government, the government crisis ended on April 25 when a minority Christian Social-Liberal Cabinet was installed. Tindemans assumed the premiership and left unchanged most of the major ministries. The new Cabinet consisted of 16 Christian Social Party members and 9 Liberals. The major newcomer in the government was majority party member Andre Oleffe who was also a leader of the Christian Workers' movement. Oleffe became economic affairs minister. Renaat van Elslande remained foreign affairs minister.

Premier Tindemans' minority government gained a narrow majority in the Chamber June 10 when the French-language federalist party, the Walloon Union, agreed to join the coalition. It was the first time one of Belgium's three federalist parties had joined the government. Tindemans had also sought to bring the other two federalist parties into the government, but the French-speaking Democratic Front, a Brussels federalist ally of the Walloon Union, and the Dutch-speaking Volksunie remained deadlocked over the language dispute in Brussels. Tindemans needed all three groups to give his Cabinet the two-thirds parliamentary majority required to pass constitutional reforms. Tindemans appointed five new Cabinet ministers June 11, including three from the Walloon Union. Among the newcomers was Walloon Union President Francois Perin, named minister of institutional reforms, and Joseph Michel, a member of the French-speaking wing of the Christian Social Party, named interior minister. The newly-enlarged government won a 108-79 vote of confidence in the Chamber June 14.

Regional autonomy law adopted. The Chamber of Representatives adopted a bill July 20, by a 109-77 vote, to set up regional assemblies and executive administrations for Wallonia, Flanders and Brussels. The Senate had passed the bill the previous week. The new bodies would have the authority only to advise the national Parliament on regional issues. Premier Tindemans had initially proposed a law that would shift full legislative power in regional matters to the new assemblies, but he lacked the two-thirds parliamentary majority required under the Constitution to make such a change.

Oil prices raised. The government May 10 increased gasoline and heating oil prices 10%, effective May 15, ending a bitter dispute with several international oil companies over their price increase demands. The dispute had begun in February when the outgoing government of Premier Leburton froze oil prices until the end of April in a move designed to win votes in the forthcoming election. (In its campaign, the Socialist Party focused on the need for stronger state control over industry.) The oil companies had demanded a price increase of $50 a ton on refined products, including a rise of 16¢-20¢ a gallon on gasoline. To protest the price curbs, some of the major multinational oil companies barred crude oil imports to Belgium, the *Wall Street Journal* reported March 12. Among the firms mentioned in the report were the British Petroleum Co. and the local subsidiary of Brussels-based Petrofina S.A., while a Belgium unit of Continental Oil Co. (U.S.) and an affiliate of the Cie. Francaise des Petroles of France were said to have suspended all distribution of petroleum products in Belgium. An interim $31 a ton across-the-board increase for refined oil products had gone into effect April 1. The May price rise, while still lower than those demanded by the oil firms, would bring the price of high octane gasoline to $1.62 a gallon.

Army reform adopted. Parliament approved a government plan to reorganize the army, it was reported Aug. 19. The current 12-month term of conscripts would be gradually reduced to six months in 1978, while the government would increase the number of professional soldiers and assign only professionals to the 10,000-man Belgian unit in West Germany. The reform was considered a first step toward creating an all-regular fighting force.

Bank discloses losses. Banque de Bruxelles, Belgium's second largest bank, disclosed Oct. 13 it had discovered "irregular, unrecorded and unauthorized" transactions by some members of its foreign exchange staff. The bank said it had given its findings to judicial authorities. A spokesman stressed that the bank's internal reserves were adequate to cover any losses. The merger of Banque de Bruxelles and Banque Lambert, subject to shareholder approval, was announced Dec. 5.

See also ALGERIA; APPOINTMENTS & RESIGNATIONS; AUTO RACING; CHILE [24]; COMMUNISM, INTERNATIONAL; EUROPEAN ECONOMIC COMMUNITY [2-4]; EUROPEAN SECURITY; FAMINE & FOOD; MONETARY DEVELOPMENTS [4, 11, 17]; NORTH ATLANTIC TREATY ORGANIZATION; OIL [26-27, 34]; SPAIN [11]; UNITED NATIONS [11]; ZAIRE

BERLIN—*See* GERMANY, WEST [8-13, 17]

BHUTAN—Jigme Singhi Wangchuk, 18, was crowned king of Bhutan June 2 in the capital city of Thimbu. The coronation took place one day after a "series of sinister plots" to assassinate him was reported. The young monarch succeeded his father, King Jigme Dorji Wangchuk, who died in 1972. According to a government announcement, more than 30 alleged conspirators had been arrested. The plotters, led by "Gyalo Thendhup, a well-known Tibetan residing in Darjeeling, India," had planned to kill the monarch, apparently to take over the country, the statement said.

BICENTENNIAL—The Senate confirmed the nomination of Navy Secretary John W. Warner, 46, as administrator of the new American Revolution Bicentennial Administration March 13. President Nixon had submitted the nomination to the Senate March 11. The appointment resulted from a reorganization of the controversial Bicentennial Commission, formerly headed by David J. Mahoney, chief executive for Norton Simon Inc. Mahoney had resigned Dec. 26, 1973 after serving a chairman for three years. Critics of the Bicentennial Commission had accused the 50-member board of allowing partisanship and commercialism to taint the planned celebrations.

BICYCLES—*See* CONSUMER AFFAIRS [8]
BIOLOGICAL WEAPONS—*See* CHEMICAL & BIOLOGICAL WEAPONS
BIOLOGY—*See* NARCOTICS & DANGEROUS DRUGS; NOBEL PRIZES; MEDICINE & HEALTH [14]

BIRTH CONTROL—G. D. Searle & Co. May 22 released a preliminary report on a large-scale British study of the effects of the oral contraceptive pill. Financed by Searle, the first company to market the pill in 1960, the study by the Royal College of General Practitioners was begun in 1968 and involved 46,000 British women. According to the report, users of the pill faced distinct, though rare, health risks including blood clots in the legs, high blood pressure and greater than normal incidences of chicken pox and other viral infections such as stomach flu. The report suggested the pill suppressed residual viral childhood immunities.

Pope Paul VI March 29 reaffirmed the church's unequivocal opposition to birth control in a message delivered during an audience for United Nations officials. A confidential Vatican document outlining a church campaign against governments and international agencies (widely believed to be U.N. groups) supporting birth control efforts had been made public March 11 by church sources opposed to the Vatican position.

A federal grand jury in New Orleans returned a seven-count indictment April 2 against the Family Health Foundation (FHF) and five of its current or former officials. The FHF was accused of defrauding the U.S. government of $2,097,000 through false claims made to the Department of Health, Education and Welfare. FHF operated family planning clinics for indigent women in all the state's parishes and was also helping medical programs in Latin America.

See also ABORTION; HUNGARY; MEDICINE & HEALTH [3, 19]; OBITUARIES [GUTTMACHER]; POPULATION; RELIGION [16]; WELFARE & POVERTY

BITTMAN, WILLIAM O.—*See* WATERGATE [21]
BLACK PANTHER PARTY—*See* CRIME [27]; RADICALS
BLACKS—*See* CIVIL RIGHTS; ELECTIONS [2]; INTELLIGENCE; POLITICS [6-8, 12]; POPULATION; PRIVACY [9-10]; RADICALS
BLIZZARDS—*See* WEATHER

BOATING—The Oxford University varsity crew team defeated Cambridge University by more than five lengths in their 149th race on the Thames River in London April 6. Oxford, which ended a six-year Cambridge victory streak, set a new record time of 17 minutes 35 seconds for the 4½-mile course.

Courageous, a 12-meter sloop, successfully defended the America's Cup Sept. 17, defeating its Australian challenger *Southern Cross*. In the best-of-seven race competition over a 23.4-mile course off Newport, R.I., *Courageous* routed *Southern Cross* 4-0 to assure U.S. retention of the 123-year-old trophy.

BOLIVIA—Opposition under pressure. Forces opposed to the conservative regime of President Hugo Banzer Suarez were under intense government pressure in early 1974. Ex-President Victor Paz Estenssoro was expelled from the country Jan. 8, six weeks after he ordered members of his Revolutionary Nationalist Movement (MNR) to withdraw from the military-civilian government. Departing for Paraguay, Paz Estenssoro said Jan. 9 that neither he nor his party had participated in the subversive activities with which they were charged. Bolivian leftists had suffered greatly as a result of the Chilean military coup. Many had been jailed, shot or dispersed to different countries by the Chilean junta, which was aided in this work by the Bolivian police. Simon Reyes, the miners' leader and Communist party official, was in a Santiago prison; ex-President Juan Jose Torres was in Argentina; and other Bolivians were hiding in foreign embassies, including Maj. Ruben Sanchez in the Honduran embassy.

Fears of Brazilian penetration. Foreign Minister Gen. Alberto Guzman said the government was worried about Brazilian penetration of Bolivia and reports from Venezuela of a Brazilian plan for territorial expansion, the news agency LATIN reported Jan. 11. The newsletter *Latin America* reported Jan. 18 that the Bolivian government was investigating allegations that Brazilian banks had been taking over land and property in Bolivia by lending money to peasants in frontier areas at high interest rates, and foreclosing when the peasants could not keep up the payments.

Food shortage, price hikes protested. Workers around the country struck and clashed with police Jan. 21-24 to protest a food shortage and sharp increases in the price of sugar, rice, flour, bread, noodles and coffee. The price hikes, some as high as 100%, were ordered by the government Jan. 21 to alleviate the food shortage, caused by producers and merchants who smuggled their wares into neighboring countries where prices were up to twice as high as in Bolivia. A general wage increase of some $20 a month was decreed along with the price increases, but was rejected by workers as too small. The government, blaming the strikes on alleged subversives, announced the arrest of members of the National Liberation Army guerrilla group, the Communist Party and the Revolutionary Left Movement. President Banzer met Jan. 25 with miners' representatives, but they rejected his offer of a 25% wage adjustment in addition to the earlier $20 increase. The government Jan. 30 crushed a six-day protest by more than 10,000 peasants against the food shortage and recent price increases. Armed farm workers on Jan. 25 had cut off sections of the roads linking Cochabamba with Santa Cruz, La Paz and Oruro, preventing supplies from getting through. Road-clearing operations began Jan. 29 and were completed the next day.

Banzer had appeared on nationwide radio and television Jan. 28 to announce a state of siege, which suspended all constitutional rights, established a strict curfew, and gave sweeping powers to the police and armed forces. Before Banzer's address, Interior Minister Walter Castro told newsmen the protest was part of a plot hatched by Bolivian and other Latin American extremists at a recent meeting in France.

As an immediate result of the unrest President Banzer made his first Cabinet changes of the year, reducing it from 18 to 16 members with the merger of the Agriculture and Peasant Affairs Ministries and abolition of the Ministry of State. Four officials resigned; two new ministers—both army officers—were named; two ministers shifted posts and the others retained their posts. Among those dismissed were Interior Minister Castro and Peasant Affairs Minister Col. Ramon Azero, held responsible for the killing of some 100 peasants in the Cochabamba protest.

Opposition to Brazilian accord. Students at San Andres University in La Paz demonstrated May 21 when Brazilian President Ernesto Geisel arrived to witness the signing of a broad economic agreement between his government and Bolivia. Complete details of the agreement were not released, but it was known to provide for Bolivia to sell Brazil 240 million cubic feet of natural gas daily for 20 years, in return for Brazilian assistance in establishing a $600 million "pole of development" in southeastern Bolivia including a gas pipeline and steel, petrochemical and cement plants. The agreement was opposed by ex-Foreign Minister Walter Guevara Arce of the Authentic Revolutionary Party (PRA); Benjamin Miguel of the Christian Democratic Party (PDC); and Ramon Claure of the MNR. The PRA and PDC based their condemnation on the fact that the agreement might provoke the loss of eastern Bolivia to Brazil. Guevara, Miguel and Claure were subsequently expelled to Paraguay. The university strike ended June 18, after the government accepted 10 demands including the dismissal of the newly appointed military rector, Col. Jose Antonio Zelaya. Writer Jorge Siles Salinas was named rector until elections could be held.

Coup attempt fails. On June 4, members of the Tarapaca armored regiment attacked the presidential palace in La Paz, and broadcast a radio communique claiming they were in control of the government. However, they retreated to their barracks and surrendered after the palace guard gave them one hour to withdraw. The government announced June 5 that the revolt had been crushed. The rebel communique was signed by Lt. Cols. Raul Lopez Leyton and Gary Prado Salmon, who reportedly had links with the MNR. The communique said the revolt was "strictly military," but MNR leader Ciro Humboldt apparently took refuge in the Peruvian embassy. (Humboldt, who had assumed MNR leadership after the January expulsion of ex-President Estenssoro, had accused the former party head of having "greatly jeopardized party unity." Humboldt had also rejected the ex-president's call for the MNR to abandon the military-civilian government.) Twenty-four armed officers, including Prado Salmon and Lopez Leyton, were dismissed from the service June 7. Government officials said Lopez Leyton had received political asylum in the Argentine embassy, while Prado Salmon and two other rebel officers had been expelled to Paraguay, according to reports June 9.

Further Cabinet changes; elections pledged. An all-military Cabinet was sworn in July 8 after President Banzer had toured Bolivian military garrisons to determine the extent of support for leaders of the attempted June coup. He reportedly had found the armed forces divided, with many officers strongly opposed to his rule. Although both MNR and FSB members were excluded from the new, all-military Cabinet, leaders of both parties expressed support for the president. Banzer submitted his resignation Aug. 30 but withdrew it later the same day at the request of the armed forces, according to the chairman of the joint chiefs of staff, Gen. Carlos Alcoreza Melgarejo. (Banzer announced July 29 that he would not run in the 1975 elections.) Banzer acted one day after one of his chief civilian supporters, Mario Gutierrez, leader of the Bolivian Socialist Falange (FSB), publicly urged that the 1975 elections be advanced and that amnesty be granted to all persons arrested or exiled in attempts to overthrow Banzer. The president opposed granting such an amnesty.

Opponents of Banzer's government were outraged by the formation Sept. 2 of the National Action Committee (CAN), a right-wing paramilitary force pledged to eradicate leftist extremism. The Christian Democratic Party charged Oct. 16 that the CAN was created by Banzer and, like the terrorist Argentine Anticommunist Alliance, was funded by the U.S. Central Intelligence Agency.

Military revolt crushed. Paratroopers under the command of President Banzer put down a revolt in Santa Cruz Nov. 7 by members of the 2nd Batallion of the army's "Manchego" Regiment, which specialized in anti-guerrilla operations, the government reported. Loyalist and rebel troops clashed several times in Santa Cruz and in Montero, 30 miles north, and loyalist jets bombed several parts of the city, officials said. Casualties were reported on both sides. The uprising was led by Gens. Julio Prado Montano and Orlando Alvarez, who were arrested, and by former Interior Minister Carlos Valverde, who escaped with other rebels into the jungles north of Santa Cruz, the government reported Nov. 8. It had charged Nov. 7 that the rebels were backed by former President Estenssoro. The armed forces officially took control of the country Nov. 9. A series of decrees issued under the state of siege, declared Nov. 7 when the rebellion began, gave the military full political and administrative powers until 1980. The elections scheduled for 1975 were canceled, and the activities of all political parties—including those that had participated in Banzer's government—were suspended. The right of assembly was revoked and the leaders of labor unions, professional associations and student groups were dismissed. Citizens over 21 years of age were required to perform civilian service for the government whenever it asked.

See also BRAZIL [2, 10]; LATIN AMERICA; MIDDLE EAST [23-26]; PERU [15]

BOOKS—National Book Awards. The 25th annual National Book Awards, given to American-authored books published in 1973 in the U.S., were presented in New York April 18. It was the second year in a row that the $1,000 fiction award was given to two authors. Thomas Pynchon's *Gravity's Rainbow* shared the prize with Isaac B. Singer's *A Crown of Feathers and Other Stories.* The other winners: **Poetry**—Allen Ginsberg for *The Fall of America: Poems of These States, 1965-71* and Adrienne Rich for *Diving Into the Wreck: Poems, 1971-72;*

History—John Clive for *Macaulay: The Shaping of the Historian;* **Biography**—Douglas Day for *Malcolm Lowry: A Biography;* **Arts & Letters**—Pauline Kael for *Deeper Into Movies;* **Children's Literature**—Eleanor Cameron for *The Court of the Stone Children;* **Philosophy & Religion**—Maurice Natanson for *Edmund Husserl: Philosopher of Infinite Tasks;* **Sciences**—S. E. Laria for *Life: the Unfinished Experiment;* **Contemporary Affairs**—Murray Kempton for *The Briar Patch: The People of the State of New York v. Lumumba Shakur Et Al;* **Translation**—Karen Brazell for *The Confessions of Lady Nijo;* Helen R. Lane for Octavio Paz's *Alternating Current* and Jackson Mathews for Paul Valery's *Monsieur Teste.*

Major book publishers charged. The Justice Department accused 21 of the nation's largest book publishers of conspiring with a British publishing association to divide the English-speaking world into exclusive territories for book sales. The antitrust suit was filed Nov. 25 in U.S. District Court in New York. Publishers Association, which, according to the Justice Department included "virtually all" of the publishing firms in Great Britain, was named an unindicted co-conspirator in the case. According to the government, the defendants had maintained an illegal market allocation agreement with the British organization since 1947, in violation of the Sherman Act. The operation of the market allocation agreement insured that U.S. copyrighted books were sold in Britain only by British publishers and that British copyrighted books were sold in the U.S. only by U.S. publishers. The division of territories applied to approximately 70 countries, all present or former Commonwealth nations. If a U.S. publisher wished to market a book in Britain or in any of those countries, rights to produce, distribute and sell the book would be sold to a British firm. Conversely, British publishers agreed not to directly enter the U.S. market.

See also CENTRAL INTELLIGENCE AGENCY; CHINA, COMMUNIST; COPYRIGHT; EDUCATION; LABOR [16]; NOBEL PRIZES; PORTUGAL [5]; POSTAL SERVICE; PULITZER PRIZES; ROCKEFELLER [11-14]; SOLZHENITSYN, ALEXANDER; UNION OF SOVIET SOCIALIST REPUBLICS [16-19]; YUGOSLAVIA [6]; ZAIRE

BOTSWANA—President Sir Seretse Khama was returned to power for another five-year term in elections Oct. 27. Khama's party, the Botswana Democratic Party, increased its majority in the enlarged 32-seat National Assembly, while the opposition People's Party and the National Front each won two seats. Khama announced an extensive Cabinet shakeup Oct. 30.

See also RHODESIA; SOUTH AFRICA [11]

BOUMEDIENNE, HOUARI—*See* ALGERIA; FAMINE & FOOD; MIDDLE EAST [7]; TARIFFS & TRADE

BOUTEFLIKA, ABDELAZIZ—*See* ALGERIA; MIDDLE EAST [24]; TARIFFS & TRADE; UNITED NATIONS [2, 5-6, 12]

BOXING—Ali dethrones Foreman. Muhammad Ali regained his world heavyweight boxing title Oct. 30, when he knocked out George Foreman in the 8th round of their 15-round championship bout in Kinshasa, Zaire. Ali, 32, was a 3-1 underdog against Foreman, 25, who had previously encountered little trouble in disposing of other challengers to his crown. (Ali was named fighter of the year Dec. 17 by the Boxing Writers' Association.) Each fighter earned $5 million in Africa's first heavyweight title bout. The government of Zaire, which sponsored the fight, reportedly lost $4.1 million because closed-circuit television revenues in the U.S. and Canada were far below the $30 million-plus estimated by the promoters. The contest, scheduled for Sept. 25, was postponed when Foreman received a gash over his eye during a sparring session Sept. 16.

Foreman had previously met Ken Norton on March 26 in Caracas, winning the bout with a barrage of punches that rendered the heavyweight contender helpless in the 2nd round. Foreman, who had been named boxer of the year by the World Boxing Association Jan. 27, and by the Boxing Writer's Association March 3, was detained in Venezuela for five days following the bout for failing at first to pay taxes accruing from the fight.

Ali had met Joe Frazier Jan. 28 in New York. The 12-round fight, in which Ali won a unanimous decision, drew a record non-title gate. The fighters were fined $5,000 each Jan. 25 for a brawl which broke out between the two after a televised interview on ABC-TV.

Foster retires. Bob Foster, who successfully defended his world light-heavyweight boxing crown 14 times, retired from the ring Sept. 16, explaining that he no longer wished to battle the world sanctioning organizations. The World Boxing Council (WBC) in Mexico City had announced Aug. 9 that it had stripped Foster of his title for failing to sign a contract to defend against John Conteh, recognized by the WBC as the top contender for the championship.

See also CRIME [30]

BOYLE, W. A. (TONY)—*See* CRIME [23]
BRANDT, WILLY—*See* EUROPEAN ECONOMIC COMMUNITY [14]; GERMANY, EAST; GERMANY, WEST [1-5, 10]
BRASCO, REP. FRANK J.—*See* CRIME [16]

BRAZIL—Geisel elected president. Retired army Gens. Ernesto Geisel and Adalberto Pereira dos Santos were elected president and vice president of Brazil, respectively, by an electoral college vote Jan. 15. Their five-year terms began March 15. Geisel had been selected to succeed by former President Emilio G. Medici. Geisel had served on the Supreme Military Court where he was known as a stern judge in cases involving alleged subversion. The generals received 400 of 497 votes in the electoral college, composed of federal and provincial legislators and dominated by the government party, ARENA. Seventy-six electors voted for the candidates of the opposition Brazilian Democratic Movement (MDB), Ulysses Guimaraes and Barbosa Lima Sobrinho. Twenty-one electors, members of the MDB's "Authentic" faction, abstained in protest. Guimaraes had denounced the indirect electoral process shortly before the vote, calling on the government to hold direct popular elections.

[2] Geisel's March 15 inaugural address praised previous military governments for "laying the solid bases of the national renovation." Although he did not promise to restore democratic rule, Geisel expressed confidence "in an even more promising future of a broad national consensus around the magnificent aim of creating a just, prosperous and sovereign state." Among those present at the inauguration were Mrs. Richard M. Nixon and Gen. Augusto Pinochet Ugarte, president of the Chilean military junta. (Pinochet was denounced March 14 by Francisco Pinto, an opposition deputy from the impoverished northeastern state of Bahia, who charged the Chilean leader with promoting a "Brazil-Chile-Bolivia-Paraguay political axis," an alliance of Latin dictatorships. Pinto was arraigned before the Brazilian Supreme Court April 4, charged with violating the article of the national security law which forbade anyone to insult the leader of a country with which Brazil enjoyed normal diplomatic relations. He was sent to prison for six months Oct. 11.)

[3] **Censorship increases.** Press censorship, briefly relaxed following Geisel's inauguration, was more strictly imposed again, it was reported May 29. The leading news magazine, *Veja,* had been placed under direct government

censorship after it published a cartoon about political prisoners which allegedly displeased the armed forces. The opposition weekly *Opiniao* had half an issue cut by censors. Newspaper executives reportedly believed the new crackdown was part of a general toughening by Geisel under pressure from military hard-liners.

[4] **Church conflict.** Among Brazil's political problems was the continuing opposition to government policies by some segments of the Roman Catholic Church. The conflict had begun the previous year when the government closed two Catholic radio stations—Radio Nove de Julho in October 1973 and Radio Palmares in mid-December. The closing of Radio Nove de Julho, a Sao Paulo station, was interpreted as retaliation against Paulo Evaristo Cardinal Arns, archbishop of Sao Paulo, an outspoken champion of the rights of peasants in the Amazon region who were being evicted from their lands by the invasion of large development companies. On Jan. 26 Eugenio Cardinal de Araujo Sales, archbishop of Rio de Janiero, denounced the government's rightist policies. He also denied allegations made by the Most. Rev. Geraldo de Proenca Sigaud, archbishop of Diamantina, who had charged infiltration of leftists, Communists and pro-Communists in the Roman Catholic clergy. Meanwhile, more than 40 Roman Catholic laymen and women were arrested during January and February as security forces continued their crackdown on dissident, church-connected intellectuals' and workers' groups. According to the *Miami Herald* Feb. 22, some of those arrested were tortured. Arns met Feb. 19 with Gen. Couto e Silva, who would head Geisel's Cabinet after March 15. In this and other meetings church officials were told that the government was prepared to end abuses by the security services, lift press censorship and lessen social inequalities, but that it also wanted the church to exercise control over the declarations of bishops and priests. The church officials reportedly replied that each bishop was responsible for his own statements.

[5] **Arrests continue.** Arrests continued through the year, with as many as 200 persons arrested during April without charges against them being disclosed. According to the London newsletter *Latin America* April 26, the arrests reflected the difficulties President Geisel was experiencing in trying to carry out a softer line on civil liberties. Geisel reportedly wanted a political deal with the Roman Catholic Church, the universities and the press to improve the government's image. However, reactionary forces in the regime, notably a group of younger army officers, opposed any move toward a political settlement, *Latin America* reported. Federal Police Chief Gen. Antonio Bandeira resigned in what was seen as a possible move by Geisel to end police abuses, it was reported March 16. But reports that political prisoners continued to be tortured and to disappear persisted. *Latin America* reported April 26 that Sergio Fleury, a police officer who was allegedly the leader of a Sao Paulo "Death Squad," participated in interrogation of prisoners. Fleury had been imprisoned in October 1973 on chages of killing a drug peddler. He had been freed early in 1974. (According to police sources in Rio, a resurgence of Death Squad activity had accounted for 27 deaths in the first seven weeks of 1974.) Fleury was acquitted Nov. 23 of killing a petty criminal in 1969.

[6] U.S. Ambassador John Crimmins strongly protested to the Brazilian government Oct. 4 the torture of a U.S. citizen by police. Frederick B. Morris, a businessman and former Methodist minister living in Recife, was arrested Sept. 30 for alleged subversive activities. He told the U.S. consul in Recife, who visited him in prison, that he had been beaten by police and tortured with electric shocks "of high intensity," according to a U.S. embassy spokesman. The consul "saw bruises and contusions on Morris' back, buttocks and wrists," the spokesman said. Brazil rejected the charges Oct. 10.

[7] A new report smuggled out of Brazil and sent to various human rights organizations alleged that 78 persons had been tortured to death in Brazil for political reasons since 1969, the *New York Times* reported Nov. 4. The document, dated February 1974, was compiled by a group of lawyers, Roman Catholic militants, relatives of political prisoners and former prisoners, according to two of its members. Independent sources including priests, professors and journalists had corroborated its information, the *Times* reported.

[8] **Opposition wins elections.** The MDB soundly defeated the government's ARENA party in federal and state legislative elections Nov. 15. The elections were the freest in more than 10 years, with opposition candidates allowed to criticize the military regime on television and at public rallies. The results were widely interpreted as a repudiation of the government's economic and social policies, and a protest against an inflation rate estimated at 33%. Nevertheless, the vote was expected to have little direct impact on national policy. The federal legislatures were virtually powerless as the result of a series of "institutional decrees" that gave the executive branch dictatorial authority. However, state governors needed the approval of state legislatures on many decisions, making some amount of change possible on the local level. Final results of the Nov. 15 elections were announced by Justice Minister Armando Falcao Dec. 5. According to the count, the MDB would hold 20 seats in the Senate and 166 in the Chamber of Deputies when the two bodies convened in March 1975. The government's ARENA party would hold the other 46 Senate and 198 Chamber seats. MDB had previously held seven seats in the Senate and 87 in the Chamber.

[9] **Indian policy denounced.** Anthropologists and political activists attending a conference in the U.S. Nov. 8 accused multinational corporations of conspiring with the Brazilian government to drive Indian tribes from the Amazon River Basin to speed the industrial development of the area. Speakers at the meeting at the Brookings Institution in Washington, D.C. charged the companies and the Brazilian regime were effectively eliminating entire tribes by displacing them from their native grounds in the mineral-rich basin. The accused corporations included Litton Industries and General Motors Corp. of the U.S., Fiat of Italy, Komatsu of Japan and Alcan Aluminium of Canada, all of which were involved in the construction of roads in the Amazon area.

[10] **Meningitis epidemic.** An outbreak of meningitis, first confirmed by the government July 23, had claimed 2,000 lives by mid-October, with the death toll continuing to mount. Health Minister Paulo de Almeida Machado told state health secretaries that some 20,000 Brazilians had contracted the disease since January. The Health Ministry had not admitted the gravity of the situation until Aug. 7. Uruguay had closed its Brazilian border Aug. 1 to prevent the spread of the disease into its territory, and Paraguay began inspecting persons crossing its border after seven cases and one death from meningitis were reported there. Peru, Argentina and Bolivia also announced special health inspections of persons entering from Brazil, it was reported Aug. 6.

[11] **Economic developments.** The cost of living and the national trade deficit rose sharply during the first five months of 1974, forcing the government to institute economic controls and to devalue the cruzeiro four times, by a total of 9.62%. The government said the cost of living rose by about 18% in January-May, but unofficial sources claimed the increase was greater. The government took a number of steps to reduce the trade deficit, which rose to a record $2.1 billion in January-May, attributable largely to the high cost of imported oil. The accelerating cost of luxury imports also was a factor. Among the government measures was a 100% surcharge on these imports, ranging from cosmetics to liquor; and a ban on credit for foreign travel.

[12] **China ties set.** Brazil and China established diplomatic relations Aug. 15, agreeing to exchange ambassadors "as quickly as possible." Brazil recognized the Communist regime in Peking as the "only legal government of China" and "took note" of Peking's claim that Taiwan was part of China. The Taiwan government suspended relations with Brazil the next day, calling its recognition of Peking an unfriendly act.

[13] **Fire takes 189 lives.** A fire which started with a short-circuit in a 12th floor air conditioner, burned through the upper floors of the modern 25-story Crensul Investment Bank killing 189 of an estimated 600 employes, Feb. 1 in Sao Paulo. Inadequate fire prevention regulations were said to have attributed to the high speed at which the fire spread. The fire lasted only 25 minutes.

See also ARGENTINA [2]; AUTO RACING, BOLIVIA; CHILE [2, 26]; COFFEE; JAPAN [10-11]; LATIN AMERICA; MEXICO [21]; PORTUGAL [7]; SOCCER; SUGAR; WEATHER

BREAST CANCER—*See* FORD, BETTY; MEDICINE & HEALTH [23-25]; ROCKEFELLER, MARGARETTA

BREZHNEV, LEONID I.—*See* CHINA, COMMUNIST; COMMUNISM, INTERNATIONAL; CUBA; DISARMAMENT; FRANCE [10]; GERMANY, EAST; GERMANY, WEST [13]; MIDDLE EAST [42, 44, 46]; UNION OF SOVIET SOCIALIST REPUBLICS [2, 3, 17, 36]

BRIDGES—*See* NEPAL

BRINEGAR, CLAUDE S.—*See* APPOINTMENTS & RESIGNATIONS; AUTOMOBILE INDUSTRY [12]; AVIATION [2]

BROADCASTING—*See* TELEVISION & RADIO

BROWN, GEN. GEORGE S.—*See* APPOINTMENTS & RESIGNATIONS; DEFENSE [13]

BUDGET—Budget tops $300 billion. President Nixon submitted a new budget to Congress Feb. 4 with total federal outlays of $304.4 billion in fiscal 1975, $29.8 billion more than in fiscal 1974. It was the nation's first $300 billion budget. Fiscal 1975 receipts were estimated at $295 billion, a $25 billion increase over the previous year. The $9.4 billion deficit was pegged primarily to an anticipated economic slowdown cutting into the normal revenue. The increase in outlays was more fixed, with approximately 90% of the increase in mandatory spending areas, such as interest on the national debt and maintenance of the Social Security system. The budget did not suggest any increase in basic tax rates, aside from the already proposed plan to tax "windfall" profits of oil companies. Total corporate income tax revenue was estimated at $48 billion. The total income tax from individuals was expected to be $129 billion. The Social Security tax yield for fiscal 1975 was put at $72.5 billion. The new budget contained few new initiatives and few cutbacks of existing programs.

Budget Receipts

(In billions of dollars for the fiscal year)

	1973 actual	1974 estimate	1975 estimate
Individual income taxes	103.2	118.0	129.0
Corporation income taxes	36.2	43.0	48.0
Social insurance taxes and contributions (trust funds)	64.5	77.9	85.6
Excise taxes	16.3	17.1	17.4
Estate and gift taxes	4.9	5.4	6.0
Customs duties	3.2	3.5	3.8
Miscellaneous receipts	3.9	5.0	5.2
Total receipts	**232.2**	**270.0**	**295.0**

Budget Outlays

(In billions of dollars or the fiscal year)

	1973 actual	1974 estimate	1975 estimate
National defense	76.0	80.6	87.7
International affairs and finance	3.0	3.9	4.1
Education and manpower	10.2	10.8	11.5
Health	18.4	23.3	26.3
Income security	73.1	85.0	100.1
Veterans benefits and services	12.0	13.3	13.6
Agriculture and rural development	6.2	4.0	2.7
Natural resources and environment	.6	.6	3.1
Commerce and transportation	13.1	13.5	13.4
Community development and housing	4.1	5.4	5.7
General revenue sharing	6.6	6.1	6.2
General government	5.5	6.8	6.8
Space research and technology	3.3	3.2	3.3
Special allowance for acceleration of energy research and development	....	....	.5
Allowances*	....	.3	1.1
Interest	22.8	27.8	29.1
Interest received by trust funds	—5.4	—6.4	—7.1
Employer share, employe retirement	—2.9	—3.5	—3.6
Total outlays	**246.5**	**274.7**	**304.4**
Budget deficit	**14.3**	**4.7**	**9.4**

*For pay raises and contingencies

Budget cut requests. President Ford reported to Congress Sept. 20 plans to postpone $600 million in Congressionally authorized spending in fiscal 1975, (ending June 30, 1975) and to postpone or rescind $19.7 billion in spending authority for following fiscal years. The Administration's spending deferral proposals covered $9 billion intended for waste treatment plants as part of the effort to clean up the nation's waters (this impoundment was in litigation); $4.4 billion in highway funds in fiscal 1975 and $6.4 billion in fiscal 1976; and much smaller amounts for several other programs. The proposals to revoke spending authority involved $456 million intended for rural electrification and telephone loans at 2% interest and $40 million for airport safety projects in Appalachia. On Nov. 26 in a message to Congress, Ford scaled down his budget-cutting plans in the face of the worsening recession. Forsaking the goal of a $300 billion budget ceiling, he set a new goal of $302.2 billion for the current fiscal year ending June 30, 1975. This required $4.6 billion worth of spending reductions, which he proposed. To attain $3.6 billion of it, Congress would be required to take 135 separate actions, including enactment of new laws. Another $979 million in savings were to be achieved through 11 actions by executive authority. The revised budget figures projected a $9.2 billion deficit from receipts of $293 billion and spending of $302.2 billion, both less than recent estimates. The deficit amount was predicated on the $4.6 billion of reductions being proposed, some $3 billion in potential revenues from federal off-shore oil leases and $1 billion in revenues from the President's previous proposal for a 5% income surtax. Another underlying assumption for the new figures was that the unemployment rate would not rise above a 6.5%-6.7% range. In giving the latter figure, Roy Ash, director of the White House Office of Management and Budget, conceded that "the conditions of the economy are changing faster than we can change the budget." The requested spending cuts of $4.6 billion were drawn largely from health, education and welfare programs ($1.7 billion), veterans' benefits ($1.1 billion) and agricultural programs ($600 million). Defense spending, which Congress already had reduced by $2.2 billion to an $83.6 billion total, would be cut by $381 million more in the Administrative revision. A staff study released by the

Congressional Joint Economic Committee Dec. 30 estimated a federal budget deficit of $23 billion in fiscal 1975.

Budget reform process OKd. A bill to revise Congressional processing of the federal budget was passed by the Senate and sent to conference with the House by an 80-0 vote March 22. The reform bill was sent to the President June 21. The final votes of approval were 401-6 by the House June 18 and 75-0 by the Senate June 21. In addition to revising the Congressional budgetary process, the bill, projected for full implementation by 1976, would change the federal fiscal year to begin Oct. 1 (instead of July 1), curb spending programs funded outside the regular budgetary process and restrict impoundment of Congressionally mandated funds by the executive branch. If the impoundment involved only deferred spending, the action could be nullified if either chamber passed a resolution calling for the expenditure. If the impoundment involved termination of a program or reduction for fiscal policy reasons, the funds could not be withheld unless both houses passed a bill to rescind the original legislation mandating the funds. The President was required under the new budget reform bill to report deferrals or request recisions. If the impoundments were not reported to Congress, they could be reported by the comptroller general and Congress could act to force release of the funds. If a president refused to comply with Congressional action to gain release of impounded funds, the comptroller general could seek court remedy. The executive branch also would be required under the reform bill to submit to Congress a "current services" budget by Nov. 10 to project spending necessary to maintain programs at existing commitment levels through the following fiscal year. A Budget Office was to be established in Congress to provide expertise and each chamber would have a budget committee. A budget resolution would be devised to set target figures for total appropriations, spending and tax and debt levels. The initial resolution, considered a tentative alternative budget to the presidential budget, was to be reported by the budget committees by April 15 and was to be cleared by Congress by May 15. A deadline of mid-September was set for final action on appropriations bills. Following that, after clearing all appropriations and other spending bills, Congress would adopt a second budget resolution by Sept. 15 affirming or revising the targets of the first resolution. A Sept. 25 deadline, before the start of the new fiscal year Oct. 1, was set for final Congressional action on the budget.

(Legislation requiring Senate confirmation of new directors and deputy directors of the OMB had been signed into law by President Nixon March 2. The President had vetoed a bill in 1973 that would have extended the confirmation requirement to the current officeholders, Director Ash and Deputy Director Frederic V. Malek. The veto was upheld by the House.)

Higher debt ceiling approved. The House approved 191-190 a $19.3 billion increase in the federal debt ceiling May 23. The deciding vote was cast by Speaker Carl Albert (D, Okla.). The bill, which was sent to the Senate, would raise the ceiling to $495 billion through March 31, 1975. The current ceiling of $475.7 billion would expire June 30, when the permanent $400 billion ceiling would apply. The Administration had requested a $505 billion level through June 30, 1975. The national debt was expected to total about $475 billion by the end of May. The close vote was attributed to general dissatisfaction with the Administration's economic policies. The Senate passed the bill June 26, and President Nixon signed it into law June 30.

See also DEFENSE [5-7]; DISTRICT OF COLUMBIA; ECONOMY, U.S. [4-5, 11-12, 20-22, 27]; EDUCATION: FOREIGN AID; HOUSING; WELFARE & POVERTY

BULGARIA—The Communist Party Central Committee announced July 3 that several important government and party officials accused of "opportunism" had been removed from their posts. Among those ousted were Politburo candidate members Ivan Abadzhiev, Kostadin Gyaurov and Venelin Kotsev and Chemical and Heavy Industries Minister Hristo Panayotov. (Kotsev also held the post of deputy premier; Abadzhiev was also a Central Committee secretary.)

Henrich Schpeter, a Bulgarian Jewish economist who had been sentenced to death on an espionage charge June 1, was released from a Sofia prison and flown to Jerusalem Aug. 22, the Israeli Foreign Ministry announced. Tel Aviv refused to provide details, but said the Israeli government had "made efforts for the release of Schpeter on humanitarian grounds." Bulgaria and Israel had maintained no diplomatic relations since the 1967 Middle East War. Schpeter, who served with the United Nations from 1966-72, had been accused of being in the pay of unspecified foreign intelligence services. However, former associates at the U.N. said that the economist had openly expressed disillusionment with the Communist regime and had been peremptorily summoned home from his U.N. post in 1972.

It was announced in Washington, D.C. that the Bulgarian government had agreed, effective Sept. 9, to stop jamming Voice of America radio broadcasts. Bulgaria had been the last Eastern European country to interfere with the transmissions.

See also COMMUNISM, INTERNATIONAL; EUROPEAN SECURITY

BURMA—Burma was established as a socialist republic under a new constitution adopted Jan. 4. The charter provided for a 451-seat, one-party, unicameral People's Assembly which convened March 2. Government in the intervening period was in the hands of a Revolutionary Council.

The government reported March 25 that ninety persons were killed and more than 160 wounded in fighting the previous week between its forces and rebel troops in southeast Burma. All but three of the dead were insurgents. A government communique implied that the rebels were based in neighboring Thailand. Government and rebel troops had clashed 15 times since February.

Former United Nations Secretary General U Thant, 65, died in New York Nov. 25 of cancer. After lying in state at U.N. headquarters, Thant's body was flown to his native Burma Dec. 1 for burial in Rangoon. Before the funeral could begin Dec. 5, thousands of students and Buddhist monks seized the coffin and took it to Rangoon University. The students said they wanted a funeral and a shrine for Thant "befitting a man of his stature." About 1,000 soldiers and policemen stormed the university campus Dec. 11 and retrieved Thant's body, which was later buried near the Shwedagon Pagoda, Burma's most sacred shrine. The action of the troops precipitated widespread street rioting as thousands of rock-throwing youths roamed the capital, looting, smashing windows and street lights, and clashing with police and troops. The government imposed martial law and a curfew in Rangoon. The rioting was regarded as an outbreak of long-smoldering resentment of many Burmese against the authoritarian regime of President Ne Win, who had seized power in 1962 from U Nu. Thant had been a close associate of U Nu, who was living in exile in India, and had long been at odds with Ne Win. More than 110 persons were reported Dec. 8 to have been sentenced to jail terms of 3-5 years in connection with the previous week's rioting.

BURUNDI—The Supreme Council approved Burundi's first Constitution July 11. Under its provisions, a single party, the Unity and National Progress Party, would define the nation's general political orientation and control the actions of the government and the judiciary. The party's leader would automatically become president of the republic. The mandate of Burundi's present president, Lt. Michel Micombero, was extended until a new president was chosen. Micombero was installed for a second seven-year term as president Nov. 27.

BUSH, GEORGE—*See* ELECTIONS [11]; POLITICS [11]; ROCKEFELLER [3]
BUSINESS—*See* AGRICULTURE; ANTI-TRUST ACTIONS; ARGENTINA [7-9]; AVIATION [1-5]; BANKS & BANKING; BUDGET; CAMPAIGN FINANCING [17]; ECONOMY [4, 12]; ENERGY CRISIS; HUGHES, HOWARD; TAXES; WELFARE & POVERTY; WOMEN'S RIGHTS
BUSING ISSUE—*See* CIVIL RIGHTS [1-8]
BUTTERFIELD, ALEXANDER—*See* AVIATION [10]; WATERGATE [98]

BUTZ, EARL L.—A remark Nov. 27 by Agriculture Secretary Earl L. Butz regarding Pope Paul VI's view on birth control raised a furor with Roman Catholic Church spokesmen in the U.S. and prompted President Ford to personally reprimand Butz and order that he issue a full "apology to any and all individuals who were offended." Butz, who led the U.S. delegation to the World Food Conference in Rome, referred to the conference delegates' meeting with the pope, who had said population control was not an acceptable method of dealing with world starvation. Butz joked, "An Italian lady told me in Rome, 'He no playa da game, he no maka da rules.'" Catholic officials protested the remark in telegrams to President Ford. He personally rebuked Butz Nov. 29 and ordered that he amend an apology issued earlier in the day because the statement was "not adequate."

See also AGRICULTURE; CANADA [29]; FAMINE & FOOD; UNION OF SOVIET SOCIALIST REPUBLICS [14]

BUZHARDT, J. FRED—*See* APPOINTMENTS & RESIGNATIONS; DEFENSE [3]; NIXON, RICHARD M.; WATERGATE [44, 47]

CABLE TELEVISION—*See* COPYRIGHT; TELEVISION & RADIO
CAETANO, MARCELLO—*See* PORTUGAL [2, 4, 7]; MOZAMBIQUE [8]
CALIFORNIA—*See* CAMPAIGN FINANCING [11]; ELECTIONS [5, 7, 9]; ENERGY CRISIS [35]; PRESS; TAXES; WATERGATE AFFAIR [13]; WOMEN'S RIGHTS
CALLAGHAN, JAMES—*See* CYPRUS [5, 6, 10]; EUROPEAN ECONOMIC COMMUNITY [10-11, 14]; GREAT BRITAIN [5]; GREECE [2]
CALLAWAY, HOWARD H.—*See* CALLEY, WILLIAM L.; DEFENSE [10]; PRIVACY [11]

CALLEY JR., WILLIAM L.—Army Lt. William L. Calley Jr., the only soldier convicted in connection with the Mylai massacre in South Vietnam in 1968, entered a military prison at Fort Leavenworth, Kan. June 26 to begin serving the remainder of a 10-year jail sentence. Calley's original 20-year term had been halved on April 16 by Secretary of the Army Howard H. Callaway. In his announcement, Callaway said there was "no reasonable doubt" that Calley had "perpetrated the acts for which he stands convicted." The sentence was reduced, however, because "of mitigating circumstances indicating that Lt. Calley may have sincerely believed that he was acting in accordance with orders he had received and that he was not aware of his responsibility to refuse such an illegal order." (On May 4 Callaway ordered Calley dishonorably discharged from the Army.)

Calley lost his bid to stay out of prison when the U.S. Court of Appeals for the 5th Circuit revoked bail June 13, after it had been granted Feb. 27 by U.S. District Court Judge J. Robert Elliot. Elliot had granted the $1,000 bail on the premise that Callaway's upcoming review might cut Calley's sentence to the point where his confinement might be longer than the sentence imposed. In revoking bail, the appellate court ruled Judge Elliot had erred. Until released on bail, Calley had been confined to quarters at Fort Benning, Ga. for two years, 11 months.

Calley's conviction was overturned by Elliott in Columbus, Ga. Sept. 25. Elliott ordered Calley's release "forthwith" from the military prison at Ft. Leavenworth. In reversing the conviction, Elliott contended that "massive adverse pretrial publicity" had made a fair trial under military law an impossibility. Elliott's decision also cited the denial of Calley's requests to call certain witnesses at his court-martial as well as the Army's charges against Calley, which the judge characterized as "improperly drawn and illegally used."

Calley was granted parole effective Nov. 19 by Callaway, who announced his action Nov. 8, describing the terms of the parole as routine. (Calley would have completed serving one-third of his 10-year prison term Nov. 19.) In a separate action, the U.S. Court of Appeals for the 5th Circuit Nov. 8 ordered Calley released on bail from Ft. Leavenworth while it reviewed the lower court decision reversing his conviction. Calley was released on a $1,000 personal recognizance bond at Columbus, Ga. Nov. 9. The Army indicated that it would press its appeal of the decision overturning Calley's conviction, although it did not intend to seek Calley's return to prison.

CAMBODIA

War Developments

In spite of heavy fighting around Pnompenh and Oudong throughout the year, no decisive military victories were achieved by either side during 1974. Hundreds of refugees fled from the area around Pnompenh's airport, following an offensive by the Khmer Rouge rebels which began Jan. 6. Scores of civilians were reported killed after being caught in the crossfire between government and insurgent troops who pushed to within five miles of the center of the capital from the west and eight miles from the north. U.S. officials described the drive as the first phase of a dry season offensive. A government force of 2,000 men was arrayed against an estimated 5,000 rebels in what Western analysts regarded as "a maximum effort" to topple the government of President Lon Nol. Government forces launched a counteroffensive Jan. 9 in an effort to trap the rebel units. The fighting was the heaviest and the closest to the city since August 1973. Rebels shelling intensified Jan. 23, when at least 35 persons were killed and more than 80 wounded. The rebel guns and rocket assaults were believed deployed about six miles from the city. A United Nations spokesman said Jan. 28 that families of some U.N. personnel were being evacuated. France had begun evacuating about 50 French women and children Jan. 18 after a rebel rocket hit a French-operated school causing one death. In spite of a brief lull in the shelling Jan. 28-30, the attacks began again Jan. 31. One of the worst occurred Feb. 11, causing the death of nearly 200 civilians. An equal number were injured as the shells fell on one of the busiest and most closely packed market and housing areas in the southern section of the city. Foreign relief officials estimated that more than 9,000 persons were left homeless as a result. (President Lon Nol declared a six-month state of emergency Jan. 30 to cope with the danger posed by the continuing attacks and reported civilian unrest.)

In February-March, government troops overran rebel positions around the capital and broke the Khmer Rouge hold on Route 4, a highway leading to Pnompenh. The fighting see-sawed back and forth in April, with a rebel victory over six government outposts southeast of the capital April 5-7. Meanwhile, on March 18, the rebels had captured the former royal capital of Oudong, 24 miles northwest of Pnompenh. It was the first major town taken by the insurgents in more than three years. At the same time, a force of about 10,000 rebels and North Vietnamese besieged the seaport town of Kampot, and advanced to within two miles of its center. The government launched a counteroffensive to recapture Oudong March 19. Heavy fighting followed during the next week, with government forces closing in on the city, only to suffer a sharp setback March 28 when the insurgents captured a besieged pagoda just north of the city. After the Cambodian defenders withdrew from the temple, government planes bombed the compound to destroy abandoned artillery and vehicles, leading to a protest rally by Buddhists in Pnompenh March 24 against destruction of historic and religious landmarks. Kampot was the scene of hand-to-hand fighting April 4 as government forces launched a counterattack, reporting success two days later. By the end of the month, the government had managed to expand its perimeter around the town. Intelligence reports said the rebels were withdrawing to the west.

Government forces suffered defeats in other areas in April, losing a government outpost at Koh Krabei, eight miles southeast of Pnompenh on April 24; and the town of Sala Lek Prem, 26 miles northwest of the capital, April 27. By July 9, however, they had recaptured Oudong, reporting that more than 1,300 rebels and 100 government soldiers had been killed in the fighting for the town since March. The same day, President Lon Nol offered peace negotiations with the rebels "without conditions," terms which represented an easing of the president's previous offer of July, 1973, in which he had said negotiations were conditioned on withdrawal of all foreign troops from Cambodia and establishment of a cease-fire. Prince Norodom Sihanouk, who headed a government in exile in Peking, said July 9 there could be no peace talks between Cambodian resistance forces and Lon Nol's government.

Heavy fighting continued Aug. 4-31. Insurgent forces Aug. 4 captured five government outposts 3-5 miles from Pnompenh. Several hundred villagers were abducted, and 40 militiamen and 15 villagers were killed after they resisted. A government drive aimed at recapturing some of the historic temples at Angkor Wat, 140 miles northwest of the capital, resulted in the recapture Aug. 26 of three temples and a district town around the ruins. The military command said the temples had been held by the rebels since 1970.

Lon Nol renewed his offer Nov. 30 to hold peace talks with the Khmer Rouge "without prior conditions." Lon Nol said "some people" had doubted his sincerity when he had first advanced his peace bid in July, contending that his offer was a ploy by his government to retain its seat in the United Nations. He called on the insurgents to test his sincere intentions by agreeing to talks.

Other Developments

Ruling council abolished. Lon Nol March 31 abolished the ruling four-member High Political Council on the ground that it was no longer needed because the two legislative chambers were now functioning normally. Another four-man advisory body was formed. The president's action prompted the immediate protest resignation of three Cabinet members. The defunct council's deputy president, Cheng Heng, said dissolution of the council meant the termination of the government and called on Lon Nol to form a new coalition regime. The new advisory body was headed by Lon Nol; its other members were Premier Long Boret, Sosthene Fernandez, chief of staff, and Sisowath Sirik Matak.

2 government officials slain. Cambodian Education Minister Keo Sangkim and his chief assistant, Thach Chea, were killed June 4 when government troops stormed a high school in Pnompenh where demonstrating students were holding the two officials hostage. Two students were killed and eight others were wounded in the ensuing two-hour clash. Police arrested more than 100 persons. The killing of the two officials climaxed five months of political unrest marked by a teachers' strike and demonstrations by students and teachers protesting inflation and government corruption. Keo and his aide were seized earlier June 4 at the Education Ministry by the students and were marched to the school. Student leaders said they had planned to hold the two men until 15 students and four teachers, arrested the previous week for demonstrating for educational reforms, were released. Police said Keo and Thach had been shot and stabbed by the students. A newsman at the scene said the two men had been fired upon by military policemen when the students used the officials as human shields.

Long Boret forms new Cabinet. Premier Long Boret resigned June 13 and was immediately called on by Lon Nol to form a new government. Long Boret announced formation of a new 16-member Cabinet June 17. The premier had quit following the resignation the previous week of several of his ministers who had protested his handling of student riots, the economy and military matters. The ministers were members of the Republican Party which did not recognize the National Assembly, claiming it was fraudulently elected. Four more ministers resigned June 7, but no reasons were given.Opposition Republican Party members refused to join Long Boret's new government, which included seven members of Lon Nol's Social-Republican Party (SRP), seven independents and two military men. Five ministers of the previous Cabinet were retained.

U.S. confirms war role in Cambodia. The U.S. Defense Department Nov. 26 confirmed that U.S. reconnaissance aircraft were providing the Cambodian armed forces with battlefield intelligence information. The statement, however, denied that this activity was in violation of the 1973 Congressional ban prohibiting the use of U.S. funds "to finance directly or indirectly" U.S. combat activity in Indochina. The department said the intelligence data was passed on to the Cambodians, with "the judgment of what should be done, if anything," left to Pnompenh.

See also APPOINTMENTS & RESIGNATIONS; FOREIGN AID; UNITED NATIONS [7]; VIETNAM, PEOPLE'S REPUBLIC OF; VIETNAM, REPUBLIC OF [4-5]; WATERGATE [21, 29, 33]

CAMEROON—*See* AFRICA; UNITED NATIONS [6]

CAMPAIGN FINANCING ABUSES & REFORMS

Major Federal Reforms Enacted

[1] **Legislation emerged from Watergate scandal.** A bill providing for a major reform of federal election campaign funding was approved in final form by the Senate Oct. 8 and House Oct. 10 and was signed into law by President Ford Oct. 15. Its provisions were effective Jan. 1, 1975, and did not apply to the Congressional elections in November. The bill, landmark legislation evolving from the abuses revealed by the Watergate scandal, provided public financing of presidential primaries and elections and set ceilings on contributions and spending in House, Senate and presidential campaigns. It was designed to eliminate undue influence of large contributors or of special interest groups. The bill's floor manager in the House, Rep. Wayne L. Hays (D, Ohio), told his colleagues Oct. 10 "if you'd adopted the limits two years ago, Watergate would never have happened." The vote in the House was 365-24. The Senate vote of approval was 60-16. A provision for public financing of House and Senate elections had been dropped in conference between the two chambers. Resolution of the issue, which had been a part of the original Senate version, had delayed final floor consideration of the bill. There was strong opposition in the House to public financing for contenders against incumbents every two years.

[2] The bill's key provisions, as cleared by Congress: (1) A presidential nominee of a major party would receive $20 million from the $1 income tax check-off fund established in 1971. If the fund were short of the amount, the nominee could raise the difference from private sources. (2) The major parties would receive $2 million each from the check-off for their national conventions. (3) Minor parties could receive the public funding in proportion to the votes

they received, if at least 5% of the total cast in previous elections. (4) Public funding for a presidential primary would be available on a matching basis to candidates who raised at least $100,000 from private sources in a way that indicated broad national support—at least $5,000 from 20 different states. Only the first $250 of any individual contribution would count toward the "seed money" required. The government would match the qualifying $100,000, plus subsequent contributions up to a $5 million total for private contributions. The candidate's spending limit for all primaries combined was $10 million but an additional $2 million would be permitted for fund-raising activities. (5) The spending ceiling for a Senate primary candidate would be 8¢ per eligible voter or $100,000, whichever was higher, in the primary and 12¢ or $150,000 in the general election. Additional funds could be spent for fund-raising expenses, and the candidate could receive at least an additional $20,000 from his political party. (6) For House candidates, the ceiling would be $70,000 in both the primary and the general elections. Another $14,000 would be permitted for fund-raising expenses, and the candidate could receive another $10,000 from his political party. (7) The ceiling on contributions by individuals would be: $25,000 to all federal candidates and their organizations in any election year; $1,000 to any one candidate for president; $1,000 to any one candidate for Congress in any one election—primary, runoff or general election—for a total of $3,000. (8) For contributions by an organization, the limit would be $5,000 to any Congressional candidate in each campaign, with a $15,000 total, and no more than $5,000 overall to a presidential candidate. (9) The ceilings on personal spending by a candidate would be $50,000 for a presidential campaign, $35,000 for a Senate race and $25,000 for a House contest. (10) An independent six-member commission would be established with subpoena and civil enforcement authority to oversee enforcement of the law. The president and the leaders of the Senate and House would appoint two members each, the appointments subject to Congressional confirmation. (11) Cash contributions of over $100, and foreign contributions, were prohibited. (12) Government contractors, as well as unions and corporations, were permitted to maintain separate funds for campaign contributions subject to the law's limitations. (13) Contributions and expenditures would have to be reported by a candidate through one central campaign committee. Regular reports to the election commission were required.

The Milk Fund Contribution Case

[3] One of the major cases of campaign funding abuse emerging from the Watergate-related investigations centered on the Associated Milk Producers, Inc. (AMPI), the nation's largest dairy producers' co-operative. Charges were raised, with increasing substantiation during 1974, that President Nixon had raised the federal support price for milk in March 1971 in return for pledges of large campaign contributions—in the AMPI case, up to $2 million—from the major dairy co-operatives. The milk fund case became a key part of the events leading to Nixon's resignation and resulted in the indictment of former Treasury Secretary John B. Connally Jr. for bribery and perjury. The final report of the Senate Watergate Committee, issued July 13, concluded that the "dual role played by many Nixon officials of both policy maker and fund raiser gave at the very least, the appearance of impropriety and provided circumstances that were ripe for abuse. Whether or not these two roles were directly tied, they *appeared* [committee emphasis] to be linked, and this had a significant impact on the approach taken by the dairymen. [Harold] Nelson [general manager of Associated Milk Producers, Inc.] said they gave the first $100,000 in 1969 because 'it appeared we were not going to get any place if we did not.' And when called

upon in March 1971 to re-affirm the $2 million pledge [made the previous September], Nelson explained that he felt he had no choice...." According to the committee, the dairy lobby eventually contributed a total of $632,500 to the Nixon re-election campaign, "including $245,000 furnished to the campaign just prior to the election."

[4] Nixon's decision, announced in March 1971, to raise federal price supports for milk, "was worth at least tens of millions of dollars to the milk producers and they spared no effort in seeking that favorable action," the report stated. However, the report continued, "price supports were just one item on the dairymen agenda. In fact, the milk producers, representing one of the wealthiest political funds in America and one of the largest groups of contributors to the 1972 campaign, had actively sought favorable action from the Nixon Administration throughout its first term on a number of matters of great financial importance to dairy farmers at the same time that they were pledging hundreds of thousands, and even millions to President Nixon's re-election campaign—with the knowledge of the President himself and with the encouragement of top presidential aides and fund raisers."

[5] According to the report, the dairymen began meeting their promised campaign obligations within one week after the price decision was announced. According to the report, an additional contribution was made during the convention "at the special request of Charles Colson. Colson testified before a state grand jury that [$5,000 in] milk money was used to pay for the break-in of the office of Daniel Ellsberg's psychiatrist." "Even before these contributions were made, the milk producers made at least one, and perhaps two, payments to [AMPI lawyer] Jake Jacobsen for [Treasury] Secretary [John] Connally's use," the report charged. Separate payments of $10,000 and $5,000 were cited. "Both Connally and Jacobsen deny that Connally ever took or used $10,000," the report acknowledged.

[6] Connally and Jacobsen were indicted on these charges by a Watergate grand jury July 29. Jacobsen pleaded guilty Aug. 7 and Connally pleaded not guilty Aug. 9. Former AMPI manager Nelson pleaded guilty July 31 to charges that he conspired to bribe Connally to help secure higher federal support prices on milk. He was sentenced Nov. 1 to four months in jail and fined $10,000. David L. Parr, former AMPI special counsel and deputy to Nelson, pleaded guilty July 23 to charges that he had authorized payment of $200,000 in illegal campaign contributions to former Vice President Hubert Humphrey and other candidates of both parties. Parr was sentenced Nov. 1 to four months imprisonment and fined $10,000. The AMPI itself was fined $35,000 in U.S. District Court Aug. 1 after pleading guilty to a six-count charge of conspiracy and making illegal campaign contributions totaling $280,900 to candidates of both parties.

ITT Antitrust Case & Campaign Fund Charges

[7] **Impeachment committee's evidence.** Two volumes of evidence on the Administration's handling of antitrust suits against International Telephone & Telegraph Corp. (ITT) were released by the House Judiciary Committee July 19 as part of its investigation into grounds for the impeachment of President Nixon. No evidence in the material published by the House committee appeared to substantiate allegations that Nixon had ordered the Justice Department to drop its appeal of an antitrust case involving ITT because of ITT's promise to underwrite the cost of the 1972 Republican National Convention, then scheduled for San Diego. No government document supported the original contention of ITT's Washington lobbyist, Dita Beard, that the two were linked. But the documents revealed

numerous meetings in the 1969-1971 period between high Administration officials and ITT executives who waged an intense lobbying campaign in an effort to have the antitrust charges dropped.

[8] The only new evidence included in the committee's information, most of it published previously, was a transcript of tape recorded conversation between Nixon and John Ehrlichman during a White House meeting April 19, 1971. George Shultz, then director of the Office of Management and Budget, was also present at the meeting, which was interrupted when Nixon telephoned then-Deputy Attorney General Richard Kleindienst, ordering him to drop a Justice Department appeal of one of the antitrust suits against ITT. Prior to the phone call, Nixon told Ehrlichman, "I don't want to know anything about the case. . . . I don't want to know about [ITT President Harold S.] Geneen. I've met him and I don't know—I don't know whether ITT is bad, good or indifferent. But there is not going to be any more antitrust actions as long as I am in this chair." In the aftermath of Nixon's phone call to Kleindienst, the Justice Department delayed bringing an appeal on the ITT case to the Supreme Court. On April 21, Nixon was persuaded by then Attorney General John Mitchell that it would be "political dynamite" to abandon the ITT appeal. Shortly thereafter, the ITT case was settled out of court, on terms considered favorable to the corporation, while the delayed appeal was still pending.

[9] **Kleindienst prosecution.** Former Attorney General Kleindienst had pleaded guilty May 16 to a misdemeanor charge that he had refused to testify "accurately and fully" before a Congressional committee investigating the Administration's handling of the ITT antitrust settlement. The guilty plea was entered in federal district court in Washington. Kleindienst received a suspended sentenced of one month in jail and a $100 fine June 7.

[10] The minor criminal offense related to Kleindienst's testimony in March and April 1972 before the Senate Judiciary Committee, which was considering his nomination to succeed Mitchell as attorney general. In his sworn committee testimony, Kleindienst had said, "I was not interfered with by anybody at the White House. I was not importuned. I was not pressured. I was not directed."

[11] **Reinecke guilty of perjury.** California Lt. Gov. Ed Reinecke (R) was convicted July 27 of one count of lying to the Senate Judiciary Committee during testimony about the alleged link between ITT's pledge of a contribution to fund the 1972 Republican Convention, then scheduled for San Diego, and the Administration's settlement of antitrust suits against ITT. The testimony was given April 19, 1972 during hearings to consider the nomination of then Deputy Attorney General Kleindienst as attorney general. Reinecke resigned Oct. 2 as California lieutenant governor and minutes later received an 18-month suspended sentence.

Kalmbach & Sale of Ambassadorships

[12] **Secret $3.9 million fund.** Herbert W. Kalmbach, President Nixon's personal attorney and one of his chief fund raisers, pleaded guilty Feb. 25 to two violations of the federal law governing campaign funds. He admitted raising $3.9 million for a secret Congressional campaign committee in 1970 and also promising an ambassador a better diplomatic post in return for a $100,000 campaign contribution. The charges, the first a felony and the second a misdemeanor, were violations of the Federal Corrupt Practices Act. Kalmbach was sentenced June 17 to a six to 18-month jail sentence and was fined $10,000. He began serving his sentence July 1. The campaign fund project, dubbed "Operation Townhouse" or "The Public Institute," was run by the White House out of a basement in a downtown Washington house, funneling secret

money to Republican House and Senate candidates in 1970 in at least 19 states, prosecutors told the court. According to the prosecutors, Ambassador J. Fife Symington Jr., a retired Maryland businessman and former state Republican Party official, offered Kalmbach donations totaling $100,000 "only on condition that he be offered an ambassadorship to one of several agreed upon European countries." At the time of the deal, Symington was ambassador to Trinidad and Tobago, a post he retained until November 1971. Kalmbach offered to return the money when the pledge was not fulfilled but Symington refused, prosecutors said. Symington was a cousin of Sen. Stuart Symington (D, Mo.).

[13] (At a press conference Feb. 25 Nixon was questioned about Kalmbach's use of the ambassadorial quid pro quo in soliciting presidential campaign contributions. In answering, the President said: "... ambassadorships have not been for sale to my knowledge, ambassadorships cannot be purchased and I would not approve an ambassadorship unless the man, or woman, was qualified clearly apart from any contribution.)

[14] **Senate Committee report on envoys.** The final report issued July 13 by the Senate Watergate Committee showed that since Nov. 7, 1972, Nixon had appointed 13 non-career ambassadors whose campaign contributions totaled $706,000. Eight of that group had each donated at least $25,000. "In fact, over $1.8 million in presidential campaign contributions can be attributed in whole or in part, to persons holding ambassadorial appointments from the President." According to the report, ambassadors in eight Western European countries were major contributors to the Nixon re-election campaign: Walter Annenberg (Great Britain)—$250,000; Shelby Davis (Switzerland)—$100,000; Ruth Farkas (Luxembourg)—$300,000; Leonard Firestone (Belgium)—$112,600; Kingdon Gould (Netherlands)—$100,900; John Humes (Austria)—$100,000; John Irwin (France)—$50,500 and Arthur Watson, Irwin's predecessor and brother-in-law, $300,000; John Moore (Ireland)—$10,442. Total figure—$1,324,442.

Hughes-Rebozo Controversy

[15] **Hughes official: gift sought from Hughes.** Richard G. Danner, an official in President Nixon's 1968 campaign and currently an employe of billionaire industrialist Howard R. Hughes, told the Senate Watergate Committee that he attended a meeting in 1968 with Nixon and Charles G. Rebozo, a friend of Nixon and a Florida banker, during which a campaign gift was solicited from Hughes. (Danner had introduced Nixon and Rebozo to each other in 1948.) The *New York Times* reported the testimony Jan. 16, the *Washington Post* Jan. 17. The *Times* reported Danner told committee investigators that Nixon personally suggested he attempt to solicit a campaign contribution from Hughes. The *Post* reported that Nixon was present at the meeting when the request was made. Danner, hired by the Hughes organization in February 1969, finally delivered a $50,000 cash payment to Rebozo in July 1970 and followed it with another $50,000 cash contribution in August of that year. Robert Maheu, a former Hughes aide, now suing the industrialist testified in a deposition given in his suit that the first $50,000 was intended for Nixon's 1968 campaign. The second $50,000, Maheu said, related to an antitrust problem Hughes was having concerning his attempts to acquire the Dunes Hotel in Las Vegas, Nev. After the second gift was received, Maheu testified, Attorney General Mitchell granted Hughes an antitrust exemption over objections of the Justice Department's antitrust division. However, the transaction was never consummated, Maheu said.

[16] The $100,000 was reported to have been returned to the Hughes organization in June 1973 after Rebozo had become the subject of an Internal

Revenue Service investigation into the contribution. It was not known whether the bills returned were the same ones given to Rebozo, however. This became a matter of controversy when it became known that Herbert Kalmbach, Nixon's personal attorney, had testified before the Senate Watergate Committee that Rebozo, at an April 30, 1973 White House meeting, had admitted disbursing part of the Hughes contribution to the President's secretary, Rose Mary Woods, and his two brothers, F. Donald Nixon and Edward C. Nixon. Kalmbach also was reported to have testified that Rebozo telephoned him in January 1974 to say that the April 30 conversation was "mistaken" and the Hughes money had never left his hands before its return. The Senate Watergate Committee's final report confirmed that the Hughes contribution had been made through Rebozo but said that many of the details remained contradictory and unclear. The committee report contained evidence that Rebozo had spent more than $50,000 of the campaign funds he collected for the Nixons' personal benefit, much of it for property improvements on their Key Biscayne, Fla. home and on a set of platinum and diamond earrings for Mrs. Nixon.

Other Developments

[17] **Further Senate Committee findings.** The Senate committee's report stated that "at least 13 corporations made [political] contributions totaling over $780,000 in corporate funds," donations that were in violation of a federal statute prohibiting campaign contributions from corporations and unions. Of this total, an estimated $749,000 was given to President Nixon's re-election campaign. (The donations Nixon received from the dairy industry were not included in this figure). These were the major illegal contributions cited: American Airlines, $55,000; American Ship Building Co., $100,000 (See below); Ashland Oil Co., $100,000; Braniff Airways, $40,000; Carnation Co., $7,900; Diamond International Corp., $5,000 to Nixon, $1,000 to Sen. Edmund S. Muskie (D, Me.); Goodyear Tire & Rubber Co., $40,000; Gulf Oil Corp., $100,000 to Nixon, $10,000 to Sen. Henry M. Jackson (D, Wash.), $15,000 to Rep. Wilbur Mills (D, Ark.); Hertz Corp., $8-9,000 in car rentals, Muskie; Lehigh Valley Cooperative Farmers, $50,000, Nixon (used to pay hush money to original Watergate defendants); Minnesota Mining & Manufacturing Co., $36,000 to Nixon, $1,000 each to Mills and Sen. Hubert Humphrey (D, Minn.); Northrop Corp., $150,000; Phillips Petroleum Co., $100,000; Gulf Resources and Chemical Corp., $114,000 (found in the possession of Watergate burglar Bernard Barker during the break-in).

[18] The report was critical of Sen. George McGovern's (D, S.D.) resolution of his presidential campaign debt. Evidence was developed, the report stated, that as McGovern's campaign finance committees were "settling bills with creditors, including corporations at 50% of their face value, these presidential committees were making substantial transfers of funds to McGovern Senatorial committees in anticipation of a 1974 contest for his re-election to this Senate seat." A total of $340,416.96 was transferred for use in the Senate campaign under these transactions, the report claimed. Debts incurred during the presidential race were reduced by $35,322.32 in negotiations with business creditors.

[19] Humphrey was cited for several apparent violations of campaign financing laws, but the committee's investigation was hampered by his refusal to be interviewed by the committee staff, and by his campaign manager's refusal to testify under oath. Humphrey also did not fully comply with the committee's request for campaign records, the report stated. Under the law in effect until April 7, 1972, the report noted, it was illegal for any individual to donate more than $5,000 in any calendar year to a presidential candidate or to any national campaign committee operating in his behalf, yet "more than $500,000 was

contributed to the Humphrey presidential campaign in 1971 and 1972 (up to April 7) in the form of donations in excess of $5,000." Humphrey was also said to have secretly accepted $25,000 from the AMPI milk co-operative. A backer of higher dairy price supports, Humphrey had denied there was a connection with the contribution. Humphrey's 1970 campaign manager, Jack L. Chestnut, was indicted Dec. 23 on charges of illegally accepting $12,000 of the AMPI money.

[20] Alleged campaign abuses also occurred in Mills' brief race for the Democratic presidential nomination. The committee said it was unable to make a complete study of Mills' campaign practices, however, because Mills ignored repeated requests from the committee for an interview and his campaign manager, like Humphrey's, refused to testify, citing his 5th Amendment rights against self-incrimination. The investigation also was limited by Mills' refusal to make a voluntary disclosure of his pre-April 7, 1972 receipts and disbursements estimated at about $200,000.

[21] Committee records published Aug. 7 showed that oil millionaire Leon Hess had made a secret $225,000 contribution to Jackson's campaign for the Democratic presidential nomination in 1972 and $250,000 to Nixon in 1972. The contribution was disguised under the names of other persons, records showed. Jackson also received $166,000 in secret cash contributions, of which more than half came from oil interests. According to the committee's records, Jackson raised $1.1 million during the campaign, nearly half of which was given by donors who also made large contributions to Nixon's campaign.

[22] In its last official action, the Senate Watergate Committee released the final report July 13 on its investigation of the Watergate and other scandals related to the 1972 presidential campaign. The committee said in an introduction to the 2,250-page report that its investigation had not been conducted, nor its report prepared, "to determine the legal guilt or innocence of any person or whether the President should be impeached. The report said the picture presented by its compilation of evidence demonstrated that "campaign practices must be effectively supervised and enforcement of the criminal laws vigorously pursued against all offenders—even those of high estate—if our free institutions are to survive." Accordingly, the report presented 35 recommendations for election campaign reform, including some endorsing legislation already passed by the Senate. Among the major proposals: (1) An independent and permanent office of "public attorney" with powers similar to those of the existing special prosecutor. (2) A federal elections commission with supervisory and enforcement powers. (3) Restrictions on domestic intelligence activities by the White House staff. (4) Extension of the Hatch Act (forbidding campaign activities by civil service employees) to cover the entire Justice Department. (5) Limits on cash campaign contributions by individuals, reforms in reporting procedures and restrictions on solicitation of campaign funds by presidential staff. (6) Tightening of laws involving use of federal agencies to aid the election of political candidates.

[23] **Steinbrenner pleads guilty, fined.** The American Ship Building Co. and its chairman, George M. Steinbrenner 3rd, pleaded guilty Aug. 23 to federal charges involving violations of the campaign contributions law. Both defendants were fined the maximum amount Aug. 30 by Judge Leroy J. Contie Jr. of federal district court in Cleveland, where American Ship Building maintained its corporate headquarters. Steinbrenner, who pleaded guilty to a two count criminal information filed by the Watergate special prosecutor, was fined $10,000 on a felony charge of conspiring to make illegal corporate contributions to the campaigns of Nixon and several Democrats—Sens. Vance Hartke (Ind.) and Daniel K. Inouye (Hawaii). Steinbrenner was the first

corporate executive to be charged with a felony as a result of an investigation conducted by the special prosecutor's office. He was also fined $5,000 for a misdemeanor charge of being an accessory after the fact to violations of the federal campaign contributions law. American Ship Building was fined $10,000 for each of two felony counts of making illegal contributions. Steinbrenner, who was also principal owner of the New York Yankees, was suspended from major league baseball for two years Nov. 27 by Bowie Kuhn, commissioner of baseball.

See also CANADA [1]; CRIME [14-15]; ENERGY CRISIS [1]; POLITICS [2, 13]; PULITZER PRIZES; VETERANS; WATERGATE [27, 74-76, 80, 98-99]

CANADA

Politics & Government

[1] **Election fund bill passed.** The first bill to limit spending and subsidize candidates in Canadian elections received final passage in Commons Jan. 3, with only two New Democrats and eight Creditistes opposed. The law would come into effect within six months. All campaign contributions of more than $100 would have to be disclosed, and an accounting would be made of all commercial services and goods obtained. National parties would be limited to total expenses of 30 cents per registered voter, roughly equivalent to the amount reported by the Liberals and Conservatives in 1972. Individual candidate spending would also be limited, depending on the size of the constituency, with the government refunding about one-third the cost to those candidates receiving at least 15% of the vote.

[2] **CBC guidelines set.** The Canadian Radio-Television Commission (CRTC) extended the Canadian Broadcasting Corporation's (CBC) radio and television licenses for five years March 31 and issued a series of directives governing the CBC's future programming and policies. Hearings on the license renewals had begun Feb. 18. Having been criticized during the hearings for the "Americanization" of its airwaves, the CBC was ordered to use Canadian programs for at least half of the TV broadcast time between 8 p.m. and 9 p.m. for a four-week average, starting Oct. 1, 1976 and also to require privately-owned network affiliates to air them.

[3] **Government toppled; new elections called.** The minority Liberal government of Prime Minister Pierre Elliott Trudeau was defeated May 8 in a 137-123 vote of no-confidence mounted in the House of Commons by the 31 members of the New Democratic Party (NDP) and the 106 Progressive Conservatives (PC). The Cabinet was formally dissolved May 9 and new elections were scheduled for July 8. The no-confidence motion was brought against the budget, presented May 6, which the PC and NDP denounced as inadequate in the face of Canada's rising inflation. It was the first time in Canadian history that a government had been ousted in a budget vote. The budget, which represented a 26% increase in government spending, had proposed: a temporary 10% surtax on corporate income; a higher tax and lower depletion allowances for oil and mining companies; increased taxes on tobacco products, liquor, wines and large-size automobiles; removal of the 12% federal clothing tax and other taxes on construction machinery, bicycles and buses; savings allowances toward housing purchases; and tax breaks for lower income groups.

[4] The budget, which included a record $22 billion spending program for fiscal 1975, had been presented in the traditional Throne Speech before Parliament Feb. 27 by Governor-General Jules Leger. At the time, Conservative Party chief Robert Stanfield had accused the Trudeau government of encouraging inflation. The Conservatives had long supported general income and price controls, which Trudeau had refused to institute, calling them "unworkable."

[5] In presenting the PC no-confidence motion during the May 8 debate, Stanfield maintained that the Liberal proposals "barely acknowledged inflation" and vowed that a Conservative government would impose an immediate 90-day freeze on wages and prices. NDP leader David Lewis then presented an additional amendment, asking the House to condemn the government for "failure to apply any measures to help pensioners or others on fixed income, to deal with the housing crisis and to remove the glaring inequalities of the tax system." The government was defeated in the vote on the NDP motion, which preceded the PC motion vote.

[6] Trudeau opened the Liberal Party election campaign May 17 with a vigorous attack on both the PC and the NDP for bringing down the government. In a whistle-stop campaign train trip through Quebec and the maritime provinces May 28-31, the prime minister criticized his opponents, particularly Stanfield, for being able only to identify the problem of inflation but not solve it. Stanfield, who mounted his campaign on the issue of inflation, was plagued by party dissension and shifts in his income-price freeze policy. Whereas he had originally advocated a firm 90-day freeze, Stanfield seemed to alter his position as early as May 11 when he said a freeze would last for "not more than 90 days" and again May 25, saying that a freeze would be "as short as possible." Stanfield encountered additional campaign problems May 27 when, for the first time in his nearly seven years as party leader, he vetoed a nominated PC candidate. The nominee, Moncton, New Brunswick Mayor Leonard Jones, was a fierce opponent of bilingualism and had refused to permit its introduction into Moncton's municipal services. The NDP released its platform May 19. Among its planks were calls for increased state competition with private enterprise, pulling Canada out of international defense organizations and $200 pensions upon retirement. NDP leader Lewis actively sought the support of the Parti Quebecois (PQ).

[7] The final weeks of the campaign before the July 8 election saw considerable interest generated in the language issue, with attention focused on Quebec, a Liberal stronghold. Underscoring the issue was the June 28 announcement by French authorities that the Quebec separatists who had kidnapped British diplomat James Cross in 1970 were now on French soil. The three men—Jean-Marc Carbonneau, Jacques Lanctot and Pierre Seguin—were members of the Quebec Liberation Front (FLQ). They had been deported to Cuba in exchange for releasing Cross, but had been deprived of valid travel papers and passports. The French authorities announced the men had entered France via Czechoslovakia June 24 "through a security error." The question of extradition immediately became an issue in the campaign. Prime Minister Trudeau announced June 24 that Ottawa would not seek extradition of the kidnappers. (French officials indicated that a Canadian request for extradition would be denied because France did not extradite persons wanted in political cases.) Trudeau was challenged on his position by Stanfield, who asserted June 25 that the government should try to get the kidnappers returned to Canada unless this was "very clearly precluded by the agreement reached at the time to save Mr. Cross's life."

[8] **Liberals win majority.** The Liberal Party of Prime Minister Trudeau was returned to power July 28 with an unexpected majority government. While the Progressive Conservatives showed gains in the West, where Liberal policies had long been opposed, it lost heavily in Ontario. Stanfield won reelection from his Halifax, Nova Scotia district. The NDP, which had held the balance of power in the previous minority government and had been responsible for the election, lost heavily in the West and in Ontario. One of the victims of the defeat was Lewis,

who lost his Toronto district seat in a liberal sweep of Ontario, the key election province. The election gave Trudeau the majority government he had lost in the 1972 election. It was only the third majority won in the nation's eight elections since 1957. Final results showed the Liberals with 141 seats (up from 109 in 1972), the PC with 95 (107), the NDP with 16 (31), the Social Credit Party (SC) with 11 (15) and one independent (down from two) in the 264-seat House of Commons. The Liberals received 43% of the popular vote, the PC 35%, the NDP 16%, the SC 5% and others 1%. About 62% of the electorate cast ballots, down from 75% in 1972.

[9] **Wiretaps curbed.** A bill to limit wiretapping and other electronic eavesdropping by government agencies and to ban all private bugging became law June 30. The law set forth for the first time specific limits and penalties for government intrusion into individual privacy. Most agencies would be required to present a detailed report to a judge in each case where surveillance was sought. The judge would have to determine that all other means had failed to obtain the necessary information before allowing the tap. All private sales of any bugging equipment were banned. The bill also included a provision requiring the government to notify subjects that they had been bugged.

[10] **Bilingualism.** The Quebec National Assembly July 30 passed the Official Language Act making French the sole official language of the province and relegating English to unofficial status and a matter of "individual rights." The Act was challenged Aug. 9 by New Brunswick Premier Richard Hatfield who asked Prime Minister Trudeau to seek a ruling by Canada's Supreme Court on its constitutionality. According to Hatfield, the Quebec law appeared to infringe on language provisions of the British North America Act (BNAA) which gave French priority in Quebec, but decreed both languages official. The BNAA had also permitted parents the choice of sending their children to either French or English-language schools. Although English speaking citizens formed a 15% minority of the province's 1,000,000 people, immigrants had opted for English education in a ratio of 8:1. A 1970 order-in-council had made French the official language of the government. Anglophones and a number of immigrant groups, which sought to protect their right to acquire knowledge of English rather than French, opposed the bill's education provisions, under which English education would be provided only for those who could demonstrate prior sufficient fluency in English to warrant English-language schooling.

[11] Trudeau said Oct. 3 that the government would not test the constitutionality of Quebec's Official Language Act, known as Bill 22. Trudeau said any challenge should be brought by a private individual rather than the federal government.

[12] The federal government Nov. 21 increased the number of civil service jobs requiring a knowledge of both French and English from 25,000 to 53,584. In the small but key executive category, 92.7% of the positions were designed as requiring bilingualism. The announcement was seen as indicating the government's commitment to making the capital the focal point of Canadian bilingualism.

[13] **Trudeau shuffles Cabinet.** Prime Minister Trudeau announced his Cabinet Aug. 8, departing from Canadian precedent by retiring several ministers to the backbenches and shifting a number of posts. The prime minister said he was introducing a new policy of frequent ministerial changes to bring needed fllexibility to his administration. Six ministers were dropped, eight shifted and four added, with Cabinet posts reduced from 31 to 29.

[14] **Stanfield quitting as PC head.** Stanfield announced Aug. 14 that he would resign as leader of the PC before the next general election. Stanfield's economic

policies received much of the blame for the party's defeat in the July 8 elections. In another development, the NDP July 17 chose Ed Broadbent, an Ontario representative, to succeed Lewis as its parliamentary leader.

[15] **Parliament opens.** Canada's 30th Parliament opened Sept. 30 with a government pledge to tackle "the serious and urgent" problem of inflation by restraining spending and expanding production. "The Canadian government doesn't intend deliberately to generate slack in the economy to order to combat inflation," the government said in its Speech from the Throne. A nationalistic tone was struck with the declaration that "further steps must be taken to enhance Canada's independence and sense of identity" and the vow to extend the domain of the Foreign Investment Review Act.

[16] **Sovereign Constitution sought.** Prime Minister Trudeau told Parliament Oct. 2 that he was "determined" to secure a sovereign Constitution for Canada and end the anomaly under which Canada's charter, the British North America Act 1867, can be amended only by the British Parliament.

[17] **Immigration rules tightened.** Stricter regulations on the entry of new immigrants were announced Oct. 22 by Minister of Manpower and Immigration Robert Andras in an attempt by the government to stem the impact of rising immigration upon Canada's rising unemployment rate. The new rules would make it more difficult for a prospective immigrant who did not have a job awaiting him or a needed skill to qualify for entry under Canada's point system for assessing applications. Sponsored immigrants would not be affected by the tighter requirements. Although he denied that racial discrimination was a factor in tightening the regulations, Andras acknowledged: "If there are racial tensions developing . . . I think they would be aggravated by the inability of the person coming to get access to decent jobs and housing." (Almost half of Canada's 184,200 immigrants in 1973 were from developing countries of South America, Africa, Asia and the Caribbean. Andras noted that more than half the total number of immigrants were settling in major cities, where severe strains on housing, jobs and social services were being felt.)

[18] **Indian and Eskimo developments.** The Ojibway Warriors Society agreed Aug. 19 to end its occupation of the 14-acre Anacinabe Park in Kenora, Ontario. The Indian group had taken over the park July 22 to call attention to grievances against the province's authorities: they claimed the park was Indian land sold illegally to the city of Kenora by the Department of Indian Affairs in 1959. About 200 Ojibway Indians living on land near Batchawana Bay, 40 miles north of Sault Ste. Marie, were given legal title, it was announced Sept. 10.

[19] A protest staged by some 200 Indians on Parliament Hill Sept. 30 turned violent as the Royal Canadian Mounted Police (RCMP) tactical squad was brought in after the Indians broke through police lines. Dozens of protesters were taken away in police vans. Twelve RCMP officers and an undetermined number of protesters were injured in the clash. The Indians were part of the Native People's Caravan, an Indian group, that occupied a vacant government building in Ottawa Sept. 29, vowing not to leave until grievances over land claims, medical care, the Indian Affairs Department, native housing and economic development for the Indian peoples were settled.

[20] About 6,000 Cree Indians and 4,600 Eskimos in the James Bay and New Quebec regions of Quebec signed an agreement in principle with the Quebec Province government Nov. 15 accepting a $150 million settlement of their land claims against the developers of the James Bay hydroelectric project. The natives had carried the suit to the Canadian Supreme Court. The agreement granted the two groups rights over more than 60,000 square miles in the region. In return, the natives agreed to suspend their lawsuit and permit the giant project to continue in a slightly modified form.

Energy Resources

[21] **Quebec oil pipe OKd.** The government decided Jan. 16 to allow an immediate start on a 520-mile oil pipeline from Sarnia, Ontario, to Montreal, to be built without public financial assistance. The $175 million project would be built by Interprovincial Pipe Line Ltd. as an extension of its present pipeline system, which brought oil from western Canada to Ontario through the midwestern U.S. Oil from the pipeline, which would be completed late in 1975, would replace about one-fourth the oil currently imported by Quebec and the Atlantic provinces, while Canadian crude oil exports to the U.S. would be cut by about 20%. The government said it still hoped to build an all-Canada pipeline to bypass the U.S. by 1980, but rejected the route at the present time, because of an estimated additional cost of $200 million and additional two-year construction time.

[22] **Macdonald in U.S.** Energy Minister Donald Macdonald visited Washington Jan. 30-Feb. 1 to discuss energy problems in Canadian-U.S. relations. Accompanied by four deputy Cabinet ministers and other experts, Macdonald met with William Simon, director of the Federal Energy Office, and other officials. Macdonald told a press conference Jan. 31 that U.S. officials had advocated a comprehensive U.S.-Canada energy agreement, but that Canada's goal of self-sufficiency of 1980 precluded such a policy.

[23] **Mackenzie pipeline proposal filed.** Canadian Arctic Gas Pipeline Ltd. filed formal application in Ottawa and Washington March 21 for permission to build a 2,625-mile natural gas pipeline from Prudhoe Bay, Alaska, through the Mackenzie Valley and southward to serve Canadian and U.S. markets. Work on the $5.7 billion pipeline, the largest project ever undertaken with private capital, would begin in late 1976 if approved by mid-1975. However, there were potential obstacles in both countries. In Washington, the Canadian Arctic pipeline plan was challenged by the El Paso Natural Gas Corp. of Houston which announced March 21 its intention to submit a competing proposal for an all-U.S. natural gas plan. The El Paso project would pipe Alaskan gas to southern Alaska where it would be liquified and shipped by tanker to the U.S. West Coast.

[24] **National oil price accord reached.** Prime Minister Trudeau and the provincial premiers met in the year's second energy conference March 27 and agreed on a new 12-15 month interim price for Canadian crude oil. Effective April 1, the per barrel cost rose from $4, the price at which oil had been frozen since late 1973, to $6.50. Trudeau and the premiers agreed that the federal government would retain all the revenues from the oil export tax to finance the subsidy to consumers in the East; gasoline and heating oil prices would rise about 8¢ a gallon in central Ontario and the West. The western oil-producing provinces of Alberta and Saskatchewan would determine for themselves how much of the $2.50 increase would go to the oil companies and how much to their own treasuries. The export price of oil would remain unchanged.

[25] **Crude export levy raised.** Ottawa increased June 1 the export surtax on western crude oil and refined products sold to the U.S. to $5.20 a barrel, pushing the cost of Canadian crude in the U.S. to $11.90 a barrel. The tax had been lowered from $6.40 to $4 a barrel in April when the Canadian price freeze on oil was lifted. Energy Minister Macdonald announced Sept. 20 that Canada had decided unilaterally to raise the price of natural gas exported to the U.S. by 67%, to $1 per thousand cubic feet, effective Jan. 1, 1975. As with oil, a two-price—domestic and export—system was set for gas.

[26] **Phase-out of oil exports to U.S.** Macdonald announced Nov. 22 that the government would begin Jan. 1, 1975 an eight-year phase-out of oil exports to the U.S. The cut, set forth in a government statement based on a report issued by

the National Energy Board (NEB), would reduce exports Jan. 1 to 800,000 barrels a day. Macdonald said a further reduction to 650,000 barrels a day would be imposed July 1, 1975 if the oil-producing provinces of Alberta and Saskatchewan concurred. Subsequent annual reductions would reduce exports to 5,000 a day in 1983. The policy contemplated a complete phase-out thereafter.

[27] Trudeau visits Washington. Prime Minister Trudeau met with President Ford in Washington Dec. 4 for inconclusive talks which centered on Canadian-U.S. oil relations. No agreements emerged and no communique was issued after the two-hour meeting. Before the meeting, an Administration spokesman said Ford was "disappointed" in Canada's decision to phase out oil exports to the U.S., but Trudeau reiterated during the talks Canada's determination to pursue a more protective and nationalistic policy on energy resources. Trudeau met with 10 U.S. senators Dec. 5 for further talks on Canadian oil pricing and supply. Sens. William Brock (R, Tenn.) and Walter Mondale (D, Minn.) expressed disappointment at Trudeau's "tough line" on Ottawa's oil policy. In a Nov. 27 letter to U.S. Secretary of State Henry Kissinger, 17 senators had accused Canada of imposing a "discriminatory tax" of $5.20 a barrel on independent refiners in the northern U.S. by charging what Ottawa called "the world price" on oil. The senators had also suggested that the U.S. retaliate with a transit tax on Canadian oil shipped through U.S. pipelines.

International Trade & Investment

[28] Meat imports restrictions. The Canadian government announced regulations, effective April 9, to limit meat and livestock imports. Temporary beef subsidies of 7¢ a pound had been instituted March 15 in another move to protect and assist the depressed national cattle market. The new import rules, disclosed by Agriculture Minister Eugene Whelan, required certification by the federal authorities of the exporting country that the animals involved had not been given the growth-stimulating hormone, diethylstilbestrol, known as DES. The drug's use as a livestock feed additive was illegal in Canada. Whelan had announced March 6 that the government was "seriously considering" the demands by Canadian cattlemen for interim tariffs and a long-term quota system to protect them against rising imports. (U.S. cattle imports had risen 14-fold in the past year, depressing the price of Canadian livestock. The all-time high prices reported in August 1973 had plummeted about 25% to $43 a hundredweight. U.S. exports totaling more than $150 million annually were immediately effected by the import restrictions. The U.S. ban on DES use had been overturned in a January court action.) The government lifted its ban on U.S. meat imports Aug. 2, announcing that Ottawa and Washington had agreed on a certification system that would assure that no cattle fed with DES growth-stimulating hormone would enter Canada. At the same time, Canada also imposed cattle and beef import quotas and set up a price support program to protect the domestic market. Removal of the import ban was expected to bring lower meat prices in Canada.

[29] U.S. sets retaliatory meat quota. President Ford imposed a quota system Nov. 16 on importation of beef and pork from Canada, charging that Ottawa had erected "unjustifiable import restrictions" against U.S. products. Ford contended that the Canadian meat restrictions "violate the commitments of Canada made to the U.S.,... oppress the commerce of the U.S. and prevent the expansion of trade on a mutually advantageous basis." Secretary of Agriculture Earl Butz said Nov. 18 that Washington was willing to drop its new quotas if Canada eliminated the restrictions on U.S. imports. Ford's decision was denounced in Commons as "totally unjustified" and some members urged that

Ottawa take further actions by restricting Canadian exports of oil or gas to the U.S.

[30] **Foreign investment controls tightened.** A 25-page list of stringent new regulations was presented March 7 as working rules under the Foreign Investment Review Act which passed Parliament by acclamation in 1973. The Act required Cabinet approval for major foreign investment or expansion into new fields. Under the new regulations, a written notice of intended acquisition would have to be submitted by the potential foreign investor to the Foreign Investment Review Agency, the newly established screening body. The notice, which would be evaluated "in terms of its overall compatibility with federal and provincial economic policy objective," would have to cite "significant benefits" for Canada as a result of the acquisition.

[31] **Trade contract with Cuba signed.** MLW-Worthington Ltd., a subsidiary of the U.S.-based firm, Studebaker-Worthington Inc., confirmed March 18 that its representative in Havana had signed a $15 million contract with Cuba for the sale of 30 locomotives. The signing of the contract was in defiance of the U.S. Trading with the Enemy Act of 1962. However, U.S. officials suggested, according to the *New York Times* March 19, that Washington would simply permit the sale without official sanction or intervention.

[32] **Closer EEC ties sought.** Canada presented a formal petition for a comprehensive trade agreement with the European Economic Community (EEC), it was reported April 25. The petition was submitted to the EEC Executive Commission and the community's nine member nations. The proposal was viewed as a major turning point in Prime Minister Trudeau's policy of making Canada less dependent on the U.S. Trudeau visited Brussels Oct. 23-25 after leaving Paris and achieved a first step toward his goal of forging closer ties with the EEC. After talks between Canada and EEC officials Oct. 24, the two parties pledged to undertake negotiations to increase trade ties. The prime minister acknowledged that this fell far short of the contractual accord sought—a preferential trade agreement that would paraphrase and individualize principles already laid down in the General Agreement on Tariffs and Trade (GATT).

[33] **Trade surplus shrinks.** Canada's overall merchandise trade surplus declined $625 million to $335 million in the first half of 1974, from $960 million a year earlier, Statistics Canada reported Aug. 22. A $1.2 billion increase in the trade deficit on finished goods which was caused by the rise in oil and other primary products prices and the deterioration of the U.S. market for Canadian automobile products was responsible for the slump. Canada showed a swing from a $501 million surplus in U.S. trade a year ago to a $65 million deficit in the first half of 1974.

[34] **Trudeau seeks closer French ties.** Prime Minister Trudeau visited France Oct. 21-23, the first Canadian prime minister to visit that country in an official capacity since Lester Pearson in 1964. Relations with France had been cool since the late French President Charles de Gaulle called for a "free Quebec" in 1967. At the conclusion of talks, it was announced Oct. 23 that the two countries had set as a goal the "rapid doubling" of trade. Two study groups were formed to examine closer Canadian-French cooperation, with one panel to study Canadian energy supplies and natural resources, notably uranium, and the other to look into industrial cooperation, particularly surface transport, aerospace and marine transportation.

Economy & Agriculture

[35] **Farmers to get more for grain, cattle.** The Canadian Wheat Board announced Feb. 23 that the prices paid to farmers for wheat and barley would be

raised March 1 by at least 50%. Minister of Justice Lang, who was responsible for the board, said initial payments for wheat would rise from $2.25 to $3.75 a bushel, while barley prices would increase as much as 75¢ to $2.25 a bushel. The price adjustments would be temporary, applying only to the remainder of the 1973-74 crop year. (Late planting because of heavy spring rains and cold weather resulted in an estimated 20% cut in the wheat crop, the Canadian Wheat Board said May 31. A June 25 assessment reported as much as a 25% reduction in the wheat harvest.)

[36] The government announced a $20 million-$25 million subsidy program Dec. 13 to help cattlemen cope with the slump in the beef industry. It also set plans to buy $10 million of low-grade beef for food aid. Farmers had been attempting to relieve a glut in the cattle market—with 15 million head, 6.1% higher than in 1973—by selling cows in the hope that prices would rise when the cattle population dropped.

[37] **Strike developments.** Canadian postal employes and airport firemen returned to work April 26, ending nationwide strikes that had disrupted services within Canada and had an impact beyond the country's borders. (Transcontinental flights from Montreal had been canceled and international service was "severely limited" due to prohibitions against flights by aircraft larger than DC-9s. Mail service was also interrupted when, at Ottawa's request, the U.S. halted all mail to Canada April 22, having instituted partial embargoes on Montreal mail April 12 and on Quebec mail April 17.) Both groups agreed to end their respective strikes pending further negotiations. The 3,750 striking members of the Seafarers' International Union returned to work April 5 after winning wage-and-benefit increases totalling 38% and a work-week reduction from 56 to 40 hours. Striking transit workers in Toronto and Montreal returned to work Sept. 4 and Sept. 19, respectively, after lengthy strikes. (The Toronto workers won an interim wage increase of 12% retroactive to July 1. In Montreal, the government had offered the workers a choice of a $600 lump-sum payment or salary indexing.) Most of the 550 striking grain handlers reported to work Oct. 11, ending their seven-week-long strike after the passage of a back-to-work order by Parliament Oct. 10. Montreal's 2,400 firefighters returned to work Nov. 3, ending a 2½-day strike during which about 20 fires caused an estimated $2 million in damages, mostly to abandoned buildings. The Montreal Firefighters' Association accepted the city's financial offer and proposal to defer negotiations on a new contract.

[38] **Lower taxes in CPI-linked indexing.** Finance Minister John Turner announced Oct. 25 that income taxes would be reduced and some 225,000 persons would be dropped from the tax rolls as a result of the tax indexing plan passed in 1973, linking income taxes to the consumer price index. The savings to taxpayers were expected to cost the government more than $750 million in revenues it would have received had the tax not been tied to the inflation rate. The program would prevent taxpayers from being pushed into higher brackets by income increases caused purely by inflation, such as raises given to compensate for a higher cost of living.

[39] **New budget presented.** Turner presented his second budget in seven months Nov. 18. It contained all the proposals, some of them slightly modified, of the earlier budget on which the government had been defeated in May and included some totally new proposals. The major proposals called for substantial reductions in personal income taxes and increases in the taxes on big corporations, including a 10% surtax on profits. An increase in the basic rate of corporation tax on production profits from minerals, oil and gas from 48% to 50% was also proposed. In recognition of the need to produce more energy

supplies, the budget proposed to reduce the federal share of the taxes on petroleum-production profits gradually from 30% to 25%, to compare with taxes on natural gas and mining profits. This was seen as a concession to the oil-producing provinces. The budget totalled $30 billion.

[40] **Unemployment, prices rise.** The November unemployment rate was 5.5%, the same figure released by the government in January. During the year the rate ranged from 4.9% in June to 5.8% in September. According to a Statistics Canada report in June, British Columbia and Nova Scotia were the only provinces to experience declines in unemployment. The sharpest increase was in Newfoundland where the rate rose from 14.4% to 17.5%. Statistics Canada reported Dec. 11 that the consumer price index had climbed to an annual rate of 12%, the highest in 26 years. Although the third quarter gross national product had increased at an average annual rate of 3.8%, to $14 billion, the increase was entirely accounted for by price rises.

See also ATOMIC ENERGY [1-2]; AUSTRALIA [16, 23]; AUTOMOBILE INDUSTRY [7]; AUTO RACING; BRAZIL [9]; CHAD; CHILE [6, 24]; EUROPEAN SECURITY; FAMINE & FOOD; FOOTBALL; HOCKEY; JAPAN [10-11]; MIDDLE EAST [26]; MONETARY DEVELOPMENTS [4-5, 17]; OIL [8, 15-26, 35]; TARIFFS & TRADE; UNION OF SOVIET SOCIALIST REPUBLICS [21]; UNITED NATIONS [11, 16]; WEATHER

CANCER—*See* FORD, BETTY; MEDICINE & HEALTH [15-16, 20-26, 32]; ROCKEFELLER, MARGARETTA

CAPE VERDE ISLANDS—*See* GUINEA-BISSAU

CAPITAL PUNISHMENT—*See* CRIME [6, 39-40]

CARAMANLIS, CONSTANTINE—*See* CYPRUS [11, 15-16, 26]; GREECE [3-7, 9, 12]

CARTER, REUBEN (HURRICANE)—*See* CRIME [30]

CASEY, WILLIAM J.—*See* APPOINTMENTS & RESIGNATIONS; BANKS & BANKING; WATERGATE [75-76]

CEAUSESCU, NICOLAE—*See* COMMUNISM, INTERNATIONAL; RUMANIA

CENSORSHIP—*See* CENTRAL INTELLIGENCE AGENCY; CHILE [11]; EDUCATION; RUMANIA; SOLZHENITSYN, ALEXANDER; URUGUAY

CENSUS, U.S.—*See* POPULATION

CENTRAL AFRICAN REPUBLIC—A plot to overthrow the government of President Jean-Bedel Bokassa was discovered in Bangui in early December, according to a Dec. 18 report from N'Djamena, Chad. Three members of the Central African Republic's police force were arrested, including Gen. Lingoupou, inspector general, who was sentenced to 10 years in prison.

See also AFRICA

CENTRAL INTELLIGENCE AGENCY (CIA)—Authors win round in CIA secrecy fight. Victor L. Marchetti and John D. Marks, authors of a book on the Central Intelligence Agency (CIA), won a round in their court battle against CIA attempts to exercise prior censorship on sections of their book considered by the CIA to be harmful to national security if revealed. In a ruling announced April 1, U.S. District Court Judge Albert V. Bryan Jr. ruled that the CIA had exceeded its authority in ordering the deletion of 168 passages from the book, *The CIA and the Cult of Intelligence*. After reviewing the excisions by the CIA, Bryan reduced the number to 15. Bryan said the CIA could not classify a fact simply because an official of the agency declared it to be so. Decisions on what was classified, Bryan said, seemed to have been made by each deputy director of the CIA "on an ad hoc basis as he viewed the manuscript." Bryan held that the CIA should have been able to produce documents or other evidence to demonstrate that the material in the book was classified. In 1972, when the book was only in outline form, the CIA had obtained a court order requiring Marchetti and Marks to submit their manuscript, when completed, to the CIA for review. Subsequently, the CIA ordered over 300 passages deleted. Taking advantage of the part of the original court order which allowed them to appeal the deletions by the CIA, the authors won a ruling by Judge Bryan Dec. 21, 1973 that the CIA had to supply evidence, justifying the deletions, to the court and other co-plaintiffs in the suit. Marchetti was a former CIA analyst and Marks a former intelligence officer for the State Department.

Minority report on CIA involvement. A report by the Senate Watergate Committee's minority staff on the CIA's involvement in the Watergate scandal was made public July 2. The 43-page document had been prepared under the direction of Sen. Howard H. Baker Jr. (R, Tenn.), the committee's vice chairman. While the preparers of the report expressly refrained from drawing conclusions, they did reveal, among other things, that the CIA had used a Washington public relations firm as a "cover" for agents outside the U.S., that the agency had destroyed its own records despite a request by Senate majority leader Mike Mansfield (D, Mont.) to keep them intact, that a CIA agent might have functioned as a domestic operative in violation of the agency's charter, that there were unanswered questions about the agency's foreknowledge of the 1971 break-in at Daniel Ellsberg's psychiatrist's office, and that a CIA employe fought within the agency against withholding data from the Watergate committee. In addition, the report detailed instances in which the CIA attempted to frustrate committee investigators by refusing to make its employes available as witnesses and by ignoring, resisting or refusing requests for documents and other materials.

CIA intervention in Chile. The CIA directly subsidized the strikes by Chilean middle class groups in 1972-73 that helped precipitate the military coup against the late President Salvador Allende, the *New York Times* reported Sept. 20. The revelations followed the disclosure Sept. 8 of an $8 million fund for CIA activities in Chile authorized by the so-called 40 Committee, a high-level intelligence panel chaired by Secretary of State Henry A. Kissinger in his capacity as national security adviser to President Nixon. (Existence of the fund was disclosed by CIA Director William E. Colby appearing before the Subcommittee on Intelligence of the House of Representatives Armed Services Committee in executive session April 22.) The Sept. 20 disclosures revealed that most of the $8 million had been used to provide strike benefits and other means of support for anti-Allende truckers, taxi drivers, shop owners and workers. This contradicted public and private claims by President Ford and Secretary Kissinger that the money had been used solely to protect opposition political parties and news media that were allegedly threatened by Allende's government. President Ford's reply to the assertions was made in a Sept. 16 press conference during which he said: "Our government, like other governments, does take certain actions in the intelligence field to help implement foreign policy and protect national security. I am informed reliably that Communist nations spend vastly more money than we do for the same kind of purposes. Now, in this particular case, as I understand it and there's no doubt in my mind, our government had no involvement in any way whatsoever in the coup itself. In a period of time, three or four years ago, there was an effort being made by the Allende government to destroy opposition news media, both the writing press as well as the electronic press. And to destroy opposition political parties. And the effort that was made in this case was to help and assist the preservation of opposition newspapers and electronic media and to preserve opposition political parties. I think this is in the best interest of the people in Chile, and certainly in our best interest."

Although he had initially rejected calls for an investigation, the wave of protests following the reports of CIA activity led Sen. J. William Fulbright (D, Ark.), chairman of the Senate Foreign Relations Committee on Sept. 17 to announce further probes. Fulbright also endorsed a proposal for a joint committee to oversee covert CIA operations abroad which was made by Senate Majority Leader Mike Mansfield (D, Mont.). A recommendation for perjury investigation was also made by the Senate Foreign Relations Subcommittee on Multinational Corporations, headed by Sen. Frank Church (D, Ida.) Church's Subcommittee had earlier investigated attempts by International Telephone and Telegraph Corp. (ITT) to subvert Allende's government. During the ITT hearings, two State Department officials—Charles A. Meyer, former assistant secretary of state for Latin American affairs, and Edward M. Korry, former ambassador to Chile—had testified under oath that the U.S. had maintained a policy of non-intervention toward Chile under Allende. They also refused to answer specific questions about what they said were privileged communications on U.S. policy toward Allende.

Domestic spying reported. The *New York Times* reported Dec. 21 that the CIA, in violation of its 1947 Congressional charter, conducted "a massive, illegal domestic intelligence operation during the Nixon Administration against the antiwar movement and other dissident groups." (The report was written by Seymour Hersh.) An extensive investigation, the *Times* said, had established that a special, top secret unit of the CIA had maintained files on 10,000 U.S. citizens. At least one antiwar congressman was among those under CIA surveillance, the *Times* said. The *Times* also said former CIA Director James Schlesinger had found evidence of dozens of illegal domestic operations by the CIA beginning in the 1950s, including "break-ins, wiretapping and surreptitious interception of mail." These activities, which were also prohibited by the agency's charter, the *Times* said, had been directed against foreign intelligence operatives in the U.S. and not dissident U.S. citizens. Richard Helms, director of the CIA during the first term of the Nixon Administration and current ambassador to Iran, issued a statement through the State Department Dec. 24 denying that "illegal domestic operations against antiwar activists or dissidents" had occurred during his stewardship of the CIA. However, in a report to President Ford Dec. 26, CIA director William Colby confirmed allegations that the CIA had engaged in the surveillance of U.S. citizens, the *Los Angeles Times* reported Dec. 31. Colby's report indicated that the CIA had compiled files on at least 9,000 U.S. citizens and had engaged in other illegal clandestine activities.

The *New York Times* reported Dec. 31 that convicted Watergate conspirator E. Howard Hunt Jr. had been the first chief of covert actions for the Domestic Intelligence Division. In an interview with the *Times,* Hunt said there had been strenuous opposition to the establishment of the Domestic Operations Division in 1962, especially from Helms, and from Thomas H. Karamessines, later the agency's head of covert operations. Continental press, the Washington news agency, was used mostly to supply news articles or propaganda to foreign clients, Hunt said. Fodor's Modern Guides, Inc., then publisher of the Fodor travel guides, was subsidized by the CIA, Hunt said. Fodor's books provided "cover" for CIA agents who posed in foreign countries as travel writers, Hunt explained. One *Times* source had said earlier the domestic spying had been directed during the Nixon Administration by James Angleton, chief of the CIA's counterintelligence department since 1954. Officially, Angleton's job was to insure that foreign agents did not penetrate the CIA. (It was reported Dec. 24 that Angleton had resigned from his post, effective Dec. 31. He also publicly denied the *Times*' allegations.)

See also Argentina [7]; Defense [7]; Laos; Peru [17]; Solzhenitsyn, Alexander; Thailand; Union of Soviet Socialist Republics [33]; Watergate [22, 30-31, 35, 49, 59-60, 80, 83, 99]

CEYLON—*See* Sri Lanka

CHAD—The government announced June 12 a decision to break diplomatic relations with West Germany and ordered Bonn's ambassador and all other West Germans in the country expelled. The move followed Bonn's negotiations with Chadian rebels who had kidnapped Christian Staewen and four others on April 21, including Staewen's wife whose death was reported April 24. Staewen, a doctor, is the nephew of West German President Gustav Heinemann. He was released June 12. In addition to payment of a $750,000 ransom, Bonn also broadcast on June 11 a rebel statement strongly critical of internal conditions in Chad.

President Ngarta Tombalbaye announced Oct. 25 that Chad would not accept any relief assistance from the U.S. and ordered returned to Washington thousands of tons of grain intended to aid the more than two million Chadians believed to be suffering from famine in the wake of the Sahel drought. Tombalbaye said the decision was reached because U.S. officials had refused to allow Chadian authorities "the right to discuss and plan the distribution of the aid." The brunt of his attack, however, was leveled against "an American journalist" who had written articles discrediting him and his government. (*New York Times* correspondent Harry Kamm had reported Oct. 6 and 10 on the state of affairs in drought-ravaged Chad, alleging that the relief program was being grossly mismanaged due to "incompetence, apathy and participation in or toleration of profiteering on the part of persons close to the national leadership.")

Canadian missionaries in Chad alleged that hundreds of Christian workers and converts were being tortured and killed in a wave of religious persecution sweeping the country as the government pursued a policy of reviving long-neglected tribal initiation rites, it was reported Oct. 26.

See also Famine & Food

CHAPIN, DWIGHT L.—*See* Watergate [77]

CHAPPAQUIDDICK INCIDENT—*See* Kennedy, Edward M.; Politics [4]

CHEMICAL & BIOLOGICAL WEAPONS—A Defense Department official told the House Foreign Affairs Committee's Subcommittee on National Security Policy and Scientific Development May 9 that the U.S. military needed a new family of nerve gases to modernize its arsenal of chemical weapons.

The Senate voted 90-0 Dec. 16 to ratify the 1925 Geneva protocol banning chemical and biological warfare. The ratification followed a Ford Administration pledge that it would "renounce as a matter of national policy" the use of tear gas and herbicides except in certain limited circumstances. The issue of whether tear gas and herbicides were covered by the 1925 protocol had delayed consideration of ratification in recent years. The executive branch's position had been that tear gas and herbicides, which the U.S. used extensively in the Vietnam war, were not covered by the international protocol. (The U.N. General Assembly had passed a resolution in 1969 declaring that the protocol banned tear gas and herbicides.) The unanimous Senate vote for ratification Dec. 16 also applied to ratification of a 1972 Geneva Biological Weapons Convention, which also had been delayed by the tear gas-herbicide issue. The convention prohibited development, production and stockpiling of bacteriological and toxic weapons.

CHEMISTRY—*See* NOBEL PRIZES

CHESS—Anatoly Karpov, 23-year-old Leningrad grandmaster, defeated Soviet grandmaster Viktor Korchnoi in a match which decided who would face Bobby Fischer in a world chess title match, it was reported Dec. 24. Fischer, an American, resigned his title in a dispute with the International Chess Foundation.

CHICAGO "SEVEN"—*See* RADICALS

CHICANOS—*See* CIVIL RIGHTS [6]

CHILDREN—*See* MEDICINE & HEALTH [34]; RELIGION [4]

CHILE—Foreign criticism of junta. The Chilean junta was severely criticized around the world as reports of arrests, sentencing without trial, and torture of political opponents mounted throughout the year. Strongest action was taken by Great Britain's Labor government March 27 which cut off aid and military sales to Chile to underscore its "desire to see democracy and human rights fully respected." Overseas Development Minister Judith Hart announced that current aid was being halted except for support for Chilean students and graduates coming to Britain, and financing for completion of one or two minor technical assistance projects. British aid to Chile in the six months ending March 31 was estimated at $1,632,680. The junta responded March 29 when Chilean Mines Minister Gen. Arturo Yovane said he would recommend suspension of all copper shipments to Great Britain. The United Nations Human Rights Commission had sent a message to the junta Feb. 28 asking it to end "all violations of human rights, committed in defiance of the principles enunciated in the United Nations Charter and in other international documents..." The Commission said it had "examined with profound uneasiness the numerous reports from diverse sources according to which flagrant and massive violations of human rights have been committed in Chile." It asked in particular that the junta release five important political prisoners—Clodomiro Almeyda, Luis Corvalan, Enrique Kirberg, Pedro Felipe Ramirez and Anselmo Sule—whose "situation has been reported as dangerous." Chile reportedly agreed to release the men. The message followed an emotional appeal to the Commission Feb. 25 by Hortensia Bussi de Allende, widow of Chilean President Salvador Allende. She asked the Commission to condemn the Chilean junta for "genocidal repression."

[2] Amnesty International had, on Jan. 18, released a statement at U.N. headquarters in New York, charging the junta with torturing and executing its opponents based on reports of conversations with prisoners and guards by an Amnesty commission team which had visited Chile in November 1973. According to the commission's findings, guards freely admitted the training of Chilean interrogators by Brazilian agents. The team had also interviewed political prisoners who showed "visible signs of torture." The commission's findings had been rejected by the junta which said team members had refused to go outside Santiago and thus could not make a well-founded judgement on Chile as a whole. A spokesman for the commission said the inquiry had been limited because of time. Amnesty charged in an 80-page report Sept. 10 that although mass executions apparently had ended, torture of political prisoners continued.

[3] The foreign ministers of Sweden, Denmark, Norway, Finland and Iceland called April 5 for more world pressure against political persecution and imprisonment in Chile.

[4] The Inter-American Commission on Human Rights, a unit of the Organization of American States, reported Aug. 2 that a team of investigators it had sent to Chile in July had found evidence that torture was used in the

interrogation of political prisoners, that persons held without charge were required to do hard labor, that Chileans sometimes disappeared for days or weeks after being seized by police or military intelligence agents, and that military courts had limited access by lawyers to their clients and had tried persons under wartime rules for acts committed before the rules were instituted in September 1973. The junta was also condemned by the International Commission of Jurists (ICJ), which asserted in a report Oct. 23 that repression in Chile was "more ubiquitous and more systematic" than at any time since the military coup. For every detainee who has been released in recent months at least two new arrests have been made," the report alleged.

[5] Mexico broke diplomatic relations with Chile Nov. 26. Mexican Foreign Minister Emilio Rabasa said Nov. 27 that the ties, strained since Chile's military coup in 1973, had "died a natural death." Venezuela agreed to represent Mexican interests in Santiago. The military junta denounced the "strange rupture" in its relations with Mexico Nov. 29, saying it "confirms the dimension of the international attack Chile is suffering."

[6] **Refugees seek asylum.** The number of Chileans seeking asylum continued to grow throughout the year. In early January, the Geneva-based Intergovernmental Committee on European Migration reported that since mid-October, 1973, 2,225 refugees had left Chile for other countries, most of them in Western Europe. Of the Communist nations, only three—East Germany, Yugoslavia and Cuba—had granted asylum. The Soviet Union, which had accepted only three persons, was reportedly bitterly criticized by Latin American leftists for refusing entrance to more refugees, many of whom were members of Chile's Moscow-line Communist Party. Among Western nations granting asylum were France, Sweden, Canada and Mexico. In Great Britain, Foreign Secretary James Callaghan said March 27 that the Labor government would "consider sympathetically" applications from Chilean refugees for settlement. Liberals and leftists in the U.K. had criticized the previous Conservative government for not accepting Chilean immigrants and for refusing asylum in Britain's embassy in Santiago to Chilean political refugees. The U.S. State Department disclosed June 12 that it had denied entry visas to 120 Chilean refugees who had requested them since the 1973 coup, saying, "The United States is not nor can it be responsible for everything that happens in Latin America. It is not nor was it responsible for the course of events in Chile."

[7] The refugees had been able to leave Chile under a program of safe-conduct passes granted by the junta. By Jan. 7, the government reported it had granted 6,462 of these, including 3,419 to Chileans hiding in foreign embassies. It claimed to have expelled 552 foreigners and allowed 605 others to leave since the coup. The French newspaper *Le Monde* reported Feb. 9, however, that the junta had decided to reject any new safe-conduct requests, though it would continue to consider those received previously. Many of those trying to leave Chile had sought sanctuary in foreign embassies, including those of France, Mexico, Colombia, Sweden, Venezuela, Panama, West Germany, Argentina and Italy. Chilean police, however, entered the Argentine embassy in Santiago, it was reported March 14, and arrested the secretary general of the Revolutionary Radical Youth, Alejandro Montesinos, who had taken asylum there. Colombia officially withdrew its ambassador from Chile May 20 and rejected the credentials of Chile's new ambassador in Bogota May 22, following the junta's refusal to grant safe-conduct passes abroad to those refugees who remained in the Colombian embassy. Chile continued to claim that five of the refugees were common criminals and ineligible for political asylum abroad. Mexico had, on April 19, withdrawn its ambassador due to a similar situation. Mexico had,

however, been able to obtain the release of former Economy Minister Pedro Vuskovic by conditioning future purchases of Chilean goods on Vuskovic's emigration. Further exit permissions were granted in June when 72 political refugees in the Mexican embassy were allowed to leave, among them former Transport Undersecretary Jaime Faivovich. They were accompanied by Mexican Foreign Minister Rabasa who had arrived in Chile May 30 on a mission to improve Mexico's strained relations with the junta. Rabasa said June 1 that he had failed in only one of his objectives—to secure the release of ex-Foreign Minister Almeyda, who was held by the junta and scheduled for trial.

Political Developments

[8] **Altamirano in Cuba.** Ex-Sen. Carlos Altamirano, the leftist most sought by the military junta, appeared Jan. 2 in Havana, where he attended celebrations marking the 15th anniversary of the Cuban revolution. Altamirano said at a press conference the next day that he had not taken political asylum in Cuba. He asserted he had left Chile with the approval of leaders of his outlawed Socialist Party, and would return when the anti-junta resistance needed him.

[9] **Christian Democrats criticize junta.**Leaders of the Christian Democratic Party made their first major criticism of the military junta's social and economic policies, but asserted they had not broken with the armed forces. The criticism was contained in a letter to the junta president, Gen. Augusto Pinochet Ugarte, from party President Patricio Aylwin and First Vice President Osvaldo Olguin. It was dated Jan. 18 and reported by the foreign press Feb. 8. "A lasting order cannot be created on the basis of repression," the letter declared. The letter denounced the "denial of any real possibility of adequate defense for accused persons; preventive detention of undetermined length for people who are not tried by competent tribunals; and the use of moral or physical pressures to obtain confessions."

[10] **Extremists executed.** Authorities Jan. 19 announced the execution of six extremists for their part in an armed attack the day before on a military jeep outside the northern city of Quillota. Six other alleged extremists, being transported in the jeep from one prison to another, were allegedly killed in the attack, and two prisoners, identified as lawyer Ruben Cabezas and former Quillota Mayor Pablo Gac, both Socialists, allegedly escaped. Other executions, torture and political arrests were reported by refugees from Chile arriving in Cuba, according to the Cuban press agency Prensa Latina Jan. 3. Eighteen Communist youths were reportedly executed Dec. 25, 1973, following the killing of three other youths Dec. 14, according to Prensa Latina.

[11] **Press censorship established.** The junta Jan. 12 established prepublication censorship of all newspapers and magazines, and suspended the right-wing newspaper *La Segunda*. Though no explanations were given, reports in the *New York Times* Jan. 13 indicated the restrictions were "to prevent the spread of alarmist news." *La Segunda* was closed for printing an article on the current cigarette shortage. Censorship was lifted on Feb. 6, but the media were ordered to continue self-censorship "to avoid distorted information." The junta earlier had abolished the left-wing press and allowed only newspapers that supported it. Easing of the restrictions followed a Jan. 22 critique of the policy in the nation's leading newspaper, *El Mercurio*. It said, among other things, that Chileans must be allowed "to face the truth." *El Mercurio* had supported the junta since the coup. Censorship was also imposed for the first time on the Christian Democratic organ *La Prensa*, it was reported Feb. 8, when an editorial on the independence of the judiciary was deleted by military officials. Directors of the paper announced Feb. 21 that it was closing for financial reasons. They denied

political pressure had been involved, although observers noted that *La Prensa* had reflected growing Christian Democratic disenchantment with the Military junta.

[12] **Senior generals resign.** Two senior army generals considered to be politically moderate resigned in February, apparently strengthening the government's hardline forces led by junta members Gen. Gustavo Leigh Guzman and Adm. Jose Toribio Merino. Gen. Manuel Torres de la Cruz, the army's new inspector general, resigned Feb. 19, and Gen. Orlando Urbina Herrera, chief of the general staff, quit the next day. Torres was replaced by Gen. Hector Bravo Munoz, who kept his job as chief of logistics. Torres had been linked with the conservative sector of the Christian Democratic Party, led by ex-President Eduardo Frei.

[13] **Toha suicide reported.** The junta announced March 15 that former Interior and Defense Minister Jose Toha Gonzalez, a close aide of Allende, had hanged himself in a Santiago military hospital. The announcement was challenged by Chilean and foreign leftists, ecclesiastical authorities and other observers, who doubted that Toha, who reportedly was dying of stomach cancer, was strong enough to hang himself.

[14] **Cardinal Silva threatened.** Raul Cardinal Silva Henriquez, archbishop of Santiago and primate of Chile's Roman Catholic Church, said in a sermon April 14 that he had received threats against his life and was being protected by bodyguards. Silva sharply criticized the military junta, asserting it had not listened to the church's protests against continuing repression. The junta asserted April 14 that Silva's life had been threatened by "leftist extremists." Chile's Roman Catholic Church issued a statement April 24, criticizing the military junta for its economic policies, political repression and violations of human rights.

[15] **Pinochet assumes executive powers.** Pinochet assumed sole executive powers as president of Chile June 26. The other three members of the ruling military junta were assigned subordinate advisory and legislative roles in his government. According to press reports, the development reflected Pinchet's growing power and the apparent failure of the collective military leadership which replaced Allende's government. A decree published June 25 proclaimed Pinochet "supreme chief of the nation" for an indefinite period, with "special powers" to: dictate decrees to "execute the law"; control the armed forces and the judiciary; name cabinet ministers, diplomats, provincial chiefs and judges; hire and fire government employes, and control the nation's budget; maintain diplomatic and commercial relations with other countries; declare a state of emergency in the event of foreign invasion or internal commotion; order the arrest and transfer of persons anywhere in Chile, and pardon convicted criminals. Legislative power was assigned to the commanders of the three armed forces and the national police. Pinochet announced sweeping changes in his Cabinet July 10, replacing eight ministers and creating two new portfolios. The entire Cabinet had resigned July 1 to give Pinochet a free hand. The new ministers—14 military officers and three civilians—were sworn in July 11. Only four members of the old Cabinet retained their posts, and three shifted portfolios. The new Cabinet maintained roughly the same military representation as its predecessor, with five ministers from the army and three each from the navy, air force and national police.

[16] **Military trials, sentences.** A court in Santiago July 30 handed down death sentences for three former officers and one civilian; and prison sentences ranging from 300 days to life for 60 other ex-officers and civilians. The trials, which began April 17, were the first of an expected series of purges against military

officials who had remained loyal to the ousted Popular Unity government. They were also the first open trials of political prisoners, following the secret court-martials of hundreds of persons. The prosecution charged the defendants had committed treason by establishing ties with the civilian Marxist parties and turning over "military secrets" to the enemy. One of the defendants was accused of turning over a map of the El Bosque air force base to the Revolutionary Left Movement (MIR). The enemy, however, was generally defined as the Popular Unity government, which the prosecution charged had lost its legitimacy by repeatedly breaking the law. The death sentences were commuted Aug. 5 to 30 years in prison.

[17] **Letelier freed; many barred from country.** Orlando Letelier, the former Chilean ambassador to the U.S. who held several Cabinet posts in the ousted Popular Unity government, was freed from prison Sept. 10 and exiled to Venezuela. His release was finally obtained by Diego Arria, governor of Caracas, who flew to Santiago to accompany Letelier out of Chile. Letelier had been held with other prominent political prisoners in the naval jail at Ritoque, on the central coast, after being imprisoned on Dawson Island in the Strait of Magellan. Osvaldo Puccio Jr., son of Allende's personal secretary, was freed and exiled with Letelier. His father remained a political prisoner. The military junta announced Sept. 20 that it would free 270 imprisoned leftists. It claimed Oct. 3 that 386 political prisoners had been released in the previous 23 days. The junta said Oct. 3 that it now held only 748 political prisoners, but unofficial reports put the total in the thousands, with a high of 60,000 reported by Popular Unity sources in Argentina Sept. 25. Pinochet said Sept. 11 that he would free nearly all political prisoners if they would leave Chile "definitively" and if the Soviet Union and Cuba released an equal number of political prisoners. The proposal was ridiculed Sept. 13 by Tass, the official Soviet news agency, which compared Pinochet to the Roman emperor Caligula in his "savage brutality and rare cynicism." Pinochet Sept. 11 lifted the state of internal war, in effect since the military coup one year before, but said the state of siege, the daily curfew and the use of military courts would be maintained "for a considerable time."

[18] **Prats assassination.** Retired Gen. Carlos Prats Gonzalez, the former Chilean army commander, and his wife were killed early Sept. 30 in Buenos Aires, Argentina, when a bomb exploded in or under their car. Prats had lived in Argentina since the coup. The couple's remains were flown to Chile Oct. 3, and they were buried in Santiago the following day as leftists inside and outside Chile accused the junta of ordering the assassination.

[19] **MIR trials, arrests, deaths.** Miguel Enriquez, secretary general of MIR was killed Oct. 5 in a shootout with police and soldiers who surrounded the house where he was hiding in the Santiago suburb of San Miguel. Carmen Castillo, an MIR militant and daughter of Fernando Castillo, former rector of the Catholic University, was wounded in the action and captured. Her ex-husband, Andres Pascal Allende, a member of the MIR central committee and nephew of the late President was wounded, but escaped. Enriquez' death reportedly left the armed resistance to the military junta in disarray. Enriquez was the only major leftist leader not in jail or exile. A number of MIR members took asylum in the Italian embassy in Santiago after his death, the government reported Oct. 11. (A total of 107 persons took asylum in the Italian embassy Oct. 6-11, according to Foreign Minister Vice Adm. Patricio Carvajal. Italy did not recognize the junta, and had not replaced its ambassador to Chile who had returned to Italy shortly after the coup.) Castillo, who was seven months pregnant, was released and exiled to France Oct. 26.

[20] Dismemberment of the MIR had begun early in January with the arrest of

51 members who represented approximately 80% of the organization's leadership. They had been tried in Temuco March 30, with 47 of the defendants sentenced to jail terms ranging from two months to 20 years on charges that included violation of the arms control and internal security laws. A second trial for 23 of the defendants opened July 29, after the first sentences had been annulled due to irregularities. On June 14 an air force court in Santiago sentenced 21 MIR members to prison terms ranging from 540 days to life for alleged subversion and infiltrating the armed forces.

[21] Authorities announced Nov. 4 that former Congresswoman Laura Allende de Pascal, sister of the late President, had been arrested in Santiago two days earlier on charges of aiding the MIR. Her husband, Gaston Pascal Lyon, was arrested without explanation Dec. 9. Interior Undersecretary Enrique Montero said security officers raiding Mrs. Pascal's home had found four grenades and a number of letters and documents linking her to the MIR. Her son, Andres, had recently assumed leadership of the guerrilla movement following the death of Enriquez. Two of Mrs. Pascal's other children charged in Mexico City Nov. 5 that their mother was being held hostage until Andres surrendered to authorities.

Economic Developments

[22] **Inflation soars.** The cost of living index rose by 20.8% during June, for a total increase of 145.6% since the beginning of 1974, the National Statistics Institute reported July 11. The government originally had vowed to keep inflation down to 100% for the year, but it had revised its goal to 200%. Economy Minister Fernando Leniz June 5 had announced big price increases for staples, and a bonus of 10,000 escudos for workers in both the public and private sector for June. The price of milk rose by 100%, cooking oil by 90%, bread by 79% and cigarettes by 115%. Leniz charged Chile had inherited its inflationary process from the ousted Popular Unity government. Pinochet announced a new plan to deal with inflation June 7. Employment in the public sector would be cut by 20%, with a moratorium on recruitment of new personnel beginning in June. All government agencies would cut spending by 15%, and no new public works would be started. Leniz June 13 announced a 20% wage adjustment for the beginning of July—coupled with a family bonus of 5,000 escudos—and a further 15% adjustment in October. He said the minimum monthly wage would be raised to 34,300 escudos.

[23] **Denationalization developments.** The U.S. firm Dow Chemical Co. said Jan. 4 that the junta had formally returned to it two Chilean affiliates "requisitioned" by the ousted government in October 1972. The units were reportedly worth more than $32 million. Cerro Corp. announced March 12 that Child had agreed to pay at least $41.9 million for its Chilean copper interests which were nationalized in 1971. The military government and Anaconda Co. of the U.S. announced July 24 that they had reached a settlement over the 1971 expropriation of Anaconda's two Chilean subsidiaries. The subsidiaries, Chile Exploration Co. and Andes Copper Mining Co., operated the Chuquicamata and El Salvador copper mines. Chile had purchased 51% of the companies in 1969 under President Frei, and had nationalized the other 49% two years later under Allende. Under the settlement, Chile immediately paid Anaconda $65 million—$59 million for the Allende seizure and $6 million for the Frei purchase—and signed $188 million worth of promissory notes guaranteed by the Chilean Central Bank. An arbitration panel Nov. 5 upheld International Telephone & Telegraph Corp.'s (ITT) claim to government-backed insurance for the 1971 seizure of its Chilean telephone company. Although the panel did not attempt to determine how much ITT could collect on its $95 million claim

with Overseas Private Investment Corp. (OPIC), an insurance agency supported by the U.S. government, the arbitrators ruled that political actions taken by the Allende government against the firm's subsidiary amounted to expropriation without fair compensation.

OPIC had rejected ITT's claim in April, 1973, alleging that in plotting against the Allende government, ITT had violated the terms of its contract with OPIC. The arbitration panel rejected that charge, terming the firm's anti-Allende activities "tentative and insubstantial." The panel noted, however, that its decision regarding the insurance claim should not be construed as a judgment of ITT's political activities within Chile or of U.S. policy toward the Allende regime. ITT said Dec. 20 that the Chilean government would pay it $125.2 million for equity and debt in the Chile Telephone Co., nationalized by the ousted Popular Unit government in 1971.

[24] **International economic developments.** The International Monetary Fund (IMF) Jan. 30 approved a stand-by arrangement allowing Chile to borrow the equivalent of $94.8 million over the next 12 months to overcome its serious foreign exchange deficit. Chile's 12 creditor nations agreed March 25 to refinance 80% of Chile's foreign debt falling due between Jan. 1, 1973 and Dec. 31. 1974. The accord, following an agreement in principle Feb. 23, covered more than $750 million, including $200 million already consolidated by the ousted Popular Unity government, according to Chilean economic adviser Raul Saez. The Netherlands, a minor creditor, had tried unsuccessfully Feb. 21 to persuade the major creditors to withhold agreement until the Chilean junta liberalized its domestic policies. The U.S., Great Britain and West Germany rejected the proposal as an "introduction of political questions in a financial negotiation." The creditor nations, known as the "Paris Club," said they would meet again in November to study Chile's request to refinance debt payments maturing in 1975. The creditors were the U.S., West Germany, Belgium, Canada, Denmark, Spain, France, Japan, the Netherlands, Sweden, Great Britain and Switzerland.

[25] A controversial $22 million loan to help finance the Chilean junta's agricultural recovery program had been "rammed through" the Inter-American Development Bank by the U.S. over the opposition of several Latin American nations, the *Washington Post* reported April 2.

Other Developments

[26] **Brazilian involvement.** Reports during early 1974 claimed private Brazilian groups had helped to overthrow the Allende government. A *Washington Post* story Jan. 8 said there was no evidence the Brazilian government participated in the activity, although the local intelligence services must have been aware of it. According to the article, by Marlise Simons, two Brazilians, Glycon de Paiva and Aristoteles Drummond, admitted helping anti-Allende forces, and said other private groups gave arms, money and political advice to Chilean opponents of Allende. De Paiva reportedly said that after Allende's election in 1970 a number of Chilean businessmen asked his advice, and he explained how civilians could prepare the conditions for a military coup against the president. According to the report, anti-Allende activists, particularly the neo-fascist Fatherland and Liberty Party, received funds and arms from Brazilians.

[27] Companies based in Mexico, Venezuela and Peru had also helped finance the middle-class strikes which helped precipitate the military coup in 1973, according to Chilean businessmen quoted by the *New York Times* Oct. 16. The businessmen were prominent members of SOFOFA, Chile's most important industrial organization. They said $200,000 donated by the foreign concerns had been channeled to striking truck owners, shopkeepers and professional groups in

the weeks preceding Allende's overthrow. Of that total, the businessmen said, $100,000 was contributed by Protexa, a Mexican manufacturing corporation with a Chilean asphalt affiliate; $50,000 by Grupo Mendoza, one of Venezuela's largest business groups, with interests in machinery imports, cement and paper production; and $50,000 by an unidentified Peruvian company. Protexa and Grupo Mendoza denied any involvement in the Chilean strikes Oct. 15. (For reports that the U.S. CIA had helped to overthrow the Allende regime, see CENTRAL INTELLIGENCE AGENCY.)

[28] **U.S. confirms jet fighters sale.** U.S. officials confirmed Oct. 7 that the U.S. had agreed to sell Chile supersonic jet fighters and close air support attack planes in a $72 million arms deal. Disclosure of the arms deal followed the defeat in the U.S. Congress of two measures to cut off military aid to Chile because of violations of human rights by its military junta. A bitter dispute had been touched off earlier in the U.S. State Department when it was learned that Secretary of State Henry A. Kissinger had rebuked the U.S. ambassador to Chile, David H. Popper, for discussing torture and other human rights issues during a meeting on military aid with Chilean officials, the *New York Times* reported Sept. 27. Some department officials contended that Kissinger was only complaining about Popper's alleged attempt to improperly link the human rights issue with proposals for additional military aid for Chile, the *Times* reported.

See also ARGENTINA [9]; BOLIVIA; BRAZIL [2]; CENTRAL INTELLIGENCE AGENCY; COPPER; FOREIGN AID; LATIN AMERICA; MIDDLE EAST [26]; NICARAGUA; PERU [15-16]; VENEZUELA

CHINA, COMMUNIST (PEOPLE'S REPUBLIC OF CHINA)—New Cultural Revolution launched. China formally launched a new Cultural Revolution-type campaign Feb. 3 whose focus was condemnation of the Chinese philosopher Confucius and the late former Defense Minister Lin Piao. Both figures were accused of attempting to restore the old regimes of their day. The Communist Party newspaper *Jenmin Jih Pao* said Feb. 2 that the campaign involved "consolidating and carrying to a higher stage" the gains of the previous Cultural Revolution of 1966-69. Wide support for the campaign was being mobilized by small groups of activists who were said to be forming "study groups" and "mass criticism groups." The theme also was being sounded by official press and broadcasts which told of mass rallies in many provinces of students, soldiers and workers. An indication that the campaign might take a violent turn was evidenced in an *Hung Chi* editorial published in major Peking newspapers Feb. 6. The editorial declared that "without destruction there can be no construction." The phrase had been used at the beginning of the Cultural Revolution and was followed two months later by attacks by the Red Guards. *Hung Chi* also cautioned against tendencies to "worship things foreign," suggesting that the drive might take on a xenophobic tinge. The ideological drive intensified in following months with attacks on literary, artistic and political figures; on"economism"; and against opponents of the campaign, some of whom were accused of "sabotage activities." Among those attacked were American author Richard Bach whose book *Jonathan Livingston Seagull* was called "idealistic claptrap," and the compositions of Beethoven and Schubert. A report March 5 told of a renewal of attacks on "economism," which was regarded as part of the reaffirmation of the Cultural Revolution. Wall posters were reported in factories denouncing the "evil tendency" to offer workers overtime payments and other incentives to spur production. (Chinese officials were assuring U.S. businessmen that the ideological drive would not damage

U.S.-Chinese trade, it was reported March 11. One American business representative, Harned Pettus Hoose, said "It was entirely business as usual" in th Foreign Trade Ministry and in the offices of the major Chinese trade corporations.)

Attacks on Communist Party officials began in March. Reuters news agency reported witnesses as saying that wall posters in Taiyuan, capital of Shansi Province, called for the removal of Hsieh Chen-hua, first party secretary and military commander of the province, and Tsao Chung-nan, deputy political commissar. In April, wall posters appeared in Anwei Province denouncing Li Teh-sheng, a member of the ruling nine-man committee of the Communist Party Politburo who was accused of being a "sworn follower" of Lin Piao. Peking city officials were assailed by posters that appeared near the municipal headquarters June 13-14. The Municipal Revolutionary Committee, which governed the capital, was accused of attempting to "keep the lid" on the drive against Lin and Confucius. The Municipal Revolutionary Committee was also accused of trying to rehabilitate former chief of state Liu Shao-chi (whose death was confirmed Oct. 31 by a Communist newspaper in Hong Kong) and former Peking Mayor Peng Chen, both of whom had been purged in the 1966-69 Cultural Revolution. One of the first official reports of violence since the start of China's ideological campaign was contained in a broadcast July 18 from Nanking, capital of Kiangsu Province. The report, monitored in Hong Kong, said gangsters and other "bad elements" had "seriously sabotaged social order" in the province. Clashes in Kiangsi June 10 and 18 and other incidents in the province in which more than 200 persons had been killed at some unspecified time were described in wall placards that went up in Peking June 24. The killings were blamed on former provincial leader Chen Shih-ching, who had risen to prominence at the end of the 1960s and dropped from view in 1972. The posters said followers of Lin Piao had tried to transform Kiangsi into a base for his faction and that there had been big output drops in some industrial and agricultural enterprises. Posters appearing in Peking June 23 charged that right-wingers armed with wooden clubs and iron bars had fought with other groups of people June 19 in Nanchang, capital of Kiangsi Province. (The ideological campaign against Lin resulted in the recent execution of about 30 persons in Canton, travelers from the southern city had reported April 17.)

The newspaper *Jenmin Jih Pao* warned the army Nov. 13 to submit unconditionally to the authority of the party. The journal said: "We absolutely must not permit the army to become an instrument in the hands of the careerists." The statement followed reports that the campaign to criticize Lin had evoked negative reactions from certain sectors of the high command. In a show of defiance, the majority of the regional military commanders were said to have refused to attend a meeting of the top party leadership in late September.

A secret Chinese document made public by a Hong Kong newspaper Nov. 14 said China's leadership had complained earlier in 1974 that the ideological campaign had caused "major weaknesses" in the country's economy. According to the report, the document said the anti-Confucius drive had resulted in a drop in coal output and in railway congestion, forcing "many enterprises to cease or reduce their production."

Government changes. The Chinese government carried out a major shakeup of its top military command, the Hsinhua press agency reported Jan. 4. Eight of 11 regional commanders were removed from their provincial posts and reassigned to other area commands. The action had the effect of reducing the power and importance of the military hierarchy and bringing it under closer civilian control.

Chiao Kuan-hua replaced Chi Peng-fei as foreign minister, the Chinese government announced Nov. 15. Chiao had headed China's United Nations delegation to the General Assembly since 1971. Chi, who had become foreign minister on the death of Chen Yi in 1972, was to be given another assignment, a Foreign Ministry spokesman said.

Chou's illness. Illness caused Premier Chou En-lai to be absent from a state banquet May 9 for visiting Senegal President Leopold Senghor, the Chinese Foreign Ministry reported. Chou's health was also mentioned by Sen. Henry M. Jackson (D, Wash.) who visited Peking July 1-6. The trip confirmed reports that Chou, 76, had been ill; but following a half-hour conference between the two men in a Peking hospital, July 7, Jackson reported Chou was "terribly sharp," "up on everything" and "most responsive." Chou appeared Sept. 30 at an official reception in Peking's Great Hall of the People, part of the ceremonies marking the 25th anniversary of Communist rule. He made a brief speech and then returned to a hospital for further treatment of a heart ailment.

Peking briefed on Soviet pact. U.S. Secretary of State Henry Kissinger arrived in Peking Nov. 25, his seventh visit to the People's Republic of China, to brief Chinese leaders on the summit meeting between President Ford and Soviet Communist Party General Secretary Leonid Brezhnev. The Peking talks also focused on Sino-U.S. relations, specifically the Taiwan issue, Chinese assets frozen in the U.S. and U.S. property claims against China. Kissinger visited with Chou En-lai Nov. 25 in a Peking hospital. The secretary of state left China Nov. 29 without having been accorded a visit with Chairman Mao Tse-tung, a gesture that was seen as an indication of Chinese displeasure at the lack of momentum in Sino-U.S. relations. In a brief communique issued Nov. 29, the U.S. and China "reaffirmed their unchanged commitment to the principles of the Shanghai Communique" and agreed that President Ford would visit China in 1975.

See also APPOINTMENTS & RESIGNATIONS; ATOMIC ENERGY [5, 10]; AUSTRALIA [2]; BRAZIL [12]; CAMBODIA; COMMUNISM, INTERNATIONAL; CUBA; FAMINE & FOOD; HONG KONG; INDONESIA; IRAN; JAPAN [14]; MACAO; MIDDLE EAST [30]; NIXON, RICHARD M.; OBITUARIES [TSO-YI]; PAKISTAN; PERU [16]; POPULATION; SOLZHENITSYN, ALEXANDER; TANZANIA; TERRITORIAL WATERS; UNITED NATIONS [6-7]; WATERGATE [40]

CHINA, NATIONALIST (TAIWAN)—U.S. Defense Department officials disclosed Aug. 7 the withdrawal in late July of a U.S. squadron of 18 F-4 Phantom jets from Taiwan, with the remaining 18-plane squadron to be pulled out in about a year. The aircraft had been sent to Taiwan in 1972 after Nationalist China had agreed to lend South Vietnam about 40 U.S.-built F-5 fighters. About 20 of the F-5s had been returned to Taiwan.

See also APPOINTMENTS & RESIGNATIONS; BASEBALL; BRAZIL [12]; CHINA, COMMUNIST; JAPAN [14]
CHINESE-AMERICANS—*See* CIVIL RIGHTS
CHOLERA—*See* WEATHER
CITIES—*See* HOUSING

CIVIL RIGHTS

Education

[1] **Congressional action on busing.** A conference committee version of a bill authorizing $25.2 billion over four years in aid to elementary and secondary schools and containing restrictions on busing of students was passed by the Senate on a vote of 81-15 July 24 and by a House vote of 323-83 July 31. Busing provisions accepted by the conferees were generally closer to the more lenient Senate bill. The final version prohibited busing for desegregation beyond the school next closest to a student's home, except—as in the Senate bill—when courts determined that more

extensive busing was necessary to protect students' constitutional rights. The final bill did not include a House provision that would have required the courts to reopen consideration of previous integration orders to bring them into compliance with the bill's restrictions. President Ford signed the bill Aug. 21.

[2] In the final week of its session, Congress resolved a 2½-month dispute over an amendment prohibiting enforcement of federal anti-discrimination laws in school systems. The amendments, sponsored by Rep. Marjorie S. Holt (R, Md.), was attached to a bill making fiscal 1975 supplemental appropriations of $8,659,352,078, more than $5 billion of it for elementary and secondary education programs. The bill was cleared by Congress Dec. 16. President Ford signed it Dec. 27. Although busing of students was not mentioned in the amendment, the provision was considered an antibusing stricture in the original version. As adopted by the House-Senate conference committee, the Holt amendment read: "None of these funds shall be used to compel any school system as a condition for receiving grants and other benefits from the appropriations above, to classify teachers or students by race, religion, sex or national origin; or to assign teachers or students to schools, classes or courses for reasons of race, religion, sex or national origin." This was approved by the House by a 212-176 vote Dec. 4. The Senate retained the amendment after adding 12 words: "... except as may be required to enforce non-discrimination provisions of federal law." Sen. James B. Allen (D, Ala.) threatened to filibuster the revision Dec. 11 after his motion to table it was rejected 60-33. A motion to invoke cloture, or limit debate, was adopted Dec. 14 for only the 24th time in Senate history. The vote, requiring a two-thirds majority to carry, was 56-27.

[3] **Court rejects cross-district busing.** The Supreme Court July 25 struck down a plan to desegregate the predominately black Detroit school system by merging it with mostly white, neighboring districts. The 5-4 decision all but banned desegregation through the busing of children across school district lines. Chief Justice Warren E. Burger, author of the court's majority opinion, was joined by Justices Harry A. Blackmun, Lewis F. Powell Jr. and William H. Rehnquist, all appointees of President Nixon, and Potter Stewart, named to the court by President Eisenhower. In his opinion Burger wrote, "No single tradition in public education is more deeply rooted than local control over the operation of schools ... local control over the educational process affords citizens an opportunity to participate in the decision-making, permits the structuring of school programs to fit local needs and encourages experimentation, innovation and a healthy competition for educational excellence." In a dissent, Justice Thurgood Marshall charged that the court's answer to this problem was to "provide no remedy at all ..., thereby guaranteeing that Negro children in Detroit will receive the same separate and inherently unequal education in the future as they have been unconstitutionally afforded in the past."

[4] **Boston busing controversy.** U.S. District Court Judge W. Arthur Garrity Jr. ruled June 21 that Boston had deliberately maintained a segregated public school system, and ordered that a state-devised racial balance plan be implemented in September. Under the state plan, the number of black-majority schools would be reduced from 68 to 40. At least 6,000 pupils, black and white (out of 94,000) would be bused. Scattered violence and successful boycotts of some schools marred the opening of Boston public schools Sept. 12 under the court-ordered busing plan. Trouble was focused in the predominantly white South Boston area. At South Boston High, a boycott proclaimed by white parents, and fear of violence, kept attendance Sept. 12-13 at fewer than 100 pupils out of the 1,500 expected to be enrolled. Buses carrying black students were stoned as they left the school on both days, although Mayor Kevin White had ordered police escorts after the first incidents Sept. 12. In another neighborhood, a bus

carrying white students was stoned as it passed through a black area. The busing plan was carried out without serious incident in most other areas of the city, and system-wide attendance was about 65% of normal. White announced Oct. 9 that 300 Massachusetts state police, 100 Metropolitan District Commission police and their supervisory personnel had been placed under the control of the city's police commissioner, Robert J. diGrazia. The police were made available by Gov. Francis Sargent following a request by White. However, outbreaks of violence continued and Sargent Oct. 15 ordered the mobilization of 450 National Guardsmen and called on President Ford to send Federal troops to Boston. President Ford declined to act on Sargent's request. Use of federal troops to deal with violence in Boston schools, Ford said Oct. 15, should be only as a "last resort." A request for U.S. troops would not be in order until Sargent had exhausted the full resources of the state, a White House statement indicated. The President had been accused by White Oct. 10 of fanning the "flames of resistance" to school integration. The mayor's criticism was in response to Ford's Oct. 9 press conference remark that he deplored forced busing to achieve school integration. By Oct. 22, a general calm, punctuated by minor racial flare-ups, had returned to the Boston schools. As the violence subsided, school attendance at all grade levels rose to a city-wide average of 75% Oct. 18. However, attendance in the Roxbury-South Boston district hovered at 28% of a projected enrollment of 3,361. (Gov. Sargent ordered a two-thirds reduction Nov. 1 in the 450-man contingent of National Guardsmen.)

[5] Judge Garrity signed a final order Oct. 30 requiring the Boston School Committee to develop by Dec. 16 a city-wide school integration plan to replace the interim court-ordered program of busing for desegregation. The new plan, which would go into effect in the fall of 1975, would free several million dollars in emergency desegregation aid from the Department of Health, Education and Welfare (HEW). In his order, Garrity urged the Committee to draft plans that would achieve desegregation with a minimum of busing and reassignment of students. Garrity Dec. 18 ordered three members of the Boston School Committee to show cause by Dec. 27 why they should not be held in civil contempt of court. In defiance of Garrtiy's Oct. 31 order, the school Committee, by a 3-2 vote Dec. 16, rejected a plan drawn up by the school system's attorneys and staff. Meanwhile, school system officials Dec. 17 decided to keep South Boston and Roxbury High Schools closed until Jan. 2, 1975. The schools had been closed Dec. 11 when a crowd of whites, angry over the stabbing of a white student by a black, trapped 135 black students in South Boston High School for four hours. Two days before at the school, four white girls had been injured in racial fighting. Garrity Dec. 27 held the three members of the committee who voted against the plan in civil contempt. On Dec. 30 Garrity ordered the committee members fined and barred from participating in school desegregation matters unless they endorsed a new integration plan by Jan. 7, 1975. The 1st U.S. Circuit Court of Appeals Dec. 19 unanimously upheld Garrity's finding that Boston had deliberately operated a segregated school system.

[6] **Culture, language bias.** Reversing a lower court decision, the Supreme Court ruled unanimously Jan. 21 that the San Francisco public school system was in violation of the 1964 Civil Rights Act if it did not provide English language instruction for 1,800 non-English speaking Chinese pupils. The U.S. Commission on Civil Rights, in the final report of a study of Mexican-American (Chicano) education, said Feb. 4 that the five southwestern states with large Chicano populations had consistently failed to provide equal educational opportunities. The commission said Chicano language and culture were largely ignored "and even suppressed" in southwestern schools: only about 4% of 1.6

million Chicano students were reached by bilingual teaching projects; courses in Mexican history were offered in fewer than 10% of the schools; and fewer than 3% offered Chicano studies. Of the 350,000 teachers in the Southwest, the report said, fewer than 5% were Chicano. The New York City board of education agreed in federal court Aug. 29 to establish a program for Spanish-language instruction in basic subjects for students unable to make adequate progress when taught in English. The same students would also be given intensive instruction in English, and efforts would be made to improve their Spanish. The agreement settled a suit filed by Puerto Rican groups charging that the school system had failed to meet the needs of its 200,000 Spanish-speaking pupils.

[7] **Justices sidestep law school quota case.** The Supreme Court April 23 declined to rule on the constitutionality of law school admissions policies giving preference to members of minority groups at the expense of white applicants. In an unsigned opinion, the court majority of five justices held that the case was moot because the student who originally brought the suit to gain admission to the University of Washington Law School was to graduate from the school in June 1974. Marco DeFunis Jr., a white Phi Beta Kappa graduate of the University of Washington, sued in 1971 after being rejected for admission by the law school and subsequently learning that 36 minority applicants—with lower predicted first year averages than his—had been admitted. A trial court, agreeing that the admissions policies violated DeFunis' right to equal protection under the law, ordered the law school to admit the defendant. The Washington State Supreme Court later reversed the order, but Justice William O. Douglas interceded, granting a stay pending U.S. Supreme Court resolution of the case. The court did not preclude a decision at a later date.

Employment Bias

[8] **State and local government.** The city of Jackson, Miss. and the U.S. Justice Department reached an agreement providing quotas for the increased placement of blacks on the municipal payroll and back pay up to $1,000 for currently-employed blacks who had been denied promotion opportunities, it was reported March 31. The accord also provided that at least one-third of city jobs would be filled by women.

[9] The U.S. Court of Appeals for the 5th Circuit April 19 upheld a lower court decision that the Alabama Department of Public Safety must revise its hiring policies so that the state's highway patrol force could become 25% black. In a related decision reported March 31, the court had found that the Mississippi highway patrol discriminated against blacks, but stopped short of ordering quota hiring. (A study by the Police Foundation, a unit of the Ford Foundation, showed that about 6% of the nation's police officers were from racial minorities and less than 2% were women, it was reported April 21.)

[10] The Justice Department obtained a consent decree June 27 setting percentage quotas for minority hiring in the Los Angeles fire department and requiring a recruiting program which would emphasize that women would be eligible for employment. The city also agreed to replace the term "fireman" with "firefighter."

[11] U.S. District Court Judge John Lewis Smith Jr. Dec. 18 ordered the Treasury Department's office of Revenue Sharing to stop making revenue-sharing payments to Chicago until the city took affirmative action to end racial discrimination in its police department.

[12] **Private industry.** The Justice Department obtained a consent decree March 20 under which seven large trucking companies would adopt percentage hiring goals for blacks and Spanish-surnamed persons. The quotas, based on

population figures, would be subject to the availability of qualified applicants in any locality. The agreement could be modified to include Indians or Asian-Americans in certain areas.

[13] Nine major steel companies, the United Steelworkers of America (AFL-CIO) and the federal government signed agreements April 15 providing back pay, totaling $30.9 million, and expanded job opportunities for minorities and women. The accord was contained in consent decrees filed in U.S. district court in Birmingham, Ala., resolving a Justice Department discrimination suit filed at the same time. The companies were: Allegheny-Ludlum Industries, Inc., Armco Steel Corp., Bethlehem Steel Corp., Jones & Laughlin Steel Corp., National Steel Corp., Republic Steel Corp., U.S. Steel Corp., Wheeling-Pittsburgh Steel Corp. and Youngstown Sheet & Tube Co. According to the Justice Department, the companies produced about 73% of the nation's raw steel and employed 347,679 workers, of whom 52,545 were black, 7,646 Spanish-surnamed and 10,175 women. The National Association for the Advancement of Colored People, which had opposed the settlement as inadequate and an obstruction to other litigation under the Civil Rights Act, filed suit in the Birmingham court April 23 to have the consent decrees set aside.

[14] Standard Oil Co. (California) agreed May 16 to pay $2 million in back wages to 160 persons between the ages of 40 and 65 who had been discharged and to rehire 120 of them. The workers had been employed in eight western states in Standard's Western Operations Division. The Labor Department, which obtained the consent decree, had charged the company with using age as a criterion for dismissal over a three-year period. The back-pay settlement was the largest under the Age Discrimination in Employment Act of 1967.

[15] The American Telephone & Telegraph Co. (AT&T) reached an agreement with the federal government May 30 providing almost $30 million in back pay and future salary adjustments to compensate for pay discrimination against managerial employes. A settlement involving nonmanagerial employes was reached in 1973. The majority of those receiving pay adjustments would be women, but the government had charged that in some cases sex discrimination worked in both directions, and that there were instances of racial discrimination. In another action, AT&T, the largest private employer in the U.S., banned discrimination against homosexuals in future hiring and retention of current jobs, it was reported Aug. 8.

[16] The Labor Department filed a suit charging Chessie System Inc., owner of the Baltimore & Ohio and Chesapeake & Ohio railroads, with illegally dismissing, demoting or denying work to 300 supervisory employes because of age, it was reported June 20. For the first time under the Age Discrimination in Employment Act of 1967, the department sought abolition of a mandatory retirement age of 62, which had been included in a revision of the company's pension plan.

[17] The Labor Department imposed mandatory minority hiring goals July 2 on building contractors and 101 construction union locals in 21 areas. The department said the unions had failed to meet employment obligations under earlier voluntary plans. Under the new orders, contractors bidding on projects receiving federal funds would be required to see that unions met percentage goals, which were based on population composition of individual cities and regions. Failure to make "good-faith" efforts could result in loss of contracts or suspension.

Other Developments

[18] **Bias suit vs Cairo, Ill. judges barred.** The Supreme Court, reversing an appellate court decision, ruled 6-3 Jan. 15 that 17 blacks and two whites from

Cairo, Ill. were not entitled to seek injunctions against local judges and prosecutors, who, the plaintiffs had charged, engaged in a pattern of setting excessive bail and meting out harsher punishments for blacks than whites. The court majority held that the complaints did not constitute a real case or controversy, the constitutional test for obtaining relief from the federal courts. Even if the petitioners had been able to prove discrimination, a five-justice majority also ruled, they could not seek federal court injunctions against such practices, since those would amount to "an ongoing audit of state criminal proceedings" in violation of federal-state harmony.

[19] **Black political convention.** About 1,700 delegates to the second National Black Political Convention met in Little Rock, Ark. March 15-17 in an atmosphere of conflict between black nationalist leaders advocating a separatist approach to political action and the more conservative leaders who favored operating within the traditional political structure. Similar divisions had marked the first convention two years earlier. A resolution calling for a black political party was defeated March 17 partly because, according to some delegates, the convention had not carried out the local organizational groundwork necessary to build an effective political unit. Among the resolutions approved was one urging creation of a black "united fund" with a goal of raising $10 million by 1976 for further convention activities, local organizations in the U.S., and projects in Africa. The convention also urged support of African liberation movements. A resolution condemning Israel as a "major instrument" of a U.S. "world strategy of monopoly" was toned down before final approval to a condemnation of black congressmen who had voted for military aid to Israel while "ignoring the plight of Arab Palestine refugees."

[20] **NYC gets new vote districts.** The New York State legislature May 29 approved a redistricting plan involving several state legislative districts in the New York City boroughs of Manhattan and Brooklyn and two Congressional districts in Brooklyn. The U.S. Justice Department had announced April 1 that the lines would have to be redrawn to eliminate racial discrimination before further elections could be held. Under the plan, Congressional districts currently represented by Shirley Chisholm and John J. Rooney, both Democrats, would be merged and redivided on a different axis. (Rooney, 70, announced June 3 that he would not seek re-relection in November. Rooney had been in the House since 1944.)

[21] **Rights unit criticizes U.S. agencies.** A report by the U.S. Commission on Civil Rights, made public Nov. 12, charged five federal regulatory agencies with failure to combat job discrimination in the industries they regulated. The study cited four agencies—the Interstate Commerce Commission (ICC), the Civil Aeronautics Board (CAB), the Federal Power Commission (FPC) and the Securities and Exchange Commission (SEC)—for not having issued rules forbidding job discrimination. The report called anti-discrimination rules issued by the Federal Communications Commission (FCC) "highly inadequate." The commission, in a report issued Dec. 16, said that the Department of Housing and Urban Development (HUD) and six other agencies with fair-housing responsibilities had done a poor job in combating housing discrimination. The report said the positive actions taken by HUD and the other agencies had "generally been superficial or incomplete and have had little impact on the country's serious housing discrimination problem."

See also BASEBALL; BASKETBALL; EDUCATION; ELECTIONS [2]; HOMOSEXUALS; INDIAN AFFAIRS; INTELLIGENCE; KENT STATE; NARCOTICS & DANGEROUS DRUGS; POLITICS [6, 8-9, 12]; POPULATION; VOTING RIGHTS; WOMEN'S RIGHTS

CIVIL SERVICE—Pay raise delay ruled illegal. The U.S. Court of Appeals for the District of Columbia held illegal Jan. 25 President Nixon's failure to grant a legislated pay increase to federal workers in 1972. The President had delayed the increase from October 1972 to January 1973 in light of the 1972 wage guidelines. The court said the 1970 Federal Pay Comparability Act required the President to adjust the federal civilian salaries to be comparable to those in private commerce or to recommend an alternative course to Congress. Although the suit was brought by the 60,000-member National Treasury Employes Union, the ruling would affect the 2.1 million federal white collar employes and cost an estimated $500 million.

Senate blocks pay-raise deferral. The Senate Sept. 19 rejected President Ford's request for a three-month deferral of a 5.5% pay increase scheduled to take effect Oct. 1 for 3.5 million federal employes. The vote was 64-35 (49 D & 15 R vs. 27 R & 8 D). The President, who had sought the deferral as an anti-inflation step, expressed disappointment but agreed "that federal employes deserve this pay increase." The increase, for 1.3 million white collar civilian employes and 2.2 million military personnel, had been recommended under 1970 legislation requiring federal pay to be comparable to that paid by private industry. Under the law, presidential modification of the increase, which had been recommended by the Civil Service Commission and the Office of Management and Budget, would go into effect unless vetoed by a majority vote of either house of Congress.

See also CAMPAIGN FINANCING [22]; CIVIL RIGHTS [8-11]; HOUSING; LABOR [2, 4, 6]; VETERANS

CLASS ACTION SUITS—*See* CONSUMER AFFAIRS [1]
CLOTHING INDUSTRY—*See* ANTITRUST ACTIONS [10]; LABOR [15]; NETHERLANDS [10]
COAL MINING—*See* ENERGY CRISIS [7]; ENVIRONMENT & POLLUTION [20]; LABOR

COFFEE—Venezuela agreed to invest several million dollars from its increased oil wealth to underwrite action by coffee producing nations to hold up world coffee prices. The commitment was announced Nov. 4 by President Alfonso Lopez Michelsen of Colombia, the world's second largest coffee producer. Venezuela would finance coffee stockpiling by small Central American countries which needed immediate income from coffee sales. Colombia and Brazil, the world's leading producer, would finance their own stockpiling. The executive board of the International Coffee Organization had voted Sept. 20 to extend for another year, until Sept. 30, 1976, the current International Coffee Agreement, which set export controls to stabilize coffee prices.

Representatives of Costa Rica, El Salvador, Nicaragua, Guatamala, Honduras, the Dominican Republic, Mexico and Venezuela met in Caracas Nov. 15-17 and agreed to form a multinational corporation to increase coffee prices on the world market. The firm, to be called Cia. Cafes Suaves Centrales, S.A. de C.V., would begin operations in January, 1975, with headquarters in Mexico City. It would be financed largely by Venezuela, which reportedly would contribute as much as $80 million to its operations. Brazil and Colombia, the world's major coffee producers, did not join the company. Coffee prices had dropped sharply in 1974.

COLOMBIA—Lopez elected president. Liberal Party candidate Alfonso Lopez Michelsen was elected president of Colombia by a landslide April 21. His four-year term of office began in August. Lopez won by more than a million votes over Alvaro Gomez Hurtado of the Conservative Party, which had shared power with the Liberals for the past 16 years under the National Front agreement. Parts of the agreement still in effect would force the Liberals to share Cabinet seats, the top administrative posts and the departmental governorships with the Conservatives. The elections were preceded by comparatively little violence, but a student-police confrontation April 19 at the National University in Bogota left two students dead and a secret police agent seriously wounded. Five persons were killed that same day in the Andean village of Yacopi, 150 miles south of Bogota. First reports said guerrillas of the Colombian Revolutionary Armed Forces (FARC) had committed the murders to frighten voters away from the polls, but police later claimed the incident was a "common hold-up." Lopez was inaugurated as president Aug. 7. Before taking the oath of office, Lopez announced a Cabinet composed of one army general and six members each of the Liberal and Conservative Parties. Lopez named one woman to the Cabinet—Labor Minister Maria Elena del Crovo—and in an unprecedented move, he named women to six of the 22 departmental governorships Aug. 8. A woman also was named economic secretary to the presidency. The Cabinet members were well received with the exception of Agriculture Minister Rafael Pardo Buelvas, who was criticized by peasants' associations. In rebuttal, Pardo said he would "be a spokesman for the peasants" and expressed agreement with Lopez' goal of changing the agrarian reform program, unsuccesful in spite of a 13-year, $300-million investment.

Leftist labor unions recognized. The government Aug. 20 granted legal recognition to the Colombian Workers Syndical Confederation (CTSC), a Communist-led labor group. The General Labor Confederation, a Christian Democratic alliance, was reported recognized Sept. 13. It was the first time in 16 years that Communist unions had been recognized. Previously, only the Colombian Workers Union, aligned with the Conservative Party, and the Colombian Workers Confederation, affiliated with the Liberal Party, had operated legally.

Emergency program. Lopez declared a state of economic emergency and issued a series of decrees to combat fiscal bankruptcy, inflation, a fall in wages, and contraband export of food. The unprecedented state of emergency was declared Sept. 17. It allowed the government to enact economic legislation by decree for 45 days, avoiding the long delays normally faced by legislation in Congress. The decrees would remain in force after the emergency period ended. A variety of measures enacted Sept. 18-Oct. 13 aimed at cutting government expenditures (seen by many as the principal cause of inflation), redistributing income, boosting agricultural production and achieving what the government called a "realistic" prices and incomes structure. The measures were initially supported by most sectors, with the exception of the CTSC, which condemned wihdrawal of wheat subsidies Sept. 18. Businessmen initially supported the decrees but began attacking the government in October, charging the tax reforms and discouragement of exports were contributing to inflation.

Landslides. Cascading earth and rocks which covered a section of highway 95 miles east of Bogota killed at least 200 persons June 28. The landslide occurred on the eastern slope of the Andes mountain range. A landslide in a shantytown outside Medellin killed at least 60 persons, it was reported Sept. 30. Some 30 persons were killed Oct. 6 when a landslide 100 miles north of Medellin buried part of a small town.

See also CHILE [7]; COFFEE; LATIN AMERICA; OIL [17]; SUGAR

COLSON, CHARLES E.—*See* CAMPAIGN FINANCING [5]; WATERGATE [21, 52, 58, 60-61, 78-82, 88, 95]

COMMODITIES—*See* MONETARY DEVELOPMENTS [26]; STOCK MARKET [5]; SUGAR; TARIFFS & TRADE

COMMON MARKET—*See* EUROPEAN ECONOMIC COMMUNITY

COMMUNISM, INTERNATIONAL—Warsaw Pact council meets. The Political Consultative Committee of the Warsaw Treaty Pact met in Warsaw April 17-18 and renewed the 20-year alliance agreement scheduled to expire in May 1975. It was the Pact's first formal meeting since January 1972. Delegations attended from the U.S.S.R., Bulgaria, Czechoslovakia, East Germany, Hungary, Poland and Rumania. Under discussion were recent East-West detentes, particularly those with West Germany and the creation of a permanent European security council by the 35 member nations.

According to observers more substantive agreements were blocked by Rumanian opposition to Soviet calls for a meeting of world Communist parties, excluding China's. (Rumania's independent policy was also evident in the final communique issued July 11 at the end of five days of meetings in Rumania between that country's Communist Party First Secretary Nicolae Ceausescu and Yugoslav Communist Party First Secretary Josip Broz Tito. The communique stressed a "nonaligned policy as an important factor in the fight against imperialism and hegemonism." Reports of a Soviet-Rumanian rift had been widely circulated during preceding weeks, but were generally discredited by the Communist Party organs of both nations. The Soviet newspaper *Pravda* July 29 had denied reports that the U.S.S.R. was pressuring Rumania to allow Soviet troops and supplies to move across the country to Bulgaria, as reported June 13 by the *Washington Post.* Although Rumania was a Warsaw Pact member, no Soviet troops had been stationed there since 1958.)

Sino-Soviet relations. China expelled three Soviet diplomats and two of their wives Jan. 19, charging them with espionage and subversion. The Soviet Union retaliated Jan. 21 by expelling a Chinese diplomat. China charged the Russians had met with a Chinese agent and another unnamed person in a Peking suburb for a mutual transfer of espionage and counterrevolutionary documents and equipment. China had not before publicly aired charges of Soviet espionage, although it had privately expressed concern over unofficial activities by the large Soviet embassy staff, according to the *London Times* Jan. 21. The Chinese imprisoned three Soviet airmen and held their helicopter after it made a forced landing in northwestern Sinkiang Province March 14. The Soviets said the aircraft had lost its bearings during a medical mission to pick up a sick soldier on the Soviet frontier. The Chinese, however, said the helicopter carried military and not first aid equipment. They announced in October that the three men would be tried on charges of espionage.

Negotiation of frontier questions also proved fruitless. Chinese sources in Moscow said talks between the two powers had been suspended because the Soviets refused to alter their negotiating position. The border talks had resumed June 25 following a proposal by Moscow May 23 to reopen the issue of frontier rivers. The Soviet Union said that China must recognize Soviet sovereignty over an island at the confluence of the Amur and Ussuri Rivers if Chinese vessels were to use "Soviet inland waterways." The Chinese Foreign Ministry dismissed the proposal May 27 as "sheer blackmail" and suggested that the border should run along the middle of the main channel. The contested territory figured in a bitter and still unresolved border dispute that peaked in 1969 in a series of armed clashes between the two sides.

Soviet Communist Party General Secretary Leonid Brezhnev Nov. 26 rejected a Chinese proposal for a nonaggression pact, declaring the Peking suggestion "absolutely unacceptable." China, in a Nov. 7 message to Moscow on the 57th anniversary of the Bolshevik Revolution, had proposed talks linking a nonaggression treaty to a separation of forces "in disputed regions." The Chinese note, regarded as the most conciliatory in tone in recent years, cited an understanding reached in a 1969 meeting between Premiers Chou En-lai and Alexei Kosygin. Brezhnev's response, delivered in Ulan Bator, Mongolia, where he was attending 50th anniversary rites commemorating Mongolia's proclamation of a people's republic, declared the Peking bid unacceptable because of the troop pullback conditions. He repeated Moscow's position that no Soviet border regions were "disputed" territory.

European Communists meet in Warsaw. Delegates from 28 European Communist Parties held a consultative meeting in Warsaw Oct. 16-18 to prepare for the first full-scale European party conference since 1967. In a final communique issued Oct. 18, the delegations agreed that the conference should be held before the middle of 1975, probably in East Berlin. Reports from the Warsaw consultations indicated that the Soviet Union had dropped its demand to convene a world Communist Party conference and demonstrated a new willingness to accept differing ideologies within the Communist bloc. A Soviet attempt to denounce China was reportedly defused when a number of delegations, including those from Italy, Yugoslavia, Hungary and Rumania, issued calls in their addresses for the recognition of the "equality" of all Communist Parties and opposed the condemnation of any single party. Attending the meeting were Communist Party delegations from: Austria, Belgium, Bulgaria, Cyprus, Czechoslovakia, Denmark, Finland, France, Great Britain, Greece, Hungary, Ireland, Italy, Luxembourg, East Germany, West Germany, West Berlin, Norway, Poland, Portugal, Rumania, San Marino, Spain, Sweden, Switzerland, Turkey, Yugoslavia and the Soviet Union. The Rumanian and Yugoslavian parties were represented for the first time, having declined to attend the 1967 conference in Czechoslovakia. The Communist Parties of Albania, Iceland and the Netherlands boycotted the meeting.

See also CUBA

COMMUNIST PARTY, U.S.—*See* RADICALS
COMMUNITY ACTION PROGRAM—*See* WELFARE & POVERTY

COMORO ISLANDS—More than 95% of the voters among the 287,000 inhabitants of the Comoro Islands chose in a Dec. 22 referendum to end 130 years of French colonial rule and become an independent nation. The French government had agreed in June to hold the referendum; parliamentary ratification of the independence vote would be required within six months.

COMPUTERS—*See* ANTITRUST ACTIONS [4-5]; PRIVACY [13]

CONGRESS—Second session convenes. The second session of the 93rd Congress convened Jan. 21. The political line-up in the Senate: 58 Democrats and 42 Republicans, with one Conservative-Republican aligned with the Republicans and one Independent-Democrat aligned with the Democrats. There were 243 Democrats, 188 Republicans and four vacancies in the House. The Senate seated Howard M. Metzenbaum (D) Jan. 21 as a member from Ohio replacing William B. Saxbe, who had resigned Jan. 3 and was sworn in as attorney general the following day.

GOP retirements in House continue. The number of Republican members of Congress planning to retire after the current session increased to 17 by mid-February. The record for such announcements in a session was 17, set by election time in 1972. The number of Democrats who had announced they would not seek re-election was 10. Among the Republican representatives retiring were: H.

R. Gross (Iowa), Craig Hosmer (Calif.), Charles S. Gubser (Calif.), Howard W. Robison (N.Y.), Henry P. Smith (N.Y.) and Wendell Wyatt (Ore.). On the Democratic side, retirement announcements were made Feb. 6 by John A. Blatnik (Minn.), chairman of the House Public Works Committee; Richard T. Hanna (Calif.); Chet Holifield (Calif.), chairman of the House Government Operations Committee; Edith Green (Ore.); and Julia Butler Hansen (Wash.).

Senators announcing plans not to seek re-election included the dean of the Senate, George D. Aiken (R, Vt.), 81, the oldest member, and the one with the longest service (since 1940). Others planning to retire were Sens. Norris Cotton (R, N.H.), Wallace F. Bennett (R, Utah), Harold Hughes (D, Iowa), Sam J. Ervin Jr. (D, N.C.) and Alan Bible (D, Nev.).

House committee reform delayed. House Democrats voted May 9 to delay action, pending further study, on a bipartisan plan to revise the set-up of House committees. The plan had been drafted by the House Select Committee on Committees, headed by Rep. Richard Bolling (D, Mo.). Reporting on March 19, the special panel had proposed limiting service by a member to one committee, specifying a sole jurisdiction for multicategory legislation, splitting the Education and Labor Committee into two separate committees and reducing the scope of the Ways and Means Committee. Backing the proposal were Speaker Carl Albert (D, Okla.) and the House Republican Policy Committee. Opposed were Rep. Wilbur D. Mills (D, Ark.), chairman of the House Ways and Means Committee, and other committee chairmen.

House reform effort rebuffed. A proposal to drastically revise the House committee structure was rejected by the House Oct. 8 by a 203-165 vote. Instead, the House approved 359-7 a rival proposal, drafted by a House Democratic Caucus committee headed by Rep. Julia Butler Hansen, that left the committee set-up largely intact. The Hansen plan called for the Ways and Means Committee to establish at least four subcommittees to handle its wide jurisdiction, which the Bolling reform plan intended to narrow by redistribution. The plan adopted retained the Internal Security Committee and the Post Office and Civil Service Committee; both would have been abolished under the Bolling plan. The Education and Labor Committee also was kept intact under the Hansen plan instead of being divided into two panels as recommended by the Bolling proposal. Some procedural changes were part of the Hansen plan: proxy voting in committees, currently condoned, would be barred; party organizational caucuses for the new Congress, generally held in conjunction with the opening session, would instead be held in December of the previous year.

House Democrats vote rules reform. House Democrats approved major reforms in committee assignments Dec. 2-5. Much of the reform was focused on the Ways and Means Committee and its Chairman Mills, for years identified as the most powerful single member of Congress. The caucus acted as Mills played out a strange personal drama, defying Congressional decorum by appearing on stage with a strip-tease dancer in Boston. [See MILLS, WILBUR D.] The action by the House Democratic Caucus capped a long-standing reform effort by liberals and reflected the heavy influx of new and younger members. The caucus consisted of 216 re-elected and 75 newly-elected representatives, the latter organized as a unit under the chairmanship of Rep.-elect Richard L. Ottinger (N.Y.), a freshman but former representative. The influx of the new members in Congress following the Nov. 5 elections reduced the average age of a member to less than 50 for the first time in the century.

The caucus voted 146-122 Dec. 2 to have committee assignments made by the party's Steering and Policy Committee, an arm of the Democratic leadership whose 25 members were appointed by the Speaker or elected to represent various regions of the country. The committee-assignment authority had been held by the Ways and Means Democrats since 1911. The caucus unanimously voted Dec. 3 to increase the membership of Ways and Means from 25 to 37 members. The Democrats would gain 10 seats and also had two existing vacancies. This would allow 12 new Democrats on the committee to be selected, presumably, to reflect the youth and reform movement in the 94th Congress. The caucus later Dec. 3 strengthened the Speaker's role by giving him, rather than the Steering and Policy Committee, the right to nominate the Democratic members of the House Rules Committee, another powerful House committee controlling the flow of legislation to the floor. Proposals in the caucus to limit the service of committee chairmen to three terms and their ages to 70 were rejected by the caucus Dec. 3. The caucus voted Dec. 4 to bar the chairman of a major committee from serving as chairman of another major committee, including a joint Senate-House committee. The caucus recessed Dec. 5 after a squabble over whether the Ways and Means Committee, with Rep. Al Ullman (D, Ore.) acting as chairman, should reorganize before its new members were seated. The committee, under reform rules adopted by the House in the current session, was to be broken down into subcommittees, a power-dispersing system eschewed by Mills during his tenure. Although a reorganization now could seat incumbents in the favored positions on the subcommittees, the freshmen members would have some protection from the newly-adopted rules of the Democratic caucus. One was that each member of a committee would be entitled to one subcommittee assignment before any member received two.

The committee established its first subcommittees Dec. 19. The six jurisdictions were health care, Social Security, trade, welfare, unemployment compensation, and oversight. The committee decided to have all tax matters, its primary jurisdiction, handled by the entire 37-member committee.

House leaders selected. Both parties in the House selected leadership for the incoming 94th Congress Dec. 2. Speaker Albert, Majority Leader Thomas P. O'Neill Jr. (D, Mass.) and Minority Leader John J. Rhodes (R, Ariz.) were renamed without opposition. Rep. Robert H. Michel (Ill.) won a contest for Republican whip replacing Rep. Leslie C. Arends (Ill.), who was retiring from Congress. The caucus chairmanship, another leadership post, was contested in both parties. The Democrats elected liberal Rep. Philip Burton (Calif.) over Rep. B. F. Sisk (Calif.), who was backed by the conservative faction. The vote was 162-111. Current caucus chairman Olin E. Teague (Tex.) did not seek re-election to the post. The Republicans re-elected Rep. John B. Anderson (Ill.) as Republican Conference (caucus) chairman. Challenger Charles E. Wiggins (Calif.) lost 52-85. The changing scene in the House also was evident when the Democrats Dec. 2 ended the 24-year reign of William M. "Fish Bait" Miller as House doorkeeper, a $40,000-a-year post with supervision over more than 300 employees. James T. Malloy, a House disbursing clerk, was given the post, with 150 votes. Miller received 77 votes and a third candidate, John Monahan, received 32.

See also ABORTION; ANTITRUST ACTIONS [12]; ATOMIC ENERGY [9, 12, 18]; AUTOMOBILE INDUSTRY [9]; AVIATION [1, 5, 10, 12, 13]; BICENTENNIAL; BUDGET; CAMBODIA; CAMPAIGN FINANCING; CANADA [27]; CENTRAL INTELLIGENCE AGENCY; CHEMICAL & BIOLOGICAL WEAPONS; CHILE [28]; CIVIL RIGHTS [1-2, 20]; CONSUMER AFFAIRS [2-3]; COPYRIGHT; CRIME [31, 39]; CUBA; CYPRUS [23]; DAYLIGHT SAVINGS TIME; DEFENSE [2-5, 7, 11-12, 15]; DISARMAMENT; DISTRICT OF COLUMBIA; ECONOMY, U.S. [4-7, 10-12, 16, 18, 20-28]; EDUCATION; ELECTIONS; ENERGY CRISIS [1-3, 10-11, 16, 18, 23-27, 31, 35, 40]; ENVIRONMENT & POLLUTION [2-3, 8-9, 14, 17, 20]; FORD, GERALD R.; FOREIGN AID; FREEDOM OF INFORMATION ACT; GAM-

CONSUMER AFFAIRS

General Developments

[1] **Court curbs class action lawsuits.** The Supreme Court ruled unanimously May 28 that plaintiffs in class action law suits had to bear the full cost of notifying all members of the class on whose behalf they were suing. Conceived as an inexpensive means for consumers to press separate small claims in court, a class action involved pooling all claims into one suit, which was then brought by a group of individuals purporting to represent the whole group. The ruling came in a suit brought against the New York Stock Exchange and two of its member firms (since merged) by a New York investor, on behalf of himself and other purchasers of odd lots—trades involving less than 100 shares of stock. The suit charged that the defendants had conspired to monopolize odd-lot trading, and had imposed excessive surcharges in violation of antitrust law. Writing for the majority, Justice Lewis F. Powell Jr. conceded that the decision might make such suits impractical or even impossible, but noted that federal court rules required notification to all identifiable parties, so that each could bring his own attorney or drop out of the suit if he preferred not be bound by its outcome.

[2] **Senate filibuster kills consumer bill.** Senate sponsors of a bill to establish an agency to represent consumer interests before other agencies said Sept. 24 the legislation was dead for the current session of Congress. Four futile attempts had been made to cut off an opposition filibuster. Another Senate filibuster had killed an effort to set up such an agency in 1972. The House had passed the bill April 3 by a vote of 293-94; rejecting, 233-176, an Administration-backed substitute bill which would have weakened or deleted most of the agency's powers. The bill had been the subject of intense lobbying on both sides. Supporters included a coalition of labor and consumer groups. On the other side were business groups such as the National Association of Manufacturers and the U.S. Chamber of Commerce. Sen. Charles H. Percy (R, Ill.), one of the chief sponsors, charged Sept. 19 that measure had been blocked "by a relatively small group of senators backed by the most powerful and lavishly funded lobbying group I've ever seen." Sen. Sam J. Ervin Jr. (D, N.C.), a leader of the filibuster, said the concept of the agency was "repugnant to the free enterprise system" and would "throw monkey wrenches into government machinery." If passed, the agency, while having no regulatory power of its own, would have been able to initiate and intervene in proceedings in regulatory agencies; to present evidence and examine witnesses; and to appeal unfavorable decisions to the courts.

[3] **Product warranties.** A bill to set federal standards for product warranties and to increase the authority of the Federal Trade Commission (FTC) was passed by 70-

5 Senate vote Dec. 18 and House voice vote Dec. 19. Warranties would not be required but sellers offering them would have to specify whether they were "full" or "limited" and explain any limitations in writing. Full warranties would entail total replacement or refund for defective products in the period covered. The FTC would be empowered for the first time to seek court redress for buyers and civil penalties of up to $10,000 against repeated offenders.

Food & Drug Actions

[4] **DES ban voided.** The U.S. Court of Appeals ruled in Washington Jan. 24 that the Food and Drug Administration (FDA) had acted illegally in 1972 and 1973 in banning the livestock growth hormone diethylstilbestrol (DES), which had been linked to cancer. The court said the drug could be marketed again until the FDA held the required hearings or the secretary of health, education and welfare concluded that "such marketing constitutes an imminent hazard to public health."

[5] **Antacid rules set.** The FDA issued final rules June requiring manufacturers of non-prescription antacid products to meet new standards for safe and effective ingredients and to limit labeling claims. The regulations limited antacid products to 13 ingredients recognized as safe and effective and required that active ingredients be listed on labels. Labels would have to include a section warning of possible harmful effects of using the product in conjunction with other drugs. Rejecting protests by some consumer groups, the FDA ruled that products containing a combination of antacids and a pain killer could still be produced. Labels, however, would have to state that the product was to be used for a combination of symptoms—headache and upset stomach—and not for upset stomach alone. The protesting groups had requested a ban on Alka-Seltzer, made by Miles Laboratories Inc., because of possible stomach hazards from the aspirin ingredient.

[6] **Food nutrient rules proposed.** The FDA June 12 proposed regulations and guidelines governing the amounts of nutrients that could be added to foods. The proposals included nutritional quality guidelines for an initial five classes of foods: ready-to-eat breakfast cereals, hot breakfast cereals, "main dish" products, "formulated meal replacements" such as diet aids and snacks, and breakfast beverage products.

[7] **Meat additives curb urged.** A panel of experts commissioned by the Agriculture Department recommended Sept. 9 that because of cancer-causing potential, sodium nitrates and nitrates should be either banned from use in processed meat products or severely restricted. The additives were used as coloring agents and to prevent growth of botulism toxins.

Other Developments

[8] **Bicycle safety standards set.** The Consumer Product Safety Commission July 2 announced mandatory safety standards for bicycles sold in interstate commerce after Jan. 1, 1975. Under the regulations, bicycle frames, steering systems, wheels and brakes would be tested for safe construction, strength and performance. The rules would also require protected edges and coverings for protruding parts, chain guards, locking devices for certain parts and improved reflector systems.

[9] **Plastics ad accord set.** The FTC announced July 29 that 25 chemical companies and their trade association—the Society of the Plastics Industry Inc.—had agreed to stop claiming that cellular plastic products were non-burning or self-extinguishing and to inform the public of fire hazards associated with the products. The agreement was the result of a class action complaint filed

in 1973. The products, primarily foamed polyurethanes and polystyrenes, were used in construction, furniture and airplane interiors.

[10] **Automotive ad tactics hit.** The FTC moved against three major auto manufacturers July 31 to halt allegedly misleading advertising on gasoline mileage. Most of the advertising had appeared during fuel shortages earlier in the year. In complaints against Ford Motor Co. and Chrysler Corp., the FTC charged that ads claiming high fuel mileage, while not necessarily false, lacked sufficient explanatory detail and in Chrysler's case were unfairly derogatory against a General Motors Corp. product. Regarding General Motors' ads, the FTC tentatively accepted a consent order under which the company agreed to stop making misleading mileage comparisons with other companies' products.

[11] **Auto recalls reported; GM fined.** Nissan Motor Corp. was recalling 63,023 1973 and 1974 Datsun autos because of a potential fire hazard, it was reported Aug. 5. General Motors Corp. (GM) warned Sept. 4 that 42,000 1974 medium-duty trucks and 500 school buses had possibly defective hydraulic brake hoses that could cause full or partial brake failure. It was reported Aug. 2 that GM had been assessed $100,000 in civil penalties for unsafe truck wheels on 200,000 1960-65 models. The case had been in the courts since 1970. (Owners of up to four million 1969 and 1970 GM products were warned of a possible steering wheel problem that could cause loss of control, it had been reported May 20. The National Highway Traffic Safety Administration said the wheel could break loose from the hub after prolonged and heavy use and advised that the cars—all in the Chevrolet line—be inspected.) The Ford Motor Co. announced Aug. 26 that it was recalling 282,000 1973 and early 1974 cars and trucks for replacement of a temperature sensing valve in the emission control system. According to the company, the valve could fail after extended use, causing the release of large amounts of nitrogen oxides.

[12] **FTC curbs pyramid selling.** The FTC ruled Aug. 21 that pyramid marketing schemes, under which distributors received bonuses for recruiting others to join the plan, were potentially fraudulent by nature and should be banned.

[13] **Credit abuses charged.** The FTC charged Sept. 11 that five major department store chains had over the past five years retained more than $2.8 million in unclaimed credit balances owed to charge account customers. The proposed complaints were filed to set the stage for possible consent agreements halting the practice. According to the FTC, customers who established credit balances would, over several months, receive statements showing the amounts in their favor. But unless the customers requested refunds or made offsetting purchases, the stores eventually cleared the accounts and kept the money. The FTC said the amounts owed individual customers were relatively small. The five chains and amounts involved were: Gimbel Brothers Inc., $1,158,000; Genesco Inc., $740,000; Carter Hawley Hale Stores Inc., $509,740; Associated Dry Goods Corp., $405,275; and Rapid American Corp., $75,000.

See also AGRICULTURE; AUTOMOBILE INDUSTRY [1, 8]; CANADA [28]; ECONOMY, U.S. [17]; ENVIRONMENT & POLLUTION [12, 18]

COOK, G. BRADFORD—*See* WATERGATE [74-76]

COPPER—The four-member Intergovernmental Council of Copper Exporting Countries (known as CIPEC, its Spanish acronym), met in Lusaka, Zambia, June 24-26. Chile, Peru, Zaire and Zambia were the four major copper-producing countries which comprised the council. In its final communique released June 26, CIPEC warned that it would move to assume a major role in controlling copper prices on the world market. The group's executive director,

Sacha Gueronik, declined, however, to reveal whether there had been agreement on a comprehensive plan for implementation of such action. The CIPEC nations produced more than 60% of the world's copper exports.

Copper prices fell from $3,000 a ton in April to $1,280 a ton in November because of world manufacturing cutbacks caused by the oil crisis, and because of Japan's decision to put its copper stockpile on the world market. CIPEC met again in Paris Nov. 18-19 and agreed to reduce foreign sales by 10% effective Dec. 1 to raise world copper prices. The move had no immediate effect on the prices, which continued to fall on the New York and London markets. Metal traders reportedly reasoned that since the exporters did not agree to cut production along with foreign sales, copper would pile up and eventually tempt them to exceed their export quotas. Chile did impose a 10% production cut, announcing Nov. 20 that it would close its Exotica mine and reduce output at other mines Dec. 1. However, the other nations of CIPEC did not follow suit.

See also AUTOMOBILES [3]; CHILE [1, 23]; ECONOMY, U.S. [7]; ZAIRE; ZAMBIA

COPYRIGHT—The Senate approved a copyright reform measure 70-1 Sept. 9, which would revise copyright provisions in effect since 1909, would require jukebox operators, for the first time, to pay a royalty fee—$8 per jukebox each year—to be divided among composers and music publishers. Cable television operators would be required to pay copyright fees for commercial television programs they picked up and relayed to distant points. The current royalty fee on records for composers would be increased from 2¢ to 3¢. The term copyright protection would be changed to the author's lifetime plus 50 years, similar to that of other countries. The provision under the current law was 28 years plus another 28 if renewed by the author or his heirs. The measure was sent to the House, where a copyright revision bill had been pased in 1967.

The Soviet Union's Copyright Agency reached major new agreements with U.S. publishers in December which would begin to normalize the previously hazy situation which left royalty payments and publishing arrangements between the two countries irregular and unpredictable. Boris Pankin, head of the Soviet agency, signed the agreements in the U.S. with representatives of several publishing concerns.

See also BOOKS; TELEVISION & RADIO

COSTA GOMEZ, GEN. FRANCISCO DA—*See* MOZAMBIQUE [4-5]; PORTUGAL [4-5, 13-19, 27-29]

COSTA RICA—Oduber becomes president. Daniel Oduber Quiros, who had been elected president of Costa Rica Feb. 3, was sworn in May 8. He succeeded Jose Figueres Ferrer, who had served since 1970. Figueres was constitutionally prohibited from running again. Oduber's National Liberation Party (PLN) won the office for the first time in 25 years, but lost its majority in the National Assembly, winning only 26 of that body's 57 seats. The National Unification Party, whose presidential candidate Fernando Trejos Escalante, ran second to Oduber, won 16 seats. The National Independent Party won seven seats; the Democratic Renovation Party, three; and the Democratic, National Republican and Cartaginesa Agrarian Union Parties, one each. The Communist Party retained its two seats. The presidential campaign had few issues aside from the 15%-25% inflation rate. (Gasoline rose from 53¢ to $1 a gallon; the Costa Rican colon had been devalued by 20% in March. There were also large price increases for products such as milk and bread.)

U.S. oil refinery bought. The legislature approved purchase by the government, for a symbolic $1, of the Atlantic coast oil refinery owned by Allied

Chemical Corp. of the U.S., it was reported April 12. The legislature stipulated that the government could not extend foreign oil companies' contracts to distribute oil products in Costa Rica, and that the government should gradually take over this service.

The government later signed an agreement with Interoceanic Liquid Transportation Co., formed by Costa Rican, Central American and European interests, to build an oil pipeline linking the nation's Atlantic and Pacific coasts, it was reported May 10. Its capacity would reportedly be 80 million tons of crude annually, earning Costa Rica $20 million a year. Construction, to begin in 1974, was estimated at $400 million. The government also took over the U.S. firm International Railways of Central America, which had run Costa Rica's main railway and docks since 1908, the newsletter *Latin America* reported Oct. 25.

North Koreans expelled. The government ordered six North Korean diplomats to leave the country after denying them permission to establish an embassy in San Jose, Foreign Minister Gonzalo Facio announced Aug. 12. The North Koreans had been in Costa Rica attempting to arrange an exchange of ambassadors between the two countries. The government accused them of making contact with leaders of an extreme leftist political party, according to the San Jose radio station Radio Reloj Aug. 12.

Campaign funds scandal. A scandal developed Aug. 15 when the San Jose newspaper *La Nacion* alleged that two state banks had illegally contributed $585,000 to Oduber's successful presidential campaign. A Congressional commission began investigating the charge Aug. 21. Former Industry and Trade Minister Gaston Kogan later admitted partial responsibility for the illicit financing, *Latin America* reported Sept. 13.

See also COFFEE; LATIN AMERICA; MEXICO [21]; MIDDLE EAST [26]; OIL [17]; SUGAR; VESCO, ROBERT L.; WATERGATE [74]

COUNCIL OF EUROPE—*See* GREECE [2]
COX, TRICIA—*See* NIXON, RICHARD M.; WATERGATE [34]
CREDIT—*See* BANKS & BANKING; CONSUMER AFFAIRS [13, 31]; HOUSING; WOMEN'S RIGHTS
CREW—*See* BOATING

CRIME

Supreme Court Decisions

[1] **Exclusionary principle limited.** The Supreme Court ruled Jan. 8 that grand juries, unlike trial juries, could use illegally obtained evidence as the basis for questioning witnesses without violating their constitutional rights. The result of the 6-3 ruling would be that a grand jury could indict a suspect, using evidence that later would be inadmissible in the suspect's trial. In so ruling, the court narrowed the so-called exclusionary principle, which was first enunciated by the federal courts in 1914 and refined by Justice Oliver Wendell Holmes in 1920.

[2] **Police search powers widened.** The court, by a 5-4 margin March 26, held that paint scrapings found in the clothing of a man arrested for attempting to break into a post office could be used as evidence against him, although the search had been made 10 hours after the arrest and without a search warrant. (The court by a 5-4 vote announced June 17 upheld a murder conviction based on evidence obtained during a warrantless search of the defendant's car parked in a commercial parking lot. Evidence in the case was a tire print and paint scrapings.)

[3] **Court voids Mitchell wiretap evidence.** The court ruled unanimously May 13 that former Attorney General John N. Mitchell failed to meet the

requirements of the Organized Crime Control Act of 1968 when he allowed his executive assistant to approve wiretap applications, rather than doing it himself or designating a specific assistant attorney general to act in his place, as required by law. In ruling that the wiretap requests approved by Mitchell's executive assistant Sol Lindenbaum were illegal, the court upheld the dismissal of a narcotics indictment against Dominic N. Giordano of Baltimore. The ruling was expected to have the same effect in 60 other narcotics and gambling cases involving 626 defendants. While the full court agreed that evidence from the wiretaps authorized by Lindenbaum were inadmissable, the four Nixon appointees to the court—Chief Justice Warren E. Burger and Justices Harry A. Blackmun, Lewis F. Powell Jr. and William H. Rehnquist—argued in a separate dissent that court-ordered extensions of the Lindenbaum-authorized taps were not improper. (In a parallel case, the court upheld by a 5-4 margin the validity of another set of wiretaps affecting 99 cases and 807 defendants. Here, wiretap applications had been authorized by Mitchell but signed by former Assistant Attorney General Will R. Wilson, who had not actually played any part in their preparation. Dissenting were Justices William O. Douglas, William J. Brennan Jr., Potter Stewart and Thurgood Marshall.)

[4] **Court bars challenges to Miranda rules.** The court June 10 upheld the rape conviction of a Michigan man who claimed that the evidence used to convict him was obtained in violation of the court's so-called Miranda rules. The 1966 Miranda ruling in essence stipulated that the 5th Amendment protection against self-incrimination restricted police interrogation of arrested suspects. In its 8-1 ruling, the court chose to narrowly interpret the Miranda ruling. Police could use evidence obtained during questioning that violated the Miranda rules, the court said, if the questioning had occurred before the Miranda rules were enunciated.

[5] **Court denies free appeal counsel.** In a decision announced June 17, the court ruled 6-3 that an indigent defendent was not entitled to free legal counsel to appeal his criminal conviction in the state and federal courts. Writing for the court majority, Justice Rehnquist conceded that an indigent defendant was somewhat handicapped compared to a wealthy defendant, but he said the state had no duty to duplicate the legal arsenal available to the defendant who could afford it. Dissenting from the ruling, which reversed a decision by the U.S. 4th Circuit Court of Appeals, were Justices Douglas, Brennan and Marshall.

[6] **Death penalty re-examination set.** The court Oct. 29, agreeing to re-examine its 1972 ruling on the constitutionality of capital punishment, took jurisdiction in the appeal of a convicted murderer, James T. Fowler, 25, of Raleigh, N.C., whose execution had been ordered for the killing of a gambling companion. After the Supreme Court ruled in 1972 that the death penalty was unconstitutional as it was then applied, the North Carolina State Supreme Court quickly reinstated capital punishment by judicial decree, ordering its automatic imposition for first degree murder, rape, burglary and arson. In 1973, the North Carolina state legislature enacted new mandatory legislation.

Government Officials

[7] **Daley aides indicted.** A 12-count indictment returned in U.S. district court in Chicago Feb. 21 charged Earl Bush with allegedly helping to arrange for the advertising firm he secretly owned to obtain an exclusive contract for display advertising at Chicago-O'Hare International Airport. Bush had been press secretary and director of public relations for Chicago Mayor Richard J. Daley from 1961 to mid-1973. Bush was convicted on 11 of the 12 counts Oct. 13. Thomas E. Keane, Democratic floor leader in the Chicago City Council for

Mayor Daley, was indicted May 2 by a federal grand jury on 18 counts of conspiracy and mail fraud. He was convicted Oct. 9 and sentenced on Nov. 18, to five years in prison and fined $27,000.

[8] **Ex-Queens DA sentenced.** Thomas J. Mackell, the former district attorney for the New York City Borough of Queens, was sentenced to six months in jail April 22. Mackell had been convicted March 2 of blocking prosecution of the operator of a $4.4 million get-rich-quick scheme, in which hundreds of Queens residents and several of his aides had invested.

[9] **Agnew associates jailed.** N. Dale Anderson, successor to former Vice President Spiro T. Agnew as Baltimore County (Md.) executive, was sentenced to five years in prison May 1. He had resigned his office April 23. A federal jury in Baltimore March 20 had found Anderson, a Democrat, guilty of accepting about $40,000 in kickbacks from engineers and architects seeking government contracts; and of failing to pay $59,000 in federal income tax for the years 1969-72.

[10] A three-judge federal court panel Nov. 25 rejected prosecution recommendations of leniency and gave prison sentences to businessmen I. H. Hammerman 2nd and Allen I. Green, who had been participants in an illegal kickback scheme involving Agnew. Hammerman and Green had pleaded guilty Nov. 11 to obstructing tax laws by delivering cash kickbacks to Agnew while he was governor of Maryland. Joseph W. Alton Jr., who resigned as Anne Arundel County (Md.) executive Dec. 2, pleaded guilty in Baltimore in federal court Dec. 6 to a charge that he participated in a scheme to extort cash kickbacks from architects and engineers seeking county contracts. He faced a maximum penalty of 20 years in prison and a $10,000 fine.

[11] **Rep. Roncallo acquitted.** Rep. Angelo D. Roncallo (R, N.Y.) was acquitted of charges of extortion and conspiracy by a federal jury May 17. According to one of the jurors, Roncallo and a co-defendant were acquitted "because of a lack of evidence and the government just never proved its case." Roncallo, who had been controller of Nassau County, N.Y., in 1970, had been accused of conspiracy to extort money from a contractor who was modernizing the town's incinerator, threatening to ruin his business if he did not pay. The *New York Times* reported Oct. 11 that the Justice Department had censured two assistant U.S. attorneys for the Eastern District of New York for their handling of the Roncallo prosecution. The Justice Department investigation of the case, the *Times* said, showed that the charges were brought in "good faith," but that the case was "poorly presented to the federal grand jury and inexpertly tried by government counsels."

[12] **N.J. officials convicted.** Nelson G. Gross, former state chairman of the New Jersey Republican Party, was found guilty by a Newark N.J. federal jury March 29 of five counts of tax fraud and perjury. Gross was sentenced to two years in prison and fined $10,000 June 16. J. Edward Crabiel, New Jersey secretary of state, was indicted July 31 on charges he had participated in a conspiracy to rig highway construction bids. The alleged crimes, the indictment said, took place from 1965 to 1970, before Crabiel took office. Crabiel, who took a leave of absence without pay from his office Aug. 9, said he was innocent. Joseph M. McCrane Jr., a former New Jersey state treasurer, was convicted by federal court jury in Scranton, Pa. Dec. 11 of four counts of assisting corporations in filing fraudulent income tax returns.

[13] **U.S. customs judge indicted.** Paul P. Rao Sr., former chief judge of the U.S. Customs Court in New York and currently a senior judge, was indicted May 14 on charges he lied to a New York state grand jury investigating an alleged scheme to bribe a state court judge to influence the outcome of a robbery

case. Rao was only the fifth U.S. judge ever indicted by a grand jury. The indictments of Rao, his son, Paul Rao Jr., and the younger Rao's law partner, Salvatore Nigrone, were announced by special New York state prosecutor, Maurice H. Nadjari.

[14] **2 sentenced in Gurney fund case.** Two Florida men received jail sentences for their roles in an illegal campaign fund scheme involving Sen. Edward J. Gurney (R, Fla.). Gurney's former aide and fund raiser, Larry E. Williams, was sentenced to a year in jail Feb. 21 after pleading guilty to charges of attempting to evade federal income taxes totaling $19,000 in 1971 and helping a government official collect a bribe. Williams had been indicted Jan. 17 by a federal grand jury for channeling a $10,000 bribe from Miami builder John J. Priestes to William F. Pelski, former director of the Federal Housing Administration (FHA) insuring office in Coral Gables and the former mayor of Pompano Beach. Priestes, currently serving a one-year jail term, received 20 FHA contracts to build subsidized housing in return for his illegal payment, according to the indictment. Pelski pleaded guilty March 19 to conspiring to defraud the government by promising FHA financing to Gurney's political contributors. He was sentenced to 18 months in prison.

[15] Gurney and six others were indicted by a federal grand jury July 10 in connection with an influence-peddling and extortion scheme to raise campaign funds. Gurney was alleged to have extorted $223,160 over a 3½ year period from Florida contractors and developers "who had matters pending before" the Department of Housing and Urban Development, promising favored treatment for them. (Gurney said July 23 that he would not seek re-election to a second term in the Senate.) Gurney was charged with one count of bribery, one count of conspiracy, one count of receiving unlawful compensation and four counts of making false statements to a grand jury in May 1973. If convicted, Gurney faced up to 42 years in prison and fines totaling $40,000. Gurney was the first senator in 50 years indicted on federal charges while holding office. (Sen. Burton K. Wheeler [D, Mont.] had been acquitted of malfeasance in 1924.)

[16] **Brasco convicted in bribery case.** Rep. Frank J. Brasco (D, N.Y.) was found guilty by a federal jury in New York City July 18 of bribery and conspiracy in connection with a scheme to obtain mail-hauling contracts for a trucking firm allegedly run by an organized crime figure. Brasco informed New York City board of elections officials that he would not seek re-election. Prosecution of Brasco on the same charges had ended in a mistrial March 19 when jurors were unable to reach a verict. Brasco was sentenced to three months in jail and fined $10,000 in New York federal district court Oct. 22.

[17] **Evers indicted for tax evasion.** Charles Evers, mayor of Fayette, Miss., was indicted by a federal grand jury in Jackson Aug. 12 on charges he evaded more than $50,000 in federal income taxes during the years 1968-70. His former wife, Nannie Laura Evers, was also charged with tax evasion in 1968 and 1969.

[18] **Podell pleads guilty to conspiracy.** Rep. Bertram L. Podell (D, N.Y.) pleaded guilty in federal district court in New York City Oct. 1 to charges of conspiracy and conflict of interest in connection with a $41,350 payment he received from a small Florida airline seeking government approval of a route to the Bahamas. The plea by Podell was not an admittance that he had accepted any bribes. He faced up to five years in prison and a $10,000 fine on the conspiracy charge and up to two years in prison and a $10,000 fine on the conflict of interest charge. Miller, head of the parent company of the now defunct airline, also changed his plea to guilty on a charge of conspiracy to pay Podell in violation of the conflict-of-interest law.

Other Crimes and Trials

[19] **Ray obtains review of guity plea.** James Earl Ray, who pleaded guilty to the 1968 slaying of civil rights leader Martin Luther King, was granted a review of his case by the 6th U.S. Circuit Court of Appeals Jan. 29. Remanding Ray's case to the U.S. District Court in Nashville for a hearing, the appellate court found merit in Ray's contention that he had not been given proper legal advice, that his lawyers had failed to investigate the case fully and that his lawyers were interested only in collecting royalties on materials written about him.

[20] **Dead hijacker's goal was White House.** Samuel J. Byck, 44, an unemployed salesman from Philadelphia, fell short of his goal to crash a hijacked jet into the White House Feb. 22, when a policeman in the Baltimore-Washington International Airport, where Byck had tried to seize a Delta Airlines jet, shot him in the chest. Wounded, Byck shot himself fatally in the head with the same gun he had used to kill an airport guard and the copilot of the jet.

[21] **Murphy kidnapping.** J. Reginald Murphy, 40, editor of the *Atlanta Constitution,* was kidnapped Feb. 20, ostensibly by members of a group calling itself the American Revolutionary Army. He was released, unharmed, Feb. 23 following payment of a $700,000 ransom by the newspaper. Six hours later police arrested William A. H. Williams, a building contractor, and his wife Betty Ruth. A Federal Bureau of Investigation (FBI) agent said suitcases with the money had been found in the Williams' Lilburn, Ga. home. Williams was found guilty Aug. 4 on charges of extortion, use of a firearm in commission of a federal felony and use of the mails to send a ransom note. He was sentenced to 40 years in prison Aug. 30. His wife was given a three-year suspended sentence for failing to report the crime. Murphy had been kidnapped when a man identifying himself as "Lamont Woods" asked help from the newspaper to anonymously distribute $300,000 worth of fuel oil to the needy. Murphy met with the man, who turned out to be Williams, on the evening of Feb. 20 supposedly to sign papers for the fuel distribution. Driving north from Atlanta, Williams pulled a gun and announced, "We're going to straighten out this damn country. We're going to stop these lying, leftist, liberal news media." Although Williams had said the American Revolutonary Army had 223 members and divisions in the Southeast and the Northeast, he said in a May 1 appearance in court that he had acted alone and that his wife was not involved. Williams was tied to the kidnapping on the basis of a tip to the FBI from a man to whom he had tried to sell $300,000 worth of non-existent fuel oil in December 1973.

[22] **Martin Luther King's mother slain.** Alberta Williams King, mother of slain civil rights leader Dr. Martin Luther King Jr., was shot and killed June 30 by a young black gunman during services in the Atlanta church of which her husband, Martin Luther King Sr., was pastor. Marcus Wayne Chenault, 23, of Dayton, Ohio, was subdued by worshippers at the Ebenezer Baptist Church, but not before he had emptied two handguns, killing Mrs. King and church deacon Edward Boykin. Chenault also wounded a church-goer. Chenault was indicted July 9 by a Fulton County grand jury. Superior Court Judge Sam P. McKenzie entered a plea of not guilty for Chenault after refusing to allow the defendant to plead no contest. A spokesman for the Justice Department said July 4 that the FBI had looked into the possibility that Chenault was part of a conspiracy, but had concluded "Chenault was acting alone and not in concert with others." Investigations into Chenault's background revealed that he became interested in 1973 in the teachings of Hananiah E. Israel, a Cincinnati resident and self-styled religious leader whose legal name was Stephen Holiman. One of the beliefs that Chenault derived from the teachings was that black ministers exploited their

congregations and deserved to be punished. Chenault was convicted of murder in Atlanta Sept. 12. The jury recommended the death penalty. Judge Luther Alverson ordered Chenault executed Nov. 8. The verdict was automatically appealed under Georgia law.

[23] **Boyle convicted in Yablonski slaying.** Former United Mine Workers (UMW) President W. A. (Tony) Boyle, 72, was convicted by a Delaware County court jury in Media, Pa. April 11 of three counts of first-degree murder in the 1969 murders of union rival Joseph Yablonski, his wife and a daughter. The conviction carried a mandatory sentence of life imprisonment. It was the fifth murder conviction obtained in the Yablonski case by special prosecutor Richard A. Sprague of Philadelphia. Three others had pleaded guilty and another, William Turnblazer, had pleaded guilty to a federal charge of conspiring to kill Yablonski. Turnblazer, 53, was sentenced May 8 in federal court in Pittsburgh to 15 years in prison. Turnblazer, a lawyer and former UMW District 19 president, was the principal witness against Boyle. He testified that Boyle had ordered the Yablonski killing and that the order was given at UMW headquarters in Washington June 23, 1969 as Boyle, Turnblazer and Albert Pass stood outside an elevator. Boyle, testifying on his own behalf, said such a meeting never took place. Pass was sentenced in Erie July 1 to three consecutive life prison terms.

[24] **Henley convicted of sex-torture murders.** Elmer Wayne Henley Jr., 18, was found guilty July 15 by a San Antonio jury of six murders in connection with a Houston homosexual-torture ring in which 27 youths were killed. Henley was sentenced to six consecutive terms of 99 years in prison Aug. 8.

[25] **"Alphabet" bombing suspect arrested.** Muharem Kurbegovic, 31, a Yugoslav alien living in the U.S. since 1967, was arrested by police Aug. 21 on the charge that he was the "alphabet bomber" who had planted the bomb that exploded in a terminal of the Los Angeles International Airport Aug. 6, killing three persons and injuring at least 35 others. The bomber had sent tape recorded messages to the news media stating that he would spell out the name of a group called Aliens of America with a series of bombings, starting with "A" for airport.

[26] **Raped woman convicted of murder.** Inez Garcia, 30, was convicted of second degree murder by a jury in Monterey, Calif. Oct. 5 for killing a man she said helped another man rape her. Garcia was sentenced to a prison term of five years to life. The case had become a cause celebre among some women's rights advocates, who contended that the trauma of rape was so great that the violent reaction by Garcia was understandable. The prosecution had contended that Garcia had not been raped and that the killing had occurred during the course of an argument.

[27] **Newton jumps bail.** The FBI issued a warrant for the arrest of Black Panther Party leader Huey Newton, who had forfeited $42,000 bail Aug. 23 when he failed to appear in municipal court in Oakland, Calif. on charges of assault. Newton had been accused of beating a tailor, who had come to his Oakland apartment to take measurements for a suit, and of shooting 17-year-old Kathleen Smith of Oakland, Calif., in the head. After the girl's death, Newton was charged with murder Nov. 1.

[28] **6 indicted in Chicago vault theft.** A federal grand jury indicted six men Nov. 7 for the theft Oct. 20 of $4.3 million in cash from a vault of the Armored Express Co. in Chicago. Police said they had recovered $1.5 million of the loot, but were not optimistic about finding the rest of the money, reported to have been deposited in secret bank accounts in the British West Indies. The burglary was the largest cash theft in U.S. history.

[29] **Coast pair guilty in tower bombings.** A truck driver and his wife pleaded guilty Nov. 13 to charges that they sought to extort $1 million from the Bonneville Power Administration by threatening to black out Portland, Ore. by dynamiting power transmission lines to the city. The couple, David and Sheila Heesch, waived grand jury indictment and pleaded guilty under an agreement with the U.S. attorney for Portland. Heesch was sentenced to 20 years in federal prison Dec. 16. His wife received 10 years.

[30] **Former boxer denied new trial.** Rubin (Hurricane) Carter, a former top contender for the middleweight boxing crown, was denied a new trial Dec. 11 by a Jersey City, N.J. judge, who said he did not believe recanted testimony by two witnesses instrumental in Carter's conviction for murder in 1967. Carter and a friend, John Artis, had been found guilty of charges that they murdered three persons in a Paterson, N.J. bar in 1966.

Police and Enforcement

[31] **U.S. offers crime data control rules.** The Justice Department proposed a new set of regulations Feb. 14 that would limit access to criminal information compiled by the FBI and state and local police agencies. The regulations, published in the *Federal Register* Feb. 14, were intended as an interim measure until Congress could pass legislation restricting the use of criminal records. The regulations were aimed at preventing government agencies and private groups from obtaining criminal information from police data banks for other than criminal justice purposes.

[32] **Philadelphia police corruption charges.** A 1,404-page report by the Pennsylvania Crime Commission, made public March 10, charged that police corruption in Philadelphia was "ongoing, widespread, systematic and occurring at all levels of the police department." The report also accused the police department and the administration of Mayor Frank L. Rizzo, who was Philadelphia police commissioner in 1967-71, of actively trying to block the 18-month investigation by arresting the commission's special agents and failing to act when presented with evidence of corruption.

[33] **Indianapolis police graft charged.** A series of articles in the *Indianapolis Star* detailing widespread corruption in the city's 1,100-man police department led to the firing of Police Chief Winston L. Churchill and Assistant Chief Donald Schaedel by Mayor Richard G. Lugar (R) March 14.

[34] **D.C. policewoman slain.** Gail A. Cobb, 24, a District of Columbia policewoman, was shot and killed by a fleeing robbery suspect she had pursued into a garage Sept. 20. According to FBI files, which dated to 1960, Cobb was the first woman police officer slain in the line of duty.

[35] **Ford takes tough law and order stand.** President Ford told the convention of the International Association of Chiefs of Police in Washington Sept. 24 that the Justice Department was initiating a new program to keep track of habitual criminals. In pursuit of this goal Ford said, he had instructed the Justice Department to undertake in cooperation with state and local governments, a career criminal impact program to target and keep track of repeat offenders. He said the effort would be similar to the program in Washington, which kept track of major repeaters, insuring "that these cases receive the most urgent attention of the prosecutors."

[36] Attorney General William B. Saxbe and Clarence M. Kelley, director of the FBI, speaking to the police chiefs Sept. 23, contended that prosecutors and the courts were responsible for the rising U.S. crime rate because they failed to convict and jail repeat offenders. Saxbe described a criminal justice study in Atlanta, which showed that of 278 adults arrested for assault, 103 were indicted,

77 went to trial, 63 were convicted and 23 were jailed. "Too often," he said, plea bargaining was used "by prosecutors to allow vast numbers of offenders at the state and local level to receive minimal punishment, if any at all." In his remarks, Kelley said "easy bail for hardened criminals," concurrent instead of consecutive sentences imposed by judges and "unreasonable plea bargaining" were undercutting law enforcement efforts. (Kelley had said Sept. 22 that the FBI needed broad wiretapping powers to properly watch revolutionaries who were responsible for many of the 2,000 bombings annually in the U.S. Noting that civil libertarians might object to legislation widening FBI electronic surveillance powers, Kelley said the bombers presented a more serious threat to U.S. society than a new wiretapping law.)

[37] **19 New York City policemen ousted.** Michael C. Codd, New York City police commissioner, Nov. 18 dismissed 19 former plain-clothes police officers after they were convicted in departmental trials of accepting bribes from gamblers totaling $240,000. Meanwhile, John Egan, retired chief of the New York police department's special investigations unit, was sentenced to 2½ years in prison Dec. 2. He had been convicted of income tax evasion for failing to report as income on his 1970 return $45,000 in bribes from narcotics dealers seeking protection against prosecution.

Other Developments

[38] **Study finds higher real crime rate.** Surveys in 13 selected U.S. cities released Jan. 29 and April 14 by the Law Enforcement Assistance Administration (LEAA) suggested that crime rates were at least twice as high as police statistics indicated. Conducted for the LEAA by the Census Bureau, each of the 13 surveys involved interviewing 22,000 residents and 2,000 businessmen about their experiences with different types of crime.

[39] **Senate OKs death penalty bill.** A bill to restore the death penalty for some crimes under certain conditions was passed by the Senate 54-33 March 13. The crimes were treason, espionage and murders involving kidnapping, hijacking, escape from custody, bombing of federal property and attacks on a president, vice president, chief justice, federal law enforcement officers or a foreign head of state. The bill would provide exemptions from the death penalty for defendants under 18 years of age, those whose judgment capacity was significantly impaired, those under "unusual and substantial duress," those whose participation in the crime was relatively minor and those who could not reasonably have foreseen the activity would "create a grave risk of causing death." Prior to passage, the Senate rejected two proposals by Sen. Edward M. Kennedy (D, Mass.) to add gun control provisions to the bill. The bill died in the House Judiciary Committee at the end of the year.

[40] According to a United Press International survey reported Aug. 15, at least 156 persons awaited execution in U.S. prisons, despite a Supreme Court ruling two years earlier that the death penalty as it was then applied was "cruel and unusual punishment." The survey found 17 states holding prisoners under capital sentences. North Carolina had the greatest number on death row wih 50, with Florida—the first state to reimpose the death penalty after the Supreme Court decision—second with 30 inmates awaiting execution. Georgia and Massachusetts each had 20 individuals who had been sentenced to death.

[41] **Oklahoma inmate treatment cited.** U.S. District Court Judge Luther L. Bohanon March 17 ordered the State of Oklahoma to stop mistreating inmates at the state prison in McAlester. He also told authorities to end racial segregation at the institution. Witnesses at a hearing called by Bohanon said that since the riots during the summer of 1973, convicts had not been provided with proper

bedding, food or heat in the cellblocks damaged during the riots. Convicts were punished arbitrarily with chemical mace and tear gas, Bohanon said. Noting that black inmates had been treated more harshly than whites, Bohanon ordered an end to all racial segregation and equal treatment for all convicts.

[42] **Convicts take over U.S. court cellblock.** Armed with only a handgun, two convicts seized control of the basement cellblock of the U.S. Courthouse in Washington July 11. Four days later, Frank Gorham Jr. and Robert N. Jones gave up, having failed to obtain an agreement with police and court officials to release their seven hostages in exchange for safe passage out of the U.S. (36 hours before the siege ended, the hostages had escaped by an elevator in the cellblock.) The take-over caused a number of court proceedings to be moved elsewhere. Among them was the "plumbers" trial involving former White House aide John D. Ehrlichman.

See also ABORTION; AMNESTY & CLEMENCY; BANKS & BANKING; BIRTH CONTROL; CALLEY, WILLIAM L.; CAMPAIGN FINANCING [3-6, 8-10, 19, 23]; CIVIL RIGHTS [9, 11, 18]; FORD, GERALD R.; GAMBLING; HEARST, PATRICIA; HORSE RACING; HOUSING; HUGHES, HOWARD; INDIAN AFFAIRS; ITALY [8]; JAMAICA; NARCOTICS & DANGEROUS DRUGS; NIXON, RICHARD M.; RADICALS; RAILROADS; ROCKEFELLER, NELSON [7, 23]; SAXBE, WILLIAM B.; STOCK MARKET [6-11]; VOTING RIGHTS

CUBA—Moves to end embargo. The U.S. Senate Foreign Relations Committee April 23 unanimously approved a resolution calling for an end to the U.S. trade embargo of Cuba and a resumption of U.S.-Cuban relations. The measure, introduced by Sen. Jacob Javits (R, N.Y.), was a rider on a State Department budget bill and was not binding on President Nixon. The resolution was passed the same day a $24.2 million agreement was signed in Buenos Aires between the Argentine subsidiaries of Chrysler Corp. and the Ford Motor Co. Special export licenses were granted by the U.S. government allowing the two firms to ship cars and trucks from Argentina to Cuba. The U.S. insisted, however, that despite granting the licenses, its policy toward Cuba had not changed, and that the U.S. continued to support the Organization of American States (OAS) sanctions against Havana. (The Cuban ambassador to Mexico, Fernando Lopez Muino had said Jan. 7 the U.S. blockade had become a "farce" because many non-Communist nations, including Japan and most Western European countries were now trading with Cuba. In addition, several Latin American nations had established diplomatic relations with Havana, he noted.)

Panama ties renewed. Cuba and Panama officially resumed diplomatic, economic and cultural relations Aug. 22, as a movement grew among Latin American nations to lift the sanctions imposed against the island in 1964 by the OAS. Other Latin nations, meanwhile, increased pressure on the OAS and the U.S. government to lift the diplomatic and economic embargo of Cuba. Mexican Foreign Minister Emilio Rabasa, a major opponent of the sanctions, met with U.S. Secretary of State Henry Kissinger June 8 and with Kissinger and President Ford Aug. 29. Cuba was discussed at each meeting. Rabasa said Aug. 29 that Kissinger did not indicate the U.S. would block moves among Latin nations to lift the sanctions. Kissinger said the U.S. would study the matter, Rabasa reported. Colombian President-elect Alfonso Lopez Michelsen and Venezuelan President Carlos Andres Perez said Aug. 3 that they intended to resume relations with Cuba. Perez, however, noted his country's "commitments" to the OAS and said he would first support an initiative to lift the OAS sanctions.

Javits, Pell see Castro. U.S. Senators Javits and Claiborne Pell (D, R.I.) visited Cuba on a personal fact-finding mission Sept. 27-30 and conferred with Premier Castro and other high government officials on the possible renewal of relations between Washington and Havana. The two senators met with Castro for three hours Sept. 29, one day after the Cuban leader delivered a blistering attack on the U.S. in a speech commemorating the 14th anniversary of the founding of the grass-roots Committees for the Defense of the Revolution (CDRs). Javits and Pell, who watched the speech on television, said they took strong exception to it in their meeting with Castro, but it did not otherwise affect their visit to Cuba. At a midnight news conference after their talk with Castro, Javits said he had forcefully outlined U.S. objections to Cuban policies, including the separation of Cuban families, expropriation of U.S. property, and alleged torture and summary executions. "I have no euphoria about settling these profound problems," Javits added. The senators visited Cuba without the sanction of the State Department, which granted them visas for the trip but twice asked them to postpone it "in the national interest," according to press reports. (The OAS foreign ministers, meeting in Quito, Ecuador Nov. 8-12, failed to lift the diplomatic and commercial embargo on Cuba. The resolution to end the embargo failed to gain the required two-thirds majority of the 21 signatories to the Rio Treaty, under which sanctions were imposed. Twelve countries voted for the resolution, three voted against, and six—including the U.S.—abstained. For further details of the meeting see LATIN AMERICA.)

Brezhnev visits. Soviet Communist Party General Secretary Leonid Brezhnev and a team of Soviet economic and political specialists visited Cuba Jan. 28-Feb. 3. They conferred with Premier Fidel Castro and other officials on a wide range of topics, including world affairs and Soviet aid to Cuba. The visit, Brezhnev's first to the island, had originally been scheduled for the end of 1973. Its postponement was attributed to Brezhnev's reluctance to jeopardize East-West detente by appearing publicly at celebrations of the 15th anniversary of the Cuban revolution. A joint Cuban-Soviet communique published Feb. 4, after Brezhnev's departure, made veiled attacks on China, suggesting that Cuba now fully supported the Soviet Union's campaign against Peking.

Venezuela, Bahamas ties set. Cuba established diplomatic relations with the Bahamas Nov. 30 and renewed full ties with Venezuela Dec. 30. Cuba officially normalized relations with the Vatican Dec. 20.

Government begins elective process. Residents of Matanzas Province elected representatives empowered to choose candidates for new municipal assemblies which eventually would cover the island, it was reported May 10. The elections began the government's first effort to give Cuba a democratic structure since the revolution 15 years ago. Matanzas was chosen first because of its small size and population. The elected assemblies had begun to operate, the *Wall Street Journal* reported Dec. 4. Premier Castro had said July 26 that the process of democratization would culminate with elections in 1976 for a national governing council. Some 50% of the delegates elected in Matanzas were members of the Communist Party, which had a national membership of only 200,000, the *Journal* reported. Although the local assemblies were charged with directing economic and cultural affairs and services within the province, they would not control transportation and industry, and would conform to national priorities and standards of health and education set by the Communist Party Politburo, the *Journal* noted.

See also ARGENTINA [2, 18]; CHILE [6, 8]; CANADA [7, 31]; HONDURAS; LATIN AMERICA; MEXICO [21]; NICARAGUA; SUGAR

CULEBRA ISLANDS—*See* PUERTO RICO
CURACAO—*See* SURINAM AND NETHERLANDS ANTILLES
CYCLONES—*See* AUSTRALIA [17]

CYPRUS—Officers lead military coup. Archbishop Makarios was overthrown as president of Cyprus July 15 by a violent military coup staged by the Greekofficered Cypriot National Guard. Although the rebels originally reported his death in the fighting, the archbishop, 60, escaped the besieged presidential palace in Nicosia and flew to London, where he began efforts to rally international support for his cause. The rebels broadcast a communique declaring the seizure of power to be an internal affair. They charged that Makarios had been leading Cyprus into civil war, apparently in reference to his opposition to Greek Cypriots fighting for enosis. The new rebel regime affirmed its support for Cypriot independence and did not indicate immediate plans to seek enosis (union of Cyprus with Greece), but Greece and Turkey reportedly mobilized their armed forces and deployed them facing Cyprus.

[2] In early July, Makarios had charged the Greek officers with supporting EOKA B, the guerrilla organization formed by the late Gen. George Grivas who had died of a heart attack at his hideout in the southern port of Limassol Jan. 27. The guerrillas, who favored enosis, had been granted an amnesty the following day. Grivas had been succeeded by George Karousos, 47, a former Greek army major. Karousos had ordered a halt to guerrilla activity, in response to the amnesty, but he was removed from his post March 1 and, according to a later report in the *New York Times*, forcibly taken to Greece. Greek army Col. Ioannis Dertilis then became new chief of EOKA B, it was reported March 15. A wave of terrorist activity followed, leading the Cyprus government to outlaw the organization April 25 and to institute a police crackdown during which 200 suspected EOKA B members were arrested. Makarios July 6 published a letter he sent to Greek President Phaidon Gizikis July 3 accusing the Gizikis regime of conspiring to seize power in Cyprus and to assassinate him. He demanded the removal of 650 Greek army officers who controlled the Cypriot National Guard, an army of 10,000-12,000 men.

[3] After the coup, the rebels July 15 named a new president, Nikos Giorgiades Sampson, 38, a Greek Cypriot newspaper publisher and former terrorist once sentenced to death by British colonial authorities for murder. Sampson held a press conference July 18 in Nicosia. He charged that Makarios' government had tortured its political opponents and "flagrantly violated" the human rights of Cypriots. The coup had been staged, he said, to avert a civil war and to save democracy in Cyprus. Asked about casualties during the coup, Sampson said "some dozens" had been killed and wounded. However, foreign diplomatic sources estimated casualties from the July 15-16 fighting at about 300. The Turkish community, which comprised about 18% of the island's population, had reportedly mobilized itself during the crisis, but was not involved in the fighting. Rauf Denktash, the elected leader of the Turkish Cypriots, told newsmen July 16 that the coup leaders "are trying to destroy all the basis for the bicommunal independence of Cyprus and to make it a part of Greece." In another interview July 18, Denktash called for international action to restore Makarios to power.

[4] **Greece, Turkey react.** Turkish Premier Bulent Ecevit charged July 15 that the military coup constituted intervention in Cyprus by the Greek government. On the same day Turkish Defense Minister Hasan Esat Isik declared Turkey's right to intervene in Cyprus to restore constitutional order under the 1960 treaty guaranteeing Cypriot independence. (Turkey, Greece and Great Britain had signed the treaty.) The threatened confrontation between Greece and Turkey, both members of the North Atlantic Treaty Organization (NATO), would endanger that force's southern flank in the Mediterranean and Aegean Seas, maintained primarily by the Greek and Turkish navies and the U.S. 6th Fleet.

[5] Greece, in its first official statement on the situation, July 16 called the rebellion an "internal affair of an independent state" and said it would respect

"the principle of noninterference." Turkish Premier Ecevit flew to London July 17 for talks with British Prime Minister Harold Wilson and Foreign Secretary James Callaghan. After two days of talks, Ecevit warned that Turkey was losing patience and he hinted at possible military action. He stressed that he hoped for a peaceful solution, but he said that time was limited because Greece was rapidly building up its position on Cyprus. Turkey had been reported rushing troops to its southern ports on the Mediterranean as early as July 16 in preparation for armed action. The Greek air force had been placed in an "advanced state of readiness," and Greek naval vessels were sailing in the direction of Cyprus, according to a July 17 report. Turkey was located only 40 miles from Cyprus, while Greece was situated about 500 miles from the island.

[6] **Other nations, UN reaction to the crisis.** Under pressure from the left wing of the ruling British Labor Party, which opposed the Greek military junta, the British government tended to support the legitimacy of the Makarios regime. On July 16 British Foreign Secretary Callaghan requested Greece to withdraw its officers from their command assignments with the Cypriot National Guard. Although, like Britain, the U.S. sought to prevent Greece and Turkey from going to war over Cyprus, it did not appear displeased at Makarios' ouster. At various meetings Secretary of State Henry Kissinger stressed that the U.S. would do nothing to jeopardize its air and sea bases in Greece. State Department spokesman Robert Anderson said July 17 that the U.S. had not yet made a decision on whether to recognize the rebel government. However, State Department officials said July 18 that the Administration believed Sampson to be unacceptable as leader of Cyprus.

[7] The United Nations Security Council met in special session July 16, but adjourned without taking any action after the U.S. and Britain declared more information was required. UN Secretary General Kurt Waldheim said the U.N. peace-keeping Force in Cyprus (UNFICYP) "cannot get involved in the internal affairs of one of the communities." The Turkish and Soviet representatives both charged the coup had been instigated by Greece, but the Greek delegate denied this. The Soviet charge d'affaires in Athens delivered a strong note to the Greek government July 16 warning that Greece would have to bear full responsibility for consequences of the coup. A Soviet statement July 17 charged that NATO had blocked any effective action on Cyprus by the U.N., adding that NATO was probably behind the coup. On the same day, according to a *New York Times* report, the Soviet Union assured Turkey of its support in defending the integrity and independence of Cyprus. At a July 17 meeting of the NATO Council in Brussels, Greece's NATO partners except the U.S., which took a neutral position, reportedly demanded Greece withdraw its officers from the Cypriot National Guard. The council also expressed "broad support" for the Makarios government. The following day Greece announced it would gradually replace the 650 Greek officers. The move fell short, however, of Turkey's demand for total withdrawal.

[8] **Turks launch invasion.** Turkey invaded Cyprus early July 20 following failure of intensive diplomatic efforts to resolve the crisis. The invasion began at dawn when Turkish jets attacked the northern port of Kyrenia, while assault troops landed by sea and air near the capital of Nicosia. Greek Cypriots staged a bloody resistance in the Nicosia area. Neither side was able to win clear control of the city. In a radio broadcast, Premier Ecevit said Turkey had decided to intervene militarily after "trying all political and diplomatic ways" to resolve the crisis. Later in the day, Ecevit called the action "a peace operation . . . to end decades of strife provoked by extremists." Ecevit cited dangers to Cyprus' independence as guaranteed by the 1960 treaty, whose provisions barred Cypriot

union with Greece as well as guaranteeing the rights and safety of the Turkish minority. About six hours after the Turkish forces landed, Greece declared a general mobilization and vowed to meet "expansionist Turkish acts" at any cost. The government rushed troops to its 90-mile northern border with Turkey in Thrace, posing the possibility of a mainland war between the two nations. U.S. State Department spokesman Anderson issued a statement July 20, after the invasion, that indicated a shift in the U.S. position on Cyprus. Anderson's statement, which said, "We regret this military action by Turkey just as we deplore the previous action by Greece that precipitated the crisis," was the first in which the U.S. had linked Greece to the coup that ousted Makarios.

[9] **Early fighting.** Heavy casualties, both civilian and military, were reported in battles between the Turks, Greeks and Greek Cypriots; and intercommunal battles erupted between Turkish and Greek Cypriots along Nicosia's U.N.-supervised "Green Line" separating the two sectors. A cease-fire arranged by U.N. peace-keeping troops on Cyprus, supposedly in effect from 5 p.m. July 20, was ignored. However, a new cease-fire was arranged for a short time July 21 to allow a British truck convoy to evacuate more than 4,000 foreign civilians, mostly Britons and Americans, from Nicosia to the British base at Dhekelia, 20 miles southeast of Nicosia. The cease-fire finally was implemented July 22 after Greece and Turkey had each brought reinforcements to the island. According to a *New York Times* report July 24, in the last hours before the cease-fire Turkish forces had consolidated their hold on the northern coast area and in Kyrenia, gaining control of the port except for a medieval castle dominating the harbor. They also tightened their control of the corridor from the coast, over the Kyrenia Mountains to the Turkish sector of Nicosia.

[10] **Cease-fire terms.** The formulation and acceptance of the truce between the belligerants was the result of intensive negotiations spearheaded by the U.S. and Britain. The U.S. had announced July 21 the Greek and Turkish acceptance of the cease-fire which had been called for by a U.N. Security Council resolution unanimously adopted the day before at an emergency session requested by Greece. Roadblocks to the cease-fire had been Turkey's demand for withdrawal of the 650 Greek officers and for new arrangements to give Turkish Cypriots more security and power on the island. British Foreign Secretary Callaghan announced in London July 22 that Turkey and Greece had agreed to begin talks with Britain in Geneva later in the week. In a television press conference the same day, Premier Ecevit said that the 10-mile corridor held by the Turkish forces from the beachhead west of Kyrenia to the Turkish enclave of Nicosia "will be a permanent base of strength for the Turkish people on the island." He said Kyrenia was "forever Turkish," although Greek Cypriots disputed Turkish control of the city.

[11] **Greek government falls.** The military junta which had ruled Greece for seven years resigned July 23 after the failure in the Cyprus coup. Former Premier Constantine Caramanlis, called from a self-imposed exile in Paris, formed a new civilian government at the request of President Gizikis. One of Caramanlis' first acts was to recognize Makarios as the president of Cyprus.

[12] **Clerides assumes the presidency of Cyprus.** Sampson, the rebel-proclaimed president of Cyprus since July 15, resigned July 23 and was replaced by a moderate, Glafkos Clerides, 55, speaker of the Cyprus House of Representatives and Greek Cypriot negotiator in the intercommunal talks. Sampson, in a radio address, said the primary objective of the coup had been to overthrow the "personal rule" of Makarios and now he believed it would be in the national interest for him to step down. Sampson, a former guerrilla assassin and a supporter of enosis, had gained no support from other nations and little backing

from the majority of Cypriots. Clerides, at his first news conference since assuming power, said July 24 that Cyprus would hold general elections in the next few months to decide if Makarios should again assume the presidency.

[13] **Cease-fire, talks fail.** Attempts to bring about an end to the fighting failed during the course of the summer in spite of a political agreement signed in Geneva July 30 by Turkey, Greece and Great Britain. Under terms of the agreement, U.N. peace-keeping forces would police mixed-population zones, and would establish security zones at "the limit of the areas occupied by the Turkish armed forces." The agreement also provided for exchange of civilian and military prisoners and pledged to begin new talks Aug. 8 aimed at re-establishing "constitutional government" on the island. Throughout the following weeks, Turkish forces continued to expand their occupation zone through a series of armed actions that met little opposition from the poorly-armed Greek Cypriot troops. By Aug. 7 the Turkish beachhead in the north extended 12 miles west of Kyrenia and about seven miles east. (Turkish forces Aug. 4 forced withdrawal of a six-man Finnish unit of UNFICYP from a village south of Kyrenia while also ordering the U.N. troops to withdraw from the Dome Hotel in Kyrenia where 650 Greek Cypriot refugees had taken asylum.) The second phase of the Geneva talks resumed Aug. 8 with Greece insisting that Turkey respect the July 30 cease-fire and halt its drive west of Kyrenia. On Aug. 10 Turkish Foreign Minister Turhan Gunes charged Greece had agreed to discuss only "a very few minor modifications" in the island's 1960 Constitution. "If that is the case, there is no point in continuing." Gunes had been insisting on the partition of Cyprus into a federation of two equal and separate states, the Turkish Cypriot one to comprise the top northeastern third of the island. On Aug. 12 Gunes proposed an alternative plan which would divide Cyprus into "cantons," six of them Turkish Cypriot, which would have their own administration, language and police forces. The cantons would be under a single national confederation. One of these cantons would encompass the Turkish-occupied area around the northern port of Kyrenia. The Greeks and Greek Cypriots, however, rejected the plan, saying they could accept additional political autonomy for the Turkish Cypriot minority, but were opposed to turning over 35% of the land to 18% of the population. Premier Ecevit Aug. 13 gave Greece 24 hours to accept the cantonal proposal. When, however, Greek Cypriot and Greek representatives requested 36-48 hours in order to consult with their governments, Turkey refused to allow the recess and the talks broke down on Aug. 14.

[14] Within a few hours after the end of the Geneva meeting, Turkish forces launched a heavy air and ground attack, fanning out from Nicosia, capturing the eastern port city of Famagusta and advancing west toward Morphou Bay. (In Ankara, Premier Ecevit blamed the renewed fighting on Greece, charging that Athens had ignored the July 30 cease-fire accord.)

[15] **U.S. denies pro-Turkey stand.** Prior to the end of the Geneva talks, the U.S. had expressed support Aug. 13 for Turkey's position. A statement issued by the State Department said: "We recognize that the position of the Turkish community on Cyprus requires considerable improvement and protection." It added, however, that the U.S. had informed all parties that it would "consider a resort to military action unjustified." Another statement was issued Aug. 14 after Turkey's renewed military action in which the U.S. said it "deplored" Turkey's use of force. It also warned that U.S. military aid would be halted if Greece and Turkey went to war. The U.S. rebuke to Turkey for its military action was the first public reproach to Turkey by the U.S. In a nationwide radio and television address the following day, Greek Premier Caramanlis said Turkey had "engaged

in these infamous actions with the toleration of those who should and could have checked her." Caramanlis' speech was delivered one day after Greece announced it would withdraw its armed forces from NATO. The government said it would remain a member of NATO's Division of Political Affairs. The decision was reportedly intended to placate Greek public opinion, which had grown increasingly anti-American during the Cyprus crisis. Premier Ecevit said Aug. 22 that Turkey could "compensate for any weaknesses" in NATO defenses in the eastern Mediterranean caused by Greece's military withdrawal from the alliance. Ecevit hinted that Turkey might provide port facilities for the U.S. 6th Fleet if Greece withdrew its facilities.

[16] **Fighting continues.** After achieving its major military goal of gaining contol of the northern third of Cyprus, Turkey unilaterally announced a cease-fire Aug. 16 and declared its willingness to resume negotiations in Geneva on the island's political future. Greek Premier Caramanlis, however, spurned both the Turkish proposal and a U.S. invitation to visit Washington and confer with President Gerald Ford. A senior Greek official later said Greece believed Washington had favored Turkey and could not serve as an impartial mediator. In spite of Caramanlis' rejection of the cease-fire, it was accepted by Cypriot President Clerides. The fighting continued for two more days, however. By Aug. 18 the Greek Cypriot government estimated that Turkish forces controlled 40% of Cyprus. Greek Cypriot refugees numbered 200,000, more than a third of that group's population. Clerides appealed for help to the United Nations High Commission for Refugees. He said Aug. 20 that a solution to the refugee problem was a condition for his participation in any new Geneva peace talks.

[17] **U.S. envoy slain.** The U.S. ambassador to Cyprus, Rodger P. Davies, 53, was shot and killed at the U.S. embassy in Nicosia Aug. 19 during an anti-American demonstration by Greek Cypriots. An embassy secretary who rushed to his aid was also shot to death. According to later reports, a burst of machine-gun fire had penetrated the window of the ambassador's office and hit Davies as he was taking shelter with other staff members in a hallway. Eyewitnesses reported that some of the persons firing at the embassy wore Cypriot National Guard uniforms. In a radio broadcast Aug. 19, Clerides denounced the killing as "an abominable crime."

[18] **Atrocity charges.** Turkish and Greek Cypriots each accused the other side of committing atrocities after the Turkish invasion July 20. A Turkish general staff communique said July 21 that Turkish communities in mountain villages in the southwest and northwest were being "incredibly, horribly exterminated" with women, children and old persons being slaughtered or seized as possible hostages against Turkish advances. About 300 Greek Cypriots released Aug. 3 from the mountain village of Timithe, southwest of Kyrenia, told stories of arson, looting, rape and arbitrary execution of civilians by Turkish troops. Turkish authorities Aug. 20 showed newsmen a mass grave in the eastern Turkish Cypriot village of Aloa where they said 57 Turkish Cypriot bodies were buried, although only seven were immediately found. A mass grave was discovered Sept. 1 in a rubbish dump in the Turkish Cypriot village of Maratha, near the eastern port of Famagusta. Officers of UNFICYP reported Sept. 3 they had uncovered the skulls of 84 victims at Maratha, whose population had totaled 93.

[19] **Peace efforts bog down.** Various diplomatic efforts to arrange renewed political talks between Greece and Turkey on the future status of Cyprus failed Aug. 24-27, with the two sides adopting opposing positions toward resumed negotiations in Geneva and a Soviet-proposed 18-nation peace conference. The Soviet Union had proposed the conference under U.N. auspices in a statement

issued by the official press agency Tass on Aug. 22. The government said the conference should be attended by the 15 member states of the U.N. Security Council as well as Greece, Turkey and Cyprus. Such a U.N.-sponsored meeting could provide "appropriate effective guarantees" that a settlement would be implemented. The U.S. State Department reacted cooly to the Soviet proposal Aug. 26 but stopped short of an outright rejection. Turkey Aug. 27 formally rejected the Soviet proposal for the expanded peace conference. The statement, issued by the Foreign Ministry after a meeting between Turkish Foreign Minister Gunes and Soviet Ambassador Vasily F. Grubyakov, denied a Soviet allegation that the Turkish intervention on Cyprus reflected an attempt to turn Cyprus into a NATO "stronghold." The letter expressed appreciation of the "constructive attitude taken by the Soviet Union since the very beginning of the Cyprus conflict," but said its suggestion to involve a large number of nations in the issue "would inevitably result in the limitation of the independence of Cyprus." Greek Cypriot President Clerides notified the Soviet Union Aug. 27 of his government's acceptance of the proposal for an expanded peace conference. The U.S.-British effort to reconvene the five-sided Geneva peace talks suffered a setback Aug. 24 when Greece informed Britain it would not attend. A Greek government spokesman said later Aug. 24 that Greece backed the Soviet proposal "in principle." Earlier Aug. 24, Greek Foreign Minister George Mavros had asserted that the British "have been able to do nothing," adding that Greece "must now take the matter to the United Nations." He made his remarks following talks with Cypriot President Clerides on a common Athens-Nicosia policy. Clerides told reporters, "We will not negotiate before a fait accompli. The Turks must pull back to the positions they held on Aug. 9," when the cease-fire lines were jointly fixed. "Secondly," Clerides said, "the Greek Cypriot refugees must be allowed to return to their homes." He warned that the Greek Cypriots would resort to guerrilla warfare rather than capitulate in the diplomatic sphere. Greek Cypriots were forming the Cyprus Liberation Army (CLA) to wage guerrilla warfare against the Turkisk occupation forces if a diplomatic settlement was not reached in the near future, a spokesman for the new group announced Aug. 27.

[20] **U.N. Council urges talks, refugee aid.** The Security Council unanimously adopted a resolution Aug. 30 urging immediate relief for the more than 200,000 refugees on Cyprus. It also called for resumed peace talks. The resolution, sponsored by Austria, Britain and France, urged the parties in the conflict to take appropriate measures to provide for the relief and welfare of the refugees and to permit those who wish to do so to return to their homes in safety. The Turkish ambassador, Osman Olcay, indicated his government would reject mass returns of displaced persons. President Clerides Sept. 9 rejected as "unacceptable" Turkey's request to Britain to allow the transfer to Turkey of 10,000 Turkish Cypriot refugees from British bases in southern Cyprus. Clerides charged that the refugees would be reshipped from Turkey to Turkish-controlled territory in Cyprus, "with the aim of altering the population composition of those areas." Turkish Premier Ecevit demanded Sept. 9 that all Turkish Cypriots who wished to move to Turkish-held areas be allowed to do so. Ecevit said "this is the only road, the realistic road" to insure the security of Turkish Cypriots.

[21] **Prisoner exchange begins.** The Greek and Turkish Cypriot communities began exchanging prisoners of war and detainees Sept. 16. A total of 245 men—116 Greek Cypriots and 129 Turkish Cypriots—were traded on the grounds of the Ledra Palace Hotel in Nicosia under the supervision of the United Nations and the Red Cross. All were reportedly in good condition. A general release of all prisoners began Sept. 23. The exchanges were suspended indefinitely Sept.

26 because of a dispute over details of the release. Agreement on the exchange had been reached by Clerides and Denktash Sept. 20.

[22] **Makarios rejects Cyprus federation.** Makarios addressed the General Assembly Oct. 1. He denounced Turkey as an "aggressor" and rejected a federation of geographically distinct Greek and Turkish Cypriot areas on the island. Such a solution, advocated by Turkey, would be "not only artificial but also inhuman" because it would require large-scale resettlement of inhabitants, Makarios said. Makarios insisted that geographic federation would be tantamount to partition, which would lead to annexation of the separate regions by Turkey and Greece.

[23] **Arms aid to Turkey opposed.** The U.S. House of Representatives voted 307-90 Sept. 24 to cut off U.S. military aid to Turkey until progress toward a military settlement on Cyprus was assured. Proponents of the amendment, which was sponsored by Reps. Benjamin S. Rosenthal (D, N.Y.) and Pierre S. du Pont 4th (R, Del.), contended that the foreign aid legislation ruled out aid to countries using it for offensive purposes. Opponents noted the State Department's concern that it would be "disruptive of negotiations we're trying to arrange." Senate approval of a military aid cut-off to Turkey was voted 64-27 Sept. 19. President Ford and Congress reached an accommodation Oct. 17 following a week-long confrontation over military aid to Turkey. Before adjourning Oct. 17, Congress cleared, after receiving assurance from Ford that he would reluctantly accept the legislation, a bill carrying amendments to continue military aid to Turkey until Dec. 10 provided that Turkey did not send U.S.-supplied implements of war to Cyprus. The vote was 191-33 in the House. The Senate approved by voice vote. Ford signed the bill Dec. 18.

[24] **POW exchange resumes.** The general exchange of all Turkish Cypriot and Greek Cypriot prisoners resumed Oct. 19 after a three-week interruption. Most of the more than 300 Turkish Cypriots freed chose to remain in the Turkish sector of Nicosia rather than return to their families in the Greek-controlled city of Limassol. Of the approximately 320 Greek Cypriots released, 141 chose to remain in their villages in the Turkish-controlled northern sector of the island. Agreement to resume the exchange had been reached in talks Oct. 14 in Nicosia between Clerides and Denktash. The exchange of prisoners was completed Oct. 28, the last of 11 such exchanges. Officials said 3,308 Turkish Cypriots and 2,479 Greek Cypriots had been traded. More than 3,000 Greek Cypriots were still listed as missing.

[25] **Turkish troop cut reported.** Turkey had withdrawn about 5,000 of its estimated 30,000-40,000 troops from Cyprus, Western diplomatic sources disclosed Nov. 12. The Turkish force reduction, reportedly begun Oct. 29, was seen as a conciliatory gesture to forestall the cutoff of U.S. aid to Turkey Dec. 10.

[26] **Greek Cypriots, Athens set strategy.** At the end of two days of talks in Athens Dec. 1, Greek and Greek Cypriot leaders announced that they had agreed on a "common line" for negotiations on the Cyprus problem. Participating in the talks were Greek Premier Caramanlis, Archbishop Makarios and Clerides. The communique said "detailed written instructions will be given to the interim president, Mr. Glafkos Clerides, to begin negotiations on the substance of the Cyprus issue." No details were disclosed. (After meeting with Makarios in London Nov. 21 for the first time since the coup, Clerides confirmed that Makarios "intends to return to Cyprus to resume his presidency" in early December.)

[27] **Makarios returns.** Makarios returned to Cyprus to resume his post as president Dec. 7. Speaking to tens of thousands of his cheering supporters assembled in front of the archbishop's residence in Nicosia, Makarios declared

that "on no account" would he "recognize and accept accomplished facts" created by Turkey's military invasion of the island in July and August. While declining to spell out his views of an acceptable settlement, Makarios expressed willingness to seek a settlement that would include "self-government" for the Turkish Cypriot minority and lead to "peaceful coexistence" between the Greek Cypriot and Turkish Cypriot communities.

See also Communism, International; European Security; Foreign Aid; Greece [1, 3-4, 12-13]; Turkey; United Nations [4]

CZECHOSLOVAKIA—The U.S. and Czechoslovakia reached preliminary agreement on the settlement of post-World War II financial counterclaims in an accord initialed July 6 in Prague by U.S. embassy Counselor Arthur I. Wortzel and Jaroslav Zantovsky of the Czechoslovak Foreign Ministry. Negotiations on the agreement, which still required approval by both governments, began in September 1973. U.S. officials had stipulated that claims settlement would have to precede steps to improve trade and economic relations.

Under a law effective July 1, the Czechoslovak security forces, including the secret police, were given extended powers to "override civil rights and liberties if the social system, the socialist state, public order or the security of persons or property require it." In its preamble, the new law stated that modifications in the 1965 law which it superseded were necessary because of "the experience of the crisis years 1968-1969" and the duty to "unmask hostile activity directed against the Czechoslovak Socialist Republic and all other anti-social elements."

Rude Pravo, the central organ of the Czechoslovak Communist Party, leveled an attack Dec. 11 against deposed reformist party leader Alexander Dubcek and his colleagues who had launched the ill-fated "Prague spring" of 1968, labeling them "liquidators of the Communist Party who plunged society and the party into fatal danger." The renewed attacks, which also appeared in the Slovak party organ, *Pravda,* were the strongest such statements since 1971 and reaffirmed the ruling regime's hardline policy opposing any trends towards liberalization.

See also Argentina [18]; Canada [7]; European Security; Obituaries [Trochta]; Portugal [24]

DAHOMEY—Lt. Col. Mathieu Kerekou proclaimed Nov. 30 that "the new society in which each Dahomean will find happiness is the socialist state" and announced eight principles to guide the country "under the doctrine of Marxism-Leninism." The nationalization of all international oil companies operating in Dahomey was announced Dec. 5 under a Cabinet ordinance which gave to a state monopoly all profits from the supply, storage, transportation and sale of petroleum products. According to a Dec. 15 report, Kerekou subsequently ordered the establishment of "Defense of the Revolution Committees" in all businesses to "protect the revolution from sabotage."

See also AFRICA

DAIRY INDUSTRY—*See* CAMPAIGN FINANCING [3-6, 19]; WATERGATE [21, 27]
DALEY, RICHARD J.—*See* CRIME [7]; POLITICS [8]
DATA BANKS—*See* CRIME [31]; PRIVACY [13]

DAYLIGHT SAVING TIME—The Senate cleared a bill Sept. 30 repealing year-round Daylight Saving Time (DST) and reinstating Standard Time, when clocks would be turned back one hour, for four winter months. DST had been instituted late in 1973 as an energy-saving step to conserve fuel and electricity consumption because of the extra hour of evening daylight. The new bill would return the nation to Standard Time the last Sunday in October through the last Sunday in February 1975. Exceptions to the DST requirement were allowed for Arizona, Hawaii and parts of Michigan, Indiana and Idaho. The vote in the Senate was by voice vote. The House had approved the bill 383-16 Aug. 19. President Ford signed the bill Oct. 5.

DEAN, JOHN W. 3rd—*See* PRIVACY [7]; WATERGATE AFFAIR [11, 15-16, 21, 25, 52, 61-62, 74-76, 94]
DEATH PENALTY—*See* CRIME [6, 39-40]
DE DIEGO, FELIPE—*See* WATERGATE [78-80]

DEFENSE—U.S. altering nuclear war strategy. Defense Secretary James R. Schlesinger said Jan. 10 that the U.S. had begun retargeting intercontinental ballistic missiles (ICBMs) from Soviet population centers to Soviet military installations. The new policy would give U.S. forces a strategic flexibility to deal with improved Soviet nuclear capabilities. Former U.S. nuclear strike plans had been aimed at deterring the Soviet Union from launching a surprise attack by ensuring that the U.S. could destroy Soviet cities even after absorbing such an attack. Schlesinger contended that the increasing size and accuracy of Soviet missiles raised the possibility that the Soviets had the strength to attack the U.S., absorb a U.S. counterattack against cities and still have enough missiles left to decimate U.S. cities. He asserted that the retargeting was not an attempt to develop a first-strike potential (which he called beyond the grasp of the U.S.), but was intended to show the Soviets that the U.S. was prepared to match them at every point in the arms race if arms limitation agreements were not reached.

[2] **Military spy ring uncovered.** A controversy between the Pentagon and the National Security Council (NSC) erupted Jan. 11 with the disclosure by the *New York Times* that a military spy ring operating within the NSC had passed highly secret information concerning U.S. diplomatic initiatives to officials in the Pentagon. The operation was reportedly stopped in 1971 following its exposure as the result of investigations by David R. Young Jr., a member of the Special White House investigative unit known as the "plumbers." The White House had initiated an investigation of leaked NSC documents concerning the India-Pakistan war of 1971 when secret NSC minutes on the situation appeared in a syndicated newspaper column written by Jack Anderson. According to Young's findings, submitted in a book-length report to President Nixon in early 1972, confidential information from the office of Henry A. Kissinger, head of the NSC, had been supplied to Adm. Thomas H. Moorer, chairman of the Joint Chiefs of Staff (JCS). Moorer admitted he had seen the reports, but said they contained no information he did not already have and that he was not aware of their source. Implicated in the ring were Rear Adm. Robert O. Welander, in 1971 liason officer between the NSC and the JCS; his chief aide, Yeoman 1.C. Charles E. Radford, who had also been on Moorer's Pentagon office staff; and Welander's predecessor, Rear Adm. Rembrandt C. Robinson, who was killed in a helicopter crash in Southeast Asia in 1972. Moorer contended that it was Radford who had leaked the information. Appearing on the National Broadcasting Co. program "Today" Jan. 18, Moorer was asked why Radford had not been punished. In answer, Moorer cited a lack of firm evidence. (Radford, a Navy stenographer often assigned to Kissinger, had retained "miscellaneous staff papers, roughs and questionnaires" from Kissinger's July 1971 trip to Pakistan and China, as well as a group of documents from a trip to Southeast Asia Radford made in September 1971, according to Moorer. The information was revealed in a letter Moorer sent Jan. 30 to Sen. John C. Stennis [D, Miss.], chairman of the Armed Services Committee which was investigating the disclosures.) Moorer reported that when he learned Radford had collected the documents in an unauthorized manner, he ordered them returned to the NSC. Moreover, Moorer denied he had any part in the pilfering of the material, saying he had "easy access" to Kissinger. In a Feb. 8 interview with Seymour M. Hersch of the *New York Times,* Radford said he had been instructed to obtain the documents by Robinson and Welander, and that they were then passed on to Moorer who, Radford believed, was always aware of his activities. Radford claimed Robinson had conveyed this fact to him on several occasions.

[3] Appearing before the Senate Armed Services Committee Feb. 20-21, Welander denied Radford's allegations. Instead, Welander suggested Radford had implicated him in order to shift the focus of a White House investigation linking the yeoman to information leaked to columnist Jack Anderson. Welander conceded he had received "a collection of tissue copies and rough drafts of staff reports, memoranda of conversations and outgoing cables" from Radford after the yeoman had returned from two secret negotiating trips to Asia, but denied

that he had any reason to doubt Radford's statements "that he acquired the documents in the regular course of his clerical duties." Radford's allegations were, on Feb. 22, supported by former JCS staff officer Marine Corps Col. James A. MacDonald (ret.) who told the *New York Times* that Welander routinely provided Pentagon officials with purloined NSC documents in the last half of 1971. J. Fred Buzhardt Jr., former chief counsel to the Defense Department, testified on the matter in secret before the Senate Committee March 7. After his testimony, Buzhardt spoke to reporters, denying allegations that the Administration had decided not to prosecute Welander and Radford for fear that disclosures involved in the prosecution would compromise the government's case against Daniel Ellsberg, who was accused of leaking the Pentagon Papers. Buzhardt said the cases against the two men were circumstantial and not prosecutable. (Earlier, Moorer had told the Committee that he had twice recommended institution of court-martial proceedings against Radford, but in both instances civilian authorities he could not identify had overruled him. Welander's post had been abolished and he and Radford were subsequently transferred to new assignments.)

[4] The Senate Armed Services Committee cleared Moorer of the spying charges, it was reported June 26. The Committee recommended that Moorer, whose tenure as head of the JCS was coming to an end, be retired with the full rank, pension and honors of an admiral. The Committee concluded that he was "not culpable" in the unauthorized transfer of the documents. A report by the Senate Armed Services Committee made public Dec. 21 condemned military spying on the NSC, but also said that the incidents in 1970 and 1971 were isolated and posed no threat to civilian control of the military. According to the report, Welander was a "cognizant participant" in the rifling of burn bags and the pilfering of papers from the briefcase of Kissinger by Radford.

[5] **Defense spending developments.** Despite "serious reservations," President Nixon Aug. 5 signed a bill authorizing $22.2 billion for military weapons research and procurement for fiscal 1975 (July 1, 1974-June 30, 1975). Nixon was critical of a provision allowing the House and Senate by concurrent resolution to disapprove a presidential decision permitting export of certain goods and technology to certain countries. Under the terms of the provision which was drafted by Sen. Henry Jackson (D, Wash.) and was aimed at the Soviet Union, the Defense Department would have the authority to recommend against exports it found not to be in the national interest. The President could overrule the Defense Department, but Congress could in turn overrule the President, in effect upholding the original Defense Department recommendation. Nixon said, "This feature provides for an unconstitutional exercise of legislative power." The Senate, by an 88-8 vote, had passed the bill July 30. The measure had cleared the House the day before by a 305-38 margin. The bill also set a $1 billion ceiling on military aid to South Vietnam for fiscal 1975. This was $600 million less than requested by the Administration.

[6] The Defense Department reported Oct. 1 that during the period from April 1 to June 30, the cost-to-completion of 42 major weapons systems increased by 13% or $16.91 billion. Presenting this information in its regular quarterly report to Congress on weapons procurement, the Pentagon estimated that all the systems, many of which were in developmental stages, would cost $143.64 billion. Of the $16.91 billion, all but $857.7 million was the direct result of inflation, the Pentagon said. The biggest increase, the Pentagon said, occurred in the B-1 bomber, the aircraft sought by the Air Force as a replacement for the B-52. (The General Accounting Office (GAO) said in a report made public June 2 that 55 new weapons systems being developed by the Pentagon had

experienced cost overruns totalling $26 billion. According to the GAO, original estimates for development of 55 new weapons had totaled $111.6 billion, but their current estimated cost had risen to $134.2 billion. Taking into account another $3.7 billion for quantity reduction, the report said, the estimated overruns reached $26.3 billion. Sen. William Proxmire (D, Wis.), who released the report, said 13 of the weapons systems had been significantly deficient in performance. Proxmire added that 24 of the systems were at least one year behind their scheduled delivery dates.)

[7] Congress approved, and sent to President Ford for his signature, legislation appropriating $82.6 billion for the Defense Department for fiscal 1975. Passed by voice vote in the Senate Sept. 24 and by a 293-59 margin in the House Sept. 23, the bill provided $4.5 billion less than the original Pentagon request of $87.1 billion. Despite the cut, the bill still ran into opposition on the House floor among members who saw it as excessively large and inflationary, and among those opposing sections of the bill containing concealed appropriations for the Central Intelligence Agency and $205 million for the F-111, aircraft not requested by the Air Force.

[8] The Defense Department Nov. 22 announced plans for consolidation of 111 domestic military installations that would result in elimination of 11,600 civilian jobs and transfer of 11,500 military personnel to other jobs. The realignment of military bases and headquarters, scheduled to begin in 1977, would result in annual savings of $300 million, which would be rechanneled into "more combat capability and effectiveness," a Pentagon spokesman said. Under the plans, only two installations would be closed—the Army's Frankford Arsenal in Philadelphia and Ellington Air Force Base in Houston.

[9] **Levy court-martial conviction upheld.** The Supreme Court June 19 upheld by a 5-3 vote the court-martial conviction of Dr. Howard B. Levy, a former Army doctor who was found guilty in 1967 of disobeying orders, "conduct unbecoming an officer and a gentleman," and "disorders and neglects to the prejudice of good order and discipline in the armed forces." The charges against Levy had stemmed from his refusal to train Vietnam-bound special forces units and making disloyal statements about U.S. policy in Vietnam. In upholding Levy's conviction, the court reversed a U.S. 3rd Circuit Court of Appeals decision that had declared the articles of the Uniform Code of Military Justice, under which Levy had been punished, unconstitutional "as measured by contemporary standards of vagueness."

[10] **Callaway calls volunteer Army a success.** Secretary of the Army Howard Callaway called the volunteer Army a success July 1. The Army had ended fiscal 1974 more than 1,000 men over the 775,000 figure authorized by Congress, Callaway said. The Air Force, it was reported June 24, had encountered no difficulties in maintaining an authorized strength of 645,000 personnel. The Navy, whose authorized strength was 551,000 persons, had also been able to meet its recruiting goals. Only the Marine Corps was clearly below strength at the end of fiscal 1974, with an estimated 6,000 fewer Marines than its planned 196,000. The Army announced Nov. 22 that its remaining 2,500 draftees had been discharged.

[11] **McDonnell Douglas profits disputed.** Sen. Proxmire convened the Housing and Urban Development, Space, Science and Veterans Subcommittee of the Appropriations Committee July 25 for testimony from members and staff of the Renegotiation Board on charges that the McDonnell Douglas Corp. had been allowed to keep $26 million in alleged excess profits on government contracts to which it was not entitled. The board, which was responsible for eliminating excess defense and aerospace profits, had ruled 4-1 June 18 that the firm had

earned $5 million in excess profits in 1967 but none in 1968 and 1969. Proxmire, chairman of the subcommittee, asked for testimony following receipt of a strong dissent by board member Godwin Chase, who asserted that the firm had failed to comply with federal regulations requiring a company doing business with the government to supply detailed financial statements. James S. McDonnell, chairman of the corporation, denied in a statement July 20 that the firm had ever been less than forthright in its dealings with the Renegotiation Board. Proxmire said Oct. 2 that the Renegotiation Board should either be reformed or abolished and its functions transferred elsewhere in the federal government.

[12] **Navy raises Grumman interest rates.** The Navy said July 30 that it had raised the interest rate on money loaned to the Grumman Corp. as advance payment for F-14 fighters produced by the aerospace firm. Members of the Tactical Air Power Subcommittee of the Senate Armed Services Committee had criticized the Navy July 24 for loaning money to Grumman at a lower rate than the one charged corporate borrowers by commercial banks. Subcommittee Chairman Howard W. Cannon (D, Nev.) asserted that Grumman was paying an effective interest rate of 2% or 3% because it had invested its "large cash balances" for profit "rather than repaying the government's loan." The Senate Aug. 13 by a 53-35 vote disapproved an agreement under which the Navy would have advanced $100 million to Grumman. Proxmire, author of the resolution to kill the advance payment, said there was "no hard evidence that Grumman will go out of business if it does not get the Navy loan." Rep. Otis Pike (D, N.Y.) disclosed Aug. 14 that the government of Iran, which had 80 F-14s on order, had offered to lend money to Grumman to insure continued production of the fighter.

[13] **U.S. MIRV, Soviet naval superiority seen.** The 1974-75 edition of the authoritative *Jane's Fighting Ships,* released Aug. 28, evaluated the Soviet Navy as "a very powerful fighting force" which "leads the world in seaborne missile armaments, both strategic and tactical, both ship and submarine launched." The U.S. Navy, it said, because of a "direct policy" of slashing its strength from 1,000 ships in 1968 to 514 in 1974, "bears a desperately heavy burden." A survey published June 18 by the Stockholm International Peace Research Institute recorded that the U.S. had nearly 6,000 independent warheads on strategic missiles, outnumbering the U.S.S.R. in deployment of both land-based and submarine missiles with MIRV warheads. The Soviet Union had about 2,200 independent strategic missile warheads, and four new ICBMs; three of them had MIRV warheads for releasing 4-7 re-entry vehicles. (Adm. James L. Holloway 3rd, chief of naval operations, Oct. 30 said the U.S. had and would continue to maintain superiority over the Soviet Union's navy.)

[14] **U.S. to use Indian Ocean base.** British State Minister Julian Amery announced Feb. 5 that the U.S. would establish a naval base on the British-held island of Diego Garcia in the Indian Ocean, 1,000 miles south of India. (The U.S. Defense Department had been operating a small communications station on the island since the spring of 1973 under agreements signed with Britain in 1966 and 1972.) Amery said that Britain had "long felt that it is desirable in the general Western interest to balance increased Soviet activities in the Indian Ocean." Opposition to the base was expressed by Australia, India, Maldives, New Zealand, Mauritius, Indonesia and the Soviet Union. The Diego Garcia base was the subject of a question put to President Ford at his Aug. 28 press conference. Referring to Ford's previously stated view favoring establishment of a U.S. Indian Ocean fleet with supporting bases, a reporter asked if the President still held that view. Ford answered by saying he favored limited expansion of the base. "I don't view this as any challenge to the Soviet Union. The Soviet Union already has

three major naval operating bases in the Indian Ocean." The Soviet Union Aug. 31 denied President Ford's assertion. A statement issued by the news agency Tass said, "In reality there exist neither three nor even one U.S.S.R. naval base in the Indian Ocean." The White House said Aug. 31 that President Ford reiterated his claim that there were three Soviet naval bases in the Indian Ocean. A Defense Department spokesman later identified them as Berbera, Somalia; Umm Qasr, Iraq; and Aden, South Yemen.

[15] **Ford rebukes general for remarks.** President Ford Nov. 14 publicly rebuked Air Force Gen. George S. Brown, chairman of the Joint Chiefs of Staff, for remarks regarded as anti-Semitic he made during a question-and-answer period following a speech at Duke University Law School Oct. 10 (published Nov. 13). Speaking at a news conference in Phoenix, Ford said Brown's comments had been a "mistake," but added that he had no intention of replacing the general as chairman of the joint chiefs. Brown's remarks had come in the context of an answer to a question concerning the strength of the Israeli lobby in the U.S. Congress. Brown said that the Jews "own, you know, the banks in this country, the newspapers. You just look at where the Jewish money is in this country." The President had summoned Brown to the White House the morning of Nov. 14 and personally reprimanded him. Brown issued a statement through the Defense Department Nov. 13, expressing regret for the remarks.

See also AMNESTY & CLEMENCY; APPOINTMENTS & RESIGNATIONS; ATOMIC ENERGY [18]; AUSTRALIA [18-19]; AVIATION [16]; BUDGET; CALLEY, WILLIAM L.; CAMBODIA; CHEMICAL & BIOLOGICAL WEAPONS; CHILE [28]; CHINA, NATIONALIST; CYPRUS [23]; ECONOMY, U.S. [5, 11, 21]; ENERGY CRISIS [2-3, 8]; FOREIGN AID; GERMANY, WEST [14-15]; GREAT BRITAIN [3]; GREECE [10-13]; ICELAND; IRAN; JAPAN [12]; KOREA, REPUBLIC OF [15]; LAOS; MIDDLE EAST [14, 39]; NIXON, RICHARD M.; NARCOTICS & DANGEROUS DRUGS; NORTH ATLANTIC TREATY ORGANIZATION; OBITUARIES [ABRAMS]; OIL [2]; PATENTS; PRIVACY [11]; PUERTO RICO; RADICALS; SOUTH AFRICA [13]; THAILAND; UNION OF SOVIET SOCIALIST REPUBLICS [33]; VETERANS; VIETNAM, REPUBLIC OF [31-33, 37-38]; WOMEN'S RIGHTS

DEFUNIS JR., MARCO—*See* CIVIL RIGHTS [7]
DELAWARE—*See* GAMBLING
DEMOCRATIC PARTY—*See* EDUCATION; ELECTIONS; POLITICS; WATERGATE [1, 77, 87-103]

DENMARK—Parliamentary passage of a bill substantially increasing sales taxes provoked strikes and protest demonstrations May 16. Tens of thousands of workers staged an unofficial strike after the Folketing (parliament) May 15 approved a tax bill introduced by the minority Moderate Liberal government of Premier Poul Hartling May 8. The legislation reduced income taxes by an average 17%, but raised sales taxes on domestic and imported consumer items by 5%-25%. Items affected included tobacco, alcohol, automobiles, gasoline, electricity and household appliances.

Hartling's government survived four no-confidence motions Sept. 20 and won approval of a compromise tax reform bill. The fiscal reform was approved by a vote of 88-41, with 48 abstentions of which 46 were cast by Social Democrats. Hartling had warned before the vote that he would call new elections if the bill failed. The legislation would reduce income taxes by 7 billion kroner ($1.13 billion), representing cuts of 10%-17%, and slash government spending by nearly 10% in the current fiscal year ending March 30, 1975. The tax reform was part of the Hartling administration's program to solve the nation's economic difficulties, including a 16% inflation rate, a 4% unemployment rate and a soaring foreign trade deficit.

An estimated 15,000 persons demonstrated in Copenhagen against membership in the European Economic Community Oct. 2, the second anniversary of the 1972 referendum which decided Denmark's entry into the community. The protesters, joined by other demonstrators in provincial towns, demanded a new referendum on continued Danish membership. According to a public opinion poll published Sept. 8, 53% of the electorate would now vote against Danish membership in a referendum.

The Foreign Affairs Ministry was reported Dec. 1 to have removed Denmark's ambassador to the United Nations, Hans Tabor, and assigned him to Ottawa, Canada, following a controversy involving the Oct. 14 U.N. vote to invite the Palestine Liberation Organization (PLO) to address the General Assembly. The statement said Tabor's actions on the PLO vote had "nothing specific" to do with his transfer, but it said the government had lost "qualified confidence in his judgment." Tabor had abstained in the Oct. 14 vote according to government instructions. But U.N. sources said he had openly supported a pro-PLO decision in consultations before the vote.

Premier Hartling Dec. 5 called general elections for Jan. 9, 1975, asserting that he preferred to go to the electorate after a majority of the parties in the Folketing had opposed the economic austerity plan of his minority Moderate Liberal government. Hartling had earlier told the Folketing that only 81 members of the 175-seat Folketing favored the anti-inflation plan presented Dec. 3, which called for a one-year freeze on prices, extension of all labor agreements though 1975, and a temporary ban on automatic wage adjustments linked to the cost of living index and introduction instead of a monthly lump sum payment to all employees. More than 100,000 workers had demonstrated Nov. 26 in Copenhagen and other cities against the government's economic policies and demanded Hartling's resignation. Workers in several cities staged wildcat strikes to protest what they called the government's inadequate measures to reduce unemployment.

See also CHILE [3, 24]; COMMUNISM, INTERNATIONAL; EUROPEAN ECONOMIC COMMUNITY [18]; EUROPEAN SECURITY; FAMINE & FOOD; NORTH ATLANTIC TREATY ORGANIZATION; MONETARY DEVELOPMENTS [4, 11, 15]; OIL [6-7, 9, 26]; POLAND; UNITED NATIONS [11]; WATERGATE [40]

DESERTERS—*See* AMNESTY & CLEMENCY
DIABETES—*See* MEDICINE & HEALTH
DIEGO GARCIA—*See* DEFENSE [14]

DISARMAMENT—U.S. gives 'mini-nuke' pledge. The chief U.S. delegate to the U.N. Conference of the Committee on Disarmament, Joseph A. Martin Jr., presented a statement to the Geneva forum May 23 in which the U.S. gave assurances that it would not develop a new generation of miniaturized nuclear weapons, known as "mini-nukes," which could be used interchangeably with conventional weapons on a battlefield. Critics of these relatively small atomic arms had argued that such weapons could make it easier to decide to cross the threshold from conventional to atomic warfare.

SALT II sessions held. Another round in the Strategic Arms Limitation Talks was held in Geneva Feb. 19-March 19 amid reports of disagreements among U.S. policymakers. The *New York Times* had reported Feb. 6 that the Joint Chiefs of Staff were more skeptical than was Secretary of State Henry A. Kissinger of the possibility of policing a limitation of multiple warhead missiles (MIRVs). Disagreements between Kissinger and Paul H. Nitze, a member of the negotiating team surfaced June 14 when Nitze resigned from the delegation where he had been a representative since 1969. Although citing Administration weaknesses due to Watergate, Nitze also was known to be the only member of the U.S. SALT team who had openly disagreed with Kissinger who, Nitze believed, was too anxious to reach an agreement with Moscow. Dr. Michael May replaced Nitze.

The SALT II talks resumed in Geneva Sept. 18 after a six-month recess. They ended Nov. 5 to permit the U.S. and Soviet delegates to consult with their governments. Under the terms of the July summit agreement signed by President Nixon and Communist Party General Secretary Leonid Brezhnev, the SALT delegations were to negotiate a new interim accord to cover the period 1975-1985. A five-year interim agreement was signed in 1972 and did not include limits on long-range bombers or on MIRVs. Western sources were doubtful that the mandated pact could be achieved before the projected date of 1975. Fundamental incompatibilities in the U.S. and Soviet positions remained unreconciled: the U.S.S.R., which in its arms programs stressed large land-based missiles, sought parity with U.S. forces, whereas the U.S., whose defense programs balanced land, sea and air forces, sought essential equivalency with the Soviet Union. The issue of U.S. nuclear forces in Europe was also unresolved, Moscow held that since these forces could be directed against the U.S.S.R., they should be taken into account in determining weapons levels, while the U.S. maintained that its European forces were a part of the North Atlantic Treaty Organization (NATO) defense and fell outside the realm of the SALT talks.

Controversy on '72 nuclear arms pact. Kissinger June 24 denied as "totally false in every detail" allegations lodged June 21 and repeated June 24 by Sen. Henry Jackson (D, Wash.) that Kissinger had engaged in a secret deal in 1972 which allowed the Soviet Union the option of deploying 70 submarine missile launchers beyond the 950 allowed it in the 1972 strategic arms agreement. In testimony later that day before the Senate Armed Services Subcommittee on Arms Control, Kissinger admitted there had been a "dispute" between the U.S. and the Soviet Union over the interpretation of the number of launchers. He also acknowledged that President Nixon had given verbal assurance to Brezhnev that the U.S. would not deploy the maximum number of missile launchers permitted it by the pact. Kissinger minimized the significance of either development. Jackson, who had been among the early critics of the 1972 agreement, claiming that it had given the Soviet Union a numerical advantage over the U.S., said June 24: "The issue here is not 70 missiles more or less. The issue is the withholding from the Congress and the American people of a secret agreement that had the clear effect of altering the terms of the SALT interim agreement."

Leaders agree to seek new arms pact. Nixon and Brezhnev signed a number of limited documents on nuclear relations July 3, none of which constituted a hoped-for breakthrough toward permanent agreements on limiting offensive nuclear weapons. In first revealing the agreements July 2, Brezhnev had observed that the arms accords "could have been broader." The communique signed by the two leaders committed their countries to negotiate a new interim accord dealing with both quantitative and qualitative limitations of strategic nuclear arms to cover the period until 1985. In a separate treaty and protocol, the U.S. and the Soviet Union agreed not to conduct any underground nuclear weapons test with a yield exceeding 150 kilotons. Senate ratification would be required for both the ABM and underground test limitation agreements. Other instruments included: Two secret protocols, to be submitted to U.S. Congressional leaders, on the dismantling and replacement of missiles under provisions of the 1972 defensive missile treaty and interim accord on offensive arms. Kissinger said they were made secret at the request of the Soviet Union, but that "they break no new ground, they change no provisions"; and an unwritten agreement in principle by Brezhnev to permit on-site inspection of explosions carried out for peaceful purposes. The signed treaty limiting underground tests called only for the use of "national means of verification" and the exchange of various data on the conduct of the tests.

Ford summit. President Ford, at a news conference Dec. 2, disclosed details of the tentative arms agreement he reached with Brezhnev at their summit meeting in Vladivostok Nov. 23-24, stressing that the agreement put "a firm ceiling on the strategic arms race." In a foreign policy statement before devoting half his news conference to the topic, Ford said major breakthroughs had been made on two critical issues: "(1) We agreed to put a ceiling of 2,400 each on the total number of intercontinental ballistic missiles, submarine-launched missiles and heavy bombers. (2) We agreed to limit the number of missiles that can be armed with multiple warheads (MIRVs). Of each side's total of 2,400, 1,320 can be so armed." Ford said these ceilings were "well below the force levels which would otherwise have been expected over the next ten years and very substantially below the forces which would result from an all-out arms race over that same period."

Kissinger, who attended all the summit meetings and who had set the foundation for the accord in October talks in Moscow with Brezhnev, had noted Nov. 24 the "very strong possibility" of reaching a final pact for signing in the summer of 1975 when the Soviet leader was scheduled to visit the U.S. Negotiations on the final accord woud be conducted at SALT II, which would resume in January 1975. Kissinger noted that the Soviet Union had made a basic concession in ceasing to insist that the U.S. forward-based fighter bomber system deployed in Europe be included in the total of U.S. strategic delivery vehicles. Strong reservations to the pact were expressed by Sen. Jackson who said Nov. 26 that setting so high a MIRV-vehicle limit "will make possible the addition of thousands of nuclear warheads," a reference to the fact that the agreement did not directly affect the number of warheads, but only the vehicles on which they could be deployed.

See also ATOMIC ENERGY [11]; CHEMICAL & BIOLOGICAL WEAPONS; DEFENSE [1]; LATIN AMERICA; NOBEL PRIZES; UNION OF SOVIET SOCIALIST REPUBLICS [2-4]

DISTRICT OF COLUMBIA—Voters in the District of Columbia approved by a substantial margin May 7 a new city charter providing for an elected mayor and council, posts currently filled by presidential appointment.

Both houses of Congress passed the fiscal 1975 appropriations bill for the District of Columbia Aug. 20. Signed into law Aug. 31, the bill provided $1,073,642,900, which was $40.5 million less than the budget request but $101 million more than the previous year funding. A separate federal payment of $221,200,000 to the city was authorized under the bill.

See also ART; CRIME [34, 42]; ENERGY CRISIS [8-9]; HOMOSEXUALS; NARCOTICS & DANGEROUS DRUGS

DOMINICA—*See* WEST INDIES ASSOCIATED STATES

DOMINICAN REPUBLIC—Joaquin Balaguer was inaugurated for his third consecutive four-year presidential term Aug. 16, amid anti-government violence and general political uncertainty. Balaguer's election came after a violent campaign in which three of the four opposition candidates withdrew and accused the government of vote fraud. A nearly complete count reported by the

Central Electoral Board May 18 gave Balaguer 924,779 votes, to 105,320 votes for retired Rear Adm. Homero Lajara Burgos of the tiny Popular Democratic Party. Widespread voter abstention was reported May 17. Opposition groups asserted May 17 that the massive abstention showed Balaguer's government no longer had a popular base.

Shopkeepers and workers in many districts of Santo Domingo struck periodically during the summer to protest the high cost of living. Santo Domingo was under strict security measures following at least 20 bomb explosions late Aug. 15. Police arrested an estimated 500 persons in connection with the blasts, which killed at least one person.

A U.S. official and six other hostages held by left-wing guerrillas for two weeks in the Venezuelan consulate in Santo Domingo were freed Oct. 9 when the terrorists accepted a government offer of safe-conduct to Panama. The seven insurgents, who claimed membership in the January 12th Liberation Movement, had kidnapped U.S. Information Service Director Barbara Hutchison outside her office in Santo Domingo Sept. 27 and taken her to the nearby consulate, where they took control of the building and seized seven more hostages—the Venezuelan consul and vice consul, a Spanish priest, and four Dominican employes of the consulate. Radhames Mendez Vargas, the guerrilla leader, told reporters over the telephone that his group would kill the hostages one by one unless the U.S. paid them $1 million in ransom and the Dominican government released 38 political prisoners. The guerrillas later issued a list of 32 other prisoners whose release they demanded. At least 10 of those prisoners and the entire organized Dominican left condemned the guerrilla action, according to press reports. The terrorists dropped the $1 million ransom demand Oct. 3 and asked for release of the political prisoners and safe-conduct for all to either Mexico or Peru. This was rejected by Balaguer and reportedly by the Mexican and Peruvian governments. Balaguer made an "absolutely final" offer of safe conduct out of the country Oct. 7, and the guerrillas accepted this the next day. Panama agreed to grant the terrorists asylum to help the Dominican government "end this unfortunate case," according to Panamanian Ambassador Alejandro Cuellar Arosemena Oct. 9. The guerrillas were flown to Panama City immediately after they freed the seven hostages, all of whom were in good condition. (The eighth hostage, a Dominican, had escaped from the consulate Sept. 28.)

See also ALUMINUM AND BAUXITE; COFFEE; LATIN AMERICA; MIDDLE EAST [23]; SUGAR

DRAFT RESISTERS—*See* AMNESTY & CLEMENCY
DRAMA—*See* THEATER
DROUGHT—*See* FAMINE & FOOD; INDIA; WEATHER
DRUGS—*See* CONSUMER AFFAIRS [5]; MEDICINE & HEALTH [3, 11-14]; NARCOTICS & DANGEROUS DRUGS

EARTHQUAKES—A sharp earthquake struck central Japan May 9, killing 30 persons and injuring 77. An earthquake, which measured 6.2 on the Richter scale of 10, struck Pakistan Dec. 28 reportedly leaving at least 5,200 persons dead. Aerial surveys revealed that at least nine towns had been flattened. All highways into the affected areas had been closed and rescue work was maintained almost exclusively by helicopter.

See also SPACE [8]

EAST GERMANY—*See* GERMANY, EAST

ECEVIT, BULENT—*See* CYPRUS [4-5, 8, 10, 13-15, 20]; TERRITORIAL WATERS; TURKEY

ECONOMICS—*See* NOBEL PRIZES

ECONOMY, INTERNATIONAL—*See* MONETARY DEVELOPMENTS, INTERNATIONAL

ECONOMY, U.S.—Statistical indicators. The Commerce Department Jan. 16, 1975, released figures for 1974 indicating that the nation was experiencing both the worst recession and the worst inflation in many years. The 1974 Gross National Product (GNP), a measure of the nation's total output of goods and services, was $1.397 trillion, which, after adjusting for inflation was a drop of 2.2% for the year. This was in contrast to a 1973 increase of 5.9%, to a market value of $1.289 trillion. The 1974 drop was the worst since 1946. The yearly inflation rate of 10.3% was the biggest since 1947. The Wholesale Price Index (WPI) increased 20.9% for the year. Measured against the 1967 base level figure of 100, the December WPI was 171.5, meaning that items which had cost $100 in 1967 currently cost $171.50. This compared to the 1973 figure of 145.3. Consumer prices, measured by the Consumer Price Index (CPI) rose 12.2% for the year, again the highest figure since 1946. At the end of 1974 the index stood at 155.4, compared to the 1973 figure of 138.5. Personal income had risen 9% from 1973, to $1.15 trillion. "Real" spendable income for the typical worker with three dependents declined 5.4% during 1974. Unemployment rose steadily through the 12-month period, from 4.8% in December, 1973, to 7.2% one year later.

[2] **Nixon economic measures.** In his annual economic message to Congress and a companion report prepared by the Council of Economic Advisers (CEA), President Nixon Feb. 1 stressed the need for policy flexibility in dealing with the

possibility of economic stagnation, prolonged inflation and the domestic consequences of international economic upheavals. On wage-price controls, the President said "We will continue our policy of progressive removal...." The message stressed "there will be no recession" in 1974, a view which was reaffirmed by CEA Chairman Herbert Stein and Treasury Secretary George P. Schultz. Their remarks, however, were qualified by an attempt to redefine the term recession. Stein said Feb. 1 that the standard definition—two quarters of declining economic output—was a "simplistic and mechanistic" guide having "no standing in the economic profession." Under Stein's definition, a recession was a "departure of the economy from its normal growth path of considerable intensity, durability and breath." Nixon re-affirmed his "no recession" pledge in a Feb. 25 press conference during which he said optimistic predictions were justified by an easing of the energy shortage and because the nation's food supply was expected to increase over the year, forcing prices down.

[3] **Midyear report.** The President presented a midyear economic report May 25 in a nationally broadcast radio address in which he said the Administration's basic economic policies would remain unchanged: opposition to a tax cut backed by Congressional Democrats, support for the Federal Reserve's "tight money" actions, efforts to increase supplies of products, and an attempt to hold the fiscal 1975 federal budget at $305 billion. During the speech, Nixon also announced the appointment of Deputy Secretary of State Kenneth Rush as counselor to the President for economic affairs, filling a policy-making vacuum left by the resignation of Shultz, announced March 1. The radio broadcast was followed, May 28, by a CEA report to Congress predicting that inflation would drop to a level "in the neighborhood of 7%" by the final quarter of 1974. Basing its prediction on the leveling off of food and energy prices, the report also called on business and labor to exert "moderation and self-restraint" in raising prices and making wage demands. A more pessimistic analysis of economic conditions was offered May 26 by Federal Reserve Board Chairman Arthur Burns who said "rampant inflation" was more a result of "awesome" federal spending levels than of the skyrocketing food and fuel costs blamed for the increase in prices by the President. [For details of the board's policy of monetary restraint during the year, see BANKS & BANKING.]

[4] **Nixon seeks restraints.** The President cut nearly $5 billion from his projected fiscal 1975 budget, he announced June 24, indicating again the Administration's conservative inflation-fighting policy of fiscal restraint. Specific areas of the budget slated for trimming were not disclosed, although Rush indicated some minor cuts could be made in defense spending for personnel and unneeded bases. Nixon's announcement followed a meeting with his top level economic advisers. Rush later told reporters that a 1974 tax cut had been ruled out, as well as a tax increase. The question of tax cuts to stimulate the economy had been in contention between the White House and Congress. Several prominent Democrats had supported passage of a cut, saying it would provide immediate help to the poor who had been hardest hit by the effects of inflation. The White House took an opposing view, saying such cuts would have an inflationary effect: increased spending would spur demand and cause higher prices. Tax incentives for business were discussed July 11 during a White House meeting with a group of corporate executives and economists. The businessmen, generally expressing support for Administration policies, also, however, asked for tax preferences such as an increase in the investment tax credit, accelerated depreciation allowances and other write-offs against federal income taxes. Later, Rush contrasted the inflationary impact of tax cuts for individuals with business proposals, saying the former meant "increased demand without increased

productivity," while the latter would be "noninflationary" if they spurred output.

[5] In a nationally broadcast address before four California business groups July 25, Nixon endorsed the Federal Reserve Board's strict credit policies, but he also acknowledged that monetary restraint could be carried to the "extreme." The Administration would work to "provide expansion of money and credit necessary to support moderate growth of the economy at reasonable prices," Nixon said, assuring the business group that "there will not be a credit crunch in which the money for essential economic activity becomes unavailable." In one of the few controversial aspects of his speech, Nixon also said, "We must re-evaluate the trade-off between increasing supplies and certain other objectives, such as improving the environment and increasing safety. These are important, but we often have a tendency to push particular social goals so fast or so far that other important economic goals are unduly sacrificed." In an official response to Nixon's speech from Congressional Democrats, Sen. Lloyd Bentsen (D, Tex.) charged the Administration with engaging in "too many trials and far too many errors" in devising economic policy. Bentsen's rebuttal, broadcast nationally July 31, said Nixon's policies were characterized by "high interest rates, tight money, slow growth—business as usual." Instead, Bentsen advocated a program to meet short and long term economic needs. Proposals included repeal of tax provisions encouraging U.S. businesses to build factories abroad, repeal of "tax shelters for unproductive investments," "selective" credit allocations that would channel investments to areas in need of funds, such as housing, creation of a cost of living force "to keep track of price increases and wage settlements," and reduced federal spending, including cuts in defense areas.

[6] **Wage-price monitoring group sought.** President Nixon asked Congress Aug. 2 to establish a "cost of living task force" that could monitor wage, price, supply and productivity developments. According to the Administration's proposed legislation, however, the new group would not have enforcement powers to delay or reduce wage and price increases—powers that had been held by the defunct Cost of Living Council. The proposal had wide bipartisan support in Congress. Joint Economic Committee members of both parties expressed support for a similar plan during hearings conducted Aug. 2 when Treasury Secretary William P. Simon was questioned about the Administration's efforts to curb inflation. In a television interview Aug. 4, Simon indicated that the White House would persist in its application of stringent policies of fiscal and monetary restraint even if the unemployment rate exceeded 6%, a level generally regarded as recessionary. Simon maintained that rising prices, rather than rising unemployment, was the nation's principal economic problem.

[7] **Cost of Living Council actions.** Controls were lifted in a number of industries, prior to the April 30 expiration of the Economic Stabilization Act. The Cost of Living Council (CLC) had freed major portions of the economy from controls, but in the negotiations leading to early decontrol releases officials had won pledges of price restraints from many important sectors of the economy. Those industries unwilling to give such pledges had been threatened with a continuation of wage and price controls after April 30, but that bargaining weapon was nullified by Congressional opposition to any form of extended controls. When the act expired, only 12.2% of consumer prices and 31.5% of wholesale prices had not been decontrolled by the CLC. Restraints had remained on machinery, steel, copper, health care and a few other industries. Only the petroleum industry would remain controlled under authority granted by the 1973 Emergency Petroleum Allocation Act, which would extend to March 1, 1975.

[8] **Senate rejects standby controls.** The Senate rejected May 1, in a 57-31 vote,

a proposal to grant standby authority to the President to reimpose wage and price controls. However, it approved, 44-41, an amendment to maintain the CLC as a wage-price monitoring agency beyond June 30, when its funding ran out, and authorized it to reimpose controls on companies that violated price restraint promises they gave to the CLC to win early decontrol. The House had already indicated opposition to any extension of controls. The CLC monitoring extension was, however, postponed indefinitely when a final vote was taken May 9. The vote came only one day after the Ford Motor Co. announced it was raising 1974 prices 3.5% despite its December 1973 pledge to the CLC. [See AUTOMOBILES] General Motors, also a party to the December 1973 pledge, raised its prices an average 2% in May. Its price rises, however, were not mainly in the base price but in optional equipment and freight charges which the CLC had called allowable.

[9] The ending of price controls was also followed May 1-2 by major price increases in the steel, copper and related industries. U.S. Steel May 2 announced an average price increase of 5.7% on "a broad range of products." Bethlehem Steel Corp. and National Steel Corp. followed suit May 6 with raises averaging 9%.

[10] **Ford economic proposals.** In his first full day in office Aug. 10, President Ford met with the government's top economic policy makers and stressed that he would pursue the budget-cutting policies devised by the Nixon Admnistration to curb rising prices. Unlike the Nixon approach, however, Ford indicated that he would seek close cooperation from Congress in choosing the areas slated for spending reductions at the outset of the budget-cutting process. In a statement issued Aug. 12, Ford strongly rebuked General Motors Corp. for its decision to raise prices on its 1975 model cars by an average of nearly 10%. [See AUTOMOBILES] Ford called on "all segments" of the economy to "exercise restraint in their wage and price actions." In line with his plea to both business and labor for restraint, Ford coupled his admonition to General Motors with an invitation to AFL-CIO President George Meany to confer with him at the White House. The "jawboning" session with Meany was held Aug. 13 as Ford intensified his efforts to use moral suasion to offset further escalation of wages and prices. Ford also met with Labor Secretary Peter J. Brennan and other department officials to discuss the implementation of programs that could deal with the expected rise in unemployment resulting from a sluggish economy. (FRB Chairman Burns had proposed earlier that a $4 billion program of public service employment be established to create 800,000 jobs at the state and local government levels if unemployment should rise above 6%. Burns told the Joint Economic Committee Aug. 6 that the plan would ease the strain of prolonged monetary and fiscal restraint. Burns also urged Congress to incorporate some enforcement powers in the bill establishing a new wage-price monitoring task force.)

[11] In a nationally televised address Aug. 12, President Ford urged Congress to cooperate with him in confronting the problems of the nation, citing inflation as the major issue. "My first priority is to work with you to bring inflation under control," Ford said. "Inflation is our domestic public enemy No. 1." The brunt of the speech was addressed to Congress for cooperation in an attack on inflation. "I do not want a honeymoon with you," he said, to an outburst of applause. "I want a good marriage." While ruling out "unwarranted cuts in national defense," which he considered "nonpartisan policy." Ford suggested that Congress exercise restraint in setting appropriations levels. Specifically, Ford said Congress should reactivate the CLC, without reimposing controls, to monitor wages and prices "to expose abuses." He also referred to Senate

Democratic Leader Mike Mansfield's (Mont.) request to convene an economic conference of members of Congress, White House consultants "and some of the best economic brains from labor, industry and agriculture." He cited the resolution to assemble a "domestic summit meeting" to plan for stability and growth in the economy. "I accept your suggestion," Ford told Congress, "and I will personally preside."

[12] **Congress OKs wage-price task force.** The House gave final approval Aug. 20 to a Senate-passed bill establishing a new wage-price monitoring agency. The cost of living task force, originally requested by President Nixon and quickly endorsed by President Ford, would lack any enforcement powers in its efforts to monitor wages, prices, profits, dividends, interest rates, the concentration of business power and antitrust practices. The legislation authorized creation of an eight-member Council on Wage and Price Stability made up of government officials. They would be aided by a four-member advisory group composed of persons outside government. Under the bill, the council's statutory authority would extend through Aug. 15, 1975. At a televised press conference Aug. 28, Ford reaffirmed his intentions to cut the federal budget for fiscal 1975 and reasserted that "wage and price controls are out, period." Federal spending would be held to levels of "less" than $300 billion, Ford said, adding that the effect of this action would be to "make our borrowing from the money market less, freeing more money for housing, for the utilities to borrow." Ford acknowledged, however, that a public works program costing $4 billion was under consideration. If restrictive monetary and fiscal policies caused the unemployment rate to rise, Ford said, "we will approach this problem with compassion and action if there is a need for it."

[13] **Meany sees slide toward depression.** AFL-CIO President Meany said Aug. 29, in a pre-Labor Day interview, that "we are in a recession now, and there is every indication that we are going into a depression." Meany said he was not optimistic that President Ford could "turn" the situation around. Meany expressed the labor federation's view that the government should move to help finance home building. Interest rates had to be reduced, he said, and he was highly critical of tight-money policies and of the stance that a balanced budget would solve all economic problems. Meany opposed wage guidelines, saying they were "just as bad as controls." According to a Gallup poll published Aug. 17, 68% of those surveyed expected the nation's economic conditions to worsen over the next six months and 46% said they believed the U.S. was heading toward a depression of the magnitude experienced in the 1930s.

[14] **Summit meeting developments.** President Ford met with advisors Aug. 20 to prepare for the economic summit conference scheduled for Sept. 27-28 in Washington. On Aug. 26 Ford set five goals for the summit. The broad aims of the meeting, according to Press Secretary J. F. terHorst, would be to "clarify" the nation's present economic situation; to identify the causes of inflation; to consider "new and realistic" anti-inflation policies; to develop a "consensus" on basic policies; and to define "hardship areas" requiring immediate attention. Nine preliminary meetings were scheduled in September for representative groups in the economy. Ford would chair two of the meetings and also would preside over the final two-day conference in Washington. An estimated 600-700 persons had been invited to participate, White House spokesmen said.

[15] In the period before the summit, conferences were held with, among others: economists, Sept. 5 and 22; union officials, Sept. 11; banking and securities executives, Sept. 20; and state and local government officials, Sept. 23. At their initial meeting the economists supported an easing of the Administration's policy of strict monetary restraint. The later meeting focused

on the target rate of growth in the money supply that should be permitted by the Federal Reserve. There was disagreement over whether federal regulations governing transportation, banking, agriculture and other areas structurally impeded anti-inflation efforts by supporting high prices, limiting competition or creating business or labor monopolies. At the meeting with union officials, over which the President presided during the morning session, the labor leaders declared wages were not responsible for the current inflationary spiral. Most of the discussion centered on the problem of rising unemployment. Among the actions Ford reported was his order to the Labor Department to speed up the spending of $350 million allocated under the Comprehensive Employment and Training Act, which would finance 85,000 public sector jobs. As the series of meetings continued, so did the debate on tight money policies. Unidentified officials of the Federal Reserve were reported Aug. 31 and Sept. 8 to have emphasized that a relaxation had already taken place. An indication of a move toward lower interest rates were seen in the downward movement of rates on federal funds—short term loans within the banking network. In the week ending July 3, the rate peaked at 13.55%, but by the week ending Sept. 6, interest had fallen to 11.5%.

[16] The Joint Economic Committee of Congress Sept. 21 presented its own report, making several recommendations. Among these was promulgation of non-inflationary pay and price guidelines on an industry-by-industry basis. If this did not work, the committee said, Congress should consider giving the Council on Wage and Price Stability authority to defer or rescind "clearly unjustified price increases." (The *New York Times* reported Sept. 25 that a number of leading economic consultants were advising their corporate clients to plan for controls. Some economists believed that sharp jumps in consumer and wholesale prices reflected precautionary price increases undertaken by business as a means of offsetting the expected controls.)

[17] President Ford was present at the economic summit conference during the entire first day of deliberations. An estimated 2,000 persons—delegates, press, diplomats, government officials and other observers—were gathered in the Washington Hilton Hotel ballroom. (The proceedings were broadcast live by public television.) The summit recommendations offered the President were generally similar to proposals originating in the preliminary economic conferences. Rather than focusing on root causes of inflation in their areas, most of the different special interests represented depicted themselves as victims of "stagflation" and sought federal help in overcoming their special economic problems. Labor leaders, led by Meany, warned that inflation cures could lead to a worsening recession and high rates of unemployment. Organized labor was especially critical of Burns and the Federal Reserve's tight money policy. Meany and others urged Ford to replace White House economic advisers who were holdovers from the Nixon Administration, and they called for a reduction in interest rates, an expanded public service jobs program, credit allocation for the housing industry, tax breaks for the poor, and an end to tax loopholes for the wealthy. Labor opposed reductions in federal spending for social programs. Banking and finance leaders supported some form of tax relief for lower income persons and tax changes to encourage savings (a proposal also backed by the housing industry). They also agreed with spokesmen for the natural resources industry that a massive energy conservation campaign should be waged. Consumer groups represented at the conference supported vigorous enforcement of antitrust laws, a rollback in oil prices and an excess profits tax on energy companies. Business and manufacturing groups urged tax incentives to spur capital investment and sought a slowdown in enactment of new environmental

and plant safety regulations. Like representatives of labor and banking and finance, they also opposed a return to wage and price controls. Agriculture and housing representatives asked for special consideration in the form of farm production incentives, higher federal food subsidy prices, credit allocation favorable to farmers, builders and building financers, eased federal credit restrictions and a special construction industry advisory panel within the Council on Wage and Price Stability. Representatives of the transportation industry also sought tax breaks, freight rate increases, relaxation of Interstate Commerce Commission regulations and the enactment of a "cost impact statement" to accompany any new government programs. [For details of the controversy over food prices during 1974, see AGRICULTURE.]

[18] Senate Majority Leader Mike Mansfield (D, Mont.) offered a specific, nine-point economic program developed by Senate Democrats to deal with what he termed an "economic emergency." Among the proposals: establishing, as needed, mandatory wage, price, rent and profit controls; beginning an equitable rationing system for energy and other scarce materials to the end that dependency on foreign sources of petroleum can be reduced and beginning, too, a stringent conservation system including measures to enforce the speed limit and to bring about a reduction of wastage in the utility and other industrial fields; developing a broader system of indexing to the end that the real incomes of wage earners can be tied to real living costs; curbing excessive profits and controlling the flow of investments abroad through the taxing power while conversely cutting taxes on Americans hardest hit by inflation, those in low and moderate income categories and those on moderate fixed incomes; creating without delay, a jobs program which puts people to work in public services and elsewhere as necessary to keep down the level of unemployment.

[19] In his closing address to the conference, President Ford renewed his commitment to fight "stagflation" with policies of fiscal and monetary restraint, but he also promised federal aid for the unemployed if anti-inflationary policies resulted in higher jobless rates. Ford also supported tax law changes; repeated his pledge to keep the federal budget for fiscal 1975 "at or under $300 billion"; and said he would soon propose a national energy program.

[20] **Asks 'total mobilization.'** President Ford presented his Administration's anti-inflation program to the nation Oct. 8 in a televised address before a joint session of Congress. Included were creation of a board to develop a national energy policy, a proposed cut in foreign oil imports by 1 million barrels a day, a 5% surtax on families earning more than $15,000 annually and on corporations, and measures to help the depressed housing industry. He proposed extending unemployment insurance for 13 weeks to those who had already exhausted their benefits. Ford also asked Congress to create a Community Improvement Corps, providing work for the unemployed on short-term projects. The program would be activated when the national unemployment rate exceeded 6%.

[21] The taxation proposal was linked to new austerity measures planned for the federal budget. Ford asked Congress to move quickly before its recess to set a "target spending limit of $300 billion for the federal 1975 budget." If agreement were reached on this ceiling level, Ford said, he would submit a number of "budget deferrals and recissions" to keep expenditures within the new limit. Budget reductions would require "hard choices," Ford said, but he promised that "no federal agency, including the Defense Department, will be untouchable."

[22] Widespread opposition to several of Ford's economic proposals quickly developed in Congress. Two features of the Administration's anti-inflation plan—the surtax and jobless aid—were attacked by members of both parties

during Congressional hearings. Other elements of the plan, such as the $300 billion spending limit for fiscal 1975 and tax reform measures, were generally endorsed by Democrats and Republicans. There was no support for the tax surcharge Oct. 9 in the House Ways and Means Committee. Opposition centered on the proposed income cutoffs of $15,000 for a family and $7,500 for an individual—floors that many members of Congress regarded as too low.

[23] Democrats responded to Ford's speech with nationally televised addresses by Senate Majority Leader Mansfield, Oct. 15, and Sen. Edward S. Muskie, Oct. 22. Rejecting Ford's program because of its close resemblance to that of the previous Administration, Mansfield called for fuel rationing; controls on wages, prices and profits; credit allocation; and a tax break for the poor. Muskie warned that if Ford's proposed voluntary methods failed, mandatory wage-price controls and gasoline rationing might be required. He also favored a minimum tax on the wealthy, charging that the surtax weighed too heavily on low and middle income wage earners.

[24] **Ford assesses policies.** President Ford said Nov. 14 that he saw "no justification" for making "any major revision" in his economic proposals to Congress, despite the repudiation of many Republicans in the Nov. 5 elections when the economy appeared to be a significant voter issue. Ford, appearing at a Sigma Delta Chi convention in Phoenix, urged Congressional action on his 5% surtax proposal, and reaffirmed his opposition to wage and price controls. Earlier in the day, he had addressed a Las Vegas convention of the National Association of Realtors, and announced that the government would free $300 million for mortgages on existing homes in order to bolster the sagging housing industry. The action marked the first time that the government had provided mortgage subsidy assistance for existing single-family houses purchased with conventional financing. The plan was modest in scope, however; an estimated 12,000 houses would be affected.

[25] In revision of Administration sentiment, President Ford's press secretary Ron Nessen, admitted Nov. 12 that the nation was "moving into a recession." Ford had resisted use of the word, although his top economic advisers, Treasury Secretary William Simon and Alan Greenspan, chairman of the Council on Economic Advisers, had conceded earlier in the week that the U.S. was undergoing a recession.

[26] **Anti-inflation panel sets program.** The Citizen's Action Committee to Fight Inflation established by President Ford unveiled its voluntary action program Nov. 11 and warned that mandatory wage and price controls would "almost inevitably" follow unless everyone cooperated in the joint effort. The program called on business people, consumers and workers to sign pledges that they would fight inflation and save energy. (In a specific anti-inflation plea, the committee asked consumers to reduce their consumption of sugar "immediately and drastically" in order to ease price pressures.) According to plans announced by committee chairwoman Sylvia Porter, state and local groups would be set up to enlist citizens in the Administration's plan to Whip Inflation Now (WIN). The voluntary program hit an immediate snag, however, when Arch Booth, president of the U.S. Chamber of Commerce and a committee member, objected to the pledge suggested for business people because it called on them to promise to "hold or reduce prices." Booth said labor groups were not asked to limit their pay demands.

[27] **Ford urges Congress act.** President Ford held a televised news conference in the Executive Office Building Dec. 2. He urged Congress to act on his pending economic proposals. "Action is more helpful than criticism," Ford said, "and every week that the Congress delays makes the prospects a little bleaker." He

asked "immediate" attention to four items: his proposed budget spending cuts of $4.6 billion, trade reform and a tax bill, and a jobs program and improved jobless benefits. The President did not foresee any gas rationing, "serious shortage" or price rise to a dollar a gallon. There was more gas in storage than a year ago and "less than the anticipated growth" in use, he said.

[28] **Ford changes policies.** President Ford told members of the Business Council Dec. 11 that the "economy is in difficult straits" and indicated that his Administration was shifting its economic policies to focus on the new threat of recession after emphasizing the fight against inflation. The new flexibility in Ford's economic program, evident in his message to the corporate executives, was in sharp contrast to his recent views. Most observers agreed that the big increase in unemployment during November was a major factor in forcing the White House to reassess its position and update its anti-inflation policies to reflect the changed conditions. Ford had declined to characterize the current economic downturn as a recession, even after his chief economic advisers conceded it. In his New York address, Ford said flatly, "We are in a recession. Production is declining and unemployment unfortunately is rising." Presidential advisers were openly discussing the possibility of asking Congress to enact a tax cut in an effort to stimulate the economy. That, too, signaled a fundamental change in White House strategy because the linchpin in Ford's economic proposals submitted to Congress in October was a tax surcharge.

[29] (Consumer confidence was at its lowest level since attitudes were first measured following World War II, according to the University of Michigan's Survey Research Center Dec. 12. Consumer confidence had been falling since 1972, analysts said, declining sharply in February at the height of the Arab oil embargo, and during October. Pessimism appeared to be growing as industry layoffs increased and sales worsened.)

[30] **U.S. Steel cuts price increase.** U.S. Steel announced Dec. 23 that it had reduced its average price increase, implemented Dec. 18, from 4.7% to 4% in response to a presidential plea for price restraint. The firm, the nation's largest steel maker, also said the average level of its steel prices would not be raised for six months, barring "unforeseen major economic events." In announcing the partial rollback, which totaled about 20% of the planned increases, U.S. Steel said the action was taken "to aid the nation in its fight against double digit inflation." In Vail, Colo., President Ford said he was pleased with the action. Just prior to U.S. Steel's announcement, its chief rival, Bethlehem Steel Corp., announced that it would meet U.S. Steel's original, higher price quotes by implementing an average "overall" increase of 2.5% for rolled steel products.

See also AGRICULTURE; ANTITRUST ACTIONS; AUTOMOBILE INDUSTRY; AVIATION; BANKS & BANKING; BUDGET; ELECTIONS; ENERGY CRISIS; FORD, GERALD R.; HOUSING; LABOR; NIXON, RICHARD M.; POLITICS; [7]; STOCK MARKET; SUGAR; TAXES; WELFARE & POVERTY

ECUADOR—Elections barred for 5 years. President Guillermo Rodriguez Lara said July 11 that elections and other political activities would remain suspended for five years, during which time his administration would carry out a national development program. Rodriguez Lara was challenged by two political groups, the National Velasquista Federation (supporters of the exiled ex-President Jose Maria Velasco Ibarra, who was overthrown by the current regime) and the Conservative Party.

Oil developments. The state oil company CEPE June 6 took over a 25% share of the operations of the Texaco-Gulf consortium in the northeastern jungle, despite the lack of a final agreement with the U.S. firms on details of the purchase. The action gave CEPE a quarter of the consortium's daily production of 210,000 barrels of crude. Production had totaled 250,000 barrels daily until May 24, when the government ordered a 16% cut to conserve oil reserves. Texaco Inc., which operated the consortium's properties, received a first compensation installment of $25 million from the Ecuadorean government July 2. The amount of the second and final payment, to be delivered by Sept. 6, would be determined by international auditors. Press reports from Quito June 5 had placed the value of the 25% share at about $48 million. Besides the Texaco-Gulf share, CEPE took over 25% ownership of the Trans-Ecuadorean oil pipeline, also administered by Texaco.

The government Oct. 8 increased the tax on the income of foreign oil companies by 8% and raised the royalty rate paid by the companies by .67%. The increases were retroactive to Oct. 1. The moves conformed with a recent decision by the Organization of Petroleum Exporting Countries (OPEC) to increase by 3.5% the taxes and royalties paid by foreign oil companies in producing nations. Crude oil accounted for 72% of the value of Ecuador's exports in January-August, it was reported Oct. 4. Exports totaled $760 million, for a favorable trade balance of $373 million during the period.

Natural Resources Minister Gustavo Jarrin Ampudia was disissed from the Cabinet Oct. 4 and replaced by Luis Salazar. Both were navy captains. According to reports, Jarrin had been under attack from conservatives for the aggressive nationalism he displayed in shaping the nation's oil policy and, since June, as general secretary of OPEC.

See also CUBA; LATIN AMERICA; OIL [5]; PERU [1, 3, 15]; SUGAR

EDUCATION—Nixon asks advance funding, consolidation. President Nixon called on Congress Jan. 24 to heed his earlier appeals to consolidate federal aid to education programs and to approve a new program providing "advance funding"—funds in one year for expenditures in the next—for elementary and secondary schools. In an education message previewing his budget, Nixon stressed the need for a revised formula for the distribution of aid to disadvantaged students focusing funds on the greatest numerical concentrations of needy children. The effort was to reach $2.9 billion by fiscal 1975 from an additional $179 million requested for fiscal 1974 and a $23 million request the next year. For college students, Nixon said the Administration would request "full funding" of $1.3 billion for the "basic opportunity grant" program, under which a student could receive up to $1,400 annually, based on need. Under the proposal, federal aid to needy college students would average $806, compared with $260 in the current fiscal year.

Democrats rebut Nixon on schools. Democratic Congressional spokesmen on education March 30 sharply criticized President Nixon's positions on federal aid to schools as divisive and obstructionist. The remarks by Sen. Claiborne Pell (R.I.) and Rep. John Brademas (Ind.) were the Democrats' "equal time" reply to Nixon's March 23 radio address. Regarding the Administration's proposals for broad consolidation of school programs, Pell agreed that some consolidation was desirable, but argued that Nixon's version amounted to "cutting out programs and cutting down services." Both Pell and Brademas accused the Administration of failing to give proper priority to education. Brademas asserted that the "rhetoric of the Nixon Administration is fine, but not the record." It was Congress, "usually with Democrats and Republicans working together," he said, that provided the "leadership" for support of education. Pell noted that Nixon had vetoed four education bills "on the grounds of extravagance," but had yet to veto a defense or space program on such grounds.

NEA-AFT merger talks fail. Merger negotiations between the nation's two largest teacher organizations—the National Education Association (NEA) and the AFL-CIO American Federation of Teachers (AFT)—broke down Feb. 27. NEA President Helen D. Wise attributed the impasse to the AFT's inflexibility on the three issues considered "paramount" by the NEA: that AFL-CIO affiliation not be required for the merged unit, guarantees of minority representation on new governing bodies, and secret ballots on a merger vote and adoption of new bylaws. In an exchange of charges the next day, AFT President David Selden said he had been willing to compromise on the minority issue but was opposed to formal quotas, which were part of the NEA constitution. Selden said he had also been willing to concede the right of NEA members to reject AFL-CIO affiliation as individuals, while retaining affiliation for the merged unit as an organization.

Albert Shanker was elected president of the AFT Aug. 21, overwhelmingly defeating Selden. Shanker was also president of the New York City United Federation of Teachers and executive vice president of New York State United Teachers, both AFT affiliates. He said he intended to hold all three positions.

W. Va. textbook controversy. An uneasy truce was reported Sept. 21 to have put at least a temporary end to an occasionally violent dispute over public school textbooks in Kanawha County (Charleston), W. Va. After several months of quieter argument, often within the county school board, picketing and protest marches had begun in earnest with the opening of school Sept. 3, resulting in boycotts, school closings and wildcat strikes by coal miners. The protests, led by fundamentalist ministers, opposed supplementary English texts alleged by protesters to be obscene, blasphemous and anti-American. A compromise agreement between protesters and the board was negotiated during the second week of demonstrations under which 90% of the disputed texts would be removed and all would be subjected to a review by an 18-member citizens' panel. Some leaders, however, continued demands for complete and final withdrawal of all the materials.

The dispute flared up again after the local school board, which had removed the books 40 days earlier, decided Nov. 8 to reinstate all but seven of them. However, in a conciliatory gesture, it passed resolutions excusing students from using books they or their parents found morally or religiously "objectionable," and forbidding teachers to "indoctrinate" students in objectionable moral or religious "values." The vote on the books was 4-1. The school board vote adopted a recommendation to reinstate the books made Oct. 29 by a citizens' review panel. The panel consisted of 18 members, but six—all of them anti-book—resigned after the panel's first meeting Oct. 8, charging they were being pressured and ridiculed by the panel's pro-book majority. Anti-book parents, backed by fundamentalist ministers, vowed to continue a school boycott that had kept attendance below 80% since the controversy began. Attendance was below 70% Nov. 12, the first school day after the board's decision, although anti-book crusaders had hoped to keep it below 50%. Anti-book picketers closed down one elementary school Nov. 12 and prevented some 30 buses from leaving their storage yard. Three buses were fired on by snipers, but no injuries were reported. Police escorts were ordered for all buses in troubled areas Nov. 13. A local strike by miners affiliated with the United Mine Workers, whose contract ran out one minute after midnight Nov. 12, contributed to the tension. Miners had staged occasional wildcat strikes to protest the new textbooks until Oct. 9, when UMW President Arnold Miller ordered them to stop.

Protests against the books continued in December despite the adoption of guidelines to give parents greater control over book selection in the future. In a speech Dec. 2, U.S. Education Commissioner Terrel H. Bell told a meeting of the School Division of the Association of American Publishers that schoolbook publishers should print "good literature that will appeal to children without relying too much on blood and guts and street language," and said they should "chart a middle course betweeen the scholar's legitimate claim to academic freedom in presenting new knowledge and social commentary on the one hand, and the legitimate expectation of parents that schools will respect their moral and ethical values on the other." Bell's statement was denounced Dec. 2 by Paul B. Salmon, executive director of the American Association of School Administrators, who asserted it fanned the flames of various schoolbook controversies around the nation.

School records controversy. A section of the 1974 education law giving parents and students access to confidential school records aroused such opposition from college administrators and teachers that its sponsor, Sen. James L. Buckley (R, N.Y.) agreed to amend it. The so-called "Buckley Amendment" barred federal education aid to institutions or agencies that denied parents the right to inspect and challenge records about their childen. This right shifted to the students when they became 18 or entered college. The amendment was aimed primarily at elementary and secondary schools, and Buckley apparently overlooked its implications for colleges and universities. Campus officials warned in October and November that the law would cause legal and administrative difficulties because it allowed students to see confidential letters of recommendation submitted by teachers and financial statements submitted by parents. Buckley's new amendment, passed Dec. 19, exempted parental financial records and confidential recommendations received before 1975 from the disclosure rule.

See also BUDGET; CIVIL RIGHTS [1-8]; KENT STATE; MEDICINE & HEALTH [16]; NIXON, RICHARD M.; RELIGION [19]; TAXES; VETERANS; WOMEN'S RIGHTS

EGYPT—Libya tied to anti-Sadat plot. Libyan leader Col. Muammer el-Qaddafi was accused April 28 of having incited a plot by a group of Islamic extremists aimed at overthrowing the government of Egyptian President Anwar Sadat. According to authorities, about 20 raiders, calling themselves the Islamic Liberation Organization, broke into the Egyptian Military Technical College in Cairo on April 18 in a plan to seize the academy, oust the government and arrest Sadat as he addressed a joint session of Parliament. Eleven persons were killed and 27 injured during the attack which was repulsed by guards and cadets at the institution. Among those arrested was the leader of the plot, Saleh Sariyah, a Palestinian who carried both Libyan and Iraqi passports. Sariyah was quoted by Egyptian newspapers on April 28 as saying that he had met with Qaddafi in Tripoli in June 1973, at which time the Libyan leader told Sariyah that the Sadat regime had to be toppled by a "popular uprising." The Libyan Foreign Ministry denied any complicity in the attack, contending it was an internal Egyptian matter. A radio broadcast from Tripoli in May, however, said that Sadat's government would be "short-lived" and accused it of the "crime of dismembering the Arab nation and relaxing under the American umbrella."

Relations between Egypt and Libya deteriorated further in the first weeks of August. A report from Cairo Aug. 7 said Sadat had sent a letter July 31 to Qaddafi and other members of Libya's ruling Revolutionary Command Council, charging that Libya had planned to blow up Sadat's retreat at Mersa Matruh, attempted to assassinate Egyptian journalist Ihsan Abdel-Kuddus and sought the return of Libyan Mirage jets serving in Egypt since the 1973 Arab-Israeli war. It was the first time Cairo had officially acknowledged the transfer of the Libyan Mirages to Egypt. The Libyan radio announced that the Council had refused to accept Sadat's letter and was returning it to him. Libyan Chief of Staff Lt. Col.

Abu Bakr Younis had warned Egypt in a letter June 17 that if the planes were not returned immediately, Libya would publicly announce that Egypt had seized them, Sadat said. Qaddafi and Sadat conferred in Alexandria Aug. 17-18 in an attempt to improve the deteriorating relations between their two countries. No official statement was issued at the conclusion of the talks in which Sheik Zayed bin Sultan al-Nahyan, president of the United Arab Emirates, served as mediator. Egypt and Libya agreed "to stop their war of words" and "liquidate the special ties existing between them and settle for good neighborly relations instead" following two rounds of high-level talks in recent weeks, it was reported Sept. 10. According to the report, President Sadat had decided to repay Libyan financial loans to Egypt "on an urgent basis" and had promised to return the Mirage jets.

Sadat gives up premiership. President Sadat Sept. 25 relinquished the additional post of premier he had assumed in March 1973 and turned the position over to his first deputy premier, Abdel Aziz Hegazi. Hegazi formed a new 37-member Cabinet but made no changes in the major ministry positions.

Egyptian war losses listed. President Sadat disclosed in an interview published in a Beirut magazine Oct. 6 that "a little more than 6,000" Egyptian soldiers had been killed in the 1973 war and that his country had lost $750 million worth of military equipment. It was the first official casualty figure given by Egypt, but conflicted with Western intelligence sources, which had placed Cairo's war fatalities at about 10,000.

U.S., Egypt exchange envoys. The U.S. and Egypt, which had formalized diplomatic relations Feb. 28, exchanged ambassadors April 19 and 20 in ceremonies held in Washington and Cairo. Under an agreement signed in Cairo Nov. 10, the U.S. was to ship Egypt 200,000 tons of wheat valued at $38.7 million, supplementing a previous accord signed in the summer providing that country with 100,000 tons of wheat.

See also AFRICA; APPOINTMENTS & RESIGNATIONS; ATOMIC ENERGY [11-12]; FOREIGN AID; GREECE [10]; IRAN; ISRAEL; MIDDLE EAST [7, 10-17, 21-22, 33-34, 37-45]; OIL [4-5, 14, 18]; PAKISTAN; SOCCER

EHRLICHMAN, JOHN—*See* WATERGATE [25-26, 52, 62, 78-103]
EISENHOWER, JULIE—*See* NIXON, RICHARD M.; WATERGATE [34]

ELECTIONS, U.S.—An anti-Republican tide attributed to the Watergate scandals and the troubled U.S. economy gave Democrats a sweeping victory in the mid-term elections held Nov. 5. Democrats won 291 of the 435 House seats, at least 61 of the 100 Senate seats (one seat remained in dispute at the end of 1974) and 36 of the 50 governorships. The net Democratic gains included 43 House seats and at least three Senate seats and four governorships. Democrats won 23 of 34 Senate races, and 27 of 35 gubernatorial races. The turnout, 38% of the voting age population, was the lowest level in any Congressional election year since 1946. After the results were evident Nov. 5, President Ford said he "accepted the verdict" and said it reflected the dominant issue of inflation. "The mandate of the electorate places upon the next Congress a full measure of responsibility of resolving this problem," he said. He pledged cooperation. "This is not just a victory, this is a mandate," House Speaker Carl Albert (D, Okla.) said Nov. 6. Democrats also strengthened their domination of state legislatures as a result of the elections. According to figures compiled by the National Legislative Conference, the Democrats controlled both houses in 37 states, the Republicans in four (Idaho, Kansas, North Dakota, Vermont). Prior to the election, the Democrats controlled both houses in 28 states, the Republicans held control in 16. The parties divided control of the legislatures in six states

(Arizona, Colorado, Indiana, Maine, New York, South Dakota). In two states—New Hampshire and Wyoming—there were ties in the Senate. Nebraska elected a nonpartisan unicameral legislature. In 16 shifts of party control of one or both houses, Democrats won 15, the GOP only one—the South Dakota house.

[2] **Women, blacks win.** A record number of black and women candidates ran for office. Women, as expected, posted gains in the elections. Rep. Ella T. Grasso (D, Conn.) was the first woman elected governor who did not first succeed her husband to office. New Yorkers elected their first woman lieutenant governor, State Sen. Mary Ann Krupsak (D). Six more women were elected to the House—Democrats Martha Keys of Kansas, Helen Meyner of New Jersey, Marilyn Lloyd of Tennessee and Gladys Spellman of Maryland, plus Republicans Millicent Fenwick of New Jersey and Virginia Smith of Nebraska. With four women in the House retiring, the net gain of two raised the total number of women representatives to 18, two short of the record 20 women in the House in 1963-64. The number of black legislators from the South increased to 97 as a result of the elections, the highest Southern black representation in state and federal legislatures since the Reconstruction era. Three were members of the U.S. House—Reps. Andrew Young (D, Ga.), Barbara Jordan (D, Tex.) and Harold Ford (D, Tenn.). There were also 10 black state senators (pre-election total, 6) and 84 black state representatives (previously 54).

[3] **Senate results.** Republicans were unseated in four races, (two involving incumbents) but seven Republican incumbents were re-elected and the party was able to retain a seat made vacant by the retirement of Wallace F. Bennett of Utah. The Democrats lost one seat in Nevada where former Republican Gov. Paul Laxalt defeated Lt. Gov. Harry Reid in a race for the office currently held by Alan Bible, who was retiring. Democratic upsets were recorded in Kentucky, Colorado, Florida and Vermont. Marlow W. Cook, Kentucky's one-term Republican senator, was easily defeated by his Democratic challenger, Gov. Wendell Ford. Another Republican incumbent, conservative Peter H. Dominick of Colorado, was decisively defeated by Gary Hart, who had managed Sen. George McGovern's presidential campaign in 1972. It was Hart's first bid for elective office. Democrats in Vermont scored a stunning upset with Patrick J. Leahy's narrow victory over Republican Rep. Richard W. Mallary. He had been regarded as the heir apparent to the safe Republican seat being vacated after 34 years by George Aiken, dean of the Senate. In Florida, a Democrat was elected to succeed Republican Sen. Edward J. Gurney, who had decided not to seek re-election to a second term after being indicted on federal charges of bribery, conspiracy and perjury. Secretary of State Richard Stone, the Democrat, defeated the Republican nominee, millionaire businessman Jack Eckerd. Fifteen Democratic incumbents were re-elected. Two had faced stiff challenges. The party retained four seats currently held by Democrats with the election of Rep. John C. Culver in Iowa to succeed the retiring Harold E. Hughes; John Glenn, who was replacing Ohio Sen. Howard Metzenbaum; Robert B. Morgan, North Carolina's attorney general, who would succeed the retiring Sen. Sam Ervin; and Gov. Dale Bumpers of Arkansas, who would replace the man he defeated in the Democratic primary, Sen. J. William Fulbright. In Utah the GOP retained Bennett's seat with Salt Lake City Mayor Jake Garn's defeat of his Democratic opponent, Rep. Wayne Owens. The race in New Hampshire to fill the seat held by retiring GOP Sen. Norris Cotton remained undecided at the end of 1974. The Republican-controlled state election commission had certified the GOP candidate, Rep. Louis Wyman, the victor by two votes, but his Democratic opponent, John Durkin, appealed the decision to the Senate where the Democratic majority was expected to support his challenge.

[4] The composition of the Senate in the 92nd Congress taking office Jan. 3, 1975, would be as below (Party designations: D—Democrat, R—Republican. Date in parentheses indicates year entered Senate. Italics indicate elected or re-elected in November 1974 for term ending 1981 unless otherwise indicated. *Incumbent. †Service began in year shown but has not been continuous.):

Ala. *John J. Sparkman (D) term ends 1979; b. Dec. 20, 1899 (1946)
James B. Allen (D) b. Dec. 28, 1912 (1969)

Alaska *Ted Stevens (R) term ends 1979; b. Nov. 18, 1923 (1968)
**Mike Gravel* (D) b. May 13, 1930 (1969)

Ariz. *Paul J. Fannin (R) term ends 1977; b. Jan. 29, 1907 (1965)
**Barry M. Goldwater* (R) b. Jan. 1, 1909 (1953)†

Ark. *John L. McClellan (D) term ends 1979; b. Feb. 25, 1896 (1943)
Dale Bumpers (D) b. Aug. 12, 1925

Calif. **Alan Cranston* (D) b. June 19,1914 (1969)
*John V. Tunney (D) term ends 1977; b. June 26, 1934 (1971)

Colo. *Floyd K. Haskell (D) term ends 1979; b. Feb. 6, 1916 (1973)
Gary W. Hart (D) b. Nov. 28, 1937

Conn. **Abraham A. Ribicoff* (D) b. April 10, 1910 (1963)
*Lowell P. Weicker Jr. (R) term ends 1977; b. May 16, 1931 (1971)

Del. *William V. Roth Jr. (R) term ends 1977; b. July 22, 1921 (1971)
*Joseph R. Biden Jr. (D) term ends 1979; b. Nov. 20, 1942 (1973)

Fla. *Lawton Chiles (D) term ends 1977; b. April 30, 1930 (1971)
Richard Stone (D) b. Sept. 22, 1928

Ga. **Herman E. Talmadge* (D) b. Aug. 9, 1913 (1957)
*Sam Nunn Jr. (D) term ends 1979; b. Sept. 6, 1938 (1973)

Hawaii *Hiram L. Fong (R) term ends 1977; b. Oct. 1, 1907 (1959)
**Daniel K. Inouye* (D) b. Sept. 7, 1924 (1963)

Idaho **Frank Church* (D) b. July 25, 1924 (1957)
*James A. McClure (R) term ends 1979; b. Dec. 27, 1924 (1973)

Ill. *Charles H. Percy (R) term ends 1979; b. Sept. 27, 1919 (1967)
**Adlai E. Stevenson 3rd* (D) b. Oct. 10, 1930 (1971)

Ind. *Vance Hartke (D) term ends 1977; b. May 31, 1919 (1959)
**Birch E. Bayh Jr.* (D) b. Jan. 22, 1928 (1963)

Iowa *Richard Clark (D) term ends 1979; b. Sept. 14, 1929 (1973)
**John C. Culver* (D) b. Aug. 8, 1932

Kan. *James B. Pearson (R) term ends 1979; b. May 7, 1920 (1962)
**Robert Dole* (R) b. July 22, 1923 (1969)

Ky. *Walter Huddleston (D) term ends 1979; b. April 15, 1926 (1973)
Wendell H. Ford (D) b. Sept. 8, 1924

La. **Russell B. Long* (D) b. Nov. 3, 1918 (1948)
*J. Bennett Johnston Jr. (D) term ends 1979; b. June 10, 1932 (1973)

Me. *Edmund S. Muskie (D) term ends 1977; b. March 28, 1914 1959)
*William D. Hathaway (D) term ends 1979; b. Feb. 21, 1924 (1973)

Md. **Charles McC. Mathias Jr.* (R) b. July 24, 1922 (1969)
*J. Glenn Beall Jr. (R) term ends 1977; b. June 19, 1927 (1971)

Mass. *Edward M. Kennedy (D) term ends 1977; b. Feb. 22, 1932 (1963)
*Edward W. Brooke (R) term ends 1979; b. Oct. 26, 1919 (1967)

Mich. *Philip A. Hart (D) term ends 1977; b. Dec. 10, 1912 (1959)
*Robert P. Griffin (R) term ends 1979; b. Nov. 6, 1923 (1966)

Minn. *Walter F. Mondale (D) term ends 1979; b. Jan. 5, 1928 (1965)
*Hubert H. Humphrey (D) term ends 1977; b. May 27, 1911 (1949)†

Miss. *James O. Eastland (D) term ends 1979; b. Nov. 28, 1904 (1943)
*John C. Stennis (D) term ends 1977; b. Aug. 3, 1901 (1948)

Mo. *Stuart Symington (D) term ends 1977; b. June 26, 1901 (1953)
**Thomas F. Eagleton* (D) b. Sept.4, 1929 (1969)

Mont. *Michael J. Mansfield (D) term ends 1977; b. March 16, 1903 (1953)
*Lee Metcalf (D) term ends 1979; b. Jan. 28, 1911 (1961)

Neb. *Roman Lee Hruska (R) term ends 1977; b. Aug. 16, 1904 (1955)
*Carl T. Curtis (R) term ends 1979; b. March 15, 1905 (1955)

Nev. *Howard W. Cannon (D) term ends 1977; b. Jan. 26, 1912 (1959)
Paul Laxalt (R) b. Aug. 2, 1922

N.H. *Thomas J. McIntyre (D) term ends 1979; b. Feb. 20, 1915 (1959)
Louis C. Wyman (R) or John Durkin (D)

N.J. *Clifford P. Case (R) term ends 1979; b. April 16, 1904 (1955)
*Harrison A. Williams Jr. (D) term ends 1977; b. Dec. 10, 1919 (1959)

N.M. *Joseph M. Montoya (D) term ends 1977; b. Sept. 24, 1915 (1965)
*Pete V. Domenici (R) term ends 1979; b. May 7, 1932 (1973)

N.Y. **Jacob K. Javits* (R) b. May 18, 1904 (1957)

*James L. Buckley (Conservative) term ends 1977; b. March 9, 1923 (1971)

N.C. *Jesse A. Helms (R) term ends 1979; b. Oct. 18, 1921 (1973)
Robert B. Morgan (D) b. Oct. 5, 1925

N.D. *Quentin N. Burdick (D) term ends 1977; b. June 19, 1908 (1960)
**Milton R. Young* (R) b. Dec. 6, 1897 (1945)

Ohio *Robert Taft Jr. (R) term ends 1977; b. June 24, 1916 (1969)
John H. Glenn Jr. (D) b. July 18, 1921

Okla. **Henry Bellmon* (R) b. Sept. 3, 1921 (1969)
*Dewey F. Bartlett (R) term ends 1979; b. March 28, 1919 (1973)

Ore. *Mark O. Hatfield (R) term ends 1979; b. July 12, 1922 (1967)
**Robert W. Packwood* (R) b. Sept. 11, 1932 (1969)

Pa. *Hugh Scott (R) term ends 1977; b. Nov. 11, 1900 (1959)
**Richard S. Schweiker* (R) b. June 1, 1926 (1969)

R.I. *John O. Pastore (D) term ends 1977; b. March 17, 1907 (1950)
*Claiborne Pell (D) term ends 1979; b. Nov. 22, 1918 (1916)

S.C. *Strom Thurmond (R) term ends 1979; b. Dec. 5, 1902 (1955)
**Ernest F. Hollings* (D) b. Jan. 1, 1922 (1967)

S.D. **George McGovern* (D) b. July 19, 1922 (1963)
*James Abourezk (D) term ends 1979; b. Feb. 24, 1931 (1973)

Tenn. *Howard H. Baker Jr. (R) term ends 1979; b. Nov. 15, 1925 (1967)
*William E. Brock 3rd (R) term ends 1977; b. Nov. 23, 1930 (1971)

Texas *John G. Tower (R) term ends 1979; b. Sept. 29, 1925 (1961)
*Lloyd M. Bentsen (D) term ends 1977; b. Feb. 11, 1921 (1971)

Utah *Frank E. Moss (D) term ends 1977; b. Sept. 23, 1911 (1959)
Jake Garn (R) b. Oct. 12, 1932

Vt. *Robert T. Stafford (R) term ends 1977; b. Aug. 8, 1913 (1971)
Patrick J. Leahy (D) b. March 31, 1940

Va. *William Lloyd Scott (R) term ends 1979; b. July 1, 1915 (1973)
*Harry F. Byrd Jr. (Independent) term ends 1977; b. Dec. 20, 1914 (1965)

Wash. **Warren G. Magnuson* (D) b. April 12, 1905 (1944)
*Henry M. Jackson (D) term ends 1977; b. May 31, 1912 (1953)

W. Va. *Jennings Randolph (D) term ends 1979; b. March 8, 1902 (1959)
*Robert C. Byrd (D) term ends 1977; b. Jan. 15, 1918 (1959)

Wis. *William Proxmire (D) term ends 1977; b. Nov. 11, 1915 (1957)
**Gaylord A. Nelson* (D) b. June 4, 1916 (1963)

Wyo. *Gale W. McGee (D) term ends 1977; b. March 17, 1915 (1959)
*Clifford P. Hansen (R) term ends 1979; b. Oct. 16, 1912 (1967)

[5] **House results.** The Democratic gain of 43 House seats gave the Democrats 291 seats, compared with the Republicans' 144 seats for the incoming 94th Congress elected Nov. 5. The majority was more than two-thirds. The Democrats gained five seats each in New York and Indiana, four each in California and New Jersey, three in Illinois, two each in Iowa, Michigan, North Carolina, Oregon, Tennessee, Virginia and Wisconsin. They gained one additional seat in each of 14 other states. The Republicans took a Democratic seat in Florida, Louisiana, Ohio, Pennsylvania, South Dakota and Maine. The losers included three ranking incumbent Republicans on committees: William B. Widnall (N.J.) of Banking and Currency, William Bray (Ind.) of Armed Services and James Grover (N.Y.) of Merchant Marine. Joel T. Broyhill (R, Va.) was rejected in his bid for a 12th term. Four Republican members of the House Judiciary Committee who had voted against impeachment of former President Nixon were defeated. The Democrats also won President Ford's home district in Michigan for the second time since 1910. The first time was Feb. 18 in a special election following Ford's departure from the district for the vice presidency.

[6] The composition of the House in the 92nd Congress taking office Jan. 3, 1975, would be as below. (Party designation: D—Democrat, R—Republican. Date in parentheses indicates year entered Senate. *Incumbent. †Service began in year shown but has not been continuous.):

Congressional District

Alabama: 4 D, 3 R [4 D, 3 R]

1. *Jack Edwards (R) b. Sept. 20, 1928 (1965)
2. *William Louis Dickinson (R) b. June 5, 1925 (1965)
3. *William Nichols (D) b. Oct. 16, 1918 (1967)
4. *Tom Bevill (D) b. Mar. 27, 1921 (1967)

5. *Robert E. Jones (D) b. June 12, 1912 (1947)
6. *John Hall Buchanan Jr. (R) b. Mar. 19, 1928 (1965)
7. *Walter Flowers (D) b. Apr. 12, 1933 (1969)

Alaska: 1 R [1 R]

At Large. Donald E. Young (R) age 41

Arizona: 1 D, 3 R [1 D, 3 R]

1. *John J. Rhodes (R) b. Sept. 18, 1916 (1953)
2. *Morris K. Udall (D) b. June 15, 1922 (1961)
3. *Sam Steiger (R) b. Mar. 10, 1929 (1967)
4. *John B. Conlan (R) b. Sept. 17, 1930 (1973)

Arkansas: 3 D, 1 R [3 D, 1 R]

1. *William Vollie (Bill) Alexander Jr. (D) b. Jan. 16, 1934 (1969)
2. *Wilbur D. Mills (D) b. May 24, 1909 (1939)
3. *John Paul Hammerschmidt (R) b. May 4, 1922 (1967)
4. *Ray Thornton (D) b. July 16, 1928 (1973)

California: 28 D, 15 R [24 D, 19 R]

1. *Harold T. (Bizz) Johnson (D) 64 (1959)
2. *Don H. Clausen (R) b. Apr. 27, 1923 (1963)
3. *John E. Moss (D) b. Apr. 13, 1913 (1953)
4. *Robert L. Leggett (D) b. July 26, 1926 (1963)
5. *John L. Burton (D) age 41 (1974)
6. *Philip Burton (D) b. June 1, 1926 (1964)
7. George Miller III (D) age 29
8. *Ronald V. Dellums (D) b. Nov. 24, 1935 (1971)
9. *Fortney H. Stark (D) b. Nov. 11, 1931 (1973)
10. *Don Edwards (D) b. Jan. 6, 1915 (1963)
11. *Leo J. Ryan (D) b. May 5, 1925 (1973)
12. *Paul N. (Pete) McCloskey Jr. (R) b. sept. 29, 1927 (1967)
13. Norman Y. Mineta (D) age 42
14. *John J. McFall (D) b. Feb. 20, 1918 (1957)
15. *B. F. Sisk (D) Dec. 14, 1910 (1955)
16. *Burt L. Talcott (R) b. Feb. 22, 1920 (1963)
17. John Krebs (D) age 47
18. *William M. Ketchum (R) b. Sept. 2, 1921 (1973)
19. *Robert J. Lagomarsino (R) age 48 (1974)
20. *Barry M. Goldwater Jr. (R) b. July 15, 1938 (1969)
21. *James C. Corman (D) b. Oct. 20, 1920 (1961)
22. *Carlos J. Moorhead (R) b. May 6, 1922 (1973)
23. *Thomas M. Rees (D) b. Mar. 26, 1925 (1965)
24. Henry A. Waxman (D) age 35
25. *Edward R. Roybal (D) b. Feb. 10, 1916 (1963)
26. *John H. Rousselot (R) b. Nov. 1, 1927 (1961)†
27. *Alphonzo Bell (R) b. Sept. 19, 1914 (1961)
28. *Yvonne Brathwaite Burke (D) b. Oct. 5, 1932 (1973)
29. *Augustus F. Hawkins (D) b. Aug. 31, 1907 (1963)
30. *George E. Danielson (D) b. Feb. 20, 1915
31. *Charles H. Wilson (D) b. Feb. 15, 1917 (1963)
32. *Glenn M. Anderson (D) b. Feb. 21, 1913 (1969)
33. *Delwin (Del) Morgan Clawson (R) b. Jan. 11, 1914 (1963)
34. Mark W. Hannaford (D) age 49
35. Jim Lloyd (D) age 52
36. *George E. Brown Jr. (D) b. Mar. 6, 1920 (1963)†
37. *Jerry L. Pettis (R) b. July 18, 1916 (1967)
38. Jerry M. Patterson (D) age 39
39. *Charles E. Wiggins (R) b. Dec. 3, 1927 (1967)
40. *Andrew J. Hinshaw (R) b. Aug. 4, 1923 (1973)
41. *Bob Wilson (R), b. Apr. 5, 1916 (1953)
42. *Lionel Van Deerlin (D) b. July 25, 1914 (1963)
43. *Clair W. Burgener (R) b. Dec. 5, 1921 (1973)

Colorado: 3 D, 2 R [3 R, 2 D]

1. *Patricia Schroeder (D) b. July 30, 1940 1973)
2. Timothy E. Wirth (D) age 35
3. *Frank Edwards Evans (D) b. Sept. 6, 1923 (1965)
4. *James P. Johnson (R) b. June 2, 1930 (1973)
5. *William L. Armstrong (R) b. March 16, 1937

Connecticut: 4 D, 2 R [3 D, 3 R]

1. *William R. Cotter (D) b. July 18, 1926 (1971)
2. Christopher J. Dodd (D) age 30
3. *Robert N. Giaimo (D) b. Oct. 15, 1919 (1959)
4. *Stewart B. McKinney (R) b. Jan. 30, 1931 (1971)
5. *Ronald A. Sarasin (R) Dec. 31, 1934 (1973)
6. Anthony J. Mofett (D) age 30

Delaware: 1 R [1 R]

At Large. *Pierre S. du Pont IV (R) b. Jan. 22, 1935 (1971)

Florida: 10 D, 5 R [11 D, 4 R]

1. *Robert L. F. Sikes (D) b. June 3, 1906 (1941)
2. *Don Fuqua (D) b. Aug. 20, 1933 (1963)
3. *Charles E. Bennett (D) b. Dec. 2, 1910 (1949)
4. *William V. Chappell Jr. (D) b. Feb. 3, 1922 (1969)
5. Richard Kelly (R) age 50
6. *C. W. Young (R) b. Dec. 16, 1930 (1971)
7. *Sam M. Gibbons (D) b. Jan. 20, 1920 (1963)
8. *James Andrew Haley (D) b. Jan. 4, 1899 (1953)
9. *Lou Frey Jr. (R) b. Jan. 11, 1934.
10. *L. A. Bafalis (R) b. Sept. 28, 1929 (1973)
11. *Paul G. Rogers (D) b June 4, 1921 (1955)
12. *J. Herbert Burke (R) b. Jan. 14, 1913 (1967)
13. *William Lehman (D) b. Oct. 5, 1913 (1973)
14. *Claude Denson Pepper (D) b. Sept. 8, 1900 (1963)
15. *Dante B. Fascell (D) b. Mar. 9, 1917 (1955)

Georgia: 10 D [9 D, 1 R]

1. *Ronald B. Ginn (D) age 38 (1973)
2. *Dawson Mathis (D) b. Nov. 30, 1940 (1971)
3. *Jack Thomas Brinkley (D) b. Dec. 22, 1930 (1967)
4. Elliot H. Levitas (D) age 43
5. *Andrew J. Young (D) b. March 12, 1932 (1973)
6. *John James Flynt Jr. (D) b. Nov. 8, 1914 (1954)
7. Lawrence P. McDonald (D) age 39
8. *Williamson Sylvester Stuckey Jr. (D) b. May 25, 1935 (1967)
9. *Phillip Mitchell Landrum (D) b. Sept. 10, 1909 (1953)
10. *Robert Grier Stephens Jr. (D) b. Aug. 14, 1913 (1961)

Hawaii: 2 D [2 D]

1. *Spark Masayuki Matsunaga (D) b. Oct. 8, 1916 (1963)

2. *Patsy Takemoto Mink (D) b. Dec. 6, 1927 (1965)

Idaho: 2 R [2 R]

1. *Steven D. Symms (R) b. April 23, 1938 (1973)
2. George V. Hansen (R) age 44 (1965)†

Illinois: 13 D, 11 R [10 D, 14 R]

1. *Ralph H. Metcalfe (D) b. May 29, 1910 (1971)
2. *Morgan F. Murphy Jr. (D) b. April 16, 1932 (1971)
3. Martin A. Russo (D) age 30
4. *Edward J. Derwinski (R) b. Sept. 15, 1926 (1959)
5. *John C. Kluczynski (D) b. Feb. 15, 1896 (1951)
6. Henry J. Hyde (R) age 50
7. *Cardiss W. Collins (D) b. Sept. 24, 1931 (1973)
8. *Dan Rostenkowski (D) b. Jan. 2, 1928 (1959)
9. *Sidney R. Yates (D) b. Aug. 27, 1909 (1949)†
10. Abner J. Mikva (D) b. Jan. 21, 1926 (1969)†
11. *Frank Annunzio (D) b. Jan. 12, 1915 (1965)
12. *Philip M. Crane (R) b. Nov. 3, 1930 (1969)
13. *Robert McClory (R) b. Jan. 31, 1908 (1963)
14. *John N. Erlenborn (R) b. Feb. 8, 1927 (1961)
15. Tim L. Hall (D) age 49
16. *John B. Anderson (R) b. Feb. 15, 1922 (1961)
17. *George M. O'Brien (R) b. June 17, 1917
18. *Robert H. Michel (R) b. Mar. 2, 1923 (1957)
19. *Thomas F. Railsback (R) b. Jan. 22, 1932 (1967)
20. *Paul Findley (R) b. June 23, 1921 (1961)
21. *Edward R. Madigan (R) b. Jan. 13, 1936
22. *George Edward Shipley (D) b. Apr. 21, 1927 (1959)
23. *Charles Melvin Price (D) b. Jan. 1, 1905 (1945)
24. Paul Simon (D) age 45

Indiana: 9 D, 2 R [7 R, 4 D]

1. *Ray J. Madden (D) b. Feb. 25, 1892 (1943)
2. Floyd J. Fithian (D) age 45
3. *John Brademas (D) b. Mar. 2, 1927 (1959)
4. *J. Edward Roush (D) b. Sept. 12, 1920 (1959)†
5. *Elwood Hillis (R) b. Mar. 6, 1926
6. David W. Evans (D) age 28
7. *John Thomas Myers (R) b. Feb. 8, 1927 (1967)
8. Philip H. Hayes (D) age 34
9. *Lee Herbert Hamilton (D) b. Apr. 20, 1931 (1965)
10. Philip R. Sharp (D) age 32
11. Andrew Jacobs Jr. (D) b. Feb. 24, 1932 (1965)†

Iowa: 5 D, 1 R [3 D, 3 R]

1. *Edward Mezvinsky (D) b. Jan. 17, 1937 (1973)
2. Michael T. Blouin (D) age 28
3. Charles E. Grassley (R) age 41
4. *Neal Smith (D) b. Mar. 23, 1920 (1959)
5. Tom Harkin (D) age 34
6. Berkley Bedell (D) age 53

Kansas: 1 D, 4 R [1 D, 4 R]

1. *Keith G. Sebelius (R) b. Sept. 10, 1916 (1969)
2. Martha E. Keys (D) age 44
3. *Larry Winn Jr. (R) b. Aug. 22, 1919 (1967)
4. *Garner E. Shriver (R) b. July 6, 1912 (1961)
5. *Joe Skubitz (R) b. May 6, 1906 (1963)

Kentucky: 5 D, 2 R [5 D, 2 R]

1. Carroll Hubbard Jr. (D) age 37
2. *William H. Natcher (D) b. Sept. 11, 1909 (1953)
3. *Romano L. Mazzoli (D) b. Nov. 2, 1932 (1971)
4. *Marion Gene Snyder (R) b. Jan. 26, 1928 (1963)†
5. *Tim Lee Carter (R) b. Sept. 2, 1910 (1965)
6. *John B. Breckinridge (D) b. Nov. 29, 1913 (1973)
7. *Carl D. Perkins (D) b. Oct. 15, 1912 (1949)

Louisiana: 6 D, 2 R [7 D, 1 R]

1. *F. Edward Hebert (D) b. Oct. 12, 1901 (1941)
2. *Corinne C. Boggs (D) age 58 (1973)
3. *David C. Treen (R) b. July 16, 1928 (1973)
4. *Joe D. Waggoner Jr. (D) b. Sept. 7, 1918 (1961)
5. *Otto Ernest Passman (D) b. June 27, 1900 (1947)
6. W. Henson Moore 3rd (R) age 35
7. *John B. Breaux (D) b. Mar. 1, 1944 (1973)
8. *Gillis W. Long (D) b. June 16, 1928 (1963)†

Maine: 2 R [1 D, 1 R]

1. David F. Emery (R) age 25
2. *William S. Cohen (R) b. Aug. 28, 1940 (1973)

Maryland: 5 D, 3 R [4 D, 4 R]

1. *Robert E. Bauman (R) b. April 4, 1937
2. *Clarence D. Long (D) b. Dec. 11, 1908 (1963)
3. *Paul S. Sarbanes (D) b. Feb. 3, 1933 (1971)
4. *Marjorie S. Holt (R) b. Sept. 17, 1920 (1973)
5. Gladys N. Spellman (D) age 56
6. *Goodloe E. Byron (D) b. June 22, 1929 (1971)
7. *Parren J. Mitchell (D) b. April 29, 1922 (1971)
8. *Gilbert Gude (R) b. Mar. 9, 1923 (1967)

Massachusetts: 10 D, 2 R [9 D, 3 R]

1. *Silvio O. Conte (R) b. Nov. 9, 1921 (1959)
2. *Edward P. Boland (D) b. Oct. 1, 1911 (1953)
3. Joseph D. Early (D) age 41
4. *Robert F. Drinan (D) b. Nov. 15, 1920 (1971)
5. Paul E. Tsongas (D) age 33
6. *Michael J. Harrington (D) b. Sept. 2, 1936 (1969)
7. *Torbert Hart Macdonald (D) b. June 6, 1917 (1955)
8. *Thomas P. O'Neill, Jr. (D) b. Dec. 9, 1912 (1953)
9. *John Joseph Moakley (D) b. April 27, 1927 (1973)
10. *Margaret M. Heckler (R) b. June 21, 1931 (1967)
11. *James A. Burke (D) b. Mar. 30, 1910 (1959)
12. *Gerry E. Studds (D) b. May 12, 1937

Michigan: 12 D, 7 R [10 D, 9 R]

1. *John J. Conyers Jr. (D) b. May 16, 1929 (1965)
2. *Marvin L. Esch (R) b. Aug. 4, 1927 (1967)
3. *Garry Brown (R) b. Aug. 12, 1923 (1967)
4. *Edward Hutchinson (R) b. Oct. 13, 1914 (1963)
5. *Richard F. Vander Veen (D) age 51 (1974)
6. Bob Carr (D) age 30
7. *Donald W. Riegle, Jr. (D) b. Feb. 4, 1938 (1967)
8. *Bob Traxler (D) age 43 (1974)
9. *Guy Adrian Vander Jagt (R) b. Aug. 26, 1931 (1966)
10. *Elford A. Cederberg (R) b. Mar. 6, 1918 (1953)
11. *Philip E. Ruppe (R) . Sept. 29, 1926 (1967)

12. *James G. O'Hara (D) b. Nov. 8, 1925 (1959)
13. *Charles C. Diggs Jr. (D) b. Dec. 2, 1922 (1955)
14. *Lucien Norbert Nedzi (D) b. May 28, 1925 (1961)
15. *William David Ford (D) b. Aug. 6, 1927 (1965)
16. *John D. Dingell (D) b. July 8, 1926 (1955)
17. William M. Brodhead (D) age 33
18. James J. Blanchard (D) age 32
19. *William S. Broomfield (R) b. Apr. 28, 1922 (1957)

Minnesota: 5 D, 3 R [4 D, 4 R]

1. *Albert Harold Quie (R) b. Sept. 18, 1923 (1958)
2. Tom Hagedorn (R) age 30
3. *William E. Frenzel (R) b. July 31, 1928 (1971)
4. *Joseph E. Karth (D) b. Aug. 26, 1922 (1959)
5. *Donald MacKay Fraser (D) b. Feb. 20, 1924 (1963)
6. Richard Nolan (D) age 30
7. *Bob Bergland (D) b. July 22, 1928 (1971)
8. James L. Oberstar (D) age 40

Mississippi: 3 D, 2 R [3 D, 2 R]

1. *Jamie L. Whitten (D) b. Apr. 18, 1910 (1941)
2. *David R. Bowen (D) b. Oct. 21, 1932 (1973)
3. *Gillespie V. Montgomery (D) b. Aug. 5, 1920 (1967)
4. *Thad Cochran (R) b. Dec. 7, 1937 (1973)
5. *Trent Lott (R) b. Oct. 9, 1941 (1972)

Missouri: 9 D, 1 R [9 D, 1 R]

1. *William L. Clay (D) b. Apr. 30, 1931 (1969)
2. *James Wadsworth Symington (D) b. Sept. 28, 1927 (1969)
3. *Leonor Kretzer Sullivan (D) age 71 (1953)
4. *William J. Randall (D) b. July 16, 1909 (1959)
5. *Richard Bolling (D) b. May 17, 1916 (1949)
6. *Jerry L. Litton (D) b. May 12, 1937 (1973)
7. *Gene Taylor (R) b. Feb. 10, 1928 (1973)
8. *Richard Howard Ichord (D) b. June 27, 1926 (1961)
9. *William Leonard Hungate (D) b. Dec. 14, 1922 (1965)
10. *Bill D. Burlison (D) b. Mar. 15, 1931 (1969)

Montana: 2 D [1 D, 1 R]

1. Max S. Baucus (D) age 32
2. *John Melcher (D) b. Sept. 6, 1924 (1969)

Nebraska: 3 R [3 R]

1. *Charles Thone (R) b. Jan. 4, 1924 (1971)
2. *John Y. McCollister (R) b. June 10, 1921 (1971)
3. Virginia Smith (R) age 63

Nevada: 1 D [1 R]

1. James Santini (D) age 36

New Hampshire: 1 D, 1 R [2 R]

1. Norman E. D'Amours (D) age 36
2. *James C. Cleveland (R) b. June 13, 1920 (1963)

New Jersey: 12 D, 3 R [8 D, 7 R]

1. James J. Florio (D) age 37
2. William J. Hughes (D) age 41
3. *James J. Howard (D) b. July 24, 1927 (1965)
4. *Frank Thompson Jr. (D) b. July 26, 1918 (1955)
5. Millicent Fenwick (R) age 64
6. *Edwin B. Forsythe (R) b. Jan. 17, 1916 (1971)
7. Andrew Maguire (D) age 35
8. *Robert A. Roe (D) b. Feb. 28, 1924 (1969)
9. *Henry Helstoski (D) b. Mar. 21, 1925 (1965)
10. *Peter Wallace Rodino Jr. (D) b. June 7, 1909 (1949)
11. *Joseph George Minish (D) b. Sept. 1, 1916 (1963)
12. *Matthew J. Rinaldo (R) b. Sept. 1, 1931 (1973)
13. Helen S. Meyner (D) age 45
14. *Dominick V. Daniels (D) b. Oct. 18, 1908 (1959)
15. *Edward James Patten (D) b. Aug. 22, 1905 (1963)

New Mexico: 1 D, 1 R [1 D, 1 R]

1. *Manuel Lujan Jr. (R) b. May 12, 1928 (1969)
2. *Harold L. Runnels (D) b. March 17, 1924 (1971)

New York: 27 D, 12 R [22 D, 17 R]

1. *Otis G. Pike (D) b. Aug. 31, 1921 (1961)
2. Thomas J. Downey (D) age 25
3. Jerome A. Ambro Jr. (D) age 46
4. *Norman F. Lent (R) b. March 23, 1931 (1971)
5. *John W. Wydler (R) b. June 9, 1924 (1963)
6. *Lester Lionel Wolff (D) b. Jan. 4, 1919 (1965)
7. *Joseph Patrick Addabbo (D) b. Mar. 17, 1925 (1961)
8. *Benjamin S. Rosenthal (D) b. June 8, 1923 (1962)
9. *James J. Delaney (D) b. Mar. 19, 1901 (1945)†
10. *Mario Biaggi (D) b. Oct. 26, 1917 (1969)
11. James H. Scheuer (D) b. Feb. 6, 1920 (1965)†
12. *Shirley Anita Chisholm (D) b. Nov. 30, 1924 (1969)
13. Stephen J. Solarz (D) age 33
14. Frederick W. Richmond (D) age 50
15. Leo C. Zeferetti (D) age 45
16. *Elizabeth Holtzman (D) b. Aug. 11, 1941 (1973)
17. *John M. Murphy (D) b. Aug. 3, 1926 (1963)
18. *Edward I. Koch (D) b. Dec. 12, 1924 (1969)
19. *Charles B. Rangel (D) b. June 11, 1930 (1971)
20. *Bella S. Abzug (D) b. July 24, 1920 (1971)
21. *Herman Badillo (D) b. Aug. 21, 1929 (1971)
22. *Jonathan Brewster Bingham (D) b. Apr. 24, 1914 (1965)
23. *Peter A. Peyser (R) b. Sept. 7, 1921 (1971)
24. Richard L. Ottinger (D) b. Jan. 27, 1929 (1965)†
25. *Hamilton Fish Jr. (R) b. June 3, 1926 (1969)
26. *Benjamin A. Gilman (R) b. Dec. 6, 1922 (1973)
27. Matthew F. McHugh (D) age 35
28. *Samuel S. Stratton (D) b. Sept. 27, 1916 (1959)
29. Edward W. Pattison (D) age 42
30. *Robert Cameron McEwen (R) b. Jan. 5, 1920 (1965)
31. *Donald J. Mitchell (R) b. May 8, 1923 (1973)
32. *James Michael Hanley (D) b. July 19, 1920 (1965)
33. William F. Walsh (R) age 60
34. *Frank Horton (R) b. Dec. 12, 1919 (1963)
35. *Barber B. Conable Jr. (R) b. Nov. 2, 1922 (1965)
36. John J. LaFalce (D) age 34
37. Henry J. Nowak (D) age 39

38. *Jack F. Kemp (R) b. July 13, 1935 (1971)
39. *James F. Hastings (R) b. Apr. 10, 1926 (1969)

North Carolina: 9 D, 2 R [7 D, 4 R]

1. *Walter B. Jones (D) b. Aug. 19, 1913 (1966)
2. *L. H. Fountain (D) b. Apr. 23, 1913 (1953)
3. *David Newton Henderson (D) b. Apr. 16, 1921 (1961)
4. *Ike F. Andrews (D) b. Sept. 2, 1925 (1973)
5. Stephen L. Neal (D) age 39
6. *Lunsford Richardson Preyer (D) b. Jan. 11, 1919 (1969)
7. *Charles G. Rose 3rd (D) b. Aug. 10, 1939 (1973)
8. W. G. (Bill) Hefner (D) age 44
9. *James G. Martin (R) b. Dec. 11, 1935 (1973)
10. *James Thomas Broyhill (R) b. Aug. 19, 1927 (1963)
11. *Roy A. Taylor (D) b. Jan. 31, 1910 (1960)

North Dakota: 1 R [1 R]

At large. *Mark Andrews (R) b. May 19, 1926 (1963)

Ohio: 8 D, 15 R [8 D, 15 R]

1. Willis D. Gradison Jr. (R) age 45
2. *Donald Daniel Clancy (R) b. July 24, 1921 (1961)
3. *Charles W. Whalen Jr. (R) b. July 31, 1920 (1967)
4. *Tennyson Guyer (R) b. Nov. 29, 1913 (1973)
5. *Delbert L. Latta (R) b. Mar. 5, 1920 (1959)
6. *William H. Harsha (R) b. Jan. 1, 1921 (1961)
7. *Clarence J. Brown (R) b. June 18, 1927 (1965)
8. Thomas N. Kindness (R) age 44
9. *Thomas Ludlow Ashley (D) b. Jan. 11, 1923 (1955)
10. *Clarence E. Miller (R) b. Nov. 1, 1917 (1967)
11. *John William Stanton (R) b. Feb. 20, 1924 (1965)
12. *Samuel L. Devine (R) b. Dec. 21, 1915 (1959)
13. *Charles Adams Mosher (R) b. May 7, 1906 (1961)
14. *John F. Seiberling, Jr. (D) age 52 (1971)
15. *Chalmers Pangburn Wylie (R) b. Nov. 23, 1920 (1967)
16. *Ralph S. Regula (R) b. Dec. 3, 1924 (1973)
17. *John Milan Ashbrook (R) b. Sept. 21, 1928 (1961)
18. *Wayne L. Hays (D) b. May 13, 1911 (1949)
19. *Charles J. Carney (D) b. April 17, 1913 (1971)
20. *James V. Stanton (D) b. Feb. 27, 1932 (1971)
21. *Louis Stokes (D) b. Feb. 23, 1925 (1969)
22. *Charles A. Vanik (D) b. Apr. 7, 1913 (1955)
23. Ronald M. Mottl (D) age 40

Oklahoma: 6 D [5 D, 1 R]

1. *James R. Jones (D) b. May 5, 1939 (1973)
2. Theodore M. Risenhoover (D) age 39
3. *Carl Bert Albert (D) b. May 10, 1908 (1947)
4. *Tom Steed (D) b. Mar. 2, 1904 (1949)
5. *John Jarman (D) b. July 17, 1915 (1951)
6. Glenn English (D) age 33

Oregon: 4 D [2 D, 2 R]

1. Les AuCoin (D) age 31
2. *Al Ullman (D) b. Mar. 9, 1914 (1957)
3. Robert Duncan (D) age 53
4. James Weaver (D) age 47

Pennsylvania: 14 D, 11 R [14 D, 11 R]

1. *William A. Barrett (D) b. Aug. 14, 1896 (1945)†
2. *Robert N. C. Nix (D) b. Sept. 9, 1905 (1958)
3. *William Joseph Green (D) b. June 24, 1938 (1964)
4. *Joshua Eilberg (D) b. Feb. 12, 1921 (1967)
5. Richard T. Schulze (R) age 45
6. *Gus Yatron (D) b. Oct. 16, 1927 (1969)
7. Robert W. Edgar (D) age 31
8. *Edward G. Biester Jr. (R) b. Jan. 5, 1931 (1967)
9. *E. G. Shuster (R) b. Jan. 23, 1932 (1973)
10. *Joseph Michael McDade (R) b. Sept. 29, 1931 (1963)
11. *Daniel J. Flood (D) b. Nov. 26, 1903 (1945)†
12. *John P. Murtha (D) age 42 (1974)
13. *Lawrence Coughlin (R) b. Apr. 11, 1929 (1969)
14. *William S. Moorhead (D) b. Apr. 8, 1923 (1959)
15. *Fred B. Rooney (D) b. Nov. 6, 1925 (1963)
16. *Edwin D. Eshleman (R) b. Dec. 4, 1920 (1967)
17. *Herman T. Schneebeli (R) b. July 7, 1907 (1960)
18. *H. John Heinz 3rd (R) b Oct. 23, 1938 (1971)
19. William F. Goodling (R) age 46
20. *Joseph M. Gaydos (D) b. July 3, 1926 (1969)
21. *John H. Dent (D) b. Mar. 10, 1908 (1958)
22. *Thomas E. Morgan (D) b. Oct. 13, 1906 (1945)
23. *Albert Walter Johnson (R) b. Apr. 17, 1906 (1963)
24. *Joseph Phillip Vigorito (D) b. Nov. 10, 1918 (1965)
25. Gary A. Myers (R) age 37

Rhode Island: 2 D [2 D]

1. *Fernand Joseph St Germain (D) b. Jan. 9, 1928 (1961)
2. Edward P. Beard (D) age 34

South Carolina: 5 D, 1 R [4 D, 2 R]

1. *Mendel J. Davis (D) b. Oct. 23, 1942 (1971)
2. *Floyd Spence (R) b. Apr. 9, 1928 (1971)
3. Butler C. Derrick Jr. (D) age 38
4. *James Robert Mann (D) b. Apr. 27, 1920 (1969)
5. Kenneth L. Holland (D) age 39
6. John W. Jenrette Jr. (D) age 38

South Dakota: 2 R [1 D, 1 R]

1. Larry L. Pressler (R) age 32
2. *James Abdnor (R) b. Feb. 13, 1923 (1973)

Tennessee: 5 D, 3 R [3 D, 5 R]

1. *James H. (Jimmy) Quillen (R) b. Jan. 11, 1916 (1963)
2. *John James Duncan (R) b. Mar. 24, 1919 (1965)
3. Marilyn Lloyd (D) age 44
4. *Joe L. Evins (D) b. Oct. 24, 1910 (1947)
5. *Richard Harmon Fulton (D) b. Jan. 27, 1927 (1963)
6. *Robin L. Beard Jr. (R) b. Aug. 21, 1939 (1973)
7. *Ed Jones (D) b. Apr. 20, 1912 (1969)
8. Harold E. Ford (D) age 29

Texas: 21 D, 3 R [20 D, 4 R]

1. *Wright Patman (D) b. Aug. 6, 1893 (1929)
2. *Charles Wilson (D) b. June 1, 1933 (1973)
3. *James M. Collins (R) b. Apr. 29, 1916 (1968)
4. *Ray Roberts (D) b. Mar. 28, 1913 (1962)
5. Alan Steelman (R) age 30
6. *Olin E. Teague (D) b. Apr. 6, 1910 (1946)
7. *W. R. (Bill) Archer (R) b. March 22, 1928 (1971)
8. *Bob Eckhardt (D) b. July 16, 1913 (1967)
9. *Jack Brooks (D) b. Dec. 18, 1922 (1953)
10. *J. J. (Jake) Pickle (D) b. Oct. 11, 1913 (1963)
11. *William Robert (Bob) Poage (D) b. Dec. 28, 1899 (1937)
12. *James C. Wright Jr. (D) b. Dec. 22, 1922 (1955)
13. Jack Hightower (D) age 48
14. *John Young (D) b. Nov. 10, 1916 (1957)
15. *Eligio de la Garza (D) b. Sept. 22, 1927 (1965)
16. *Richard Crawford White (D) b. Apr. 29, 1923 (1965)
17. *Omar Burleson (D) b. Mar. 19, 1906 (1947)
18. *Barbara Jordan (D) b. Feb. 21, 1936 (1973)
19. *George H. Mahon (D) b. Sept. 22, 1900 (1935)
20. *Henry B. Gonzalez (D) b. May 3, 1916 (1961)
21. Robert Krueger (D) age 39
22. *Robert (Bob) Randolph Casey (D) b. July 27, 1915 (1959)
23. *Abraham Kazen Jr. (D) b. Jan. 17, 1919 (1967)
24. *Dale Milford (D) b. Feb. 18, 1926 (1973)

Utah: 2 D [2 D]

1. *K. Gunn McKay (D) b. Feb. 23, 1925 (1971)
2. Allan T. Howe (D) age 47

Vermont: 1 R [1 R]

At large. James M. Jeffords (R) age 40

Virginia: 5 D, 5 R [3 D, 7 R]

1. *Thomas N. Downing (D) b. Feb. 1, 1919 (1959)
2. *G. William Whitehurst (R) b. Mar. 12, 1925 (1969)
3. *David Edward Satterfield III (D) b. Dec. 2, 1920 (1965)
4. *Robert W. Daniel Jr. (R) b. March 17, 1936 (1973)
5. *W. C. (Dan) Daniel (D) b. May 12, 1914 (1969)
6. *M. Caldwell Butler (R) b. June 22, 1925 (1973)
7. *James Kenneth Robinson (R) b. May 14, 1916 (1971)
8. Herbert E. Harris II (D) age 48
9. *William Creed Wampler (R) b. Apr. 21, 1926 (1953)†
10. Joseph L. Fisher (D) age 60

Washington: 6 D, 1 R [6 D, 1 R]

1. *Joel M. Pritchard (R) b. May 5, 1925 (1972)
2. *Lloyd Meeds (D) b. Dec. 11, 1927 (1965)
3. Don Bonker (D) age 37
4. *Mike McCormack (D) b. Dec. 14, 1921 (1971)
5. *Thomas Stephen Foley (D) b. Mar. 6, 1929 (1965)
6. *Floyd V. Hicks (D) b. May 29, 1915 (1965)
7. *Brock Adams (D) b. Jan. 13, 1927 (1965)

West Virginia: 4 D [4 D]

1. *Robert H. Mollohan (D) b. Sept. 18, 1909 (1953)†
2. *Harley O. Staggers (D) b. Aug. 3, 1907 (1949)
3. *John Slack (D) b. Mar. 18, 1915 (1959)
4. *Ken Hechler (D) b. Sept. 20, 1914 (1959)

Wisconsin: 7 D, 2 R [5 D, 4 R]

1. *Les Aspin (D) b. July 21, 1928 (1971)
2. *Robert William Kastenmeier (D) b. Jan 24, 1924 (1959)
3. Alvin J. Baldus (D) age 48
4. *Clement J. Zablocki (D) b. Nov. 18, 1912 (1949)
5. *Henry S. Reuss (D) b. Feb. 22, 1912 (1955)
6. *William A. Steiger (R) b. May 15, 1938 (1967)
7. *David R. Obey (D) b. Oct. 3, 1938 (1969)
8. Robert J. Cornell (D) age 54
9. Robert W. Kasten Jr. (R) age 32

Wyoming: 1 D [1 D]

At Large. *Teno Roncalio (D) b. Mar. 23, 1916 (1967)

[7] **Governorships.** The trend of the 1974 gubernatorial elections was clearly Democratic. Of the 35 contests for governor, 27 were won by Democrats, seven by Republicans and one by an independent candidate in Maine. The Demcrats took nine statehouses from the GOP, but surrendered five of their own—one of them to the independent James B. Longley—for a net gain of four seats. The Republicans lost control of nine previously held governorships and recaptured four from the Democrats for a net loss of five statehouses. By winning the gubernatorial races in California, New York and Massachusetts, the Democrats controlled the governorships of eight of the 10 most populous states. Democratic incumbents were returned in Pennsylvania, Texas and Florida, while the Democrat-held states of Illinois and New Jersey did not have elections. In the other two of the 10 most populous states, Ohio and Michigan, Republicans were elected by narrow margins. Control of statehouses passed from the GOP to the Democratic Party in Arizona, California, Colorado, Connecticut, Massachusetts, New York, Oregon, Tennessee and Wyoming. Republicans wrested governorships from Democrats in Kansas, Ohio and South Carolina.

[8] The list of governors after the elections was as below (Party designation: D—Democrat, R—Republican. Italics indicate elected or re-elected in Nov. 1974.

Date in parentheses indicates year office was assumed. *Incumbent. †Service began in year shown but has not been continuous. Unless indicated, governors serve four years):

Ala. **George C. Wallace* (D); b. Aug. 25, 1919 (1963)†
Alaska *Jay S. Hammond* (R); age 51
Ariz. *Raul H. Castro* (D); b. June 12, 1916
Ark. *David Pryor* (D); b. Aug. 29, 1934
Calif. *Edmund G. Brown Jr.* (D); age 36
Colo. *Richard D. Lamm* (D); age 39
Conn. *Ella T. Grasso* (D); b. May 10, 1919
Dela. **Sherman W. Tribbitt* (D) term ends 1977; born Nov. 9, 1922
Fla. **Reubin Askew* (D); born Sept. 11, 1928 (1971)
Ga. *George Busbee* (D); age 47
Hawaii *George R. Ariyoshi* (D); age 48
Idaho **Cecil D. Andrus* (D); b. Aug. 25, 1931 (1971)
Ill. *Daniel Walker (D) term ends 1977; born Aug. 6, 1922
Ind. *Otis R. Bowen (R) term ends 1977; b. Feb. 26, 1918
Iowa
(two-year term)
**Robert Ray* (R); born Sept. 28, 1928 (1969)
Kansas
(two-year term)
Robert F. Bennett (R); age 47
Ky. *Wendell H. Ford (D) term expires 1975; b. Sept. 8, 1924 (elected to Senate, Lt. Gov. Julian Carroll succeeds)
La. *Edwin W. Edwards (D) term ends 1976; b. Aug. 7, 1927 (1972)
Me. *James B. Longley* (Independent); b. April 22, 1924
Md. **Marvin Mandel* (D); b. April 19, 1920 (1969)
Mass. *Michael Dukakis* (D); age 40
Mich. **William G. Milliken* (R); b. March 22, 1922 (1969)
Minn. **Wendell R. Anderson* (D); b. Feb. 1, 1933 (1971)
Miss. *William Waller (D) term ends 1976; b. Aug. 21, 1926 (1972)
Mo. *Christopher S. Bond (R) term ends 1976; b. March 6, 1939 (1972)
Mont. *Thomas L. Judge (D) term ends 1976; b. Oct. 12, 1934 (1972)
Neb. **James J. Exon* (D); b. Aug. 9, 1921 (1971)
Nev. **Mike O'Callaghan* (D); b. Sept. 10, 1932 (1970)
N.H.
(two-year term)
**Meldrim Thomson Jr.* (R); b. 1912 (1973)
N.J. *Brendan T. Byrne (D); b. April 1, 1924 (1973)
N.M. *Jerry Apodaca* (D); age 40
N.Y. *Hugh L. Carey* (D); b. April 11, 1919
N.C. *James E. Holshouser Jr. (R) term ends 1976; b. Aug. 8, 1934 (1972)
N.D. *Arthur A. Link (D) term ends 1976; b. May 24, 1914 (1972)
Ohio *James A. Rhodes* (R); b. Sept. 13, 1909 (1963)†
Okla. *David L. Boren* (D); age 33
Ore. *Bob Straub* (D); age 54
Pa. **Milton J. Shapp* (D); b. June 25, 1912 (1971)
R.I.
(two-year term)
**Philip Noel* (D); b. June 6, 1931 (1973)
S.C. *James B. Edwards* (R); age 47
S.D. **Richard F. Kneip* (D); b. Jan. 7, 1933 (1971)
(two-year term)
Tenn. *Ray Blanton* (D); b. April 10, 1930
Texas
(two-year term)
**Dolph Briscoe* (D); age 51 (1973)
Utah *Calvin L. Rampton (D) term ends 1976; b. Nov. 6, 1913 (1972)
Vt.
(two-year term)
**Thomas P. Salmon* (D), b. April 19, 1932 (1973)
Va. *Mills E. Godwin (R) term ends 1977; b. Nov. 19, 1914 (1966)†
Wash. *Daniel J. Evans (R) term ends 1976; b. Oct. 16, 1925 (1964)
W.Va. *Arch A. Moore (R) term ends 1976; b. April 16, 1923 (1972)
Wis. **Patrick J. Lucey* (D); b. March 21, 1918 (1971)
Wyo. *Ed Herschler* (D); age 56

[9] **Special elections.** Earlier in the year Democrats had won four of five special elections to fill seats in the House that had been held by the GOP. Observers attributed the Democratic gains to the Watergate scandals. Democrat John P. Murtha won a narrow victory over GOP candidate Harry Fox Feb. 5 in a special election in Pennsylvania's 12th District. The seat had been held for the last 24 years by John P. Saylor (R), who died in October 1973. Murtha won the regular election in November. Democrat Richard F. VanderVeen was elected to Congress Feb. 18 from Michigan's 5th District (a seat held by Republicans since 1910 and for the past 25 years by Gerald R. Ford who vacated it in 1973 to become vice president), by defeating Republican Robert VanderLaan by a comfortable margin. VanderVeen won re-election in November. Democrat

Thomas A. Luken won a special election March 5 in Ohio's 1st District, defeating Willis D. Gradison Jr. The traditionally-Republican seat had been held by William J. Keating who resigned Jan. 3 to become president of the *Cincinnati Enquirer*. Both candidates were former Cincinnati mayors. Gradison recaptured the seat from Luken in the Nov. 5 election. The GOP retained its hold on California's 13th District March 5 when Robert J. Lagomarsino won a majority of votes against seven Democratic opponents. The Republican incumbent, Rep. Charles M. Teague, had died Jan. 1. J. Robert Traxler (D) defeated James M. Sparling Jr. (R) in a special election April 16 in Michigan's 8th District. It was the first time a Democrat had won the seat since 1932. President Nixon had campaigned for Sparling in the district April 10. Traxler retained the seat in the November elections.

[10] **Key primary results.** Three primary elections received national attention during the year. In Ohio Democratic primary May 7, former astronaut, John H. Glenn Jr. easily defeated incumbent Sen. Howard M. Metzenbaum who had been appointed to the seat in December 1973. Sen. J. W. Fulbright (D, Ark.) was defeated by Gov. Dale Bumpers May 28. Fulbright had been a member of the Senate for 30 years and chairman of the Senate Foreign Relations Committee since 1959. Orval Faubus, governor of Arkansas from 1954 through 1966, was defeated in the gubernatorial primary by former Rep. David H. Pryor. Georgia Lt. Gov. Lester Maddox lost a Democratic runoff primary for the gubernatorial nomination Sept. 3 to George Busbee, the majority leader of the State House of Representatives.

[11] **General election campaign.** The primary question in 1974's off-year election was the affect Watergate and related revelations would have on Republican candidates. The party position was expressed early in the year when, on Feb. 22, House Republican Leader John J. Rhodes (Ariz.) said, "The official Republican Party had nothing whatsoever to do with the disgraceful abuses that took place in 1972." Attacking the Democrat-controlled Congress, Rhodes added the only way to "get Congress off dead center is to change the guard." Concern over the issue was also expressed by Vice President Gerald Ford at a rally in Millburn, N.J. on March 23 at which he said predictions by some Democrats of a gain of between 50 and 100 seats in the House were "not impossible." President Nixon, however, maintained an optimistic view, citing "peace and prosperity" as the "two great issues" in the upcoming campaign. Nixon also pledged to campaign for Republican candidates. In a survey of 11 Republican senators seeking re-election, the Associated Press reported March 27 that only Sen. Henry Bellmon (Okla.) had asked Nixon to campaign for him. Seven reported they did not want Nixon to campaign for them. Two said he could campaign for them but they were not going to ask him. In an interview May 19, National Chairman George Bush admitted he was "more concerned than ever" about the political fallout from Watergate. It "can't possibly help us," he said.

[12] For the Democrats, the campaign theme was expressed March 9 by Democratic National Chairman Robert S. Strauss: "Run on the issues... the Nixon leadership." A meeting of Democratic governors in Chicago April 21-22 focused primarily on the November elections and the 1976 presidential election. Optimism about the November results, because of an expected Watergate fallout against Republican candidates, was so high that a fear of beneficial underdog status for the Republicans surfaced at the meeting, which was attended by 15 of the 32 Democratic governors. As Gov. Thomas P. Salmon (Vt.) put it, "We've almost reached the point where the President and the Republican Party could achieve certain benefits from the martyrdom people now perceive in Watergate and its preempting of other national events."

[13] After his ascension to the Presidency, Ford attempted to deflect attention from Nixon and Watergate by concentrating on economic issues and by supporting candidates of either party who stood for fiscal restraint, according to an Aug. 30 announcement by Press Secretary J. F. terHorst. Ford's theme of an "inflation-proof" Congress was expressed in a speech to the Republican National Committee Sept. 16. In a speech at a Republican fund-raising dinner in Burlington, Vt. Oct. 7, Ford stressed the virtues of the two-party system, which he suggested was imperiled by a drift away from political partisanship "in the wake of Watergate." "We need two strong parties... to serve as the twin pillars of democracy," he said. In other campaign appearances, Ford stressed the dangers of a "veto-proof Congress" which he warned might become a "legislative dictatorship." Ford also stressed his own anti-inflation program which, he said, demanded prompt action from Congress.

See also CAMPAIGN FINANCING [1-2]; VOTING RIGHTS

ELIZABETH II, QUEEN—*See* AUSTRALIA [13]; GREAT BRITAIN [4, 6, 18]; GRENADA; IRELAND, NORTHERN [15]; MALTA

ELLSBERG, DANIEL—*See* CAMPAIGN FINANCING [5]; DEFENSE [3]; WATERGATE [15, 21, 24, 26, 31, 59, 62, 78-86]

EL SALVADOR—The ruling National Conciliation Party (PCN), whose disputed victory in the 1972 presidential election precipitated an abortive military coup, won the March 10 Congressional and mayoral elections. Unofficial returns reported by the *Miami Herald* March 13 gave PCN 32 legislative seats, to 14 for the National Opposition Union (UNO), 4 for the Salvadorean People's Party and 2 for the United Independent Democratic Front. The PCN won a majority of the 261 mayoralty posts at stake. UNO spokesmen charged vote fraud less than 24 hours after the balloting. The elections were preceded by an upsurge of left-wing guerrilla activity.

See also COFFEE; LATIN AMERICA; OIL [17]; SUGAR

EMMY AWARDS—*See* MUSIC; TELEVISION & RADIO

ENERGY CRISIS (U.S.)—**Congress probes crisis, oil profits.** Several subcommittees in the House and Senate probed various aspects of the energy crisis during January and February. Sen. Henry Jackson (D, Wash.), chairman of the Senate Permanent Subcommittee on Investigations, charged Jan. 11 that there is a "total lack of public confidence in the oil industry, in the federal agencies charged with regulating the industry, and in the validity of the spiraling costs of gasoline and heating oil. People are not going to make sacrifices unless they get some straightforward answers about the extent of the shortage and who is benefiting from the shortage." In testimony Jan. 16 before a House Select Committee on Small Business subcommittee, chaired by Rep. John D. Dingell (D, Mich.), four energy policy experts said the oil industry had been able to reap advantages from the fuel shortage by keeping the government "in the dark" about their supply and price information. They also criticized tax credits given multinational oil companies for royalties paid to foreign governments. (Rep. Les Aspin [D, Wis.] had charged Jan. 1 that 413 directors, senior officials and stockholders of 178 oil and gas companies had contributed $4.98 million to President Nixon's re-election campaign. Because of these donations, nearly 10% of Nixon's total campaign receipts, Aspin said, "President Nixon's hands are tied, preventing him from dealing effectively with the current energy crisis. After their massive contributions, there is little he can do to control them.")

[2] Hearings held Jan. 21-23 by the Senate Permanent Investigations Subcommittee provided a forum for airing of charges that the fuel shortage had been

contrived, that oil industry profits were excessive, particularly during the period of the Arab embargo, and that at least one major oil company had cut off supplies to U.S. military forces during the Middle East crisis at the order of Saudi Arabia. Oil executives from seven major companies—Exxon, Texaco, Mobil, Gulf, Shell, Standard Oil (California) and Amoco, a subsidiary of Standard Oil (Indiana)—testified in rebuttal over the three-day period. The subcommittee had laid the groundwork for the hearings, which opened as Congress reconvened to begin work on the stalemated emergency energy bill, by asking the oil companies to respond to questionnaires about their business operations. Sen. Jackson, sponsor of the emergency energy legislation, said at the opening of testimony that Mobil and Gulf had been the only companies to comply in full. Despite the lack of cooperation from the industry in providing complete information on the extent of the fuel shortage, the subcommittee concluded that at the end of 1973, inventories in all petroleum products held by the seven companies were 5.5% higher than at the end of 1972. Oil officials, who did not challenge the assertion, insisted that the fuel crisis was real. They attributed their favorable position to "prudent management" and mild winter weather, but cautioned the public not to be misled. The full effects of the Arab embargo would be felt within a few weeks as crude oil stocks dropped rapidly, industry officials warned. Under harsh questioning from several openly skeptical senators, the oil executives denied they had withheld fuel from the market to force up prices during the shortage period. During the hearing Jan. 22, Jackson disclosed that a subcommittee staff report showed that the seven major oil companies increased their profits by 46% during the first nine months of 1973 when sales rose by only 6%. Sen. Abraham Ribicoff (D, Conn.) charged that the nation's tax structure permitted the oil industry to reap windfall profits. According to Ribicoff, Texaco had paid U.S. income taxes of only 1.7% and Gulf only 2% because of the depletion allowance and foreign tax credit contained in the U.S. tax code. Texaco and Gulf spokesmen said that their total worldwide taxes amounted to 51% and 52% of their entire income. Sen. William Proxmire (D, Wis.) charged that the tax provision allowing such wide discrepancies between foreign tax payments and U.S. payments was a "gigantic loopole" costing citizens $2 billion-$2.5 billion a year.

[3] Jackson said Jan. 23 that he had documentary evidence that Exxon had cut off fuel supplies to U.S. military forces abroad at the bidding of the Saudi Arabian government. Jackson said he based his charges on the Dec. 1, 1973 issue of *Business Week* and corroboration from "independent [government] documentation." According to the magazine, Saudi Arabia's King Faisal ordered U.S. companies participating in the Arabian American Oil Co. (Aramco) to cease supplying U.S. troops with fuel derived from Saudi crude oil. Faisal threatened to "retaliate against any breach by extending the oil embargo to the company involved and the country in which the violation took place," *Business Week* stated. Spokesmen for Aramco members—Exxon, Mobil, Standard Oil (California) and Texaco—denied personal knowledge of the alleged shutoff but said they would check further on the charge. Jackson labeled the action a "flagrant act of corporate disloyalty to the U.S. government." The Pentagon had admitted publicly in October 1973 that Navy ships had been denied their usual source of Arab oil, a fact which had prompted the Administration to invoke the Defense Production Act to insure an adequate supply of fuel for national security purposes.

[4] **Final fuel allocation rules.** The Federal Energy Office's (FEO) final fuel allocation rules were published Jan. 15 and became effective immediately. Noting that industrial and public service users were favored over those requiring

fuel for home heating and private automobiles, Deputy FEO Administrator John C. Sawhill said that the allocation program's aim was "to preserve jobs rather than to have homes at 75 degrees." Private homeowners could obtain only enough oil sufficient to heat residences at temperatures that were six degrees lower than average settings in 1972. Oil suppliers would be allowed to deny deliveries to those refusing to cooperate. Violators of the regulation could be fined up to $2,500. Gasoline supplies during the first three months of 1974 would be 20% below projected demand, according to Sawhill, necessitating limits on pleasure driving. Sawhill also released details of the Administration's contingency plan for gasoline rationing, insisting, however, that no decision had been made on whether to adopt the plan and voicing hope that rationing could be avoided.

[5] The FEO Feb. 14 ordered petroleum refiners to increase their production of jet fuel by 6% in order to supply the nation's airlines with fuel promised under the Administration's allocation program.

[6] **Truckers' protests.** The Administration announced a series of proposals Jan. 30 that were designed to offset a threatened shutdown of the nation's major highways by independent truckers. Representatives of 77 trucking groups had called for a nationwide shutdown to begin Jan. 31, but delivery interruptions and violence had already occurred in Ohio and Pennsylvania and other areas of the northeast. Reports of gunfire, beatings and rocks thrown at moving trucks marred the protests by dissident truckers as the strike approached. Under the Jan. 30 plan announced by W. J. Usery Jr., a special assistant to President Nixon and director of the Federal Mediation and Conciliation Service, the Interstate Commerce Commission was preparing regulations that would permit independent owner-operators to recover the difference between present fuel prices and those set May 15, 1973. Truckers would be allowed to pass through the higher fuel costs in their contracts with trucking firms. The carriers in turn would be compensated with higher government-set trucking rates. The strike, which was loosely organized by a coalition of 18 regional groups, was successful in halting deliveries of perishable goods and other items throughout much of the nation. As the effectiveness of the strike mounted, reports of violence also increased. As in past protests by independent truckers, the level of violence was highest in Ohio and Pennsylvania—the nexus of the nation's trucking system and home territory for most militant drivers—but incidents involving gunfire, stoning, beatings, burned rigs, and bomb threats also were reported in at least 20 states. Two deaths were reported—a driver was killed in Pennsylvania when a boulder was dropped on his cab, causing him to crash; another person was shot to death in Delaware. The National Guard was called up in Ohio, Pennsylvania, Maryland, Michigan, Kentucky, West Virginia and Florida to patrol the highways and provide convoy protection to non-striking drivers. Most of the independent truckers returned to the highways Feb. 11, indicating their acceptance of a strike pact negotiated with the aid of Pennsylvania Gov. Milton J. Shapp (D) and Administration officials. There were pockets of resistance to the agreement in New Jersey and areas of the Mid-west, government officials said, but truck traffic was reported at near normal levels across the rest of the country. The pact provided for a 6% surcharge on freight rates to cover increased fuel costs

[7] A violence-marred three-week wildcat strike, which crippled southern West Virginia coal mines and forced major steel producing firms to cut back production, ended March 18 after Gov. Arch A. Moore Jr. suspended a controversial rule banning gasoline sales to motorists with more than a quarter tank of gasoline. More than 27,000 miners, many of them long distance

commuters, had protested the allocation order. Gunfire injured two pickets and one bystander March 13, forcing Moore to withdraw the gasoline rule for 30 days.

[8] **Gasoline shortage worsens.** Calls mounted during February from governors and members of Congress for a nationwide gasoline rationing program but FEO Director William Simon continued to resist, suggesting instead that states adopt regional plans to deal with spot shortages. The worsening gasoline shortage was particularly severe in urban areas and in the Northeast, where the strike by independent truckers had interrupted the delivery of already scarce gasoline supplies. Evidence of the uneven nature of the shortage and the allocation program's ineffectiveness in redistributing the dwindling supplies could be seen in New Jersey, where two-three hour waits at gasoline stations were common while motorists in much of the rest of the country faced no lines and few limits on their purchases. By Feb. 15, five states and the District of Columbia (and adjacent areas of northern Virginia) had joined Oregon and Hawaii in implementing a form of rationing that based distributions on odd and even numbered license plates. To blunt criticism about its inaction, the FEO Feb. 16 allowed half the nation's gasoline stations to raise gasoline prices 1¢ a gallon, effective March 1. The markup was authorized only for those stations whose allocations had been reduced at least 15% from their supply level in the 1972 base period. The action, coming on top of the regular price adjustment allowed dealers at the beginning of each month, was expected to cost motorists $500 million a year. Sawhill admitted that the agency acted in response to threats by many gasoline stations to shut down their operations entirely to protest what they considered the government's discriminatory restraints on profits. The number of gasoline stations closing permanently as a consequence of the fuel crisis had risen sharply, with independent dealers very hard hit by the dwindling supply. (According to a nationwide survey of retail gasoline stations published Sept. 26, nearly 20,000 service stations went out of business during the 12-month period ending June 30. According to Audits and Surveys Inc., a marketing research firm, the number of gas stations dropped from 215,880 to 196,130.)

[9] Simon issued further revisions of the government's gasoline allocation program Feb. 22 and 23 as state officials and station dealers continued to voice dissatisfaction with the distribution system. Supplementary allocations to meet an emergency situation in February were expanded in a ruling announced Feb. 22. Gasoline deliveries for Washington, D.C. and 24 states were increased to total 10% of the month's basic supply. Two other states were allowed a total of 6% in additional gasoline. (South Carolina was the only new state added to the group already scheduled to receive extra gasoline supplies.)

[10] **Senate, House pass energy bill.** The Senate Feb. 19 passed the emergency energy bill in the form that the legislation had been reported out of House-Senate conference committee Feb. 6. The vote was 67-32. The House acted Feb. 27 on the same measure, approving it 258-151. Parliamentary maneuvers, which had delayed final votes on the bill for several weeks, characterized its eventual passage in both houses. Although the revised version was reported out Feb. 6, no action was taken immediately because Republicans and senators from oil producing states opposed another provision in the bill that would mandate a rollback, to $5.25 a barrel, in the price of crude oil from "new" wells and "stripper" wells producing less than 10 barrels a day. The current price of "new" oil, which was not under price controls, was $10.35 a barrel. The bill would allow the President subsequently to raise the ceiling price of oil to $7.09 a barrel, unless Congress disapproved within 30 days. Also included in the

emergency legislation was authority for the FEO to order further energy conservation measures subject to a six-month time limit and veto by either house of Congress; standby authority for the President to order gasoline rationing; authority for regulatory agencies to make fuel saving cutbacks in transportation; authority for the FEO to make generating plants convert from oil to coal burning; authority for the FEO to order increased domestic oil production; authorization for increased unemployment compensation for those laid off as a result of the fuel crisis; grants of limited immunity from antitrust prosecution for retailers and the oil industry, under close government supervision; requirements for energy producers to file product information reports with the FEO; authorization for a delay in certain 1976 auto emission requirements; authority for issuing loans to homeowners and small businessmen to make energy conservation improvements.

[11] **Energy bill vetoed, Nixon upheld.** President Nixon vetoed the emergency energy bill March 6. In action the same day, the Senate sustained the veto on a 58-40 vote that was eight short of the two-thirds majority required to override the President's action. Despite the veto, there was no indication that the issue was dead. Shortly after the Senate vote, the House voted 218-175 to insert a price rollback measure, nearly identical to the rollback provision in the original bill, into a bill that would establish a Federal Energy Administration. (Under the price amendment, producers of less than 30,000 barrels a day of "new" crude oil would be exempt from the rollback provision.) In his veto message, Nixon said the bill would "set domestic crude oil prices at such low levels that the oil industry would be unable to sustain its present production of petroleum products, including gasoline. It would result in reduced energy supplies, longer lines at the gas pump" and increased unemployment. The next day the House reversed itself and voted 216-163 March 7 to reject a measure setting a ceiling on the price of "new" oil. The measure was rejected after Rep. John Anderson (R, Ill.) cited an apparent loophole—refiners producing less than 30,000 barrels a day would have been exempt from the price ceiling, according to the bill. Anderson said Standard Oil Co. (Ohio) produced only 25,000 barrels a day and would qualify for an exemption. Other supporters of the rollback were persuaded that an excess profits tax, currently under consideration in committee, was a preferable method for dealing with the oil industry's windfall profits.

[12] **Gasoline allocations increased.** Simon told the National Governors Conference in Washington March 7 that "every state will receive a greater supply of gasoline in March than in February, even when the February emergency allocations to the states are included." Nationwide, the average state allocation would be 89% of the base period, but Simon promised that by April, the equalization process would be completed and no state would receive more than 95% of its 1972 base level (February allocations had ranged from 61% to more than 100% of the consumption levels in 1972.) By the time Simon had announced yet another readjustment in his much criticized gasoline allocation program, the supply situation had stabilized somewhat from its chaotic condition in February. Emergency fuel allocations covered the critical spot shortages that were in evidence at the end of the month and new deliveries became available for March, but the price of gasoline continued to rise.

[13] **Arabs lift U.S. embargo.** The oil embargo against the U.S. was lifted March 18 by seven of the nine Arab oil-producing countries: Algeria, Saudi Arabia, Kuwait, Qatar, Bahrain, Egypt and Abu Dhabi. [For details on the decision see OIL] As a result of the Arab action, President Nixon announced several basic energy policy decisions in a speech before the National Association of Broadcasters March 19. He flatly ruled out the need for compulsory gasoline

rationing and rescinded an order banning Sunday sales of gasoline, effective March 24. Nixon said he had directed the FEO to increase fuel allocations to industry and agriculture "so that they can have the necessary energy to operate at full capacity." He also pledged to increase gasoline allocations to the states "with the purpose of diminishing . . . and eventually eliminating" lengthy lines at gasoline stations.

[14] As the direct impact of the embargo lessened and the indirect price consequences became widespread, analysts began to examine the effects of the Arab oil embargo and warn that further shortages could be expected. Because of the embargo, the nation's economic output declined by $10-$20 billion during the first quarter of 1974, according to a report issued Sept. 2 by the FEA. The curb on oil imports also caused the civilian labor force to shrink by about 500,000 persons. An estimated 80% of the industrial layoffs could be "traced to the decline in demand for automotive or recreational vehicles." The embargo also caused a loss in state and federal gasoline taxes, used to finance road maintenance, education and other budgt areas. The FEA estimated that this reduction in gasoline consumption resulted in a $700 million loss in tax money. Increased energy prices also caused the Consumer Price Index to move sharply higher, the FEA added.

[15] Another analysis of the embargo was prepared by Harvard Business School Professor Robert B. Stobaugh for the Senate multinationals subcommittee. The study, released July 25, concluded that it was a misconception to believe that the import curb was widely violated—the embargo was nearly 100% effective in cutting off the supply of oil imported to the U.S. Crude oil imports were reduced from 1.2 million barrels a day in September 1973 to 19,000 barrels a day in January and February. The study also refuted charges that major oil companies contrived the winter fuel shortage in order to raise prices. Oil available for consumption in the U.S. dropped 6.1% during the worst four-month period of the embargo, compared with a 3.4% worldwide drop in supplies, the report said.

[16] **Aramco profits probed.** The Senate Subcommittee on Multinational Corporations resumed hearings on the oil industry March 27. Aramco, a consortium owned jointly by the Saudi Arabian government and four U.S. oil companies—Texaco, Exxon, Mobil and Standard (California), was the focus of the Congressional investigation into the relationship between sharply higher industry profits and sharply reduced oil supplies. According to preliminary figures made public by the subcommitee for the first time, Aramco's gross income in 1973 totaled $8.7 billion and profits equaled $3.2 billion. (Another $1.1 billion was paid in royalties and $3.9 billion when to the Saudi government in taxes. U.S. taxes came to $3 million in 1973, $5 million in 1972 and $4 million in 1971.) These figures compared with revenues of $4.6 billion in 1972 and $3 billion in 1971. Profits in 1972 had totaled $1.7 billion and $1.1 billion in 1971. Aramco officials said the figures, which were based on documents submitted by company auditors, were "grossly misleading" because they were based on the "posted" price rather than on the actual market value of oil.

[17] **Oil companies report quarterly profits.** Oil companies reported continued high earning levels in the first quarter of 1974. When measured in percentage gains over the first quarter of 1973, profits rose as much as 748% at Occidental and as little as 29% at Standard (Ohio). According to the *New York Times* May 1, the 20 major oil companies showed a 79% gain in first quarter profits which totaled $3.3 billion. Among the reports: Occidental Petroleum Corp., up 748% (over the first period of 1973) to $67.8 million (net income), announced April 23; Royal Dutch/Shell Group of Companies, up 178% to $776.1 million on revenue

of $7.61 billion (up 94%), reported May 9; Phillips Petroleum Co., up 150% to $108.6 million (operating earnings) on gross revenue of $1.15 billion (up 69%), announced April 30; Texaco Inc., up 123.2% to $589.4 million on revenue of $2.49 billion, announced April 23; Atlantic Richfield Corp., up 86.7% to $93.9 million on revenue of $1.56 billion (up 56%), announced April 30; Standard Oil Co. (California), up 92% to $292.9 million on revenue of $3.91 billion (up 110%), announced April 25; Cities Service Co., up 87% to $68.8 million on revenue of $703.2 million (up 34%), announced April 30; Sun Oil Co., up 85% to $90.8 million, announced April 16; Standard Oil Co. (Indiana), up 81% to $219 million on 55% gain in revenue, announced April 22; Gulf Oil Corp., up 76% to $290 million on revenue of $4.16 billion, announced April 22; Mobil Oil Corp., up 66% to $258.6 million on revenue of $4.4 billion (up 57%), announced April 29; Shell Oil Co., up 52% to $121.8 million on revenue of $1.89 billion (up 46%), announced April 25; Exxon Corp., up 39% to $705 million, announced April 23; Standard Oil Co. (Ohio), up 29% to $22.6 million on revenue of $482.9 million (up 27%), announced April 18.

[18] **Federal Energy Administration created.** President Nixon May 7 signed into law the first of his energy proposals to pass Congress. It was a bill establishing the Federal Energy Administration (FEA), which would replace the FEO created by executive authority Dec. 4, 1973. The legislation authorized the FEA to administer an emergency energy rationing plan and gasoline allocation programs for the states, but powers granted to the new agency were more limited than Nixon had requested. The FEA administrator was specifically empowered to impose energy conservation measures, prohibit unreasonable profits and develop export/import policies for energy resources. The law gave the FEA a two-year existence and required the President to submit the names of those nominated for top FEA posts to the Senate for consideration. The measure, which had passed the Senate Dec. 19, 1973, was approved by the House March 7. Final action came May 2 when the Senate adopted a conference report on the bill, already approved in the House April 29. (The FEO was not dismantled and replaced by the FEA until the beginning of fiscal 1975, on July 1. There had been confusion in press reports about the FEA's effective functioning date since early May, when Congress had passed the bill establishing the new agency.)

[19] **Crude oil price changes proposed.** The FEO issued proposed changes May 16 for its petroleum price regulations. One of the revisions, which would disallow some of the costs oil companies had claimed for crude and refined products purchased abroad from their affiliates, could result in a price rollback by a number of oil companies because these overseas costs had been used to compute domestic prices under government guidelines. Use of these "transfer prices" to the "disadvantage of American consumers" "may explain in part the significant increases in international profits reported by the major oil companies," FEO Administrator Sawhill said. Sawhill revealed April 25 that a joint FEO-IRS investigation was considering 47,000 cases of alleged price gouging by the energy industry at the wholesale and retail level. The evidence indicated that U.S. consumers may have been overcharged by as much as $100 million, Sawhill said. He added that $14.2 million in wholesale and retail refunds had been ordered as a result of price violations uncovered during the continuing investigations.

[20] **'73 oil price increase disputed.** Consumer advocate Ralph Nader made public June 7 internal documents from the Cost of Living Council (CLC) indicating that the CLC had authorized a $1 a barrel increase in the price of "old" oil despite the objections of its staff and an independent consultant hired by the CLC. The new information was obtained from the CLC when Nader

invoked the Freedom of Information Act. The documents pertained to the CLC's decision, announced Dec. 19, 1973, to allow a $1 increase to $5.25 a barrel in the price of crude oil that was produced in the U.S. at pre-1972 production levels. "Old" oil was then and remained subject to Administration price controls. According to the newly released documents, the CLC staff felt that the increase was "arbitrary" and unjustified. Since production of domestic oil already was near maximum levels, the staff paper declared, no additional increase in oil supplies could be expected as a result of the price hike.

[21] **New natural gas price set.** The Federal Power Commission (FPC) June 24 authorized a single national price for "new" natural gas pumped from wells that began operation after Jan. 1, 1973. The ruling, which the FPC termed a "landmark decision," affected new gas sold in interstate commerce and replaced the FPC's current policy of setting ceiling prices for separate geographic areas under limited term and emergency sales rate procedures. The new rate—42¢ per 1,000 cubic feet—eventually would mean sharply higher prices for gas wholesalers and consumers. The average price of gas sold nationwide, including gas that the FPC had said could be sold at prices above the regulated ceiling level, was 27¢ per 1,000 cubic feet in March. Fear was growing that some areas of the country would experience a shortage of natural gas supplies during the coming winter that would be at least as severe as the previous year's shortage of oil. The FPC warned June 12 that the nation's chronic gas shortage had worsened in the last 12 months, and within a few months, supplies would fall short of demand by 10%, equivalent to the loss of about 330 million barrels of oil. The shortage could become a "severe crisis" over the next five years, according to the FPC. (Natural gas accounted for more than 31% of the nation's energy supplies.)

[22] The General Accounting Office (GAO) charged Sept. 14 that the FPC used "improper" procedures in granting price increases for natural gas. After completing its 10-month investigation of the agency, the GAO also said the FPC had failed to safeguard against conflict of interest by employing officials who held stock in companies regulated by the agency.

[23] **Geothermal energy program.** A bill for a geothermal energy research program was approved by the Senate Aug. 20, the House Aug. 21 and President Ford Sept. 3. The bill called for a management team to be set up to coordinate a federal effort in locating and evaluating geothermal resources, determining technical problems and establishing demonstration projects exploring the commercial potential of producing electric power from underground heat. The bill authorized agreements to be made with utilities and municipalities to build geothermal facilities for commercial energy. Appropriations of $50 million were authorized for guarantees on loans to acquire resources and build facilities.

[24] **'Double-dip' pricing, conflict of interest controversies.** Controversy developed over an FEA regulation written in January at the height of the Arab oil embargo after Sawhill said the agency rule permitted oil companies to overcharge consumers by $100 million in 1974. In a letter Sept. 13 to Sen. Jackson, chairman of the Permanent Investigations Subcommittee, Sawhill said a continuing investigation of about 10 major oil companies revealed that they had profited from the agency's "double recovery" rule which, until it was revised in May, allowed refiners to double their costs on the volume of crude oil they were required to sell to other refiners under the government's oil-allocation rules. Unwarranted profits based on this practice, known in the oil industry as "double-dipping," could total up to $300 million, Sawhill said. The controversy had its origins in the agency's oil swap rule, which required large refiners to share their supplies of crude oil with independent refiners, whose supplies were

limited and higher priced, in order to increase domestic production of petroleum products. Sawhill also said the Federal Bureau of Investigation (FBI) was examining a possible conflict of interest involving the role of Robert C. Bowen, a Phillips Petroleum Co. engineer who had served with the FEO for a year on leave from Phillips. Bowen had returned to work for Phillips in June after he was dismissed by Sawhill because an independent investigation of Bowen's possible conflict of interest was forwarded to the Justice Department for review. The probe, conducted by the General Accounting Office, had been requested by Rep. Charles Vanik (D, Ohio), because of reports that Bowen had been responsible for drafting price regulations. Attorneys for the FEA testified Sept. 25 before the House Small Business Committee that Bowen and his superior at the agency, William A. Johnson, then FEO assistant administrator for policy analysis, had ignored their warnings that the double recovery regulation would result in unwarranted profits to some oil companies. Phillips netted profits of about $52 million from the double dipping practice, according to Rep. John D. Dingell (D, Mich.), chairman of the subcommittee. William N. Walker, former FEO-FEA general counsel, identified Bowen as the "key party" in drafting the crude oil allocation rule. Assistant Attorney General Henry Petersen was questioned Oct. 3 about the Justice Department's decision, made public Aug. 30 in a letter to Rep. Vanik, that prosecution of Bowen for conflict of interest violations was "not warranted." Petersen told Vanik the criminal investigation "had been completed" and showed only that a "violation, if any [committed] by Mr. Bowen was inadvertent and technical."

[25] **Solar energy developments.** A Solar Heating and Cooling Demonstration Act was signed by the President Sept. 3. As cleared by Congress—the Senate approved it Aug. 12, the House Aug. 21—the bill established a five-year, $60 million program to explore technology to use solar energy to heat and cool buildings. The Solar Energy Research, Development and Demonstration Act of 1974 was passed by the House Oct. 9 and Senate Oct. 11 and signed into law by President Ford Oct. 26. An appraisal of solar energy resources was to be made on a regional and national basis. Demonstration projects were authorized. The research and development program was to be conducted in the various solar energy areas, including ocean thermal power conversion, wind power conversion and solar heating and cooling of buildings. The conference report on the bill specified that it was the intent of Congress that the authorizations were separate from those of the Solar Heating and Cooling Demonstration Act.

[26] **Ford proposals.** In an Oct. 8 televised address before a joint session of Congress, President Ford presented an anti-inflation program which included a series of energy proposals. "We have a real energy problem," Ford said. "One third of our oil, 17% of America's total energy, now comes from foreign sources we cannot control—at high cartel prices costing you and me $16 billion more than just a year ago. The primary solution has to be at home." Ford named Interior Secretary Morton to head a newly established National Energy Board charged with developing a national energy policy. "His marching orders are to reduce imports of foreign oil by 1 million barrels per day by the end of 1975, whether by savings here at home or by increasing our own sources," Ford said. In his legislative requests, Ford asked Congress to give priority to four areas involving the deregulation of natural gas, increased use of the naval oil reserves in California and Alaska, amendments to the Clean Air Act, and passage of strip mine legislation that would "insure adequate supply with common sense environmental protection." Ford also said he would seek new legislation requiring the use of cleaner coal processes and nuclear fuel in new electric plants

and "the quick conversion of existing oil plants." Ford proposed setting a target date of 1980 for "eliminating oil-fired plants from the nation's base loaded electrical capacity."

[27] In a press conference the following day, the President was asked why he had not proposed mandatory gasoline taxes or rationing to conserve fuel. Ford said this had been considered but found to be potentially "harmful to people," especially those "less able to pay." As for rationing, "we believe," he said, "that the American people will respond to our volunteer program," which was "far preferable and more in the traditions of the American system."

[28] Arthur Burns, chairman of the Federal Reserve Board, Nov. 27 criticized President Ford's fuel saving program, which relied on voluntary measures, and urged the Administration to adopt an "austerity policy" on energy conservation. Among the mandatory conservation efforts Burns supported was a "sizable" gasoline tax increase. "We have been lecturing the rest of the world [on cutting fuel consumption] while our own practices leave much to be desired," Burns said. He noted that although Britain, Italy, France, Japan, West Germany and other nations had raised gasoline taxes, "we haven't touched the tax on gasoline." Burns also said he favored a tax on imported oil and a tax on autos based on horsepower or weight. He called for faster development of domestic energy sources and an increase in U.S. oil storage capacity to mitigate the impact of any new embargo on oil supplies.

[29] **FEA acts on crude oil transfer costs.** The FEA issued two regulations Oct. 28 dealing with the transfer costs paid by some international oil companies for crude oil imported from foreign affiliates. Under current price controls, these transfer costs could be passed on to consumers. The new regulations could result in an oil price rollback if evidence of overcharging were found. Of the 4 million barrels of oil imported to the U.S. daily, an estimated 3 million barrels of crude oil were bought by refiners from foreign affiliates, the FEA said. FEA Administrator Sawhill said the agency was suspicious that some foreign affiliates were inflating the transfer costs because some of the international oil companies had been paying "significantly higher" landing prices than independent refiners.

[30] **Policy making group revamped.** President Ford Oct. 29 announced the appointment of a "new team that will be in charge of the energy problem," under the direction of Interior Secretary Morton as head of the Energy Resources Council. All of Ford's nominees, who would require Senate confirmation before taking up their new posts, had formerly served in the Nixon Administration. The reorganization was announced at a presidential news conference. Federal Energy Administration Director Sawhill was the principal victim of the administrative shakeup. Ford, announcing Sawhill's resignation, said he would be replaced by Andrew E. Gibson, who had previously served President Nixon as maritime administrator and as assistant secretary in the Commerce Department. Ford also named Robert C. Seamans Jr. to head the new Energy Research and Development Administration; Dixy Lee Ray to the new post of assistant secretary of state for oceans and international, environmental and scientific matters; and William A. Anders to serve as chairman of the new Nuclear Regulatory Commission. Seamans was a former secretary of the Air Force who had left the Nixon Administration in May 1973 to head the National Academy of Engineering. Ray was currently chairman of the Atomic Energy Commission (AEC). Anders, a former astronaut, was also a member of the AEC. Ford denied that he had any "major policy differences" with Sawhill but said that Morton, who had overall charge for determining national energy policy, had the "right" to "make recommendations for those that will work with him on the council." Morton later said Sawhill "lacked a sense of working together." Sawhill had

been outspoken in his call for increased energy conservation. He had publicly advocated the use of mandatory energy saving measures, such as a sharp increase in the gasoline excise tax.

[31] President Ford Nov. 12 withdrew Gibson's nomination after controversy developed over the disclosure that Gibson's former employer, Interstate Oil Transport Co., had agreed to pay him $1 million over 10 years under a financial agreement negotiated when he joined the firm. Gibson had already collected about $120,000 in pay and was due to receive $88,000 annually over a 10-year period. The withdrawal was at Gibson's request.

[32] **Project Independence blueprint.** The FEA formally presented its 800-page "Blueprint for Project Independence" to the interagency Energy Resources Council Nov. 13. The study, in preparation for seven months at a cost of $5 million, originally had been intended to serve as a master plan for the nation's energy policy, but differences within the Nixon and Ford Administrations over energy affairs had resulted in a lack of continuity on policy matters and had diluted the report's impact as a policy setting document. Although President Nixon had set national self-sufficiency in energy needs as the major goal of Project Independence when it was announced in November 1973, designers of the FEA blueprint rejected the idea, opting instead for a goal of independence from "insecure" foreign oil by 1985 and emphasis on strict conservation measures to reduce the volume of energy imports. The report called for a major conservation effort including adoption of a 15¢ a gallon federal tax on gasoline; a mandatory fuel economy standard requiring that cars get at least 20 miles to the gallon; a 25% tax credit for insulating existing housing and a 15% tax credit for improving the energy efficiency of commercial buildings; national heating, cooling and lighting standards for all commercial buildings; efficiency standards for electrical appliances.

[33] There were two alternatives to strict conservation programs, according to the study. One was intensive exploration and drilling for oil and natural gas, but the FEA noted that environmental hazards, as well as the social and financial costs of the operation, posed strong drawbacks to this approach. Another choice was establishment of a 1 billion barrel stockpile of oil in underground salt caverns. Maintenance costs for the stockpile were estimated at $1.4 billion a year.

[34] **Ford, GM officials back gas tax.** Proponents of the gasoline tax increase won support from unlikely sources—officials of the nation's two largest auto makers. Henry Ford 2nd, chairman of the Ford Motor Co., said Nov. 22 that he favored cutting fuel consumption by imposing a 10¢ a gallon increase on the federal gasoline tax. Thomas A. Murphy, chairman of General Motors Corp., said Dec. 2 that he supported voluntary fuel conservation measures, but added that he believed the Administration "ought to consider" a gasoline tax increase if it were necessary to reduce oil imports.

[35] **Offshore leasing hearings delayed.** Interior Secretary Morton announced Nov. 25 that the government would scale down plans to lease oil drilling rights to 10 million offshore acres as opposition to the project mounted from officials in coastal states. Morton also said that hearings on a draft environmental impact statement related to the leasing project would be postponed until February 1975. Hearings had been scheduled during December in California, Alaska and New Jersey. Morton made the disclosures in a meeting with Sens. John V. Tunney and Alan Cranston, both California Democrats, Burt Pines, attorney for the city of Los Angeles, and Richard Maullin, energy adviser to California's Gov.-elect Edmund G. Brown Jr. Tunney criticized the Administration's plan to lease the acreage under a "bonus bidding" system, which would permit the government to sell the leases "without knowledge of their worth." Under a "royalty

bidding" system, the government would be entitled to a fair price for any oil discovered in the area. A Senate study group also was critical of bonus bidding. "The precipitous leasing of so many acres in a single year [could] cause coastal states and communities environmental harm and create administrative, financial, and technical problems beyond the capability of the federal government and the oil industry to handle," the report concluded. President Ford had met with 23 governors of coastal states Nov. 13 to seek support for the government's accelerated leasing schedule. Ford sought to allay the governors' fears about possible environmental damage to the coastline. "The greatest danger to our coasts from oil spills is not from offshore production but instead from greatly expanded tanker traffic that would result from increasing imports," he said. One of Ford's few supporters in the group was Louisiana Gov. Edwin W. Edwards (D), who said offshore drilling was "essential." Thirteen Atlantic coastal states had filed suits claiming that they already controlled the Outer Continental Shelf beyond the three mile boundary as part of their territorial grants from the king of England. States currently derived no direct benefit from offshore drilling—revenue from the sale of leases went directly to the U.S. Treasury.

[36] **Price equalization plan adopted.** Regulations that would equalize the cost of crude oil among refiners and the cost of fuel oil among distributors were adopted by the FEA Dec. 2. The regulations would allocate low-priced domestic oil proportionately among all refiners with the aim of eliminating the price disparities that existed between refiners with greater access to cheaper domestic oil and those which depended on the higher-priced domestic oil and imported supplies. Although the rules were not expected to cause any net change in the nationwide price of oil, areas of the East, which relied heavily on imported supplies, were expected to benefit from the rules because the burden of using high price oil would be shared by all parts of the nation. The new regulations, which would take effect gradually over the next two months, were designed to replace the two-tiered price control system for domestic "old" and "new" oil. (Old oil came from wells drilled prior to 1972 and was subject to federal price control; new oil came from wells developed after that point and was not controlled.)

[37] **FPC raises gas price ceiling.** The FPC Dec. 4 raised its recently adopted uniform price for natural gas to 50¢ per 1,000 cubic feet, an 8¢ increase over the previous national ceiling price of 42¢. The new rate, which was made retroactive to June 21, applied to gas sold on an interstate basis to pipeline companies by producers from "new" wells that began operations after Jan. 1, 1973, or that were switched from the intrastate market after that date.

[38] **15 oil firms roll back prices.** Fifteen oil companies agreed to price rollbacks totaling about $77 million to correct alleged overcharges to customers, the FEA announced Dec. 17. The FEA also disallowed about $375 million in "banked" costs claimed under a controversial ruling, since revised, permitting the oil industry to make a double recovery on costs. These expenses could have been passed on to consumers. The FEA ordered price rollbacks of $10 million from Standard Oil Co. (Ohio), $6.9 million from Exxon Corp. and $600,000 from Mobil Oil Corp. The remaining adjustments were settled voluntarily or through consent agreements.

[39] **Zarb confirmed as FEA administrator.** Frank G. Zarb, 39, associate director of the Office of Management and Budget specializing in energy matters, was confirmed Dec. 11 as administrator of the FEA succeeding Sawhill. (The nomination had been submitted to the Senate Dec. 2.) President Ford had announced his selection of Zarb, a former investment banker, Nov. 25.

[40] **New energy sources.** A bill outlining the program for non-nuclear energy development was adopted by the House Dec. 16 and Senate Dec. 17. The bill cited a goal of a $20 billion program over a 10-year period administered by the newly established Energy Research and Development Administration (ERDA). Under the bill, ERDA would have the authority to establish federal-private corporations to operate pilot plants utilizing new energy sources. Congress could veto projects funded with $25 million or more of federal money. The agency could make loans to private contractors and give financial awards to inventors. The chief issue during the legislative process concerned patent rights. Congress decided to continue the basic federal policy of reserving patent rights to the government on federally-financed research by private contractors. License to the technology generally would be granted on a non-exclusive basis, but the bill permitted granting of some exclusive licenses to outsiders.

See also APPOINTMENTS & RESIGNATIONS; ATOMIC ENERGY [14-18]; AUTOMOBILE INDUSTRY [12]; BUDGET; CANADA [21-27]; DAYLIGHT SAVINGS TIME; ECONOMY, U.S. [2-3, 7, 17-20]; ENVIRONMENT & POLLUTION [5, 16, 20]; FINLAND; FRANCE [17-19]; GREAT BRITAIN [19, 22-25]; JAPAN [6-8]; LABOR [10-13]; LIBYA; MEXICO [1, 4-5]; MONETARY DEVELOPMENTS; NETHERLANDS [1-5]; NIXON, RICHARD M.; OIL; SCIENCE; UNION OF SOVIET SOCIALIST REPUBLICS [5, 8]; UNITED NATIONS [3]

ENVIRONMENT & POLLUTION

Air Pollution

[1] **Construction review rules set.** The Environmental Protection Agency (EPA) issued final rules Feb. 14 under which the EPA and state and local agencies would review major construction projects for their impact on air quality, primarily from automobile congestion. According to EPA Administrator Russell E. Train, the regulations were aimed at new shopping centers, highways, sports arenas and airports. The rules would apply to projects begun after Jan. 1, 1975, but the EPA was to begin advance review July 1 to provide lead time to developers. State and local agencies would eventually take over complete administration of the review program. (See [7] below)

[2] **Air law developments.** The Nixon Administration sent to Congress March 22 a group of air pollution law amendments designed, according to the Administration, to meet the demands of the energy crisis. The proposed amendments to the Clean Air Act of 1970 represented a compromise between the White House Office of Management and Budget (OMB), which had backed sweeping revisions, and EPA Administrator Train, who had opposed too drastic a weakening of air quality standards. Two revisions opposed by Train remained in the package, but Train said that under the compromise he would be allowed to speak against them in Congressional hearings. The first would revoke the requirement that the EPA set standards to prevent significant deterioration of air—primarily in rural areas—that was already cleaner than required by national standards. The OMB and federal energy officials had argued that the law prevented industrial development in such regions. The second would allow power plants to substitute less expensive methods than "scrubber" systems for control of sulfur oxide emissions. The proposal would permit the use of tall smokestacks for dispersion of pollutants into the upper air or temporary plant closings when pollution levels became high. (The Ford Administration, reversing the Nixon position, supported the EPA, the *Wall Street Journal* reported Nov. 29.)

[3] By voice votes in the House June 11 and in the Senate June 12, Congress approved and sent to President Nixon a compromise version of a bill setting rules for conversion to coal by oil- and gas-burning plants and extending to the

1977 model year the EPA's strict standards for auto exhaust emissions. Plants which converted to coal voluntarily between Sept. 15, 1973 and March 15, 1974, or converted afterwards under Federal Energy Administration order, would be exempt from strict compliance with state emission rules, if emissions did not exceed EPA standards set for the affected air quality region.

[4] **EPA proposes retreat on air rules.** The EPA Aug. 16 proposed regulations under which states would have the primary role in setting air pollution standards for areas where the air was cleaner than required by current federal regulations. Courts had ruled in 1972 and 1973 that states could not allow "significant deterioration" of existing clean air. The thrust of the proposed regulations would be to give states the option in setting priorities between industrial growth and the preservation of clean air. State designations would be subject to EPA approval, but only to the extent of determining whether states had followed proper procedures in setting the designations. State designations of federally-owned lands would have to be cleared by the federal agency involved. The proposal dealt only with land use and industrial development; other pollutants such as auto emissions were not covered.

[5] **Utility scrubbers called adequate.** The EPA said in a report released Sept. 25 that the "scrubber" technique for removing sulfur gases from power plant emissions had been found to be efficient and reliable. The EPA said its findings could clear the way for burning plentiful high-sulfur coal while maintaining the standards of the Clean Air Act. (Scrubbing involved passing smokestack gases through a liquid spray to remove most sulfur oxides and particulate matter.)

[6] **Court upsets EPA leaded gas curb.** The U.S. Circuit Court of Appeals for the District of Columbia Dec. 23 set aside the EPA's regulations requiring removal of most lead from gasoline over a three-year period beginning Jan. 1. The suit had been brought by several oil refiners who argued that the EPA had not demonstrated a basis for its contention that leaded gasoline presented a hazard to public health.

[7] **EPA delays some clean air standards.** The EPA Dec. 24 postponed for six months, until July 1, 1975, the enforcement of the construction review. The decision to suspend the rules followed Congressional intervention in the form of a prohibition against EPA expenditure of any funds on "indirect source" enforcement in the current fiscal year, ending June 30, the *Wall Street Journal* reported Dec. 26. (See [1] above)

Water Pollution

[8] **GAO reports on clean water program.** The General Accounting Office (GAO) reported to Congress Jan. 16 that 1972 legislation to clean the nation's waterways was being seriously undermined by lack of funding. Citing the legislation's target date of 1985 for "zero discharges" into the waterways, the report estimated that $543 million additional federal funding was required to develop the technology for industry to meet the target. Since the funding level currently was about $12 million a year, "it could take more than 45 years" to attain the technology, the GAO pointed out, and another 5-7 years to implement it.

[9] **Waste treatment funds impounded.** President Nixon ordered the impoundment of $3 billion of the $7 billion authorized by Congress for the construction of sewage treatment plants in fiscal 1975 beginning July 1. The order was contained in a letter to EPA Administrator Train dated Jan. 1 and made public by the EPA Jan. 10. An EPA spokesman said the impoundment would set the pollution control effort "back a year or two." Nixon explained his action as an effort "to control spending in order to avoid renewed inflation or a requirement for increased taxes." Congress had anticipated Nixon's action with a

bill to ease the effect of possible impoundments of $3 billion or $4 billion. The measure, cleared by voice votes Dec. 21, 1973, set an allocation formula under which no state would receive less sewage treatment aid than in fiscal 1972. Nixon signed the bill Jan. 4. The U.S. Court of Appeals in Washington Jan. 24 upheld a 1973 district court ruling that the Administration had been illegally withholding $6 billion in sewage treatment funds for fiscal 1973 and 1974. The appeals court emphasized that it was not ordering that the money be spent but that it be allocated to states so that pollution control projects could be planned. The court said it was expressing no opinion as to whether funds could be impounded at one of the later steps in the spending process. The Supreme Court announced April 29 that it had agreed to decide whether President Nixon had acted illegally on the impoundment issue.

[10] **River nutrients pollution up.** An EPA study of 22 river systems, reported Jan. 18, found significant increases in concentrations of such nutrients as phosphorus and nitrogen in the 1968-72 period compared with the previous five years. At the same time, sewage and other bacterial pollutants—which had been the subject of more stringent control measures—had decreased. The EPA noted that nitrogen and phosphates could enter rivers naturally from land erosion, as well as from industrial sources and detergents. Among the most polluted rivers, the report said, were the Hudson, lower Mississippi, lower Ohio and lower and middle Missouri. The upper Missouri, Columbia, Snake, Willamette, upper Mississippi and lower Colorado were the cleanest.

[11] **Atlantic sludge dumping to continue.** Richard T. Dewling, director of the EPA's surveillance and analysis division, said Feb. 11 that the agency had tentatively decided to continue allowing the dumping of sewage sludge off the New York—New Jersey coast, despite reports that sludge had been found perilously close to Long Island beaches. The EPA disclosed March 22 that it had designated two areas off the New York and New Jersey coasts for dumping sewage sludge as possible replacement sites for the disputed area. The new sites would range up to 70 miles offshore. Dewling said that in response to complaints of shore pollution from the present dumping site, the EPA had begun monitoring beaches in the two states and water surrounding the site.

[12] **Ore plant ordered closed; order overruled.** U.S. District Court Judge Miles W. Lord of Minneapolis April 20 ordered the Reserve Mining Co. to halt discharges of industrial wastes from its Silver Bay iron ore processing plant into Lake Superior and the air. After a trial lasting almost nine months, Lord ruled that asbestos and other fibers in the wastes posed substantial cancer hazards to five communities in Minnesota and Wisconsin using Lake Superior as a drinking water source. The immediate effect of the order was the closing of both the plant, which processed taconite, a low-grade iron ore, and the company's taconite mine inland from the lake. But a three-judge appeals panel, acting on an appeal by the company, issued a temporary stay of Lord's order April 22 and allowed the plant to resume operations pending a hearing May 15. Lord rejected company objections that closing the plant would cause severe economic hardship in the area, ruling that people in Duluth, Minn. should not be "continuously and indefinitely exposed to a known human carcinogen in order that the people in Silver Bay can keep working." Lord also noted that he had repeatedly encouraged the company to devise an alternative method of disposing of the wastes on land. The company had failed to do so, Lord said, and had engaged in delaying tactics while continuing the taconite dumping. The Supreme Court July 9 denied without comment a petition by Minnesota, Michigan and Wisconsin to overrule the appeals court order which had allowed Reserve Mining Co. to continue dumping taconite wastes into Lake Superior.

[13] **Steel industry water rules issued.** The EPA June 14 announced effluent

guidelines for the steel industry, as required by water pollution control legislation passed in 1972. The rules required that new plants meet discharge ceilings when they began operations, and that existing plants meet one set of standards by July 1977 and a stricter set by July 1983. The EPA estimated total capital costs of plant upgrading at $267 million through 1983.

[14] **Drinking water bill cleared.** A $156 million, three-year program to safeguard drinking water was cleared by Congress Dec. 3. Final action was by voice votes in the Senate Nov. 26 and House Dec. 3. President Ford signed the bill Dec. 16. National standards for safe drinking water were to be set at the federal level by the EPA, which could seek compliance by court action if the primary enforcement, assigned to the states, were neglected. The bill also permitted citizen suits against public water systems to gain compliance with the standards. Each state was guaranteed eligibility for at least 1% of the federal grants authorized under the program.

Other Developments

[15] **Pesticides and herbicides.** The EPA said June 24 that because of insufficient evidence of potential harm to humans, it would not press legal motions to ban the herbicide 2,4,5-T, widely used domestically and, according to some evidence, the possible cause of deaths following defoliation operations in South Vietnam. The EPA said its legal challenges were being withdrawn because after more than three years of research, it had found that unreliable analytical techniques were being used. The EPA Nov. 19 proposed a ban on almost all uses of two widely sold pesticides, chlordane and heptachlor, because of their cancer-causing potential. The agency said the pesticides appear to pose "substantial questions of safety amounting to an unreasonable risk to man and the environment."

[16] **Ford scores no-growth approach.** In his first environmental policy message, President Ford said Aug. 15 that the "zero economic growth" approach to conserving natural resources "flies in the face of human nature" and must be compromised to meet economic and energy needs. Ford said the previous winter's energy crisis had demonstrated the need for more coal mining, offshore oil exploration, oil shale development and nuclear power plant construction. Ford contended that meeting energy needs did not mean "that we are changing our unalterable course to improve the environment, and it doesn't mean that we are retreating or giving up the fight." He added, however, that "it does mean stretching the timetable in some cases," adjusting some long-range goals "to accommodate the needs of the immediate present," and some "trade-offs."

[17] **Threats to ozone layer reported.** Two separate studies reported Sept. 26-27 that inert gases used as propellants in widely-used aerosol sprays were chemically broken down by sunlight and acted as a catalyst in destruction of the stratospheric ozone layer, which serves as a shield against harmful ultraviolet rays. The destructive action by these chlorofluoromethane gases added to concern about the essential ozone layer, which was also said to be threatened by nitric oxides from nuclear explosions and supersonic aircraft. The *New York Times* reported Sept. 26 that Harvard University scientists had calculated that even if use of such gases (widely known under the trade name Freon) were halted as soon as practicable, the lingering effects would cause a 5% depletion of ozone by 1990. If use of the gases continued to increase at the present rate, the ozone level would be down 7% by 1984 and 30% by 1994. In a study reported in the Sept. 27 issue of *Science* magazine, three University of Michigan scientists said that if emissions from Freon gases were halted immediately, ozone destruction would peak around 1990 and remain "significant" for several decades afterwards. Dr. Fred Ikle, director of the Arms Control and Disarmament Agency (ACDA), had warned

that a nuclear war might result in the destruction of the ozone layer. Addressing the Council on Foreign Relations in Chicago Sept. 5, Ikle said nuclear explosions produced nitric oxide molecules that interacted with and destroyed the ozone. Six scientists testifying before the Public Health and Environment Subcommittee of the House Commerce Committee Dec. 11 urged Congress to appropriate funds to conduct an intensive study of the potential threat to the earth's ozone shield posed by the aerosol gas Freon.

[18] **Vinyl chloride exposure curbed.** The Labor Department Oct. 1 issued final rules designed to curb workers' exposure to vinyl chloride, a basic material in manufacture of plastic products. The substance, a gas processed from solid polyvinyl chloride, had been shown to induce angiosarcoma, a rare and incurable form of liver cancer. Beginning Jan. 1, 1976, workers would be required to wear respirators if concentrations exceeded a limit of one part per million (ppm) parts of air, averaged over eight hours. During 1975, respirator use would be optional up to 25 ppm. The old limit in effect before the April emergency action had been 500 ppm. The Consumer Product Safety Commission (CPSC) Aug. 16 had announced a ban on the use of vinyl chloride as a propellant in household aerosol sprays. In a series of actions April 3-24 involving other aerosol products containing vinyl chloride, the EPA and the Food & Drug Administration (FDA) had ordered recalls and banned further sales of some brands of cosmetics, medicinal products and deodorants (FDA), and 29 brands of indoor pesticides (EPA). The EPA added five more pesticides to the banned list, it was reported May 29.

[19] **CEQ sees costly pollution fight.** In its fifth annual report issued Dec. 12, the White House Council on Environmental Quality (CEQ) estimated overall national expenditures for pollution control would total $325 billion during 1973-1982, more than $50 billion above the estimate of costs during the 1972-1981 decade. According to the report, prospective expenditures for pollution control efforts attributable only to federal laws would total $194.8 billion for the 1973-1982 decade, including both capital and operating costs.

[20] **Ford pocket vetoes strip-mining bill.** A bill to regulate strip-mining of coal on federal lands was cleared by Congress Dec. 16 and sent to President Ford despite his threat to veto it. President Ford pocket vetoed the bill Dec. 30. Congressional passage had been preceded by a long struggle over the measure in committee. A two-month deadlock had developed in the House-Senate conference over the rights of surface-rights owners. The bill would require the coal companies to obtain the consent of farmers and ranchers with surface rights prior to any mining. A fair market price would be determined by three appraisers, which the land owner could accept or reject. Another controversial feature of the bill was a fee to be applied against all coal mined in the U.S.—strip and underground mining. The fee would be 10% of coal's value at the mine mouth, or 35¢ a ton, whichever was smaller. The revenue was to be used to reclaim the more than a million acres of abandoned stripmined land, to reimburse local communities for adverse mining impact and to build miners' facilities. The bill basically required coal strip mines to prevent environmental damage and restore mine land to its "approximate original contour." President Ford vetoed the bill on the ground it would slow the production of coal "when the nation can ill afford significant losses from this critical energy source" that would increase U.S. dependence on foreign oil.

See also ATOMIC ENERGY [14-20]; AUTOMOBILE INDUSTRY [1, 8, 10]; BUDGET; CONSUMER AFFAIRS [4]; ECONOMY, U.S. [5, 17]; ENERGY CRISIS [26-28, 33, 35]; MEDICINE & HEALTH [21]; NIXON, RICHARD M.; SHIPS & SHIPPING; TERRITORIAL WATERS; UNION OF SOVIET SOCIALIST REPUBLICS [3]; VIETNAM, REPUBLIC OF [39]

EQUAL RIGHTS AMENDMENT—*See* WOMEN'S RIGHTS

ERVIN JR., SEN. SAM J.—*See* CONGRESS; CONSUMER AFFAIRS [2]; ELECTIONS [3]; WATERGATE [43, 62]

ESPIONAGE—*See* BULGARIA; CENTRAL INTELLIGENCE AGENCY; COMMUNISM, INTERNATIONAL; DEFENSE [2-4]; FREEDOM OF INFORMATION ACT; GERMANY, EAST; GERMANY, WEST [1-5]; NEW ZEALAND; OBITUARIES [GOLD]; PRIVACY [12]; THAILAND

ETHIOPIA—Military unrest forces reforms. Mutinies and protests in the Ethiopian army forced the government of Emperor Haile Selassie to undertake a series of drastic reforms during the early part of 1974. A mutiny by troops in Asmara, the country's second largest city, Feb. 26 forced the Emperor's Cabinet to resign. Selassie sought to maintain control by naming a new premier and raising army wages Feb. 28. The mutiny broke out when the 10,000-man 2nd Division of the 46,000-man army seized control of Asmara to press demands for pay increases, better living conditions and the resignation of several ministers from the Cabinet of Premier Aklilou Habte Wold. The mutineers claimed that Aklilou had failed to control inflation. He and 19 other ministers resigned Feb. 27 and Selassie appointed former United Nations Ambassador Endalkachew Makonnen premier Feb. 28. Selassie also announced appointment of a new army commander, Lt. Gen. Selassie Berebe, and a new minister of defense, Lt. Gen. Abiye Abebe. According to press reports March 1, rebel forces had imposed "a form of martial law" in Addis Ababa and were stopping cars to check identity papers, in a reported effort to keep former Cabinet ministers from leaving the country. The army uprising followed a week of civilian rioting in Addis Ababa during which five persons were killed and almost 1,000 arrested, according to the *London Times* Feb. 24. Although a curfew imposed March 1 was lifted March 4, and troops had generally withdrawn from Addis Ababa by March 2, military and civilian protests continued, culminating in a general strike March 7, the first in the nation's history. The Confederation of Ethiopian Labor Unions, representing 80,000-100,000 members, called the strike after it had rejected an offer by Premier Endalkachew to take its demands under consideration. The union said the strike would continue until its demands were met. The strike was called to press demands for a trebling of the minimum wage to $1.50 a day, pension plans, a social security system, protection from the rising cost of living, and the right to strike. Public transportation, airports, docks and unionized industries ceased to function and, as a result, many non-unionized enterprises came to a standstill. The strike ended March 11 after the government agreed to act on the 16 demands submitted March 7. Price controls, educational reforms, the right to strike and a review of the minimum wage level were among the government's concessions.

[2] **Reform program begun.** Selassie agreed March 5 to call a constitutional convention that could lead to the replacement of his absolute monarchy by a more democratic government. In a television broadcast March 5, the emperor called for constitutional reforms to make the premier "responsible to Parliament" and to further "define and clarify the institutional relationships between different branches of the imperial Ethiopian government." Under the current Constitution, adopted in 1955, the emperor had almost absolute power. Selassie's proposals were followed April 8 by further programs announced by the government. The program, in the form of a White Paper, the first of its kind ever issued in Ethiopia, envisaged a constitutional monarchy and stressed Ethiopia's adherence to the nonaligned nations movement. On the issue of land reform, a "land-to-the-tiller" policy was adopted, although the means by which the policy was to be implemented was not specified.

[3] **Strikes multiply, economy threatened.** In spite of the promised reforms, a wave of strikes continued through April as transportation, telecommunication and hospital workers, journalists and students caused a series of disturbances. Religious dissension was added to the general unrest April 20 when as many as 50,000 Moslems demonstrated in Addis Ababa to demand an end to religious discrimination. They said Ethiopia should become a secular state and called for equal participation in administration. None of the country's 14 provincial governor's was Moslem and there were no Moslem army generals, they pointed out. (Although no official figures existed, it was estimated that about half of Ethiopia's 26 million people were Moslems.) As violent demonstrations and strikes continued to threaten stability in the crisis-torn country, Premier Endalkachew said April 19 that he might have to declare a national state of emergency. Acceding to military pressure, Makonnen announced April 18 that security forces had been ordered to place Cabinet ministers of the former government under house arrest. Arrests began with a series of raids April 26 in Addis Ababa. Police and armed forces units arrested more than 200 civilian and military officers, whom they cited for corruption. Among those arrested April 26 who were held in 4th Division headquarters were former Premier Aklilou, ousted army Deputy Chief of Staff Lt. Gen. Haile Baikedagne, ousted Police Commissioner Lt. Gen. Yilma Shibeshi, the former commander of the emperor's bodyguard and the former ministers of commerce, information, justice and the interior. Communications Minister Assefa Ayene was reported arrested May 2, the first member of the present Ethiopian Cabinet affected by the anti-corruption purges mounted by the army.

[4] **Addis Ababa under military control.** The army's 4th Division seized virtual control of Addis Ababa June 28, taking over the country's two radio stations and beginning a new round of arrests of prominent persons. Troops maintained their loyalty to Selassie and declared June 29 that their actions were being taken "to find a solution to the problems of the whole country." No fighting was reported, but the Imperial Bodyguard cordoned off the emperor's residence July 2. Troops arrested more than 80 prominent Ethiopians, including some of the emperor's closest associates, in Addis Ababa June 28—July 16 and were seeking some 200 other conservatives whom they wanted to bring to trial for "corruption, maladministration and misuse of authority." The Armed Forces Committee (AFC) said July 4 that the arrests were being carried out with Selassie's consent. The Committee released a list July 3 of 27 high officials whose arrest was sought. By July 18, 25 of the 27 had either given up or been arrested. Defense Minister Abiye surrendered to 4th Division troops July 16. The surrender July 12 of Ras (duke) Mesfin Sileshi, reputed to be the richest man in Ethiopia after the emperor and one of Selassie's closest associates, removed the threat that an armed movement would be assembled to oust the reformist troops. As president of the powerful Patriotic Association and one of the country's largest landholders, the duke had under his command a provincial force of some 50,000 men. (Military forces numbered about 60,000, according to a July 8 report.)

[5] **Endalkachew ousted.** Amid moves by the armed forces to strengthen their control over the government, Endalkachew was ousted as premier July 22. A military commentary broadcast July 24 said that Endalkachew shared responsibility for the government's failures to implement reforms and would face the same charges as other officials arrested in recent weeks. Michael Imru, a relative of the emperor, was named July 22 to replace Endalkachew The new premier had held a Cabinet post but had been in Geneva since May as head of the Ethiopian mission to the United Nations there. Endalkachew was arrested by

the military Aug. 1 after being under house arrest since his ouster as premier. Also arrested were nine other prominent figures, including a royal adviser, three generals and two Supreme Court judges.

[6] **New Constitution drafted, emperor weakened.** A 30-member panel appointed in March presented the draft of a new Consitution to Premier Michael Aug. 6. The proposed charter would bring Ethiopia closer to a constitutional monarchy, providing for a premier elected by and responsible to Parliament and establishing a system of governmental checks and balances. (Under the present Constitution, the premier was appointed by the emperor.) Michael said the draft would be submitted to Emperor Haile Selassie after being studied by the new provisional Cabinet approved by the emperor Aug. 3. The new Cabinet contained 12 members of the previous government of Endalkachew.

[7] The emperor's Crown Council, Court of Justice and military committee were abolished by the AFC Aug. 16. The military committee was transferred to the Ministry of Defense in order to integrate the Imperial Bodyguard with the other armed forces entities. The Imperial Bodyguard had been considered the sole military faction loyal to the emperor. However, a number of guards participated in an unannounced parade of military troops and equipment through the capital Aug. 16. The show of strength, which included repeated flyovers by U.S.-provided jet fighters, was seen as a warning to the shrinking opposition to the AFC and its program of reforms. On Aug. 25 the AFC announced that the emperor's residence, the Jubilee Palace, had been nationalized and renamed the National Palace. The emperor's other estates in the country's 14 provinces were also nationalized, as was the National Resources Co., which owned millions of dollars worth of real estate throughout the country. The Ethiopian Transport Co. was nationalized Aug. 27, with the AFC accusing the shareholders, most of whom were related to the emperor, of using it to enrich themselves illegally. In an Aug. 27 announcement, the AFC said the emperor had been ordered not to leave the capital, a directive that was tantamount to house arrest, diplomatic sources acknowledged. The committee had abolished the Ministry of the Imperial Court Aug. 25 and placed the palace under the authority of a government-appointed manager. The criticism being directed against the monarchy heightened Aug. 27 when a report was released which implicated the emperor in the government cover-up of the drought that claimed the lives of more than 100,000 peasants in 1973.

[8] **58 years of rule by Selassie ended.** Emperor Haile Selassie, who ruled Ethiopia for 58 years, was peacefully deposed Sept. 12 by the AFC, which said the 82-year-old monarch had been taken to a palace in Debre Zeit, 19 miles outside Addis Ababa, for his "personal safety." Confronted with the deposition, Selassie, who had ruled as regent since 1916 before being crowned emperor in 1930, was quoted by a military spokesman as saying: "I accept the present change in Ethiopia and acknowledge that such changes are also taking place elsewhere in the world." The AFC asked the emperor's only son, Crown Prince Asfa Wossen, to return to Ethiopia and be crowned as a figurehead with no powers, thus preserving—at least in name—the 2,000-year-old monarchy. The crown prince had lived in Geneva since suffering a stroke that left him partially paralyzed in 1972. Demonstrations and strikes were banned and tanks assumed positions at key points in the capital where all remained calm. Parliament was dissolved and the Constitution suspended. It was announced that a provisional military government would rule until elections were held. Lt. Gen. Aman Michael Andom, defense minister in the outgoing civilian government and chief of staff of the armed forces, was named head of the Cabinet; he would also retain his military and ministerial posts. Michael Imru, premier in the outgoing

government, was named minister of information; Zewde Gabre-Selassie would continue as foreign minister, the committee said. The AFC announced a domestic policy pledging equality for all Ethiopians and promised that land reform would be given priority. The nation, according to the AFC, would continue a foreign policy of non-alignment.

[9] **Post coup developments.** The military government encountered its first vocalized opposition Sept. 16 when 1,000 students sought to demonstrate in the capital to call for creation of a civilian government. The armed forces blocked the demonstration but permitted a rally to be held in a university stadium. A violent demonstration against the government was broken up Sept. 19. Tanks had been withdrawn from Addis Ababa Sept. 13. Gen. Aman held his first press conference Sept. 20 and said the fate of Selassie would be left "up to the Ethiopian people to decide what to do with him." Shooting erupted between rival military factions in Addis Ababa Oct. 7 when tanks and armored vehicles were sent to the army engineering corps barracks to arrest leftist officers considered too radical by the Provisional Military Government. Several persons were reported killed or wounded.

[10] **Famine conditions.** Wollo Province, where more than 100,000 persons were reported to have starved to death in 1973, had been declared a disaster area and placed under martial law Aug. 30. A bill, passed by wide majorities in both houses of Parliament, placed the entire province under the administration of the Relief and Rehabilitation Commission which was set up to deal with the drought that now threatened more than half the country. A Harar Province official said Oct. 18 that one million people faced starvation in 12 of the eastern province's 13 districts. A grave water shortage also threatened, particularly in the Dagabur district, where more than one-third of the estimated 300,000 inhabitants lacked adequate water supplies. As much as $2.50 was being charged for a barrel of water in that district, he said, and more than 80% of the cattle and camels had succumbed, depriving the nomadic population of its livelihood. According to a *Washington Post* report Oct. 23, almost total crop failure was observed in parts of northern Eritrea, Ethiopia's northernmost province. Complicating the relief efforts was an emerging dispute between Ethiopian and international relief agencies over the nature and extent of the crisis. Most international relief groups were closing down their emergency feeding stations in Ethiopia, according to an Oct. 23 *Washington Post* report, in the wake of the dispute and other pressing international demands for assistance. A serious factor was Addis Ababa's reported reluctance to tap its available resources—including over $300 million in gold and foreign exchange holdings—to purchase grain for relief.

[11] **60 former officials executed.** The provisional military government announced Nov. 24 the execution Nov. 23 of 60 former officials, including Lt. Gen. Aman who was ousted Nov. 23 as head of the 120-member ruling military council; former Premiers Endalkachew and Aklilu; and Rear Adm. Esikinder Desta, former naval commander and grandson of Selassie. No statement was issued on the status of Selassie himself. The executions were announced over a government radio broadcast which described the step as "an act of justice." Most of those executed had been declared responsible for the cover-up of the famine in Wollo Province where more than 100,000 had reportedly died. Others, the broadcast said, had been found "guilty of outrage to incite civil war and disrupt Ethiopia's popular movement and of attempts to... plunge the country into a blood bath." The death of Gen. Aman, 51, aparently established Maj. Mengistu Haile Mariam, 36, as the effective leading power in the country. Mengistu's identity had been publicly revealed for the first time Nov. 17 when he was identified as first vice chairman of the provisional military council and head of

its inner Cabinet. According to Reuters reports, Aman had been involved in a power struggle with Mengistu and was placed under house arrest Nov. 22 after he refused to sign an order dispatching 5,000 troops to his native Eritrea Province where separatist activities were mounting.

[12] The 120-member Provisional Military Administrative Committee, known as the Dergue, Nov. 28 elected Brig. Gen. Teferi Benti, 53, to serve as its chairman, filling the post left vacant by Aman's death. Teferi, a relatively obscure general who was not himself a member of the Dergue, would serve, officials indicated, as a powerless figurehead and carry out the military council's decisions, the *Washington Post* reported Nov. 28. He was believed to be popular with the 2nd and 3rd army divisions garrisoned in Eritrea and Harar Provinces, within which potential opposition was seen to the 4th division Addis Ababa units which carried out the mass executions Nov. 23. The Dergue also announced Dec. 6 a shuffle of 14 top civilian and military posts, a move apparently aimed at purging opponents. Foreign Minister Zewde, a cousin of the deposed emperor, was relieved of his post and replaced by Kifle Wodajo, ambassador to Washington. In a New York press conference at the United Nations that day, Zewde said he did not plan to return to Ethiopia for the time being.

[13] **Selassie cedes fortune; fate unclear.** The military government announced Nov. 30 that Selassie had signed a letter authorizing the transfer of "all his personal and family fortune," estimated unofficially at $1.5 billion, to aid victims of Ethiopia's devastating drought and famine. Though the Dergue said Selassie had signed over his fortune, most of which was believed in Swiss banks, "of his own free will," diplomats speculated that he was bargaining for his life. Amid rumors that the Dergue was planning the execution of the deposed emperor and others in detention, the military council Dec. 3 issued a statement guaranteeing that all would receive humane treatment and fair trials. Responding to the Nov. 23 summary executions, the United Nations General Assembly had addressed a "solemn appeal" to the Dergue Nov. 27 to spare the lives of those presently in detention. The Organization of African Unity issued a similar appeal, it was reported Nov. 30. The ruling military council announced Dec. 20 that Ethiopia would become a socialist state with major industrial nationalizations, farm collectivization and a one-party system. The 120-man military committee said the sole political organization, to be called the Supreme Progressive Council, would have as its goal "national progressive unity." On Dec. 21 the military council launched its rural development program with a rally in Addis Ababa attended by tens of thousands of university undergraduates, high school students and teachers who were to be sent into the countryside to help collectivize farms and eradicate "alcohol, luxury, prostitution and illiteracy."

[14] **Eritrean rebellion continues.** The Moslem separatist movement in the province of Eritrea continued its rebellion against the central government during 1974, clashing with government troops before and after the new military government took power in Addis Ababa. The Eritrean Liberation Front (ELF) abducted an American nurse, Deborah Dortzbach, from a provincial hospital in Ghinda May 27. A Dutch nurse seized at the same time died during a forced march following the abduction. Dortzbach, who was six months pregnant, was later released. Twenty-three Eritrean members of the Ethiopian Chamber of Deputies resigned Aug. 16 to protest the government's alleged neglect of the province. They charged that Eritrean prisoners had not been released under a July 3 amnesty and said the military was conducting massacres in the province. Premier Michael called for a "peaceful dialogue" with the ELF Aug. 20 as a step toward improving the province's relations with the central government.

[15] Ethiopian government troops, backed by air force jets and artillery, were fighting large-scale battles against ELF rebels, it was reported Oct. 17. Government aircraft had begun raids on rebel sites Oct. 15, according to an Agence France-Presse report which also noted that three army battalions had been sent to the northern region of Eritrea Province. Sustained combat was reportedly taking place just outside the provincial capital, Asmara. ELF leader Osman Saleh Sabbe said Oct. 15 that the movement was making efforts to broaden Arab and European support for an independent Eritrea. He revealed that Saudi Arabia, Kuwait and Abu Dhabi were providing the ELF with "material support." The military government was reportedly concentrating troops in Eritrea Province, with two brigades of about 5,000 men under orders to join the 2nd Division troops already stationed there, according to a Nov. 27 report. A dispute over the way in which the secessionist movement in Eritrea would be dealt with had figured significantly in the developments leading to the death of Lt. Gen. Aman. The recent troop reinforcements indicated that a hard-line position, maintained by Dergue Vice Chairman Maj. Mengistu had prevailed, leading to speculation that a full-scale guerrilla war could emerge.

See also AFRICA; APPOINTMENTS & RESTRICTIONS; ARCHEOLOGY; FAMINE & FOOD

EUROPEAN COAL & STEEL COMMUNITY—*See* TARIFFS & TRADE

EUROPEAN ECONOMIC COMMUNITY (EEC)

Agricultural Policy & Developments

[1] **Farm prices to rise 8.5%.** Agricultural ministers of the member governments of the European Economic Community agreed in Brussels March 23 on an average 8.5% increase in minimum guaranteed price supports for farmers in 1974-75. Britain's new Labor government was granted special concessions permitting subsidies that would protect British consumers. The increases, backdated to March 1, were agreed upon at the three-day meeting that ended March 23 after several earlier unsuccessful bargaining sessions. The higher support prices, which meant that EEC Commission officials would intervene to buy surpluses at a higher price level, were lower than most commodity prices in the current open market so that intervention was necessary in only a few cases.

[2] **Beef imports banned temporarily.** EEC agriculture ministers July 16 approved a ban on most imports of beef from nonmember countries until Nov. 1. The action would replace the current program under which beef importers had to match purchases from abroad with purchases from EEC stockpiles. An earlier temporary curb on French and Italian beef imports had been instituted Feb. 20 and extended to Belgium and Luxembourg two days later, but the measure had expired at the end of March. The ministers, meeting in Brussels, also approved other measures, including sales of beef to poor persons at cut-rate prices; special premiums on a monthly rising scale to farmers for delaying slaughter of their cattle until February, when supply was normally lowest.

[3] **Farmers' protests.** The agricultural ministers' decisions came after mounting demonstrations by cattle raisers and farmers in France and Belgium to press demands for aid to bolster their sagging incomes. Aside from the import of cheap agricultural products, the farmers were protesting the restriction on prices for their own goods under anti-inflation programs, coupled with soaring production costs, particularly sharp increases in the cost of farm machinery. Belgian farmers argued that the action by the EEC ministers failed to help other livestock producers or crop farmers.

[4] **France, Belgium act to calm farmers.** In the face of the continuing wave of

farmers' unrest, France and Belgium took separate government actions to aid their agricultural sectors after the EEC ministerial decisions July 16. The French Cabinet approved an "immediate salvage plan" July 17, which provided price support measures, including subsidies for livestock producers, storage aids for cheese farmers, grants to egg producers and credits to farmers hit by soaring production costs. (The French government July 12 had increased by 12% the threshold price for lamb and mutton imports, a move designed to halt cheap imports.) EEC Commissioner for Agriculture Pierre Lardinois announced Aug. 1 that the Commission had initiated legal proceedings against the French government over its agricultural measures. He said the subsidies violated EEC free trade rules. In Belgium, amid continuing farmers' protests, the government July 31 approved a $40 million plan that would reduce farmers' taxes and provide direct government payments for meat producers and farmers in the poorer rural districts.

[5] **Bonn accepts 5% farm price hike.** European Community foreign and agricultural ministers reached agreement Oct. 2 on an interim special 5% increase in the community's minimum guaranteed prices for its farmers, resolving a crisis threatened by a West German government veto of the hike. The 5% increase was in addition to the 8.5% granted in March. At an emergency meeting in Luxembourg, Bonn agreed to the 5% price boost, retroactive to Oct. 1. In return, the other ministers agreed to the West German demand of an overall study of the strengths and deficiencies of the EEC's agricultural policy, with a view toward eventual reform of the system. The European Commission Oct. 21 announced measures aimed at cutting consumption and exports of grain in anticipation of reduced cereal imports from the U.S.

Energy & Financial Crisis

[6] **Britain ends veto on energy action.** Britain Jan. 30 lifted its procedural veto blocking formulation of a common energy policy for the EEC. British Foreign Secretary Sir Alec Douglas-Home, announcing the move at a meeting of the nine EEC foreign ministers in Brussels, said it was designed "to get things moving again" in a wide range of community business, including the deadlocked regional aid fund for economically backward areas. Britain had previously said that progress toward creating the regional fund was a condition for moving toward a common energy policy. The British concession followed one by West Germany Jan. 23 that more than doubled their previous proposal for the total amount of the fund—to 1.4 billion units of account for three years (1 UA equals $1 U.S. before the 1971 devaluation), still substantially less than what the Commission or Britain had proposed. The end of the British procedural veto came amid growing concern over divisiveness in the community. The EEC Commission issued an unprecedented declaration Jan. 31 warning that the community was in a state of crisis because of its inability to reach agreements on such issues as monetary, energy and regional aid policy.

[7] **Arabs offered cooperation plan.** The EEC offered March 4 to explore long-term economic, technical and cultural cooperation with 20 Arab nations. The joint offer was approved at a meeting of EEC foreign ministers in Brussels. The pro-Arab move omitted mention of cooperation on political and oil questions. According to reports, France had wanted to include those issues. Three initial steps were envisaged as part of the plan: diplomatic contacts in Bonn between the Arabs and West German Foreign Minister Walter Scheel, current president of the EEC Council of Ministers; establishment of joint working groups to discuss possible areas of cooperation; and eventually an EEC-Arab ministerial meeting. (A permanent joint commission was formed by the EEC and the Arab League in Paris July 31 to begin work on the program.)

[8] **Community to back joint oil loans.** The finance ministers of the EEC, meeting in Luxembourg, agreed Oct. 21 to apply for a joint loan of up to $3 billion, mainly from oil-producing countries, to help members cover balance of payments deficits caused by soaring costs of oil imports. The $3 billion figure, including principle and interest, would be for a minimum of five years. The nine members would jointly guarantee the loans, with the three big powers—France, West Germany and Britain—each assuming 22% responsibility for loans by any member. In case of multiple defaults, each member woud gurantee a maximum of double its normal share.

[9] **10-year energy goals set.** European Community energy ministers Dec. 17 decided on joint objectives for energy use by 1985. They agreed to reduce the 10-year growth in their nations' domestic energy consumption from a projected 50% to 35% and to cut dependence on imported energy supplies from the 1973 level of 63% to 40%-50%. The plan called for reducing the share of oil in energy production from 61% to 41%-49%, through increased use of nuclear power and natural gas. Among other actions, the ministers agreed to require oil companies to report twice a year on their energy imports and decided to create a joint fund of nearly $50 million to encourage oil exploration and development in Europe. Britain stressed it would cooperate on a joint energy policy but insisted it would retain full national control of its North Sea oil and natural gas resources. The statement on energy goals came out well after an EEC summit meeting in Paris declared that the nine nations were prepared to negotiate with the oil producing countries. No specific terms were disclosed.

Renegotiation of Britain's Membership

[10] **Labor government sets demands.** Foreign Secretary James Callaghan, in his first major foreign policy address for Britain's new Labor government, told the House of Commons March 19 that Britain would not seek a confrontation with the EEC in trying to renegotiate its membership terms. But he warned that Britain would not "carry forward further processes of integration" of the community pending the outcome of its talks. Britain would seek satisfaction of its needs within the existing community rules, he said, and would raise the question of amending the EEC's basic Treaty of Rome only if Britain's demands were not met. The government's two major goals in renegotiation would be wider access to European markets for traditional food suppliers such as Australia, New Zealand, the U.S. and Argentina and a reduction in Britain's contribution to the EEC budget. French Foreign Minister Michel Jobert, speaking to Gaullist members of the National Assembly March 17, had rejected Britain's right to renegotiate its EEC membership terms, but said "there can be adaptation to passing conditions for this or that country."

[11] On April 1, on the first day of a two-day meeting of foreign ministers in Luxembourg, Callaghan reiterated his warnings, saying that unless "certain errors were put right" in Britain's membership terms, the government would seek a national referendum to authorize Britain's withdrawal from the community. If renegotiations were successful, he said, the British public would be asked to register approval for continued membership.

[12] **Party stiffens terms.** At its annual conference in London Nov. 27-30, the Labor Party overrode government leadership and adopted a resolution setting stringent demands for Britain's continued membership in the European Community. It called for revisions in the EEC's basic treaty, a move opposed by all other community members, and demanded the right of the British Parliament to reject any EEC orders, to control the entry of workers into Britain, determine its own taxation policy and nationalize any company operating there.

[13] **EEC Paris summit on problem.** Leaders of the nine EEC countries held a

formal summit meeting in Paris Dec. 9-10 and moved toward compromise on the divisive issue of Britain's terms of membership. The summit asked the European commission to devise a "corrective mechanism" that could ease financial burdens of membership for countries in economic difficulty. The issue had sparked a bitter exchange between French President Valery Giscard d'Estaing and British Prime Minister Harold Wilson, with the French president objecting to Britain's demands for a cut in its contribution to the community budget. The European leaders also gave final approval to a development fund for depressed regions, agreed to meet three times a year and agreed to suspend the rule of unanimity on decisions not considered vital to any member's national interest.

Relations with U.S. and Other Countries

[14] **Kissinger backs consultation offer.** En route to Moscow for talks with Soviet leaders, Secretary of State Henry A. Kissinger stopped in West Germany March 24 to confer with Chancellor Willy Brandt and Foreign Minister Walter Scheel. Kissinger said later he had "welcomed" recent proposals by the West German government to strengthen consultation between the U.S. and the EEC and had encouraged Bonn to pursue the ideas with its European partners. The West German proposal called for a U.S. representative to meet regularly with the EEC's political consultation committee, which prepares important decision papers for the community's ministers. German officials had discussed the proposal with French government aides in Paris March 20 and with Britain's Foreign Minister Callaghan in Bonn March 22. (French Foreign Minister Jobert April 2 vetoed the German plan.

[15] **U.S. accepts tariff cut offer.** The U.S. and the EEC announced agreement May 31 on European tariff cuts to compensate the U.S. for trade losses resulting from the enlargement of the EEC in 1973. The accord, reached after 18 months of sometimes bitter negotiations, averted a threatened trade war between the U.S. and the community in which the U.S. threatened to take retaliatory tariff action. William D. Eberle, Nixon's special representative for trade negotiations, said the tariff cuts would affect U.S. agricultural and industrial exports worth $750 million-$1 billion. The tariff cuts, some effective immediately and others to take effect in stages starting Jan. 1, 1975, covered more than 20 products, including tobacco (cut from 15% to 14%), oranges (reduced from 15% to rates ranging from 13-4% depending on the season), excavating equipment (cut from 11% to 9%); kraft paper (cut in stages from 12% to 8% by 1979) and grapefruit.

[16] **Trade & aid talks with developing nations.** The EEC and 44 developing nations, in ministerial-level talks held in Kingston, Jamaica July 25-27, agreed on key principles to govern their future trade relations. Participants in the talks included the African nations associated with the EEC under the Yaounde Convention and independent Commonwealth countries deemed eligible for association in Britain's treaty of accession to the EEC. Agreement was reached on the broad lines of a plan to stabilize export commodity earnings of the 44 developing nations, with the EEC to compensate for any drop in world prices below agreed reference prices.

[17] EEC development aid ministers agreed Oct. 3 to jointly contribute $150 million to aid the 25 developing nations worst hit by the quadrupled price of oil imports. The decision was reached at a meeting in Luxembourg. The EEC would give $30 million to the United Nations emergency fund set up for this purpose, while the remaining $120 million would go directly to the affected countries.

[18] **Australian accord on tariff cuts.** After 18 months of negotiations under the auspices of the General Agreement on Tariffs and Trade, agreement was reached

between the Australian government and the EEC on a package of tariff reductions and other concessions to compensate Australia for the loss of concessions in Britain, Denmark and Ireland as a result of the expansion of the community in 1973, it was reported July 31. Australia's existing tariff concessions to the original six EEC members would be extended to the nine-member community and supplementary arrangements would affect about $A240 million of Australian exports.

[19] **Greek association pact reactivated.** The EEC Dec. 2 reactivated its association agreement with Greece which had been suspended because of the 1967 Greek military coup. EEC foreign ministers agreed to release $56.7 million in unspent financial aid and to open talks with the new Greek government on additional financial aid and agriculture cooperation. Greek Coordination Minister Panayotis Papaligouras told newsmen he had told the ministers that Greece wanted full membership in the EEC "as soon as possible."

See also CANADA [32]; DENMARK; FAMINE & FOOD; GREAT BRITAIN [3]; GREECE [2, 6]; ITALY [6-7]; MIDDLE EAST [23, 26]; MONETARY DEVELOPMENTS; NORTH ATLANTIC TREATY ORGANIZATION; OIL [27]; SPAIN; URUGUAY

EUROPEAN SECURITY—The Conference on Security and Cooperation in Europe resumed in Geneva Jan. 15 after a holiday recess. The 35 nations attending the conference were: Austria, Belgium, Bulgaria, Canada, Cyprus, Czechoslovakia, Denmark, East Germany, Finland, France, Great Britain, Greece, Hungary, Iceland, Ireland, Italy, Liechtenstein, Luxembourg, Malta, Monaco, Netherlands, Norway, Poland, Portugal, Rumania, San Marino, Spain, Sweden, Switzerland, Turkey, U.S.S.R., U.S., Vatican, West Germany and Yugoslavia. The Conference adjourned April 5 after achieving a last-minute success with a preliminary agreement on the principle of frontier inviolability. Moscow hailed the frontier agreement and stressed its significance with the claim that "peace in Europe is dependent upon it." (The West accepted the inviolability principle, the *New York Times* reported April 24, after the Bonn delegation at the talks withdrew a clause that would have asserted the right to peaceful change of borders through negotiation, thus making future reunification of the two Germanys possible; the present agreement would insure a divided Germany.) The meeting resumed April 23, with no progress in the following weeks. According to the *New York Times* May 26, the West had expected Soviet concessions on human rights issues in exchange for having met Soviet frontier inviolability demands. However, by adjournment July 26, a compromise agreement had been reached calling for acceptance of the explicitly-stated principle of sovereignty, a determination which appeased both Eastern and Western parties at the conference. The Conference resumed full-scale negotiations in Geneva Sept. 9 and recessed Dec. 20 with optimism expressed by both Eastern and Western delegations that the talks could conclude in 1975 with the summit conference advocated by the Soviet bloc. (The Soviets had advocated the summit meeting to ratify the final documents issued as a result of the negotiations. The West had initially demanded Soviet concessions on human rights in exchange for such a meeting.) Western sources at the talks said Nov. 28 that the Soviet Union had joined in a tentative agreement to facilitate emigration to help reunite families separated by frontiers.

The conference on reduction of forces in Central Europe resumed Jan. 17 in Vienna. The Netherlands delegate, acting as a spokesman for the Western nations at the conference, had said Jan. 14 that the members of the North Atlantic Treaty Organization (NATO) still supported an initial reduction by U.S. and Soviet troops alone, limited to ground forces. The Czechoslovak delegate told a news conference Jan. 17 that the Warsaw Pact countries continued to insist that the initial reductions should include troops of all 11 participating governments, and should cover nuclear and air forces as well. NATO had called for an eventual reduction of 225,000 Warsaw Pact troops in return for a 77,000-troop NATO reduction, to achieve a mutual level of 700,000 troops, with smaller cuts in the first stage. The Warsaw Pact nations had called for an equal percentage reduction by both sides. The 11 full participants were the U.S., Canada, Britain, Belgium, Luxembourg, the Netherlands, West Germany, the U.S.S.R., Poland, Czechoslovakia and East Germany. In addition, eight nations on the periphery of Central Europe attended as observers. They were Norway, Denmark, Italy, Greece, Turkey, Hungary, Bulgaria and Rumania. The conference recessed April 9 with Eastern and Western participants entrenched in the positions they had reiterated in January. The talks resumed in May but recessed again July 17 without having reconciled conflicting views. The talks began again in Vienna Sept. 24.

See also COMMUNISM, INTERNATIONAL; DISARMAMENT; FRANCE [10]; GERMANY, WEST [5, 15]; ICELAND; NORTH ATLANTIC TREATY ORGANIZATION; UNION OF SOVIET SOCIALIST REPUBLICS [2]

EVERS, CHARLES—*See* CRIME [17]

EXPORT-IMPORT BANK—*See* APPOINTMENTS & RESIGNATIONS; BANKS & BANKING; NARCOTICS & DANGEROUS DRUGS; RUMANIA; SOUTH AFRICA [13]; UNION OF SOVIET SOCIALIST REPUBLICS [5, 7, 8]; ZAIRE

FAIRNESS DOCTRINE—*See* TELEVISION & RADIO

FAMINE & FOOD—Massive famines predicted. Dr. Norman E. Borlaug, Nobel Peace Prize-winning developer of high-yield grains, warned that 20 million people in developing countries might die in the next year as a result of fertilizer shortages and climate shifts, it was reported Jan. 26. Borlaug said Arab oil cutbacks had drastically curtailed fertilizer production, which required heavy energy use and which used petroleum by-products as a base. Japan had cut nitrate fertilizer output by half since the oil crisis began in October 1973. Most of the deficit was expected to hit India, Indonesia and Southeast Asia. A worldwide southward migration of monsoon rains was reported to be a major factor in droughts in West Africa, India and Latin America, according to a Jan. 24-25 meeting of climate and food experts at the Rockefeller Foundation in New York.

Sub-Sahara drought worsens. Addeke H. Boerma, director general of the Food and Agriculture Organization (FAO) of the United Nations, said Jan. 23 that the drought in the sub-Sahara region of West Africa was worse than at the same time in 1973. He warned that pledges of aid received so far would not be enough to prevent widespread starvation and malnutrition. The nations most affected were Mauritania, Mali, Senegal, Upper Volta, Niger and Chad, with large stretches of northern Nigeria also affected.

U.S. increases drought aid. The U.S. Agency for International Development said Feb. 4 that U.S. aid to the Sahel region in West Africa would total $81 million in 1974, in addition to $47 million spent in 1973. About $20 million would be spent for rehabilitation, including construction of food warehouses as a first step. (The Sahel was a 2,600-mile semi-desert strip across Africa below the Sahara.)

Drought and famine unrelenting. As many as 100,000 persons were estimated to have died and millions more were starving in the drought-stricken Sahel. The deaths were estimated in *Disaster in the Desert,* a report issued March 3 by the Carnegie Endowment for International Peace. The League of Red Cross Societies issued an appeal March 8 for renewed efforts to help save the two million people, mostly of the cattle-breeding Tuareg tribe, starving in Niger alone. Drought was also taking a heavy toll in eastern Africa. A March 20 *Washington Post* report cited more than 4 million Ethiopian drought victims whose fate was made more precarious by the attempts of the recently overthrown

Cabinet to conceal the devastation and famine plaguing the country. United Nations sources reported that at least 100,000 had perished in 1973 in the drought-stricken northern provinces of Tigre and Wollo. Throughout the Sahel and eastern Africa, a number of problems, chiefly the embryonic state of transportation and communications infrastructures, were thwarting attempts to provide relief.

Rains hit Sahel drought belt. The sub-Saharan Sahel region of western Africa, stricken by drought for six years, was being swept by heavy rains, an FAO spokesman said in Rome Aug. 22. The rains caused floods which forced thousands of persons to flee their homes and obstructed relief efforts by destroying roads and isolating villages. The FAO estimated that over 3.5 million head of cattle had perished in the region in 1973. Estimates of the human death toll ranged from tens of thousands to one million in the six main Sahel states. Estimates on refugees ranged from 250,000 to five million. International relief workers, cited by the *New York Times* July 15, said the grain needs of the region totaled about 3.5 million tons a year. Before the drought had begun, the region produced about 2.5 million tons of grain and imported about one million tons annually. Major pledges of grain during November 1973-October 1974 were made, according to the report, by: the U.S., 216,769 tons; the European Economic Community, 110,000; France, 74,000; West Germany, 35,000; World Food Program, 33,957; Belgium, 13,400; Denmark, 13,000; Britain, 10,000; the Soviet Union, 10,000; North Korea, 8,000; Hungary, 5,000; and Sweden, 3,500.

U.N. food conference. The 10-day United Nations World Food Conference opened in Rome Nov. 5, attended by more than 1,000 governmental and private delegates from 130 countries. U.S. Secretary of State Henry Kissinger, addressing the conference Nov. 5, set as its objective that "within a decade no child will go to bed hungry, that no family will fear for its next day's bread, and that no human being's future and capacities will be stunted by malnutrition." This objective would require at least a minimum doubling of food production in the next 25 years, and improvement of its quality, he said. Kissinger called on the conference to organize a reserves coordinating group, composed of all major exporters and importers, to negotiate an international system of nationally held grain reserves. An information system to share data on reserves, working stocks and crop prospects, should be established, he said. Kissinger also proposed preference for nations that contributed in the distribution of reserves, and sanctions against those refusing to cooperate. Kissinger also emphasized the "special responsibility" of prosperous oil exporting nations to extend aid to poor nations hardest hit by soaring petroleum prices over the last year. U.S. Agriculture Secretary Earl Butz, in his address to the conference Nov. 6, implicitly called into question Kissinger's proposals for world food reserves. Butz said no grains currently existed for "an internationally coordinated" food stockpile, unless citizens of developed nations paid more to eat less. However, he held out hopes of "substantially larger production" as a result of the opportunity for the farmer "to gain increased returns from the market." Although he indicated willingness to accept a future reserves system, he said he opposed reserves of such a size that they would depress prices, destroy farmer incentives and mask deficiencies in national production efforts. Butz, as well as Kissinger, ran into considerable opposition from other members of the U.S. delegation, who, according to news reports, wanted the U.S. to make a firm commitment on additional food aid. The Ford Administration wanted to avoid specific figures, according to a senior member of the delegation, because it would drive up commercial grain prices in the U.S. In another dispute, Sen. Mark O. Hatfield (R, Ore.), one of the Congressional advisers, was reported to have said at a delegation strategy session

Nov. 6 that Americans should reduce their consumption of food, particularly meat, to help make more available for starving persons around the world. Butz countered that reducing U.S. meat consumption would not effectively divert grain to developing nations. Animal forage was not edible for humans, Butz said, and even if it were, it could not be transferred immediately because someone would have to pay for it.

The Saudi Arabian spokesman said Nov. 6 that his nation was mistakenly considered rich and asserted it suffered, along with other oil-producing nations, from many social and economic problems. Saudi Arabia had done more than its share to help developing countries, he insisted. Alberto Vignes, Argentine foreign minister, said Nov. 6 that the U.S. had exploited developing nations and should pay food in reparation. Algerian President Houari Boumedienne expressed a similar view the same day.

The conference ended Nov. 16 with approval of the broad outlines of a program to "end the scourge of hunger and malnutrition." It agreed to establish a new United Nations agency to supervise food programs, but it failed to take concrete action to provide immediate food relief for the millions of persons threatened with starvation. The new agency, called the World Food Council, would be established by the U.N. General Assembly and would report to the Assembly through the U.N. Economic and Social Council (ECOSOC). The food council would be composed of officials at ministerial or plenipotentiary level, who would meet at various times a year to coordinate existing and new policies concerning food production, nutrition, food security and food aid. It would have a full-time secretariat in Rome, whose staff would be drawn from the FAO. The formula establishing the council represented a compromise between the developed nations, who wanted ECOSOC to create and control the coordinating body, and the developing nations, who favored establishment and control of the body by the General Assembly, where each nation had one vote and the developing countries had numerical superiority. The conference Nov. 16 approved several new programs to be supervised by the projected council. Details and machinery would be formulated later. They included: An international agricultural development fund, originally proposed by Arab nations, including major oil producers, to channel investment toward improvement of agriculture in the developing countries, with voluntary contributions to come from traditional donors and from new wealthy developing nations, mainly the oil producers; a fertilizer-aid program to provide increased supplies to developing nations and to help them build new and improved plants; a pesticide-aid program; an irrigation, drainage and flood control program; a nutrition-aid program; and a call for "achievement of a desirable balance between population and the food supply." Earlier, the conference pledged to create an internationally coordinated system of nationally-held grain reserves, a 10-million-ton a year food aid program for poor nations, and an early-warning system of data-sharing to disseminate information about climatic or other threats to food supplies or sudden increases in demand. (The Soviet Union, which was not a member of the FAO, initially expressed strong reservations on the last proposal.)

FAO Director General Boerma organized a private meeting Nov. 6 with principal grain producing nations, including the U.S., Soviet Union and China, and major importers, including India, to tackle the problem of short-term food relief. Boerma produced an FAO paper which estimated the grain storage in South Asia and sub-Sahara Africa, as of Oct. 15, at 7 million-11 million tons, which at current prices would cost about $2 billion, and in 20 other countries, mainly in Africa, at 1.3 million tons. The neediest countries were India, 3.4

million-7.4 million tons; Bangla Desh, 1.9 million; Sri Lanka, 200,000; Tanzania, 500,000; and Pakistan, 1 million. A similar meeting was held Nov. 13, at which the U.S. reportedly questioned the accuracy of the FAO figures, estimating instead that the crop need of the five most threatened nations was 10.5 million tons, of which six million had been met and the rest was "in sight" if financing were found. The Soviet Union was absent from the meeting.

President Ford Nov. 15 rejected a request by the U.S. delegation at the World Food Conference to announce an immediate doubling of U.S. humanitarian food aid in fiscal 1975 to 2 million tons, valued at $350 million, for nations facing famine. Announcing the decision in Rome, Butz said the increase "would have a bullish effect on the market." He cited budget constraints tight supplies and pressure on already inflated U.S. consumer food prices.

The U.S. and other major grain exporting nations agreed Nov. 29 to supply 7.5 billion tons of new food aid, worth $1.8 billion, over the next eight months to nations threatened with mass starvation; but they failed to agree on how to finance the food shipments. The grain exporting nations at the meeting included Canada, Australia, Argentina and the nine-nation European Economic Community. Among the grain importers were India, Bangla Desh, Pakistan and Tanzania. The Soviet Union and China, who had attended earlier meetings, were absent.

See also AGRICULTURE; ALGERIA; ARGENTINA [17]; CHAD; ETHIOPIA [11]; FOREIGN AID; INDIA; NIGERIA

FARM LABOR—*See* LABOR [4, 6]; MEXICO [18]

FEDERAL BUREAU OF INVESTIGATION (FBI)—*See* CRIME [22, 36]; ENERGY CRISIS [24]; FREEDOM OF INFORMATION ACT; HEARST, PATRICIA; INDIAN AFFAIRS; PRIVACY [3]; RADICALS; ROCKEFELLER, NELSON [13]; WATERGATE [22, 26, 31, 35, 59-61, 99, 101]

FEDERAL COMMUNICATIONS COMMISSION—*See* APPOINTMENTS & RESIGNATIONS; CIVIL RIGHTS [21]; TELEVISION & RADIO

FEDERAL TRADE COMMISSION—*See* ANTITRUST ACTIONS [3, 6, 8]; CONSUMER AFFAIRS [3, 9, 12-13]

FIELDING, DR. LOUIS J.—*See* WATERGATE AFFAIR [15, 59, 62, 78-86]

FIGUERES, JOSE—*See* VESCO, ROBERT L.

FIJI ISLANDS—*See* AUSTRALIA [16]

FILMS—*See* MOTION PICTURES

FINLAND—The government had published the first part of its anti-inflation program, it was reported July 2. Measures included housing aid, savings stimulants, continuation of strict price controls beyond Sept. 1 when they were to be eased, and establishment of an import price control office. (A short-term total price freeze was replaced at the end of March by strict price controls that would be eased gradually over the next two years, it was reported March 14. The price curbs were demanded during negotiations for the central wage agreement which went into effect for two years at the end of March, providing for increases, including fringe benefits, of 10.4%-12% in 1974 and 10.8%-11.9% in 1975.)

Foreign Minister Ahti Karjalainen, at the end of a two-day official visit to West Germany, signed Sept. 19 with his Bonn counterpart, Hans-Dietrich Genscher, a joint declaration regulating issues left unsettled when the two nations established diplomatic relations in January 1973. In the declaration, both nations renounced the use of force against each other; West Germany agreed to respect Finland's policy of neutrality; and some of the financial and legal issues resulting from World War II were settled, with further Finnish demands to be postponed and regulated as provided in a 1953 agreement on

German foreign debts. Karjalainen's visit was the first by a Finnish foreign minister to West Germany. He had made the first official visit by a Finnish foreign minister to East Germany May 27-29, ending the trip with a joint communique reaffirming friendly relations between the two countries.

Finland and the Soviet Union signed a 10-year energy cooperation agreement Oct. 16 providing for the delivery to Finland of two 440 megawatt nuclear power stations which would go into operation in 1981-82. The agreement was signed in Helsinki by Jermu Laine, Finland's foreign trade minister, and S. A. Skachkov, chairman of the Soviet State Committee for Foreign Economic Relations, during a visit to Finland Oct. 14-17 by Soviet President Nikolai Podgorny. Podgorny was in Finland primarily for observance of the 30th anniversary of the Soviet-Finnish armistice agreement. The sixth five-year trade agreement between Finland and the Soviet Union was signed Sept. 12 in Helsinki. It provided for total bilateral trade of about 9 billion rubles ($12.33 billion), about double the amount actually traded under the 1971-75 accord, initially set at 2.5 billion rubles.

See also CHILE [3]; COMMUNISM, INTERNATIONAL; EUROPEAN SECURITY; OIL [26]

FIRES & FIREFIGHTING—*See* BRAZIL; CIVIL RIGHTS [10]; CANADA [37]; KOREA, REPUBLIC OF [16]; LABOR [2]
FISHING—*See* INDIAN AFFAIRS; NORWAY, PERU [1, 12]; TERRITORIAL WATERS
FLOODS—*See* FAMINE & FOOD; WEATHER
FLORIDA—*See* CRIME [14-15, 40]; ELECTIONS [3, 5, 7]; ENERGY CRISIS [6]; PRESS; WOMEN'S RIGHTS
FOOD—*See* AGRICULTURE; ANTITRUST ACTIONS [3, 9]; BUTZ, EARL; CONSUMER AFFAIRS [6]; FAMINE & FOOD; NIGERIA; OIL [2]; PERU [15]; POPULATION; SCIENCE; TANZANIA; UNITED NATIONS [3]; VENEZUELA; WEATHER
FOOD & DRUG ADMINISTRATION—*See* CONSUMER AFFAIRS [4-6]; ENVIRONMENT & POLLUTION [18]; MEDICINE & HEALTH [13, 19]
FOOD STAMP PROGRAM—*See* WELFARE & POVERTY

FOOTBALL—World Football League developments. In preparation for its first season, scheduled to begin in July, the World Football League (WFL) held a draft for graduating college football players Jan. 22-23. Anticipating the expiration of contracts of players currently in the National Football League (NFL) or the Canadian Football League (CFL), the WFL held a second draft March 18 to assign negotiating rights for NFL and CFL players. As of March 26, WFL organizers had granted franchises in Birmingham, Ala., Boston, Chicago, Detroit, Florida (Jacksonville), Honolulu, Houston, New York City, Philadelphia, Portland Ore., Southern California (Anaheim), Toronto and Washington-Baltimore.

U.S. District Court Judge David S. Porter May 14 refused to grant the NFL an injunction prohibiting the WFL from signing NFL players. In ruling against the Cincinnati Bengals, Porter said the signing by the WFL of Bengal players Bill Bergey and Steve Chomyszak would not significantly hurt Cincinnati, as its management had asserted. Porter also held that such an injunction would harm the goal of fostering "free competition in the market place for the sports dollar." (A three-judge panel on the U.S. 6th Circuit Court of Appeals upheld Porter's ruling Aug. 27.) In Dallas June 24, a Texas state appeals court judge reversed a lower court injunction against WFL recruitment of NFL Dallas Cowboy players. A team could assure itself of the continued services and loyalty of its players by offering them long-term contracts and other financial inducements, Judge Harold Bateman said. If a club failed to do so, it had no legal ground for complaint if its players "looked elsewhere for their future careers . . . when their present contracts with the club expire." According to a *Washington Post* survey reported Aug. 30, the WFL listed 53 players currently playing out NFL contracts prior to moving to the WFL.

The president of the WFL, Christopher B. Hemmeter, said Dec. 6 that the financially troubled organization would collapse if new owner-investors were not found by March 1975. Hemmeter, co-president of the league's Hawaii franchise, was named WFL president Nov. 22. (Gary Davidson, the first WFL commissioner, resigned Oct. 29 under pressure from team owners.) An Associated Press survey of WFL finances, reported Nov. 20, confirmed Hemmeter's view that the league faced possible dissolution because of financial problems. According to the AP, the league lost more than $20 million in its first year. Officials of the WFL Dec. 13 approved a reorganization plan that required owners planning to field teams in 1975 to post $750,000. The money was reportedly intended for use as payment of salaries still owed players and coaches from the 1974 season. The requirement also was expected to drive potentially insolvent owners from the WFL.

The Birmingham (Ala.) Americans won the first WFL championship, the World Bowl, Dec. 5, defeating the (Orlando) Florida Blazers 22-21 at Legion Field in Birmingham.

NFL amends rules to enliven games. The NFL announced April 25 that it had made radical changes in its rules in an effort to enliven its games. Approved by the owners of the 26 NFL franchises, the alterations were the most sweeping since 1933 when the league moved the goal posts from the end line of the end zone to the goal line. NFL Commissioner Pete Rozelle denied the changes were a reaction to incursions by the WFL, although he conceded that the WFL hastened the alterations. Among the revisions: A sudden death period of 15 minutes was added to break ties; kickoffs were to take place on the kicking team's 35-yard line, rather than the 40, to encourage runbacks by the receiving team; the goal posts were returned to the end line of the end zone (10 yards back) to discourage field goals, which some critics had said were making the game dull.

Striking NFL players end walkout. Player representatives of the NFL Players' Association voted Aug. 27 to end a strike by veteran players that had begun July 1. They agreed to play out the regular season, even in the absence of a collective bargaining agreement with the team owners. The strike centered around what the Players' Association called "freedom issues" but what the owners insisted were really questions of money. The association had asked that players be allowed to move freely from team to team without any of the current restrictions in the trade, draft and waiver systems. The association also sought elimination of disciplinary actions, including fines and curfews, as well as a limit on the number of working hours during training camp. The association asked for substantial increases in minimum salaries, exhibition game pay and postseason playoff money.

NFL reserve system ruled illegal. U.S. District Court Judge William T. Sweigert Dec. 20 ruled in San Francisco that the NFL's contract and reserve system, which bound a player to a team indefinitely, was illegal. The sweeping decision came in an antitrust suit brought against the NFL by Joe Kapp, a former New England Patriots quarterback, who had retired rather than sign a standard NFL player contract. Sweigert held that the NFL's Rozelle Rule was "patently unreasonable and illegal." The rule required a team to compensate another team—with players or money—if it signed a free agent who formerly had played with the other team. When teams did not agree on a price, the commissioner of the NFL (currently Pete Rozelle) would unilaterally determine just compensation.

Dolphins repeat as Super Bowl victors. The Miami Dolphins won their second straight Super Bowl Jan. 13, defeating the Minnesota Vikings 24-7 at Rice Stadium in Houston. Unable to stop Miami fullback Larry Csonka, who rushed for a Super Bowl record of 145 yards, and incapable of putting together a sustained offensive effort against the Dolphin defense, the Vikings were hopelessly behind 24-0 in the fourth quarter before quarterback Fran Tarkenton ran four yards for Minnesota's only score of the game. Csonka was named the game's most valuable player.

College bowl games. Cotton Bowl, Dallas, Tex., Jan. 1, University of Nebraska defeated University of Texas, 19-3; Rose Bowl, Pasadena, Calif., Jan. 1, Ohio State University over the University of Southern California, 42-21; Orange Bowl, Miami, Fla., Jan. 1, Penn State University defeated Louisiana State University 16-9; Liberty Bowl, Memphis, Tenn., Dec. 16, University of Tennessee defeated Maryland 7-3; Tangerine Bowl, Orlando, Fla., Dec. 21, Miami of Ohio topped Georgia 21-10; Sun Bowl, El Paso, Tex., Dec. 28, Mississippi State defeated North Carolina 26-24; Gator Bowl, Jacksonville, Fla., Dec. 30, Auburn upset the University of Texas 27-3; Sugar Bowl, New Orleans, La., Dec. 31, University of Nebraska defeated the University of Florida 13-10.

See also OBITUARIES [BROWN]

FORD, BETTY—President Ford's wife Betty successfully underwent major surgery Sept. 28, a radical mastectomy, when her right breast was removed after detection of cancer. Her physicians reported Sept. 30 that microscopic traces of cancer had been found in two of the 30 lymph nodes removed during the operation. There was "no clinical evidence" that cancer had spread to other areas and the doctor said they were "optimistic for a prolonged survival." Her postoperative course was reported Oct. 1 as "excellent." The operation was performed at the Bethesda Naval Medical Center. Mrs. Ford, 56, had entered the center Sept. 27 after a lump had been detected in her right breast during a routine gynecological examination Sept. 26.

See also MEDICINE & HEALTH [23-25]; POLITICS [1]

FORD, GERALD R.—Gerald Rudolph Ford, 61, was sworn is as the 38th President of the United States at 12:03 p.m. Aug. 9. Ford, who had become the first non-elected Vice President of the United States Dec. 6, 1973 when he replaced Spiro T. Agnew, became the first non-elected President and the first President to fill a vacancy left by resignation. The oath of office was administered by Chief Justice Warren E. Burger (who had hastily returned to Washington from a European vacation) in the East Room of the White House. According to the terms of the Constitution, Ford was to serve the remaining 2½ years of the second term of Richard M. Nixon and would be eligible for only one full term of office. Following his swearing-in, Ford made a brief address to those gathered in the East Room and to a national television audience. He noted that he was "acutely aware that you have not elected me as your President by your ballots. So I ask you to confirm me as your President with your prayers." He added that, if he had not been chosen by secret ballot, neither had he "gained office by any secret promises." Noting that "truth is the glue" holding together "not only our government, but civilization itself," Ford vowed "openness and candor" in all his public and private acts as President. He stated that the "long national nightmare" of Watergate was over and asked that its "wounds" be bound up. "Before closing," he said, "I again ask your prayers for Richard Nixon and his family. May our former President, who brought peace to millions, find it for himself."

The nation reacted soberly to the events culminating in the swift, smooth transfer of power to Ford. Liberals and conservatives, Republicans and

Democrats, labor and business leaders, religious and civil rights spokesmen joined in public support of Ford Aug. 9. Representatives of the nation's governors, mayors and county officials sent a joint telegram Aug. 9 pledging their "fullest cooperation and assistance" in "reuniting the nation and restoring its sense of common purpose and direction." Members of Congress predicted Aug. 8 (before the Nixon resignation, but after announcement of it) that there would be an extended "honeymoon" between Congress and the White House, erasing antagonism and suspicion that had characterized relations between Congress and the Nixon Administration. World leaders greeted the replacement of Nixon by Ford with some expressions of concern over the policies of the new President, who was largely unknown in foreign capitals. In the Soviet Union, commentators emphasized that the change in U.S. Presidents would not affect relations between Moscow and Washington. Western European leaders expressed confidence that relations between their countries and the U.S. would not change significantly, but officials questioned Ford's ability to conduct complex economic and financial affairs. Israel expressed confidence in continued U.S. friendship, but Arab leaders voiced concern that Ford might lean too heavily in Israel's favor in Middle East affairs. South Vietnamese officials expressed hope that Ford would follow Nixon's policies in Indochina.

After his swearing-in Aug. 9, Ford met with a bipartisan group of Congressional leaders and the Nixon Administration's top economic advisers. The latter were told that control of inflation was a "high and first priority of the Ford Administration." Ford also met Aug. 9 with the senior members of the Nixon White House staff, still intact except for Press Secretary Ronald L. Ziegler, who resigned and accompanied Nixon to California. Ford asked the staff to remain through the transition and appealed for their "help and cooperation." Gen. Alexander M. Haig Jr., chief of staff, pledged the same loyalty to Ford "in our hour of common cause." Ford Aug. 9 named a four-member committee of his own to oversee the transition: former Gov. William W. Scranton (R, Pa.); Donald M. Rumsfeld, ambassador to the North Atlantic Treaty Organization; Interior Secretary Rogers C. B. Morton; and former Rep. John O. Marsh (D, Va.), a member of Ford's vice presidential staff.

The chief of that staff, Robert T. Hartmann, was named a counselor to the President Aug. 9. Hartmann, 57, chief of the Washington bureau of the *Los Angeles Times* (1954-64) joined Ford's staff in 1966. (Marsh was named a counselor Aug. 10.) Ford also appeared in the White House press room Aug. 9 to introduce his new press secretary, J. F. terHorst, 52, former Washington bureau manager of the *Detroit News*. "We will have an open, we will have a candid Administration. I can't change my nature after 61 years," Ford said. In his first full day as President Aug. 10, Ford met with the Nixon Cabinet and asked its members, as well as all federal agency chiefs, to remain in their posts in the name of "continuity and stability." He also met with the National Security Council and announced he was seeking suggestions from Republicans and Democrats for the choice of a vice president.

In a nationally televised address Aug. 12, President Ford urged Congress to cooperate with him in confronting the problems of the nation, citing inflation as the major issue. "My first priority is to work with you to bring inflation under control," Ford said. "Inflation is our domestic public enemy No. 1. To restore economic confidence, the government in Washington must provide leadership. It does no good to blame the public for spending too much when the government is spending too much." In a well-received appearance (his speech was interrupted 32 times with applause) before an evening joint session, the new President announced several opening moves on the economic front, pledged an open Administration in domestic and foreign policy and declared his belief in "the absolute necessity of a free press." He also pledged protection of individual privacy and declared his dedication to be President of "all the people." "There will be no illegal tappings, eavesdropping, buggings, or break-ins by my Administration," he asserted.

Ford poll rating down. The Gallup Poll found President Ford's popularity rating declining in early December to a 42% approval rating, with 41% disapproving of the way he was handling his job. The results, published Dec. 26, were based on a sampling taken Dec. 6-9 and were said to reflect concern over the nation's economy. Ford's ratings compared to approval ratings of 48%-32% in mid-November, 47%-33% in early November and 55%-28% in mid-October (sampling Oct. 18-21) after Ford's explanation to Congress of his pardon to former President Nixon. Prior to that, his low point had been 50%-28% in late September.

White House trespasser surrenders. A man dressed like an Arab and claiming to be armed with explosives kept White House security guards at bay for four hours a few feet from the White House Dec. 25 before surrendering peacefully. The man, carrying satchels, gained entry to the grounds by ramming a car through a White House gate about 7:07 a.m. President Ford and his family were in Vail, Colo. for the holidays. The man, identified as Marshall Hill Fields, 25, a former taxicab driver and son of a deceased U.S. diplomat, eventually asked that a radio station broadcast his desire to speak with the Pakistani ambassador. When he heard it on his car radio, he surrendered and was found to possess, not explosives, but highway flares. He was taken to a hospital for observation.

See also ABORTION; AMNESTY & CLEMENCY; ANTITRUST ACTIONS [12]; APPOINTMENTS & RESIGNATIONS; ATOMIC ENERGY [9, 12, 18]; AUSTRALIA [22]; AUTOMOBILE INDUSTRY [1, 8, 11]; AVIATION [2]; BUDGET; BUTZ, EARL; CANADA [27, 29]; CENTRAL INTELLIGENCE AGENCY; CHINA, COMMUNIST; CIVIL RIGHTS [1-2, 4]; CRIME [35]; CUBA; CYPRUS [16, 23]; DAYLIGHT SAVINGS TIME; DEFENSE [7, 14-15]; DISARMAMENT; ELECTIONS [1, 5, 9, 11, 13]; ENERGY CRISIS [23, 25-31, 35]; ECONOMY, U.S. [10-28]; ENVIRONMENT & POLLUTION [14, 16, 20]; FAMINE & FOOD; FRANCE [18]; FREEDOM OF INFORMATION ACT; GREECE [12-13]; HOUSING; JAPAN [14]; KOREA, REPUBLIC OF [13, 15]; LABOR [4-5]; LATIN AMERICA; MEXICO [5, 18]; MONETARY DEVELOPMENTS [19-20]; NARCOTICS & DANGEROUS DRUGS; NIXON, RICHARD M.; NORTH ATLANTIC TREATY ORGANIZATION; OIL [2, 28-29]; PAKISTAN; PENSIONS; POLAND; POLITICS [1, 11]; PORTUGAL [27]; PRIVACY [6]; ROCKEFELLER, NELSON [1, 3, 5, 29-32]; SHIPS & SHIPPNG; SUGAR; TAXES; TRANSPORTATION; UNION OF SOVIET SOCIALIST REPUBLICS [1, 10, 14, 29]; UNITED NATIONS [3]; WATERGATE AFFAIR [3, 19, 23, 43, 64-73, 90]; WOMEN'S RIGHTS

FOREIGN AID—Foreign aid request. President Nixon submitted a $5.18 billion foreign aid program to Congress April 24. A substantial part of the program—$900 million—was directed to the Middle East, including Egypt for the first time since 1967. In his special message to Congress, the President said "increased foreign aid will be a vital component to our diplomacy in maintaining the momentum toward a negotiated settlement which will serve the interests of both Israel and the Arab nations." Of the total, $3.6 billion would be for economic aid and $1.6 billion for military aid. Other large items, in addition to the Middle East aid, were $1.06 billion for international financial organizations and $939.8 million for reconstruction in Indochina. The latter included $750 million for South Vietnam, $110 million for Cambodia, $55 million for Laos and the remainder for regional programs. The funds would be in addition to about $1.4 billion of military aid for Indochina handled separately under the defense budget. The funds were also separate from $390 million for

Cambodia and $90 million for Laos requested under the military section of the new aid program. The Middle East aid sought by the President consisted of $350 million for Israel, $250 million for Egypt, $207.5 million for Jordan and $100 million for "a special requirements fund" to be applied "for new needs that may arise" as peace negotiations continued.

Foreign aid bill cleared. A foreign aid authorization of $2.69 billion for fiscal 1975 was approved by the Senate Dec. 17, 49-41, and the House Dec. 8, 209-189. It was signed Dec. 30 by President Ford. The bill contained a provision to suspend military aid to Turkey immediately, unless there was substantial progress toward a Cyprus settlement, but the President was permitted to delay the cutoff until Feb. 5 if he determined it would aid negotiations. The total authorization was $55 million less than the budgeted request. It included $1.1 billion for Middle East countries, $617 million for Indochina. Military aid comprised $600 million of the total. Food and nutrition programs were authorized $500 million. Special restrictions were put on aid to Cambodia (a $377 million ceiling, with no more than $200 million of that in military aid), Chile (a $25 million ceiling, with no military aid or sales), South Korea (a 145 million ceiling on military aid, or $165 million if progress were reported in observance of human rights) and India (a $50 million ceiling). Pending passage of an appropriations bill, funding for the foreign aid program was continued at its current annual rate of $3.48 billion. A resolution to this effect was passed by the House Dec. 18 and Senate Dec. 19.

See also AFRICA; ATOMIC ENERGY [1-4, 9, 11-12]; CAMBODIA; CHAD; CHILE [1]; CYPRUS [15, 23, 25]; DEFENSE [5]; EUROPEAN ECONOMIC COMMUNITY [16-17]; FAMINE & FOOD; INDIA; MIDDLE EAST [38-39]; MONETARY DEVELOPMENTS [5, 8-9]; NICARAGUA; OIL [18-21, 31]; TANZANIA; UNITED NATIONS [3]; VIETNAM, PEOPLE'S REPUBLIC OF; VIETNAM, REPUBLIC OF [10, 17, 34-38]; WEATHER

FRANCE

Government & Politics

[1] **Pompidou dies.** President Georges Jean Raymond Pompidou, 62, died at his private Paris apartment April 2. Alain Poher, president of the French Senate, automatically became interim president. Under the Constitution, presidential elections had to be held within 20-35 days. Pompidou, a protege of the late Charles de Gaulle, became de Gaulle's premier but was dismissed from that post in 1968. However, when de Gaulle retired, Pompidou was elected in 1969 as the second president of the Fifth Republic, which was created by de Gaulle in 1958. The government had long denied that Pompidou was seriously ill. Royalty, presidents, premiers and dignitaries of more than 80 countries attended a memorial mass for the late president celebrated in Notre Dame Cathedral April 6. Pompidou had been buried April 4 near his country home in Orvilliers, 31 miles west of Paris. Among those attending was U.S. President Richard Nixon. After the mass Nixon held a series of private talks with leaders from France, Italy, Great Britain, West Germany, Denmark, the Soviet Union and Japan. Nixon was criticized by the French press for detracting from the solemnity of the occasion by holding political discussions.

[2] **Mitterrand, Giscard d'Estaing candidates.** Socialist Party leader Francois Mitterrand and Finance Minister Valery Giscard d'Estaing announced their candidacies for the presidency April 8. They joined 10 other major and minor aspirants in the election scheduled May 5, with a runoff May 19 if no candidate won an absolute majority. Mitterrand represented a united left led by his Socialists and the large Communist Party. Giscard d'Estaing, leader of the Independent Republicans, of the ruling three-party coalition, challenged two other government candidates, Gaullist (UDR) ex-Premier Jacques Chaban-

Delmas and centrist ex-Premier Edgar Faure. The presidential candidacies of 12 persons—11 men and one woman—were approved by the Constitutional Council April 19, following the closing of the presidential lists April 16. Eighteen other candidacies were rejected as frivolous. Publication of the final candidates' list followed withdrawal from contention of Faure, further unsuccessful attempts by Gaullists to derail the campaign of Chaban-Delmas, the decision of the Reformers' Movement not to field a candidate, and the entry into the race of Jean Royer, the populist postal services minister and mayor of Tours. Interior Minister Jacques Chirac had joined three other Gaullist Cabinet ministers April 14 in appealing to Premier Pierre Messmer to re-enter the presidential race and in asking for anti-leftist candidates to withdraw. The appeal was endorsed by 39 members of the National Assembly, but it received little other support. Messmer endorsed Chaban-Delmas April 21.

[3] **Mitterrand faces Giscard in runoff.** Mitterrand won more than 43% of the vote and Giscard d'Estaing nearly 33% in the first round of presidential elections May 5. Because neither gained the 50% required for a first-round victory, the two would face each other in the second and decisive ballot May 19. Former Premier Chaban-Delmas, the official candidate of the Gaullist Union of Democrats for the Republic (UDR), won slightly more than 15% of the vote, ending 16 years of Gaullist rule. The other nine candidates shared the remaining votes. Premier Messmer, who reluctantly supported Chaban-Delmas in the first round, announced his "total support" for Giscard d'Estaing May 5. Chaban-Delmas said he was "resolutely opposed" to Mitterrand's candidacy because of the "presence of the Communist Party" in the United Left alliance and "the dangers of the common program." However, he refrained from specifically endorsing Giscard d'Estaing. The UDR executive bureau and the 190 Gaullist members of the National Assembly May 6 endorsed Giscard d'Estaing for the second round, declaring that the party's main objective was to "bar the road to Marxism."

[4] Mitterrand and Giscard d'Estaing debated each other in the first such live television encounter in a French presidential campaign May 10. A public opinion poll taken after the debate showed that Giscard had edged slightly in front of his opponent. Among the major debate points: Mitterrand charged that although France had prospered in recent years, the poor had not gained their equal share of the growing wealth; he demanded drastic anti-inflation measures, including a ceiling on food prices. Giscard d'Estaing cited increased numbers of automobiles and television sets owned by French workers to show how the workers' lot had improved. Mitterrand defended his intention to include Communists in a new Cabinet, saying he wanted "to become the president of all Frenchmen, and there are five million of them that voted Communist." Giscard d'Estaing reiterated one of his major campaign themes: the "danger in having Communists at the helm in key ministries." Giscard d'Estaing also criticized Mitterrand's stated plans to nationalize certain key industries, one of the major points in the common program between the Communists and Socialists. The Radical Party followed the advice of its leader, Jean-Jacques Servan-Schreiber May 14 by endorsing Giscard d'Estaing for president.

[5] Giscard d'Estaing was elected president of France by narrowly defeating Mitterrand in the runoff election May 19. Nearly final results indicated that Giscard d'Estaing had won 50.66% of the approximately 26,175,067 votes cast, compared with 49.33% for Mitterrand. Nearly 88% of the registered voters cast ballots, a record turnout. Giscard d'Estaing was sworn in May 27. Later that day he named Interior Minister Chirac, 41, as his premier, and the next day he announced a new Cabinet which sharply reduced Gaullist influence. Giscard dispensed with much of the pomp and protocol of the traditional French presidential inauguration. He walked to the Elysee Palace for the ceremony

dressed in a plain business suit and then walked up the Champs-Elysee to lay a memorial wreath at the Tomb of the Unknown Soldier under the Arch of Triumph. The Cabinet announced May 28 by Giscard contained only three holdovers from the Messmer Cabinet and only five Gaullist ministers, including Chirac, half the previous number. Nonpolitical technocrats were appointed to head four posts: Jean Sauvagnargues, French ambassador to West Germany, was appointed foreign minister; Jean-Pierre Fourcade, who had worked for some years under Giscard at the Finance Ministry before resigning for a private banking position, was named economics and finance minister.

[6] **Servan-Schreiber fired on A-tests.** Reform Minister Jean-Jacques Servan-Schreiber was dismissed from his post June 9, hours after he publicly criticized the government's decision, announced June 8, to resume atmospheric nuclear testing in the South Pacific during the summer. At a news conference in Nancy June 9, Servan-Schreiber charged that the present government had "not been consulted" and had been presented with "a fait accompli" by the military. He acknowledged that he had not included nuclear testing in his terms for joining the Giscard government. A communique issued from the presidential palace said Servan-Schreiber's news conference statements were "in contradiction with the fundamental principle of ministerial solidarity" and that therefore the president, at Premier Chirac's request, was dismissing Servan-Schreiber.

[7] **New social welfare program set.** The Cabinet adopted a social reform program June 19. The basic minimum wage for the 600,000 lowest-income wage earners was increased 7.57% to the equivalent of $1.30 an hour, effective July 1 (the increase meant that the minimum wage had risen 23% over the past year); family allowances to persons with at least one child were increased 12.2%; minimum government-paid old-age allowances were raised 21.12%, to about $3.50 a day; and other retirement pensions were increased 6.7%. The cost to the government of the program was estimated at around $500 million in 1974 and $1 billion in 1975. At his first presidential press conference July 25, Giscard d'Estaing said he would press ahead with various domestic reforms. Among the changes he envisaged: a law to provide control of political party expenditures and enable government financing of election campaigns; and an increase in capital gains taxes so they would be subjected to the same taxation as ordinary income. He also said he would not permit prosecution of women for illegal abortions, pending revision of the law. Some reforms had already been carried out. The National Assembly voted nearly unanimously June 25 to lower the voting age and the age of majority from 21 to 18. About 2.4 million French youths would be affected. The Senate adopted the measure at the end of June. Giscard July 16 appointed Francoise Giroud, 58, a leading feminist and editor in chief of the weekly news magazine *L'Express,* to a new junior Cabinet post as secretary of state for the status of women. Giscard d'Estaing had promised creation of the post during his election campaign. The National Assembly, by a 289-186 vote July 28, gave final approval to a government bill that would divide ORTF, the state-owned French radio and television organization, into independent and competing units still under government control. The Senate had approved the bill earlier that day.

[8] **Communists, Socialists in rift.** Socialist gains in National Assembly by-elections caused a rift between the Communist and Socialist parties, partners in the United Left alliance. In the two rounds of by-elections held Sept. 29 and Oct. 6, four of six former Cabinet ministers seeking to regain their seats, vacated when they joined the government under the late President Pompidou, were elected, but with reduced majorities. The Socialists and Left-wing Radicals each won a seat. Among the Gaullists elected was former Premier Messmer, who won in the first round. The central committee of the Communist Party, in a front-page article in their

newspaper *L'Humanite* Oct. 8, said the Socialist "campaign designed to demonstrate that only a non-Communist candidate could defeat the candidate of the government" was undermining their alliance. Socialist Party leader Mitterrand, during a congress of the Socialist Party Oct. 12-13, said he "totally adhered" to the alliance with the Communists. But at the same time, the congress adopted a program that proposed creation of an enlarged Socialist Party that would provide close coordination between political action and labor struggles.

[9] **Separatist developments.** The government Jan. 30 banned four separatist movements, three of which had claimed responsibility for bomb attacks and other violence. Those connected with violence were the two rival Breton groups, the Liberation Front of Brittany (FLB—ARB) and the left-wing Liberation Front of Brittany for National Liberation and Socialism (FLB-LNS), and the Corsican Peasant Front for Liberation (FPCL). The fourth was the Basque association "Enbata," which linked several political and cultural groups among the French-speaking Basques of southwest France. Premier Messmer warned March 26, at the close of a two-day visit to Corsica, that the government would quell "without pity" any resort to violence for political ends in the island and would combat "any attack on the unity of the French Republic." Earlier March 26, a bomb blast attributed to Corsican militant autonomists had damaged a government building in Bastia a few hours after Messmer left it. A few days before Messmer arrived on the island, a bomb had destroyed part of a French jet airliner at Bastia airport March 22 and another explosion March 18 damaged the French Foreign Legion headquarters at Corte. Six bombs exploded in Ajaccio, capital of Corsica, and elsewhere on the island the night of July 8-9, causing heavy damage but no injuries.

[10] **Moscow, Paris broaden cooperation.** Soviet Communist Party General Secretary Leonid Brezhnev and President Giscard d'Estaing concluded broad agreements Dec. 5-7 indicating a closer alignment of Soviet-French positions and interests during three days of talks at Rambouillet, a Paris suburb. In the final joint communique issued Dec. 7, France and the Soviet Union stated that "a good basis has been created for the early conclusion" of the 35-nation Conference on Security and Cooperation in Europe (CSCE) being held in Geneva and urged "the signature of its final documents at the highest level," calling a summit-meeting conclusion, advocated by Moscow, "an essential element for the procedure of detente in Europe."

[11] **Abortion reform approved.** The National Assembly, by a 277-192 vote, gave final approval Dec. 20 to a government-sponsored bill liberalizing a 1920 law which outlawed nearly all abortions. A group of deputies immediately filed a suit with the Constitutional Council challenging the constitutionality of the new law. The Senate had approved the bill 182-91 Dec. 15.

The Economy

[12] **$1.5 billion loan floated.** France floated a $1.5 billion Eurodollar loan, the biggest single such borrowing ever raised by a government, the weekly newsletter Euromarket News reported Feb. 14. The loan had been oversubscribed within days, according to Euromarket. In announcing plans to float the loan, Finance Minister Giscard d'Estaing had said Jan. 31 that it was needed to reduce the expected $4 billion trade deficit caused mainly by higher Arab oil prices and to prevent the franc from dropping too far below its pre-float parity. (France had, on Jan. 19, announced a de facto devaluation of the franc, estimated at 4%-5%, by allowing it to float for six months.) Citing the need to simplify the foreign exchange market, Giscard announced March 20 that the two-tier exchange system with differing commercial and financial franc rates would be ended March 21. The system had been introduced in August 1971 to protect the franc against currency speculation.

[13] **Labor protests mount.** Labor unrest in the face of increased living costs resulted in a series of protests in the spring. The Bank of France called in police March 7 to prevent striking clerks and other bank employes from interfering with transactions. The workers had begun their job action a week before. Bank clerks, who also staged protest marches in Paris in March, continued their work stoppages into April, and were joined at the end of March by stock exchange clerks. The unrest reached at least a dozen industrial companies, it was reported March 30. Truck and car manufacturing workers, textile workers at Rouen, shipyard workers at Saint-Nazaire, coal miners in the Lorraine and gas workers in the Lacq field staged strikes and job actions. A short respite in France's labor problems was indicated May 20 by Georges Seguy, head of the Communist-led General Confederation of Labor (CGT). He said the union was prepared to negotiate with government and employers for "the essential social demands," but added that new labor action would be launched if the demands were not satisfied.

[14] **Austerity plan presented.** An economic austerity plan designed to cut the nation's current 19% annual inflation rate by two-thirds and restore the payments balance within 18 months was announced by the government June 12. The program included an 18% increase in corporate taxes for 1974, and income surtax increases of 5%-15% on a sliding scale for the nation's top 1.5 million taxpayers. Part of the income surtax would be reimbursed in 1975. Among other measures, a special 10% capital gains tax on 1974 real estate profits was ordered, credit curbs maintained and government spending cut. In an attempt to restore the payments balance by reducing the annual oil import bill by 10%, the government program raised fuel prices and curbed consumption. It increased the gasoline tax by 3%-5%, bringing the price of premium gas to $1.40 a gallon, with the increased revenue to be spent maintaining mass transport fares at current levels.

[15] **Jobless plan agreed.** An agreement under which workers dismissed by a company for "economic reasons" would receive 90% of a full year's gross wages (equivalent to total net take-home pay) was signed in Paris Oct. 14 by representatives of all the trade unions and the National Council of French Employers (CNPF). The accord, which fulfilled one of President Giscard d'Estaing's election promises, was among the most generous ever achieved by workers in any country. It covered some 20 million workers. Wage earners, who lost their jobs through business failure or structural changes, including declared bankruptcies or liquidations, would receive the year's salary, providing equivalent jobs or suitable retraining programs were not refused. A special fund would be established, with funds provided by the government and the balance to be paid by the CNPF (80%) and the workers (20%).

[16] **Wave of labor unrest.** A general strike, called by the CGT and the French Democratic Labor Confederation (CFDT), was staged Nov. 19 to protest President Giscard d'Estaing's economic austerity program. The unions charged that the government had refused to negotiate pay increases that reflected cost of living inflation. The strike disrupted national broadcasting, transportation, hospital, bank, school, utility and other services, but participation was limited. There were only spotty stoppages in the private sector. Government spokesman Andre Rossi said he had "very exact figures" that only 800,000 workers of a total 20 million struck. France had been engulfed in labor unrest for over five weeks. A wildcat strike among poorly paid Paris mail sorters had begun Oct. 14 and spread nationwide, halting all mail deliveries. The government used the police Nov. 14 to remove strikers occupying postal sorting offices.

Energy Developments

[17] **Energy plan announced.** In an effort to reduce French oil consumption, the Cabinet adopted an energy plan March 6 that set limits on home heating, cut

spending on highways and provided for construction starts of 13 nuclear power plants through 1975. The program was designed to save 10 million tons of oil a year. As part of an emergency program to conserve France's fuel, the Cabinet Sept. 25 set a "definitive" limit on spending for oil imports in 1975 and ordered reductions in industrial and home heating consumption. Expenditure on oil imports during 1975 would be limited to a maximum F51 billion ($10.7 billion), representing a 10% reduction, at prevailing prices, from the volume of oil imports in 1973. A national fuel consumption agency would be created to supervise rationing of heavy industrial fuel to factories and other users.

[18] **Oil conference planned.** U.S. President Gerald Ford and President Giscard d'Estaing conferred on the French Caribbean island of Martinique Dec. 15-16 and reached compromise agreements on energy, gold and other issues. The accords, reached, according to the communique, in an atmosphere of "cordiality and mutual confidence," represented a sharp departure from the conflicts that had marked U.S.-French relations in recent years. In the joint communique issued Dec. 16, the U.S. agreed to participate in the French-proposed conference of oil producing and exporting nations "at the earliest possible date," with a "preparatory" producer-consumer meeting to be held in March 1975 to work out procedural issues for the conference. In exchange, France agreed to "intensive consultations among consumer countries in order to prepare positions for the conference," a concession to the U.S. demand for a unified front among oil consuming nations. The presidents also agreed "it would be appropriate for any government which wished to do so to adopt current market prices as the basis of valuation for its gold holding." Noting that this would enable nations to align the fixed price with the much higher market price, Secretary of State Henry A. Kissinger later said that he did not foresee the U.S. making such an adjustment soon. But Giscard d'Estaing said France would act quickly. (The French revaluation of its gold reserves at the 1975 market value was announced Dec. 20. The move increased the dollar value of the reserves from about $4.2 billion to $18-$19 billion.) Resolving a long dispute between the two nations, France agreed to pay the U.S. $100 million to compensate for financial losses incurred when France expelled U.S. forces and bases committed to the North Atlantic Treaty Organization from its territory.

[19] **Energy deals with Iran, Libya.** As part of its campaign to obtain secure oil supplies, France signed major energy agreements with Iran and Libya in mid-February. The accord with Iran, signed Feb. 9, provided for collaboration in energy development and industrialization expected to be worth $3 billion-$5 billion. Oil deliveries to France were not mentioned in the agreement, although French objectives were seen as assuring long-term energy supplies and offsetting increased oil costs with sales of industrial equipment and know-how. In the deal with Libya, France agreed to provide technical and economic aid in exchange for Libyan oil in an agreement in principle signed in Paris Feb. 19 at the end of a week-long visit by Libyan Premier Abdel Salam Jalloud. The shah of Iran, on an official visit to France June 24-26, placed orders worth an estimated $4 billion-$5 billion over 10 years within the framework of the economic accord signed in February. Under an agreement signed June 27 by foreign ministers of both countries, Iran agreed to make a $1 billion advance deposit with the Bank of France to cover the orders, a payment that would substantially ease France's oil-related balance of payments deficit. Under the contracts, France would supply Iran with five 1,000-megawatt nuclear reactors worth about $1.1 billion. The other agreements cited in a joint communique issued June 27 provided for France to build a subway in Teheran, supply a steel plant to be built by Creusot-Loire, build a liquified natural gas plant with other nations, participate in construction of a natural gas pipeline and build 12 large tankers through a

French-led consortium. The communique also said Iran would increase its oil shipments to France, but did not specify the amount. (Iran currently supplied 12% of France's oil.) At a press conference in Paris June 27, the shah confirmed that the French accord also involved military sales but declined to give details other than the purchase of fast motor boats. At the end of a three-day visit to Teheran, Premier Chirac announced Dec. 23 that he had signed economic agreements with Iran worth $6 billion. One of the major agreements called for installation of the French color television system, which had been vying with the West German system for the contract.

See also ALGERIA; APPOINTMENTS & RESIGNATIONS; ATOMIC ENERGY [5-7, 10]; AUTO RACING; AVIATION [10, 15]; BELGIUM; CAMBODIA; CANADA [7, 34]; CHILE [6-7, 19, 24]; COMMUNISM, INTERNATIONAL; COMORO ISLANDS; CYPRUS [20]; DISARMAMENT; EUROPEAN ECONOMIC COMMUNITY [2-4, 8, 10, 13-14]; EUROPEAN SECURITY; FAMINE & FOOD; GABON; GERMANY, WEST [7, 12]; ITALY [7]; MARTINIQUE; MAURITANIA; MIDDLE EAST [26]; MONETARY DEVELOPMENTS [4, 8, 11, 14, 16, 17, 19, 23]; MOROCCO; MOUNTAIN CLIMBING; NIGER; NORTH ATLANTIC TREATY ORGANIZATION; OIL [3, 11, 23, 26-27, 29, 34]; PAKISTAN; PORTUGAL [25]; SAUDI ARABIA; SENEGAL; SOUTH AFRICA [13-14]; SPAIN [8, 11, 13]; SWITZERLAND; TENNIS; UGANDA; UNION OF SOVIET SOCIALIST REPUBLICS [17]; UNITED NATIONS [6, 9, 11, 16-19]; URUGUAY; VIETNAM, REPUBLIC OF [26]; ZAIRE

FREEDOM OF INFORMATION ACT—President Ford vetoed a bill Oct. 17 amending the 1966 Freedom of Information Act to give freer public access to govenment data. Ford said the bill was "unconstitutional and unworkable" and a threat to U.S. "military or intelligence secrets and diplomatic relations." Ford objected to the bill's authority to the courts to declassify secret documents "in sensitive and complex areas where they have no expertise." He had no objection for courts "to inspect classified documents and review the justification for their classification," he said, but the law should read that the courts would have to uphold the classification "if there is a reasonable basis to support it." In the bill, the burden of proof was on the government to justify a secrecy classification. The President also objected to a provision that agency investigatory files, including those of the Federal Bureau of Investigation, be made public on request unless the agency could prove that disclosure would be harmful to the national interest. The Senate had approved the final version of the bill by voice vote Oct. 1, the House by 349-2 vote Oct. 7. The House voted to override Ford's veto 371-31 on Nov. 20. In the Senate, Nov. 21, the vote was 65-27 (three more than the required two-thirds majority).

See also ENERGY CRISIS [20]; PRIVACY [9-10]

FRENCH WEST INDIES—*See* MARTINIQUE

FULBRIGHT, SEN. J. WILLIAM—*See* CENTRAL INTELLIGENCE AGENCY; ELECTIONS [3, 10]

GABON—President Omar Bongo signed a protocol agreement July 10 with the Societe des Mines de Fer de Mokambo (Somifer), giving Gabon 60% control of the iron ore venture which was half owned by the Bethlehem Steel Corp.

Bongo met with French Premier Jacques Chirac in Paris June 19 and later said France had agreed to pay Gabon "a large sum" following Gabon's decision in February to increase uranium prices. It was reported May 15 that the two countries had signed new cooperation treaties which included the continuation of a French military presence in Gabon, but excluded any reference to Gabonese supplies of uranium to France.

See also AFRICA; OIL [5]

GAMBIA—*See* SENEGAL

GAMBLING—Attorney General William B. Saxbe told representatives of 13 states at a meeting in Washington Sept. 6 that he would seek permanent injunctions against their states' lotteries unless they obtained Congressional exemption from federal anti-lottery laws within 90 days. The state-operated lotteries, Saxbe said, violated sections of federal gambling laws prohibiting interstate transportation of lottery tickets, broadcasting of lottery information and advertisements, use of the mails by lottery agencies and sale of lottery tickets in federally chartered banks. States operating lotteries were Maryland, Connecticut, Delaware, Illinois, Maine, Massachusetts, Michigan, New Hampshire, New Jersey, New York, Ohio, Pennsylvania and Rhode Island. On Dec. 20, Congress cleared and sent to the White House, a bill to exempt state lotteries from much federal anti-gambling regulation. Broadcasting and publication of lottery information would be permitted in the states with lotteries.

See also BAHAMAS; HORSE RACING

GANDHI, INDIRA—*See* ATOMIC ENERGY [3]; BANGLA DESH; INDIA
GASOLINE SHORTAGE—*See* ENERGY CRISIS [4, 6-15, 27-28, 32-34]
GAS WARFARE—*See* CHEMICAL & BIOLOGICAL WEAPONS
GENERAL ACCOUNTING OFFICE (GAO)—*See* AGNEW, SPIRO T.; DEFENSE [6]; ENERGY CRISIS [22]; ENVIRONMENT & POLLUTION [8]; UNION OF SOVIET SOCIALIST REPUBLICS [5, 14]
GENERAL AGREEMENT ON TARIFFS & TRADE (GATT)—*See* CANADA [32]; EUROPEAN ECONOMIC COMMUNITY [18]

GENERAL SERVICES ADMINISTRATION—*See* PATENTS; WATERGATE [69-70, 73]
GENETICS—*See* INTELLIGENCE; MEDICINE & HEALTH [31-34]
GEORGIA—*See* CRIME [40]; ELECTIONS [10]; OBSCENITY & PORNOGRAPHY; WEATHER; WOMEN'S RIGHTS
GEOTHERMAL ENERGY—*See* ENERGY CRISIS [23]

GERMANY, EAST (GERMAN DEMOCRATIC REPUBLIC)—The U.S. and the German Democratic Republic established formal diplomatic relations Sept. 4, 25 years after the creation of the East German state. Ambassadors were named by both governments: former Sen. John Sherman Cooper (R, Ky.) for the U.S. and Rolf Seiber, a professor of economics, for East Germany. Permanent embassies were opened Dec. 9. The diplomatic ties became possible after East Germany agreed for the first time to hold discussions, scheduled to begin in several months, on the possible compensation of Jewish victims of Nazism.

Premier Horst Sindermann had arrived in Moscow May 12 for two days of talks with Soviet Communist Party General Secretary Leonid I. Brezhnev, Premier Alexei N. Kosygin and Deputy Premier Nikolai K. Baibakov, chairman of Gosplan, the state planning committee. A communique issued May 13 stated that the meetings had permitted the two countries to approach "certain international problems concerning bilateral cooperation," an apparent reference to the recent spy scandal in West Germany which resulted May 6 in the resignation of Chancellor Willy Brandt. (Gunter Guillaume, a high Brandt aide, was revealed to be an East German spy.) The Soviet Union was known to be displeased with the West German events, for Brandt's Ostpolitik (policy of improving relations with East Europe) had been a fundamental element in Soviet foreign policy. However, East German Communist Party First Secretary Erich Honecker implied that the Russians were in on the spy case when, in remarks May 12, he noted that "all strategic and tactical questions of foreign and defense policy [between the Soviet Union and East Germany] are constantly coordinated."

The East German Volkskammer (parliament) unanimously approved a new Constitution Sept. 27. From it was removed all mention of the concept of the eventual reunification of the two Germanys, a principle still maintained in West Germany's Constitution and policy. The bill amending East Germany's 1968 Constitution went into effect Oct. 7. The constitutional amendment bill also added an article which proclaimed that East Germany was "linked irrevocably and forever" with the Soviet Union.

See also APPOINTMENTS & RESIGNATIONS; AUSTRALIA [20]; CHILE [6]; COMMUNISM, INTERNATIONAL; EUROPEAN SECURITY; FINLAND; GERMANY, WEST [1-5, 10-13]; OBITUARIES [BRAUN]; PORTUGAL [24]; SWIMMING

GERMANY, WEST (FEDERAL REPUBLIC OF)

Government & Politics

[1] **Brandt aide in spy scandal.** Gunter Guillaume, 47, an aide to Chancellor Willy Brandt, was arrested in Bonn April 25 on suspicion of being a spy for East Germany. Also arrested was Guillaume's wife, Christel, 46, and several others. Chief Federal Prosecutor Ludwig Martin said the suspect had made a statement admitting being an officer in the East German army and being in collaboration with the East German Ministry of State Security. Guillaume had come to West Germany as a refugee in 1956 and joined the Social Democratic Party (SDP) in Hesse in September 1957. He began work at the chancellor's office in early 1970 and had been personal assistant to Brandt since Feb 1, 1973. Guillaume was said to be a moderate Socialist.

[2] **Brandt resigns.** Brandt unexpectedly resigned May 6, citing the spy scandal as the reason for his action. In a letter of resignation to President Gustav Heinemann, Brandt assumed responsibility for "negligence" in allowing Guillaume to become a top member of his staff. Brandt asked Heinemann to name Foreign Minister Walter Scheel, also vice chancellor, as head of a caretaker government until the Bundestag (lower house of parliament) elected a new chancellor. Scheel became acting chancellor May 7. Brandt, however, remained head of the SPD. The SPD May 7 nominated Finance Minister Helmut Schmidt, 55, to become the new chancellor. The Free Democratic Party, junior partner in the federal coalition government, indicated its support for Schmidt, assuring his selection May 16. Another factor in the resignation surfaced May 8 when Brandt said in a televised speech that "there were indications my private life would be drawn into speculation about the case." Although he gave no details, Brandt added that it was "grotesque" to maintain that his resignation stemmed from fear of being blackmailed. Two right-wing opposition newspapers owned by Axel Springer had published reports charging that Guillaume had damaging information on Brandt's private life and had threatened to disclose it if he were brought to trial. Horst Ehmke, minister of research and technology, asked Schmidt May 8 not to include him in a new Cabinet. Ehmke had headed Brandt's Chancellery office in 1970 when Guillaume joined the staff, and he had been charged since the arrest with failing to investigate Guillaume's background thoroughly. In an address to a conference of SPD officials in West Berlin May 11, Brandt called reports that he resigned because of a love affair with a Communist woman spy "an evil slanderous campaign of defamation." The government May 10 had denied press reports that an East German woman spy had been paid about $160,000 in public funds not to publish a book about an affair she had with Brandt in the 1950s when he was president of the Berlin City Council.

[3] An independent investigating commission issued a report Nov. 18 blaming structural weaknesses and a breakdown in communication among West Germany's three security services for employment of Guillaume. The commission absolved Brandt of direct blame for the spy scandal but criticized Ehmke, and the security services for giving "speed precedence over caution" in granting secret clearance to Guillaume.

[4] **Scheel elected president.** Walter Scheel was elected president of West Germany May 15 to succeed Heinemann, who was retiring. Scheel won 530 of the 1,036 votes in the presidential electoral college, compared with 498 votes for his only opponent, Richard von Weizsaecker, the candidate of the opposition Christian Democratic Union (CDU). There were five abstentions and three absences. The vote demonstrated that the governing coalition of the FDP and the SPD had withstood bitterness between the two parties provoked by the recent spy scandal. The two parties had quarreled over who should take responsibility for the scandal, with Brandt's Social Democrats angry over the role of Interior Minister Hans-Dietrich Genscher, a Free Democrat. The Social Democrats felt that Genscher should be held responsible for the security services. According to reports, Genscher had advised Brandt to retain Guillaume in his position as a close personal aide so his contacts could be discovered. The electoral college was composed of members of both houses of Parliament and an equal number of representatives from the 10 state legislatures. Scheel was sworn in July 1.

[5] **Schmidt sworn in as chancellor.** Helmut Schmidt, was formally elected and sworn in as chancellor May 16. The vote in the Bundestag was 267-255 in favor of Schmidt, with one Social Democrat absent and apparently three others breaking ranks to vote with the opposition. Three opposition deputies were absent. The Bundestag president, Annemarie Renger-Loncarevic, administered

the oath of office. Schmidt had the reputation of being strongly pro-U.S. and an "atlanticist," a supporter of the North Atlantic Treaty Organization. An unidentified aide said Schmidt was "not very interested in Ostpolitik," Brandt's policy of developing relations with Communist Europe. Schmidt delivered his coalition government's policy address to Parliament May 17. Declaring that his government's theme would be "continuity and concentration," he pledged to pursue the "social-liberal policies" begun under Brandt. Schmidt indicated his intention to smooth over recent difficulties with the U.S., stating that "The security of Western Europe will, within the foreseeable future, remain dependent on the military and political presence of the United States in Europe." His coalition Cabinet was sworn in May 17. The 15-member government, two fewer than Brandt's, had only five new persons. Eleven ministers belonged to the SPD and four to the FDP. The most significant change was the appointment of Genscher as foreign minister and vice chancellor. He replaced Scheel. The Social Democrats had also tried to gain control of the Interior Ministry but the FDP withstood the pressure and the top post went to Werner Miahofer, a Free Democratic minister without portfolio in the outgoing Cabinet.

[6] **Local and state elections.** The SPD suffered setbacks in state and local elections in March. The most severe rebuff occurred in elections for the Hamburg State Senate March 3, when the SPD lost the absolute majority it had held since 1957. With 45% of the vote, down from 55.3% in the 1970 state elections, it won 56 seats in the 120-seat legislature. The opposition CDU won 40.6% of the votes, compared with 32.8% in 1970, winning 51 seats; and the FDP won nearly 11%, up from 7.1% in 1970, for 13 seats. The SPD narrowly retained control of the Lower Saxony State legislature in coalition with the FDP in elections June 9. The SPD had won a one-seat majority on its own in 1970 elections. The opposition Christian Democrats increased their vote percentage over the 1970 elections by 3.2%, winning 48.9% of the votes and 77 seats; the Social Democrats won 43% of the votes, a loss of about 3%, and 67 seats; and the Free Democrats increased their vote percentage from under 5% to 7.1%, winning 11 seats. The FDP did not have any seats in the last legislature because it had failed to get the required 5% of the votes. The SPD lost ground in elections for the state legislatures of Hesse and Bavaria Oct. 27. The CDU scored major gains over the SPD in Hesse, emerging as the strongest single party in the state for the first time since 1946. But the SPD, in coalition with the FDP, would retain control of the legislature. According to early returns, the CDU increased its 1970 vote 7.6%, to 47.3%, winning 53 seats. The SPD obtained 43.2% of the vote, down from 45.9% in 1970; the SPD and FDP won a total of 57 seats. In Bavaria, the Christian Social Union, led by Franz Josef Strauss, retained its absolute majority in the state legislature. It increased its vote share to a record 62.1%, winning 132 seats, eight more than in 1970.

[7] **Klarsfeld sentenced for kidnapping.** Beate Klarsfeld, 35, a German-born non-Jewish Nazi hunter married to a French Jew, was sentenced to two months' imprisonment by a Cologne court July 9 for her part in an abortive kidnap attempt in 1971 against Kurt Lischka, head of the Paris Gestapo during World War II. She was released pending appeal. The trial, protested by the Israeli government July 8, was marred by courtroom demonstrations by Klarsfeld's French supporters until the judge barred the public. During the trial Klarsfeld said the kidnapping had been designed to focus attention on the freedom still enjoyed by Nazi war criminals in West Germany.

[8] **Berlin court president slain.** Gunter von Drenkmann, 64, president of West Berlin's highest court, was shot dead at his home Nov. 10 by a group of men believed to be left-wing extremists. Police said they suspected the killers

were members of the "Red Army Faction" acting in revenge for the death of a leader of the Baader-Meinhof urban guerrilla group in prison Nov. 9. The prisoner, Holger Meins, died after a two-month hunger strike, which he had begun Sept. 13 along with some 40 other members of his group to protest their alleged isolation in jail. Meins, in pretrial detention since 1972, had been indicted with Andreas Baader, Ulrike Meinhof, Gudrun Ensslin and Jan-Carl Raspe Oct. 2 on charges of complicity in several murders, bombing attacks and bank holdups. The trial was scheduled for the spring of 1975 in Stuttgart. The Red Army Faction claimed responsibility for the murder of von Drenkmann, who had no direct connection with the Meins case, and threatened more murders, it was reported Nov. 12.

[9] Meinhof, 40, a ringleader of the Baader-Meinhof urban guerrilla group, was sentenced to eight years in prison by a West Berlin court Nov. 29 for complicity in attempted murder in connection with helping another terrorist, Baader, escape from jail in 1970. A person was shot and wounded in the incident. Another defendant, Horst Mahler, a former lawyer serving a 12-year term for robbing a bank, was sentenced to two years' imprisonment; and Hans Jurgen Backer was acquitted.

Relations with East Germany

[10] **Berlin traffic harassed.** East Germany imposed strict traffic controls between West Berlin and West Germany for about 12 hours Jan. 26, in an apparent violation of the 1971 four-power Berlin accord. The East German government said Jan. 28 that the extra roadblocks and unusually thorough searches of passengers and cars resulted from a search for criminals. Chancellor Brandt had conferred with West Berlin officials in West Berlin Jan. 27 about the incidents, which were the first since the four-power pact went into effect in June, 1972. Egon Bahr, West German representative in East Berlin, said Jan. 27 that East Germany was trying "to restrict, narrow and slow down" the process of establishing full diplomatic relations with West Germany. East German agents again interfered with traffic from West Germany to West Berlin Feb. 1. East Germany had also threatened to bar officials of the new West German environmental protection office in West Berlin from reaching the city by rail or road, it was reported Feb. 10.

[11] **Two Germanys set diplomatic exchange.** East and West Germany signed an accord in Bonn March 14 establishing permanent diplomatic missions in one another's capitals. Although the missions would not have the diplomatic status of embassies, they would perform many of the same functions. The agreement was concluded by Gunter Gaus, a state secretary in the Bonn Chancellery, and Kurt Nier, East German deputy foreign minister. Both sides made significant concessions on issues which had impeded the progress of the talks. The Federal Republic of Germany (West Germany), which was prohibited by its Constitution from treating the Democratic Republic of Germany (East Germany) as a foreign country, agreed to attach its representative to East Germany's Foreign Ministry yielding to East Germany's demand that Bonn conduct inter-German affiairs in accordance with international norms. The other major impasse was cleared by East Germany which, like all Warsaw Pact members, had refused to recognize West Germany's formal rights to ties with West Berlin and had never entered into any treaties that included West Berlin. In the final accord, however, East Germany agreed to the inclusion of a note that said West Germany's representative in East Germany "would represent the interests of (West) Berlin, conforming to the Sept. 3, 1971 four-power agreement on Berlin." The 1971 accord had affirmed that although West Berlin would "continue not to be a constituent part" of West Germany, its ties with West Germany would "be maintained and developed." East

and West Germany exchanged permanent representatives June 20. West Germany's representative, Gunter Gaus, was accredited in East Berlin and East Germany's Michael Kohl was received in Bonn.

[12] **Environment office opening sparks harassment.** The Soviet Union issued a warning July 20 that it would take "appropriate measures" if West Germany went ahead with announced plans to open an environmental office in West Berlin. The German Democratic Republic said July 21 that, should the office be opened, staff members would be prevented from using the highways between West Germany and West Berlin. Despite threats and traffic blockades, the environmental office was opened in West Berlin July 25. East German border guards at Marienborn July 30 stopped an agency official from entering the city. The U.S., Britain and France Aug. 5 delivered separate protest notes to the U.S.S.R. Foreign Ministry urging that the border harassment be discontinued. A U.S. State Department spokesman said Aug. 7 that harassment had ended and that access to West Berlin and the environment office was no longer being hampered.

[13] **Berlin gains seen in Moscow visit.** Chancellor Schmidt concluded three days of talks with Soviet Communist Party leader Leonid Brezhnev in Moscow Oct. 30, declaring that some progress had been made on the issue of West Berlin's links to West Germany. At a press conference in Moscow, Schmidt said the two sides had agreed "in principle" on West German construction of a 1,200 megawatt nuclear power plant at Kaliningrad on the Soviet-Polish border, with the electricity feeder line from the station to run through West Berlin to West Germany. The chancellor also said accord had been reached which would permit Bonn to represent West Berlin interests in some long-range economic projects. During the three days of talks, Soviet leaders did not indicate they had eased their objection to Bonn representing West Berlin's legal institutions in Eastern Europe or to a West German environmental office in West Berlin.

Foreign Relations

[14] **Radio sales to Arabs defended.** The government rejected a U.S. complaint that the Munich electronics firm Telemit Corp. had illegally manufactured and sold U.S.-designed military radio equipment to Arab nations, including Syria and Libya, the *Washington Post* reported Feb. 10. The U.S. had invoked a 1956 agreement with Bonn on "patent and technological interchange for defense purposes" to demand that the German government compel Telemit to cease unauthorized manufacture of a walkie-talkie developed in the U.S. for military use. The West German government replied that the equipment was also used for civilian purposes and did not come under the scope of the 1956 military technology agreement. Telemit contended that it had so changed and improved the design of the U.S. radio that it no longer resembled it.

[15] **U.S. troop cost accord signed.** The U.S. and West Germany signed a final agreement April 25 under which Bonn would pay $2.218 billion to offset the costs of stationing 197,000 U.S. troops in Germany. The new agreement covered the two-year period ending June 30, 1975. Under the accord, Germany would buy $1.03 billion worth of U.S. arms and $843 million in low-interest U.S. Treasury securities, spend $225 million to modernize U.S. barracks in West Germany and exempt U.S. forces from $8 million in airport landing fees and real estate taxes.

[16] **Iran projects.** West German business firms and Iran signed 24 preliminary agreements for more than $2.2 billion of industrial projects, including a $1.2 billion oil refinery at the Persian Gulf port of Bushire, a steel plant and petrochemical complex, it was reported May 2. The announcement followed a

conference in Iran attended by more than 100 West German businessmen. The preliminary accord on the petrochemical complex was signed by the West German chemical producers Hoechst AG and Bayer AG with the Iranian National Petrochemical Co. The steel accord was signed by the Iranian National Steel Corp. and five German steel manufacturers, including Fried. Krupp. (The Economics Ministry disclosed Dec. 2 that Kuwait had purchased a 14.6% share in Daimler-Benz, West Germany's second largest automobile manufacturer after Volkswagen and maker of the Mercedes car.)

[17] **West Berlin restricts Jewish immigrants.** The West Berlin government announced new regulations Dec. 3 to restrict the "undiminished influx" of Jewish refugees from the Soviet Union and Eastern Europe. More than 540 immigrants had settled in West Berlin since August 1973, a spokesman said. Under the new rules, immigrants must obtain valid entry visas, a regulation applied to the entry of all foreigners. Most Jewish refugees to West Berlin had entered as tourists, who were allowed to stay six months, and then sought to settle. These regulations also provided that those Jews who could prove German ancestry would be allowed to remain under the German resettlement laws.

See also ALGERIA; AUTO RACING; BANKS & BANKING; BELGIUM; CHAD; CHILE [7, 24]; COMMUNISM, INTERNATIONAL; EUROPEAN ECONOMIC COMMUNITY [5-7, 14]; EUROPEAN SECURITY; FAMINE & FOOD; FINLAND; FRANCE [19]; IRAN; ITALY [6-7]; MAURITANIA; MEXICO [19]; MIDDLE EAST [26, 34]; MONETARY DEVELOPMENTS [4, 8, 10, 14-17, 19, 22]; NORTH ATLANTIC TREATY ORGANIZATION; OBITUARIES [GISEVIUS]; OIL [11, 23, 26, 34]; POLAND; PORTUGAL [22]; PRIVACY [11]; SOCCER; SOLZHENITSYN, ALEXANDER; SUDAN; SWITZERLAND; TERRITORIAL WATERS; UNION OF SOVIET SOCIALIST REPUBLICS [11]; UNITED NATIONS [11]

GHANA—*See* ALUMINUM AND BAUXITE; APPOINTMENTS & RESIGNATIONS

GISCARD d'ESTAING, VALERY—*See* ATOMIC ENERGY [7]; EUROPEAN ECONOMIC COMMUNITY [13]; FRANCE; MONETARY DEVELOPMENTS [11]; OIL [27]

GIZIKIS, PHAIDON—*See* CYPRUS [2, 11]; GREECE [3-4]; MIDDLE EAST [28]; ZAIRE

GOLD—*See* FRANCE [18]; ITALY [6]; MONETARY DEVELOPMENTS; SOUTH AFRICA [2, 10]

GOLDBERG, ARTHUR J.—*See* ROCKEFELLER, NELSON [2, 12-14]

GOLF—Miller sets new earnings mark. By posting his eighth triumph of 1974 in the Kaiser International open in Napa, Calif. Sept. 29, Johnny Miller set a new record for money won on the Professional Golfers Association (PGA) tour in a single season. The first prize of $30,000 in the Kaiser open boosted Miller's earnings to $346,933, breaking the old record of $320,542 set by Jack Nicklaus in 1972. Miller was also the first pro to win eight tournaments in a year since Arnold Palmer in 1960. The PGA Oct. 24 announced it had selected Miller as top player of 1974.

Player wins second Masters. Gary Player of South Africa won his second Masters golf tournament April 14 in Augusta, Ga. His four-round total of 278 earned him $35,000.

Irwin wins U.S. Open. Hale Irwin won the U.S. Open at Winged Foot Golf Club in Mamaroneck, N.Y. by two strokes June 16. Irwin posted a seven-over-par total of 287 for 72 holes. Irwin earned $35,000.

Trevino captures PGA title. Refusing to succumb to a challenge by Jack Nicklaus, Lee Trevino fired a final-round, one-under-par 69 to win the 56th PGA national championship at Tanglewood Golf Club in Clemmons, N.C. Aug. 11. Trevino's four-round total of 276, one shot better than Nicklaus, earned him $45,000.

GOVERNMENT SECRECY—*See* FREEDOM OF INFORMATION ACT

GREAT BRITAIN

Government & Economy

[1] **State of emergency continues.** The early part of the year saw a deepening of Great Britain's economic crisis as a result of labor disputes in the coal, electrical power and railroad industries, aggravated by the shortage of oil. Faced with crucial energy shortages, the government had, on Nov. 13, 1973, declared a state of emergency; and, the following month, had announced a three-day workweek for most industries and businesses, effective Jan. 1, 1974. Workers in the electrical industries were protesting the declining margin between their pay and that of unskilled workers. The situation had been aggravated when the nation's 270,000 coal miners banned overtime to support their demands for sharp pay increases. The economic crisis worsened Jan. 10 when many rail engineers walked off their jobs in protest against management-ordered disciplinary action. The engineers' union ordered its members back to work the next day, but threatened a one-day strike for the following week unless pay negotiations were resumed. The union also suspended its work-to-rule campaign, but maintained its ban on Sunday, overtime and rest-day working. Talks held Jan. 14 between Prime Minister Edward Heath and leaders of the Trades Union Congress (TUC) failed to resolve the pay dispute with the coal miners. Temporary registered unemployment caused mainly by the coal shortage and three-day workweek, rose to 915,000 Jan. 8, with the Midlands industrial region hardest hit. Steel production had been running at 50% of normal capacity since Dec. 22, 1973 because of coal shortages. The government ended its power restrictions on the steel industry Jan. 17 and hinted that it would extend the three-day workweek to four days.

[2] Leaders of the National Union of Mineworkers (NUM) Feb. 5 ordered a strike to begin Feb. 10 because of the government's refusal to increase its pay offer to the miners. The union leaders demanded a 30%-40% increase. The strike call came one day after Heath and leaders of the TUC, whose 10 million members included the 270,000 miners, failed to agree on a proposal made by Heath Jan. 30 that the miners accept the current offer of about 16.5% and await the findings of a new impartial board. The coal miners began their nationwide strike Feb. 10 amid government warnings that the shutdown of mines would have a devastating effect on the faltering economy already hit by the three-day workweek. The strike and the Conservative government's anti-inflation policies were the major issues in the opening days of the three-week general election campaign. The special public inquiry into additional wages for miners on the basis of "relativity" began Feb. 18.

[3] **Elections called.** Prime Minister Heath Feb. 7 ordered Parliament dissolved and called a general election for Feb. 28, 16 months earlier than required, after leaders of the coal miners decided to widen their overtime ban to a full strike. Heath made a last-minute appeal to the miners to delay their strike, set to begin Feb. 10, until after elections, but the union leaders rejected the request Feb. 8. The Labor Party program, issued Feb. 8, called for controls over "key" commodities and services, but said a Labor government would rely on voluntary restraint by unions to curb wage increases; pledged to renegotiate the terms of Britain's entry into the European Economic Community (EEC) and to hold a referendum on the new terms; said it would expel the U.S. Polaris bases

on British soil; and promised to nationalize more industries, as well as Britain's share of offshore North Sea oil and gas resources. The Conservative Party issued its manifesto Feb. 10, defining the choice for voters as one "between moderation and extremism." The platform defended the government's mandatory wage and price policy and envisaged a new provision to force unions to pay strike benefits to their members' families rather than leave that as a government responsibility. The manifesto of the Liberal Party, issued Feb. 12, called for a penalty tax for either employers or employes who contributed to inflation and for a permanent prices and incomes policy with dividends, prices and wages limited to an agreed ratio of increase. Labor Party leader Harold Wilson called for a special tax on windfall profits Feb. 16, one day after publication of official figures showing a 20% increase in food prices since January 1973.

[4] **Elections result in deadlock.** General elections held Feb. 28 resulted in Britain's worst political crisis in over 40 years. Neither the ruling Conservative Party nor the Labor Party won a majority in the 635-seat House of Commons. But the Laborites gained a slight edge over the Conservatives in the new Parliament. Heath did not resign when he met with Queen Elizabeth March 1. In an apparent effort to seek additional support that would help keep the Conservatives in office, Heath conferred with Liberal Party leader Jeremy Thorpe March 2. Details of the meeting were not disclosed.

[5] Composition of the new House of Commons (number of seats in the previous 630-seat Parliament in parentheses): Labor 301 (287), Conservatives 296 (323), Liberals 14 (11), others 24. Hard-line Northern Ireland Protestants won 11 of the province's 12 seats in the Commons, emerging as the fourth largest group in the deadlocked new Parliament. Gerard Fitt, leader of the Catholic Social Democratic and Labor Party, was the only Ulster representative elected who supported power-sharing between Protestants and Catholics in the newly-formed provincial executive. Heath resigned March 4 after he failed to win the Liberals' support for a coalition government; Labor Party leader Wilson was immediately named prime minister. Wilson's new Cabinet: Prime minister—Harold Wilson; lord president of the Council and leader of the House of Commons—Edward Short; foreign—James Callaghan; home affairs—Roy Jenkins; Exchequer—Denis Healey; employment—Michael Foot; defense—Roy Mason; lord chancellor—Sir Elwyn Jones; energy—Eric Varley; agriculture and fisheries—Frederick Peart; social services—Barbara Castle; industry—Anthony Wedgwood Benn; environment—Anthony Crosland; secretary of state for Scotland—William Ross; chancellor of the Duchy of Lancaster—Harold Lever; trade—Peter Shore; prices and consumer protection—Shirley Williams; secretary of state for Northern Ireland—Merlyn Rees; secretary of state for Wales—John Morris; education and science—Reg Prentice; lord privy seal—Lord Shepherd (named March 7).

[6] **Wilson outlines policy.** The program of the minority Labor government, read to the new Parliament by Queen Elizabeth II in her Speech from the Throne March 12, called for a "fundamental renegotiation" of the terms of Britain's membership in the EEC but omitted most of its pledges to nationalize additional sectors of the economy. In a more cautious statement than Labor's campaign pledge for "full public ownership" of North Sea oil and gas resources, the government's program spoke only of exploiting the North Sea resources to confer "maximum benefit to the community." Except for national ownership of land for urban development, there was no other mention of industries slated for nationalization in Labor's election platform. Wilson pledged that any extension of public ownership within industry would be submitted to a parliamentary vote. The queen's speech promised repeal of the Industrial Relations Act, which regulated trade union activity and was opposed by labor, and its replacement by

a new conciliation and mediation service for securing wage increases on a voluntary basis; establishment of "fair prices" for certain key foods and introduction of food subsidies "where appropriate"; repeal of a Conservative government measure imposing higher rents in some public housing; and increase in pensions and social security benefits.

[7] **Mine strike settled.** Leaders of NUM and the new Labor government agreed March 6 on a pay settlement that would end the nationwide miners' strike and send the workers back on the job March 11. The settlement, providing for an overall 30% increase in wages that would cost the equivalent of about $230 million, nearly doubled the 16½% increase worth $100 million offered by the Heath government. The contract was approved by rank-and-file members. It was effective March 1, 1974, rather than Nov. 1, 1973 as initially demanded by the union. The Trades Union Congress reiterated March 6 a promise made to Heath that the miners' settlement would not be used as a precedent for higher wage claims by other unions. Because of the coal settlement, the new energy secretary, Eric Varley, March 7, canceled the three-day workweek, effective midnight March 8. The government March 11 ended the state of emergency declared in November 1973. The National Coal Board (NCB) March 11 announced coal price increases, effective April 1, of 28%-48%, which would total over $620 million.

[8] **'75 budget introduced.** The new Labor government March 26 presented a budget for fiscal 1975 (April 1, 1974-March 31, 1975) that raised a variety of taxes, increased food subsidies and raised prices for some essential goods and services. The basic income tax rate, on income up to about £4,000, was increased from 30% to 33%, while the highest income rate was raised from 75% to 83%. As a tax relief for low wage-earners, the government raised the standard tax exemption allowance. Healey estimated that the new rates would exempt 1.5 million workers from taxes. The standard corporate tax rate was increased to 52%, and company tax payments in 1974 would have to be accelerated. All foreigners working in Britain would have to pay British tax on at least half their income, closing the loophole under which foreigners were exempt if their earnings were not brought into the country. Large increases in indirect taxes were set for numerous products, including cigarettes, liquor, wine and beer. To raise the revenues of nationalized industries, the government announced price increases of an average 25% for the British Steel Corp., 30% on home electricity rates, 15% on rail freight, 12.5% on rail passenger fares and 15%-20% on telecommunications charges. Defense spending was cut by £50 million. Certain basic foods would be subsidized, including milk, in addition to a bread subsidy announced March 20.

[9] **Economic indicators drop.** Continued anxieties over the state of Britain's economy, fed by the payments and trade deficits, business insecurity over the Labor government's nationalization plans and soaring inflation, caused the London stock market to drop to a new 15-year low June 24, with the Financial Times Industrial Index closing at 248.3 The index dropped 24.4 points the previous week in what was described as one of the market's weakest performances on record. The market had fallen over 50% in the last two years, according to one report. The pound dropped more than 2¢ June 24, closing at around $2.355, its lowest level in more than two months. The government had reported June 21 that the retail price index in May rose 1.4%, bringing the rise to a postwar record of 16% in one year. Some 60 strikes, many of them wildcat, were under way as unions sought wage increases tied to the inflation index, it was reported June 18.

[10] **Interim budget presented.** In a turnabout from the budget presented in

March, the government July 22 announced tax cuts and other measures designed to slow price rises and bolster public confidence in the economy. The value-added tax (VAT) would be reduced from 10% to 8% effective July 29; food subsidies would be increased by £50 million ($119 million); local property tax relief would be granted; dividend controls would be relaxed, permitting companies to increase dividends from the current 5% to 12.5%; and regional employment premiums would be doubled, a move designed to stimulate employment in regions of high unemployment. Chancellor of the Exchequer Healey, who presented the interim budget to the House of Commons, said the VAT reduction and other measures should reduce retail prices by more than 1.5% in the next three months. This would curb the automatic "threshold" wage increases triggered by rises in the cost of living index.

[11] **Shipbuilders to be nationalized.** Secretary for Industry Anthony Wedgwood Benn announced plans July 31 to nationalize the nation's biggest shipbuilding, ship-repairing and marine engineering companies. He told the House of Commons that fair compensation would be paid. A White Paper on the subject would be published later this year. Thirteen shipbuilding companies and 13 ship-repairing companies and specialized diesel-makers would be nationalized. The promised White Paper, entitled "The Regeneration of British Industry," was presented Aug. 15. It proposed establishment of a National Enterprise Board to supervise government take-overs of private firms. It would have the power to take a controlling interest in a company "by agreement" and would provide investment capital in exchange for shares. If the government decided to nationalize a company, the acquisition would require parliamentary authorization and "fair compensation to existing shareholders." The White Paper also recommended a program of three-year planning agreements under which major private companies, in consultation with trade union representatives and government officials, would submit operating plans to cover investment, price policy, employment and other factors. Sectors to be nationalized were North Sea Oil, shipbuilding, aircraft manufacturing and various port industries, with an extension of state control envisaged for road haulage and construction.

[12] **Wealth redistribution taxes proposed.** Two tax proposals, aimed at redistribution of wealth, were outlined by Chancellor of the Exchequer Healy Aug. 8. One tax was a wealth levy on assets exceeding £100,000 ($237,000). The second proposal was for a capital transfer tax on gifts exceeding £15,000, which would replace existing estate duty provisions. Designed to close estate tax loopholes under which the rich put their wealth into trusts or gave it to their children before they die, the capital transfer tax would be retroactive to March 26.

[13] **Labor relations bill approved.** The House of Commons July 30 gave final approval to the Trade Union and Labor Relations Bill, which repealed the Industrial Relations Act of the former Conservative government. The Conservative and Liberal opposition had used their numerical superiority to force a number of restrictive changes in the bill. The government had repeatedly been defeated on votes during its three-month consideration. The bill's major clause provided for abolition of the National Industrial Relations Court and the Registry of Trade Unions and Employers' Associations. It retained provisions of the Industrial Relations Act concerning unfair dismissals. One of the successful opposition amendments removed protection from unions for inducing breaches of commercial contract.

[14] The annual conference of the TUC voted Sept. 4 to support the Labor

government's "social contract," an informal agreement which called for voluntary wage restraint by unions in exchange for social and economic reform by the government.

[15] **Second 1974 election held.** Prime Minister Wilson announced Sept. 18 that general elections would be held Oct. 10. It would be the first time in 50 years that two general elections had been held in a year. In a television address, Wilson appealed to the nation to give his Labor Party a majority in Parliament, asserting that his government "has the policies for our national recovery" from "the gravest economic crisis since the war."

[16] Divisions in the Labor Party over Britain's membership in the EEC became an issue in the election campaign when two ministers (Shirley Williams and Ray Jenkins) said they would resign from the government if Britain withdrew from the community as a result of a national referendum.

[17] The Labor Party won a three-seat majority in Parliament in general elecions held Oct. 10. The Labor Party won 319 seats, a gain of 18, while the Conservatives took 276, a loss of 20, and the Liberals won 13, a loss of 1. The remainder of the seats in the 635-member House of Commons went to (seats won in the February vote in parentheses): Northern Ireland's Protestant Unionist Party 10 (11); Ulster's Catholic Social Democratic and Labor Party 1 (1); Scottish Nationalists 11 (7); Welsh Nationalists 3 (2); and others 2. The Labor Party won 11,452,510 votes, compared with 10,405,387 for the Conservatives. Labor's share of the popular vote was 35.9%, compared with 37.3% in February; Conservatives polled 35.9%, compared with 38.1%; and Liberals 18.3%, as against 19.3%. Enoch Powell, a right-wing defector from the Conservative Party, won a seat under the banner of Ulster's Unionist Party.

[18] **Policy speech stresses nationalization.** The new Labor government outlined a legislative course that would extend nationalization of private industry, in line with the Labor Party's election campaign pledges and pre-election White Papers. The policy speech was read at the opening of the recently elected Parliament by Queen Elizabeth II in her traditional Speech from the Throne Oct. 29. The speech, which contained few surprises, reiterated government plans to nationalize the aircraft, shipbuilding and offshore oil industries, establish a national enterprise board and foster planning agreements between management and labor. It omitted mention of nationalizing Britain's remaining privately-owned ports.

[19] **Budget triples gasoline tax.** The Labor government presented its third budget of the year Nov. 12, providing for a threefold increase in the tax on gasoline and measures to ease the liquidity squeeze on corporations. Delivering the budget message to Parliament, Chancellor of the Exchequer Healey said the government's main tasks now were to promote investment so that productivity would increase, and to protect the balance of payments against its growing oil-related deficit. Healey said the government planned to phase out subsidies for most of the deficit-ridden nationalized industries. The first big increase for consumers would be the tripling, effective Nov. 18, of the value-added tax on gasoline, from 8% to 25%. This would raise the price of medium grade gasoline about 16¢, to $1.15 a U.S. gallon. To stimulate industry, which had been caught in a cash crunch, the government eased price controls and provided tax relief, which together were expected to amount to some £1.5 billion ($3.45 billion). Companies would be permitted to pass along to consumers up to 80% of any increases in labor costs, compared with the present 50%, and 17½% in investment costs. They would also be permitted to deduct from taxable income some of the inflation-caused inventory appreciation profits.

[20] **Major defense cuts planned.** The government announced plans Dec. 3 to

reduce defense expenditures by £4.7 billion (about $11 billion) over the next decade, reducing the defense share of Britain's gross national product from 5½% to 4½%. The proposals would reduce the armed forces, now totaling about 354,000, by 35,000, half of them from the Royal Air Force.

[21] **Arabs deny sterling sales.** Sheik Ahmed Zaki al-Yamani, Saudi Arabia's petroleum minister, Dec. 14 blamed U.S. oil companies, not Arab oil producers, for the sharp drop in the British pound in the first half of December. Yamani said the U.S. partners in the Arabian-American Oil Co. had sold "huge amounts" of sterling after being notified that they would have to make all future oil payments in dollars. Until now, Saudi Arabia had accepted about 25% payment in sterling.

Oil and Energy

[22] **Self-sufficiency by 1980 predicted.** In a report to Parliament May 21, Energy Minister Eric Varley estimated that Britain would be self-sufficient in oil by 1980 because North Sea oil production would be in the range of 100-140 million tons a year (equal to about 2-3 million barrels a day). The production estimate represented a sharp increase over the 70-100 million ton forecast in the Energy Department's 1973 report, an indication of the accelerating pace of Britain's North Sea discoveries.

[23] **North Sea oil control planned.** The Labor government July 11 announced its plans to gain a majority interest in North Sea oil development, giving the nation a greater share of the profits and more control over production. The proposals provided for an additional tax on continental shelf profits and closing of various tax loopholes; creation of a Scottish-based national oil corporation which would obtain a majority interest in future licenses granted for North Sea fields, while companies currently operating in the North Sea would be "invited" to talk about majority state participation in existing leases. The program also called for extension of government powers to control offshore operations, including production; and immediate creation of a Scottish development agency to use offshore oil revenues to promote Scotland's economy, while a similar body would be established for Wales as oil development proceeded in the Irish Sea.

[24] **North Sea oil output plans cited.** In an attempt to reassure worried companies about commercial prospects in the North Sea, Energy Secretary Varley disclosed in the House of Commons Dec. 6 that the government would not curb the development of oil discoveries made up to the end of 1975; on finds made after 1975, he said he saw no production controls at least until 1982. He also said companies would be permitted to recover 150% of their capital investment in any field before production cuts were imposed.

[25] **Government aids Burmah Oil.** The government announced Dec. 31 that the Bank of England would guarantee a $650 million one-year loan to Britain's second largest oil company, Burmah Oil, which said it expected to show a big 1974 loss in its oil tanker operations. In exchange, the Bank of England would acquire Burmah's "unpledged" shares in the British Petroleum Co. (BP) and Shell Transport & Trading Co., the British unit of the Royal Dutch/Shell group.

Other Developments

[26] **Ambush of princess fails.** Princess Anne and her husband, Capt. Mark Phillips, escaped unharmed when a gunman fired shots into their limousine near Buckingham Palace in a kidnap attempt March 20. Ian Ball, 26, was charged and held without bail the next day. Ball was ordered indefinitely committed to a mental hospital May 22 after he pleaded guilty in London's Old Bailey court to the attempted kidnapping of Princess Anne and attempted

murder charges. Lord Widgery, England's chief justice, said he had decided against life imprisonment because of evidence that Ball was mentally ill.
[27] **Major bank incurs losses.** Lloyds Bank, one of Britain's four largest banks, announced Sept. 2 it had incurred losses of about £33 million ($76 million) because of "irregularities" in foreign exchange transactions at a branch in Lugano, Switzerland.

See also APPOINTMENTS & RESIGNATIONS; ATOMIC ENERGY [10]; AUSTRALIA [13, 16]; AUTO RACING; AVIATION [15]; BOOKS; CANADA [61]; CHILE [1, 6, 24]; COMMUNISM, INTERNATIONAL; CYPRUS [3-4, 6, 9-10, 13, 19-20]; DEFENSE [14]; EUROPEAN ECONOMIC COMMUNITY [1, 6, 8-14, 18]; EUROPEAN SECURITY; FAMINE & FOOD; GREECE [2]; GRENADA; IRAN; IRELAND, NORTHERN; JORDAN; KUWAIT; MALTA; MAURITANIA; MEDICINE & HEALTH [34]; MIDDLE EAST [14, 26, 29, 34]; MONETARY DEVELOPMENTS [4, 8, 10-11, 17, 19, 23]; MOROCCO; NOBEL PRIZES; NORTH ATLANTIC TREATY ORGANIZATION; OBITUARIES [GLOUCESTER]; OIL [3, 11, 23, 25-26, 33-34]; PAKISTAN; SEYCHELLE ISLANDS; SOUTH AFRICA [13]; TARIFFS & TRADE; TENNIS; TERRITORIAL WATERS; UGANDA; UNION OF SOVIET SOCIALIST REPUBLICS [25, 28]; UNITED NATIONS [6, 11]; URUGUAY; WEST INDIES ASSOCIATED STATES

GREECE—Junta replaced by civilian regime. The military junta of Greece, in an attempt to take over control of the island of Cyprus by deposing its president, Archbishop Makarios, instead provoked a Turkish invasion that resulted in the loss of more than one-third of that island's territory. The failure of the attempted coup resulted in the resignation July 23 of the military regime in Athens after seven years of near-absolute power.
[2] Opposition to the dictatorship had grown steadily both within and outside Greece. The Council of Europe had adopted a measure Jan. 17 condemning the Greek government for continuing to violate basic human rights. They also called on members of the North Atlantic Treaty Organization (NATO) and the European Economic Community (EEC) to exert pressures on the military regime to restore democracy. The newly-elected Labor government of Great Britain had, on March 14, announced cancellation of a four-day visit by a cruiser and frigate to Greece. The Greek Foreign Ministry called the cancellation "an intervention in the domestic affairs of Greece." British Foreign Secretary James Callaghan said, however, "we have to differentiate ourselves from dictatorships." Within Greece, the junta fought opposition with arrests, exile and censorship. George Mavros, acting leader of the Center Union Party which had won a majority in Greece's last parliamentary elections in 1964, was arrested March 16 for welcoming Britain's cancellation of a navy visit on the grounds that there was no democracy in Greece. Mavros was released May 15.
[3] Faced with the failure of its attempt to manipulate the Cyprus coup, the military regime in Athens resigned July 23. Immediately after consultation with civilian leaders, President Phaidon Gizikis summoned former Premier Constantine Caramanlis back to Athens from his self-imposed exile in Paris. The junta's announcement of its resignation was broadcast at 7 p.m. The announcement was cheered by thousands of Greeks who flooded Athens streets. The ruling junta had called a meeting of "national emergency" that afternoon with civilian and political leaders to discuss the political crisis. Among those attending the meeting, presided over by President Gizikis, were representatives of every major non-leftist group, many of whom had been arrested, jailed or exiled under the military regime. The junta's leader, Brig. Gen. Demetrios Ioannides, was not present. The radio announcement and the resignation of Premier Adamantios Androutsopoulos and his Cabinet followed the meeting,

during which Gizikis asked the civilian leaders to set aside their differences in order to lead the country out of its political and economic problems.

[4] Caramanlis returned to Athens July 24 and was sworn in immediately. Caramanlis was founder of the conservative National Radical Union (NRU) and had been its leader until he entered voluntary exile in 1963 after being defeated in national elections by liberal Center Union Party (CUP) leader George Papandreou. Announcing his Cabinet July 24, Caramanlis said he sought a "government of national unity," and, though he named an essentially center-and-right government, he pledged July 25 that it would be "reinforced with new political forces." Recently-exiled CUP leader Mavros was appointed deputy premier and foreign minister. Lt. Gen. Gizikis, a member of the deposed junta, was asked to remain in the office of president for the time being. The junta's strongman, Brig. Gen. Ioannides, was placed under "comfortable house arrest." Andreas Papandreou, son of the late Premier George Papandreou and exiled head of the leftist Panhellenic Liberation Movement, said July 23 that the new government represented no real change in Greece and asserted that "the Americans and the Greek armed forces" remained in control. The new civilian government announced July 24 a "full and unreserved" amnesty for political crimes and said that it recognized Archbishop Makarios as "the legal head of Cyprus." Ex-King Constantine said July 24 that he hoped to return to Greece. According to Aug. 21 reports, Constantine announced he would be willing to return to Greece to assume a symbolic role as monarch and would shun any political function. The issue of the restoration of the monarchy was held in abeyance by the civilian government when it restored the 1952 Constitution Aug. 1. The government restored freedom of activity Sept. 23 to all political parties and legalized the long-banned Communist Party.

[5] The 88-member Council of Appeal Judges Nov. 1 ordered the prosecution of former President George Papadopoulos and 48 junta associates, including Brig. Gen. Ioannides, on charges of high treason for organizing and carrying out the military coup of April 1967. The charges were formally laid by Athens' chief prosecutor Nov. 5. If convicted, the military officers could face the death penalty. Premier Caramanlis had been severely criticized for not acting more decisively against the members of the defunct military regime; the unexpected arrests and exiles were expected to give him support in the Nov. 17 elections.

[6] The government announced Oct. 2 that parliamentary elections would be held Nov. 17 and that a referendum on the future of the monarchy would be held within 45 days after the elections. Caramanlis resigned as premier Oct. 8 and was named to head a caretaker government until the elections. Leftist leader Papandreou had announced the formation Sept. 3 of the Panhellenic Socialist Movement, a new party which was seen as a major political threat to Premier Caramanlis. His party's platform included a call for abolition of the monarchy and the pursuit of a nonaligned policy, including termination of all political and economic alliances which "undermined Greek independence." He included the European Common Market in this category. Caramanlis announced the formation of a new party, New Democracy, Sept. 28 which, he said, would be broadly based to dissociate itself from "the misleading labels of right, center and left." The liberal Center Union Party, headed by Foreign Minister Mavros, announced Oct. 7 that it would merge with a new organization called the New Political Forces, composed of Social Democrats who had struggled against the dictatorship. Mavros resigned from the government Oct. 15 to concentrate on the campaign. Career diplomat Demetrios Bitsios replaced him as deputy premier and foreign minister Oct. 17.

[7] Caramanlis' New Democracy Party (NDP) received 54.37% of the popular

vote Nov. 17. The NDP victory signaled a rejection of leftist and liberal parties and personalities, according to news reports Nov. 15-18. Caramanlis' overwhelming victory gave the NDP 220 of the total 300 seats under the complex electoral representation law passed in September. The Center Union-New Political Forces Party (CUP) headed by Mavros took 20.42% of the vote to win 60 Parliamentary seats. Papandreou's Panhellenic Socialist Movement (Pasok) secured 12 seats, having failed, with only 13.58% of the vote, to qualify for the second distribution of seats. The United Left, the Communist Party coalition, won 9.45% of the vote and obtained 8 Parliamentary seats. The extreme right-wing National Democratic Union (NDU) got 1.1% of the vote and other small splinter parties drew 1.08%, securing no Parliamentary seats.

[8] Greek voters rejected by more than a 2-1 margin the restoration of the 142-year-old monarchy and elected to remain a parliamentary republic, voting in favor of "uncrowned democracy" in a national referendum Dec. 8.

[9] The draft of a new Constitution, proposing a strong presidential-form parliamentary republic was made public by the government Dec. 23. The text was immediately criticized by opposition parties as authoritarian. The draft was proposed to replace the 1952 Constitution voided by the abolition of the monarchy in a national referendum Dec. 8. The draft constitution gave the president, who would also be commander in chief of the armed forces, the power to name and dismiss the premier and Cabinet ministers, dissolve parliament and veto legislation. The president would be chosen by a two-thirds majority of Parliament. The draft was widely described as "Gaullist" in view of the broad powers accorded the president.

[10] **Relations with U.S.** The U.S. postponed substantive talks with Greece on further implementation of the 1973 naval base agreement, it was reported Jan. 15. The initial stage of the accord had already been put into effect, with the stationing of a destroyer squadron at Eleusis and the settlement of 1,500 Navy dependents in the Athens area. State Department opposition to the accord involved a belief that the new regime was unstable or excessively nationalistic, and had barred U.S. transshipment of arms to Israel while allowing Soviet overflights of military supplies to Egypt and Syria. Some U.S. Navy admirals also were reported to oppose the accord, out of distrust of foreign bases. Implementation of a plan to station an aircraft carrier in Megara Bay was deferred for at least a year because of delays in concluding arrangements with the new Greek government, it was announced March 15.

[11] The White House announced Aug. 13 that Henry J. Tasca would be replaced as U.S. ambassador to Greece and nominated Jack B. Kubisch, assistant secretary of state for inter-American affairs, to the post. Tasca had been ambassador since 1970. Kubisch took up his post Sept. 19. With the July 24 restoration of civilian rule and the lifting of censorship, many Greek newspapers and politicians had demanded Tasca's removal from office.

[12] Public and official actions reflected growing anti-U.S. sentiment throughout Greece. Waves of demonstrations surged in Athens, Salonika and Crete where thousands vocally denounced the U.S. role in the Cyprus crisis for which Washington was held to blame because of its past support of the Greek military junta that had mounted the Cyprus coup. Greeks believed the U.S. supported Turkey's invasion of the island. Although additional guards were stationed at the U.S. embassy and other American installations, the embassy refrained from officially condemning the protests. The civilian government of Premier Caramanlis took several steps to express its displeasure with Washington which paralleled the public sentiment. Caramanlis Aug. 16 rejected an invitation to confer in Washington with President Ford. All U.S. military

flights to and from Greece were banned Aug. 16. The restriction was eased Aug. 17 to require advance request for such movements, but even that proviso was in contrast to the freedom with which the flights had previously operated.

[13] The new Greek government sent notes to its NATO allies Aug. 30, informing them of its desire to begin talks on the future of foreign military installations in Greece. The notes came in the wake of the Cyprus crisis and Athens' announced withdrawal from the military sector of NATO. That step was formally confirmed in a note to President Ford Aug. 30, and was described as a reassertion of Greek sovereignty over its entire territory, air space and territorial waters.

See also ALUMINUM & BAUXITE; APPOINTMENTS & RESIGNATIONS; AUSTRALIA [23]; COMMUNISM, INTERNATIONAL; CYPRUS; EUROPEAN ECONOMIC COMMUNITY [19]; MIDDLE EAST [28]; NORTH ATLANTIC TREATY ORGANIZATION; OIL [26]; TERRITORIAL WATERS; TURKEY; ZAIRE

GRENADA—Dame Hilda Bynoe resigned as governor of the British West Indies associated state of Grenada in a dispute with Premier Eric Gairy, it was reported Jan. 17. The resignation added to growing unrest on the island as Grenada prepared for full independence, set for Feb. 7. Gairy had asked Britain to dismiss Bynoe, the only woman serving as a governor in the British Commonwealth, after she threatened to resign following antigovernment demonstrations. One man died and several were injured Jan. 21 in clashes between government supporters and opponents in St. George's, capital of Grenada. Half of Grenada's businesses had been closed since Jan. 1 as part of a general strike to force Gairy to resign because of his alleged dictatorial methods and his handling of police brutality. Leo de Gale, former chairman of the Public Service Commission, was sworn in Jan. 24 as acting governor to replace Bynoe. De Gale was authorized Jan. 29 to represent Britain at independence celebrations after London canceled a scheduled visit by Prince Richard of Gloucester, a cousin of Queen Elizabeth, because of the unrest.

Grenada became an independent nation Feb. 7, ending more than 200 years of British colonial rule. In a radio address delivered shortly after midnight, Gairy appealed for an end to the conflict that had beset the island since November 1973. Gairy made his peace appeal a few hours after police arrested Maurice Bishop, 28, a leader of the opposition leftist New Jewel Movement and son of a man allegedly killed by police in an anti-government demonstration Jan. 21. Other members of the movement were reported in hiding. At an independence day reception Feb. 6, Gairy justified the arrest by saying there was evidence that the movement was "planning something for today." (Bishop, released on bail Feb. 8, was re-arrested on a charge of "inciting to grievous bodily harm," the *Miami Herald* reported April 10.)

Gairy said March 9 that the strikes, organized by the Committee of 22, had cost Grenada more than $100 million. The dockworkers had posed the gravest threat to the prime minister, blocking fuel supplies and depriving the government of its vital revenue from customs duties. The strikes lost momentum when electricity and telephone workers ended their six-week stoppage after running out of money. Shops and businesses had begun reopening for the same reason, after many were looted by secret police, the London newsletter *Latin America* reported March 15. The secret police also looted factories, threatened priests, searched churches and schools for arms, and attacked anyone they suspected of opposing Gairy, according to *Latin America*.

See also UNITED NATIONS [2]

GROSS NATIONAL PRODUCT—*See* ECONOMY, U.S. [1]

GUATEMALA—Presidential election dispute. Charges of fraud followed the presidential election March 3. According to press reports, government officials had admitted the victory of retired Gen. Efrain Rios Montt of the National Opposition Front (FNO). However, on March 6 the government announced that retired Gen. Kjell Laugerud Garcia of the ruling Nationalist Coalition was the winner. Official results gave Laugerud 260,313 votes, 41.2% of the total; Rios Montt 225,586 votes, or 35.7%; and Col. Ernesto Paiz Novales of the Revolutionary Party 145,967 votes, or 23.1%. Since no candidate won an absolute majority, the outgoing Congress, dominated by the government, proclaimed Laugerud the winner March 12. Rios Montt challenged the proclamation and said: "A regime of absolute illegality has begun in Guatemala." The FNO and the Revolutionary Party had charged before the election that the government was planning vote fraud on Laugerud's behalf.

Rios Montt was ordered back to active military duty March 15 after he gave up efforts to organize nonviolent resistance to the government. "My supporters have not responded adequately to my call for nonviolent resistance," Rios Montt said March 14. "They want me to call the people onto the streets, but I refuse to order people to their deaths." The government sent Rios Montt to Europe, naming him Guatemalan military attache in Madrid, it was reported April 15.

Post-election violence continued March 27 with the murder of Mario Monterroso Armas, a Guatemala City radio newscaster who had supported the opposition Christian Democratic Party in the disputed vote. Political violence continued throughout Guatemala in April-June. The victims included supporters of both the government and the opposition, and common criminals executed by the self-styled "Death Squad."

Laugerud was inaugurated president of Guatemala for four years July 1. He succeeded retired Gen. Carlos Arana Osorio, who had chosen Laugerud as his successor. Laugerud announced an economic austerity program, ordering the pay of federal deputies cut from $500 to $350 monthly and refusing to continue paying for their bodyguards with state funds. However, he proposed no major changes in the country's social and economic structure. Laugerud named a Cabinet which included only one member of the Nationalist Coalition, the right-wing political alliance which backed his candidacy in the disputed March 3 election. This reflected the armed forces' total loss of patience with the coalition's major parties, the National Liberation Movement (MLN) and the Democratic Institutional Party (PID), which had feuded openly since the election, according to the London newsletter *Latin America* July 5.

See also COFFEE; LATIN AMERICA; OBITUARIES [ASTURIAS]; OIL [17]; SUGAR

GUINEA—President Ahmed Sekou Toure was re-elected Dec. 27 to a third consecutive seven-year term; there was no opposition candidate.

See also ALUMINUM AND BAUXITE

GUINEA-BISSAU (PORTUGUESE GUINEA) & CAPE VERDE—Portugal signed an agreement with the African Party for the Independence of Guinea-Bissau and the Cape Verde Islands (PAIGC) Aug. 26 which set Sept. 10 as the date upon which the Portuguese colony would become independent. The agreement was signed in Algiers by Portuguese Foreign Minister Mario Soares and Guinea-Bissau Vice Minister of Defense Pedro Pires. Under the agreement, which formally ended 11 years of guerrilla warfare and signaled the close of five centuries of colonial rule, Lisbon agreed to withdraw all of its armed forces from the territory by Oct. 31. (A de facto cease-fire had gone into effect in May. The pact also specified that the question of Cape Verde's political future would be decided by a referendum to be held on the islands. The United Nations Security

Council had unanimously recommended Aug. 12 that Guinea-Bissau be admitted to the U.N.; Portugal lent its support to the recommendation. Official recognition of Guinea-Bissau was extended that day by the nine member nations of the European Community, bringing the total number of countries recognizing Guinea-Bissau to over 100. Formal recognition of the independence of the Republic of Guinea-Bissau came on Sept. 10, as Portuguese Provisional President Antonio de Spinola handed the documents terminating five centuries of colonial rule to Pires. Pires said Aug. 29 that Guinea-Bissau would follow a policy of nonalignment. The new nation's President was Luis de Almeida Cabral, leader of the PAIGC. The U.S. recognized Guinea-Bissau and offered to establish diplomatic relations, the State Department announced Sept. 10. The Portuguese government announced Dec. 18 the Cape Verde Islands independence in July 1975. PAIGC would be the only local political group permitted to participate in the transitional government.

See also AFRICA; AUSTRALIA [20]; UNITED NATIONS [2]

GUN CONTROL—*See* CRIME [39]
GURNEY, SEN. EDWARD J.—*See* CRIME [14-15]; ELECTIONS [3]

GUYANA—The government purchased the two Graphic newspapers, including the country's leading daily, the *Guyana Graphic,* it was reported Oct. 4. This gave it control of the entire daily press except for the *Mirror,* run by the People's Progressive Party (PPP) of former Prime Minister Cheddi Jagan. According to the newsletter *Latin America* Oct. 18, the Graphic's owner agreed to sell after extensive harassment from the government.

Prime Minister Forbes Burnham said Dec. 16 that the local bauxite operations of Reynolds Metals Co. of the U.S. would be nationalized on Jan. 1, 1975, whether or not the government and the firm had agreed on a just compensation price. Guyana and Reynolds, which were negotiating the compensation price, were also involved in a dispute over Reynolds' refusal to pay $7 million in back taxes, it was reported Nov. 15.

See also ALUMINUM & BAUXITE; SUGAR; UNITED NATIONS [15]

HAIG JR., ALEXANDER M.—*See* APPOINTMENTS & RESIGNATIONS; FORD, GERALD R.; NORTH ATLANTIC TREATY ORGANIZATION; PRIVACY [3]; WATERGATE [34-36]

HAITI—Thirty-eight Haitians were rescued from a foundering boat off the Florida coast in January. The refugees had all asked for political asylum, but had been rebuffed by the U.S. Immigration and Naturalization Service, which jailed 100 of them and moved to deport them all. The U.S. claimed the Haitians had not been active in politics and only wanted to improve their economic prospects. Defenders of the refugees, asserted that if the refugees returned to Haiti, many of them would face death or imprisonment at the hands of the government of President Jean-Claude Duvalier. Fifty-three Haitians reached the coast of Florida in a small sailing boat at the end of September, bringing to nearly 1,000 the number of refugees who had illegally fled Haiti for the U.S. in the past two years, it was reported Oct. 25. The refugees, like their predecessors, were jailed to await deportation. Illegal Haitian immigrants were also under pressure in the Bahamas, where the government ordered them to register for voluntary return to Haiti. Seventy-five refugees were returned to Haiti Aug. 9 in the first flight under the Bahamian repatriation program.

See also ALUMINUM & BAUXITE; LATIN AMERICA

HALDEMAN, H. R.—*See* WATERGATE [28, 35, 47, 52, 60-62, 87-103]
HATCH ACT—*See* CAMPAIGN FINANCING [22]
HEAD START PROGRAM—*See* WELFARE & POVERTY
HEALTH—*See* MEDICINE & HEALTH
HEALTH, EDUCATION & WELFARE DEPARTMENT—*See* APPOINTMENTS & RESIGNATIONS; BIRTH CONTROL; CIVIL RIGHTS [5]; INTELLIGENCE; MEDICINE & HEALTH [7, 16-17]; WELFARE & POVERTY; WOMEN'S RIGHTS

HEARST, PATRICIA—Patricia Hearst, 19, granddaughter of the late newspaper publisher William Randolph Hearst, was kidnapped from her Berkeley, Calif. apartment Feb. 5 by at least two women and two men who were later identified as members of the Symbionese Liberation Army (SLA), a radical terrorist organization. In a tape recorded message received April 3 she said she had "chosen to stay and fight" with the SLA for the "freedom of the oppressed people." Miss Hearst was linked to the armed robbery of a San Francisco bank April 15 when bank photographs showed her to be a participant. She was charged with the crime on June 6 by a San Francisco grand jury. In spite of a Christmas appeal by her parents asking her to return home, by the end of the year Miss Hearst's whereabouts were still unknown. The SLA had been linked with the Nov. 6, 1973 ambush-slaying of Oakland school superintendent Marcus A. Foster. Arrested for the crime in January were Joseph M. Ramiro and Russell Little. A ballistics report indicated a pistol found in Ramiro's possession was the gun that had killed Foster.

The kidnappers made their first demand known in a letter to radio station KPFA Feb. 12. Accompanying the letter was a tape recording of Miss Hearst's voice saying she was all right and asking her father to meet her abductor's demands. The kidnappers demanded that Hearst provide $70 worth of top quality free meat, vegetables and dairy products over a four-week period—commencing Feb. 19—to "all people [in California] with welfare cards, Social Security pension cards, food stamp cards, disabled veteran cards, medical cards, parole or probation papers and jail or bail release slips." In addition to the tape recording of Miss Hearst's voice and the food-distribution demand, KPFA received a second tape recording, whose speaker called himself Field Marshal Cinque of the SLA and said he was black and father of two children, who was "quite willing to carry out the execution of your daughter to save the life of starving men, women and children of every race." (Cinque was later identified as escaped convict Donald D. DeFreeze. Also named as an SLA leader was Thero M. Wheeler who had escaped from Vacaville State Prison in August 1973.) Hearst said Feb. 13 that it was impossible to meet the demand. Later he said, "We'll set up some kind of food distribution system," but he warned "we can't meet the cost." (Estimates of the cost of giving $70 worth of food to all California's needy ran as high as $400 million.)

On Feb. 19 Hearst announced a $2 million food giveaway program, following the receipt, three days earlier, of a second tape recorded message from his daughter. A coalition of activist groups was to aid in the food distribution. Accusing her father of "throwing a few crumbs to the people," Miss Hearst and Cinque—on a tape recording received Feb. 21—demanded another $4 million worth of food to be added. Hearst denied his financial capability to meet the latest demand, but the Hearst Corporation said it would donate the money, if Miss Hearst was released unharmed. In the tape, Cinque also warned against injury to "our captive soldiers," Ramiro and Little, who pleaded not guilty to the murder charges against them Feb. 25. The food giveaway began Feb. 22, but the program suffered from improper distribution and planning, with fights breaking out among those waiting for the food. It resumed again on Feb. 28 in a more orderly and rapid manner. After 17 days of silence, another tape from Miss Hearst was received again demanding the additional $4 million in food.

The April 3 message in which Miss Hearst said she chose to remain with the SLA also contained remarks by Cinque who said the young woman was free to leave at any time but refused to go. It said she had been "accepted into the ranks of the people's army as a comrade and fighter." Although Randolph Hearst refused to believe his daughter was acting of her own free will, the bank robbery photographs and reports by eyewitnesses indicated she "absolutely was a participant." Also identified in the photographs were DeFreeze, Nancy Ling Perry, Patricia M. Soltysik and Camilla C. Hall. The robbery netted $10,960. An April 24 tape in which Miss Hearst denied she had been brainwashed, revealed she had taken the name "Tania," which was the name of a woman who had been the collaborator of and mistress to the late Argentine revolutionary Ernesto Che Guevara de la Serna.

Six members of the SLA died in a gun battle and ensuing fire that erupted after police surrounded their Los Angeles hideout May 17. Patricia Hearst was not present during the shootout. A team of medical examiners from the Los Angeles County coroner's office identified the charred bodies found in the house as DeFreeze, Perry, William L. Wolfe, Soltysik, Angela Atwood and Hall. Los Angeles police had been alerted to the SLA group's whereabouts by the mother of one of the women living in the house in which the SLA members later died. On the basis of the tip, 150 heavily armed police surrounded the house. With everyone in place, a police sergeant shouted on a bullhorn, "Come out with your hands up. The house is surrounded." The police waited, repeating the order five minutes later. When there was no response, an officer crept near the house and lobbed a canister of tear gas inside. Gun fire immediately erupted on both sides. The battle continued for at least an hour with both sides expending over 1,000 rounds of ammunition. Finally, smoke began to pour from the house, the byproduct of a fire started by a tear gas cannister or an ignited SLA gasoline bomb. Flames rapidly engulfed the stucco house and soon the gunfire from within ceased.

A San Francisco federal grand jury indicted Patricia Hearst June 6 on charges of armed bank robbery in connection with the San Francisco bank theft. Meanwhile, Los Angeles radio station KPFK received a tape recording June 7 in which Miss Hearst affirmed a commitment to the SLA and a determination to continue the terrorist fight. According to police, the tape also contained the voices of William and Emily Harris, who along with Miss Hearst were thought to be among the only surviving members of the SLA.

A spokesman for the Federal Bureau of Investigation (FBI) conceded Nov. 29 that police had reached a dead end in their search for Patricia Hearst.

HEART DISEASE—*See* MEDICINE & HEALTH [26-30]
HELMS, RICHARD—*See* CENTRAL INTELLIGENCE AGENCY; WATERGATE [99]
HERBICIDES—*See* ENVIRONMENT & POLLUTION [15]; VIETNAM, REPUBLIC OF [39]
HEREDITY—*See* INTELLIGENCE; MEDICINE & HEALTH [33-34]; NARCOTICS & DANGEROUS DRUGS
HEROIN—*See* NARCOTICS & DANGEROUS DRUGS

HIGHWAYS—A bill increasing the federal weight limit for trucks on interstate highways was passed by both houses of Congress Dec. 18. The Senate vote was 67-27, the House approved it 307-67. The new limit was 80,000 pounds, an increase of 6,720 pounds from the previous limit. The bill would also make the temporary nationwide 55 m.p.h. speed limit permanent. To provide incentive for enforcement of the limit, Congress authorized the Transportation Department to reduce a state's federal highway fund allotment by 10% if it found enforcement lax.

See also ENERGY CRISIS [6]; TRANSPORTATION

HIJACKINGS—*See* CRIME [20]; JORDAN; LIBYA; MIDDLE EAST [29, 34]; MOROCCO; UNION OF SOVIET SOCIALIST REPUBLICS [22]; VIETNAM, REPUBLIC OF [41]
HISTORY—*See* PULITZER PRIZES

HOCKEY—The Philadelphia Flyers became the first expansion team to win the National Hockey League's (NHL) Stanley Cup, defeating the Boston Bruins 1-0 May 19 to win the best-of-seven championship finals 4-2. Notable for its record number of penalties, the series was highlighted by the goaltending of Flyer goalie Bernie Parent, who held the Bruins to less than half their regular season average of

4.5 goals a game. Parent was awarded the Conn Smythe Trophy as the outstanding player in the series. To reach the finals, Philadelphia eliminated the New York Rangers in semi-final competition. Boston had defeated the Chicago Black Hawks in the other semi-final series.

The Houston Aeros defeated the Chicago Cougars 6-2 to win the World Hockey Association (WHA) championship Avco Cup May 19. The Cougars were no match for the high-scoring Aeros, who captured the first three games of the best-of-seven series 3-2, 6-1 and 7-4. Gordie Howe, 46, who came out of retirement to play for the Aeros with his sons Mark and Marty Howe, set a four-game WHA playoff record with nine assists. In semifinal play, Houston had defeated Minnesota and Chicago had downed Toronto.

The NHL and the WHA announced Feb. 19 that they had settled out of court a $50 million suit filed by the WHA against the NHL. Under the terms, both leagues agreed to respect each other's player contracts, compete in a limited number of exhibition games and drop all court claims and counter-claims. The NHL also agreed to pay $1.75 million in legal expenses incurred by the WHA and not to oppose use of NHL arenas by WHA clubs.

The Soviet Union won its 13th World Ice Hockey championship April 20 by defeating Sweden 3-1 in Helsinki, Finland. They also defeated Team Canada 3-2 Oct. 6 to win their best-of-eight series 4-1. Three games ended in ties.

HOMOSEXUALS—The city council of New York City, by a vote of 22-19 May 23, defeated a measure which would have banned discrimination in housing, employment and public accomodations because of "sexual orientation." The bill was the first to come to a floor vote in the council after 3½ years of controversy in committees. Observers said a key factor in the bill's defeat was the strong opposition by the Roman Catholic Archdiocese of New York. The Minneapolis City Council had approved an ordinance March 29 banning discrimination in education, public accomodations, housing and jobs on the basis of "affectional or sexual preference." In a special election May 7, voters in Boulder, Colo. defeated by a 2-1 margin an amendment to the city charter which would have prevented job dismissals on grounds of homosexuality. According to the Associated Press May 8, laws banning various forms of discrimination against homosexuals had been passed in Detroit, San Francisco, Seattle and Washington, D.C.

See also CIVIL RIGHTS [15]; CRIME [24]

HONDURAS—The government Jan. 15 nationalized all cutting rights and export of timber in a first step toward taking full control of the valuable lumber industry. President Oswaldo Lopez Arellano had said Jan. 1, in a speech announcing his national development program, that the lumber industry would be nationalized gradually. He had asserted that "the nation's forest resources have been improperly exploited in the light of the nation's interest." There were 119 lumber companies operating in Honduras, including Italian, Arab, Cuban and U.S. concerns. Among the U.S. firms were the major banana companies (bananas were Honduras' chief export, and lumber was next in importance).

President Lopez Arellano announced a 15-year national development plan to provide "important changes" in a number of fields including agriculture, industry and labor, it was reported Jan. 18. The plan, an apparent departure from the military government's conservative economic posture, would establish "agricultural communities" in an apparent cooperative venture; support collective bargaining for trade unions, and a minimum wage; gradually nationalize forestry resources and their exploitation; end lucrative mining concessions to foreign companies; and promote investment in new industries, with carefully controlled government incentives.

Hurricane Fifi struck Honduras Sept. 19 and 20, leaving devastation unparalleled in the country's history. Conflicting reports estimated the death toll at 1,000-10,000. A Honduran official Oct. 3 placed the number of dead at 5,000 with 100,000 homeless and damage at $450 million. Some 182 communities were reported damaged or destroyed. The village of Choloma was destroyed when an avalanche of debris tore through the north Honduran town Sept. 20, killing an estimated 2,800 persons and leaving it under 12 feet of mud. By Sept. 25 tons of supplies were reported to have been poured into the country. Seven nations sent 15 planes and seven helicopters to aid relief efforts. However, distribution had been hampered by poor roads, deficient organization and a shortage of fuel. Thousands were reported to be on the brink of starvation. Widespread looting was reported Sept. 25, particularly in isolated villages. The Honduran Student Federation had charged Sept. 28 that the government's National Emergency Committee (COPEN) was hindering international aid to the hurricane victims. The *Miami Herald* Oct. 14 printed allegations by U.S. medical missionaries returning from Honduras that government officials were confiscating relief supplies for sale on the black market.

See also COFFEE; LATIN AMERICA; OIL [17]; SUGAR

HONG KONG—Hong Kong returned five illegal immigrants to China Nov. 30 and another 12 Dec. 1. It was the first such action since 1968 and represented a reversal of the government's policy of permitting refugees from China to remain in the British crown colony. The government announced Nov. 30 that it would no longer accept refugees found illegally entering from China because of the strain put upon Hong Kong's welfare resources and rising unemployment. As of Nov. 29, 7,121 illegal migrants from China were listed as having arrived in the colony since Jan. 1, compared with 6,139 for all of 1973.

See also CHINA, COMMUNIST

HORSE RACING—Willie Shoemaker, winner of 6,624 races, established a personal mark March 30 when he rode Miss Musket to victory in the $100,000 Fantasy Stakes at Oakland Park in Hot Springs, Arkansas. For Shoemaker, 42, it was the 100th time he had won a stakes race with a purse of $100,000 or more.

A New York City federal jury convicted two gamblers June 1 of conspiracy and sports bribery in connection with a scheme to fix superfecta races at two New York harness racing tracks. Discontinued in 1973 after the alleged fixing was uncovered, the superfecta involved picking the first four finishers in correct order. The convicted men, Forrest Gerry Jr. and Richard Perry, each faced sentences of up to five years in prison and fines of $10,000. Thirteen harness drivers, who also had been indicted, were acquitted.

Little Current, ridden by Miguel Rivera, won the final two legs of thoroughbred horse racing's 1974 Triple Crown, capturing the Preakness and Belmont Stakes. The first leg of the Triple Crown, the Kentucky Derby, was won by Cannonade. Chris Evert scored a 3½ length victory in the Coaching Club American Oaks at Belmont Park in Elmont, N.Y. June 22, becoming the third thoroughbred race horse to win the Filly Triple Crown. Jorge Velasquez was the jockey over the 1½ mile Belmont course, as he was in the Mother Goose Stakes at Belmont May 26 and the second division of the Acorn Stakes at Belmont May 11. Capping Chris Evert's triple crown win was a 50-length victory in a 1¼-mile match race with Miss Musket at Hollywood Park in Inglewood, Calif. July 20. Velasquez was Evert's jockey for the $350,000 winner-take-all contest. (Chris Evert was owned by Carl Rosen, who designed clothes for Chris Evert, the tennis player.)

HOSPITALS—*See* VETERANS

HOUSE OF REPRESENTATIVES—*See* CONGRESS

HOUSING—Housing slump. Rising materials prices, tight money policies and high interest rates were reflected in an almost-constant drop in new housing starts through the year. The January figure for new units was at an annual seasonally-adjusted rate of 1,486,000, rising slightly by April to 1,626,000. Lack of mortgage money, however, caused a drop in May to 1,450,000, a figure which was 37.8% below that of May 1973. The slump worsened during August, when housing starts dropped 15% from July and were off 45% from August 1973, prompting a housing industry spokesman to label it the "worst housing slump since the depression." The Commerce Department announced Dec. 17 that the number of new housing starts declined in November to a seasonally-adjusted annual rate of 990,000 units, the lowest since December 1966. The November rate was 10.5% below the level set the previous month, which was revised downward, and 40.9% below the level registered in November 1973.

The worsening situation was the subject of a meeting between Administration offcials and representatives of the housing and construction industries in Atlanta Sept. 12. Industry spokesmen warned that they had become both the "victim of inflation" and the "scapegoat" of the Administration's anti-inflation policies aimed at monetary and fiscal restraint. Alan Greenspan, chairman of the Council of Economic Advisers, responded that there was little the Administration could do to aid the housing industry until inflation eased. Conference delegates, who included representatives of construction unions, builders, construction suppliers and thrift institutions, agreed that little upturn in the housing industry could be expected before early 1975. To spur that recovery, they sought an easing of the Federal Reserve's tight money policies, expanded use of government funds to provide mortgage money at below-market levels, and tax breaks on savings to encourage increased deposits at savings institutions, which were the chief sources of mortgage funds. Maximum interest rates on federally insured mortgage loans had been raised from 8.75% to 9% July 5. Officials said the increase was required to boost the availability of loans. With interest ceilings on the government program so low, lenders had been bypassing federally insured mortgages and investing in the higher yield short-term money market.

Home mortgage aid. A Home Purchase Assistance Act to authorize an infusion of $7.75 billion in federal money into the home mortgage market was cleared by Congress Oct. 15 and sent to President Ford, who had requested such legislation Oct. 8. Ford had said then he planned to release $3 billion of the financing immediately. The President signed the bill Oct. 18, although he objected to its "rigid, illogical interest ceiling" as inadequate to offset borrowing costs. An interest rate ceiling was set by the bill of one-half percentage point above the average yield on Treasury bonds, or 8.25% at the time of enactment. The secretary of housing and urban development would set the rates, within the ceiling, at which the Government National Mortgage Association (Ginnie Mae) would buy mortgages made to home buyers, using Treasury borrowings. The individual mortgages purchased in the new program were not to exceed $42,000, and 75% of the mortgages were to be on new homes. A major feature of the legislation was extention of Ginnie Mae's authority to purchase conventional mortgages (those not backed by any government agency, such as the Veterans Administration [VA] and the Federal Housing Administration [FHA]). The latter comprised less than 20% of the mortgage market. The Administration had favored a higher interest rate ceiling of 9.5%.

Omnibus aid bill approved. President Ford Aug. 22 signed an $11.1 billion housing and community development bill containing broad revisions in the formulas for distribution of federal aid. Most of the money ($8.6 billion over three years), as well as the major departure from previous programs, lay in provisions authorizing locally-administered block grants for community development to replace categorical aid plans such as Model Cities and urban renewal. The funds would be allocated on the basis of population, degree of overcrowding and poverty (weighted double in the formula). During the three-year-period, no community would receive less than the total previously granted under the categorical programs. A separate provision esablished a $1.23 billion rent subsidy program for low-income families under which tenants would pay 15%-25% of gross income towards local fair market rentals, with the difference subsidized. The FHA mortgage ceiling for single-family homes was increased from $33,000 to $45,000, and down payment requirements were reduced. The fiscal 1975 Housing and Urban Development (HUD) appropriation bill was passed by both houses Aug. 22 and signed by President Ford Sept. 4. The HUD budget was $3,014,519,000, which included $197 million for the urban renewal program.

Political hiring at HUD charged. The Civil Service Commission recommended March 19 that three key HUD officials be dismissed and six others suspended for using a "special referral unit" to circumvent civil service regulations and favor politically well-connected job applicants. The commission did not identify the nine officials or disclose the number of employes hired under the illegal system. The accused officials would have the opportunity for hearings before a final commission decision. The commission noted that it was proper for job candidates to be referred by political sources, but said HUD officials had asked about applicant's political affiliations and had used the information to discriminate.

See also Banks & Banking; Civil Rights [17]; Crime [14-15]; Economy, U.S. [5, 17, 20, 24]; Veterans

HOUSING & URBAN DEVELOPMENT DEPARTMENT—*See* Civil Rights [21]; Crime [14-15]; Housing; Population

HUGHES, HOWARD—Howard R. Hughes, the billionaire recluse, was indicted by a Las Vegas, Nev. federal grand jury July 29 on stock manipulation charges in connection with his acquisition of Air West, a California-based regional airline. A similar indictment against Hughes and three others was dismissed Jan. 30 by a federal judge, who ruled that it had not been drawn correctly. The new indictment also named as defendants Robert A. Maheu, the former chief of Hughes operations in Nevada; Chester C. Davis, chief counsel for Summa Corp., which was known as the Hughes Tool Co. at the time of the alleged crime; and David B. Charney, a television and motion picture executive. According to the indictment, which charged stock manipulation, wire fraud and conspiracy, the alleged actions occurred in the fall of 1968, when Hughes made an offer of $22 for each share of Air West common stock. Hughes gained 52% acceptance of his offer from stockholders, but was not successful with the company's board of directors, who rejected the proposal Dec. 28, 1968, three days before it was to expire. The four defendants, the indictment charged, then employed fraudulent means to induce the recalcitrant directors to change their minds by driving down the price of Air West stock.

U.S. District Court Judge Bruce Thompson Nov. 14 dismissed the conspiracy and stock manipulation charges against Hughes and the other defendants. Thompson, who had previously dismissed a similar indictment, commented that "we can find no statute or regulation which renders the alleged conduct of the defendants criminal."

A Los Angeles federal jury July 1 ruled in favor of Maheu in his libel suit against Hughes. Maheu's suit stemmed from a statement by Hughes during a 1972 telephone news conference that he had dismissed Maheu as a staff aide because Maheu "stole me blind." Hughes, who employed Maheu from 1953 until his firing in 1970, had convened the unusual press conference to disclaim any connection with a purported biography by Clifford Irving. The jury Dec. 4 awarded Maheu $2,823,333 in damages. The jury also awarded Summa Corp. $47,743 of its original $4.4 million countersuit against Maheu. Summa had charged Maheu with improperly diverting that amount.

See also CAMPAIGN FINANCING [15-16]

HUMPHREY, SEN. HUBERT H.—*See* CAMPAIGN FINANCING [6, 17, 19]

HUNGARY—A new, restrictive abortion law went into effect Jan. 1, in an attempt by the government to raise the low birth rate. Following the lead of Rumania and Bulgaria, Hungary abolished a mid-1950s law that allowed abortion on demand. The new law restricted the practice to women who were over 40, who already had three or more children, who became pregnant through rape, or who were single or had been separated from their husbands for six months, and to couples with no home of their own. A special commission would rule on cases where maternal or fetal health was endangered.

Pope Paul VI Feb. 5 removed Jozsef Cardinal Mindszenty from his honorary position as Roman Catholic primate of Hungary and archbishop of Esztergom in an apparent attempt to improve church-state relations with Hungary. (According to reports, denied by the government, Hungarian officials had told the Vatican that vacant bishophrics could not be filled, nor religious education of children conducted, so long as Mindszenty formally retained his position.) The 81-year-old cardinal, who had been living in Vienna since 1971, had not exercised his pastoral functions since his arrest by the Communist government in 1948. He had spent seven years in jail and 15 years in asylum at the U.S. legation in Budapest.

Two prominent figures in the Hungarian Socialist Workers' Party, Rezso Nyers, chairman of the Economic Policy Committee, and Gyorgy Aczel, chairman of the Cultural Policy Committee, were moved to lower-echelon positions in a "personnel shift" carried out during Central Committee plenum meetings March 20-21. Nyers, architect of Hungary's economic reform system instituted in 1968, and Aczel were close associates of party First Secretary Janos Kadar.

See also ARGENTINA [18]; COMMUNISM, INTERNATIONAL; EUROPEAN SECURITY; FAMINE & FOOD

HUNGER—*See* FAMINE & FOOD; WELFARE & POVERTY
HUNT JR., E. HOWARD—*See* CENTRAL INTELLIGENCE AGENCY; WATERGATE [13, 21, 24, 28, 59, 62, 78, 80, 95, 97, 102]
HURRICANES—*See* HONDURAS; WEATHER
HUSTON, TOM CHARLES—*See* PRIVACY [9]

I

ICELAND—A coalition Cabinet headed by conservative Independent Party leader Geir Hallgrimsson was sworn in Aug. 28, nearly two months after general elections resulted in a sharp setback for the leftist coalition government of Premier Olafur Johannesson. Hallgrimsson had been summoned by President Kristjan Eldjarn Aug. 27 to form a government. Hallgrimsson quickly named a coalition Cabinet with outgoing Premier Johannesson's Progressive Party. Einar Agustsson, a Progressive Party member, was retained as foreign minister, while former Premier Johannesson was named justice and commerce minister. Matthias Mathiesen of the Independence Party was given the Finance Ministry. Hallgrimsson had pledged during the campaign to maintain the U.S. presence, on behalf of the North Atlantic Treaty Organization, at the Keflavik air base, while the leftist coalition had urged early withdrawal of the Americans. The conservatives had also promised to introduce stringent measures to curb inflation currently running at a 40% annual rate. The government crisis began May 6 when the Liberal Left quit the three-party government to protest the government proposals to abolish cost-of-living wage increases and impose a ceiling on pay rises. The conservatives won 25 seats in the June 30 elections, an increase of three. Before the 1971 elections which brought the leftist coalition to power, the conservatives had governed for 12 years in coalition with the Social Democrats. The big loser in the elections was the Liberal Left, which decreased its representation from five seats to two. The Communists won 11 seats, a one-seat gain, while Johannesson's Progressives retained their 17 seats. The Social Democrats dropped from five seats to four.

The U.S. and Iceland reached an agreement Sept. 26 under which Washington would withdraw 400 technicians from the 3,300-man American contingent at the military air base in Keflavik. Icelanders would replace the departing U.S. personnel.

See also CHILE [3]; COMMUNISM, INTERNATIONAL; EUROPEAN SECURITY; MIDDLE EAST [26]; NORWAY; TERRITORIAL WATERS

ILLINOIS—*See* ELECTIONS [5]; GAMBLING; LABOR [13]; NARCOTICS & DANGEROUS DRUGS; WEATHER; WOMEN'S RIGHTS

IMMIGRATION & EMIGRATION—*See* ALGERIA; AUSTRALIA [16]; CANADA [17]; GERMANY, WEST [17]; HAITI; ISRAEL; MIDDLE EAST [17, 24]; POLAND; POPULATION; SWITZERLAND

INDIA—Food crisis. A severe economic crisis, marked by food shortages, provoked a series of riots and demonstrations in India throughout the year. Protest actions were especially violent in the states of Maharashtra, Gujarat and Bijar. The first outbreak occurred Jan. 2 when a 24-hour strike in Bombay closed factories, railways, restaurants and markets. Rioting, looting and arson in Gujarat State, during January, left 27 persons dead and an unspecified number injured. In Bihar State, 22 persons were killed March 17-19 during riots protesting food shortages, rising prices and alleged political corruption. The action was led by students who had pledged to topple the government. About 2,000 students were confined to dormitories on the university campus at Patna after outbreaks of arson and looting had been reported March 20-22. More than 600 students and demonstrators were arrested. In an action aimed at speeding up food production, the Indian Cabinet decided March 28 to abandon government control of wheat distribution. The old policy, adopted in April 1973, was designed to keep the price low and stable. Instead, the cost of wheat increased by 36% in one year and shortages, hoarding and a black market developed. In announcing repeal of the program, Agriculture Minister Fakhruddin Ali Ahmed said the government would permit "wholesalers to operate under a system of licensing and control" which would, in effect, end the nationalization of the wheat trade.

A poor harvest forced India to purchase 1.8 million metric tons of foreign food grain during the year, Economic Affairs Minister M. G. Kaul announced Aug. 1. Domestic farmers had brought only 2.9 million metric tons of wheat to market by that date, compared with 4.3 million for the same period in 1973. The crisis was further pointed up Aug. 12 by Food Minister Chidambara Subramaniam, who told Parliament that the government was having difficulty distributing wheat to the cities, where about a third of the population lived. The system under which the government purchased food for its ration shops in the cities was said by officials to be failing because of inflation, shifting policies, hoarding, corruption and the failure of state governments to deal with farmers. A prolonged drought and severe power shortages intensified the famine situation in the northern and central sections of the country in September. A West Bengal minister said 15 million people in rural areas were either starving or living on one meal a day. Another report said more than 500 people had died of malnutrition in West Bengal. (In Assam, the food problem had worsened because of an influx of refugees from neighboring Bangla Desh, according to state legislators there who estimated the total number of deaths in that state as 15,000.) The situation continued to worsen as the year ended. A dispatch from New Delhi Oct. 4 told of widespread hunger in the states of Orissa, Gujarat, Rajasthan, Madhya Pradesh, West Bengal, Uttar Pradesh and Bishar. Virtually half the state of Madhya Pradesh was affected by the drought, with 70%-80% of the rice harvest lost. In West Bengal, more than 1,000 persons were said to have starved to death in the previous two months, according to a report published by the *Washington Post* Oct. 15.

State governments fall. The food shortages and economic upheaval resulted in government changes, particularly in Gujarat State where, on Feb. 9, the government collapsed and the state was placed under central presidential rule. The state capital, Ahmadabad, had been placed under martial law Jan. 28 after more than two weeks of rioting and looting to protest rising prices. A new wave of rioting broke out March 2, however, when protestors demanded dissolution of the suspended state assembly, while also protesting new elections. The protest was based on the fear that Chimanbhai Patel, the state's chief minister who had resigned on Feb. 9, might resume power if the assembly was reconvened. Patel had been accused of corruption and mishandling food distribution. Patel was expelled from the Congress Party on March 2 after being accused of "anti-party" activities. In response to protesters' demands, the state assembly was dissolved March 15. It was the first time since India's independence that a popular revolt had forced the resignation of a state government and dissolution of its legislature. A similar protest occurred Nov. 4 in Bihar State when thousands of students demonstrated in the capital city of Patna, demanding dissolution of the state government on the grounds of corruption. Police used tear gas to disperse the marchers, estimated at 5,000. Leader of the Patna demonstration was Jayaprakash Narayan, who had conducted other anti-government demonstrations in other parts of India. Narayan met Nov. 1 with Prime Minister Indira Gandhi who said she "would look into his demands."

Another result of the economic crisis was an overhaul of her cabinet by Prime Minister Gandhi. The shift, involving the key defense, food, finance and home affairs ministries, underlined the government's concern with food shortages, increasing inflation and urban tensions. Among the major changes: Defense Minister Jagjivan Ram was named agriculture minister; Chidambaram Subramaniam, who had headed the industrial development and agricultural ministries, was appointed finance minister; the outgoing finance minister, Y. B. Chavan, took over as foreign minister, replacing Swaran Singh, who was named defense minister.

Labor and the economy. A nationwide rail strike that had started May 8 was officially ended May 28 by union officials who conceded that the government's mass arrest of their leaders and workers had crushed the walkout. The government had begun making arrests May 2 in an attempt to prevent the strike, accusing union leaders and workers of inciting to violence and preparing for the walkout while negotiations were in progress. An estimated 20,000-50,000 persons had been imprisoned. The government said it would not negotiate until the strike was ended. The union had demanded double wages, a bonus, shorter working hours, cheaper food rations and reinstatement of employes dismissed for union activities. The government rejected the demands on the grounds that granting the salary hikes would cost the nation $700 million. An estimated $1.5 billion-$2 billion had been lost in production and trade disruption as a result of the walkout.

On July 6 Prime Minister Gandhi announced a series of inflation-fighting decrees. One edict limited the distribution of dividends to 12% of the share value, or one-third of the total profits. The announcement resulted in a sharp drop in stock prices and led to the closing of stock markets throughout the country. Two other decrees impounded 50% of the cost-of-living allowances due wage earners and curbed company profits. The allowances were to be deposited in a special fund with the government-owned Reserve Bank of India, with repayment to employes after two years in five annual installments at 11% interest.

International trade developments. Iran agreed to provide India with large amounts of economic assistance following discussions by Prime Minister Gandhi in Teheran April 28-May 2 with Shah Mohammed Riza Pahlevi and Premier Amir Abbas Hoveida. Iran had, on Feb. 22, agreed to supply India with oil on credit and to invest $300 million in a joint project to develop India's iron ore export. Under terms of the second accord, Iran was to grant India soft loans to increase its production of iron ore and aluminum, both of which would be traded for Iranian oil; Iran would finance increased Indian output of cement, steel, paper, chemicals and sugar; an Indian-Iranian shipping line would be established to serve the ports of both countries and others in Asia; and India would provide Iran with technicians, engineers, professors and doctors to help Teheran carry out its development plans. Indian-Iranian relations were further expanded after the Shah's visit to New Delhi Oct. 2-4. A joint communique issued Oct. 4 included a demand that the Indian Ocean serve as a "zone of peace" devoid of big power rivalries. Speaking at a news conference Oct. 3, the shah had urged creation of a new grouping of Indian Ocean nations to "secure our shipping lanes" and exclude "non-regional powers."

U.S. Ambassador Daniel P. Moynihan and Indian Finance Minister M. G. Kaul signed an agreement in New Delhi Feb. 18 for the disposal of $3 billion worth of rupees accumulated by the U.S. through the sale of food to India. Part of the money was given as a grant for agricultural development and social welfare projects; the remaining $1 billion was to be used by the American embassy in New Delhi to support educational, cultural and other programs.

A consortium of 13 industrial nations pledged June 14 to provide India with $1.4 billion in aid over the next year. At the conclusion of a two-day meeting in Paris, the group agreed that "substantial new commitments of aid to India were required in present conditions in the current year so as to maintain imports at minimum levels. Without aid India will not be able to surmount present difficulties and maintain any momentum of economic development."

See also ALUMINUM & BAUXITE; APPOINTMENTS & RESIGNATIONS; ATOMIC ENERGY [1-4]; BANGLA DESH; BHUTAN; CUBA; DEFENSE [14]; FAMINE & FOOD; FOREIGN AID; NEPAL; OBITUARIES [MENON]; PAKISTAN; PORTUGAL [26]; SIKKIM; TENNIS; WATERGATE [40]; WEATHER

INDIANA—*See* ELECTIONS [1, 5]; WEATHER; WOMEN'S RIGHTS

INDIAN AFFAIRS—Wounded Knee trial. Charges against militant Indian leaders Dennis Banks and Russell Means were dismissed by a federal district court judge Sept. 16 after he strongly criticized government conduct of the case. The charges—assault on government officers, conspiracy and larceny—stemmed from the 1973 occupation of Wounded Knee, S.D. Ending a lengthy trial, which had begun Feb. 12, marked by delays and courtroom outbursts, Judge Fred J. Nichol accused chief prosecutor, R. D. Hurd, of deceiving the court, charged the Justice Department with being more interested in getting a conviction or mistrial than in seeing justice done, and said the Federal Bureau of Investigation (FBI) had "stooped to a new low" in dealing with witnesses and evidence. Leading directly to the dismissal was the illness of a juror Sept. 13, the day after the jury had begun deliberations. In a decision which Nichol termed "incredible," the Justice Department refused to allow the case to be decided by the 11 remaining jurors, a procedure that would have been possible only with the agreement by both sides. The defense had been willing to proceed with the 11 jurors. Nichol's lecture cited incidents involving Louis Moves Camp, an FBI informer and a principal government witness. Nichol noted that Moves Camp had been paid substantial witness fees and "relocation" expenses, and that he had been accused of raping a teen-age girl after a night of tavern visits with FBI agents. Nichol noted that the rape charges had been dropped and hinted that the FBI had arranged for such action to be taken.

Richard Wilson, an opponent of Wounded Knee defendant Means' militant American Indian Movement (AIM), was re-elected president of the Oglala Sioux tribe Feb. 7, defeating Means by the final, but unofficial, margin of 1,709-1,530. A tribal council generally sympathetic to Wilson was also elected.

Voting rights suit filed. The Justice Department Jan. 23 filed its first suit to protect Indian voting rights, charging that a 1972 Arizona redistricting plan discriminated against voters on the Navajo reservation in Apache County. According to the department, there were 23,994 Indians and 8,304 non-Indians in the county, but Indians were a majority in only one of the three districts. The suit asked immediate redistricting of the three districts.

Fishing rights upheld. U.S. District Court Judge George H. Boldt ruled in Tacoma, Wash. Feb. 12 that most Washington state fishing regulations could not legally be applied to 14 Indian tribes in the western part of the state, since Indian fishing rights were already guaranteed by treaties.

INDIAN OCEAN—*See* AUSTRALIA [2, 21]; DEFENSE [14]; INDIA; SEYCHELLE ISLANDS; SOMALIA; SOUTH AFRICA [13-14]

INDOCHINA WAR—*See* AMNESTY & CLEMENCY; CAMBODIA; KENT STATE; LAOS; OBITUARIES [ABRAMS]; RADICALS; THAILAND; VETERANS; VIETNAM, PEOPLE'S REPUBLIC OF; VIETNAM, REPUBLIC OF

INDONESIA—President Suharto Jan. 28 assumed command of the state security agency and abolished the posts of personal presidential assistant. Four of his aides were dismissed. Suharto took the action in response to the student rioting during the visit of Japanese Premier Kakuei Tanaka Jan. 14-16, the government said. The students were protesting Tokyo's alleged economic exploitation in Southeast Asia. The Jakarta military garrison reported Jan. 18 that 11 persons had been killed and 105 injured and that 659 vehicles, most of them Japanese-made, were burned or badly damaged in the rioting. Among those arrested were leaders of student groups accused of fomenting the anti-Japanese and anti-government disturbances. A government security official said 410 more suspects were being sought. In defiance of a ban against demonstrations, more than 1,000 students at universities in Bandung staged protests Jan. 21 against the arrest of the student leaders. In a related development, the government Jan. 23 announced a series of measures to curb the business activities of Chinese merchants, who were also the target of demonstrators during the Tanaka visit, and to eliminate corruption in government. Effective April 1, all foreign investments, most of which were controlled by the Chinese, were to be shared jointly with Indonesians, who were to have at least 51% control. The anti-corruption measures prohibited government officials from makng gifts of government funds.

See also ATOMIC ENERGY [5]; AUSTRALIA [2]; AVIATION [14]; DEFENSE [14]; FAMINE & FOOD; JAPAN [10]; OIL [5-6, 8]; PAKISTAN; PORTUGUESE TIMOR; UNITED NATIONS [6, 15]

INFLATION—*See* BANKS & BANKING; ECONOMY, U.S.; HOUSING; MONETARY DEVELOPMENTS [19]; NIXON, RICHARD M.; WELFARE & POVERTY

INSURANCE—The Senate May 1 approved legislation that would establish a naional no-fault auto insurance system. According to the bill, passed 53-42, states with no-fault plans already in effect or approved by September 1975 would be required to meet federal minimum standards. (An estimated 20 states had adopted the no-fault system in some form, but only 12 had enacted strong legislation, Senate supporters of the federal plan said.) The federal no-fault program would be imposed automatically on states not meeting the deadline. The bill would also allow states the option of including recovery for damage to property in new no-fault laws or allowing that coverage to remain under the tort, or fault, system. Under the bill, motorists would be required to purchase car insurance that guaranteed payment of minimum benefit levels for bodily injury to all accident victims regardless of who was at fault. The payment level was defined as all reasonable medical and rehabilitation expenses, plus up to $25,000 in compensation for the victim's lost earnings. Traditional "pain and suffering" benefits were restricted. The bill had the backing of major auto insurers, though it was also the subject of intensive lobbying efforts against passage by groups representing the nation's lawyers. The House had taken no action on no-fault legislation.

See also ANTITRUST ACTIONS [1-3]; MEDICINE & HEALTH [1-10]; WOMEN'S RIGHTS

INTELLIGENCE—A study by a University of Pennsylvania anthropologist, released Jan. 20, indicated that whites scored higher than nonwhites on intelligence tests because of environmental factors rather than genetic differences between races. The study, conducted in the Pittsburgh public school system by Dr. Peggy Sanday and financed by the Department of Health, Education and Welfare, said test score differences were a function, among other factors, "of middle-class social integration." Dr. Sanday said her information, combined with data from other studies, suggested that IQ differences between racial groups was "exclusively a matter of environment," while differences within racial groups was determinant on both genetics and environment.

INTER-AMERICAN DEVELOPMENT BANK—*See* CHILE [25]; LATIN AMERICA; NICARAGUA; VENEZUELA

INTEREST RATES—*See* BANKS & BANKING; ECONOMY, U.S. [5]; HOUSING; STOCK MARKET [3]

INTERNAL REVENUE SERVICE—*See* ANTITRUST ACTIONS [1-3]; ENERGY CRISIS [19]; PRIVACY [6-10]; TAXES; WATERGATE [13, 21-22, 25, 31]

INTERNATIONAL COMMISSION OF JURISTS—*See* CHILE [4]; UGANDA; URUGUAY

INTERNATIONAL COURT OF JUSTICE—*See* ATOMIC ENERGY [6]; SPANISH SAHARA; TERRITORIAL WATERS

INTERNATIONAL MONETARY FUND (IMF)—*See* CHILE [24]; ITALY [1, 6]; MONETARY DEVELOPMENTS; OIL [21, 30-31]; VENEZUELA

INTERNATIONAL TELEPHONE & TELEGRAPH CORP. (ITT)—*See* ANTITRUST ACTIONS [1-3]; CAMPAIGN FINANCING [7-10]; CENTRAL INTELLIGENCE AGENCY; CHILE [23]; PUERTO RICO; WATERGATE [21-22, 27]

INTERSTATE COMMERCE COMMISSION—*See* APPOINTMENTS & RESIGNATIONS; CIVIL RIGHTS [21]; ENERGY CRISIS [6]; RAILROADS

INVENTIONS—*See* PATENTS

INVESTORS OVERSEAS SERVICES—*See* VESCO, ROBERT L.

IRAN—Dispute with Iraq. A long-running border dispute between Iran and Iraq erupted again on Feb. 10, with heavy casualties on both sides. The dispute involved Iraqi occupation of three small islands at the entrance to the Persian Gulf; and other navigational rights in the Shatt el-Arab waterway. The two countries also had been at odds over Kurdistan, an ethnic region that straddled their northern border. The Kurds, led by Gen. Mustafa al-Barzani, had been seeking self-rule and were said to have received arms and other assistance from Iran. (An Iraqi military offensive against the Kurdish rebels forced about 100,000 Kurdistan civilians to flee to Iran between March and September. Many found refuge in camps set up by the Iranians.) Iran and Iraq had severed diplomatic relations in 1971, but restored them in October, 1973. During the February outbreak, both nations blamed each other for provoking the action. An Iranian military spokesman said Feb. 11 the fighting had broken out when an Iraqi armored force opened fire on the Iranian frontier posts opposite Badra, five miles inside Iraq. Iraq, however, claimed the Iranians had shelled Badra, and that Iranian planes had flown deep into Iraqi airspace. On a complaint by Iraq, the United Nations Security Council met Feb. 15 and 20 to take up the question. During the latter meeting, it was reported both countries were considering a proposal to have a U.N. mission go to the area to study the problem. Fighting resumed again on March 4-6, with both sides again claiming attack by the other. Iran brought its charges to the U.N. Security Council on March 6. The new fighting coincided with Iraqi offers of autonomy to the Kurds. The offer was rejected by Gen. Barzani who asserted it failed to meet Kurdish demands for self-rule. On May 21 U.N. Secretary General Kurt Waldheim informed the Security Council that Iran and Iraq had agreed to a cease-fire, the prompt and simultaneous withdrawal of troops along their disputed border, resumption of peace talks and acceptance of U.N. mediation efforts. The council approved the pact by a 14-0 vote May 28. China did not participate. Iraq reported Dec. 16 that Iranian forces using U.S.-made Hawk missiles downed two Iraqi planes Dec. 14 and 15 over the northern part of the country near Iran. The U.S. State Department Dec. 17 denied the Iraqi charge that Hawk missiles had been used to down their planes. The department said that although Iran was equipped with a Hawk radar and firing system, the missiles themselves had not yet arrived. Iran said Dec. 17 that its "artillery" had shot down the Iraqi planes but claimed they were in Iranian air space.

U.S. sells warplanes. Iran agreed to an American offer whereby it would purchase 30 F14A fighter planes at a cost of $900 million, it was reported Jan. 10 by Grumman Aerospace Corp., manufacturer of the jet aircraft. Twenty-four of the planes were to be delivered in 1976 and six in 1977. In June Iran ordered an additional 50 planes at a cost of about $950 million. Delivery of these was to start in 1978.

U.S. investments to be increased. Iran's ambassador to the U.S., Ardeshir Zahedi, said his government planned to spend several billion dollars in the U.S. within the next five years on equipment for developing Iranian agriculture and technology and on training personnel, according to an interview published in the *New York Times* Dec. 21. Zahedi said the U.S.' nuclear power expertise and equipment would account for part of Iran's outlay. The groundwork for the U.S.-Iranian cooperation referred to by Zahedi had been laid in talks Secretary of State Henry A. Kissinger had held in Iran Nov. 1-2.

Iran acquires Krupp interest. Iran's acquisition of a 25.04% interest in the steel and engineering division of the Krupp works for an estimated $75 million was announced simultaneously July 17 in Teheran and Essen, West Germany.

Iranian loans. The World Bank, Egypt and Great Britain received loans from Iran in 1974. The World Bank borrowed $200 million for 12 years at an annual 8% interest rate. Egypt received $1 billion in loans and credits for projects which included importation of Iranian buses, road building equipment and machine tools; the reconstruction of Port Said by an Iranian-Egyptian firm; and Iranian participation in a multinational project to construct an oil pipeline between Suez City and Port Said. Great Britain was granted $1.2 billion, to be paid in three annual installments. The funds would be used to assist Britain's failing government-owned industries.

See also AUSTRALIA [21]; BELGIUM; DEFENSE [11-12]; FRANCE [19]; GERMANY, WEST [16]; INDIA; IRAQ; MONETARY DEVELOPMENTS [5]; NETHERLANDS [1]; OIL [3, 5, 8, 15-16, 19-20, 28-29, 35]; PAKISTAN; UNION OF SOVIET SOCIALIST REPUBLICS [40]

IRAQ—Iraqis battle Kurds. Fighting erupted between Iraqi troops and Kurdish tribesmen in the northern part of the country March 13 after the Kurds rejected the government's March 11 proposal for autonomy and rebelled against the Baghdad regime. Iraq was reported March 18 to have mobilized 48,000 troops against an estimated 20,000 rebels in preparation for a counterdrive. Baghdad had given the Kurds until March 26 to accept the government plan before the offensive would begin. It was rejected by Gen. Mustafa al-Barzani, head of the Kurdish rebels. The Kurdish Democratic Party had asked for wider autonomy, including veto power over legislation in Baghdad pertaining to Kurdistan, and inclusion of the oil-rich areas of Kirkuk and Mosul in the new Kurdish region. Baghdad had opposed this, saying it was tantamount to secession. Under the government proposal, the Kurdish language would have official status, the region would elect a legislative council and executive council and the region's new boundaries would be drawn on the basis of a new census. The central government would retain strong authority. By March 17 the Kurdish rebels had seized control of a large area bordering Turkey and Iran, including a number of Iraqi border posts. News reports published April 1 indicated heavy fighting had erupted, with 8,000 government soldiers cut off in the Kurdistan mountains. A government decision to halt virtually all civilian supplies to the region resulted in a Kurdish blockade of Iraqi bases at Spilek and Sakho. The Kurds were circumventing the blockade by receiving supplies across the Syrian, Turkish and Iranian borders. Iraqi jets went into action on April 12. Two days later Iraqi armored columns converged on rebel troops near Kirkuk, but were said to have been thrown back with heavy losses. On April 9 Vice President Saddam Hussein accused the United States of supplying arms to the Kurds. The State Department denied the charge. In a March 29 interview with the *New York Times*, Barzani said the Kurds had failed to receive "serious, large-scale or solid aid," despite appeals to the West. The fighting escalated in April following an announcement by the Voice of Kurdistan radio that the rebels had launched an all-out war against Iraq in response to the arrest and execution by the government of 11 prominent members of the Kurdish Democratic party sometime after March 11. Nineteen captured Iraqi officers were executed by a Kurdish firing squad in retaliation April 21.

Barzani charged Iraq with conducting a "war of genocide" against its Kurdish minority in a letter delivered to United Nations Secretary General Kurt Waldheim June 7. The letter was referred to the U.N. Human Rights Commission. The Kurds claimed the Iraqis had bombed 15 towns and 204 villages in the Kurdish region in April-May, killing 1,534 civilians and wounding about 3,500. A Barzani aide also claimed that Soviet pilots were flying missions against the rebels in support of government troops. About 100,000 Kurdistan civilians were reported to have crossed into neighboring Iran between March and September in an attempt to escape the fighting.

The war continued through the summer. According to a July 17 report, Iraq, using most of its 90,000-man army, backed by reservists and irregulars, had driven the rebels back into the mountains along the Turkish and Iranian borders. By Sept. 23 Iraqi troops were reported to have captured virtually every city and town in Kurdistan. Barzani said Sept. 22 that the rebel forces faced a possible major setback that would give the government control of more of Kurdistan than they had in 13 years. Kurdish officers confirmed Iranian and Soviet arms aid to the combatants Sept. 23, reporting that the Russians had provided government forces with 8,000 military advisers, including pilots who reportedly had flown an undetermined number of missions against Kurdish villages, while Teheran had supplied the insurgents with rifles, artillery pieces and ammunition. Israel gave the rebels several medium-range artillery pieces, Kurdish officers said.

See also DEFENSE [14]; IRAN; MIDDLE EAST [9, 22, 27, 30, 46]; OIL [4-5, 15, 38]; RHODESIA; UNITED NATIONS [6]

IRELAND, NORTHERN (ULSTER)—The Ulster Executive, the new administrative body responsible for running Northern Ireland, took office in Belfast Jan. 1. The executive body had been proposed in a British White Paper in March, 1973, as part of a plan for power-sharing by Protestant and Catholic parties. The plan provided for creation of a Cabinet composed of 12 members (later reduced to 11) with Great Britain retaining responsibility for security, justice, foreign relations and some financial matters. All other functions were assumed by the Executive and a newly-elected assembly. Former Prime Minister Brian Faulkner was named head of the Executive Board. Faulkner was also the leader of the Protestant Unionists, who had agreed to the power-sharing proposals and who received a majority of the Executive posts. The Faulkner group was opposed by dissidents within their own party and by the Provisional IRA; although the major Catholic party, the Social Democratic and Labor Party (SDLP) gave its support. The new government had, in 1973, entered an accord with the Republic of Ireland known as the Sunningdale agreement in which the Irish government acknowledged Northern Ireland as a separate entity but did not specifically say it was part of Britain. (Irish courts had accepted the constitutionality of the agreement, ruling that it did not violate the republic's goal for an ultimately united Ireland.)

[2] Faulkner resigned Jan. 7 as leader of the Unionists after the party's ruling council refused to support creation of a proposed Council of Ireland, a consultative body providing links between the Belfast and Dublin governments. The vote represented a victory for Protestant hard-liners. It had, however, no binding effect, and Faulkner vowed to pursue his policies, saying he would continue as chief of the governing Executive. After his party resignation, Faulkner called on the Irish Republic to crack down on IRA terrorists, saying ratification of the Sunningdale agreement and establishment of the Council of Ireland were contingent on progress against terrorism. The first meeting of the new Northern Ireland Assembly Jan. 22 was disrupted when hard-line Protestants, threatening to wreck implementation of the 1973 White Paper, traded blows with moderate Assembly members. The Assembly adjourned after a few minutes as police carried out or escorted 18 shouting protesters from the chamber. Among those forcibly removed was the Rev. Ian Paisley, head of the United Loyalist Action Group, formed in 1973 to fight the White Paper proposals. (Earlier, the Unionists had elected MP Harry West to replace Faulkner as party head.)

[3] The Executive and the moderate Protestants supporting it suffered a serious blow Feb. 28 when, in elections for the British Parliament, a coalition of three extreme rightist Protestant groups won 11 of the 12 Northern Ireland seats. Paisley indicated March 1 that the Protestant hard-liners would form a separate bloc in the new British Parliament with the goal of renegotiating Ulster's constitution to end the Catholic-Protestant coalition and halt formation of the Council of Ireland. Although the Ulster Assembly itself was dominated by moderates, Paisley maintained it did not represent the will of the majority because more than 60% of the votes cast in the British elections were for anti-Assembly candidates.)

[4] An attempt to appease the hard-liners was made March 13 by Irish Republic Prime Minister Liam Cosgrave in a statement to the Dail (Parliament) in Dublin. Cosgrave declared that "Northern Ireland is within the United Kingdom, and my government accept this as fact." Cosgrave added that "the factual position of Northern Ireland within the United Kingdom cannot be changed except by a decision of the majority of the people of Northern Ireland."

Although Cosgrave's statement was accepted by some elements within the Republic, opposition came both from the Sinn Fein, the political arm of the IRA, and from Dail member Vivian de Valera, who said the statement came dangerously close to recognizing the right of a section of the Irish people to secede from the Irish nation. Protestant hard-liners in Northern Ireland said Cosgrave's statement made "no difference" because he had not withdrawn the Republic's claim to ultimate sovereignty over Ulster. On April 26, the rightist leaders announced their own plans for the future of Northern Ireland. Among their proposals: rearming the police as a paramilitary group; rejection of the Council of Ireland; dismantling of the power-sharing Executive.

[5] **Ulster Executive falls.** A crippling 14-day strike organized by the newly-formed Ulster Workers Council (UWC) of right-wing Protestant trade unionists resulted in the fall of the Executive May 28. The British government temporarily resumed direct rule over Northern Ireland following the resignation of Faulkner and his coalition. Faulkner blamed the events on the failure of the British government to open a "dialogue" with the UWC, whom British Prime Minister Harold Wilson had described in a televised speech May 25 as "thugs" and "bullies." The strike, designed to force repudiation of the Sunningdale agreement, began May 15, one day after the Northern Ireland Assembly had approved in principle the establishment of the Council of Ireland. Many of the workers who struck were reportedly intimidated by the Ulster Defense Association. The most serious disruption came from a walkout at the main power stations, which reduced electricity supplies by 40%. By May 20 nearly 100 barricades sealed off Protestant quarters and cut off entrances and exits from Belfast. Electricity service was cut to about six hours a day, mail service was halted, trucking ceased, all factories were shut and downtown stores were closed. Britain dispatched 500 more troops to the province May 20, bringing the total there to over 16,000. The troops and police, however, were under orders to avoid clashes with the Protestants. Though rightist politicians were not directly involved in organizing the strike, they had issued a statement May 19 expressing support. Britain intervened May 27; troops occupied 21 gasoline stations and two oil storage depots to assure supplies for essential services. Catholic members of the Executive had threatened to resign unless the British government intervened in the strike. In an attempt to undermine support for the walkout, the coalition Executive May 22 scaled down plans for the Council, agreeing it would be initially limited to consultative meetings of ministers from both states. Further moves, including creation of a consultative assembly composed of members of the two Irish legislatures, and transfer of some government functions, would be postponed until after new provincial elections in 1977 or 1978. The concession was immediately rejected by the UWC.

[6] Following the resignation of the Executive, the UWC suspended the strike May 29 without achieving one of its major goals: a promise by the British government for new Assembly elections in which the militants believed they could win a majority. A few hours later, the British government suspended the Assembly for four months and recalled Parliament from recess to debate the crisis. The decision was announced by Britain's secretary of state for Ulster, Merlyn Rees, who said the Assembly would remain in existence but its functions would be assumed by the British Parliament and Ulster administrators. Belfast returned to working order May 30, with electricity, gas and public transport virtually normal, shops and streets open, and many factory workers back on the job. The Belfast Chamber of Commerce and Industry estimated that the strike had cost the province more than $190 million. The call for troop withdrawal

was rejected, however, by British Prime Minister Wilson in a June 4 speech before the House of Commons. Any pullout by the British, he said, involved risk of a "holocaust."

[7] The British government issued a White Paper July 4 calling for new Ulster elections to choose members of a constitutional convention which would draft a new constitution for the province. The government said no new Executive could be formed from the suspended Assembly; it pledged to play "no part" in the convention, although results would require British parliamentary approval; and it stressed the need for power-sharing among Protestant and Catholic groups. The convention would have 78 members elected by proportional representation. A bill to implement the White Paper proposals was published July 5. Aside from the provisions for the convention, it gave Britain's secretary of state the powers granted Northern Ireland's Assembly in 1973. The bill provided that the Ulster Assembly remain suspended pending its dissolution when new elections were held.

[8] **Terrorism unabated: toll mounts to 1,141.** Civil unrest continued unabated in Northern Ireland during 1974, with 1,141 persons listed as killed in terrorist incidents since the campaign began in the province in 1969 (*London Times* report Dec. 27). The shootings and bombings carried out both by Catholic and Protestant extremist groups brought new calls for action to suppress the terrorism, and a growing extension of terrorist bombings to Britain involved Britons in the Northern Ireland problem more directly than ever before. The following were some of the major terrorist actions carried out during the year:

[9] Eleven persons were killed and 14 wounded Feb. 4 when a 50-pound bomb blew up a busload of British servicemen and their families as they were traveling through Yorkshire, in Britain's Midlands. The dead included an entire family—a soldier, his wife, and two children—and seven other soldiers. Police suspected the IRA was responsible for the blast.

[10] Explosions ripped the main shopping streets in Armagh, Lisburn and Bangor and several buildings in Belfast Mar. 29-31. Four men were killed in bomb blasts at a Catholic bar in north Belfast March 29 and a retaliatory blast at a Protestant bar the following day. A fifth victim, found shot in the head, was believed murdered by a disciplinary squad of the IRA. Nine more persons were killed by IRA bombings in Belfast April 9.

[11] After a lull of a month, the IRA resumed its attacks June 13 when four incendiary bombs exploded in downtown Belfast department stores and a car bomb wounded a British military policeman. Car bombs exploded in Armagh, Londonderry and elsewhere June 18-20. Twenty-two bomb attacks on more than a dozen towns and villages were reported.

[12] A 20-pound bomb exploded at the Houses of Parliament in London June 17, damaging the 900-year-old Westminster Hall. Eleven persons were injured, none seriously. Police laid responsibility to the Provisional wing of the IRA. The House of Commons and the House of Lords, both some distance from the hall, were not damaged.

[13] A bomb exploded without warning in a tourist-packed cellar armory at the Tower of London July 17, killing one person and injuring at least 36 others, many of them children. The police declined to attribute blame for the blast. The explosion occurred in the White Tower, the oldest of the 13 structures comprising the Tower of London.

[14] Bombs exploded in two crowded bars in Birmingham Nov. 21, killing 19 persons and injuring 184, many of them teenagers. Two of the injured died later.

Although the IRA disclaimed responsibility for the blasts, the British public blamed the Irish terrorists. The attack was the worst in the series of bombings that had hit Britain in the past two years. Thirty Britons had been killed in almost 50 major bomb attacks and 200 minor ones, according to the *Washington Post* Nov. 23. The explosions followed a warning broadcast Nov. 17 by David O'Connell, chief of staff of the IRA Provisional wing, that bombings in Britain would be increased unless the government issued a statement of intent to withdraw its troops from Northern Ireland. He made the statement in a television interview taped in Ireland Nov. 15.

[15] **Britain approves IRA ban.** The House of Commons approved without opposition Nov. 29 a government bill outlawing the IRA and giving the police wider anti-terrorist powers, including authority to detain suspects for up to seven days without bringing charges and to curb travel between Britain and the Irish Republic. Queen Elizabeth signed the bill later that day. Police staged raids Nov. 30-Dec. 4, detaining at least 45 persons as bombing suspects in London and Birmingham. British Home Secretary Roy Jenkins signed at least six expulsion orders against IRA suspects Nov. 30. The House of Commons, by a 369-217 vote Dec. 11, rejected hanging as a penalty for persons convicted of "acts of terrorism causing death." The recent increase of terrorism had brought strong pressure, mainly from the opposition Conservative Party, for restoration of the death penalty, which was formally abolished in 1969.

[16] **Compensation to Londonderry riot dead.** The British Defense Ministry announced it would pay more than $92,000 compensation to relatives of 13 men killed by British troops during the "Bloody Sunday" riots in Londonderry, Northern Ireland in January, 1972, it was reported Dec. 20. An official inquiry had found the victims innocent of charges that they carried bombs or firearms when shot.

[17] **IRA sets Christmas truce.** The Provisional wing of the IRA began an 11-day Christmas truce at midnight Dec. 22. In announcing the ceasefire Dec. 20, the IRA said it could become permanent if the British government gave an adequate positive response. As conditions of the temporary truce, the IRA demanded that the British army and Ulster police cease all "aggressive military activity." Protestant hard-liners criticized the truce Dec. 20, saying it amounted to a surrender to the IRA. Britain announced Dec. 31 it would release 20 suspected terrorists—17 IRA members and three Protestants—detained in Northern Ireland; it allowed 50 more prisoners to leave for a three-day parole and freed 100 other convicted terrorists whose terms expired before the end of March 1975. Britain's secretary of state for Northern Ireland, Merlyn Rees, pledged that if the IRA permanently halted its campaign of violence, Britain would gradually free all detainees and reduce its army activity.

See also GREAT BRITAIN [5]; IRELAND, REPUBLIC OF

IRELAND, REPUBLIC OF—Prime Minister Liam Cosgrave, in a Jan. 1 congratulatory telegram to the new Ulster Executive of Northern Ireland, vowed to join it in defending "democratic institutions against violence" and promised that "those who seek to undermine or wreck these institutions would find no refuge here." Invoking an 1861 act, the government announced Jan. 2 that persons accused of murder in Northern Ireland and seeking refuge in the republic would be tried by special criminal courts in Dublin.

William Fox, 36, a Protestant senator was found shot to death near the Northern Ireland border March 12. It was the first political murder recorded in the republic since 1927. Responsibility for the killing was claimed by the Ulster

Freedom Fighters (UFF) a Protestant extremist group that charged Fox with ties to the IRA. Five men were captured, convicted and given life imprisonment for the murder in June.

Bridget Rose Dugdale, a British heiress and university lecturer, was convicted in Dublin in June of an IRA-connected art theft. She was sentenced to nine years for receiving 19 paintings, valued at about $20 million, following their April 26 theft from the home of millionaire Sir Alfred Beit. Her group had threatened to burn the paintings unless four IRA guerrillas were transferred from jail in England to Northern Ireland, and the equivalent of $1.2 million in ransom was paid. Dugdale had been arrested May 4 and the paintings recovered. After a second Dublin trial, Dugdale was sentenced to another nine years concurrent term for hijacking a helicopter in an abortive attempt to bomb a police station in Northern Ireland in January.

A new Protestant group, calling itself the Young Militants Association, claimed responsibility in June for a series of car bombings in Dublin and Monaghan May 17 which killed 30 persons and injured about 200 others. The group warned it would retaliate in the Republic for IRA bombings in Northern Ireland. The government May 18 recalled its 340 soldiers serving with United Nations forces in the Sinai Desert as part of the effort to intensify security along the border with Northern Ireland. Officials promised tighter security measures, including new border checkpoints and severe Dublin traffic restrictions. Prime Minister Cosgrave announced plans in the Dail June 27 to form a force of unarmed vigilantes under police control in every town and village. The force would watch out for possible car bombs.

Nineteen Provisional IRA guerrillas escaped from the maximum security prison at Portlaoise, 50 miles southwest of Dublin, Aug. 18 by blasting open the doors of the jail with high explosives. They fled in cars hijacked at gunpoint. One of those who escaped was identified as Kevin Mallon, a Provisional leader who escaped by helicopter from Dublin's Mountjoy prison in October 1973 and was later recaptured.

Erskine Hamilton Childers, 68, fourth president of the Irish Republic and the nation's first Protestant head of state, died Nov. 17 after 18 months in office. He had suffered a heart attack Nov. 16 while delivering a speech. Cearbhal O'Dalaigh, 63, a European Court judge and former chief justice of Ireland, was sworn in Dec. 19 as the fifth president of the Republic.

See also AUSTRALIA [16]; COMMUNISM, INTERNATIONAL; EUROPEAN ECONOMIC COMMUNITY [18]; EUROPEAN SECURITY; NOBEL PRIZES; IRELAND, NORTHERN; OIL [26]

IRON ORE—*See* ENVIRONMENT & POLLUTION [12]; INDIA; VENEZUELA
ISLAM—*See* AFRICA; OIL [18]; RELIGION [17]
ISLAMIC DEVELOPMENT BANK—*See* OIL [21]

ISRAEL—War debate. The Arab attack on Israel in 1973 caused major military and governmental changes in that country during 1974, following bitter disputes over Israel's state of preparedness, approval of troop disengagement plans with Egypt, and withdrawal to pre-1967 frontiers. The Knesset (Parliament) approved the troop disengagement plan Jan. 22 by a 76-35 vote following sharp debate in which right-wing Likud Party members denounced the accord as a surrender. Maj. Gen. Ariel Sharon, who had led the division task force that crossed the west bank of the Suez Canal during the war, was one of the critical Likud Party members. At a news conference Jan. 20, Sharon also charged that his division had managed to achieve victory "notwithstanding omissions and errors, failures and mistakes, the loss of nerves and control." Although the Israeli Cabinet, on Jan. 27, expressed full confidence in Sharon's superior, chief of staff Lt. Gen. David Elazar, a judicial commission investigating conduct of the war found that Elazar "bears responsibility for what happened on the eve of the war both with regard to the assessment of the situation and the Israeli Defense Force's preparedness." The report recommended dismissal of Elazar and other top army officers, while at the same time clearing Premier Golda Meir and Defense Minister Moshe Dayan of responsibility. Elazar resigned April 2 asserting that, contrary to charges, a defense plan had been drawn up to deal with the eventuality of an attack by Egypt and Syria. Though the judicial commission report said Dayan "was not required to issue orders additional to or different from those proposed to him by the General Staff," Elazar argued that Dayan had to approve all operational plans since he was the "authority above the chief of staff." (Maj. Gen. Mordechai Gur was chosen by the Cabinet April 14 to succeed Elazar as chief of staff. Gur, who assumed his post the next day, had been commander of the northern front.) The initial findings of the panel, headed by Chief Justice Shimon Agranat, precipitated a political storm in the country, with both wings of the governing Labor Party and the opposition Likud charging the report was unduly severe on the military and too lenient with the government leadership.

Debate over the report, and demands for Dayan's resignation, led to the fall of the government April 10 and the selection, 10 days later, of Labor Minister Yitzhak Rabin, a member of the Labor Party, as premier-designate. In addition to the war debate, Meir had also been in conflict with the National Religious Party (NRP) who had demanded a change in the government's Law of Return. The law, which conferred automatic Israeli citizenship on any Jew wishing to reside in Israel, also accepted converts to Judaism made by Reform or Conservative rabbis. The NRP demanded that conversion be recognized only when it occurred within the Orthodox branch of the religion, thus denying citizenship to converted Reform or Conservative members. Dayan, too, had been the subject of severe criticism when, on Feb. 17, a group of 3,000 demonstrators called for his resignation as defense minister, charging him with responsibility for Israel's "failures" in the October war. In an attempt to halt the crisis, Meir had formed a new 22-member coalition Cabinet on March 10, after receiving a 62-46 vote of confidence from the Knesset.

With the judicial commission report, however, divisions occurred within Meir's Labor Party, leading the premier to announce her "irrevocable" decision to resign. The decision came after a closed-door session of parliamentary members of the party during which the meeting became deadlocked over whether Dayan should accept responsibility for the mistakes that led to Israeli setbacks at the beginning of the war. Dayan and his supporters argued that the entire government shared collective blame and should quit. Under the Israeli system, Rabin was officially designated by President Ephraim Katzir April 23 to try to form a new coalition government, within a 42-day period. If he failed during that time, national elections would be called. (Rabin had been chief of staff from 1963-1967 and had played a prominent role in Israel's victory in the 1967 war.)

The first native-born Israeli to head his country's government, Rabin succeeded in forming a new Cabinet on May 28. It was composed of members of the Labor Party, two Independent Liberals and one Civil Rights Movement member. The NRP, which had been in the previous government, had decided May 6 not to join the Rabin Cabinet because it would not include the right-wing opposition Likud and because there was no indication Rabin would agree to change the Law of Return. The new Cabinet contained 15 holdovers from Meir's government, but excluded three key members, among whom was Dayan who had refused to serve because of the inclusion of the dovish Civil Rights Movement. The Knesset approved Rabin and his Cabinet June 3 by a 61-51 vote with 5 abstentions. It was the closest vote of confidence ever registered. (Rabin's majority was increased Oct. 30 when the NRP decided to join the government after accepting a compromise formula on the religious question which would provide for a Cabinet committee to examine the problem. The NRP decision, however, immediately prompted the withdrawal of the Civil Rights Movement Party which advocated a program of separation of religion and state.) Outlining his policy in June, Rabin reiterated the outgoing government's opposition to a return to the pre-1967 boundaries; to establishment of a Palestinian state on the West Bank; and to negotiation with Palestinian commando groups. Rabin's associates later explained that this left open the possibility that the Palestinians could be represented at Geneva by a delegation who had no connection with commando groups, preferably within that of Jordan.

West bank controversy. Israeli squatters July 25 began a drive to open the entire West Bank to Jewish settlers. They were removed from the area near Nablus July 29 by Israeli troops, but, in October, gathered about 5,000 members or supporters of the NRP for another try. Security forces, anticipating the intrusion, had set up barricades to block the move, but about 500 demonstrators managed to break through the lines near Ramallah before being forcibly evicted by the soldiers. (Although officials of the NRP supported the squatters in principle, they opposed establishment of the settlements.) Government action continued through mid-October, with troops clearing out squatters near Jericho, Tel Shilo, north of Jerusalem, and Tulkarm, northeast of Tel Aviv. The squatters maintained their settlement rights were based on the fact that the West Bank was part of the biblical land of Israel. The government announcd Nov. 24 it planned to construct a major new industrial center and housing for its workers in the occupied West Bank between Jerusalem and Jericho and several smaller projects on the eastern outskirts of Jerusalem. Information Minister Aharon Yariv announced the decision after it was adopted at a Cabinet meeting. He said the timing of the move was "coincidental," implying that it was not related to the resolution of the United Nations General Assembly declaring that the Palestinian people had the right to independence and sovereignty and to return to their former homes in the West Bank and in other parts of Israel.

Riots protest devaluation. The government Nov. 9 devalued the Israeli pound by 43% and announced other austerity measures, including a wage freeze, higher taxes, import curbs and sharp increases in the cost of basic foods to cope with the country's economic crisis brought on by the October 1973 war. The Cabinet's decision precipitated riots in Tel Aviv and elsewhere Nov. 10-11 as demonstrators protested the dramatic rise in food prices. The devaluation was part of a series of steps taken by the government to combat an inflation rate which had driven up the general price index about 50% in a year and a half. As a result of defense outlays for the October war, Israel faced a 1974 balance-of-trade deficit of $3 billion, compared with $1 billion in 1973. Measures enacted in July had included a sharp cutback in government spending and public construction, $600 million in new taxes and a freeze on half of the 20% cost-of-living increase that all wage earners had been scheduled to receive in July. Israelis were also required in 1974 to make a compulsory war loan of 10%-20% of their income. Rioters protested the measure in Tel Aviv, Haifa and Ashdod, where port employes staged work stoppages Nov. 11.

Israel may forego U.S. A-reactor. Israel informed the U.S. that it was not presently interested in Washington's offer of an atomic power plant, but dropped its objections to Egypt's receipt of one from the U.S., it was reported by the U.S. State Department Dec. 16. The Israeli position was outlined by Foreign Minister Yigal Allon in talks with Secretary of State Henry A. Kissinger in

Washington Dec. 9. Officially Israel said it was not prepared to make the relatively large commitment required in building the atomic power plant. Administration officials, however, were said to believe the reason for Israel's lack of interest was its reluctance to place all its atomic facilities, including the Dimona reactor capable of producing plutonium weapons, under international inspection as called for by the U.S. plan. A writer for the *New Scientist*, Nicholas Valery, reported in the magazine's Dec. 12 issue that Israeli President Ephraim Katzir's meeting with science journalists Dec. 1 left the impression that his country "must be assumed to possess a quite effective nuclear force" in the 20 kiloton range. Israel "could possess at least six such devices and possibly as many as 10" on the basis of "the plutonium production rate of its two nuclear reactors," Valery reported.

See also Atomic Energy [11-12]; Aviation [14]; Banks & Banking; Bulgaria; Civil Rights [19]; Defense [15]; Ford, Gerald R.; Foreign Aid; Germany, West [17]; Greece [10]; Iraq; Middle East; Oil [4, 6, 13-14]; Religion [12-13]; Union of Soviet Socialist Republics [9-13, 20, 22, 25-31]; United Nations [4, 8-10, 16-19]; Watergate [40]

ITALY—Governmental crisis. Italy had three new governments during the year, bringing the total to 37 since World War II. Premier Mariano Rumor resigned on March 2, reassumed office on March 15, resigned again on June 10, returned to the government on the 20th, and left office again Oct. 3. The last government of the year was formed Nov. 23 by Aldo Moro who had been Rumor's foreign minister. The government crises focused on a dispute over ways to end Italy's severe economic problems, chief among which was an unprecedented 9.2 trillion lire deficit projected for Italy's 1974 budget. Italy also suffered a massive balance of payments deficit, running at $1 billion a month in the period from January-May. Inflation was rising at an annual rate of 20%. Precipitating the March 2 crisis was a promise by Treasury Minister Ugo La Malfa and by Guido Carli, governor of the Bank of Italy, to the International Monetary Fund (IMF) that Italy would curb domestic credit and government spending in return for a standby credit of 1 billion Special Drawing Rights (SDRs) ($1.2 billion) from the IMF. The credit was sought to support the declining value of the lira and help finance Italy's expected 1974 trade deficit. La Malfa's economic proposals were opposed by Budget and Economic Planning Minister Antonio Giolitti, a Socialist, who said it would increase unemployment and economic stagnation and prevent investment in social reforms. (Both the Socialists and the Republicans were part of the four-party center-left coalition of Rumor's government.) After expressing full support for La Malfa, the Republican Party pulled out of the coalition March 1. Rumor submitted his resignation the next day and then, on the request of President Giovanni Leone, agreed on March 6 to try again.

[2] The new coalition formed on March 15—receiving final parliamentary approval March 27—was composed of members from the Christian Democratic, Socialist and Social Democratic Parties. The Republican Party declined to participate, but promised support in Parliament. The Communists, who had been relatively tolerant of Rumor's previous government, denounced the new one as inadequate to meet the nation's economic problems. They also objected to Christian Democratic leadership, particularly party secretary Amintore Fanfani, for ignoring efforts to avoid a national referendum on divorce, scheduled for May 12. The continuing deadlock over economic policies caused Rumor's second resignation of the year June 10. Treasury Minister Emilio Colombo, a Christian Democrat, called for tighter curbs which were again opposed by the

Socialists. According to the *New York Times* June 11, leading central bankers said after the annual meeting of the Bank for International Settlements in Basel, Switzerland, they would grant aid only if Italy adopted more stringent economic restrictions to reduce domestic demand and curb imports. After three days of political consultation, President Leone rejected the resignation June 13 because of the nation's grave economic situation. He urged the coalition "to make every effort to reach an accord." The Cabinet became operational again June 20 after the three parties agreed on an austerity program June 19. In the negotiations to revive the coalition, the Socialists had suggested that the government consult the Communist Party before important decisions were made. Unidentified sources reported June 19 that Rumor had said he planned to consult "with the opposition," apparently the Communists, whenever he thought it necessary. The Communist Party—the largest Marxist movement in the Western World, and Italy's second largest political force—intensified its bid for more power in September. The party, in an editorial in its newspaper *L'Unita* Sept. 1, asserted that the government needed its cooperation to resolve the nation's social and economic problems. Party spokesman Armando Cossutta said Italian Communists were aware of the need to "act within the framework of a specific international, geographic and political reality,"—interpreted as a willingness to retain membership in the North Atlantic Treaty Organization. The Rumor government had sought and received Communist help for parliamentary passage of a fiscal austerity program, the *New York Times* reported Sept. 6.

[3] The continuing dispute over economic policy, a political dispute between coalition members, and a conflict over reported right-wing plots finally fragmented Rumor's government Oct. 3. The main Cabinet dispute involved differences between Socialists and Christian Democrats over economic policy. However, the most recent political quarrelling occurred between Socialists and Social Democrats. Mario Tanassi, leader of the Social Democrats and finance minister, had accused the Socialists Oct. 1 of sabotaging the coalition. He called for new general elections, in the apparent hope of reducing Socialist representation in the legislature. Another strain in the coalition had developed when Socialist Budget Minister Antonio Giolitti had criticized Christian Democratic Defense Minister Giulio Andreotti Sept. 30 for failing to inform the Cabinet of reports of planned right-wing coups. Andreotti had forwarded material gathered by the intelligence service to the judiciary. The crisis was resolved Nov. 23 when Moro formed a 25-member minority government of Christian Democrats and Republicans which was then approved by President Leone. Parliamentary support for the new coalition was pledged by the Socialists and Social Democrats, both partners in Rumor's Cabinet, giving the minority government 371 votes in the 630-seat Chamber of Deputies. The leader of the Republican Party, Ugo La Malfa, was named deputy premier, and Republican Bruno Visentini became finance minister. Rumor took over Moro's post of foreign minister. In two significant shifts, Interior Minister Paolo Emilio Taviani was replaced by a fellow Christian Democrat, Luigi Gui, a close associate of Moro. Arnaldo Forlani, a Christian Democrat, was named defense minister, replacing Giulio Andreotti, who became minister of budget and economic planning.

[4] **Economic crisis.** Leaders of the labor front, composed of Italy's three major trade unions, announced June 28 they would launch four-hour regional work stoppages to protest the government austerity program which the unions contended placed a heavier burden on wage earners than on other classes. The partial stoppages represented a victory for the moderates in trade union echelons. Militant labor groups, particularly the metal workers and building

trade unions, had pressed for a general strike. On July 6, however, the government issued emergency decrees, implementing an earlier program, which called for steep tax and price increases. The new measures introduced a one-time surtax on motor vehicles and residential and office property; increased the value-added tax (a levy imposed on the value of each stage in the production and distribution of goods) from 6% to 18% on beef and other basic consumer goods and from 18% to 30% on luxury goods; boosted gasoline prices (premium gas increased from $1.60 a gallon to $1.85); and raised property taxes. Also increased were some bus fares and utility rates, income tax rates for higher income brackets and the tax exemptions of lower wage groups. Stricter controls against tax evasion were also ordered. The decrees, effective immediately, required parliamentary approval within 60 days.

[5] The government July 31 abandoned its year-long price freeze on certain basic consumer items and replaced it with a new system of "administered" and "supervised" prices. Under the new program, the Interministerial Price Committee would administer prices on such basic items as pasta, bread, vegetable oils, beef, milk, sugar and soaps and detergents; the committee reserved the right to supervise the prices of other items. The policy change followed a report by government statisticians that the cost of living rose 16.8% over the 12-month period through June, with food up 13.9%. A severe scarcity of pasta products, Italy's basic food, was reported Aug. 29 in many parts of the nation. Hoarding, panic buying, speculation and black marketing created the shortage, which developed after the government authorized local officials to fix new price ceilings on pasta, in some areas amounting to a 50% increase. The Industry Ministry reconsidered its policy and ordered a temporary suspension of the price increases in provinces where they had not yet gone into effect, creating wide price differentials between regions. The retail price was increased 23% on Sept. 5.

[6] The IMF April 10 had announced approval of a standby credit to Italy of 1 billion Special Drawing Rights (SDRs) ($1.2 billion) on condition the nation adopt measures to stabilize the lira and reduce the payments deficit. Other IMF loans: $621 million, Aug. 31; $540 million in various currencies, Sept. 24; and $314.9 million from the fund's special "oil facility," Sept. 29. West Germany agreed Aug. 31 to grant Italy a $2 billion credit to help ease its economic and financial crisis. A small portion (estimated by news reports as one-fifth or one-sixth) of Italy's gold reserves would be used as collateral for the loan, with the value set at 80% of the average international free market rate over the previous eight weeks, or about $120 an ounce. Italy's gold reserves exceeded 2,000 tons. In announcing the loan, West German Chancellor Helmut Schmidt said his government would also support a plan for a new loan to Italy by the European Economic Community (EEC).

[7] A nationwide strike of farmhands for more pay on April 23 came amid scattered protests that month from farm groups protesting meat and milk prices they contended were driven down by imports from the EEC. In an attempt to halt the imports, farmers had blockaded border points between Italy and France, Switzerland, West Germany and Austria. The government, April 30, imposed a 50% surcharge on all imports of manufactured goods, including those from EEC countries. The measure was in compliance with the EEC's Treaty of Rome, the government said, which allowed member nations to take "necessary measures" in the case of a sudden balance of payments crisis.

[8] The Banca Privata Italiana, a Milan bank formed in August by the merger of two banks controlled by Sicilian-American financier Michele Sindona, was ordered liquidated, the Bank of Italy announced Sept. 28. The Bank said it took the action after discovery of irregularities and "losses of such a size as to exceed

considerably both the reserves and the capital of the enterprise." The Bank pledged deposits would be fully reimbursed, except those held by shareholders. (Sindona, who also owned 21.6% of the Franklin New York Corp., which filed for bankruptcy on Oct. 16, had been excluded from management of his Italian banking network by the state-controlled Banco di Roma, it was reported Aug. 6. Banco di Roma then formed Banca Privata Italiana by merging two Sindona banks, Banca Unione and Banca Privata Finanziaria. A consortium of four Milan banks had been formed Sept. 17 to save the Banca Privata. The consortium would be responsible for reimbursement of depositors.) The Bank of Italy had filed with the Milan public prosecutor's office four complaints charging possible wrongdoing by Sindona, it was disclosed Sept. 17. A Milan magistrate announced Oct. 9 that he had issued an arrest warrant for Sindona on charges of falsifying accounts and illegally dividing profits in connection with the activities of the defunct Banca Unione.

[9] **Divorce repeal defeated.** In a landmark national referendum held May 12-13, the electorate voted overwhelmingly to retain the controversial three-year-old divorce law opposed by the Roman Catholic Church. According to final results announced May 13 by Interior Minister Taviani, 59.1% voted against repeal of the law, 40.9% voted in favor. More than 32 million valid ballots were cast, representing an 88.1% turnout. The Catholic church hierarchy May 14 expressed "deep regret" over the defeat of its antidivorce stand, but pledged "due respect" for the will of the majority. The law permitted termination of a marriage after a legal or de facto separation of five-seven years or if one party had been sentenced for a grave crime. Since the law went into effect in December 1970, 66,000 persons had been granted divorces.

[10] **Extremist activity.** Mario Sossi, Genoa's deputy public prosecutor, who had been kidnapped by the extreme leftist Red Brigade April 18, was released by his abductors May 23. Police had reported May 6 that the kidnappers threatened to kill Sossi unless eight members of the Maoist "October 22" group were released from jail and flown to Cuba, North Korea or Algeria. Sossi had headed the prosecution of the group. A Genoa court had agreed to the kidnappers' demand, however the Supreme Court June 18 overturned the decision after Genoa's chief public prosecutor appealed the decision of his home court.

[11] A bomb exploded at an anti-Fascist rally in the northern industrial town of Brescia May 28, killing six persons and injuring 94. The rally, attended by 3,000 workers and students, had been called by a local anti-Fascist committee to protest "obscure Fascist schemes" in connection with recent violence in the city in which left-wing cooperatives and trade union buildings had been bombed. Spokesmen for the neo-Fascist Italian Social Movement-Naional Right Wing denied responsibility. A four-hour general strike was staged the next day by Italy's three major trade unions who were protesting the blast. During the demonstrations, the neo-Fascist offices in Brescia were attacked. Police also raided extreme leftist and rightist organizations, arresting a doctor said to have been connected with the bombing the previous day and uncovering, in a remote mountain area about 50 miles north of Rome, a cache of arms and about $600,000 thought to be obtained through kidnap ransoms. The Cabinet May 30 ordered the formation of a special anti-terrorist unit to combat extremist violence. In raids in the Milan area and north of Rome, it was reported June 2, police captured documents and maps indicating that the Brescia bombing was part of a planned rightist terrorist offensive aimed at forcing a military takeover and bringing in a neo-Fascist government. Defense Minister Andreotti pledged July 4 to reform the counterespionage service amid reports that more than one person involved in recent terrorist incidents had been an informer for the service,

which knew of the plans but did not act against them. Declaring that secret service files on Italian citizens were illegal, Parliament announced the destruction Aug. 10 of about 33,000 portfolios on private citizens and about 7,500 other documents.

[12] A bomb exploded on a crowded express train Aug. 4, killing 12 persons. A neo-Fascist terrorist group, the Black Order, claimed responsibility. The explosion occurred as the train, which originated in Rome and was bound for Munich, West Germany, emerged from a tunnel between Florence and Bologna. In a note Aug. 5, the Black Order said government members who were "bringing Italy under Marxism by dissolving our organizations" must bear responsibility for the deaths. Two neo-Fascist boxers, Angelo Rossi and Riccardo Ardillo, were arrested in Rome Sept. 4 for allegedly using threats or violence to force a key witness to give false testimony about the train bomb explosion.

[13] Gen. Vito Miceli, 58, head of the Italian military espionage secret service until August, was arrested in Rome Oct. 31 on charges of plotting a military coup in December 1970. The general issued a statement asserting he was the innocent victim of "incredible political and judicial machination." The arrest warrant, issued by a Padua magistrate, charged Miceli with actively participating in the plot, believed directed by the late neo-Fascist Prince Junio Valerio Borghese, and protecting the alleged conspirators. Earlier, Oct. 10, police had arrested eight persons, including two carabinieri and police officers, on charges of political conspiracy and armed insurrection in connection with the 1970 coup plot. Four right-wingers had been arrested on charges of plotting in September to murder leading Italian politicians in an effort to provoke a left-wing backlash which would force the army, aided by armed right-wing groups, to stage a coup, the Interior Ministry announced Oct. 10. Those on the execution list, according to informed sources, included Defense Minister Andreotti, Interior Minister Taviani and Communist Party leader Enrico Berlinguer. Andreotti confirmed press reports that right-wing terrorists had planned to poison Italy's water supply and assassinate prominent personalities, it was reported Oct. 25.

See also ALBANIA; ART; AUTO RACING; BRAZIL [9]; BUTZ, EARL L.; CHILE [7, 19]; COMMUNISM, INTERNATIONAL; EUROPEAN ECONOMIC COMMUNITY [2]; EUROPEAN SECURITY; HONDURAS; MAURITANIA; MEXICO [19]; MIDDLE EAST [26]; MONETARY DEVELOPMENTS [4, 17]; MOROCCO; NORTH ATLANTIC TREATY ORGANIZATION; OIL [23, 26, 34]; SAN MARINO; SWITZERLAND; TENNIS; UNITED NATIONS [15]; YUGOSLAVIA [9-10]

IVORY COAST—President Felix Houphouet-Boigny announced a Cabinet shuffle July 24, including creation of two new ministries—for commerce and for water and forests. Two military officers were appointed secretaries of state for the interior and for the navy. No military personnel had previously held Cabinet posts.

See also AFRICA

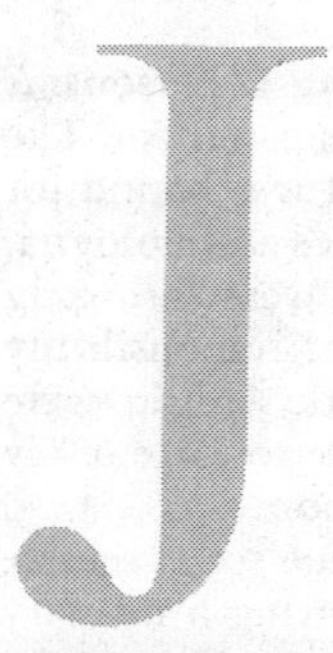

JACKSON, SEN. HENRY M.—*See* CAMPAIGN FINANCING [17, 21]; CHINA, COMMUNIST; DEFENSE [5]; DISARMAMENT; ENERGY CRISIS [1-3, 24]; OIL [30]; UNION OF SOVIET SOCIALIST REPUBLICS [9-14, 29]

JACOBSON, JAKE—*See* CAMPAIGN FINANCING [5]

JAMAICA—The legislature enacted a tough and controversial gun control law in response to a wave of murders and other violence, it was reported April 12. The law, called the Suppression of Crime Act, established a special court to deal with firearms offenses. It provided for secret trials, no bail, and indeterminate prison sentences for convicted offenders. It also empowered security forces to conduct searches without warrants and to seize property. The law was passed unanimously, but it was opposed by the Jamaican Bar Association, the Caribbean Bar Association and others concerned with civil liberties. The government defended the law by citing a dramatic drop in crimes involving firearms since its enactment, it was reported May 28. The law was drafted in response to a general wave of crime and violence that had reached "almost anarchical proportions," according to the *Jamaica Daily News*.

The Jamaican government and Kaiser Aluminum & Chemical Corp. of the U.S. reached a preliminary agreement Nov. 20 for the government to buy a 51% interest in Kaiser Bauxite Co., the Kaiser subsidiary in Jamaica, and all the land owned by Kaiser in Jamaica. Initial reports said Jamaica would pay $15 million for its interest in Kaiser, but did not quote a price for Kaiser's land, which totaled 40,000 acres. The settlement followed a dispute between the government and all foreign bauxite companies operating in Jamaica over a 700% tax increase imposed on the firms in June.

See also ALUMINUM & BAUXITE; MEXICO [21]; SUGAR

JAPAN

Politics & Government

[1] **LDP set back in upper house elections.** Japan's ruling Liberal Democratic Party (LDP) lost eight seats in elections held July 7 for half of the 252-seat House of Councilors, the upper chamber of the Diet (parliament). Although LDP's strength was reduced to 126 seats, it would still be in control of the house because it was assured of the support of at least one of several conservative

independents. The Democratic Socialist Party lost one seat, while all other parties gained. Composition of the new House of Councilors: LDP 126, Socialist Party 62, Komeito 24, Communist Party 20, Democratic Socialist Party 10 and Independents 10. The LDP received 39% of the popular vote, the Socialists 26% and the Communists 12%. Three leading members of Premier Kakuei Tanaka's Cabinet resigned July 12 and 16 following demands within the LDP for organizational reform in the wake of the party's setback in the election. Those who resigned were Deputy Premier Takeo Miki, Finance Minister Takeo Fukada and State Minister Shigeru Hori.

[2] **Tanaka resigns under fire.** A magazine article Oct. 10 accusing Tanaka of amassing a fortune during his political career stirred a controversy which, on Nov. 26, caused the premier to resign. The article, printed in the *Bungei Shunju*, was the result of an investigation of reports that Tanaka had spent $10-$16 million in his 1972 campaign to become LDP president and thus premier. According to the article, unspent campaign money had been used by Tanaka to purchase real estate and stock holdings in half a dozen chemical and transportation companies. Although Tanaka first denied any conflict between his business and political activities, his resignation statement said he was leaving office to take "moral and political responsibility" for causing the controversy. Tanaka asserted, "I've done nothing illegal."

[3] **Miki elected premier.** Takeo Miki was elected premier by the Japanese Parliament Dec. 9. He formed a new 21-member Cabinet after Tanaka's Cabinet resigned earlier in the day. Miki's assumption of the premiership had been assured when the leaders of the ruling LDP selected him as its president Dec. 2 by a consensus in preference to two other rivals, Takeo Fukuda and Masayoshi Ohira. LDP's Parliament members ratified the decision Dec. 4. Parliament's election of Miki was along party lines, with the lower House of Representatives balloting 278-205 and the Upper House of Councilors 130-110. Among the major Cabinet appointees was Michio Nagai, editorial writer for the newspaper *Asahi Shimbun* and a U.S. college graduate, who was named minister of education. He was the first non-parliamentarian in a Japanese Cabinet in 17 years. Miki had announced that he would appoint highly qualified persons, regardless of their factional orientation within the LDP.

[4] Miki disclosed a listing of his personal finances Dec. 26, explaining that he was doing so "in consideration of the fact that I have taken power in the prevailing circumstances." Miki said he owned land, houses and stocks worth $1,078,400.

Energy & the Economy

[5] **Strike wins 30% pay increase.** About 6 million transport and other workers staged a nationwide strike April 11, ending the walkout two days later after accepting pay increases averaging 30%. Those receiving the increases were employes of public and privately-owned railroads, postal and telephone services. The unions had launched their campaign Feb. 18 with an anti-inflation rally staged in Tokyo. Union leaders addressing 30,000 followers blamed the government, big business and international oil companies for Japan's soaring inflation. An estimated 527,000 government and private-industry workers had staged a 24-hour nationwide strike March 1. The job action was in defiance of a Cabinet warning Feb. 28 that the government would take stern action against the "illegal" strike.

[6] **Oil firms, executives indicted.** The Tokyo High Public Prosecutor's office May 28 indicted the Petroleum Association of Japan, 12 oil companies and 17 senior oil executives on charges of conspiracy to fix prices and to control 1973

refinery production. One foreign firm, the Japanese affiliate of Shell International Petroleum Co., was among the 12 firms indicted. The executives went on trial Dec. 20. The 12 companies, which supplied more than 90% of the Japanese market, were accused by the Fair Trade Commission (FTC), after a three-month investigation, of tripling their prices through a cartel. The FTC indictment charged that the Japanese oil industry had conspired to raise oil prices fives times during 1973. Among the increases cited were a 93% boost in the wholesale price of gasoline from $7.94 to $15.31 a barrel.

[7] (The government had authorized March 16 a 64% increase in the average wholesale price of petroleum products and established new retail ceilings for gasoline and certain types of motor oil. The government also froze indefinitely the domestic prices of 53 industrial products and 148 consumer products to prevent the oil price rise from spurring a new round of inflation.)

[8] **OECD report cites inflation.** Inflation in Japan had reached "unprecedented and clearly intolerable rates," according to an Organization for Economic Cooperation and Development (OECD) report released in Paris Aug. 11. Rising import prices, world shortages and the failure of supply to keep pace with consumer demand were cited as causes by the report. It said the temporary oil embargo imposed by the Arabs in October 1973 resulted in sharp industrial production cuts in the first quarter of 1974. Increased oil prices had brought a marked deterioration of Japan's balance of payments deficits, rising from an annual rate of $2.5 billion in the second half of 1973 to $10 billion in the first quarter of 1974, according to the OECD. The report added that consumer prices, which had increased 11.7% in 1973, jumped at a yearly rate of 24.5% in the first quarter of 1974.

[9] **Government fears depression.** Emei Yamashita, vice minister of international trade and industry, warned Oct. 16 that as long as Japan tried "to restrain inflation, we have to take it for granted that a kind of depression will come in 1975." The minister predicted a shrinkage in the country's economic activity for the remainder of the year and a small growth rate in 1975. The crisis would come in the late spring when labor launched its annual drive for wage increases, Yamashita said. Yamashita cited a growing unemployment problem in the country, noting that the rate of joblessness had begun to rise in May from its normal level of less than 1% to the current 1.5%. (Prices on the Tokyo Stock Exchange dropped to their lowest level in 2½ years Oct. 9 as the 225-share index sagged 191.78 points to 3,355.13. The index had stood at over 4,000 in August.)

Foreign Relations

[10] **Tanaka tours.** Premier Tanaka made a five-nation tour of Southeast Asia Jan. 7-17 and also visited Mexico, Brazil, the U.S. and Canada, Sept. 12-26. The Premier's Asian tour was greeted by violent anti-Japanese disturbances in Thailand, Indonesia and Malaysia. He also visited the Philippines and Singapore. Tanaka was greeted by anti-Japanese demonstrations by Thai students on his arrival in Bangkok Jan. 9. He met with a student delegation the following day and was handed a letter demanding that Tokyo provide assurances that Thais would benefit from Japanese investments in their country and that Japanese firms would stop exploiting Thai workers. Following discussions on economic policy in Singapore Jan. 11, Tanaka visited Malaysia Jan. 12-14 where he refused to meet with a delegation of students, provoking an anti-Japanese demonstration in Kuala Lumpur. Eight persons were killed in demonstrations in Jakarta Jan. 15 during which the Japanese embassy was attacked and other Japanese property in the city was damaged. Although President Suharto expressed regret over the

incidents, the Japanese government filed a protest, requesting that measures be taken to protect Japanese lives and property in Jakarta and that compensation be paid. Returning to Tokyo on Jan. 17, Tanaka made a major address to Parliament in which he asked Japanese to pay heed to criticism leveled against their country in order to "improve our mutual relationships."

[11] The premier was in Mexico Sept. 12-16, Brazil Sept. 16-20, the U.S. Sept. 20-23 and Canada Sept. 23-26. His discussions in Ottawa with Prime Minister Pierre Elliott Trudeau centered on plans to expand trade between the two countries, giving Japan "a non-United States window into North America," according to a Trudeau aide.

[12] **U.S. atomic arms dispute.** Testimony by a retired U.S. admiral that American warships were routinely entering Japanese ports with nuclear weapons aboard raised a storm of controversy in Japan Oct. 7. The alleged action constituted a possible violation of the U.S.-Japanese mutual security treaty. The testimony was given Sept. 10 by Rear Adm. Gene R. La Rocque before the Military Applications Subcommittee of the Joint Atomic Energy Committee and was made public Oct. 6. La Rocque, a former captain of the Seventh Fleet flagship, had said in his testimony: "Any ship that is capable of carrying nuclear weapons carries nuclear weapons. They do not unload when they go into foreign ports such as Japan or other countries." A U.S. government explanation handed Japanese Ambassador Takeshi Yasukawa in Washington Oct. 11 did not deny that atomic weapons had been brought into Japan, but merely said the U.S. "adheres" to its "undertakings" with Japan. This was a restatement of a 1960 U.S.-Japanese agreement that the temporary entry into Japan of U.S. nuclear weapons did not constitute a "major change" of forces and equipment, as cited in the mutual aid pact, and was therefore not subject to prior consultation. There also was said to exist a secret U.S. National Security Study Memorandum written in 1969 which reputedly stated there was a U.S.-Japanese "transit agreement" permitting the U.S. to bring nuclear weapons into Japan temporarily but not to deploy them there. Foreign Minister Toshio Kimura denied Oct. 14 the existence of a written or oral agreement allowing the U.S. to do so without Japan's permission.

[13] **Ford visits Japan.** President Ford became the first U.S. chief executive to travel to Japan when he visited that country Nov. 18-22. A joint communique issued at the conclusion of talks held Nov. 19-20 between Ford and Premier Tanaka and other U.S. and Japanese officials reaffirmed the "friendly and cooperative relations" between the two countries. The president's visit to Japan was the first leg of an eight-day Asian tour that was to take him to South Korea and Vladivostok, Siberia, where he was to meet Soviet Communist Party Chairman Leonid I. Brezhnev.

[14] **Chinese trade & airline pact.** Japan and China signed a most-favored-nation trade agreement in Peking Jan. 5, the first since the two countries had normalized relations in 1972. The accord went into effect Jan. 10. Also discussed during the Peking meeting was an aviation agreement providing for direct flights between China and Japan and discontinuance of Japan's air service to Taiwan. Taiwan's China Air Lines would be permitted to continue flights to Japan, but would be required to operate through a Japanese agent. A draft of the agreement was approved by the LDP executive board Feb. 9 and signed by both nations in Peking April 20. Nationalist China retaliated by immediately severing all civil aviation ties with Japan and barring Japanese planes from Taiwan's airspace. Under the China-Japan accord, a major realignment of world flight patterns was achieved by giving China the right to fly its aircraft to Japan and

on to Canada and the U.S. and Latin America; and by giving the Japanese transit rights through China to the Middle East and Western Europe. The Japanese Parliament approved the treaty May 8.

See also Appointments & Resignations; Atomic Energy [5]; Australia [22]; Baseball; Chile [24]; Cuba; Earthquakes; Famine & Food; Indonesia; Korea, Republic of [2-5, 8, 10]; Kuwait; Libya; Middle East [14, 26]; Monetary Developments [4, 10-11, 14, 17, 19]; Netherlands [11-13]; Nobel Prizes; Oil [11, 23, 26]; Peru [10]; Tariffs & Trade; Union of Soviet Socialist Republics [39]; United Nations [11, 15]; Uruguay; Vietnam, People's Republic of; Weather

JAWORSKI, LEON—*See* Saxbe, William B.; Watergate [7, 41-42, 50-57, 67, 71, 91]

JEWS—See Argentina [14]; Bulgaria; Defense [15]; Germany, East; Germany, West [7, 17]; Religion [1-2, 17]; Saxbe, William B.; Union of Soviet Socialist Republics [9-13, 25-31]

JOHN BIRCH SOCIETY—*See* Press; Privacy [10]

JOHNSON, DONALD E.—*See* Appointments & Resignations; Veterans

JORDAN—After repeated denials, Jordan confirmed that it had sold 41 British-built Centurion tanks and a missile system to South Africa in violation of its supply contracts with Britain, British officials reported Sept. 20.

A Jordanian airliner en route from Amman to Aqaba was hijacked Nov. 6 by two of its four security guards and flown to Benghazi, Libya, after Lebanon and Cyprus refused it permission to land. The hijackers were given Libyan asylum and the jet returned to Jordan with its crew and passengers.

See also Appointments & Resignations; Foreign Aid; Israel; Middle East [7, 18, 20, 22, 27, 33, 35, 38, 40-41]; Oil [19]

JOURNALISM—*See* Press

JUDICIARY—ABA proposes new review court. A committee of the American Bar Association (ABA) proposed that a new national division of the U.S. Circuit Courts of Appeals be created to screen cases appealed to the Supreme Court, the *New York Times* reported Jan. 20. The ABA plan was offered as an alternative to the national buffer court plan advanced by a panel of legal scholars appointed by Chief Justice Warren E. Burger. Both plans aimed at cutting the Supreme Court's caseload by screening out 90% of the litigation reaching it, but the Burger plan had aroused opposition in legal circles because it curtailed the traditional right of litigants to appeal to the Supreme Court. The new proposal modified but did not reduce this access.

Disqualification rules for judges. A bill setting forth the circumstances requiring disqualification of a federal judge from a case was passed by the House Nov. 18 and Senate Nov. 21 and signed by the President Dec. 6. Disqualification was required in any proceeding in which a question could reasonably be raised about a judge's impartiality. The bill specified a number of such circumstances. The measure was the first federal law on judicial disqualification.

See also Civil Rights [18]; Crime [13, 36]

JURIES—*See* Crime [1]

JUSTICE DEPARTMENT, U.S.—*See* Antitrust Actions; Appointments & Resignations; Aviation [3]; Books; Campaign Financing [7-10, 22]; Civil Rights [8, 10, 12, 20]; Crime [3, 11, 31]; Energy Crisis [24]; Indian Affairs; Radicals; Saxbe, William B.; Television & Radio; Watergate [30-31, 61]

K

KALMBACH, HERBERT—*See* CAMPAIGN FINANCING [12-13, 16]; WATERGATE [21, 62, 99]
KANSAS—*See* ELECTIONS [1, 7]; WEATHER
KELLY, CLARENCE M.—*See* CRIME [36]; RADICALS

KENNEDY, EDWARD M.—Sen. Edward M. Kennedy (D, Mass.) told the *Boston Globe* Oct. 28 that "ugly speculation" about the conduct of Mary Jo Kopechne and himself was one of the worst aspects of the 1969 tragedy on Chappaquiddick Island, Mass. when Miss Kopechne drowned after a car driven by Kennedy fell off a narrow bridge into a tidal pond. The speculation was "completely untrue," Kennedy said in the interview. "The defamation or attempted defamation of her character is one of the aspects I regret most deeply." In the interview, he also recalled "my own anguish and anxiety of that evening, the thoughts that went through my mind, my sense and feeling that somehow it had been almost miraculous that I had escaped from that car and I had not given up hope all night long that by some miracle Mary Jo would have escaped from the car as well." In reporting on the accident to the police across the channel, which he swam, nearly drowning: "By the time that I arrived on the other shore, I was absolutely spent. Absolutely exhasted. And just saying I just can't do it. I just can't do it. I just can't do it. I remember walking up towards the Shiretown Inn and walking through the front entrance and just going up to my room... My conduct was irrational and indefensible and inexcusable and inexplicable... but it was this mental state of mind." The *Globe* reported that Miss Kopechne's parents had received $140,923 from Kennedy's insurance company as a settlement, the amount based on an actuarial estimate of earning potential.

See also AMNESTY & CLEMENCY; CRIME [39]; KISSINGER, HENRY A.; MEDICINE & HEALTH [1, 9-12]; POLITICS [4]; VIETNAM, REPUBLIC OF [34-36]

KENT STATE—U.S. District Court Judge Frank J. Battisti acquitted eight former Ohio National Guardsmen Nov. 8 in Cleveland of charges stemming from the shooting deaths of four students at Kent State University May 4, 1970. Battisti ruled that U.S. prosecutors had failed to prove charges that the guardsmen had willfully intended to deprive the slain students and nine other wounded students of their civil rights. "At best," Battisti said, "the evidence...would support a finding that the amount of force used by the defendants was excessive and unjustified." The eight accused men were James D. McGee, William E. Perkins, James E. Pierce, Lawrence A. Shafer, Ralph W. Zoller, Mathew J. McManus, Barry W. Morris and Leon H. Smith.

The Supreme Court had ruled April 17 that the parents of the dead students could sue Ohio officials of the National Guard. The 8-0 decision reversed lower court decisions holding state officials immune from such suits. Writing for the court, Chief Justice Warren E. Burger said the well-established constitutional prohibition against suing a state provided "no shield for a state official confronted by the claim that he has deprived another of a federal right under the color of state law." Federal civil rights guarantees, he concluded "would be drained of meaning were we to hold that the acts" of state officials have "the quality of supreme and unchangeable edict, overriding all conflicting rights..." and were unreviewable by the federal courts.

KENTUCKY—*See* ELECTIONS [3]; ENERGY CRISIS [6]; WEATHER

KENYA—Asians' departure demanded. President Jomo Kenyatta Feb. 24 ordered all unauthorized non-citizen traders in Kenya to leave the country as soon as their businesses were turned over to Kenyan nationals. More than 1,000 foreign businessmen, mostly Asians, had been commanded to close their establishments in 1973 as part of the government's Kenyanization program.

Swahili made official language. President Kenyatta declared July 4 that henceforth Swahili would be the official language of Kenya and ordered that all government business, including parliamentary debate, be conducted in it. He also said that voting rights would no longer be linked to passing an English test.

Bank, college strikes prompt ban. Kenyatta announced a total ban on all strikes Aug. 16 saying that the government had noted "with grave concern" the recent strikes in educational and commercial establishments. Some 5,000 bank workers had struck July 29 demanding a 20% pay increase to meet spiraling costs. They returned to work Aug. 2 after the Kenyan Bankers Association warned that all strikers would be fired if they did not. Several banks were unable to conduct business during the strike. (Finance Minister Mwai Kibaki had announced new taxes on luxury items in Kenya June 12, in an effort to reduce the expected balance of trade deficit of $150 million, the worst in the country's history. Gasoline prices were raised for the third time since the October 1973 Middle East war.)

The University of Nairobi and Kenyatta College closed Aug. 14 because of a strike begun Aug. 8 by students protesting the loan system, staff shortages and the government's ban on the university students' union.

4 Cabinet ministers lose in election. Four Cabinet ministers and nine assistant ministers were defeated Oct. 14 in Kenya's second elections since independence in 1963. About half the incumbents lost their bids to retain membership in Parliament, with more than 700 candidates vying for the 152 elected seats. Voting was reported as heavy in the one-party election in which all candidates represented the ruling Kenya Africa National Union. President Kenyatta and Vice President Daniel Arap Moi ran unopposed from their election districts. All members of the Kenya executive branch must also be members of Parliament. (Kenyatta's victory had been assured Sept. 20 when the Election Control Commission declared him the only valid candidate. Kenyatta had imposed a ban Aug. 21 on former Vice President and opposition leader Oginga Odinga, preventing him and all other former members of the outlawed Kenya People's Union from running in the elections.)

Kenyatta adjourns Parliament. President Kenyatta Nov. 6 adjourned Parliament within an hour of swearing in the 172 members, 152 of whom were elected in October. No reason was given, but reports indicated that Kenyatta's action followed a dispute, mounted by John Seroney, a member of Parliament critical of the president, over the election of a deputy speaker.

Americans expelled in mine claim dispute. One of two U.S. geologists expelled from Kenya in a dispute with the government over ownership of a ruby mine they had discovered brought a court suit in Nairobi Oct. 4 in an attempt to maintain the pair's interest in the mine. The initiator of the suit, John Saul, had been expelled from Kenya June 18 on seven hours notice on a government order alleging that he was involved in gemstone and ivory smuggling. His colleague, Elliot Miller, had gone into hiding when a similar order was issued for his deportation, but he left the country Sept. 28. According to Sept. 27 and Oct. 4 reports, Saul and Miller had staked claims to a rich vein of rubies they discovered in Tsavo National Park earlier in the year and had enlisted some Kenyan officials as partners in a company to exploit the mine. The officials reportedly exerted pressure to acquire an ever-increasing percentage of the company. Saul was deported when he countered a demand for 80% interest with an offer to the Kenyans of 72%. President Kenyatta's wife and niece were in the group demanding Kenyan control of the mine, it was reported. Another figure in the controversy was a Greek businessman with Kenyan citizenship, George Criticos, who filed his own claim on the mine within days of Saul's expulsion. Criticos, according to the reports, was a close friend of the president and a business partner of Kenyatta's wife. Kenya announced Dec. 4 that it had revoked the license it had granted Criticos to work the ruby mine. According to a *Washington Post* report that day, the mine's registration had been shifted to one of Kenyatta's sons and it was being worked by a company in which the president's wife was a co-director.

See also AFRICA; AUTO RACING; UGANDA; UNITED NATIONS [6, 15]

KENYATTA, JOMO—*See* KENYA
KEY BISCAYNE ESTATE—*See* CAMPAIGN FINANCING [16]; WATERGATE AFFAIR [29, 70]
KIDNAPPINGS—*See* ARGENTINA [7-9]; CRIME [21]; DOMINICAN REPUBLIC; ETHIOPIA [14]; GREAT BRITAIN [26]; HEARST, PATRICIA; MEXICO [7-16]; MOROCCO; NETHERLANDS [11-13]; NICARAGUA
KING JR., DR. MARTIN LUTHER—*See* CRIME [19, 22]

KISSINGER, HENRY A.—Secretary of State Henry Kissinger, 50, and Nancy Maginnes, 39, were married March 30 in Arlington, Va. Following a private wedding, the couple flew to Mexico for a 10-day honeymoon.

Kissinger topped the list of most admired Americans for the second year in a row, according to a Gallup poll released Dec. 29. (Following him were Billy Graham, President Ford, Sen. Edward Kennedy (D, Mass.), Gov. George Wallace (D, Ala.) and Vice President Nelson Rockefeller.)

See also AVIATION [6]; CANADA [27]; CENTRAL INTELLIGENCE AGENCY; CHILE [28]; CHINA, COMMUNIST; CUBA; CYPRUS [6]; DEFENSE [2]; DISARMAMENT; EUROPEAN ECONOMIC COMMUNITY [14]; FAMINE & FOOD; FRANCE [18]; IRAN; ISRAEL; KOREA, REPUBLIC OF [10]; MIDDLE EAST [3, 5-10, 12, 37-43]; MONETARY DEVELOPMENTS [19]; NIXON, RICHARD M.; NORTH ATLANTIC TREATY ORGANIZATION; OIL [4, 23-25, 28-29, 31, 34]; PAKISTAN; PANAMA; PORTUGAL [27]; PRIVACY [1-5]; ROCKEFELLER, NELSON [9-10]; SOLZHENITSYN, ALEXANDER; TARIFFS & TRADE; UNION OF SOVIET SOCIALIST REPUBLICS [2, 8, 10]; VIETNAM, REPUBLIC OF [34-36]; WATERGATE [26, 83]

KLEINDIENST, RICHARD—*See* CAMPAIGN FINANCING [8-11]; WATERGATE [103]

KNIEVEL, EVEL—Motorcycle stuntman Evel Knievel unsuccessfully attempted to rocket 1,600 feet across Snake River Canyon in Twin Falls, Idaho, when a tail parachute deployed prematurely on take-off Sept. 8, sending the vehicle into the canyon. Knievel was rescued at the edge of the river at the bottom of the canyon by a helicopter rescue team, with minor injuries. His craft, the Sky-Cycle X-2, had been propelled from a 108-foot launching track and streaked 1,000 feet above the canyon before the drogue chute, which released immediately instead of at 2,800 feet, caused it to turn belly-up and plummet downward. A main chute then deployed, allowing a safe landing. The event was preceded by a saturation publicity campaign which promoted tickets for viewing in person and on closed-circuit movie screens. Money from these sources as well as Evel Knievel buttons, dolls and skycycles reportedly grossed between $10 and $20 million. Reports of rowdyism and looting at the scene were widespread, much of it attributed to motorcycle gangs.

KOREA, PEOPLE'S REPUBLIC OF (NORTH KOREA)—North sinks ROK fishing boat. Two North Korean gunboats Feb. 15 sank a Republic of South Korea fishing boat and captured another in the Yellow Sea in a contested area about 40 miles off North Korea, the South Korea Defense Ministry said. Twelve fishermen were reported missing and feared drowned and 13 were captured. North Korea acknowledged the sinking of the South Korean vessel Feb. 16, but charged that it was a "spy ship" sent "to intrude in the coastal waters of our side in a premeditated act of provocation." South Korea denied the allegation and called the loss of its boats an "illegal act of piracy." It demanded a North Korean apology, compensation for the sunken vessel and return of the seized ship and bodies of the dead fishermen.

Buildup reported in North. An official of the U.S. Defense Department said Feb. 22 that North Korea's military forces had carried out a "major" redeployment in the direction of the South Korean border in the past few months.

North asks U.S. peace talks. North Korea called on the U.S. March 23 to enter into talks with Pyongyang to replace the Korean armistice agreement of 1953. South Korea would be excluded from the discussions. The proposal, in a letter sent to the U.S. Congress, was made by Foreign Minister Ho Damin in a speech before the legislative Supreme People's Assembly, which approved the plan March 25. The principal points of the plan as outlined by Ho: North and South would not invade each other and would eliminate all danger of direct conflict; both sides would halt the arms race; the insignia of the United Nations forces would be removed from foreign troops (U.S.) serving in South Korea, who should be withdrawn "at the earliest possible date"; and guarantees would be given that no foreign power would turn Korea into a military or operational base after the pullout of all foreign troops from the South. The U.S. State Department responded to the North Korean proposal March 25: "We continue to feel the North Korean problem must be settled by the two Korean sides." The proposal, the department, said, "seems to be a reformulation of proposals made a year ago." South Korea denounced the plan following a Cabinet meeting March 25. A government statement said North Korea must abide by the truce agreement and accept an earlier South Korean proposal for a non-aggression pact.

ROK patrol boat sunk. A South Korean patrol boat was sunk by three North Korean gunboats in a sea battle June 28 ON the east coast, just south of the North Korean border. The fate of the 29 men aboard was not known. The vessel, on a routine fisheries protection mission, was surrounded by the gunboats and sunk by shellfire, the South Korean Defense Ministry reported. Planes from both sides appeared on the scene but made no contact. South Korea accused the North of an unprovoked attack, claiming that its ship was in international waters. The Communists charged that the vessel had violated North Korean waters and was sunk in self-defense. Some survivors were captured, the North Koreans said.

Troops clash on border. North and South Korean troops exchanged gunfire Nov. 15 after ROK soldiers discovered a tunnel dug by the Communist forces about 1,000 yards south of the Demilitarized Zone. The North Koreans opened fire with machine guns as a squad of Seoul troops checked the tunnel, two-thirds of a mile long and 18 inches below the surface. The South soldiers fired back and the exchange continued for more than an hour. South Korean Defense Minister Suh Jong Chul charged that the tunnel and others like it "were not designed to smuggle a few dozen agents or subversives to the South but to stealthily send down a large force and stage a big-scale attack." A U.S. and ROK officer were killed and five U.S. military men were seriously injured Nov. 20 when an explosion, apparently set off by a mine, ripped through the tunnel as they were inspecting it.

See also AUSTRALIA [20]; COSTA RICA; FAMINE & FOOD; KOREA, REPUBLIC OF

KOREA, REPUBLIC OF (SOUTH KOREA)

Park Assassination Attempt

[1] **Park escaped assassin; wife slain.** The wife of President Chung Hee Park was fatally wounded Aug. 15 by an assassin's bullet intended for her husband. Park was delivering a Liberation Day address to an audience of 1,500 in a Seoul theater when the assailant ran down the center aisle firing a pistol. Mrs. Park, who was sitting on the stage behind her husband, was struck in the head by one of the bullets. The president escaped injury as his bullet-proof podium deflected the second shot. A 17-year-old girl participating in the program was killed by a stray bullet. The assassin was seized after being wounded by security guards who returned fire. After the turmoil subsided, Park completed his speech and then went to the hospital where his wife had been taken. She died six hours later.

[2] The assailant was identified as Mun Se Kwang, 22, a Korean living in Osaka, Japan. He reportedly had entered South Korea Aug. 6 on a Japanese passport falsely obtained in the name of a friend. According to Japanese news reports, Mun was a member of the Osaka branch of the Korean Youth League, an anti-Park organization of Korean residents in Japan. However, league officials said Aug. 15 that Mun had left the group in 1968.

[3] **South Korea accuses Japan, North Korea.** South Korean government officials accused Japan of complicity in the slaying and of failure to properly investigate the incident. In an Aug. 30 interview with Japanese Ambassador Torao Ushiroku, Park demanded that Tokyo control what he called "criminal groups" in Japan aimed at his overthrow. South Korean investigators had, on Aug. 16, also charged that Park's assassination had been plotted by North Korean President Kim Il Sung. The day before, Japanese police in Osaka, arrested a Japanese woman, Mikiko Yoshii, who was suspected by police of having helped Mun obtain the forged passport in her husband's name. Japanese police also reported they had found a document at Mun's home indicating that he had planned the slaying for a year. Kim Il Du, South Korea's chief investigator, told newsmen Aug. 17 that Kim Il Sung had ordered the killing of Park and that North Korean agents had then recruited Mun in

September 1972, assigning him to the mission in November 1973. According to Kim Il Du, Mun received his final orders from an agent aboard a North Korean ship calling at Osaka in May and made his way into South Korea Aug. 6. North Korea denied it was linked to the plot.

[4] **Mrs. Park's slayer sentenced.** A court in Seoul Oct. 19 sentenced Mun to death for the attempted assassination of President Park and the slaying of Park's wife. Mun had admitted at the opening of his trial Oct. 7 that he had attempted to kill Park on orders from two North Korean agents operating in Japan. One of the agents was a leader of a group of Korean residents in Japan, which supported North Korea. Mun had met the other agent aboard a North Korean cargo ship in Osaka, who had told him that Kim Il Sung had personally ordered the assassination.

[5] **Japanese dispute settled.** South Korea and Japan formally settled their dispute on Sept. 19. Representatives of both countries, negotiating since Sept. 12, worked out an agreement under which Japan extended expressions of regret over the incident, pledged a full government investigation, and promised to prevent a recurrence of any activity aimed at overthrowing the South Korean government. Prior to the agreement, the Japanese embassy and Japanese-owned businesses in Seoul had been the target of South Korean demonstrations Sept. 6-12.

[6] **Cabinet shuffled.** President Park Sept. 18 replaced nine of his 20 ministers in a major Cabinet shakeup aimed at solidifying national unity in the wake of the assassination attempt. The new ministers were: Hwang San Duk, justice; Yu Ki Chun, education; Shin Do Sang, national unification; Lee Won Kyong, culture and information; Nam Duk Woo, economic planning; Kim Yong Whan, finance; Choe Kyong Nok, transport; Kim Jae Kyu, construction; and Chang Sung Tae, communications.

Government Actions & Dissent

[7] President Park proclaimed two presidential emergency measures Jan. 8 aimed at curbing mounting opposition to his Constitution, adopted under martial law in 1972. The first measure prohibited opposition to the Constitution and efforts to repeal it. It also banned any actions barred by the emergency measures as well as criticism of the decrees. The second decree established emergency courts-martial to deal with those who violated the first measure, with imprisonment up to 15 years as the sentence for proven violators. In proclaiming the measures, Park cited "reckless and thoughtless action" aimed at overthrowing the present political structure.

[8] A series of arrests of dissidents followed. On April 25 the South Korean Central Intelligence Agency (KCIA) announced 240 persons were being questioned in connection with an alleged plot by the National Democratic Youth and the Student League to overthrow Park's government. (The League had been outlawed April 3 following student protest rallies in Seoul. The demonstrations had prompted Park to issue an emergency decree outlawing activist student organizations and threatening a possible death penalty for violators of the new law.) The KCIA report said the League planned to set up a pro-Communist "labor-farmer regime" following Park's fall. Trial of the dissidents, which had started June 15, was concluded July 11, 13 and 15 when a military court in Seoul handed sentences against 55 persons, including two Japanese who were accused of participating in the League plot. Of the 21 persons sentenced July 11, seven received the death penalty, including To Ye Jong, head of the defunct People's Revolutionary Party. Eight received life terms and six were given 20 years. Seven more defendants were sentenced to

death July 13, including the nation's best known poet, Kim Chi Ha. Seven received life terms, 12 were sentenced to 20 years and six others to 15. The two Japanese, Yoshiharu Kayakawa and Masaki Tachikawa, were sentenced to 20 years. (Japan and South Korea recalled their ambassadors from each other's countries on July 14.) The death sentences of Kim Chi Ha and four other dissidents were commuted to life terms July 20 because, according to Defense Minister Suh Jong Chul, the defendants had shown repentance during their trials. Kang Shin Ok, the lawyer who had defended Kim and others at their trials, calling the proceedings a farce, was reported by associates to have been arrested July 26. He was sentenced to 10 years on Sept. 4.

[9] More than 2,000 South Korean Roman Catholics attended a mass in Seoul July 25 to protest the jailing of the Most Rev. Daniel Chi Hak Soun, bishop of the Wonju see east of the capital. Chi had been seized July 23 after reading a statement denouncing "violence, intimidation and fraud" under Park's rule. Chi was sentenced to 15 years on Aug. 12.

[10] Secretary of State Henry A. Kissinger said July 24 that the U.S. would continue to provide South Korea with economic and military assistance even though it disapproved of its repressive policies. Testifying before a Senate Appropriations subcommittee on the Administration's foreign aid requests, Kissinger said such aid was necessary because South Korea's strategic position was "very critical to Japan" and to Asian security in general.

[11] In what was believed a move to ease oppositon to the government, Park removed two of the emergency decrees Aug. 23. The measures were the Jan. 8 edict prohibiting all discussion, criticism and demands for revision of the 1972 Constitution which gave the president unlimited power and the April 3 directive barring dissent against the government and its policies, with penalties ranging from five years to death. Two other measures were retained: the Jan. 8 decree that established secret courts-martial and authorized arrests without warrant; and a Jan. 14 decree that cut taxes for low-income persons, raised taxes on luxury goods and increased import tariffs. Park said judicial proceedings would continue against persons already arrested under the Jan. 8 and April 3 decrees.

[12] New Democratic Party (NDP) leader Kim Yong Sam warned Park Oct. 7 that unless he revised the Constitution to eliminate government repression, "there will be demands outside the normal political arena" and that the NDP would join in the "struggle." Speaking to the National Assembly, Kim, who had been elected NDP president Aug. 23, implied that Park should resign.

[13] Protests against Park were intensified Oct. 9-20 in anticipation of the upcoming visit by President Ford. The Oct. 9 demonstration in Seoul in which about 5,000 Roman Catholics participated was the largest anti-government outburst since Park had imposed martial law in 1972. The march followed Park's warning Oct. 8 that he would not tolerate street demonstrations or demands that his powers be curtailed. The demonstrators were among 15,000 persons who had gathered at an outdoor protest mass on the grounds of a seminary. The marchers, attempting to move into the streets of the city, were stopped by police. Seoul police used tear gas Oct. 10 to break up a demonstration of about 1,500 rock-throwing students, who were demanding the immediate release of all political prisoners and a new Constitution. About 1,000 university students took to the streets of Seoul Oct. 14 to resume their protests. They were joined that day by about 400 students in Kwangju, 150 miles south of the capital, and about 50 students in Pusan, on the southeastern coast.

[14] South Korean newspapers Oct. 24-25 joined the growing protests against

the government and demanded an end to government censorship and harassment of reporters. Reporters and editors of *Dong-A Ilbo,* the country's largest and most influential newspaper, struck Oct. 24 when the publishers rejected their demand to print a front-page statement calling for press freedom, withdrawal of police agents from newspaper offices and an end to arbitrary arrests of newsmen. The strike was called off 11 hours later after the publisher acceded to the staff's demands. Another newspaper, *Hankook Ilbo,* also voted to suspend publication until the government had rescinded its ban on printing certain stories.

Other Developments

[15] **Ford visits South Korea.** President Ford visited South Korea Nov. 22-23 on the second stop of his eight-day Asia tour. A communique issued Nov. 22 based on talks Ford held with President Park reaffirmed that the U.S. had "no intention to withdraw United States forces" from South Korea and supported Seoul's moves to conduct negotiations with North Korea aimed at unifying Korea, the communique said. Ford and Park discussed the modernization program of South Korea's armed forces and agreed that its implementation was vital to the country and to the peace of the Korean peninsula. Ford reaffirmed the U.S.' willingness to help South Korea share the financial burden of further development of its defense industry. Demonstrations had been staged in Seoul before Ford's arrival to protest his visit and to emphasize opposition to Park's repressive government.

[16] **107 die in Seoul hotel fires.** Hotel fires Oct. 17 and Nov. 3 caused the deaths of 107 persons in Seoul. Nineteen persons were killed Oct. 17 when a fire struck a downtown tourist hotel before dawn. A fire Nov. 3 gutted the sixth floor of a downtown hotel, killing 88 persons, most of them inside a discotheque where 72 bodies bodies were reported found.

[17] **Korea command upheld.** The U.N. General Assembly's Political Committee Dec. 9 adopted a resolution providing for maintenance of the U.N. military command in South Korea. It subsequently rejected a proposal for removal of all foreign troops stationed in South Korea "under the United Nations flag." The successful resolution urged North and South Korea to resume their interrupted peace talks, and asked the Security Council to consider dissolution of the U.N. command in South Korea "in due course." The command, which once consisted of forces from 16 countries, now consisted mainly of U.S. and South Korean troops.

See also APPOINTMENTS & RESIGNATIONS; FOREIGN AID; RELIGION [5]; UNITED NATIONS [4]; WEATHER

KOSYGIN, ALEXEI N.—*See* GERMANY, EAST; RHODESIA; RUMANIA
KROGH, EGIL—*See* WATERGATE [62, 78-80, 83]
KURDISTAN—*See* IRAN; IRAQ

KUWAIT—Kuwait signs Gulf, BP pact. Kuwait signed an agreement Jan. 29 permitting it to purchase immediately a 60% share of the Kuwait Oil Co., jointly owned by Gulf Oil Corp. and British Petroleum Co. Ltd. The agreement would later provide Kuwait with virtually total control of the firm. According to details of the accord disclosed by the Kuwaiti government Jan. 31, Kuwait would pay $112 million for 60% of the company's operations. There was no provision for Gulf and BP to buy back the majority control. The 60% acquisition would cover all operations, including exploration, production and refining. A new firm would be formed that would be headed by a Kuwaiti. It would operate under a joint-management committee of Kuwaitis and Gulf and BP personnel.

The Kuwaiti Parliament and Cabinet ratified the agreement May 14. An increase in the 60% share was to be negotiated after Dec. 31, 1979. The agreement was retroactive to Jan. 1.

Gulf, BP pay higher prices. Gulf and BP disclosed July 18 that they had agreed to pay $10.95 a barrel for Kuwait government participation oil during the third quarter of 1974, under threat of having their access to that oil cut off permanently. Payment of the higher price—which amounted to 95% of Kuwait's posted price of $11.55 a barrel—was criticized by the U.S. and British governments, which feared it would cause new increases in world oil prices, it was reported July 20. The price was raised again by $1.14 per barrel for one million barrels of oil a day during October-December as a result of a tax and royalty hike announced by Kuwait Oct. 1. A Gulf spokesman said the royalty rate for the fourth quarter would rise from 14.5% to 16.7%, and that the tax rate would be boosted from 55% to 65.75%, bringing Kuwait an additional 3.5% total revenue in accordance with the Sept. 13 resolution of the Organization of Petroleum Exporting Countries (OPEC).

Kuwait cuts oil output. Kuwait had reduced its oil production in August and planned further cuts, Oil Minister Abdel Rahman Atiki said in an interview published Aug. 21 by the Beirut weekly magazine *As Sayad*. Atiki did not disclose the extent of the production drop, but current output was about 2.55 million barrels a day, 15% less than in the pre-embargo days of September 1973. The minister asserted that "if prices are determined by supply and demand, then we shall reduce the supply of our crude oil to increase the demand on it." Kuwait, Atiki said, was not convinced by the arguments of consumer nations that lower oil prices would end chaos in the world economy.

Kuwait controls Arabian Oil Co. Kuwait and the Japanese-owned Arabian Oil Co. signed a "participation" agreement Aug. 25 giving Kuwait 60% of the company's shares and assets. Under the terms of another accord, Kuwait was to sell Arabian Oil all of the government's share of crude until the end of the third quarter of 1974 at $10.95 a barrel.

Kuwait buys into British firm. In what was believed to be the first purchase by an oil country of a major stake in a Western industrial enterprise, Kuwait bought a more than 10% interest in St. Martin's Property Corp., a British firm with large commercial real estate holdings in London. Kuwait acquired 2.1 million shares in the corporation Sept. 11 and an additional 100,000 shares Sept. 12. Kuwait had entered a $248 million bid for St. Martin's Sept. 6. St. Martin's had rejected as inadequate a $175 million offer made earlier by the Commercial Union Assurance Co. of Britain.

See also ETHIOPIA [15]; GERMANY, WEST [16]; MONETARY DEVELOPMENTS [5]; OIL [4-6, 14-15, 18-19, 29, 35]

LABOR

Government Actions

[1] **Minimum wage raised.** President Nixon signed new minimum wage legislation April 8. He had vetoed a similar bill in 1973. The minimum wage would be increased in stages to $2.30 an hour and coverage would be extended to 7-8 million workers not previously covered. The basic minimum wage, applying to 36 million nonfarm workers, would rise from $1.60 to $2 an hour May 1, to $2.10 Jan. 1, 1975 and to $2.30 Jan. 1, 1976. For another 19 million nonfarm workers covered under amendments to the basic legislation in 1966, the minimum wage would be $1.90 on May 1, $2 in 1975, $2.10 in 1976 and $2.30 in 1977. For the more than 500,000 farm workers whose current minimum was $1.30, the new minimum would be $1.60 May 1, $1.80 Jan. 1, 1975, $2 in 1976, $2.20 in 1977 and $2.30 in 1978.

[2] Minimum wage coverage would be extended to an additional seven million workers in federal, state and local government (about 5 million employees), domestic service and retail and service employees of chain store operations. Overtime coverage would be extended in 1975 to local policemen and firemen who worked more than 240 hours in 28 consecutive days.

[3] **'74 wage gains topped 1973.** Major collective bargaining agreements negotiated during the first nine months of 1974 for 4.1 million workers exceeded wage gains won in 1973, according to the Labor Department Oct. 25. During the nine-month negotiating period, wage increases won in the settlements averaged 9.6% for the first year of the contract, compared with 5.8% in 1973, and 7.2% over the life of the contract, compared with 5.1% in 1973. Cost of living provisions were adopted in 110 settlements, affecting more than 600,000 workers, during the first nine months of 1974. It was estimated that escalator clauses currently covered 5 million workers in major bargaining units (49% of the total).

[4] **Regulation of farm labor contractors.** A bill to tighten regulation of farm labor contractors (crew leaders) in dealing with farmers and migrant farm workers was approved by the Senate Nov. 22 and House Nov. 26 and signed by President Ford Dec. 9. The President had vetoed the legislation previously when it contained an unrelated provision for promotion of certain federal employees. The new version did not contain the provision.

[5] **Jobs program, jobless aid enacted.** Congress cleared in the final days of the session a package of bills to authorize an emergency public service jobs program and to extend unemployment compensation coverage. The bills were signed Dec. 31 by President Ford.

[6] A bill adopted Dec. 18 by a 346-58 House vote and Senate voice vote authorized $2.5 billion in fiscal 1975 for state and local governments to hire jobless workers for community service work in education, health, sanitation, day care, recreation and similar programs. The same bill extended jobless compensation to about 12 million workers not currently covered, primarily farm workers, domestics and state and local government workers. The extension was on a one-year basis and would provide eligibility for up to 26 weeks of compensation in areas of high unemployment.

[7] Companion legislation was prepared to provide an additional 13 weeks of emergency unemployment compensation benefits for unemployed workers who had exhausted their regular benefits. The Senate approved the final form of the bill by an 84-0 vote Dec. 16. The House cleared the bill for the President Dec. 19.

[8] A bill to appropriate $4 billion in fiscal 1975 to fund the emergency program was passed by both houses Dec. 19. More than $2 billion of it was allocated for the jobless compensation provisions. States and communities would receive $875 million for the public service jobs aspect. Another $125 million was channeled for stimulation of pulic works projects in depressed areas.

Strikes & Settlements

[9] **Automobile industry.** Agreement on a new two-year contract was reached Oct. 1 by negotiators for American Motors Corp. (AMC) and the United Auto Workers (UAW). The strike-ending agreement was ratified by the union membership Oct. 6 and the strikers, who had walked out Sept. 16 when the old contract expired, returned to work Oct. 7. Negotiations for the new pact had begun July 25. The new pact, covering about 15,000 workers, would raise the AMC wage and benefit package to that set in the Big Three negotiations in 1973. Wages for an assembler would rise from about $5 an hour to $5.91, all but 19¢ of it cost-of-living boosts built into the base pay rate. Supplemental unemployment benefits, a 30-years-and-out retirement plan, pension and insurance plans were also made equivalent to Big Three standards. The economic package generally was agreed on before the strike, which was largely a confrontation over the company's effort to drop from the new pact certain provisions unique to AMC, such as the profit-sharing plan adopted in 1961.

[10] **Coal industry.** United Mine Workers President Arnold R. Miller signed a new national coal contract Dec. 5 and officially ended the miners' 24-day strike begun Nov. 12. The return to work was set to begin at 12:01 a.m. Dec. 6. Miller announced that 56% of the 79,495 miners voting on the new pact had approved it. It was the first contract in the union's history to be subject to rank-and-file ratification. About two-thirds of the union's 120,000 members had voted. The contract with the Bituminous Coal Operators Association would provide for a 54% increase over the three years in the $8.11 average hourly compensation. The increase included wages and fringe benefits and assumed an 8% annual rate of inflation, or the maximum increments written into the contract in the cost-of-living escalator clause.

[11] Aside from the miners, more than 23,000 workers in affected industries, notably railroad and steel, were idled by the strike, a much lower figure than estimated by government officials prior to the strike. The majority of these layoffs, about 18,000, were at U.S. Steel Corp., which cut back its cokemaking operation by about 50% because of the strike. Soft coal production the week

before the end of the strike dropped to 4,310,000 tons nationwide; a year earlier it had been 11,525,000 tons.

[12] Union leadership and management of the industry had reached agreement on a new contract Nov. 13, but encountered unexpected resistance from the union's 38-member bargaining council, the first step in the ratification process prior to submission to the rank and file membership. The council Nov. 20 refused to approve the proposed contract, asking for "some minor adjustments." Treasury Secretary William E. Simon intervened in the process Nov. 24 because of the "very serious economic implications" of the strike. Agreement on a revised contract was reached later Nov. 24. The major revision was in wages and a vacation provision. The original terms for wage increases of 9% the first year, 3% the second and 3% the third year of the contract were changed to 10%, 4% and 3%. Quarterly cost-of-living increments to be initiated in the second year were to begin February 1975. Instead of splitting two basic weeks of vacation as proposed in the original agreement—one in the summer and one at Christmas, when absenteeism traditionally was high—the contract would permit the miners to take the two weeks in the summer, as in the past. The revised contract was put before the UMW bargaining council Nov. 26. It rejected it by a vote of about 2-1, reportedly on the wage issue. Miller said he believed the members of the union "should have the right to express their will." He reconvened the council, which reversed itself and approved the contract. Before-the-strike wages for miners were $42-$50 a day.

[13] A return to work by all 120,000 members of the UMW was delayed by a separate strike by the union's mine construction workers. A new contract for the 4,500 construction workers had not been resolved when the union signed its new national pact Dec. 5. The return to work set for Dec. 6 was blocked in some areas by construction workers' picketing. The idling figure caused by the pickets was estimated at 35,000-50,000, concentrated in Alabama, West Virginia, Virginia, Pennsylvania and Illinois. A tentative agreement for the construction workers was reached Dec. 18, ratification by the union members was announced Dec. 22, and the return to work came Dec. 23.

[14] **Dock workers.** Dock workers in Baltimore voted final ratification Sept. 5 of a new three-year labor contract covering some 35,000 longshoremen from Portland, Me. to Hampton Roads, Va. The master contract, between the AFL-CIO International Longshoremen's Association and the Council of North Atlantic Shipping Associations, had been worked out in negotiations June 21. It called for an increase of $2.72 an hour, $1.90 to be applied to wages and 82¢ to pension and welfare funds. The base hourly wage rate would rise from the current $6.10 to $8 in the third year of the new pact. Rank-and-file union approval was announced Aug. 21 for the ports of New York-New Jersey, Boston, Providence, Philadelphia and Hampton Roads. But the pact was rejected by the Baltimore dock workers, who were seeking a guarantee of more hours pay for workers called to a job and more hours of guaranteed pay annually. Under the new pact, the guaranteed annual pay, negotiated in 1964, ranged from a total of 2,080 hours in New York-New Jersey docks to 1,250 hours in South Atlantic ports. The Baltimore dock workers, whose guaranteed pay would remain 1,900 hours, approved the new pact Sept. 5. The settlement was the first by the ILA without a strike in some 30 years. The union had conducted eight major strikes since 1942. Negotiators for the AFL-CIO International Longshoremen's Association and Great Lakes stevedoring companies reached agreement Dec. 20 on their first master contract for some 12,000 longshoremen and 65 employers. It called for wage and fringe benefits to be boosted a total of $2.72 to the $10.57 level ($7.80 in wages) by 1977.

[15] **Farah Manufacturing Co.** The 21-month strike against Farah Manufacturing Co. and the 19-month nationwide boycott of Farah trousers were ended Feb. 24 when Farah recognized the AFL-CIO Amalgamated Clothing Workers of America (ACWA) as bargaining agent for its nearly 8,000 employes. (Farah had been denounced by a National Labor Relations Board [NLRB] judge Jan. 28 for flouting the NLRB act and "trampling on the rights of its employes.") A three-year contract was approved by the union membership March 7. The pact called for general wage increases of up to 80¢ an hour and pay rates ranging up to $4.75 an hour (pre-contract wages ranged from $1.70 to $2.40 an hour). The pact also included standard overtime, seniority and arbitration provisions and fringe benefits of eight holidays, up to three weeks vacation, company-paid insurance, medical coverage and maternity benefits.

[16] **Harper & Row.** Some 300 employees of Harper & Row Publishers Inc. struck in New York June 17. The 17-day strike was the first against a major publishing house. It ended July 3 with an accord, reached with the help of a state mediator, on a three-year contract for the independent union involved calling for a total $61 weekly gain in wages over the period, $30 of which was in cost-of-living raises. The pre-strike average weekly pay was $190.

[17] **Steel Industry.** Agreement on a new three-year contract was reached April 12 by negotiators for the AFL-CIO United Steelworkers of America (USW) and the major steel companies. Negotiations were conducted under terms of an Experimental Negotiating Agreement (ENA) signed in 1973, a no-strike agreement calling for binding arbitration of unresolved contract issues. Representatives of both sides—R. Heath Larry, top industry negotiator and vice chairman of U.S. Steel Corp., and USW President I. W. Abel—endorsed the operation of ENA, which was incorporated into the contract for utilization in the 1977 negotiations. This would carry the no-strike status between the union and steel firms into 1980. A $150 lump-sum payment guaranteed by ENA to each of the 386,000 workers covered by the negotiations was part of the accord worked out April 12. Minimum wage increases of 3% in each contract year also were guaranteed under ENA.

[18] The wage agreement reached April 12 called for increases of more than 10% over the three-year period of the pact, a total of 60.9¢. These included a 28¢-an-hour boost May 1, a 16¢-an-hour increase Aug. 1, 1975 and another a year later. The base pay would also receive a 39¢-an-hour injection May 1 from the cost-of-living (COL) adjustments under the existing contract. The new pact would have an improved COL formula, effective May 1, to provide a 1¢-an-hour hike for every .35 point rise in the consumer price index (previous boost point was .4).

[19] The new contract did not include the cost-of-living escalator for pension benefits previously negotiated by USW with the container and aluminum industries. But it did include a flat 5% "inflation adjustment" for those retiring after July 31. Beginning in the third contract year, the adjustment would be applied in the regular monthly pension checks until the contract expired.

[20] In addition to U.S. Steel, the pact covered Bethlehem Steel, Republic Steel, National Steel, Jones & Laughlin Steel, Armco Steel, Youngstown Sheet and Tube, Inland Steel, Wheeling-Pittsburgh Steel and Allegheny Ludlum Industries Inc.

See also Appointments & Resignations; Automobile Industry [5-9]; Canada [37]; Civil Rights [8-17]; Crime [23]; Economy, U.S. [10, 13, 15, 17]; Education; Energy Crisis [6-7]; Football; Housing; Panama; Pensions

LABOR DEPARTMENT, U.S.—*See* Civil Rights [14-17]; Environment & Pollution [18]; Pensions; Welfare & Poverty

LANDSLIDES—*See* COLOMBIA; WEATHER
LAND USE—*See* ENVIRONMENT & POLLUTION [4]

LAOS—The 1973 truce agreement, intended to end the 20-year war in Laos, was implemented in 1974 with the signing of neutrality accords and the formation of a coalition government. On Jan. 17 government and Pathet Lao representatives signed a pact aimed at neutralizing the Laotian royal and administrative capitals of Luang Prabang and Vientiane. Under terms of the agreement, both sides would be authorized to have 1,200 men in the administrative capital and 600 in the royal capital. There would be a joint command staff which would make decisions on a unanimous basis. Other Laotian and Pathet Lao troops would be banned from areas within nine miles of the centers of Luang Prabang and Vientiane. Each side would be responsible for its own section in each city. The agreement was extended Feb. 6 with creation of a joint police force to patrol the streets of both cities: 1,000 for Vientiane and 500 for Luang Prabang.

A coalition government of neutralists, rightists and pro-Communist Pathet Lao was established April 5 after dissolution of the neutralists-rightist government of Premier Souvanna Phouma. A decree bringing about the change was signed in Luang Prabang by King Savang Vatthana. The Cabinet was installed in Vientiane April 6. The king appointed Souvanna to head the new government as premier and formally installed Souvanna's half-brother, Prince Souphanouvong, the Pathet Lao leader, as president of the National Political Council, an advisory body. The council was comprised of 42 members—16 Pathet Lao, 16 Vientiane representatives and 10 members acceptable to both factions. The Cabinet consisted of 12 ministers—five each from the Vientiane and Pathet Lao sides and two ministers agreeable to both wings. Under terms of the political protocol signed in Vientiane Sept. 14, 1973, the council was empowered to advise and "activate" the Cabinet on foreign and domestic problems. The Cabinet's function was to carry out the "recommendations" of the council.

Fighting erupted in southern Laos April 7, two days after formation of the coalition government. About 200 North Vietnamese and Pathet Lao troops attacked along a section of Route 13 about 175 miles southeast of Vientiane and several miles inland from the Mekong River border with Thailand. In another action, the Pathet Lao forced a government unit to abandon a position north of a large army base at Seno, in the southern panhandle. The Communist troops also forced government troops to retreat from positions April 10 near the Se Bang Fai River, midway between the provincial capitols of Thakhek and Savannakhet. Laotian troops were said to have been ready to counterattack, but Premier Souvanna Phouma reportedly rejected the idea.

Laos' tripartite ruling National Political Council was formally inaugurated in Luang Prabang April 25. In its first political crisis, the government decided May 3 to postpone the scheduled May 11 opening of the legislative National Assembly because of "present political circumstances." No specific reason was given for the cancellation, but it was known that the Pathet Lao had requested the delay, a move assailed at a meeting of 40 deputies later in the day.

Thailand's last military contingent withdrew from Laos May 22, ending Bangkok's more than 10 years of direct military involvement in the Laotian fighting. The pullout occurred 13 days ahead of the June 4 schedule for withdrawal of all foreign forces under terms of the Laotian peace accord. The 10-year U.S. military role in Laos came to an end June 3 with the departure of the last of its military and paramilitary forces from the country. About 460 American embassy and foreign aid officials and some military attaches were to remain.

Premier Souvanna, who had suffered a heart attack July 12, appointed Deputy Premier Phoumi Vongvichit of the Pathet Lao faction to serve as acting premier while he recuperated in France, it was reported Aug. 6. (He returned Nov. 1 and announced the following day that he had not yet fully recovered and would require further convalescence.) The government had decided July 10 to dissolve the National Assembly at a Cabinet meeting after Premier Souvanna threatened to resign when right-wing ministers attempted to attach conditions to the dissolution. The premier's threat ended the feud and the Cabinet unanimously recommended sending its decision to King Savang Vatthana. Souvanna had decided to dissolve the Assembly after two members had attempted to stage a protest July 9 against the continued presence of North Vietnamese forces in Laos.

The first exchange in Laos of war prisoners since the Laotian cease-fire began Feb. 22, 1973 was carried out Sept. 19 as the Vientiane and Pathet Lao factions traded 350 North Vietnamese, Thai and Laotian captives in a ceremony in the village of Phong Savan. The POW's included 150 Thai irregulars recruited by the U.S. Central Intelligence Agency (CIA) to fight for the Laotian government, 173 North Vietnamese, who were on the side of the Pathet Lao, 20 Royal Lao troops and seven Pathet Lao. The last known U.S. captive in Indochina, Emmet James Kay, had been released by his Pathet Lao captors Sept. 18 and flown to the Philippines. The Pathet Lao Sept. 29 released another 54 Thai and 44 Royal Laotian army prisoners.

See also FOREIGN AID; THAILAND; VIETNAM, PEOPLE'S REPUBLIC OF; VIETNAM, REPUBLIC OF [5]

LARUE, FREDERICK C.—*See* WATERGATE [21]

LATIN AMERICA—OAS retains Cuba sanctions. The Organization of American States (OAS) upheld its diplomatic and commercial embargo of Cuba at a meeting of hemispheric foreign ministers in Quito, Ecuador Nov. 12. The OAS had voted unanimously Sept. 20 to consider the question after it had been proposed Sept. 6 by representatives of Costa Rica, Colombia and Venezuela. (The OAS sanctions had been imposed in 1964 because of Cuba's alleged interference in the internal affairs of Venezuela. Venezuela's representative, Jose Maria Machin, said Sept. 19 that his country now had "no grievance to air" with Cuba. Paraguay and Uruguay charged before the Permanent Council that Cuba was still interfering in their internal affairs, it was reported Sept. 21.) At the November meeting, a resolution to lift the embargo failed to gain the required two thirds majority of the 21 nations which signed the Inter-American Treaty of Reciprocal Assistance, or Rio Treaty, under which the sanctions were imposed. Twelve countries voted for the resolution, three voted against, and six—including the U.S.—abstained. The favorable votes were cast by Argentina, Colombia, Costa Rica, Ecuador, El Salvador, Honduras, Mexico, Panama, Peru, the Dominican Republic, Trinidad & Tobago and Venezuela. Chile, Paraguay and Uruguay voted against the resolution, and Brazil, Bolivia, Haiti, Guatemala and Nicaragua joined the U.S. in abstaining. The U.S. refused to take part in the debate on the embargo, and was criticized for it by supporters of the resolution, particularly Venezuelan Foreign Minister Efrain Schacht Aristeguieta and Colombian Foreign Minister Indalecio Lievano. The chief U.S. delegate, Undersecretary of State Robert S. Ingersoll, explained Nov. 12 that the U.S. had remained silent "because we wished to avoid even the appearance of influencing by our remarks or our actions the outcome of this meeting. We have not voted no and we have not worked against the resolution." The 12 supporters of the resolution issued a statement Nov. 12 assailing the embargo as "anachronistic, ineffective and inconvenient."

The question of trade with Cuba had arisen earlier in the year when, on Feb. 25, more than 200 Argentine businessmen and government officials traveled to Havana to consolidate agreements which included Cuba's purchase of 44,000 vehicles—worth $130 million-$150 million—from Argentine subsidiaries of General Motors, Ford and the Chrysler Corp. These contracts required the approval of the U.S. government which had a regulation forbidding U.S. companies to sell goods to Cuba. In preparation for a general assembly of OAS nations in Atlanta, Ga. April 19, the U.S. had agreed the day before to issue export licenses for delivery of the vehicles. The U.S., however, insisted that its approval of the licenses did not presage a change in its Cuba policy. Officials said the decision responded to threats by Argentina to nationalize the U.S. subsidiaries if they were not allowed to sell to Cuba. The assembly closed May 1 wth the delegates ordering an investigation of charges that multinational corporations based outside Latin America were interfering in the political and domestic affairs of hemispheric nations.

The Commission on United States-Latin American Relations, an independently financed organization of U.S.businessmen, scholars and former government officials, sent a report to President Ford Oct. 29 urging him to end the U.S. trade embargo of Cuba and make other major changes in U.S. policy toward Latin America. The report warned that if the U.S. did not end its policy of isolating Cuba, it might become the isolated nation "as one Latin American country after another renews relations" with Havana. "Economically, the U.S. embargo is ineffective," the report added. "It may serve as much to deny American manufacturers a chance to compete for exports as it does to deprive the Cuban regime of supplies."

Economic security statement issued. A meeting of Latin American foreign ministers in Mexico City Feb. 21-23 resulted in the issuance the following day of the Declaration of Tlatelolco (after the site of the Mexican Foreign Ministry which hosted the talks). The declaration called for "a system of collective economic security" and a "frank and realistic relationship with the United States," adding the U.S. "accepts a special responsibility" for the economic development of Latin America. The U.S. pledged to maintain present aid levels; press for trade preferences for underdeveloped countries; avoid measures which would "restrict access" of Latin exports to U.S. markets; and facilitate transfer of U.S. technology to Latin nations.

IDB approves special fund. The governors of the Inter-American Development Bank (IDB) held their 15th annual assembly in Santiago, Chile April 1-3, with nearly 1,000 delegates from 44 countries attending, including U.S. Treasury Secretary George Shultz and 10 members of the U.S. House of Representatives. At their last session, the governors approved a Venezuelan proposal to create a special trust fund, administered by the bank without U.S. veto power, to finance regional natural resource development projects normally ignored by international lending agencies. The trust fund, suggested by Venezuelan President Carlos Andres Perez in March, reportedly would total at least $500 million.

Ayacucho declaration signed. Representatives of eight Latin American countries, including four heads of state, met in Ayacucho, Peru Dec. 9 and signed a declaration of political and economic solidarity. Military leaders of the countries signed a separate document pledging to limit armaments and stop acquiring offensive weapons. All of the signatories—Peru, Venezuela, Panama, Bolivia, Argentina, Chile, Colombia, and Ecuador—had been involved in frontier clashes in the past and some still claimed territory in neighboring countries.

'Banana war' developments. The conflict between members of the fledgling Union of Banana Exporting Countries (UPEB) and the U.S. firms United Brands Co. and Standard Fruit & Steamship Co. intensified during May-August. (UPEB nations accounted for 60% of the world's banana production.) The trouble stemmed from an UPEB decision in March to impose an export tax of up to $1 per 40-pound crate on the producing companies. Standard and United Brands retaliated by halting exports and cutting production in three of the four countries which actually imposed the tax—Costa Rica, Honduras and Panama—prompting charges by Panamanian officials that the firms were plotting against those nations' governments. Leaders of the affected nations met several times to discuss the companies' action. Representatives of all UPEB countries except Ecuador met in Panama July 15-17 and agreed to formally constitute UPEB by Sept. 17. Ecuador did not participate or impose the export tax because it said that as an oil producer, it was not suffering from the rise in world oil prices—the chief reason given by UPEB members for trying to increase their banana export revenues.

The Panamanian government and United Brands Sept. 4 resolved their tax dispute. The company had paid the tax under protest, depositing $3.9 million in escrow in the state-run National Bank of Panama while it contested the tax in court. Panama, which had refused payment in bank certificates, seized the funds late in July and United Brands suspended its Panamanian operations. United Brands agreed to resume production and exports, and to pay back wages and taxes for the period of suspended operations. In return, Panama agreed to an unspecified reduction in the banana tax. The parties also agreed to eventual purchase by Panama of the properties of United Brands' Panamanian subsidiary, Chiriqui Land Co. Chiriqui valued its assets at $100 million, but the government put the book value at $44 million, according to press reports. Chiriqui, the largest landowner in Panama and the third largest employer, had a local monopoly on bananas. Bananas accounted for 87% of Panama's agricultural exports and about 47% of its total exports, with earnings of $63.8 millon in 1973, according to the Associated Press Sept. 5.

Representatives of Panama, Colombia, Costa Rica, Guatemala and Honduras signed the UPEB constitution in Panama City Sept. 17, formally establishing the banana producers' organization. Ecuador's refusal to take full membership was seen as seriously weakening UPEB because Ecuador was the world's major banana producer.

See also specific countries; COFFEE; CUBA; FAMINE & FOOD; OIL [17]; POPULATION; SUGAR; UNITED NATIONS [16]

LAW ENFORCEMENT ASSISTANCE ADMINISTRATION—*See* APPOINTMENTS & RESIGNATIONS; CRIME [38]
LAWYERS—*See* AGNEW, SPIRO T.; CRIME [5]; WATERGATE [3]
LEAD—*See* AUTOMOBILES [3]; TARIFFS & TRADE

LEBANON—Armed militiamen of Lebanon's right-wing Phalangist Party and Palestinian guerrillas clashed outside Beirut July 29-30 in the worst outbreak of fighting in the country since May 1973. The fighting, involving guerrillas from the Tal al-Zaatar refugee camp, was marked by an exchange of rocket fire by both sides on a road to Dekwaneh, northeast of Beirut. Police and guerrilla sources said at least four persons were killed and 15-20 wounded. The Phalangists, whose militia totaled 5,000 men, had called for the re-establishment of Lebanese government control over the 15 Palestinian refugee camps in the country. The clashes were halted by a truce arranged in talks held by Premier Takieddin Solh.

Premier Takieddin Solh and his Cabinet resigned Sept. 25 following a dispute involving security problems arising from a proliferation of guns among civilians. President Suleiman Franjieh Oct. 24 designated Rashid Solh as premier; he formed a new 18-member Cabinet Oct. 31, which included five ministers of the previous government. Solh, a cousin of Takieddin Solh, was an independent member of Parliament. The resignation of Takieddin Solh had been assured by the decision of four Cabinet members to quit over government adoption Sept. 19 of a law that canceled all licenses for carrying firearms by civilians. The measure, applying to Lebanese civilians and Palestinian guerrillas, was endorsed following a threat by Interior Minister Bahji Takieddin and Petroleum Minister Tawfik Assaf to resign unless the proposal for strengthening law and order was adopted.

See also APPOINTMENTS & RESIGNATIONS; MIDDLE EAST [10, 22, 29-36]; OIL [19]; YEMEN

LESOTHO—Hundreds of supporters of the opposition Congress Party had been shot or beaten to death in the two months since the unsuccessful January attempt to overthrow the National Party (NP) government of Premier Leabua Jonathan, the *London Times* reported March 5. The police and the NP's irregular militia, known as the Peace Corps, carried out the murders and sacked a number of villages according to the report. Congress Party Treasurer Shakhane Mokhehle was reported arrested Jan. 8.

See also SOUTH AFRICA [11]

LEVY, DR. HOWARD E.—*See* DEFENSE [9]
LIBEL—*See* HUGHES, HOWARD; PRESS; TELEVISION & RADIO

LIBYA—Oil developments. Libya announced Feb. 11 the total nationalization of three U.S. oil firms—Texaco Inc., the California Asiatic Oil Co., a subsidiary of Standard Oil of California, and Libyan American, a subsidiary of Atlantic Richfield Co. Libya had taken 51% contol of the three firms along with several others Sept. 1, 1973. The government had warned at the time the companies would come under complete Libyan control unless they agreed to terms of nationalization. All Royal Dutch Shell operations in Libya were nationalized under a government law passed March 30. Under an agreement signed in Tripoli April 16, Libya gained 51% control of the operations of Exxon Corp. and Mobil Oil Corp. Libya ordered Exxon to stop all its oil production in the country, affecting a daily output of 225,000 barrels, or 17% of Libya's total petroleum production, it was reported Oct. 10. Two other smaller operations also were directed to close—W. R. Grace & Co. and Atlantic Richfield.

British Petroleum Co. (BP) accepted about $40.4 million from Libya as compensation for the nationalization of the firm's property in 1971, the company announced Nov. 25. Libya had agreed that it owed BP $144.8 million, but deducted counterclaims of $104.4 million, which reflected "taxes, royalties and other claims" by Libya, the company said. BP had filed an original compensation claim of $580 million.

Qaddafi threatens Arab revolt. Libyan leader Muammar el-Qaddafi threatened Feb. 10 to arm and train guerrillas to overthrow the leaders of Tunisia, Egypt and Algeria "if [Arab] unity cannot be brought about by normal means." He said the people of those three countries would pressure their leaders to achieve this unity. The Libyan leader also referred to the aborted efforts of his country to merge with Egypt and later with Tunisia. [See EGYPT and TUNISIA] He accused those states of paying only lip service to their peoples' "irreversible determination" to achieve Arab unity. The editor of the official Libyan news agency ARNA later denied that Qaddafi had called for a revolt against Tunisia, Algeria and Egypt.

Change in Qaddafi role. The Libyan government announced April 6 that Col. Qaddafi had been relieved of all political powers so he could "devote all his time to popular organization and ideological action." He remained commander in chief of the armed forces. The government decree, circulated among foreign embassies in Tripoli and dated April 2, said the 11-man ruling Revolutionary Command Council had agreed that Qaddafi give up "work related to political, executive and traditional affairs, in addition to relieving him from all protocol matters, including greeting heads of state... and receiving ambassadors." The decree stated that Premier Abdul Salam Jalloud would take over all the functions performed by Qaddafi. The statement said the decree "does not affect the authority and obligations" of the Revolutionary Command Council. Two Libyan Cabinet ministers said April 7 that the government changes were routine and formal.

Libya frees hijackers. Libya released four guerrillas who had hijacked a Japan Air Lines jet in 1973 after it left the Netherlands, and then blew it up at a Libyan airport, a Palestine Liberation Organization (PLO) spokesman confirmed Aug. 14. The men, three Palestinians and a Japanese, had arrived in Damascus Aug. 13, the spokesman said. A Beirut newspaper said Qaddafi had personally decided to free the hijackers following requests from PLO Chairman Yasir Arafat and other Palestinian guerrilla leaders.

See also AFRICA; EGYPT; FRANCE [19]; GERMANY, WEST [14]; JORDAN; MIDDLE EAST [28, 34]; MONETARY DEVELOPMENTS [5]; MOROCCO; OIL [4-8, 10, 18-19, 35]; SUDAN

LIDDY, G. GORDON—*See* WATERGATE [62, 78, 80-81, 95, 101]
LIECHTENSTEIN—*See* BANKS & BANKING; EUROPEAN SECURITY
LITERATURE—*See* BOOKS; NOBEL PRIZES; PULITZER PRIZES
LITTLE LEAGUE BASEBALL, INC.—*See* BASEBALL; WOMEN'S RIGHTS
LIVESTOCK—*See* AGRICULTURE; ANTITRUST ACTIONS [9]; CANADA [28-29, 36]; CONSUMER AFFAIRS [4, 7]; FAMINE & FOOD
LON NOL—*See* CAMBODIA; UNITED NATIONS [7]
LOTTERIES—*See* GAMBLING
LOUISIANA—*See* ELECTIONS [5]; WEATHER
LUMBER—*See* HONDURAS

LUXEMBOURG—Premier Pierre Werner submitted the resignation of his coalition Cabinet May 27, one day after his conservative Christian Social Party suffered an unexpected setback in general elections. According to unofficial results, the Christian Social Party won 18 seats in the Chamber of Deputies, compared with 21 in the previous election in 1968, while its coalition partner, the Democratic Party (generally known as the Liberal Party), increased its representation from 11 to 14 seats. The Socialists were the big winners, raising their representation from 12 to 17 seats. Gaston Thorn, who had been foreign minister in Werner's Cabinet, was sworn in as premier June 18 by Grand Duke Jean. Thorn was the leader of a new center-left coalition that excluded the Christian Socialists from the government for the first time in over 50 years. The new government's program, presented to Parliament July 4, included an anti-inflation program, a large increase in family allowances, creation of an ombudsman, liberalization of divorce and abortion legislation and an end to telephone tapping.

See also COMMUNISM, INTERNATIONAL; EUROPEAN ECONOMIC COMMUNITY [2]; EUROPEAN SECURITY; MONETARY DEVELOPMENTS [11]; NORTH ATLANTIC TREATY ORGANIZATION; OIL [26]; UNITED NATIONS [11]

M

MACAO—Government changes. Gen. Francisco Rebelo Goncalves was named acting military commander of Macao June 3, replacing Col. Manual Mesquita Borges who, with his deputy, had been dismissed that day. About half of the 500 Portuguese troops stationed in Macao, a small colony on the southern coast of China, had demonstrated in their barracks June 1-2, denouncing senior officcers and shouting, "We want to go home." A new interim governor, Lt. Col. Manuel Maia Goncalves, was installed in Macao Oct. 14.

MADEIRA—*See* PORTUGAL [4, 7]
MAGRUDER, JEB STUART—*See* WATERGATE [96, 101]
MAINE—*See* ELECTIONS [1, 5, 7]; GAMBLING; WOMEN'S RIGHTS
MALAWI—*See* MOZAMBIQUE [4]; SOUTH AFRICA [11]

MALAYSIA—Prime Minister Abdul Razak's ruling National Front coalition was returned to power in general elections Aug. 24, winning at least 120 seats in the 154-member Parliament, while the Chinese Democratic Action Party won nine. The front also retained control of 10 of the 12 state assemblies in voting for the legislative bodies.

See also JAPAN [10]

MALDIVE ISLANDS—*See* DEFENSE [14]

MALI—New Constitution. More than 99% of the electorate voted approval of Mali's new Constitution in a June 2 referendum. Article 78 of the Constitution decreed that the Military Committee of National Liberation (which seized control in 1968) would "define and conduct the politics of the state for the next five years." Other amendments said that a chief of state would be elected by universal suffrage and that a national assembly and a single political party would be established. The government carried out numerous arrests in Bamako of persons who had voted against approval of the new Constitution, the French newspaper *Le Monde* reported June 26.

See also AFRICA; FAMINE & FOOD

MALTA—Base abolition plan offered. The government of Prime Minister Dom Mintoff had presented to Parliament a seven-year plan to make Malta economically independent of foreign military bases on its territory by 1980, it was reported Oct. 30.

Republic proclaimed. Malta became a republic Dec. 13, and Governor General Sir Anthony Malmo was sworn in as its first president. The 55-member House of Representatives, by a vote of 49-6, had approved constitutional amendments Dec. 12 establishing the republic and barring the Roman Catholic Church, Malta's official church, from making political statements. Malta would continue to recognize Queen Elizabeth II of Britain as the symbolic head of the Commonwealth. She had also been queen of Malta until the proclamation of the republic.

See also EUROPEAN SECURITY

MANSFIELD, SEN. MIKE—*See* AMNESTY & CLEMENCY; CENTRAL INTELLIGENCE AGENCY; PRIVACY [3]; WATERGATE [49, 68]

MARDIAN, ROBERT—*See* WATERGATE [87, 93, 96, 103]

MARIJUANA—*See* NARCOTICS & DANGEROUS DRUGS

MARTINEZ, EUGENIO—*See* WATERGATE [78, 80, 83, 86]

MARTINIQUE—At least one person was killed and three were injured in the French West Indies island department of Martinique Feb. 14 when police fired at demonstrators during labor unrest. Four policemen were injured.

See also FRANCE [18]

MARYLAND—*See* AGNEW, SPIRO T.; CRIME [9-10]; ENERGY CRISIS [6]; GAMBLING

MASSACHUSETTS—*See* CIVIL RIGHTS [4-5]; CRIME [40]; ELECTIONS [7]; GAMBLING; POLITICS [4]

MASS TRANSIT—*See* TRANSPORTATION

MAURITANIA—President Mokhtar Ould Daddah anounced Nov. 28 the nationalization of the Miferma iron ore mining corporation. Miferma's ownership had been 56% French, 19% British, 15% Italian, 5% German and 5% Mauritanian. The president said the owners would be fully compensated for the takeover.

See also AFRICA; FAMINE & FOOD; OIL [19]; SPANISH SAHARA; UNITED NATIONS [6]

MAURITIUS—*See* AFRICA; DEFENSE [14]

McCARTHY, EUGENE J.—*See* POLITICS [3]

McGOVERN, SEN. GEORGE—*See* CAMPAIGN FINANCING [18]; ELECTIONS

MEANY, GEORGE—*See* ECONOMY, U.S. [10, 13, 17]; POLITICS [8]

MEAT—*See* AGRICULTURE; CANADA [35-36]; CONSUMER AFFAIRS [7]; EUROPEAN ECONOMIC COMMUNITY [2]; FAMINE & FOOD

MEDICAID & MEDICARE—*See* ABORTION; MEDICINE & HEALTH [2-6]

MEDICINE & HEALTH

Government Actions

[1] Action on a national health insurance bill began with a presentation of a plan to Congress by President Nixon on Feb. 6. Other versions of a national health plan also were presented during 1974 by Sen. Russell B. Long (D, La.) and Sen. Abraham Ribicoff (D, Conn.), and by Sen. Edward M. Kennedy (D, Mass.) and Rep. Wilbur D. Mills (D, Ark.).

[2] Nixon's proposal, which was based on the existing private health insurance industry, was to be paid for by employers and employes. A government-subsidized program was to replace Medicaid and extend such coverage to non-working families with an annual income below $7500, who were to pay a small premium, and to families with income below $5,000 and persons with high medical risk, whose deductibles and copayments were to be less. The plan was voluntary and to be available to every American. Nixon

estimated that the program would cost an additional $6.4 billion a year in federal funds and an additional $1 billion in state funds. Increased Medicare coverage for the aged was to be offset by increased charges.

[3] Under the President's proposal benefits included physicians' care in and out of the hospital except regular check-ups for adults; outpatient prescription drugs; treatment for mental health, alcoholism and drug abuse within certain limits; eye, ear and dental care for children up to age 13; prenatal and well-baby care; family planning services; 100 days of nursing home care; home health services; blood and other services, such as X-rays and laboratory tests. The states were to have the responsibility for reviewing insurance premium rates and physician charges and for setting hospital fees covered by the plan. All full-time employes were to be offered the basic plan, or one supplementing the basic benefits, the latter requiring approval. The employer would pay 65% of the premium costs, the employe the remainder, for the first three years of the plan. These costs were put at $600 for a family and $240 for an individual. After three years, the employer share would rise to 75%.

[4] A family would pay a deductible of $150 per person, up to a family limit of $450, and a separate $50 deductible for outpatient drugs, in annual medical expenses, plus 25% of medical expenses covered by the plan. If payments reached $1,500 in a year, the plan would absorb further costs that year.

[5] The plan for the unemployed and poor would replace most of the current Medicaid program. It would be operated under federal guidelines by the states, which would pay 25% of the increased costs of the program.

[6] In the program for the elderly, Medicare would be expanded to cover outpatient drugs and mental health services. A ceiling of $750 was set for the maximum annual cost to the individual, but the aged would have payments increased over the current program. Hospital and other care would require an initial $100 deductible, a separate $50 deductible for outpatient drugs and payment of 20% of all medical bills up to the $750 limit. Currently, Medicare patients paid $84 as the average cost of the first day of hospital care, then received 59 days of hospitalization free. A $90 annual premium also would be required from the aged.

[7] Hearings on the plan by Mills' House Ways and Means Committee began April 24. The opening witness was Health, Education and Welfare (HEW) Secretary Caspar W. Weinberger. Mills questioned the major role for private companies under the Nixon bill. Weinberger said this would save money. Although cautious about cost estimates, the Secretary said the Administration program would cost about $60 billion annually in payments by employers, employes and the federal government.

[8] Ribicoff and Long testified before the committee April 25. Ribicoff said: "Let's not do a program that's completely indigestible, but do a program one step at a time and see if it works." The Long-Ribicoff plan, covering illnesses costing more than $2,000 a year, would be financed by a payroll tax and administered through the Social Security system.

[9] Nixon stated his willingness May 20 to compromise with Congress on the plan in order to facilitate passage of the legislation in 1974, but remained adamant on allowing the patient to choose a doctor and in basing the program on the private health insurance industry. Although finding merit in both the Long-Ribicoff and Kennedy-Mills programs, Nixon said both proposals involved too much direct administration by the federal government.

[10] The Kennedy-Mills plan offered generally the same coverage provided by the Administraion proposal, although the benefits would be somewhat greater and the cost to employes somewhat less. The financing was different, however,

involving a 3% payroll tax from the emloyer and 1% from the employe. It also would be compulsory.

[11] **Drug actions.** The Health Subcommittee of the Senate Labor and Public Welfare Committee heard testimony in February and March on abuses in the drug industry concerning medicines which were incorrectly prescribed, not needed or ordered by brand—rather than generic names—as a result of drug company promotion campaigns.

[12] In testimony before the subcommitte on March 8, former drug salesmen told of being under great pressure to sell but under little pressure to educate physicians and pharmacists on the hazards and limitations of their drugs. Drug company executives March 12 defended industry marketing practices, contending they were intended to provide doctors with balanced information on the good and bad points of their products. Salesmen, however, had told the subcommittee of promotional campaigns involving gifts to pharmacists, hospital officials and doctors who ordered or prescribed large amounts of their companys' products. During the hearings, Sen. Kennedy, chairman of the subcommittee, charged that adverse drug reactions killed 30,000 persons annually and that 50,000-100,000 deaths a year could be attributed to treatment-resistant bacteria which had emerged, in part, because of misuse and overuse of antibiotics. On May 2 Kennedy released statistics showing that in 1973, 20 leading drug concerns had given health professionals promotional gifts valued at $14 million.

[13] Eleven staff scientists of the Food and Drug Administration (FDA), testifying before the subcommittee Aug. 15, charged that their superiors in the agency had harassed, transferred and overruled them when they had produced adverse findings on drugs needing final FDA approval before being marketed. Testimony revolved around staff members' findings against Cylert, a drug made by Abbott Laboratories for use on hyperkinetic children. Dr. Carol Kennedy, the FDA staff member who first recommended against the drug, said she had been subsequently transferred to another section of the agency. Her findings had been backed by three outside consultants who had been named to FDA panels created to review staff work. One of the consultants, Dr. Gerald Solomons of the University of Iowa said, "Professional personnel who had been involved and enthusiastically supported our findings [against the drug] were reassigned to other projects." Dr. Richard Crout of the FDA's Bureau of Drugs testified Aug. 16 there were "real misconceptions" among the 11 staff members and three consultants testifying Aug. 15. Disapproval of a drug "commonly [was] not a permanent turndown," as adverse reports were often re-reviewed in the light of new information, he said. HEW Secretary Weinberger Aug. 24 announced a "full review" of FDA procedures and practices with regard to evaluations of new drugs.

[14] **National Resarch Act signed.** President Nixon July 12 signed into law the National Research Act, which created a commission to monitor the use of human subjects in biomedical research and established a biomedical research training awards program. The bill had been passed by the Senate 72-14 June 27 and by the House 311-10 June 28. The first U.S. legislation ever to consider the ethical questions of medical research, the act aimed at developing guidelines for research involving humans.

[15] **Cancer, diabetes research funding set.** President Nixon July 23 signed into law a bill extending the National Cancer Act through 1977. The bill, which authorized $2.8 billion for cancer resarch for fiscal 1975-77, was approved by voice vote in the House July 9 and the Senate July 10. One section of the act required Senate confirmation of all future directors of the National Institutes of Health. The President also signed into law July 23 legislation

authorizing for fiscal 1975-77 $41 million for new diabetes research centers and for establishment of a national commission to formulate long-range plans to combat diabetes.

[16] **HEW study on alcholism.** An HEW report on alcohol and health made public July 11 indicated that alcoholic abuse among high school students had risen sharply.The study, prepared by the National Institute on Alcohol Abuse and Alcoholism also contained the finding that heavy drinkers ran far greater risk of getting certain kinds of cancer—of the mouth, throat region, esophagus and liver—than nondrinkers. Despite its negative findings, the report did not condemn moderate use of alcohol, which it defined as no more than three ounces of whiskey, a half bottle of wine or four glasses of beer a day, all with meals and the hard liquor in diluted form. For reasons not clear, the report said, moderate drinkers tended to outlive nondrinkers.

[17] **Senate study assails nursing homes.** A report by the Long-Term Care Subcommittee of the Senate Special Committee on Aging, made public Nov. 19, strongly criticized the HEW for laxity in the enforcement of laws and administrative standards intended to end abuses in the nation's nursing homes. Federal policy on nursing homes was confusing and incoherent, the report charged. It was especially critical of HEW, which, the report said, was "reluctant to issue forthright standards to provide patients with minimum protection."

[18] **NIH Controversy.** Six prominent scientists Dec. 17 issued a statement deploring the forced resignation of Dr. Robert S. Stone, director of the National Institutes of Health (NIH). In their statement the scientists also criticized the abrupt dismissal in December 1972 of Stone's predecessor, Dr. Robert Q. Marston. Stone's resignation was not immediately officially announced. In their statement the scientists cited "unwarranted and counterproductive political control."

[19] **FDA ends Dalkon IUD sales moratorium.** The FDA Dec. 20 ended a six-month moratorium on sale of the intrauterine contraceptive device (IUD), the Dalkon Shield. The FDA said A. H. Robbins Co., manufacturer of the device, had agreed to register all new users of the shield, as well as follow their progress. Data to be reported to the FDA by Robbins was to include the number and kind of adverse reactions, the rate at which the device was expelled by women and other details. Robbins had withdrawn the shield from the market in May and June when evidence linked its use to 11 fatal and 209 nonfatal infections. Some 2.2 million women had been fitted with the Dalkon Shield since it was first marketed in 1970.

Cancer Research

[20] **Beef linked to colon cancer.** The National Cancer Institute reported Jan 28 that a five-year study in Hawaii indicated that the incidence of cancer of the colon was statistically higher among persons who ate large amounts of beef than among non-beef eaters. Dr. Ernst L. Wynder, addressing a science writers' seminar in St. Augustine, Fla. March 25, said a low-fat, low-cholesterol diet might protect against cancer of the colon and rectum, the second largest source of cancer deaths in the U.S.

[21] **Cancer-link focus in water study.** The Environmental Protection Agency (EPA) issued a report Nov. 8 stating that 66 organic chemicals, some suspected of being carcinogenic (cancer-causing), were present in treated Mississippi River water used by New Orleans and nearby communities. EPA Administrator Russell E. Train simultaneously ordered an immediate nationwide study of chemical contaminants in drinking water.

[22] **Safe drinking water.** A bill to set federal standards for safe drinking water was passed by the House 296-85 Nov. 19. It went to conference with the Senate, which had passed a similar measure by voice vote in 1973. The bill was opposed by the Administration because of the expansion of federal authority into state and local areas and by some oil interests because of an underground-protection provision. It received added impetus for passage following recent reports that up to 66 cancer-causing agents had been found in drinking water in New Orleans, Cincinnati and Washington.

[23] **Breast cancer surgery debate.** Breast cancer surgery on Betty Ford, wife of President Ford, and on Margaretta Rockefeller, wife of Vice President-designate Nelson A. Rockefeller, resulted in widespread public discussion of the disease, which afflicted 90,000 U.S. women and resulted in the deaths of 30,000 others in 1973. New findings concerning treatment also increased public interest.

[24] Despite the high incidence of occurrence of breast cancer, its treatment remained in dispute. A study released by the National Cancer Institute Sept. 29 found that a radical mastectomy, the operation performed on Mrs. Ford, was unnecessary in many cases. The study also found that chemical therapy could "drastically" reduce the incidence of recurrence of breast cancer. The report said that radical mastectomies, which produced life-long pain, weakness and periodic swelling of the arm, were not required for patients whose lymph nodes were cancer-free. By changing normal procedures, surgeons could order immediate laboratory tests on the lymph nodes, the report said. If the tests failed to show malignancy in the nodes, the surgeons could limit treatment to the less disfiguring, less traumatic simple mastectomy—amputation of the breast only. (Normal procedure was to remove the lymph nodes and conduct tests afterward.) Currently, 95% of all women undergoing breast cancer surgery received radical mastectomies.

[25] The American Cancer Society Oct. 17 took a cautious view of the institute study, pointing out that it had three more years to run before anything definitive could be said about the relative effectiveness of the simple mastectomy.

Other Medical Developments

[26] **Smoking.** HEW reported June 28 that it had new evidence linking cigarette and pipe smoking to cancer, emphysema, bronchitis and coronary heart disease. The Agriculture Department reported Sept. 14 that per capita cigarette consumption by U.S. adults was climbing back to the level it had reached prior to the surgeon general's 1963 report. Figures for the year ending June 30 reported a level only 2% below that of 1963.

[27] **Heart research.** The National Center for Health Statistics reported July 6 that the U.S. death rate from coronary heart disease had fallen 10% since 1963, compared with a 19% rise during 1950-1963. Despite the drop, however, heart disease remained the leading cause of death in the U.S.

[28] Researchers at the Boston University School of Medicine reported June 6 that men who exhibited high degrees of so-called Type A behavior were twice as likely to have heart attacks as men who did not. Type A personalities were described as those who strived to achieve, were perfectionist, tense, unable to relax, active and energetic. The four-year study had involved 2,750 men who were free of heart disease at its inception.

[29] **Extra heart implanted by Barnard.** Dr. Christiaan Barnard, the South African surgeon who performed the first heart transplant operation in 1967, achieved another medical breakthrough Nov. 25, implanting a second heart in the chest of a 58-year-old-man to ease the burden on the man's own heart. The

new heart, from a 10-year-old girl killed in an accident the day before, was attached to the left ventricle of Ivan Taylor's heart after a third of the patient's diseased left ventricle had been cut out.

[30] **Longest survivor of transplant dies.** Louis B. Russell Jr., 49, longest surviving recipient of a transplanted heart, died Nov. 27 in Richmond. According to doctors, Russell's new heart developed beating rhythms too irregular to sustain life. Electronic pacemakers were unable to stabilize the abnormal fluctuations, the doctors said. Russell, an Indianapolis school teacher, had received the new heart in 1968. Statistics in the Organ Transplant Registry of the National Institutes of Health showed that 259 heart transplant operations had been attempted on 253 patients since 1967. Of those 52 patients had survived longer than one year.

[31] **Genetics.** A committee of scientists endorsed by the National Academy of Sciences urged colleagues throughout the world to observe a temporary ban on certain types of experiments involving genetic manipulation of bacteria, it was reported July 18. Such a moratorium should be declared, the ad hoc panel said, because gene-transplantation experiments might accidently increase the resistance of some micro-organisms to drugs or led to the spread of some types of cancer-causing virus.

[32] The panel especially urged caution in experiments with the bacterium Escherichia Coli (E. Coli), which was commonly found in the human digestive tract. A genetically hybrid E. Coli, the committee warned, "might possibly become widely disseminated among human bacterial, plant and animal populations with unpredictable effects."

[33] Scientists at the Massachusetts Institute of Technology (MIT) reported Sept. 10 that they had synthesized and deciphered the chemical structure governing the turning-on of heredity instructions in a gene. (The gene, the basic unit of heredity, comprises an helexical double strand of deoxyribonucleic acid [DNA]. In any one gene, the sequence of the DNA's chemical sub-units determines instructions for a living cell. The sum of coded chemical messages in all the genes of a cell gives it complete instructions, determining what the cell can do and what it can become.) The MIT team of researchers reported to the American Chemical Society that it deciphered what it believed to be most or all of the "on" signal for a gene they had succeeded in synthesizing in 1973.

[34] **'Test-tube' babies.** British obstetrician Dr. Douglas Bevis told colleagues at the annual meeting of the British Medical Association (BMA) July 15 that he knew of three babies—one in England and two on the European continent—that had been concieved in laboratory test tubes and then implanted in their mothers' wombs. Bevis said the implantation technique involved removal of an unfertilized ovum from the mother's fallopian tubes and subsequent fertilization in a test tube, after which it was then implanted on the lining of the womb.

See also ABORTION; AVIATION [12]; BIRTH CONTROL; BRAZIL [10]; BUDGET; ECONOMY, U.S. [7]; ENVIRONMENT & POLLUTION [15]; FORD, BETTY; NARCOTICS & DANGEROUS DRUGS; NIXON, RICHARD M.; NOBEL PRIZES; OBITUARIES [SUTHERLAND]; ROCKEFELLER, MARGARETTA; SPACE [1-3]; UNION OF SOVIET SOCIALIST REPUBLICS [3]; VETERANS; WEATHER; WOMEN'S RIGHTS

MEIR, GOLDA—*See* ISRAEL; MIDDLE EAST [2, 4-5, 30]; WATERGATE [40]
MENINGITIS—*See* BRAZIL [10]
MENTAL ILLNESS—*See* MEDICINE & HEALTH [3, 6]
METZENBAUM, HOWARD M.—*See* CONGRESS; ELECTIONS [3, 10]; ROCKEFELLER, NELSON [28]

MEXICO

Oil & Economic Developments

[1] **Oil investment set.** The government announced plans to invest $5.5 billion in the oil and electricity industries in 1974-76, it was reported Jan. 10. An official said Mexico should be self-sufficient in oil by the end of July. Mexico currently imported about 8% of its oil—45,000 barrels a day—from the U.S. and Venezuela. The state oil firm Pemex planned to open 2,000 wells in 22 states by 1976, boosting production from 550,000 barrels a day to more than 700,000 barrels daily.

[2] **Price controls decreed.** President Luis Echeverria Alvarez decreed a broad system of price controls Oct. 3 over strong objections from private business and industry. The move was aimed at stemming the accelerated inflation rate, estimated by the government at 25% and by organized labor at 42.5%. The prices of 29 staple foods were frozen at Sept. 1 levels and those of 170 other products were placed under strict controls. The price of a controlled product could not rise unless a 5% increase in production costs was demonstrated and government permission obtained. The controlled products included industrial items such as chemicals and metals and consumer goods such as clothes and appliances.

[3] In a preamble to the decree, Echeverria said his objective was to "protect the purchasing power of the weakest sectors of the country, which are the ones most severely affected by inflation." Observers said he sought to protect the real value of 22% wage increases granted to Mexico's workers Sept. 13.

[4] **New oil deposits found.** The discovery of important new oil deposits in southeastern Mexico was reported by U.S. officials Oct. 11 and confirmed by the Mexican government the next day. U.S. officials said reserves of up to 20 billion barrels of crude oil had been found in the Mexican states of Chiapas and Tabasco, near the Gulf of Mexico. One official said the area might be as rich in petroleum as the Persian Gulf. Mexico confirmed the discovery Oct. 12 but claimed the 20 billion barrel estimate was wildly exaggerated.

[5] Reports of the discovery raised hopes in the U.S. that Mexico, which recently became a net oil exporter, might sell its new oil at prices below those set by the Organization of Petroleum Exporting Countries (OPEC). However, Horacio Flores de la Pena, Mexico's national patrimony minister, said Oct. 15 that Mexico sought observer status in OPEC and that it would sell its oil "at OPEC prices." (Mexico had nationalized its oil industry in 1938.) Asked how much of Mexico's oil exports might go to the U.S., Flores replied: "It will depend on the price offered by the United States compared to that offered by other countries." President Echeverria said Oct. 19, on the eve of a meeting with President Ford, that Mexico would not make any concessions to the U.S. regarding oil.

Terrorism & Unrest

[6] Mexico experienced anti-government rebellions, student riots, guerrilla attacks, bombings, kidnappings and peasant land occupations through the year, with the most severe disturbances occurring January-March.

[7] At least four persons were killed and 20 wounded when 200 students, organized into five attack groups, clashed with police in Sinaloa State Jan. 17. In Teoloyucan (Mexico State) more than 330 citizens stormed the municipal palace Feb. 4, demanding that a popularly elected neighborhood council take control of the town. They were evicted by police who wounded 10 persons and arested 10. Citizens of Tecolutla (Veracruz State) had occupied their municipal palace Feb. 1 and held a "people's trial" for Gov. Rafael Murillo Vidal and

state congressmen on various charges including illegally deposing the elected mayor who opposed the ruling Revolutionary Institutional Party. Students and workers in Merida (Yucatan State) rioted after Efrain Calderon Lara, leader of an independent trade union group, was kidnapped and killed, it was reported Feb. 22. The London newsletter *Latin America* reported March 29 that State authorities were involved in the murder. The director for public security and seven of his associates were arrested on assassination charges, it was reported May 12.

[8] There were also a series of kidnappings, among them: Raymundo Soberanis Otero, uncle of the Guerrero governor, who was taken Jan. 19 by members of the Sept. 23rd Communist League. League members asserted Feb. 26 that Soberanis had been executed "for being a bourgeois," but the body was not found. Vincente Ruedo Saucedo was released Feb. 11, two weeks after his abduction by members of the Revolutionary Armed Forces. A ransom of $240,000 had been paid.

[9] A mutilated body found in the desert near Hermosillo (Sonora State) July 8 was positively identified two days later as that of John Patterson, a U.S. vice consul who disappeared March 22 after leaving his consulate with an unidentified man. A note delivered to the consulate said he had been kidnapped by the People's Liberation Army and demanded a $500,000 ransom. Patterson's wife, Ann, subsequently said she had attempted to deliver the ransom money but had been unable to make contact with the abductors. Mexican authorities July 10 asserted Patterson's kidnappers were not left-wing guerrillas, as some early reports had suggested, but persons from the U.S. seeking ransom. California resident Bobby Joe Keesee had been arrested in San Diego May 28 and indicted by a local grand jury June 7 on charges of causing Patterson's kidnapping.

[10] Sen. Ruben Figueroa, kidnapped by left-wing guerrillas May 30, was freed Sept. 8 during an alleged shootout between his captors and pursuing army troops. Figueroa, a local gubernatorial candidate who advocated amnesty for rural insurgents, was kidnapped May 20 when he went into the mountains to negotiate a truce with the Poor People's Party, led by Lucio Cabanas. He had been the object of what was described as the largest military operation in three decades when some 16,000 troops—one-third of the Mexican army—moved into the mountains of Guerrero State June 27 to search for him. A June 13 communique from Cabanas called on Mexican workers and peasants "to destroy the capitalist and exploitative regime." [See below]

[11] There were conflicting reports on the method of Figueroa's release, with the government maintaining he had escaped during a gun battle between soldiers and insurgents. Another report in the left-wing magazine *Por que?* said Figueroa had been ransomed by his family and was being returned in the care of a group of peasants who were attacked by the soldiers to give the appearance that Figueroa was being "saved." The magazine was closed by the government Sept. 9 before it could print its account.

[12] Cabanas was killed in a battle with soldiers Dec. 2 in the mountains of northern Guerrero State, where he and his followers had operated since 1967. Eleven other rebels died with Cabanas Dec. 2, and another 17 were killed fighting with troops Nov. 30, according to officials. Two soldiers were reported killed in the clashes. Cabanas and his small band had been pursued by nearly half the Mexican army since late June.

[13] Despite Cabanas' death, terrorism by his followers and other rebels continued. Alleged members of the September 23rd Communist League robbed two banks in Mexico City Dec. 11, killing five policemen and taking nearly

$200,000. Members of Cabanas' Poor People's Party reportedly kidnapped Josfah Munoz, a business executive and close friend of Figueroa, Dec. 17. At least 19 bombs had been exploded Nov. 16-18 at banks, department stores and newspaper and government offices in Mexico City, Guadalajara and Oaxaca.

[14] In an incident which acutely embarrassed the government, guerrillas of the left-wing People's Revolutionary Armed Forces (FRAP) kidnapped President Echeverria's father-in-law, Jose Guadalupe Zuno Hernandez, and held him for 11 days, during which Zuno made a tape recording praising his abductors and denouncing Echeverria's administration.

[15] Zuno, a former Jalisco State governor who remained powerful in Mexican politics, was seized in Guadalajara Aug. 28. A FRAP communique Aug. 30 threatened his execution unless the government paid a $1.6 million ransom, freed 10 political prisoners and flew them to Cuba, and authorized publication of a FRAP political statement in leading newspapers. The government refused to negotiate with the guerrillas or meet their demands, in accordance with a policy set by Echeverria in 1973. Zuno was released Sept. 7. At a press conference the next day, he denied making the tape recording under duress and repeated his criticism of the government, which he said had "fallen under the control of the reactionary forces of the world."

[16] The government announced the arrest of one of Zuno's alleged abductors Sept. 3 and 14 more Sept. 26.

Foreign Relations

[17] **Desalting plant bill signed.** President Nixon June 24 signed a bill authorizing construction of a $155.5 million desalting plant to clean up Colorado River waters flowing into Mexico. The plant would be the largest of its kind in the world.

[18] **Ford, Echeverria meet at border.** President Ford and President Echeverria met at the border Oct. 21. During the day-long discussions, the officials visited both sides of the border. At a concluding joint news conference in Tubac, Ariz., Ford affirmed support for Mexico's proposal for a United Nations economic charter to protect developing countries. No formal agreements were signed during the day but there was agreement to set up a new joint panel to study the problem of increased illegal traffic of Mexican workers to the U.S. On the problem of increased illegal traffic in heroin, Ford promised more equipment and personnel to help Mexico stem the flow.

[19] **Echeverria tours Europe.** President Echeverria left Mexico Feb. 1 for official visits to West Germany, Austria, Italy and Yugoslavia. Among the goals of the tour was to secure European support for Echeverria's proposed United Nations charter of economic rights and duties of nations.

[20] Echeverria had an audience with Pope Paul VI, a decision which stunned Mexico, the only Catholic country not to have relations with the Vatican (over a century) according to the London newsletter *Latin America* Feb. 1.

[21] **Echeverria on Latin tour.** President Echeverria visited seven Latin American countries July 10-31, conferring with their leaders in an attempt to promote Mexican trade, hemispheric economic integration and an end to the political and commercial blockade of Cuba. He stopped in Costa Rica, Ecuador, Peru, Argentina, Brazil, Venezuela and Jamaica. The highlight of the trip was a five-day stay in Brazil, where Mexico sought increased commercial and technological cooperation.

See also ARCHEOLOGY; CHILE [5-7, 27]; COFFEE; CUBA; DOMINICAN REPUBLIC; JAPAN [10-11]; LATIN AMERICA; OBITUARIES [SIQUERIOS]; PERU [10, 12]; SUGAR; UNITED NATIONS [11]

MICHIGAN—*See* ELECTIONS [5, 7, 9]; ENERGY CRISIS [6]; GAMBLING; WEATHER

MIDDLE EAST

[1] **Fighting continues.** Fighting continued in the disputed Golan Heights area in the first part of the year, coming to a formal halt following the signing of a disengagement agreement in Geneva, May 31. [See below]. However, Israel and Syria accused each other in August of plotting further military action. In November, in response to what it called a Soviet arms buildup in Syria, Israel massed its troops along the frontier.

[2] Syrian Foreign Minister Abdel Halim Khaddam had said Feb. 3 that Syria was deliberately fighting a "war of attrition" on the Golan Heights in order to "paralyze" Israel's economy by forcing it to keep its reserves mobilized. On March 8 Israeli Premier Golda Meir said that Israel had received "reliable information from diplomatic sources that Syria had a plan" to renew the war to recapture the territory it had lost to Israel in the October 1973 conflict. Meir implied that the Soviet Union was contributing to the tension as a result of Foreign Minister Andrei A. Gromyko's visit to Damascus which was followed by a joint Soviet-Syrian communique March 7 warning of a possible outbreak of war.

[3] Sporadic fighting had been erupting along the Heights during the first months of the year. Israel reinforced its troops in that area April 2 as defense officials expressed fear that the unabated tank and artillery clashes with Syria presaged a possible all-out attack by the Syrians. As of April 3 there had been 23 consecutive days of fighting. Israeli jets April 6 went into action for the first time since the October war, striking twice at Syrian forces that crossed the truce line in the Golan Heights. The fighting centered around Mount Hermon, the strategic peak located at the frontiers of Israel, Syria and Lebanon. The Israelis had held positions at the 7,200-foot level of the mountain since the 1967 war, lost them to the Syrians in the first day of the October war and regained them 15 days later. The latest fighting was an attempt by the Syrians to retake the area through commando assaults up toward the peak and by attempting to land troops on the summit via helicopter. Israeli and Syrian jets engaged in dogfights April 19 for the first time since the October war. Damascus acknowledged the loss of one of its aircraft, while Tel Aviv admitted the loss of two of its jets. On Mount Hermon the Israelis appeared April 24 to be holding their positions on the peak, but the Syrians were said to have gained several strategic positions. Syrian forces intensified their attacks on Israeli positions in the Heights April 30-May 8. The unabated combat was marked by Israeli air and artillery attacks on Palestinian commandos and Syrian units inside Lebanon. The Israelis attributed the upsurge to a Syrian attempt to pressure the negotiations as U.S. Secretary of State Henry Kissinger arrived in Jerusalem that day to start his shuttle diplomacy. [See below] The Syrian attacks subsided May 3 as Kissinger arrived in Damascus, but the tempo of the attacks picked up again May 5. The fighting, which had lasted for 81 consecutive days, ended a half hour after the signing of the disengagement agreement May 31.

Israel-Syria: Diplomatic Moves

[4] Meir, expressing interest Jan. 30 in negotiations between Israel and Syria on military disengagement, said Israel had no intention of retaining Syrian territory captured in the October war. But she reiterated Israel's opposition to entering into discussions until Syria provided a list of its Israeli prisoners and permitted International Red Cross officials to visit them. Syria's position was that it would submit the list, but would not permit Red Cross visits until

progress had been made in the talks, an offer which was rejected by the Israeli Cabinet Feb. 4.

[5] Kissinger flew to Damascus Feb. 26 and to Jerusalem Feb. 27. As a result of the trip, he was able to give Meir a roster of 65 Israeli POW's held by Syria along with Assad's assurances that International Red Cross officials would be permitted to visit the captives starting March 1. Israeli officials said the release of the list and the promise of Red Cross visits fulfilled Israeli's conditions for holding talks with Syria. A U.S. official said an understanding had been reached that the 65 Israeli prisoners and the 386 Syrians held by Israel would be exchanged as soon as a disengagement accord was arranged.

[6] Following preliminary settlement of the prisoner issue, Israel presented a disengagement plan calling for a demilitarized zone between Israeli and Syrian front lines within the territory captured by Israel. United Nations troops would be stationed in the zone, while both sides would thin out their forces and weapons. The plan, carried to Assad by Kissinger March 1, was called unacceptable by the Syrians. Assad challenged Israel's claim to the Golan Heights March 8 and said Syria would continue its state of belligerancy "until all the Arab territory is liberated." U.S.-sponsored indirect negotiations on disengagement began March 29 as Israeli Defense Minister Moshe Dayan submitted his country's formal proposal in talks with Kissinger in Washington. Although the plan was not publicly disclosed at the time, it was known that in addition to establishment of the "buffer zone" the plan provided for withdrawal of Israeli troops from the 300-square mile Syrian territory seized in the October war. Syria's proposals were presented to Kissinger in Washington April 13 by military intelligence chief Brig. Gen. Hikmat Khalil al-Shihabi. The Syrian proposals were transmitted to Israeli Ambassador Simcha Dinitz the following day. Dinitz later told newsmen that Damascus' proposal had "room for give and take" but represented no breakthrough.

[7] Kissinger continued his shuttle diplomacy through April and May with trips to Geneva for conferences with Soviet Foreign Minister Gromyko; to Algiers, meeting with President Houari Boumedienne; and to Egypt for conferences with President Anwar Sadat. The visits were an attempt to enlist the cooperation of all three countries in reaching an Israeli-Syrian accord. Kissinger arrived in Jerusalem May 2. On arriving at the airport in Tel Aviv, he sought to reassure the Israelis that the U.S. was not pressuring them to make concessions to reach an agreement with Damascus. Additional meetings followed May 3-14 with Israel, Syria, Jordan, the U.S.S.R. and Saudi Arabia as Kissinger flew back and forth carrying proposals and counter-proposals to both sides. The crucial issue in the negotiations centered on how far the Israeli forces would withdraw. Among the Israeli proposals was the return of the now uninhabited town of Quneitra on the Golan Heights. Israel, however, insisted on retaining three strategic hills near the town because they overlooked Israeli settlements and because of their military importance in preventing any possible Syrian advances. An apparent breakthrough was reached May 18, following Kissinger's meeting with Assad in Damascus, on the location of the demarcation line dividing Israeli and Syrian forces. A final agreement was officially announced by President Nixon May 29. It was signed by Syria and Israel in Geneva May 31.

[8] Among the principal points in the agreement: Israel would return to Syria the 300 square mile salient captured in the October 1973 war plus a strip of the Golan Heights seized in the 1967 war, including the town of Quneitra. The Israelis would withdraw about 350 yards from Quneitra but would retain three hills overlooking the town and Israeli settlements. Quneitra would be included in a ¼ mile-wide U.N. buffer zone that was to be manned by 1,250 armed troops

called the United Nations Disengagement Observer Force (UNDOF). All territory east of Israel's demarcation line would be under Syrian administration and Syrian civilians would be permitted to enter this region. The exact delineation of the detailed map and the implementation of the disengagement of forces was to be worked out by the two sides in stages, with the discussions starting 24 hours after signing of the agreement. The pullback of forces was to be completed within 20 days. War prisoners were to be returned within 24 hours after signing of the agreement. The bodies of all dead soldiers held by both sides were to be returned within 10 days. It was revealed May 30 that the U.S. had agreed to conduct aerial reconnaissance to assure implementation of the disengagement agreement and to support Israeli retaliation for any Palestinian commando attacks. Middle East peace conference sources in Geneva revealed May 31 that a verbal agreement had been given to Kissinger by Assad that Palestinian guerrillas would not infiltrate into Israel across the Syrian border. It was understood that Assad's assurance represented a vital breakthrough in reaching the final pact. Informed of the Syrian statement, Israel reportedly dropped its demand for formal guarantees that Damascus halt guerrilla activities from Syrian territory.

[9] Syria and Israel began their three-stage withdrawal of forces from the Golan Heights battlefront June 5, hours after their representatives signed a procedural accord in Geneva settling the precise lines of troop and weapons disengagement and demarcating the United Nations buffer zone. The buffer zone established by the pact ran from Mount Hermon in the north to the southern end of the Golan Heights, varying in width from 500 yards to six miles. Military sources in Tel Aviv said that Israeli troops were destroying bunkers and other installations as withdrawals began, in an operation believed to be similar to the Israeli pullback from the Suez Canal in January. First UN troops arrived in Quneitra that day. The troop disengagement was completed June 25. Israel and Syria exchanged their prisoners of war June 1 and 6. Israel received 68; Syria, 392 Syrians, 10 Iraqis and six Moroccans. Israel and Syria charged each other with brutality, torture and mistreatment of prisoners following the release, although Israeli POW's said in interviews June 7 that their condition improved considerably after the first Red Cross visit.

[10] Israeli Defense Minister Shimon Peres told the Israeli Cabinet Aug. 2 that the Syrians had installed 160-mm. mortars in the limited forces zone on the Golan Heights and that Syria was still arming terrorists operating in Lebanon. Peres also said that as a result of Soviet arms shipments, Syria's military forces were now stronger than they were at the time of the 1973 war. Further charges were lodged against the Syrians Aug. 13 when Israel accused that nation of bringing troops into Quneitra and sending planes into the airspace of the U.N. buffer zone. The next day Syria retaliated by accusing Israel of planning a new war, citing a mobilization of reservists and the massing of troops and arms. (Israel had announced Aug. 11 that it planned to conduct a one-day mobilization test.) Fears of resumed fighting followed an Israeli mobilization Nov. 14, which included a shift of troops to the Syrian and Lebanese borders. The Israeli embassy in Washington was said to have informed the State Department that day that the action was the result of intelligence reports that Syria was massing artillery and tanks near the Golan Heights and that large shipments of Soviet arms had arrived in the Syrian port of Latakia. Israeli concern had been further heightened by speculation that Syria might not agree to extension of the UNDOF mandate, due to expire Nov. 30. Kissinger was reported to have sent cables Nov. 15 to the heads of state of Syria, Egypt and Saudi Arabia. The Syrians and the Egyptians quickly cabled back that they had no plans to launch

a war against Israel. King Faisal of Saudi Arabia said he would use his influence to calm the situation. The danger of a flare-up subsided Nov. 17 after the U.S. informed Israel that Syria had no intention of attacking. Despite the easing of tensions, Syrian and Israeli forces remained on alert. On Nov. 29 the UNDOF mandate was extended through May 21, 1975.

Israel-Egypt Agreements

[11] Israeli forces Jan. 2-3 imposed a blockade of food and other nonmilitary supplies for the Egyptian III Corps trapped on the east bank of the Suez Canal and for the city of Suez on the west bank in retaliation for Egyptian firing on an Israeli bulldozer two miles north of the truck-unloading point at Suez. The United Nations Emergency Force (UNEF) Jan. 4 announced the lifting of the blockade following U.N. intercession with the Israeli army and government. The blockade came during intensified fighting around Suez City and on the east bank of the canal. Egyptian troops advanced beyond the cease-fire lines several times during the fighting and Jan. 8 blocked UNEF movements, barring an Austrian UNEF unit from entering Port Said at the northern end of the canal and from using a road on the eastern side of the waterway. Israeli forces Jan. 11 again blocked the flow of nonmilitary supplies to Suez City and to the III Corps in retaliation for the shelling of Israeli positions near Ismailia, about 50 miles north of Suez. The blockade was lifted Jan. 12, but fighting Jan. 15 prevented U.N. vehicles from bringing supplies to the Egyptians.

[12] Egypt and Israel Jan. 18 signed a two-part accord to separate their military forces along the Suez Canal. The agreement, which had been announced simultaneously Jan. 17 in Jerusalem, Cairo and Washington, had been negotiated through the mediation of Secretary of State Kissinger, who had held separate meetings with Egyptian and Israeli officials, shuttling between Aswan (where Egyptian President Sadat was recovering from bronchitis) and Jerusalem Jan. 11-17. The accord consisted of a troop withdrawal treaty, and a secret pact on the limitation of troops and arms in the disengagement zones. The text of the separation accord was accompanied by a map delineating the zones of disengagement. Israel was to abandon its bridgehead on the west bank of the canal and withdraw its forces 14-20 miles from the east bank. In the southern sector, the Israelis would be deployed immediately west of the Mitla and Gidi Passes, which controlled the routes into the heart of the Sinai Peninsula. The Egyptians were to remain on the east bank in a 5-7½ mile-wide zone. Both forces would be separated by a 3½-5 mile buffer zone patrolled by UNEF troops. Israeli and Egyptian military representatives were to work out details of the disengagement process within five days, with the pullback itself to be completed within 40 days. The accord pledged that Israel and Egypt scrupulously would "observe the cease-fire" and stressed that the agreement was only the first step toward a permanent peace. The accord was approved by the Israeli Knesset (Parliament) Jan. 22. Following signing of the agreement, President Sadat toured Arab states Jan. 18-23 to rally support for the accord. He termed the tour a "complete success."

[13] The Egyptian and Israeli chiefs of staff Jan. 24 completed details of the troop separation agreement after four days of meetings at Kilometer 101 under the direction of UNEF Commander Lt. Gen. Ensio Silasvuo. The troop withdrawal formally got under way Jan. 25, although Israel had begun moving troops and armor on the west bank to new positions in the Sinai Jan. 23. By Jan. 28 Israeli forces had withdrawn their siege of Suez City. Israeli troops completed their second phase of withdrawal Feb. 4, moving their last rear-guard unit about 5-6 miles north of the Cairo-Suez road. About 600 troops of the UNEF moved

into the area and turned over the newly evacuated territory to the Egyptians Feb. 5. UNEF troops started to move into the proposed buffer zone Feb. 4, as the armies of Egypt and Israel began reducing their forces in the zones on either side of the buffer strip. UNEF soldiers completed their deployment in the northern part of the buffer zone Feb. 21 as Israeli troops completed their withdrawal from the west bank of the canal. East bank territory held by the Israelis was turned over to UNEF troops March 4, and UNEF buffer-zone deployment was completed the same day.

[14] The Egyptian government newspaper *Al Ahram* reported Feb. 7 that Egypt had begun work on clearing the Suez Canal of sunken ships, mines and shells which had blocked it since the 1967 war. Egypt and the U.S. March 18 reached a formal agreement authorizing the U.S. Navy to help clear the canal of unexploded ordnance, with the assistance of British naval ships. The U.S. share of the $170 million cost of clearance operations was estimated at about $10 million, with Japan pledging $140 million in soft loans. The U.S. State Department said that the U.S. also had agreed to provide technical advice and to train Egyptian personnel in clearing explosives from the waterway and its banks.

[15] The U.N. Security Council April 8 approved 13-0 (China and Iraq not voting) a resolution extending the UNEF from its current expiration date of April 24 to Oct. 24. The Council first had taken up the matter April 4-5, but had delayed final action because of a dispute involving Soviet efforts to require Israel to permit free movement inside its zone for all UNEF troops, including the 824-man Polish contingent. Israel opposed the entry of troops from countries it regarded as "unfriendly" and feared that the admission of the Polish forces would be followed by a Soviet request for similar access. The mandate was again extended Oct. 23 to last through April 24, 1975.

[16] Egypt hardened its position on the reopening of the Suez Canal, declaring Nov. 13 that it would remain closed to international shipping after clearing operations were completed in the spring of 1975 unless "there had been a complete Israeli withdrawal east of the canal so as to make the waterway safe and the cities safe against Israeli surprise attack."

[17] Egypt called on Israel Dec. 13 to "freeze" its population and suspend immigration for the next 50 years as a condition for peace in the Middle East. The statement, indicating a hardening of the Egyptian position, was expressed by Foreign Minister Fahmy. Fahmy's statement was in response to remarks made by Israeli Premier Yitzhak Rabin in a television interview Dec. 12 in which he said Israel wanted to avoid a new war but was capable of inflicting 10 times more destruction on Arab cities than the Arabs could carry out against Israeli civilian targets. Fahmy said Rabin "fails to understand the situation in the Middle East. Sooner or later, Israel has no alternative but to recognize the Palestine Liberation Organization (PLO) as representative of the Palestinian people, or face expulsion" from the U.N. [See below] Fahmy said Israel must also pay compensation for the destruction resulting from the "aggressive wars" it had conducted against the Arabs in the past 26 years and for its "exploitation of raw materials, including oil from Sinai."

Palestinian Question

[18] **Hussein backs Palestinians.** In a major policy shift, King Hussein of Jordan agreed May 1 to the presence of a separate PLO delegation at the Geneva peace conference on the Middle East and recognized the PLO as the exclusive representative of the Palestinian people. Hussein had previously insisted that the Palestinians be part of the Jordanian delegation. There were indications, however, that Hussein retained the right to ask that the Israeli-occupied West Bank be

returned to his country. The PLO had demanded the area be turned over to Palestinian control.

[19] **PLO plans future moves.** The Palestinian National Council met in Cairo June 1-9 to press demands to be represented at Geneva and to map plans for a future Palestinian state. The 150-member council served as the PLO parliament, the group representing the various factions of the nationalist movement. Among major actions taken at the nine-day conference was an instruction to the Palestinian leadership to make "the national rights of the Palestinian people" a topic of discussion at Geneva. There were two versions of the phrase "national rights." Minimally it meant the right of the Palestinians to establish a "national Palestinian authority" on any part of the West Bank or Gaza Strip that might be evacuated by Israel. Palestinian radicals, however, regarded the phrase to mean replacement of the state of Israel by a "secular democratic state" in all of Palestine in which Moslems and Jews might have equal rights.

[20] **Conflicting Israeli views.** Two Israeli attitudes toward the PLO were expressed by Israeli Information Minister Aharon Yariv July 12 and Premier Rabin July 15. Yariv said Israeli-PLO talks could be held if the PLO would acknowledge the existence of Israel and end its hostile acts. Rabin, however, declared such PLO revision of it views as unlikely, saying he saw "no reason why Israel should negotiate with any organization... that has as its aim the destruction of the state of Israel." Rabin stressed the Palestinian problem could only be settled within the framework of negotiations between Israel and Jordan which, he said, administered the territory in which the great majority of Palestinians lived.

[21] **Egyptian-PLO controversy.** A split appeared in the Arab world over who should represent the Palestinians with the issuance of a joint statement July 18 by Egyptian President Sadat and King Hussein. The statement recognized the Jordanian king as representative of the Palestinians in his nation and the PLO as their representatives elsewhere. The communique, issued after three days of talks in Cairo, also asserted the PLO should have a separate delegation at Geneva and called for troop disengagement on the Jordanian-Israeli front, which the Palestinians had opposed for fear the evacuated areas would revert to Jordanian rather than Palestinian control. The statement was immediately rejected by leaders of the PLO's five guerrilla groups. The Egyptians seemed to reverse their position Aug. 5 with an official declaration that "Egypt is committed to the principle that the West Bank should not be returned to Jordanian civil and military authorities...."

[22] **PLO gains support.** Egypt and the Soviet Union expressed support Oct. 18 for the seating of the PLO as a full participant at Geneva and for the creation of a Palestinian state as a condition for a Middle East peace settlement. The statement was contained in a joint communique issued after Egyptian Foreign Minister Fahmy's visit to Moscow Oct. 14-18. (Egypt, Syria and the PLO had agreed, during a Cairo meeting Sept. 21, that the PLO was "the sole representative of the Palestinian people." As a result, Jordan Sept. 22 said it had 'frozen" its participation in the Geneva conference, but intended to raise the issue at the Arab summit conference in Morocco in October.) Meanwhile, a split had developed in the PLO with the Sept. 26 announcement by the Popular Front for the Liberation of Palestine (PFLP) that it had withdrawn from the PLO Executive Committee, along with the Popular Front for the Liberation of Palestine-General Command and the Iraqi-sponsored Arab Liberation Front. The reason given for the withdrawal was the PLO policy of establishing a Palestinian state in the West Bank and Gaza Strip. The PFLP advocated the "liberation" of all of Palestine, the destruction of Israel and the overthrow of

Hussein. (The two factions had openly clashed during June 23 fighting at three refugee camps in and around Beirut, resulting in the death of 20 guerrillas and the wounding of 17 others. The Palestinian news agency WAFA said the clashes were "the result of a misunderstanding.") The summit meeting of 20 Arab heads of state was held in Rabat, Morocco, Oct. 26-28. Among it results was unanimous adoption of a five-point resolution recognizing the PLO as the "sole legitimate representative of the Palestinian people" and calling for creation of an independent Palestinian state "on any Palestinian land that is liberated" from Israeli occupation, meaning the West Bank and the Gaza Strip. Sayed Nofal, deputy secretary of the Arab League who read the text to newsmen, said Hussein accepted the summit decision "without any reservations." In a broadcast Oct. 30, Hussein hailed the Arab summit decision as "a triumph of the Arab nation's will," saying it was made "in a climate of serenity, brotherliness and frankness."

[23] **General Assembly recognizes PLO.** The General Assembly Oct. 14 recognized the PLO as "the representative of the Palestinian people" and invited it to participate in the Assembly's debate on Palestine, scheduled to begin the week of Nov. 3. A resolution to this effect was approved by a vote of 105-4 with 20 abstentions. The U.S., Israel, the Dominican Republic and Bolivia voted against the measure, but many other nations in the Western bloc voted for it, including most members of the European Economic Community. John A. Scali, the chief U.S. delegate, noted that the PLO would be the first nongovernment organization to participate in the General Assembly, and asked: "Have we created a dangerous precedent that may return to haunt this Assembly?" Israeli Ambassador Yosef Tekoah denounced the resolution as "the surrender of the U.N. to murder and barbarism," and said it "sabotages peacemaking efforts." The vote would "encourage international terrorism," Tekoah charged.

[24] The General Assembly opened debate Nov. 13 on "the Question of Palestine." PLO leader Yasir Arafat delivered the opening address, declaring that his group's goal remained the creation of a Palestinian state that would include Moslems, Christians and Jews. Tekoah denounced Arafat's speech in rebuttal, asserting that his proposal would mean the destruction of Israel and its replacement by an Arab state. He reiterated his government's policy of refusing to permit the PLO to take over any territory relinquished by Israel. In his speech, Arafat outlined the historical reasons for the Palestine problem, attributing it to a "Zionist scheme" to bring Jewish immigrants into the country as part of a wave of colonialism in Africa. Arafat appealed to the Assembly "to aid our people in its struggle to attain its right to self-determination." Concluding his address, the PLO chief said: "I have come bearing an olive branch and a freedom fighter's gun. Do not let the olive branch fall from my hand." On instructions of Assembly President Abdelaziz Bouteflika of Algeria, Arafat was accorded the honor of chief of state, being seated in an armchair, a U.N. status symbol for such dignitaries.

[25] At its Nov. 14 session, the General Assembly voted 75-23 (18 abstentions) to limit each nation to one major speech in the current debate on Palestine. The restriction was believed to be the first of its kind in U.N. history. The decision was opposed by the U.S. and Israel. U.S. Ambassador Scali called it a "deeply disturbing trend." Tekoah denounced it as a move to "muzzle Israel's freedom to speak." The Assembly rules still permitted Israel the right to reply, but Tekoah noted that these responses were customarily limited to 10 minutes and depended on the discretion of the Assembly president. The new ruling affected Israel more than the others since there were 20 potential Arab speakers, while Israel alone spoke for its case in the debate, Tekoah said.

[26] The General Assembly concluded its debate on the Palestine question Nov.

22 by approving two resolutions declaring that the Palestinian people had the right to independence and sovereignty, and granting the PLO observer status in U.N. affairs. The resolution on rights was adopted by an 89-8 vote, with 37 abstentions. The negative ballots were cast by Israel, the U.S., Norway, Iceland, Bolivia, Chile, Costa Rica and Nicaragua. The resolution on PLO status was passed by a 95-17 vote, with 19 abstentions. Most Western European countries joined the U.S., Canada and Israel in voting against the second resolution. France, Japan and some Latin American countries abstained. The resolution on sovereignty affirmed "the inalienable rights of the Palestinians to return to their homes and property from which they have been displaced and uprooted." The resolution did not mention Israel. The delegates of France, Britain and Italy had urged in debate Nov. 20 that any Middle East peace settlement must guarantee Israel's right to exist. The statements represented a common position worked out by the nine countries of the European Economic Community. Their position had first been presented by the West German delegate in the Nov. 19 Assembly session.

[27] **West Bank Arabs support PLO.** Palestinian demonstrations were held Nov. 13 in the Israeli-occupied West Bank in support of Arafat and the PLO to coincide with Arafat's appearance before the General Assembly. In an apparent gesture supporting Arafat's address to the U.N., King Hussein Nov. 13 decreed an amnesty for about 100 political prisoners, most of whom were Palestinian guerrillas and members of Arafat's Al Fatah. Arafat laid claim to Jordan, as well as to the West Bank and all of Israel, according to a letter he had sent to the Jordanian Student Congress in Baghdad, Iraq, it was reported Nov. 11. He was quoted as saying: "Jordan is ours; Palestine is ours, and we shall build our national entity on the whole of this land after having freed it of both the Zionist presence and the reactionary-traitor presence."

Terrorist Activities & Counter-Raids

[28] **Greeks condemn, expel 2 Arabs.** A Greek court in Athens Jan. 24 sentenced Shafik Hussein el Arida, a Palestinian, and Tallal Khaled Kaddourah, a Lebanese, to death for the Aug. 5, 1973 grenade attack at the Athens airport in which five persons died. Each of the Arabs was convicted on five counts of committing a "particularly odious crime" and also received a 27-year prison term for attempted murder and illegal possession and use of arms. The Greek government Feb. 3, however, promised to commute the two death sentences after three Pakistani guerrillas, describing themselves as members of the Moslem International Guerrillas, seized a Greek freighter in Karachi, Pakistan Feb. 2 and threatened to blow up the ship and kill two hostage crewmen unless Greece freed the two convicted commandos. (The hostages were released Feb. 3.) The death sentences were commuted to life imprisonment April 30, and Greek President Phaidon Gizikis later granted the Arabs a full pardon. The two guerrillas were deported from Greece to Libya May 5 at the request of the Libyan government, which pledged that they would be "held answerable for their actions."

[29] **Arabs hijack British plane.** Two armed Arab guerrillas March 3 hijacked a British Airways jetliner shortly after takeoff from Beirut, Lebanon on a scheduled flight from Bombay to London. The hijackers, who allegedly said they were members of the PLO, ordered the pilot to fly to Athens, but Greek authorities refused permission to land; and the plane was then forced to land at Amsterdam's Schiphol airport. After all 92 passengers and 10 crewmen were permitted to leave, the plane was set afire. The two hijackers were arrested, and their action was condemned March 3 by the PLO in Beirut. They were sentenced to five-year prison terms June 6.

[30] **Qiryat Shemona.** Three armed guerrillas, apparently infiltrating from Lebanon, crossed the border April 11 into the Israeli town of Qiryat Shemona, stormed a four-story apartment building, forced their way into apartments and began shooting indiscriminately, killing 18 persons—including eight children and five women. All three infiltrators were killed when explosive-laden knapsacks they were carrying ignited after being hit by Israeli fire, according to Israeli accounts. Sixteen persons, most of them soldiers, were wounded in the attack. The Lebanese-based Marxist PFLP-General Command, a splinter group which April 11 claimed credit for the attack, demanded the release from Israeli prisons of 100 prisoners, including Kozo Okamoto (serving a life sentence for a 1972 attack on Lod airport in Israel). Although Lebanese Premier Takieddin Solh April 11 supported the commandos' claim that the raid was launched from within Israel, Premier Meir insisted that the guerrillas had infiltrated from Lebanon. In retaliation for the attack, Israeli forces April 12 crossed into southern Lebanon and raided the villages of Dahira, Yaroun, Muhebab, Blida, Ett Taibe and Aitarun. According to an Israeli communique, buildings in the towns were blown up after their inhabitants were evacuated; but a Lebanese communique said that the raiders had blown up 24 houses and a power station in Ett Taibe, kidnapped 13 civilians and killed two women while blowing up a house in Muhebab. The Israelis, who did not encounter the Lebanese army in the operation, said "the action was intended to harm villages whose residents had given assistance to terrorists." Following the raid, Beirut April 15 requested the U.N. Security Council to consider the attack. The Council met April 15-16 and 18, and April 24 approved 13-0 (China and Iraq not voting) a resolution condemning Israel for "violation of Lebanon's territorial integrity." The resolution deplored "all acts of violence," but made no mention of the Qiryat Shemona attack. The Council earlier had defeated 7-6 (2 abstentions) a U.S. amendment which would have mentioned the Qiryat Shemona attack.

[31] **Young hostages die in attack.** Twenty-five Israelis, all but four of them teenaged school children, died as a result of an attack by three Palestinian commandos May 15 on the village of Maalot, five miles from the Lebanese border. Israeli military forces retaliated May 16, carrying out damaging air strikes against Palestinian refugee camps and suspected guerrilla bases in southern Lebanon. The Beirut-based Popular Democratic Front for the Liberation of Palestine, ([PDFLP], a breakaway PFLP group), headed by Nayef Hawatmeh, took credit for the attack. The three guerrillas, who were said by Israel to have infiltrated from Lebanon, burst into a high school at Maalot, where about 90 students from other towns on an excursion were sleeping. Israeli troops stormed the building after a breakdown in negotiations with the guerrillas who were seeking the release of 20 commandos imprisoned in Israel in return for the lives of the youths. Sixteen children were killed immediately and five of 70 injured students died later. Israel claimed the children were shot by the guerrillas, all of whom were slain themselves in the exchange of fire with the soldiers. One Israeli soldier was killed. Before taking over the school, the commandos had burst into an apartment in Maalot and killed a family of three. In reprisal for the attack on Maalot, Israeli jets May 16 carried out two separate attacks in southern Lebanon, bombing and strafing Palestinian targets from the foothills of Mount Hermon to the coastal city of Saida. Initial casualty figures reported by Lebanese and Palestinian commando authorities said 21 were killed and 134 wounded. It was the heaviest Israeli air attack ever carried out in Lebanon.

[32] **Raids continue.** In succeeding months, Palestinian terrorists continued their attacks on Israeli settlements. Palestinian guerrillas Nov. 19, infiltrated an

apartment building in the northern Israeli town of Beit Shean, killing four civilians before they were shot dead by an Israeli assault squad. Nineteen others were injured, most of them by leaping from windows to escape the terrorists. Enraged by the attack, a crowd of Israelis seized the bodies of the gunmen and threw them into a bonfire. Israeli authorities said leaflets in the terrorists' possession showed they were PDFLP members and had probably crossed into Israel from Jordan after setting out from Syria. (The PDFLP was the same organization which had attacked Maalot.) PDFLP chief of operations Abou Leila warned the raids would continue until Israel agreed to negotiate with the PLO. There also were numerous other incidents, among them a Dec. 22 grenade attack on a bus carrying Christian pilgrims from the U.S. A 16-year-old U.S. girl had her leg amputated as a result. The Palestinian activities, especially those originating in Lebanon, had caused the Israeli government June 20 to announce that its airstrikes and other actions against Lebanese towns represented a new policy of pre-emptive attacks against the commandos. Their purpose was to disrupt the guerrilla forces by striking at their headquarters and to pressure the Lebanese government to curb the commando activities. The new pre-emptive policy resulted in a continuing series of attacks on Lebanon, including: raids on the ports of Tyre, Saida and Ras a-Shak, July 8; an attack by Israeli troops on Bustan, July 18; bombings of Khreibe and Rachaya el Fakkhar, Aug. 7 and 9 and numerous other jet attacks and ground clashes with guerrillas throughout the rest of the year. On Dec. 10 PLO offices in Beirut were blasted by rockets fired from the roofs of parked automobiles. Several hand grenades were thrown into a crowded Tel Aviv movie house in retaliation. (There was some speculation that the Beirut attack may have been carried out by Palestinian dissidents opposed to the PLO.) In apparent retaliation, Israeli planes Dec. 12 carried out a heavy raid against what Israeli officials described as PLO military installations near Beirut, although Lebanese authorities said the planes had hit refugee camps.

[33] **Arabs offer Lebanon aid.** Israeli Defense Minister Peres had urged Lebanon June 21 to "take constructive steps toward sealing her frontier with Israel against the passage of terrorists setting out to commit murderous acts." Lebanese Premier Solh had said his country had no intention of curbing the Palestinians and that Israeli attempts to divide the Lebanese and the Palestinians were bound to fail. Offers of help to the Lebanese were forthcoming from the PLO, Libya, Syria, Egypt and Jordan. Israel's chief of staff, Lt. Gen. Mordechai Gur, warned Lebanon June 27 not to accept outside Arab military assistance if it wanted to avoid becoming a new area of combat. The PLO was reported to have informed Solh June 30 that its forces would stop using Lebanon as a base for attacks against Israel to spare the country retaliatory Israeli raids. Egypt and Syria were said by Palestinian sources July 1 to have pressured the guerrillas to halt their forays across the border in a move to preserve the cease-fire with Israel. The Arab League defense council was reported to have agreed at a meeting in Cairo July 3-4 to provide Lebanon and the PLO in that country with financial assistance to strengthen their defenses against Israeli air and ground attacks. The conferees also were said to have agreed to pressure the U.S. to restrain Israel from attacking Lebanon and the Palestinian refugee camps there.

[34] **Hijacking.** Four Palestinian terrorists hijacked a British Airways passenger jet in Dubai Nov. 22; forced it to fly to Tunis after a refueling stop in Tripoli, Libya; killed one hostage Nov. 23 and finally surrendered Nov. 25. They voluntarily turned themselves over to the PLO for trial, Tunisian authorities reported Dec. 7. (The PLO had arrested 26 persons in Beirut and in other Arab countries for their alleged involvement in the incident. Arafat was said to have ordered his group to prevent any dissident Palestinian units from carrying out acts of terrorism in foreign

countries. He wanted the organization to concentrate its physical assaults solely against Israel.) The hijackers, reportedly angered at what they considered trickery by the Tunisians, on Nov. 23 had shot and killed a West German hostage in public view from behind the open doorway of the jet. The hijackers were demanding the freedom of 13 other Palestinian guerrillas imprisoned in Cairo, plus two others held by the Netherlands. The Dutch prisoners plus five held by the Egyptians were released, were rearrested again on the hijackers' surrender Nov. 25, and were finally placed under PLO custody—along with the hijackers—on Dec. 7.

[35] **West Bank developments.** Arabs staged violent demonstrations in West Bank towns Nov. 16-19 in an intensified campaign of opposition to the Israeli occupation and in support of the PLO. The unrest spread to East Jerusalem for the first time. Thousands of Arab students rioted Nov. 16 in Jenin, Nablus, Halhul and Hebron, hurling stones at Israeli policemen. A 16-year-old girl was killed in Jenin. Scores were injured and at least 50 were arrested in the three towns. Police arrested 33 persons during rioting in Hebron and Jenin Nov. 17 and closed schools in the towns indefinitely. Hundreds of youths had built roadblocks at Jenin and hurled stones at passing vehicles. Israeli authorities Nov. 21 deported five prominent Palestinian activists from the West Bank to Lebanon on charges of inciting the recent demonstrations in the area and of being members of "hostile organizations." The Israelis also imposed economic sanctions on Ramallah, cutting its trade with Jordan, where most of its produce was sold. The action was taken in reprisal for a pro-PLO general strike called by the town's merchants. Travel between Ramallah and Jordan also was banned. Israeli Information Minister Yariv announced Nov. 23 that his government was willing to consider a plan to grant the West Bank's 700,000 Arabs local autonomy in gradual steps. Eventually this plan could lead to a federated status under which relations between the West Bank and Israel and Jordan could finally be worked out. He reiterated his government's refusal to deal with the PLO.

[36] **Israelis sentence Capucci.** A Jerusalem district court Dec. 9 sentenced the Most Rev. Hilarion Capucci, archbishop of the Greek Catholic Church of East Jerusalem, to 12 years in prison after convicting him on three counts of smuggling arms into the West Bank for Palestinian guerrillas and making contacts with foreign agents. Capucci had been arrested at his home in Jerusalem Aug. 18 as he was about to leave for a religious conference in Beirut. Police disclosed he had been under surveillance since 1973. They said he had first been detained and then released Aug. 8 after being intercepted by police as he was about to leave for Nazareth, in northern Israel. A search of his car turned up large quantities of weapons and dynamite. It was thought he had brought back the weapons after a visit to Lebanon. According to Israeli officials, Capucci had told his interrogators that he had been forced into Al Fatah service through blackmail, it was reported Aug. 23. The Archbishop was said to have claimed that Al Fatah officials in Lebanon had threatened him with physical violence and with disclosure of actions that might jeopardize his position in the church. During the trial, which had started Sept. 20, the prosecution charged that Capucci had met frequently with Al Fatah leaders in Beirut and had used his car to transport weapons on trips between Lebanon and Israel. Capucci's conviction was denounced by Syria, Lebanon and the PLO which said it would try to rescue the prelate. The Vatican Dec. 10 expressed "pain and grief," saying that sentencing would only aggravate the situation in the Middle East.

U.S. Actions

[37] **Kissinger negotiates moves.** The U.S. and Egypt announced Feb. 28 the immediate resumption of full-scale diplomatic relations severed in 1967. The

announcement was made in Cairo and Washington after President Sadat had met that day with U.S. Secretary of State Kissinger.

[38] **Nixon tours Mideast.** President Nixon visited five Middle East nations June 12-18. On the first stop of the tour Nixon signed an accord with Egyptian President Sadat June 14 in which the U.S. agreed to provide Egypt with nuclear technology for peaceful purposes under agreed safeguards. The agreement was part of a wide-ranging declaration of friendship and political and economic cooperation signed by the two leaders at the conclusion of Nixon's three-day visit to Egypt. White House Press Secretary Ronald Ziegler said the agreement would not enable Egypt to develop military nuclear capability. The U.S. had similar cooperative atomic agreements with about 35 countries, including Israel. The other three sections of the joint statement outlined general principles of bilateral relations, stressing cooperation to attain a peaceful resolution of the Arab-Israeli dispute, and established a Joint Cooperation Commission and working groups to implement the commission's objectives in the economic, scientific and cultural fields. Nixon concluded his trip to the Middle East with visits to Saudi Arabia, Syria, Israel and Jordan June 14-18. The remainder of the President's visit to the region was highlighted by a joint announcement in Damascus June 16 by Nixon and President Assad of resumption of U.S.-Syrian diplomatic relations, and by Nixon's pledge in Jerusalem June 17 of long-term military and economic aid to Israel and the promise to that country of nuclear technology for peaceful purposes, similar to that made to Egypt earlier during the trip.

[39] **U.S. to aid Israeli air force.** Nixon Administration officials disclosed June 29 that they had advised Israel that the U.S. would provide it with a new generation of fighter-bombers if necessary to help modernize its air force. The assurances had been conveyed to Israeli Defense Minister Peres during talks in Washington June 24-26 with Secretary of State Kissinger and Defense Secretary James R. Schlesinger. The Israelis were said to be seeking $1.5 billion annually in U.S. military aid over a five-year period, much of it in grants because of Israel's heavy indebtedness. President Nixon June 29 waived repayment of $500 million in credits to Israel for replacing military equipment after the October 1973 war.

[40] **U.S. holds pre-Geneva talks.** U.S. officials in Washington opened an intensive month of negotiations with Israeli and Arab leaders to seek a formula for further progress toward a Middle East settlement as a forerunner to resumption of the Geneva peace talks. Israeli Foreign Minister Yigal Allon met Aug. 1 with Kissinger, Schlesinger and Vice President Ford. Allon informed Kissinger that Israel was prepared to negotiate with either Jordan or Egypt in the next stage of peace discussions. President Ford and Kissinger held meetings in Washington Aug. 12-18 with Egyptian Foreign Minister Fahmy and King Hussein. Fahmy arrived in Washington Aug. 11. After a week of talks with Ford and Kissinger, Fahmy and the secretary signed a joint communique Aug. 19 that said the two sides "agreed that the Geneva peace conference on the Middle East should resume its work as soon as possible . . . with the question of other participants from the Middle East area to be discussed at the conference." This meant that the role of the Palestinians would not be taken up beforehand. King Hussein's meeting Aug. 16-18 with Ford, Kissinger and Schlesinger concentrated on Jordan's demand for disengagement of Israeli and Jordanian troops along the Jordan River as the next stage in Middle East peace moves. A joint statement issued by Ford and Hussein Aug. 18 announced agreement to work for such an accord. The king warned Aug. 17 that his government would boycott the resumption of the Geneva peace conference unless Israel withdrew from at least

part of the West Bank or if the PLO was given "the responsibility at the outset to negotiate for the return of lost territories." Israeli Premier Rabin conferred in Washington Sept. 10-13 with Ford, Kissinger and Schlesinger. The U.S. officials sought to obtain from Rabin a strong commitment to continue negotiations toward a Middle East peace settlement and to determine whether those talks should be between Israel and Egypt, or Israel and Jordan. At the conclusion of the discussions, Rabin suggested that the U.S. and Israel were concentrating on new talks between Egypt and Israel as a fruitful follow-up to the troop separation accords that Israel had reached with Egypt and Syria. In exchange for relinquishing Egyptian territory in the Sinai, Israel wanted a state of "non-belligerency" with Cairo, the premier said. Appearing on NBC-TV's "Meet the Press" Sept. 15, Rabin explained this to mean an end to all Egyptian military, diplomatic and economic action against Israel.

[41] **Kissinger resumes peace mission.** Kissinger visited seven major capitals of the Middle East Oct. 9-15 in an effort to create a framework for resumption of Arab-Israeli peace negotiations and to discuss high petroleum prices with oil-producers of the region. The secretary's first stop was Cairo, where he conferred Oct. 9-10 with President Sadat. Egyptian sources reported Oct. 12 that Sadat had informed Kissinger that Egypt would refuse to grant any political concessions in exchange for a new partial Israeli withdrawal from the Sinai. Any agreement on additional Israeli pullbacks would be an extension of the January military disengagement agreements and not an interim political accord, as the Israelis reportedly have suggested, according to the sources. Kissinger held meetings in Damascus Oct. 11 with Syrian President Assad and Foreign Minister Khaddam. The secretary then flew to Jordan and conferred with King Hussein in Amman later Oct. 11 and in Aqaba Oct. 12. The Secretary arrived in Israel Oct. 12. Before leaving the next day, Kissinger announced he had reached agreement with Israeli leaders on "the principles and procedures" that might be followed in the next round of Arab-Israeli talks. Correspondents aboard Kissinger's jet were later told that the principles would essentially provide that any agreement between Israel and Egypt and Israel and Jordan would have to include further Israeli territorial concessions in exchange for Arab moves that would improve Israel's security. Kissinger returned to Cairo and Damascus Oct. 14 to inform Presidents Sadat and Assad of his discussions with the Israelis and the Jordanians. Kissinger revisited five Middle East capitals Nov. 5-7. Kissinger conferred with President Sadat in Cairo Nov. 5-6 and received the Egyptian leader's endorsement for a "second stage" of discussions with Israel on the further withdrawal of its forces from the Sinai Peninsula despite the recent Arab summit conference's backing of the PLO. Sadat was said to have told Kissinger that Egypt could not meet Israel's request for a statement of nonbelligerency in exchange for relinquishment of more Sinai territory because that would seem too much like a peace accord. Cairo would not agree to such a pact until Israel withdrew from all Arab territories, Sadat said. Kissinger received similar backing for his peace efforts from King Faisal at a meeting with the Saudi Arabian monarch in Riyadh later Nov. 6. The secretary flew to Amman Nov. 7 and met with Hussein, who reportedly informed him that the Arab summit decision giving the PLO sole authority over any part of the West Bank given up by Israel left his country with no political role in negotiations over the territory. Syrian President Assad was said to have informed Kissinger at their meeting Nov. 7 that the Rabat talks gave the Palestine problem first priority in steps toward peace. Kissinger replied that giving PLO authority over West Bank territories in effect ruled out Arab recovery of the area because of Israel's refusal to deal with the guerrilla organization. On arriving in Tel Aviv later Nov. 7 for the start of a two-day visit,

Kissinger assured the Israelis in an airport statement that "since I have been here last, there has been no change in American policy on any of the issues before us."

[42] **Arabs report U.S.-Soviet plan.** Arab diplomatic sources in Beirut reported Nov. 28 that Ford and Soviet Communist Party General Secretary Leonid Brezhnev had reached an agreement in the Vladivostok summit meeting Nov. 23-24 on a formula to break the Middle East diplomatic impasse. Israel expressed doubt Nov. 29 that such a plan had been broached, and the U.S. government issued a denial. Under the reported plan, the Soviet Union would attempt to persuade Arafat to recognize the right of Israel to exist as an independent state, while the U.S. would try to convince Israel to drop its refusal to negotiate with the PLO.

[43] **U.S.-Israeli talks.** Israeli Foreign Minister Allon conferred in Washington Dec. 9 with Ford and Kissinger to review the possible next step in Middle East peace negotiations, including a second round of Israeli-Egyptian talks on further disengagement of Israeli troops from the Sinai Peninsula. A spokesman who had participated in the discussions said Allon and Kissinger had drawn up general principles that would be conveyed by the U.S. to Egypt and other Arab countries. Allon said the talks did not center on a possible pact with Egypt alone "but with the entire Middle East because each one of the countries there are candidates for political progress." Addressing newsmen in Washington Dec. 11, Allon reiterated his government's refusal to conduct negotiations with the PLO.

Soviet Actions

[44] **Egypt to end reliance on Soviet arms.** President Sadat announced April 18 that Egypt would no longer depend on the Soviet Union as its main supplier of arms and that it would seek the military equipment from other countries. The Soviet Union had become Egypt's sole provider of weapons in 1955 when the late President Gamal Abdel Nasser negotiated a deal for arms that were first delivered through Czechoslovakia. Addressing a joint session of the People's Assembly and the Arab Socialist Union, Sadat said he had made the decision after Soviet Communist Party Chairman Brezhnev had ignored four of his requests in the past six months for arms delivery. Sadat also said Egypt intended to retain its policy of nonalignment and "positive neutrality." He praised the U.S. for its peace efforts in the Middle East, but said Cairo "does not want to be friendly with the United States at the Soviet Union's expense or vice versa." Sadat said April 21 that Egypt had decided to end its exclusive reliance on the Soviet Union for arms because Moscow had been using the supply of its equipment as an "instrument of policy leverage to influence Cairo's actions."

[45] **U.S.S.R. backs Palestinians.** The Soviet Union expressed support Oct. 18 for the creation of a Palestinian state as a condition for a Middle East peace settlement and for the seating of the PLO as a full participant at any Geneva peace conference. The statement was contained in a joint communique issued after Egyptian Foreign Minister Fahmy's visit to Moscow Oct. 14-18.

[46] **Brezhnev cancels Middle East visit.** Brezhnev indefinitely called off a scheduled visit to Egypt, Syria and Iraq, it was announced in Moscow Dec. 30. No official reason was given, but speculation ranged from Brezhnev's ill health to serious diplomatic differences between Moscow and Cairo over a common approach to resolving the Middle East problem. The announcement was made by the Soviet press agency Tass at the end of a three-day visit to Moscow by Egyptian Foreign Minister Fahmy and Gen. Mohammad Abdel Ghany el-Gamasy, war minister.

See also AFRICA; ALGERIA; ATOMIC ENERGY [11-12]; AVIATION [14]; BULGARIA;

MILLS, REP. WILBUR D.—U.S. Park Service police in Washington stopped a car at 2 a.m. Oct. 7 for speeding without lights on. One of its five occupants was Rep. Wilbur D. Mills (D, Ark.), 65, chairman of the House Ways and Means Committee, who was bleeding from facial scratches and, like the other occupants, according to the police, "appeared to have been drinking." Another passenger was identified as Annabel Battistella, 38, a stripper known as Fanne Foxe, who leaped into the nearby tidal basin. Police rescued her and drove the group home.

Mills denied participating until park police identified him as being at the scene. Then, Oct. 10, he explained his wife had remained home because of a broken foot during a party for Gloria Sanchez, one of the car's occupants, a visiting Argentine cousin of the Battistellas, who were friends of the Mills. Mr. Battistella was not one of the car's occupants. Mills said his face was cut when his glasses broke as he tried to stop Mrs. Battistella, who had become ill during the evening, from jumping out of the car. Despite meetings of his committee, Mills remained secluded until Oct. 16, when he returned with Mrs. Mills to Little Rock to campaign against Judy Petty (R), 31, his first general election opposition in his 36-year House career. (Mills was returned to his seat.)

After the election, while the Democrats deliberated the distribution of power in the House, the chairman of its Ways and Means Committee was re-establishing a liaison with Foxe, now billed as the "Tidal Basin Bombshell." Mills appeared on stage with her before her act at the Pilgrim Theater in Boston Nov. 30. As the House Democratic Caucus assembled Dec. 2, Speaker Albert was quoted as saying, "I feel sorry for Mr. Mills." There were reports that Mills had been told by colleagues that he could no longer serve as chairman of Ways and Means. Mills entered the Bethesda (Md.) Naval Medical Center Dec. 3 without public explanation. He was reported under heavy sedation and undergoing tests. A reporter asked Albert Dec. 4 whether Mills would no longer be Ways and Means chairman. "I think that is an accurate statement," Albert replied.

Mills informed Albert Dec. 10 that he was stepping down as chairman of the Committee, a position he had held since 1958. According to Rep. Joe D. Waggonner Jr. (D, La.), Mills had told him he was "bone tired" and "worn out" and "in no condition to continue as chairman."

Mills declared Dec. 30 he was an alcoholic, pledged "total abstinence" and affirmed his intention to remain in Congress. In a statement issued from his office, Mills said his stay in the hospital made him realize he had developed "a severe drinking problem" in recent years. He said he had been "a sick man" and even suffered "blackouts from time to time—periods during which I have had no knowledge of what I was doing." Mills apologized for any embarrassment he caused his family, constituents or colleagues.

Foxe pleaded not guilty to charges of indecent exposure in a Florida nightclub, it was reported Dec. 21. She announced she was quitting the striptease business Dec. 13.

See also CAMPAIGN FINANCING [17]; CONGRESS; MEDICINE & HEALTH [1, 7, 9-10]

MINIMUM WAGE—*See* LABOR [1-2]
MINING—*See* LABOR [10-13]; MAURITANIA; TERRITORIAL WATERS
MISSILES—*See* DEFENSE [1, 13]; DISARMAMENT
MITCHELL, JOHN N.—*See* CAMPAIGN FINANCING [8-10, 15-16]; CRIME [3]; PRIVACY [2]; TELEVISION & RADIO; WATERGATE [21, 62-63, 74-76, 87-103]
MODEL CITIES PROGRAM—*See* HOUSING
MONACO—*See* AUTO RACING; EUROPEAN SECURITY

MONETARY DEVELOPMENTS, INTERNATIONAL—An already-shaky international monetary situation was dealt several severe blows in 1974 by the drastic increases in the price of Middle East oil and the resulting accumulation of petrodollars by the oil-producing nations. [See also OIL, ENERGY]

[2] **IMF meets as crisis deepens.** Representatives of the International Monetary Fund's (IMF) member nations met in Rome Jan. 14-18 to discuss the planned overhaul of the world's currency system. But the question of reform was quickly overshadowed by the sudden disruption in the patterns of trade and currency circulation caused by oil price rises that drove the price of gold to record levels and the British pound to new lows. Large deficits in balance of current accounts faced all of the world's oil-importing nations, rich and poor alike. At the conclusion of the conference, a communique was issued stressing "the importance of avoiding competitive depreciation and the escalation of restrictions on trade and payments." During the conference, IMF Managing Director Johannes Witteveen proposed that the IMF borrow money directly from the oil-producing nations to meet the needs of any nation facing an unmanageable payments deficit. (According to estimates prepared by the Organization of Economic Cooperation and Development [OECD], developing countries would be required to spend $10 billion more in 1974 over 1973 to pay for their oil supplies. This was a figure equivalent to the annual aid provided them by richer nations. Arab spokesmen at the meeting expressed guarded approval for Witteveen's plan and the final communique urged that this proposal be explored. At the meeting's end, however, nations which had been divided on the issue of a systematic overhaul of monetary arrangements, also appeared to be in basic conflict over a strategy for dealing with rising oil prices and the payments crisis.

[3] The attempt to reform the monetary system hinged upon efforts to make the IMF's unit of currency, Special Drawing Rights (SDRs)—or paper gold—the basis for all international transactions, replacing gold and the dollar (the current reserve currency). A step in the direction of increased use of SDRs was taken by the IMF with the Jan. 23 announcement that the Bank for International Settlements (BIS) had been permitted to hold SDRs, the first institution permitted to do so. The new arrangement called for IMF member countries to obtain currency from the BIS with the assurance that the BIS would use the same amount of SDRs to obtain currency from the participant. To insure an active exchange of payments, the transactions would be required to occur within a six-month period.

[4] **IMF sets reform goals.** The IMF's Committee of 20 adopted interim rules dealing with reform of the international monetary system and postponed for "some time" efforts to devise a permanent solution to the currency crisis. Agreement on the interim guidelines was reached at the group's sixth and final

meeting, held June 12-13 in Washington. An "outline of reform" describing long-range plans for modernizing the monetary system was published June 14. Final agreement on a permanent framework of reform promoting financial harmony and stability had eluded the committee and its deputies since their work, subject to a two-year deadline, had begun in September 1972. "Economic vicissitudes have dictated changes in objectives, approach and timing," IMF officials explained. Instead of designing a thoroughly revised monetary structure, they resigned themselves to drawing up a plan that featured the "managed float"—a device that had been adopted on a temporary basis in early 1973 to deal with recurrent instability in exchange rates. One of the measures adopted would set a new value for SDRs. Effective July 1, the value of one SDR would be based on a "basket" of the currencies of the U.S. (33%), West Germany (12.5%), Great Britain (9%), France (7.5%), Japan (7.5%), Canada (6%), Italy (6%), the Netherlands (4.5%), Belgium (3.5%), Sweden (2.5%), Australia (1.5%), Spain (1.5%), Norway (1.5%), Denmark (1.5%), Austria (1%), and South Africa (1%). According to the IMF, "The currencies included in the SDR basket are those of the 16 countries that had a share in world exports of goods and services in excess of 1% on average over the 5-year period 1968-72. The relative weights for these currencies were set broadly proportionate to the share of these countries in international transactions, using as proxy for this purpose average exports of goods and services in the period 1968-72 but modified, particularly with respect to the United States, in recognition that the proxy does not necessarily provide an adequate measure of a currency's real weight in the world economy in all cases. Accordingly, the U.S. dollar was assigned the weight of 33% of the basket. The IMF will collect exchange rates of the basket currencies daily in order to calculate a daily rate of the SDR in terms of each of the 16 currencies."

[5] Decisions also were made setting a higher interest rate on the SDR and new rates of remuneration and charges in the IMF's general account. Another interim proposal called for establishment of a temporary "oil facility" providing loans to member nations hard hit by increased fuel costs. According to the IMF, 3 billion units of SDRs already had been pledged by Abu Dhabi, Canada, Iran, Kuwait, Libya, Oman, Saudi Arabia, and Venezuela. The money would be available for four-seven year terms at about 7% annual interest. (The "oil facility" was established Aug. 22. Seven oil producing nations agreed to lend the IMF $3.4 billion until Dec. 31, 1975.)

[6] The committee also published an "outline of reform" describing the general form a permanently reformed monetary system would take. Highlights of the long-term reform proposals: the central feature of the new system would be a "stable but adjustable" currency exchange rate system: most countries would maintain fixed "par values" and intervene frequently to maintain those rates within an agreed upon margin on either side of the value to correct balance of payments deficits and surpluses. Countries in financial troubles could seek IMF approval to make major adjustments by instituting floating exchange rates. "Objective indicators" would be used to warn governments when to make adjustments in its exchange rates. No agreement was reached on the question of "automatic" adjustments, under which nations would be compelled to institute changes. The question of sanctions and degrees of pressure that could be used by the IMF against member nations refusing to make adjustments also remained a matter of dispute. "Convertibility" would be restored to the new monetary system, allowing nations to turn in their dollar holdings for "primary" reserve assets, such as gold or SDRs. SDRs would replace gold or the dollar as the main reserve asset and also would serve as the "numeraire" or standard of value in which currency values were expressed. Although it was agreed that gold would

have a reduced role in the new system, its ultimate place in an overhauled monetary structure was not resolved. Disagreement also was expressed on the means required to control the growth of total world reserves or "liquidity."

[7] **IMF, World Bank discuss oil-money crisis.** The IMF and the World Bank held their annual joint meeting in Washington Sept. 30-Oct. 4. A number of proposals were debated dealing with the need to "recycle" the vast amount of money earned by oil exporting countries and the huge sums paid for oil by importing countries, but no conclusive agreements were reached. The new IMF Ministerial Council, which replaced the Committee of 20, met Oct. 3 and called on Witteveen to draw up proposals on recycling, enlargement of IMF member quotas, the role for gold in a new monetary system, and the desirability of a link between the distribution of SDRs issued by the IMF and assistance provided to developing countries. The latter two questions had dominated the 1973 annual meeting in Nairobi and were not resolved during a year of conferences.

[8] Participants at the conference were divided over the need for, among other things, a proposed expansion in the credit program. U.S. Treasury Undersecretary Jack F. Bennett said that worldwide economic distortions caused by higher oil prices could be alleviated by a reduction in price. The U.S. also was opposed to a new recycling mechanism, Bennett said, preferring to deal with the problems of massive transfers of funds by relying on Eurocurrency markets and an increase in investment by oil exporting countries through non-banking channels. West German Finance Minister Hans Apel tended to support the U.S. position, but he also called for "the creation of a specialized investment institution operated jointly by the oil-producing and oil-consuming nations" as an additional means of redistributing the new oil revenues. The need for an expanded recycling program was supported by Witteveen who said Oct. 4 that "it would be neither realistic nor prudent to expect the private short-term money markets—principally the Eurodollar market—to continue playing as large a role in the recycling process as they have in the past." This view was supported by most of the conference participants, including Great Britain, France and the developing nations. (The strain on the Eurodollar had been revealed in an Aug. 19 announcement by the World Bank which cited figures showing that governments and other borrowers had floated loans on the Eurodollar market for $19.7 billion during the first six months of 1974. This was only slightly less than the $22 billion borrowed during all of 1973. Interest rates also rose sharply during the first half to 13.38% for six-month deposits as of June. According to the bank, demand "remained strong" partially because of the "greater need of a number of countries for external finance arising in part from higher oil costs." Of the total publicized loans, 66% went to industrialized nations [compared with 51% in 1973], 30% to developing countries [41% in 1973] and 3% to other borrowers.)

[9] World Bank President Robert S. McNamara told the conference Sept. 30 that the poorest nations "are the principal victims" of worldwide inflation. Large increases in aid from developed nations were required to prevent a worsening of their plight, he said. McNamara said he had recommended that total World Bank lending over a five-year period be increased from $16 billion to $36 billion—a 125% absolute rise in credit commitments that actually represented only a 40% increase because of the effects of inflation. (McNamara did not mention that his proposal had been rejected by the World Bank directors, who approved only a one-year commitment of funds.)

[10] **Currency and gold fluctuations.** The dollar registered sharp gains on the European exchange markets in January as a result—according to most analysts—of the widespread belief that the U.S. would be the country least affected by increases in Middle Eastern oil prices and disruptions in fuel

supplies. Another factor was the Jan. 7 decision of the Bank of Japan to suspend its intervention in support of the yen rate of 280 to the dollar. The result was an immediate de facto devaluation of 6.7% as the yen went to 299. In Europe, the heaviest pressure was felt by the British pound and the West German mark. In London, Jan. 16, the pound closed at $2.1760.

[11] In a move that reflected France's "go it alone" policies and the IMF's inability to allay deepening financial fears, Finance Minister Valery Giscard d'Estaing announced Jan. 19 that the French government would undertake a de facto devaluation of the franc (estimated at 4%-5%) by allowing it to float for six months. Giscard d'Estaing conceded that the government's action presented one major "drawback." "It means a temporary halt in the progress of the European economic and monetary union," he said. The five remaining European Economic Community nations that had beeen participating in a joint float announced Jan. 21 that they were determined to "maintain the existing margins" between the West German, Dutch, Belgian, Luxembourg, and Danish currencies. The group also announced extended plans to facilitate a coordinated monetary policy. (Norway and Sweden also indicated a desire to remain associated with the joint float.) On the first day of the float, the financial franc lost 4% against the dollar, closing at 5.35 francs. (The Bank of France intervened to prevent a drastic drop in the franc's value by selling $150 million in currency reserves.) The dollar was strong against most currencies (closing at 2.84 West German marks). The pound closed at $2.173 after falling 1.45¢. Gold closed at $142 an ounce in Zurich and $152.16 in Paris. Massive intervention by the governments of Japan and France was required Jan. 23 to check their currencies' drop against the dollar. The Bank of Japan was reported to have spent at least $650 million to maintain the rate of 300 yen to the dollar. But an end to the U.S. credit curbs caused the dollar to take a tailspin against most currencies Feb. 4, trading off at 2.748 marks, and 4.9963 commercial francs. Gold dropped to $133.50 an ounce on the London bullion market. In the only exception to its decline, the dollar gained against the pound, trading at $2.2653.

[12] In three actions designed to eliminate controls on the flow of dollars abroad, President Nixon Jan. 29 had ended the interest equalization tax on the purchase of foreign securities by U.S. citizens by reducing the tax rate to zero; the Commerce Department lifted restraints on direct investments abroad by U.S. companies; and the Federal Reserve Board removed limits on lending and investment abroad by U.S. banks and financial institutions. According to the Treasury Department, the Administration abolished the barriers to credit outflow, which had been in effect since the mid-1960s, because of "the recent improvements in the U.S. balance of payments position [and] the strong position of the dollar in the exchange market," as well as a desire to lessen the burden of other nations imperiled by large payments deficits.

[13] At the beginning of the year, the flight from European currencies was felt on the gold market: the price in London closed at $122.25 Jan. 7 and $124 Jan. 9. It gained dramatically through the month, closing at $136.58 on the Paris bullion market Jan. 18, the highest price ever recorded. The price continued to climb in February, in a burst of speculative trading reflecting investors' fears that worldwide inflation and uncertainties about monetary reform would persist. The oil crisis was also a factor in the heavy trading. Middle East states were believed to be using their massive foreign currency reserves accumulated from quadrupled oil prices to invest in metals and other basic commodities. By mid-February the price of gold stood at $149-$152 an ounce.

[14] The dollar exhibited unusual weakness over the March-June period. The wave of selling reflected a general fear that inflation would further undermine

paper currencies; as well as specific U.S. difficulties, such as high interest rates, shrinking trade and payments surpluses, the continued outflow of dollars from U.S. banks and Nixon's political troubles. The dollar closed at 2.645 West German marks March 13 and continued to drop during the rest of the month. On March 19, the dollar traded at 280.9 yen in Tokyo. On March 21, following a French decision to abandon its two-tiered exchange system, the dollar closed at 4.7975 French francs. The dollar moved lower during April. On April 2, the dollar was worth 4.7775 French francs, 2.532 marks and 274.25 yen. The dollar's slide continued during May, hitting values of 627.67 lira May 6; 2.3925 marks and 4.7825 French francs May 13; but rallying slightly May 30 to levels of 2.54 marks and 280.83 yen. The U.S. Federal Reserve System revealed June 5 that the government had intervened actively in support of the dollar from February to April. An estimated $4.27 million in foreign currencies (mostly borrowed West German marks) was sold.

[15] Austria announced a de facto revaluation of the schilling May 16 when the government withdrew as an unofficial participant in the five-member joint float. Although other participants in the float reaffirmed the partnership, West Germany was forced to intervene May 17 in support of the Danish, Swedish and Norwegian currencies to offset any consequent instability. (The dollar traded at 17.65 schillings May 17.)

[16] Trading in gold was active on major European markets from March to June. Gold traded at a record high of $179.50 an ounce on the London bullion market April 3 following the death of French President Georges Pompidou. In Paris, where gold prices were ordinarily higher than elsewhere, the political uncertainty caused the price to soar to $197 an ounce April 3. The record London price exceeded the previous high of $175 an ounce set Feb. 26. Rumors that the official price of gold would be advanced beyond the current level of $42.22 an ounce also sparked trading in the metal. Gold prices sagged, however, during most of the next two months, declining to $154 an ounce in London and $158.41 in Paris May 28. The price rose abruptly May 30 in London to $162 an ounce on news that the U.S. Senate had approved a bill allowing private U.S. citizens to own gold. There were wide fluctuations in the price of gold June 5 when rumors of a realignment of the West German mark and the French franc boosted London gold prices from an opening $154.50 to $165 at the close.

[17] Several compromises appeared to be developing around the question of gold's role in a reformed monetary structure. An informal, but significant, agreement was reached in Washington June 11 by finance ministers representing the Group of 10 nations—the U.S., Great Britain, West Germany, Japan, Canada, Belgium, the Netherlands, Italy, Sweden and France. It was agreed that nations could use their gold reserves as collateral in arranging international loans and that the lender would set the value of the security. Should the borrower default, it was expected that payment in gold would be at a price near the market level. This meant, in effect, that nations would be able to sell gold at prices nearer the market quotes and far above the current official price of $42.22 an ounce. The action promised an informal increase in the value of gold and provided a temporary solution to the oil price crisis without formally raising the official price of gold and enhancing its long-term value as a fundamental reserve. The Group of 10 agreement, which was announced June 12 by the U.S. Treasury Department, was regarded as an important compromise by the U.S., which adamantly opposed the use of gold as the principal reserve asset, and by European nations, which sought to use their large gold reserves in meeting their current balance of payments problems. The compromise was precipitated by Italy's urgent need to secure large loans to meet its vast trade bills. Other

nations, such as France and Japan also were straining to overcome payments deficits and desirous of using their ready reserves.

[18] Gold prices hit a six-month low July 4, closing at $129 an ounce in London, a result, observers said, of world economic uncertainties and speculative purchases of gold on margin. Prices jumped to $158 an ounce July 29 when impeachment articles against President Nixon were voted by the Judiciary Committee of the U.S. House of Representatives. The Aug. 1 London price of $159.40 reflected investor fears that the U.S. was entering a period of political instability.

[19] Events in Washington continued to exert a strong influence on the position of the U.S. dollar in foreign markets. The dollar gained on nearly all markets Aug. 7 in the wake of President Nixon's release of key tape transcripts and reports that he was being pressured to resign by members of his party. In Frankfurt, Aug. 8, the dollar reached its highest level since March, closing at 2.5998 marks. These advances flowed Aug. 9, the day of President Nixon's resignation, as the dollar traded at 2.6 marks in Frankfurt, 4.765 francs in Paris and 2.9745 Swiss francs in Zurich. The dollar also moved higher in Tokyo. There followed a brief drop in the dollar's value reflecting what some observers believed was uncertainty over the direction of President Ford's policies. The dollar rebounded, however, Aug. 12 and 13 as investors were reassured by Ford's stated determination to curb runaway inflation and his firm moves to reassure world leaders that basic U.S. foreign policy would remain unchanged and that Secretary of State Henry Kissinger would remain at his post. The dollar hit a five-month high of 2.6175 marks in Frankfurt and also registered strong gains in Paris and London.

[20] President Ford signed legislation Aug. 14 ending a 40-year ban on the sale and purchase of gold by private citizens. The bill had been cleared by the House July 31 after it accepted a Senate amendment providing that no existing law could conflict with the new measure. The ban on private ownership would be lifted Dec. 31, or earlier if authorized by President Ford.

[21] The price of gold, which had been stable during August and September, advanced steadily through October and early November, reaching an all-time high of $190.50 an ounce in London Nov. 18 as speculators increased their holdings in the metal. Demand for gold was expected to be heavy in the U.S., where the stock market was in a pervasive decline and investors were seeking a safe, high yielding return on their purchases. A combination of other factors also contributed to the gold price rise: interest rates had been reduced in the U.S. and elsewhere, making currency less attractive to investors; there was continued uncertainty about currency fluctuations because of widespread economic problems and the disruptive effects of petrodollars on international markets; political unrest in the Mideast stirred new fears of war; and the dollar exhibited a general weakness.

[22] As the price of gold hit new highs Nov. 18, the dollar moved downward. The drop was in response to the West German government's statement that it would not oppose an upward revaluation of the mark as a means of reducing the country's large balance of payments surplus. According to other analysts, the dollar's weakness also was related to tensions in the Middle East as oil producing nations diversified their currency holdings. There was fear that the U.S. might freeze Arab funds in the event of hostilities, analysts said. Central bankers met in Basel Nov. 11 and agreed that the central banks of West Germany, Switzerland and the U.S. would intervene if necessary to support the dollar. Although there was some central bank intervention in foreign exchange

markets during the next week, the dollar's downward trend was not reversed until Nov. 20 when Switzerland imposed a 12% annual tax on new foreign deposits in an effort to stem the flow of petrodollars. The value of the Swiss franc had gained so much strength in recent weeks because of these investments that the government feared its trade and tourist policies would be threatened by an overvalued franc. The dollar's recovery was brief. Its value plunged again on news that five prominent West German economists had advised their government to allow the mark to float freely upward. Falling U.S. interest rates also discouraged holders of the dollar, causing them to seek higher yielding currencies.

[23] The pound sterling sank to its lowest level ever recorded Dec. 12 in the wake of Saudi Arabia's decision that it would no longer accept British currency in payment for oil. About 25% of Saudi Arabia's payments had been in sterling, with the balance in dollars. Central bank intervention was required Dec. 12 to prevent the pound from falling below $2.309. The dollar also was weak against most major currencies, closing at 4.5025 French francs Dec. 12.

[24] U.S. Treasury Secretary William E. Simon disclosed Dec. 3 that the U.S. would sell 2 million ounces of its gold reserves at public auction Jan. 6, 1975. The action was taken, Simon said, because of fears that lifting of the gold ownership ban on Dec. 31 would have an "adverse effect on our efforts to bring inflation under control." Experts had feared a "gold rush" when U.S. citizens could legally buy, sell and hold gold, leading to a further weakening of the stock market and other private markets for investments. The gold, which represented less than 1% of the total 276 million ounces held in the U.S. gold stockpile, was officially valued at the "official" rate ($42.22 an ounce) at about $84.4 million. However, gold sold at the public auction would be purchased at or near the open market rate. Simon said domestic and foreign investors would be able to bid on the metal, which would be sold in 400 ounce bars. Disclosure of the U.S. plan to sell 2 million ounces of gold in January caused gold prices to fall sharply Dec. 3. On the London market, prices dropped $9 an ounce, but recovered to close at $174.25.

[25] The price of gold soared to a record level of $197.50 on the London bullion market Dec. 30 in anticipation of heavy sales to U.S. citizens Dec. 31 when the 41-year-old ban against gold ownership was lifted. Trading was light, however, on the four U.S. bullion markets authorized to trade in gold and the price fell to $186 an ounce in late trading Dec. 31 on the London market.

[26] Trading was slow Dec. 31, the first day the U.S. citizens could legally buy, sell and hold gold. Four major commodity exchanges traded a total of 6,541 gold future contracts calling for delivery of gold valued at about $108 million. Major banks reported few customers for the metal. The nation's two largest commercial banks, Bank of America and First National City, had announced Dec. 26 that they would not deal in gold because of the heavy costs involved in buying, selling and holding gold, as well as the investment risks. On the Commodity Exchange in New York where trading was heaviest, gold futures for January delivery traded as high as $190.50 an ounce, but closed at $182.50.

See also BANKS & BANKING; EUROPEAN ECONOMIC COMMUNITY [6-11]; FRANCE [12]; GREAT BRITAIN [9-10, 21]; IRAN; ISRAEL; ITALY [1, 3-8]; JAPAN [8]; OIL; TARIFFS & TRADE

MONEY—*See* BANKS & BANKING; ECONOMY, U.S.; MONETARY DEVELOPMENTS
MONGOLIA—*See* COMMUNISM, INTERNATIONAL
MONITOR, U.S.S.—*See* SHIPS & SHIPPING

MOORER, ADM. THOMAS H.—*See* DEFENSE [2-4]

MOROCCO—6 sentenced to die. A court in Kenitra sentenced to death Jan. 18 six defendants accused of aiding the "March 3 plot," which allegedly attempted to overthrow the government of King Hassan II in 1973. (Defense lawyers said Aug. 28 that the six men had been executed.) Three other defendants were given life sentences in solitary confinement and four others ordered jailed for 30 years. Another 62 defendants, who were believed to be in exile in France, Algeria and Libya, were sentenced to death in absentia Jan. 28. The *New York Times* reported Jan. 27 that 1,500 people had been charged in connection with alleged subversive plots since 1971, while hundreds more were being held without trial.

Government shuffled. King Hassan II reorganized the Moroccan Cabinet April 26, changing 13 Cabinet posts and appointing seven new ministers. While the political complexion of the government remained unchanged, the personnel shifts revealed a trend toward the naming of younger, university-educated men to administrative posts. The reorganization fell short, however, of changes indicated in a March 3 speech in which King Hassan had promised to set a date for the election of parliamentary representatives, as specified by the Constitution. Among the new appointments was that of Dr. Ahmed Laraki, a fomer premier and ex-ambassador to the U.S., who was named minister of state for foreign affairs.

'Moroccanization' of oil firms. The government approved a decree April 4 calling for the "Moroccanization," or government majority control, of firms distributing refined petroleum products. American, Italian and British companies would be affected by the decision.

Harsh penalties set for hijacking. Premier Ahmed Osman signed a law making hijacking a major crime in Morocco, it was reported July 31. (Four Moroccan government officials were killed in a 1973 Arab commando attack on an aircraft at Rome airport.) Under the new law kidnappers would face sentences of from five years to life, and would risk the death penalty if the hostage were tortured. The government also tightened drug curbs, raising the minimum penalty from three months to five years and the maximum fine to the equivalent ot $120,000 for drug trafficking.

See also AFRICA; ALGERIA; MIDDLE EAST [9, 22]; OIL [19]; SPANISH SAHARA

MORTGAGES—*See* BANKS & BANKING; HOUSING; VETERANS

MORTON, ROGERS C. B.—*See* ENERGY CRISIS [30-31]; FORD, GERALD R.; WATERGATE [19]

MOTION PICTURES—Academy Awards. *The Sting*, a dramatic comedy about a pair of 1930s confidence men, won seven Academy Awards in the 46th annual presentation by the Academy of Motion Picture Arts and Sciences in Los Angeles April 2. *The Sting* won awards for best picture, best director (George Roy Hill), best screenplay, best score and achievements in costume design, film editing, art direction and set decoration. Other awards: **actor**—Jack Lemmon (*Save the Tiger*); **actress**—Glenda Jackson (*A Touch of Class*); **supporting actress**—Tatum O'Neal (*Paper Moon*); **supporting actor**—John Houseman (*The Paper Chase*); **foreign language film**—*Day for Night;* **best original score and best song**—Marvin Hamlisch (*The Way We Were*); **best achievement in sound**—Knudson and Newman (*The Exorcist*); **best screenplay based on a work in another medium**—Peter Blatty (*The Exorcist*); **cinematography**—*Cries and Whispers;* **short subjects (animated)**—*The Bolero;* **documentary features**—*The Great American Cowboy;* **documentary short subjects**—*Princeton: A Search for Answers.* Four special awards were given: the Irving Thalberg Award—Lawrence Weingarten; the Jean Hersholt Humanitarian Award—Lew Wasserman; an honorary award to Henri Langlois; and a special award to Groucho Marx for all the Marx brothers.

Cannes film festival. U.S. films were awarded three of the top five prizes at the 27th Cannes International Film Festival, May 24 in Cannes, France. The awards were: **Film**—*The Conversation*, directed by Francis Ford Coppola (U.S.). **Actor**—Jack Nicholson in *The Last Detail* (U.S.). **Actress**—Marie Jose Nat in *Les Violons du Bal* (France). **Grand jury prize**—Carlos Saura, director of *La Prima Angelica* (Spain). **Special jury prize**—Pier Paolo Pasolini's *A Thousand and One Nights* (Italy). **Best screenplay**—Hal Barwood and Matthew Robbins for *Sugarland Express* (U.S.). Charles Boyer was awarded an "homage" for his role in Alain Resnais' *Stavisky*.

N.Y. Film Critics. *Day for Night* (*La Nuit Americaine*) won three Film Critics Awards in presentations Jan. 9: best film; Francois Truffaut was named best director; and Valentina Cortese was awarded the prize for best supporting actress. The other winners were: **best actress**—Joanne Woodward (*Summer Wishes, Winter Dreams*); **best actor**—Marlon Brando (*Last Tango in Paris*); **supporting actor**—Robert De Niro (*Mean Streets*); **screen-writing**—Lucas, Katz and Huyck (*American Graffiti.*)

See also OBITUARIES [DE SICA, DE WOLFE, GOLDWYN, MOOREHEAD]; OBSCENITY & PORNOGRAPHY

MOTORCYCLING—*See* KNIEVEL, EVEL

MOUNTAIN CLIMBING—13 die in Soviet mountain range. Thirteen climbers on various expeditions perished while traversing mountains in the Soviet Pamir mountain region, all caught in a series of avalanches and snowstorms which struck the area during the 30-day period ending Aug. 10. Among the dead were eight Soviet women scaling Lenin peak, the third highest in the Soviet Union, Aug. 7; and an American, Jon Gary Ullin, 31, who died in an avalanche July 24th on nearby 19th Party Congress Peak. Veteran climbers called it the worst weather in 25 years.

The Americans, allowed in the Pamirs for the first time, were part of a 10-nation international mountaineering camp based in the Alai valley among the Pamirs. Twelve Americans successfully negotiated 23,404-foot Lenin Peak.

Mt. Everest avalanche kills 6. Tons of snow buried the leader of a French mountaineering expedition, Gerard Devoussoux, and five guides on Mt. Everest, it was reported Sept. 12. The tragedy ended an attempt to put the first Frenchman atop the world's highest peak.

MOZAMBIQUE—The takeover of the Portuguese government April 25 by a military junta led by Gen. Antonio de Spinola began a series of developments that led to the signing of an agreement on Sept. 7 under which Mozambique would gain full independence on June 25, 1975. The new government would be formed by the Front for the Liberation of Mozambique (FRELIMO), which had been fighting for that nation's freedom from Portugal for 10 years.

[2] Clashes between the FRELIMO forces and Portuguese troops had increased through 1973 and the early part of 1974. Insurgent activities had spread from the northern and northwestern regions to central Mozambique, concentrating on attacks on railway connections, white-owned farms near the Rhodesian border and, in some instances, African villages considered unsympathetic to the rebels.

[3] The change of government in Portugal did not bring about an immediate cessation of fighting. Although Portuguese Socialist Party leader Mario Soares

called for complete independence for all Portuguese African territories, Spinola opposed such a move, preferring the territories remain in federation with Portugal. One of Spinola's first moves was to dismiss the territory's governor and to appoint Col. David Ferreira as acting governor. Ferreira issued decrees April 29-30, releasing political prisoners, lifting press censorship, dissolving the Popular National Action Party, Mozambique's only legal political party, and suspending the territory's legislative assembly. Imprisoned members of guerrilla liberation movements were not released. While generally approving of the coup that toppled Portugal's dictatorship, FRELIMO leaders vigorously opposed federation.

[4] Portugal's chief of the general staff, Gen. Francisco da Costa Gomes returned from a May 10-13 "fact-finding mission" to Mozambique and expressed fears in a televised speech May 14 that Portugal would not be able to hold Mozambique because of deteriorating military, political and economic conditions there. (FRELIMO guerrillas had resumed fighting May 8, attacking a bus in the north, killing at least six passengers; and causing another death the next day when they blew up a train on the Beira-Malawi line.)

[5] The conciliatory tone of Costa Gomes appeal spurred the momentum of a mounting "white backlash" movement that found its chief political expression in a new party calling itself the Independent Front for Western Continuity, whose Portuguese acronym, FICO, means "I stay." FICO supporters demonstrated in the capital May 4-5 against Portuguese abandonment of Mozambique. Violent demonstrations between blacks and whites broke out in Lourenco Marques May 11 and in Beira May 12. FRELIMO issued a statement May 10, stressing that it was not waging a racial war, but was "struggling against Portuguese colonialism for Mozambique's independence." Rebel leader Samora Moises Machel called May 8 for a "general offensive" until the territory's right to independence was acknowledged.

[6] A major group emerging was the United Group of Mozambique, GUMO, a multi-racial party seeking "gradual autonomy" for the territory and presenting itself as "FRELIMO without the violence." In remarks reported May 11, GUMO Vice President Joanna Simiao, a black African, stressed that FRELIMO was the most important element in Mozambique's political future.

[7] The first formal contact between Lisbon and FRELIMO took place June 5-6 in Lusaka, Zambia. (Zambia, Tanzania and Zaire had taken an active role in helping chart plans for the peaceful attainment of independence by the Portuguese territories.) The talks ended sooner than expected, apparently because of FRELIMO's insistance that Portugal acknowledge Mozambique's right to independence before meaningful talks on a cease-fire could begin.

[8] Henrique Soares de Melo, a Mozambique lawyer, was sworn in as governor of Mozambique June 11 in Lisbon. Although a vigorous opponent of former Premier Marcello Caetano, his appointment was favored by neither blacks nor liberal whites in Mozambique, according to the French newspaper *Le Monde* May 29.

[9] Groups of armed white civilians had begun patrolling the streets of Inhaminga in central Mozambique amid fears that FRELIMO would launch an intensified attack, according to a July 5 report. A major railway junction on the line connecting Tete, site of the Cabora Bassa dam, with Beira, Inhaminga had been hit frequently by guerrilla raids in recent weeks. A Portuguese military communique issued July 7 said that 18 members of the security forces, 45 FRELIMO rebels and 36 African civilians had been killed in fighting during June.

[10] Although a de facto cease-fire was in effect in several regions, according to a

FRELIMO announcement Aug. 3, the insurgents continued military action, capturing the central Mozambique town of Morrumbala July 12 after three days of fighting, and staging five bomb attacks on the Tete railroad July 11-25. Racial violence disrupted the northern port of Antonio Enes Aug. 10. Right-wing groups attacked the Lourenco Marques office of the daily newspaper *Noticias* Aug. 15. The news agency Reuters reported that five political groups had merged Aug. 24 to form the National Coalition of Mozambique as a challenge to FRELIMO.

[11] Soares resigned as governor July 25 after three members of the Lisbon military junta arrived to set up a new military administration that would lead to self-rule. (The Portuguese Council of State had issued a constitutional law July 17 abolishing an article of the old Constitution that made the overseas territories integral parts of Portugal.)

[12] A final round of talks, beginning Sept. 5 in Zambia ended two days later with agreement on decolonization procedures under which Mozambique would be ruled by a transitional Portuguese-FRELIMO government until June 25, 1975, when independence would be granted and a government formed by the insurgent group. A white backlash movement calling itself the "Dragons of Death," which disrupted Lourenco Marques Sept. 7-10 with a series of riots, was put down by police and Portuguese troops, as was an attempt to seize the port city of Beira. Over 100 persons were killed in the disturbances. Although FRELIMO took no part in quelling the uprising, one of its leaders, Samora Machel, had warned Sept. 9 that his forces would take up arms against the movement if it wasn't put down by Portuguese troops. Machel also reiterated FRELIIMO's advocacy of a multiracial society.

[13] Two representatives of Spinola were sent to Lourenco Marques Sept. 9 for talks with the white rebel leaders who subsequently announced their readiness to negotiate with FRELIMO in the hope of forming a coalition government. According to Sept. 11 reports, the white resistance movement had collapsed amid fears of a nationwide bloodbath resulting from overt racial conflicts. With the Portuguese government's strong affirmation of its FRELIMO pact, hopes for substantial troop defections and aid from Lisbon were destroyed, rendering the movement impotent. (The "Dragons of Death" had been joined by FICO and the black National Coalition Party to form an association calling itself the Movement for a Free Mozambique.)

[14] (The United Group of Mozambique [GUMO] had joined forces with FRELIMO July 6, according to the French newspaper *Le Monde* Aug. 23.)

[15] The transitional government assumed office in Lourenco Marques Sept. 20. Joaquim Chissano, FRELIMO's security operations chief and third-ranking leader was sworn in as premier in the government. (Adm. Vitor Crespo had been appointed Portuguese high commissioner to supervise the transitional phase Sept. 10.) The new nine-man Cabinet included five blacks and four whites; one of the six ministers appointed by FRELIMO was of Indian origin.

[16] Among the points made in a FRELIMO statement issued after the installation: strikes would be banned in Mozambique; tribalism, regionalism and racialism were deemed "a grave threat" and "those who deviate from this line will not be tolerated;" all national institutions would be "decolonized;" and whites were promised "tranquility" and urged to make "a positive contribution to the national reconstruction of our country." In a gesture which FRELIMO described as "the symbolic end" to the 10-year war for independence, the liberation movement freed 197 Portuguese soldiers from a camp in southern Tanzania and flew them to Mozambique Sept. 19. (Portugal began withdrawing its troops Oct. 8.)

[17] Premier Chissano sought in a Sept. 22 statement to stem the tide of white emigration, saying that there was "room for everybody in Mozambique" and urging all, except those with "guilty consciences," to remain or return. According to a Sept. 22 Reuters report, up to 25,000 persons—10% of the white population—was estimated to have left Mozambique since the signing of the Sept. 7 pact; 1,000 were reportedly leaving each day by train for South Africa as hundreds more departed by air and road, according to the *New York Times* Sept. 21.

[18] More than 1,200 persons were arrested in the wake of violent racial clashes in Lourenco Marques, Portuguese army sources said Oct. 27. The government announced Dec. 21 that an additional 77 persons, mostly whites, had been arrested in recent days for obstruction of "the decolonization process."

See also AFRICA; PORTUGAL; SOUTH AFRICA [5, 11]

MURPHY, J. REGINALD—*See* CRIME [21]

MUSIC—National Academy of Recording Arts & Sciences. The 16th annual Grammy Awards were presented March 2 by the National Academy of Recording Arts and Sciences. Stevie Wonder, a blind singer-composer, won four of the top 10 awards and dedicated his pop vocal prize to Jim Croce, a singer killed in a 1973 plane crash. The winners: **record of the year**—*Killing Me Softly With His Song* (Roberta Flack); **album of the year**—*Innervisions* (Wonder); **song of the year**—*Killing Me Softly With His Song* (Gimbel and Fox, writers); **best new artist**—Bette Midler; **best jazz performance**—*God is in the House* (Art Tatum); **best jazz performance, group**—*Supersax Plays Bird* (Supersax); **best jazz performance, big band**—*Giant Steps* (Woody Herman); **best pop vocal, female**—*Killing Me Softly With His Song* (Flack); **best pop vocal, male**—*You Are the Sunshine of My Life* (Wonder); **best pop vocal, group**—*Neither One of Us* (Gladys Knight and the Pips); **best rhythm and blues vocal, female**—*Master of Eyes* (Aretha Franklin); **best rhythm and blues vocal, male**—*Superstition* (Wonder); **best rhythm and blues vocal, group**—*Midnight Train to Georgia* (Knight and the Pips); **best rhythm and blues song**—*Superstition* (Wonder, writer); **best classical vocal, soloist**—*Puccini: Heroines* (Leontyne Price); **best country vocal, male**—*Behind Closed Doors* (Charlie Rich); **best country vocal, female**—*Let Me Be There* (Olivia Newton-John); **best country song**—*Behind Closed Doors* (Kenny O'Dell, writer); **best instrumental**—*Dueling Banjos* (Weissburg and Mandell); **best Broadway score**—*A Little Night Music* (Stephen Sondheim, writer); **best soul gospel**—*Love Me Like a Rock* (Dixie Hummingbirds); **best gospel**—*Release Me From My Sin* (Blackwood Brothers); **best opera recording**—*Bizet: Carmen* (Leonard Bernstein and Thomas Mowery); **best comedy album**—*Los Cochinos* (Cheech and Chong).

See also CHINA, COMMUNIST; COPYRIGHT; OBITUARIES [ELLINGTON, ELLIOT, KRIPS, MILHAUD, OISTRAKH]; PULITZER PRIZES; TAXES

MUSKIE, SEN. EDMUND S.—*See* CAMPAIGN FINANCING [17]; WATERGATE [77]

MY LAI MASSACRE—*See* CALLEY, WILLIAM L.

NADER, RALPH—*See* ANTITRUST ACTIONS [1]; ENERGY CRISIS [20]; PATENTS; PRIVACY [9-10]
NAMIBIA—*See* SOUTH WEST AFRICA

NARCOTICS & DANGEROUS DRUGS—Opium exports damage U.S.-Turkish relations. U.S. Ambassador to Turkey William B. Macomber Jr. was recalled to Washington July 5 "to review the situation" arising from the Turkish government's announcement July 1 formally lifting the 1971 ban on opium poppy cultivation. The U.S. had sought to dissuade Turkey from the move since Ankara's decision in March to begin germinating poppy seeds for autumn sowing. Opium poppy farming had been halted in 1971 under pressure from the U.S., with guarantees of American funds to offset state and individual financial losses in Turkey where an estimated 100,000 families were dependent upon poppy cultivation. At that time, authorities had concluded that approximately 80% of the illegal heroin entering the U.S. each year originated in Turkey. In announcing resumption of poppy farming, Turkish Foreign Minister Turhan Gunes said, "There is a limit to the sacrifices Turkey can make for other people and nations." In July the Turkish government announced "stringent measures to prevent illegal poppy growing and drug-trafficking." The crop would be used only to "feed the international pharmaceutical industry." (The United Nations International Narcotics Control Board said in its 1973 report released Feb. 25 that growing demand and dwindling stocks had created a temporary shortage of opium for medical use.) Despite a Turkish statement July 7 inviting U.S. assistance in helping to control the flow of illegal opium from Turkish poppy fields, U.S. authorities remained unconvinced of Turkey's ability to implement adequate controls once cultivation resumed. In a retaliatory action for the lifting of the ban, the U.S. State Department July 2 said Turkey would not be given the approximately $20 million remaining of the original $35.7 million promised by the U.S. in 1971 when the poppy ban was instituted.

The U.S. Senate July 11 voted to suspend all aid to any country that failed to impose sufficient safeguards to prevent the illegal diversion of opium to the U.S. This move was directed chiefly at Turkey. The House of Representatives Aug. 21 approved a bill that would prohibit the Export-Import Bank from extending loans to Turkey until the growing of opium poppies was halted.

(Congressional actions against Turkey were also being taken to suspend aid because of Ankara's use of U.S. military equipment in the invasion of Cyprus. [See CYPRUS])

The Turkish government's decision "in principle" to adopt a new method of harvesting opium poppies was welcomed Sept. 20 by the U.S. State Department, which in recent weeks had been seeking to soften Congressional demands to cut off aid to Turkey. Under the new collection system, the entire poppy pod, rather than merely the opium sap, would be collected by the government. This would, if effective, prevent illegal diversion of opium for production of heroin. Some 90,000 farmers Oct. 2 began to plant their first opium poppy crop in two years. Agriculture officials said 100,000 tons of seed were being distributed in seven provinces.

Army drug drive. U.S. District Court Judge Gerhard A. Gesell ruled Jan. 14 that methods used by the Army to check for drug abuse among non-commissioned soldiers in Europe were unconstitutional. Under the Army program, soldiers had been subject to middle-of-the-night, mass strip searches and examination of their private property by inspectors. Forced to enter 60-day drug rehabilitation programs, drug abusers faced discharge or courts martial if their commanders determined they had not successfully completed the program.

The Court of Military Appeals ruled in Washington July 5 that an Army program requiring a soldier to undergo urinalysis for detection of drugs violated a soldier's rights when the evidence was "used for disciplinary action or for administrative elimination proceedings at which a soldier could be subjected to a general discharge." "Laudable as the program may be," the court said, it had to overturn the court-martial conviction of Army Pvt. Robert J. Ruiz, who had refused to cooperate on the grounds of possible self-incrimination leading to a less-than-honorable discharge. In this case, the right involved under the Code of Military Justice was similar to the constitutional right against self-incrimination, the court reasoned. Subsequently, James R. Schlesinger, secretary of defense, July 18 announced the suspension of the testing program becuse of the "legal cloud" created by the decision. A Pentagon spokesman indicated Aug. 2 that since the inception of the urinalysis program in June 1971, 5.4 million persons had been tested. Of these, 71,209 (1.3%) had been found to be drug users.

Illinois drug raiders acquitted. An Alton, Ill. federal district court jury April 2 acquitted 10 undercover narcotics agents of charges they conspired to deprive victims of mistaken drug raids of their civil rights. Subsequently, all other charges stemming from the April 1973 raids were dropped by the Justice Department. The agents built their trial defense on the argument that they had mistakenly raided six homes in three southeastern Illinois communities in the belief that the occupants were armed and dangerous drug dealers and users. Civil actions brought against the agents by the raid victims were still pending.

Marijuana safety debated. Heavy use of marijuana could have the effect of depressing the production of male sex hormones and sperm in men, researchers reported in the *New England Journal of Medicine* April 18. Using 20 men who were heavy smokers and 20 men in the same 18-28 year age group who did not smoke marijuana, scientists at the Reproductive Biology Research Foundation in St. Louis found that heay smokers had blood levels of the male sex hormone testosterone that were 44% lower than nonsmokers. Heavy smokers were also discovered to have diminished sperm counts. However, researchers cautioned that the sample was small, the study did not deal with casual marijuana smokers, and the subjects of the study supplied their own marijuana, whose potency was unmeasured.

The Attack, the quarterly newsletter of the New York State Drug Abuse

Control Commission (DACC) issued Nov. 15, criticized recent reporting of marijuana research. The newsletter quoted Dr. Thomas E. Bryant, president of the Drug Abuse Council, a private oranization concerned with information, policy evaluation and research funding in the drug abuse field. Calling some recent reports on the effects of marijuana "exaggerated and misleading," Bryant said "some researchers are drawing conclusions about the harm of marijuana which far exceed the data presently available." Bryant pointed to the HEW marijuana report to Congress in 1973, which said there was "no convincing evidence" that chromosomal abnormalities arise from marijuana use.

Dr. Robert L. DuPont, director of the White House Special Action Office for Drug Abuse Prevention, said in testimony before the Senate Labor and Public Welfare Committee's Subcommittee on Alcoholism and Narcotics Nov. 19 that elimination of penalties for possession and use of marijuana would lead many persons to the incorrect conclusion that the drug was safe. DuPont said he and the Ford Administration opposed the abolition of legal penalties for marijuana use. DuPont, who said he was appalled by the large number of marijuana arrests—420,000 in 1973—in the U.S. each year, said he believed prison terms for users were wrong, despite their probable deterrent value. Instead of prison, DuPont advocated fines for use or possession of small amounts, penalties that would not stigmatize users as criminals. DuPont also testified on the new HEW report to Congress titled "Marijuana and Health." Scientific research indicated, DuPont said, that the effects of marijuana on the body might be more deleterious, widespread and persistent that previously suspected. However, DuPont cautioned that findings on the hazards of marijuana were preliminary, in some cases contradictory. Evidence to date left more questions unanswered than answered, he said. According to the report, studies not involving humans had shown that a major chemical component of marijuana might interfere with cells' normal mechanism for intake of amino acids, the building blocks of proteins and of nucleotides. (Nucleotides were the sub-units of DNA, deoxyribonucleic acid.) DuPont also said researchers had determined that persons under the influence of marijuana demonstrated poorer than normal automobile driving performances. Such persons were slower to brake, slower to start and exhibited lessened ability to concentrate, he said. Favorable effects of marijuana were also noted in the report: reduction in aggressive behavior, the drug's value as a sedative and pain killer, and its use in treatment of glaucoma.

'No-knock' drug searches barred. President Ford signed into law Oct. 28 a bill repealing laws permitting federal and District of Columbia agents to make "no-knock" drug searches of private dwellings—searches where the agents did not knock and identify themselves before entry. Authorization for such entries had been enacted in 1970 in federal drug control legislation and in a D.C. criminal procedure act. The new bill, passed by the House Oct. 15 and Senate Oct. 16, also made it a federal crime to kill an agent of the Drug Enforcement Administration.

See also Crime [3]; Medicine & Health [3]; Mexico [18]; Morocco; Nixon, Richard M.; Pulitzer Prizes; Turkey

NATIONAL ACADEMY OF SCIENCES—*See* Medicine & Health [31-32]; Science; Vietnam, Republic of [39]
NATIONAL AERONAUTICS & SPACE ADMINISTRATION—*See* Space
NATIONAL GUARD—*See* Civil Rights [4]; Kent State
NATIONAL SECURITY COUNCIL—*See* Defense [2-4]; Rockefeller, Nelson [32]
NATURAL GAS—*See* Algeria; Bolivia; Canada [23-25]; Energy Crisis [21-22,

26, 37]; EUROPEAN ECONOMIC COMMUNITY [9]; FRANCE [19]; NETHERLANDS [4]; NICARAGUA; NORWAY; OIL [11]; UNION OF SOVIET SOCIALIST REPUBLICS [40]; VENEZUELA

NAZIS—*See* GERMANY, WEST [7]

NEBRASKA—*See* ELECTIONS [1]; WOMEN'S RIGHTS

NEPAL—The Nepal Foreign Ministry said 142 people were believed to have drowned when a suspension bridge collapsed on the Indian-Nepal border, it was reported Nov. 26.

NERVE GAS—*See* CHEMICAL & BIOLOGICAL WEAPONS

NETHERLANDS

Oil & Energy

[1] The Arab oil embargo imposed on the Netherlands eased slightly in January, according to an announcement by Premier Joop den Uyl. Refinery production had risen from 68% to 76% of capacity; and 12.5% more oil had arrived in the port of Rotterdam during the first week of January than in the first week of December 1973. The mayor of Rotterdam announced Jan. 1 that non-Arab nations, including Iran, Nigeria and Venezuela, were openly sending more oil to the Netherlands

[2] The First Chamber (upper house of Parliament) Jan. 8 adopted a Special Powers Act giving the government authority to control wages, prices, rents, dividends and layoffs caused by the energy crisis. The lower house had approved the bill in December 1973.

[3] Gas rationing, which went into effect Jan. 12, was abolished Feb. 4 and replaced by a ban on Sunday pleasure driving every other week. February reports indicated the gap between supply and demand had fallen to 15%. Gasoline prices rose, however, on March 1, reflecting increases in the cost of crude oil. The price of super gasoline was increased nearly 4¢ a liter to 35¢, while a similar raise boosted the price of regular gas to 34¢ a liter. (One U.S. gallon equals 3.79 liters.) Fuel oil prices for domestic use were also increased.

[4] NAM, the Dutch partnership of Shell and Esso, struck oil in the Netherlands sector of the North Sea, it was reported April 27. There was also an earlier natural gas find in the area.

[5] Economics Minister Ruud Lubbers announced that the Netherlands would build three more nuclear power stations of 1,000 megawatts each by 1985, it was reported Sept. 28. He said the new stations would reduce annual crude oil imports by five million tons, aiding the balance of payments by more than $333 million a year.

The Economy & Politics

[6] The government Jan. 22 announced new measures to tighten price controls, retroactive to Jan. 18. The measures were taken under the new Special Powers Act. [See above] All businesses regardless of size would be required to give prior notification to the government of planned price increases; industry would have to wait eight weeks before raising prices to cover cost increases, service businesses had to wait six weeks and the retail trade sector four weeks. Labor cost increases, however, could be passed on immediately. In a related austerity measure, the government had decided to freeze 750 million guilders ($247.5 million) of its 51 billion guilder budget for 1974, it was reported Jan. 20. The biggest cuts were in education, road construction, defense and housing construction.

[7] Government-determined wage increases, also granted under the act, went into effect April 1 following the March 19 failure of union and management

representatives to reach agreement. The measures included a flat-rate pay rise of slightly over $5 a month for all employes in addition to the $9 a month rise ordered by the government earlier in the year. Employers were also told to grant an advance payment to compensate for the cost-of-living increase. The government also announced an increase in annual personal income tax exemptions, effective July 1, more generous tax write-offs on buildings and a resumption of tax write-offs for capital goods.

[8] The ruling Labor Party polled 27.9% of the vote in nationwide provincial council elections March 27, a 2% gain over the general elections in late 1972. The right-wing Liberal Party also improved its standing, becoming the nation's second largest party with a gain of 4½% to 18.9%. The Labor Party gains contrasted with losses by most of the other parties in the coalition government.

[9] In her traditional Speech from the Throne opening the new session of Parliament Sept. 17, Queen Juliana announced government plans to increase expenditures 23% in 1975. The budget set spending at 62.8 billion guilders ($23.2 billion), compared with 51.07 billion guilders in 1974; revenue was estimated at 58.2 billion guilders, doubling the deficit to 4.6 billion guilders. Natural gas prices for export and domestic consumption would be raised, giving the government additional revenue with which to fund its programs; and the 1974 balance of payments surplus was estimated at 4 billion guilders. New or expanded programs included increased unemployment relief and a plan to create 45,000 new jobs; implementation of equal pay for women, to start Jan. 1, 1975; and a one-third increase in development aid, with a target in four years of 1½% of the national income.

[10] Dutch companies acquired control of two major U.S. firms during 1974. The Dutch firm Seamar Holland, N.V., purchased operating control of Bond Industries Inc., owners of the Bond clothing chain in the U.S., it was announced Oct. 10. Thyssen-Bornemisza, the Netherlands-based international industrial holding company, purchased about 3,687,000 shares, or 92%, of the common stock of Indian Head Inc., a U.S. packaging, textile and automotive group, it was reported Aug. 21.

Terrorist Activity

[11] **Extremists stage Hague embassy siege.** Four Japanese members of the underground extremist organization, the Japanese Red Army, surrendered Sept. 18 to Palestinian guerrillas in Damascus, Syria, where they had flown after releasing hostages whom three of the Japanese terrorists had held at gunpoint for four days at the French embassy in The Hague. The action by the three terrorists had won the release of a comrade from a French prison. Syria promised safe conduct for the terrorists to a country of their choice and left them in the custody of the Palestine Liberation Organization (PLO).

[12] Three of the terrorists had seized 11 hostages at the French embassy Sept. 13 and initially demanded a $1 million ransom and release of Yutaka Furuya, who had been arrested by French customs officials July 26 with three false passports, $10,000 in counterfeit money and documents that reportedly revealed plans for a terrorist campaign in France and elsewhere in Europe. Furuya was flown under police escort to Amsterdam's Schiphol Airport Sept. 13. The gunmen freed two women hostages Sept. 16 and released the other nine captives Sept. 17, including French Ambassador to the Netherlands Jacques Senard, after Furuya was freed and the French provided a Boeing 707 jet. Three of the hostages were freed at the embassy in The Hague and six at the airport.

[13] **Prison hostages rescued.** Dutch Marines stormed a prison chapel at Schveningen, near The Hague, Oct. 31 and rescued 15 hostages held by four

convicts, including a Palestinian guerrilla, since Oct. 26. No one was injured in the raid. The convicts, who had earlier released seven hostages—mainly women and children—had demanded freedom for another imprisoned guerrilla and an airplane to leave the country.

See also AVIATION [6, 14]; CHILE [24]; COMMUNISM, INTERNATIONAL; ETHIOPIA [14]; EUROPEAN SECURITY; LIBYA; MIDDLE EAST [29, 34]; MONETARY DEVELOPMENTS [4, 11, 17]; NORTH ATLANTIC TREATY ORGANIZATION; OIL [6-7, 9, 23, 26, 34]; SOCCER; SURINAM & NETHERLANDS ANTILLES; WATERGATE [40]

NETHERLANDS ANTILLES—*See* SURINAM
NEVADA—*See* ELECTIONS [3]; WOMEN'S RIGHTS
NEVAS—*See* WEST INDIES ASSOCIATED STATES
NEW GUINEA—*See* PAPUA NEW GUINEA
NEW HAMPSHIRE—*See* ELECTIONS [3]; GAMBLING; POLITICS [5]
NEW JERSEY—*See* CRIME [12]; ELECTIONS [5]; ENERGY CRISIS [6-8, 35]; ENVIRONMENT & POLLUTION [11]; GAMBLING
NEW LEFT—*See* RADICALS
NEWSPAPERS—*See* PRESS
NEW YORK CITY—*See* ANTITRUST ACTIVITIES [10]; CIVIL RIGHTS [6, 20]; CRIME [8, 16, 37]; HOMOSEXUALS; OBITUARIES [HOGAN]; RADICALS; RELIGION [5]; TRANSPORTATION
NEW YORK STATE—*See* ELECTIONS [1-2, 5, 7]; ENVIRONMENT & POLLUTION [11]; GAMBLING; POPULATION
NEW YORK TIMES—*See* CHAD; PRESS

NEW ZEALAND—Prime Minister Kirk dies. Prime Minister Norman E. Kirk, 50, died of a heart seizure in a hospital in Wellington Aug. 31. Deputy Prime Minister Hugh Watt assumed governmental powers until the ruling Labor Party caucus in Parliament elected a new leader. The party caucus met Sept. 6 and chose Finance Minister William Edward Rowling, 46, to succeed Kirk. Health Minister Robert J. Tizard was selected as deputy prime minister. Kirk had become prime minister when the Labor Party won the November 1972 elections.

Rowling shuffles Cabinet. Premier Rowling announced Sept. 10 a major reshuffling of his Cabinet, assuming the additional post of foreign minister. Among the other changes: finance, Deputy Prime Minister Tizard, former health minister; defense, former Housing Minister Walter A. Fraser; labor and state services, Arthur J. Faulkner; works and development, former Deputy Prime Minister Hugh Watt; and railways and electricity, Ronald Bailey, the only new Cabinet member.

Soviet embassy aides leave. Two members of the Soviet embassy in Wellington, First Secretary Dimitri Razogovrov and administrative staffer U. F. Pertsev were forced to leave New Zealand Oct. 8 and 12 following New Zealand government complaints that they had engaged in activities incompatible with their official status. The men were said to have had contacts with William Ball Sutch, former head of the Department of Industries and Commerce, who went on trial on charges of violating the Official Secrets Act. Sutch pleaded not guilty to charges of obtaining information useful to an enemy and said "my sole motive in meeting with any person from the Russian embassy was to find out what they had to say."

See also ATOMIC ENERGY [5-7]; DEFENSE [14]; EUROPEAN ECONOMIC COMMUNITY [10]; TARIFFS & TRADE; VIETNAM, PEOPLE'S REPUBLIC OF

NICARAGUA—Somoza re-elected. Anastasio Somoza Debayle, the nation's strongman, was elected to a second presidential term by an overwhelming margin

Sept. 1. His major opponents called the election a farce. The official ballot count Sept. 4, with 826 of the 2,728 electoral tables reporting, gave Somoza 216,158 votes against 11,997 for his lone adversary, Edmundo Paguaga Irias of the Conservative Party. Paguaga conceded defeat Sept. 2 and pledged to lead "strong opposition" to Somoza's administration in Congress. Members of Nicaragua's bicameral legislature also were elected.

Somoza had been barred from another presidential term by the 1950 Constitution's electoral provisions. He resigned in May 1972. Since then the country had been ruled by a civilian triumvirate which included Paguaga, although Somoza had retained full power as "supreme commander of the armed forces." A new Constitution permitted his nomination by the Liberal Party in April, 1974. Nine of the 10 opposition groups had been excluded from the election by a new law which required each of them to obtain the signatures of 5% of the electorate. In addition, 27 major opposition leaders—three from each of the excluded groups—had been deprived of their political rights after they issued a manifesto, titled "There is No One to Vote For," calling the election a farce and urging voters to boycott it. The 27 were accused of violating the Constitution (which made voting mandatory) and "endangering the welfare of the state." A Managua police judge Aug. 13 stripped them of the rights to vote, run in elections and make political statements.

Oil and gas search. President-elect Somoza said the government had awarded 30 oil and gas exploration concessions to foreign companies, including Texaco Inc. and El Paso Natural Gas Co. of the U.S., it was reported Oct. 11. The firms, spurred by the discovery of substantial oil deposits in Mexico, were exploring Nicaragua's Pacific and Caribbean coasts. Explorers had already found seven apparent gas structures in the Pacific, one of which was "about seven times the size of the North Sea structure," Somoza said.

Somoza inaugurated. Somoza assumed the presidency Dec. 1 in a ceremony attended by four Central American presidents and representatives of more than 40 other countries. He immediately announced a six-year program to invest $6 billion in the reconstruction of Managua, the earthquake-ravaged capital, and in other development projects. The program had the support of the World Bank, the Inter-American Development Bank, the U.S. Agency for International Development and other organizations, Somoza said.

The inaugural ceremony was marked by unprecedented security measures. Many foreign delegates at the inaugural reportedly had objected when a member of the Chilean military junta, Gen. Cesar Mendoza, was accorded the honors of a chief of state.

Somoza reappointed most of the Cabinet after his inaugural, replacing only three ministers. The new Cabinet: Government (interior)—Jose Antonio Mora Rostran; foreign—Alejandro Montiel Arguello; finance—Gen. Gustavo Montiel; education—Leandro Marin Abaunza; works—Armel Gonzalez Espinosa; health—Adan Cajina Rios; economy, industry & trade—Juan Jose Martinez Lopez; economic integration—Ricardo Parrales; agriculture & livestock—Klaus Sengelman; labor—Julio Cardoze; planning—Ivan Osorio Peters; presidential secretary—Carlos Dubon Alvarado.

Guerrillas free prisoners, fly to Cuba. Eight guerrillas of the left-wing Sandinista Liberation Front invaded a party at the home of a wealthy Managua businessman Dec. 27 and seized a number of prominent officials. Through the mediation of the Roman Catholic archbishop of Managua, the guerrillas subsequently negotiated the release of more than a dozen imprisoned comrades, payment of a large ransom, and safe-conduct to Cuba. The hostages were freed Dec. 30 and the guerrillas and released prisoners were flown to Havana accompanied by the archbishop, Msgr. Miguel Ovando y Bravo, the papal nuncio in Managua and the Mexican and Spanish ambassadors to Nicaragua. Because of strict press censorship, there was some confusion as to how many prisoners were released and how much ransom was paid. Most foreign reports put the freed prisoners at 14 and the ransom at $1 million.

The party invaded by the Sandinistas was at the home of Jose Maria Castillo, a former agriculture minister, who was killed when he apparently tried to resist the guerrillas. Two or three guards at the home (reports varied) were also killed. The Sandinistas took more than 30 hostages—including Foreign Minister Alejandro Montiel Arguello and Ambassador to the U.S. Guillermo Sevilla Sacasa—but they missed Turner Shelton, the U.S. ambassador and guest of honor, who had already left.

See also COFFEE; LATIN AMERICA; MIDDLE EAST [26]; OIL [17]; SUGAR

NIGER—Military ousts president. The army staged a successful coup d'etat in Niger's capital, Niamey, April 15, overthrowing President Hamani Diori who had ruled the former French colony since its independence in 1960. The takeover was led by Lt. Col. Seyni Kountche, chief of staff of the 2,500-man army. Two soldiers were killed in the coup. Diori was placed under house arrest. His wife was reported killed.

A 12-member military government was formed April 17 with Kountche installed as president and minister of development. In seizing power, he suspended the Constitution, dissolved the National Assembly, banned all political groups and imposed a curfew. A total of 37 political prisoners was released. Students demonstrated in support of the new regime.

According to an analysis in the French newspaper *Le Monde* May 5-6, the coup was precipitated by: Diori's failure to call a national congress of the Nigerian Progressive Party (Niger's only politial party) since 1960 when Niger gained independence, imparting a "no party system" structure to political life; Diori's unwillingness to appoint younger men to key government posts; and the widespread dislike and disapproval of Diori's wife.

French troops ordered withdrawn. Niger's new military government May 16 demanded the departure of the French military detachment stationed at Niamey, declaring that "the presence of foreign troops constituted an affront to sovereignty." The commander of the French detachment had been expelled from the country April 29.

See also AFRICA; APPOINTMENTS & RESIGNATIONS; FAMINE & FOOD

NIGERIA

Government

Disputed census results were among the factors leading to unrest during 1974 in Nigeria, where population figures determine allocation of federal development funds and political representation. (Results of the last census, taken in 1963, led to political conflict following allocation of seats in the national assembly; they also contributed to events leading to the abortive 1967 Biafran secession attempt.) The 1973 census, released May 12, 1974, showed that two-thirds of Nigeria's nearly 80 million people lived in the nation's six predominantly Moslem northern provinces. The results were disputed on July 7 by Chief Obefami Awolowo, a prominent Yoruba leader, in a speech at the University of Ite where he was a chancellor. The chief challenged figures that showed the population of the six northern states had increased during the ten-year period from 29.8 million to 51.38 million, while the six southern states' population had risen from 25.86 million to only 28.38 million. The results also provoked renewed demands for creation of additional states by the Ibo, whose population was concentrated in the East Central State.

Rumors about the potential for armed conflict over actions taken as a result of the census figures were among the factors reported leading to the postponement of the return to civilian rule originally set for 1976. In a nationwide broadcast to mark Nigeria's 14th anniversary of independence, Gen. Yakubu Gowon, the head of state, announced Oct. 1 that "the Supreme Military Command has decided" that such a date would be "unrealistic" because "a precipitate withdrawal [of the military government] would certainly throw the nation back into confusion." Gowon stressed that his regime had not abandoned the idea; however, he also said that a ban on political activities, due to be lifted that month, would remain in force.

Gowon also said the system by which federal revenues were allocated to the states would be revised. Under the present system, the revenues were distributed unevenly, with mineral royalties giving the oil-rich Rivers and Mid-West States more than nine times the per capita amount given to the West and North-East States. Under the new proposal, the pool of royalties would be divided so that half would go to the states in equal proportions and half would be distributed according to population. The government also agreed to surrender its share into the distributable pool. Gowon also announced Nigeria's second national development plan, due to end Sept. 30, was extended to March 31, 1975.

The Economy

Drought in Nigeria's North-East State led the government to announce a plan to set up a 250,000 ton grain reserve to prevent future food shortages, it was reported Feb. 6. In another measure, announced July 6, the army and police were deployed to help distribute relief material.

The Ministry of Mines and Power issued a decree, back-dated to April 1, announcing the country's assumption of a 55% interest in five oil exploration companies operating there, it was reported May 19. Nigeria's total daily output was 2.3 million barrels. Nigeria had previously held no interest in either of the two U.S. companies included in the takeover—Gulf Oil Corp. and Mobil Oil Corp. Spokesmen for the firms said the 55% figure would be accepted only if an entire participation package could be negotiated. Such an agreement had been reached with the Royal Dutch Shell Group/British Petroleum Co. joint venture.

(Gulf Oil Corp. had announced in March that it would invest over $975 million in a proposed Nigerian liquefied gas project. The U.S. was expected to provide the major market for the 500 million cubic feet of gas to be produced daily. Lagos estimated that the gas project would cost the Nigerian government $1.169 billion.)

Nigeria's economy grew at a rate of 10.2% annually during the 1970-74 development plan, it was reported Aug. 10. Planners had predicted a rate of 8.3%. According to the Ministry of Mines and Power, about 85% of the nation's budget would be funded by oil revenues, it had been reported July 30. With 1973 oil revenues totaling $3.3 billion and 1974 earnings expected to reach $8 billion, a budget surplus in excess of $2 billion was anticipated. Nigeria could afford, the ministry said, to halve oil production and still maintain its economy for another 20 years with petroleum earnings. Daily output was scheduled to reach three million barrels a day within the next five years.

See also AFRICA; FAMINE & FOOD; NETHERLANDS [1]; OIL [5, 8, 20, 35]

NIXON, EDWARD C.—*See* CAMPAIGN FINANCING [16]
NIXON, F. DONALD—*See* CAMPAIGN FINANCING [16]

NIXON, MRS. PATRICIA—*See* BRAZIL [2]; CAMPAIGN FINANCING [16]; NIXON, RICHARD; WATERGATE [34]

NIXON, RICHARD M.—Richard Milhous Nixon, 61, resigned as 37th President of the United States Aug. 9 at 11:35 a.m. A single sentence message—"Dear Mr. Secretary: I hereby resign the office of the President of the United States. Sincerely, Richard Nixon"—was handed to Secretary of State Henry A. Kissinger. The presidential resignation—the first in the nation's history—followed Nixon's admission that he had participated in the Watergate cover-up and that he had kept knowledge of this participation from investigating bodies, his own counsel and the public. The admission had destroyed what remained of Nixon's support in Congress against a tide of impeachment that already was swelling. [*For details of Nixon's resignation, pardon, etc. see* WATERGATE AFFAIR.]

State of the Union address. President Nixon, delivering the State of the Union message in person before a joint session of Congress Jan. 30, reviewed the accomplishments of his five years in office and outlined 10 goals for accomplishment in 1974. In characterizing the progress made by his Administration, the President lauded the withdrawal of U.S. troops from Southeast Asia, moves toward detente with the Soviet Union and the People's Republic of China, advances in the war against drug abuse, the end of the military draft, improvement in the quality of the environment, increases in agricultural production and the growth of personal prosperity for Americans. He also pledged that there would be no recession, that inflation would be checked and that the back of the energy crisis would be broken. After concluding his address, Nixon added that "one year of Watergate is enough" and it was time to get on with the "great issues" outlined in his address. [For details, see WATERGATE AFFAIR 4] The 10 goals outlined by the President were "key areas in which landmark accomplishments" were possible in 1974. They covered: (1) resolution of present and future energy problems—assigned first priority; (2) moves toward world peace by negotiation with the great powers and by assisting in achievement of a just and lasting settlement in the Middle East; (3) checking price rises without recession and moving the economy "into a steady period of growth at a sustainable level"; (4) establishing a high-quality system of health care for every American; (5) making states and localities more responsive to the needs of citizens; (6) developing better transportation in towns and cities; (7) reforming the systems of federal aid to education; (8) beginning the task "of defining and protecting the right of personal privacy for every American"; (9) moving toward reform of the welfare system; and (10) "together with other nations of the world," establishing "the economic framework within which Americans will share more fully in an expanding world-wide trade and prosperity in the years ahead, with more open access to both markets and supplies."

Stolen 'copter lands at White House. Army Pfc. Robert K. Preston, 20, a Fort Meade helicopter maintenance man who had been dropped from an Army helicopter pilot school five months earlier for "deficiency in the instrument phase," was apprehended by White House security men Feb. 17 after the helicopter he was piloting landed 100 yards from the White House. Preston was taken to a hospital for treatment of minor shotgun pellet wounds incurred when the Army "Huey" helicopter he had commandeered from Fort Meade was struck by shotgun blasts from the Executive Protection Service. The landing at the White House occurred at 2 a.m. Neither President Nixon nor any member of his family was at the White House. Preston was sentenced to one year at hard labor and fined $2,400 Aug. 29.

Gifts to family acknowledged. The White House May 14 acknowledged that Mrs. Nixon and her daughters, Julie Eisenhower and Tricia Cox, had received gifts of jewelry from the Saudi Arabian royal family, but accused the *Washington Post* (which had reported the story May 13) of blowing the story "completely out of proportion." According to the *Post*, the gifts, received in 1969, 1971 and 1972, included a matched set of emeralds and diamonds valued at $52,400, diamond and ruby earrings, a diamond watch bracelet, a diamond and ruby pin (for Julie) and a diamond and sapphire pin (for Tricia). The gifts were received from King Faisal and two of his half brothers and reportedly kept in Mrs. Nixon's bedroom wall safe until March 28, when they were sent to a gifts unit in the Executive Office Building after the *Post* attempted to verify reports of the jewelry's existence. Federal law (based on Article 1 of the Constitution) prohibited anyone related to a government official from accepting gifts valued at more than $50. Regulations implementing the law required that state gifts be "deposited" with the State Department's chief of protocol, who was authorized to keep records of all items received by officials. In commenting on the gifts May 14, White House Counsel J. Fred Buzhardt Jr. termed the jewelry "private gifts," but said that the family had intended to "turn them over" when Nixon left office. (Following disclosure of the gifts to the Nixon family, dozens of valuable gifts to U.S. officials and their families from foreign countries flowed into the protocol office. Some of the gifts had been received as early as 1968. State Department officials attributed the delays in turning over the gifts to the "weakness" of the law, which was considered to be "vague, ambiguous" and lacking in sufficient enforcement procedures.)

Nixon's leg ailment. The disclosure that President Nixon had a leg ailment diagnosed as phlebitis was confirmed at the White House June 24. The disclosure was broadcast earlier that day by CBS News. The President's physician, Maj. Gen. Walter K. Tkach told reporters Nixon first noticed his left leg was swollen the weekend before he departed for the Middle East on June 10 but did not reveal it to Tkach until he had reached Salzburg, Austria, on June 11. Although the White House had first characterized the condition as "mild," Tkach revealed July 4 that the ailment was life-endangering since it involved clotting as well as inflamation and there had been "an outside chance" that the clot could have broken loose during the trip and caused death by reaching the heart or lungs. Tkach reported Sept. 12 that Nixon had suffered a recurrence of phlebitis in his left leg with a new blood clot present and the leg "swollen and painful." Tkach had flown from Washington to California to provide continuity of treatment for Nixon, who was residing at San Clemente. Nixon had remained isolated from the public since his resignation, and the state of his health had become a recurring news topic, with conflicting reports. Nixon's health and the weight attached to it by President Ford in granting Nixon a pardon had brought persistent questions at White House press briefings. Nixon was found to have a blood clot in his right lung and his doctor, John C. Lungren, announced Sept. 25 that it was "a potentially dangerous situation" but was "not critical at this time." "There's a very good chance of recovery," he said. "It will take some time." Nixon was hospitalized at Memorial Hospital Medical Center in Long Beach, Calif. Sept. 23. Nixon was released Oct. 4.

Nixon went into life-endangering medical shock after a surgical operation Oct. 29 and remained in critical condition after a stabilization of vital life signs was achieved. Nixon had been readmitted to the Memorial Hospital Medical Center Oct. 23 because of complications in his phlebitis condition. Defects in the veins of the left leg, detected by a venogram, led to the second hospitalization, which was expected to last "a few days," according to Lungren. A new clot, said to be an "active" one, was discovered late Oct. 28 and a 70-minute operation was performed by Dr. Eldon Hickman and a team of physicians at 5:30 a.m. Oct. 29 to put a plastic clamp (a Miles clip) on a vein in the pelvis to prevent the clot from moving, if it broke loose in the leg, to the lungs, where it could cause death. Nixon's post-operative condition was "stable" and he was "recovering in a normal manner." But at 12:45 p.m. Nixon suddenly went into vascular shock. Countershock treatment was administered for three hours until a stable vascular condition was restored. Nixon remained on the critical list under intensive care. Nixon press aide Ronald L. Ziegler told reporters Oct. 30 "there's no question about the fact that we almost lost President Nixon yesterday afternoon." Nixon was released from the hospital Nov. 14 to recuperate at his San Clemente estate. [For details of attempts to secure Nixon's testimony at the cover-up trial see WATERGATE AFFAIR 92, 100]

See also AGNEW, SPIRO T.; AGRICULTURE; APPOINTMENTS & RESIGNATIONS; BICENTENNIAL; BUDGET; CAMPAIGN FINANCING; CUBA; DEFENSE [2, 5]; DISARMAMENT; ECONOMY, U.S. [2-6]; EDUCATION; ELECTIONS [9, 11]; ENERGY CRISIS [6, 11, 13, 18, 32]; ENVIRONMENT & POLLUTION [2-3, 9]; FORD, GERALD R.; FOREIGN AID; FRANCE [1]; LABOR [1-2]; MEDICINE & HEALTH [1-10, 14-15]; MEXICO [17]; MIDDLE EAST [7, 38-39]; MONETARY DEVELOPMENTS [12, 14, 18-19]; NORTH ATLANTIC TREATY ORGANIZATION; OIL [4, 23]; POLITICS [10]; POSTAL SERVICE; PRIVACY [1-7, 9,]; PULITZER PRIZES; RAILROADS; ROCKEFELLER, NELSON [3-5, 16]; SCIENCE; STOCK MARKET [1]; SUPREME COURT; TARIFFS & TRADE; TELEVISION & RADIO; UNION OF SOVIET SOCIALIST REPUBLICS [1, 3-6, 9, 17, 26]; VETERANS; VIETNAM, REPUBLIC OF [35]; WATERGATE; WELFARE & POVERTY

NOBEL PRIZES—The 1974 Prizes were awarded Oct. 3-15 by the Swedish Royal Academy of Science in five fields—literature, medicine, economics, physics and chemistry. The peace price, which drew criticism in 1973 when it was awarded to U.S. Secretary of State Henry Kissinger and North Vietnam's Le Duc Tho for their efforts in resolving the Vietnam war, was again disputed, this time for one of its two choices, former Premier Eisaku Sato of Japan. (The peace prize, which carried an equal monetary value with the other Nobels of about $124,000 was decided by a committee of the Norwegian Storting [parliament] rather than the academy.)

Peace—The Nobel Peace Prize committee Oct. 8 awarded the 1974 prize to Sato, 73, and to Sean MacBride, 70, of Ireland, United Nations commissioner for South-West Africa. Sato was cited for his role in the signing of a treaty to halt the spread of nuclear weapons. It was revealed Oct. 11 that a worldwide drive had been mounted on Sato's behalf, by the chairman of Japan's largest construction company and a former U.N. ambassador, Toshikazu Kase. The campaign had taken 14 months and involved publication of a special book written by a ghost writer, to meet one of the requirements for the award but which never went on sale to the public. MacBride, who was foreign minister of Ireland (1948-51), was honored for his work on behalf of human rights. In his United Nations post, he had supervised efforts by South-West Africa to gain independence from South Africa.

Medicine—Three scientists, whose innovations began the modern science of cell biology nearly 30 years ago and who had made major contributions since to understanding the inner workings of living cells, shared the 1974 Nobel Prize for Medicine or Physiology, it was announced Oct. 10. The winners were Albert Claude, 75, who headed the Jules Bordet Institute in Brussels; George Emil Palade, 61, of the cell biology section of the Yale University School of Medicine; and Christian de Duve, 57, who held appointments at both Rockefeller University and the University of Louvain in Belgium.

Economics—The 1974 Nobel Memorial Prize in Economic Science was awarded Oct. 9 to Gunnar Myrdal and Friedrich A. von Hayek, two 75-year-old social economists who had won international recognition for differing views. Myrdal was a visiting professor at the City University of New York on leave from Stockholm University in his Swedish homeland; von Hayek was a visiting professor at Salzburg (Austria) University having retired, under the school's mandatory policy, from the University of Chicago. Myrdal advocated deep government involvement in the economy, while von Hayek favored a hands-off governmental policy.

Literature—Eyvind Johnson, 74, and Harry Edmund Martinson, 70, Swedish writers regarded as literary giants in their own country but virtually unknown aboard, were named by the Swedish Academy Oct. 3 as co-winners of the 1974 Nobel Prize in Literature. The choices were immediately attacked by literary figures and critics, who noted that neither had earned an international reputation and contended that their selection smacked of favoritism within the Swedish academy. The authors had written scores of novels, short stories, poem and other writings but only a half-dozen had been published in English.

Physics—Two British radio astronomers, Sir Martin Ryle, 56, and Antony Hewish, 50, were awarded the 1974 Nobel Prize for Physics, it was announced Oct. 15, the first time the prize was given in that field. The two were honored for their pioneering work in radioastrophysics. Ryle, director of a radio telescope outside Cambridge (England), was cited for his work in developing advanced techniques for using telescopes in observing detail in celestial bodies. Hewish, a professor at the University of Cambridge, was cited for his part in the discovery of mysterious energy sources, made up of condensed stars, known as pulsars.

Chemistry—Paul J. Flory, 64, a professor at Stanford University (Palo Alto, Calif.), won the 1974 Nobel Prize in Chemistry for his work in macromolecules, it was announced Oct. 15 by the Royal Swedish Academy. Flory was cited for "fundamental achievements, both theoretical and experimental," in the field of macromolecules which included plastics and such biological compounds as protein, nucleic acids, cellulose and rubber.

See also SOLZHENITSYN, ALEXANDER

NO-FAULT AUTO INSURANCE—*See* INSURANCE

NORTH ATLANTIC TREATY ORGANIZATION (NATO)—Kissinger, Nixon score European allies. In mid-March U.S. Secretary of State Henry A. Kissinger and President Nixon were sharply critical of America's NATO allies. Kissinger told a group of congressmen's wives in Washington March 11 that the biggest current U.S. foreign policy problem was getting the cooperation of European allies. He issued a milder statement the next day after Europeans expressed dismay over his unusually blunt words. In what he thought was a private session unattended by the press, Kissinger said "the biggest problem American foreign policy confronts right now is not how to regulate competition with its enemies ... but how to bring our friends to a realization that there are greater common interests than simply self-assertiveness." Referring to U.S. complaints over what it considered French obstacles to a united policy by oil-consuming nations in the current energy crisis, Kissinger said the U.S. objected when European "independence takes the form of basic hostility to the U.S." and when "in a crisis which can only be dealt with cooperatively the Europeans deliberately adopt a competitive posture." He said Europe's most serious problem was that "there have been very rarely, fully legitimate governments in any European country since World War I." In a follow-up statement issued March 12 after his remarks stirred sharp controversy, Kissinger acknowledged "real and serious" problems in the alliance but promised that the U.S. would use "patience and goodwill" in seeking to overcome them. He said "our overriding objective is to preserve the unity of the West."

In a nationally televised question and answer period at a meeting of business executives in Chicago, Nixon warned March 15 that the U.S. might reduce its troop levels in Europe if the European Economic Community (EEC) tried to "gang up against the U.S." in economic and political matters. Stressing that the U.S. was "indispensable to the security of Europe," both in the presence of American troops in Europe and in the U.S. nuclear umbrella, he said "the Europeans cannot have it both ways. They cannot have the U.S. participation and cooperation on the security front and then proceed to have confrontation and even hostility on the economic and political fronts."

Declaration on Atlantic relations approved. Foreign ministers of the 15 member states of NATO met in Ottawa June 18-19 and approved a 14-point declaration of principles that affirmed the "common destiny" of the allies. Alliance relations had been strained by political, economic and military disagreements. [See below] The declaration was formally signed in Brussels June 26 at a meeting of heads of state of the NATO members. The key section of the declaration, Article 11, stated that the alliance members "are firmly resolved to keep each other fully informed and to strengthen the practice of frank and timely consultations by all means which may be appropriate on matters relating to their common interests." Disputes over consultations had contributed to a deterioration of relations between the U.S. and its NATO allies. Delegates to the Ottawa meeting acknowledged that the passage on this issue had been the last and most difficult to be drafted. The U.S. had sought a stronger commitment to consultations, preferring language which would have imposed a legal obligation upon members to consult. France, in particular, had opposed any such binding language and ultimately secured U.S. compromise on this point. The declaration itself developed from a call issued by U.S. Secretary of State Kissinger in April 1973 in which he proposed an Atlantic Charter. (Although Kissinger had envisioned a single charter, Europeans had insisted on a separate document for U.S.-Common Market relations.)

Among the other points covered by the declaration: The mutual-defense provisions were potentially increased geographically when members agreed that "the area of application of the treaty" could include the Middle East. New emphasis was placed on the deterrent role of Britain and France, as Western Europe's two nuclear powers, who would "undertake to make the necessary contribution" through the use of deterrent or actual force if that became necessary for mutual security. The U.S. agreed to maintain its troop levels in Europe and to implement defense actions "should the need arise." The members agreed "to work to remove sources of conflict between their economic policies and to encourage economic cooperation with one another."

The declaration was signed in Brussels June 26 by government leaders of the 15 member states. In remarks upon his arrival the day before, President Nixon said, "Without the alliance, it is doubtful that detente [with Russia] would have begun." He also pledged not to reduce U.S. forces "unless there is a reciprocal action" by Moscow. (Nixon attended the NATO meeting en route to his June 27-July 3 summit meeting in the Soviet Union.) In an address June 26, West German Chancellor Helmut Schmidt said the worst problems facing the alliance were not political, but economic, an assessment with which, it was reported later, other heads of state concurred. (The economic disagreements had surfaced in March when Kissinger told a group of Congressional wives in Washington that European "independence takes the form of basic hostility to the U.S." Kissinger was referring to U.S. complaints over what it considered French obstacles to a united policy by oil-consuming nations.)

NATO's internal conflicts also had been reflected in the subdued atmosphere which marked the observance in Brussels April 4 of the 25th anniversary of the alliance. In June, at a Brussels meeting of European defense ministers, Norway said it would not accept foreign bases or nuclear weapons on its soil except in case of war or threat of war. However, some progress was made when U.S. Secretary of Defense James Schlesinger received support for the new U.S. nuclear "counterforce" strategy against Soviet missiles which was replacing the "countercity" strategy previously employed.

Defense reductions scheduled. The Netherlands revealed plans July 9 to go ahead with a ten-year program of extensive man-power and equipment cuts in its military forces, despite strong criticism by its NATO allies and its earlier promise not to make the cuts. According to a Dutch Defense Ministry spokesman July 12, the planned reductions were expected to be implemented regardless of NATO's reaction, saving an estimated $300 million over four years.

Haig named NATO commander. The appointment of White House chief of staff Alexander M. Haig Jr. as supreme commander of NATO was announced by the White House Sept. 16. Haig, who resigned his commission as a four-star general to serve in the White House under former President Nixon, returned to active duty to assume the NATO post, effective Dec. 15. President Ford also named him commander of U.S. forces in Europe, effective Nov. 1. Gen. Andrew J. Goodpaster, 59, currently held the posts. Prior to the announcement, NATO's defense planning committee met in Brussels and unanimously approved the Haig appointment. Some objection had been voiced in Congress and reportedly within NATO to Haig's appointment.

Haig denied Sept. 17 a report in the *New York Times* that day that he had been instrumental in persuading Ford to grant a pardon to Nixon before it might be too late to avert Nixon's physical and mental collapse. His denial was supported by Ford who said, "Al Haig never discussed with me the mental or physical condition" of Nixon prior to the pardon decision.

In Dec. 15 ceremonies at Supreme Headquarters Allied Powers Europe, located in Casteau, Belgium, Haig took over as supreme commander of NATO forces in Europe. At a news conference earlier that day, Haig defended the adequacy of his combat experience, noting that he had served in the Korean and Vietnam wars. Haig was the first officer without military experience from World War II to assume the NATO supreme command. In Nov. 1 ceremonies in Stuttgart, West Germany, Haig had taken over as commander in chief of U.S. forces in Europe.

NATO ministers meet. Foreign and defense ministers of the member nations held their semi-annual meetings in Brussels Dec. 9-13. At the sessions held Dec. 10-11 by the NATO defense ministers, U.S. Secretary of Defense Schlesinger warned the allies against any "stampede" to cut back military strength for economic reasons in the belief that U.S. military power would be sufficient to protect them. Although the defense ministers of 10 European NATO members—Great Britain, West Germany, Belgium, Denmark, Greece, Italy, Luxembourg, the Netherlands, Norway and Turkey, the so-called "Eurogroup"—had announced at a Dec. 9 meeting plans to increase arms during 1975, these additional forces would be the result of budgetary decisions taken at least three years ago; Schlesinger's appeal was to avoid reductions in forthcoming budgets. (Great Britain had recently announced a planned reduction in its military budget.)

See also Appointments & Resignations; Cyprus [4, 7, 15]; Disarmament; European Security; Ford, Gerald R.; France [18]; Germany, West [5, 15]; Greece [2, 13]; Iceland; Italy [2]; Portugal [27-29]; Territorial Waters; Yugoslavia [10]

NORWAY—Oil Developments. The government published a White Paper Feb. 15 outlining a restricted role for foreign oil companies in the oil and gas fields in Norway's sector of the North Sea. Foreign firms would be subject to close government control; they would be confined mainly to contracting for exploration and drilling and would be authorized as operators only in exceptional cases. No new concessions would be granted in the next few years south of the 62nd parallel in the North Sea, the White Paper proposed. The Norwegian state oil company Statoil would become an independent operator and would be favored in exploitation of fields north of the 62nd parallel. Production would be held at "a moderate tempo" to protect oil and gas resources and to permit gradual absorption by the Norwegian economy. Private foreign and domestic groups would be allowed "reasonable" profits.

The Industry Ministry announced Aug. 29 that a discovery, reported April 17, by a group headed by the government-owned Statoil and Mobil was the biggest oil and gas field in Norway's sector of the North Sea. The ministry said the field contained reserves of at least 2 billion barrels of oil and 50 billion cubic meters of natural gas. The new field was located 95 miles west of the Sognefjord estuary, and bordered the British sector. The field, which displaced Ekofisk as Norway's biggest, was renamed Statfjord after previously being called "Norwegian Brent," after the adjoining British field.

Indications of extensive petroleum deposits were found separately during 1974 by Soviet and U.S. scientists at two widely separated sites in the Norwegian Sea, off the coasts of Norway and Iceland. The U.S. research ship Glomar Challenger, which had been drilling into the ocean floors for six years, had found indications of oil and natural gas in deep holes drilled in August-September at the so-called Voring Plateau, which extended westward some 400 miles off the northwestern coast of Norway, the French newspaper *Le Monde* reported Oct. 10. The Norwegian government protested the ship's activity on an "extension of the continental shelf," asserting it had denied the ship permission to drill. The U.S. National Science Foundation, which subsidized the project, said the area was an "international zone."

According to the London *Times* Oct. 7, the area was part of the Norwegian shelf, whose outer limit had never been fixed. Norway laid claim to a shelf that extended as far out as drilling could be conducted. The other oil find was made by Soviet scientists aboard a research ship northeast of Iceland, according to an Oct. 28 *New York Times* report. They discovered oil-bearing sediment at the southwestern end of the Jan Mayen Ridge, which extended toward Jan Mayen Island in the Norwegian Sea.

Fishing changes sought. The government announced Sept. 26 a three-phase extension of its fisheries limits off northern Norway in 1975 to preserve fish stocks and avert collisions between trawlers and other types of fishing gear. Under the plan, Norway would establish, effective Jan. 1, 1975, "pocket zones" outside the existing 12-mile fishing limit which would bar all trawlers both domestic and foreign; Norway would then extend its fishing limits from 12 to 50 nautical miles after consultation with the countries affected; ultimately, the government sought a 200-mile economic zone for coastal states. Jen Evensen, minister of state with responsibility for negotiations on fishing limits, disclosed Oct. 24 that Norway claimed 5,320 square nautical miles as non-trawling zones.

Barents Sea talks with U.S.S.R. The Soviet Union and Norway held formal negotiations in Moscow Nov. 25-29 on the delineation of their disputed boundary on the continental shelf of the Barents Sea between the Norwegian island of Spitsbergen and the Soviet islands of Novaya Zemlya off the U.S.S.R. mainland. Extensive oil and gas deposits were believed to exist in the area.

See also Chile [3]; Communism, International; European Security; Middle East [26]; Monetary Developments [4, 11, 15]; Nobel Prizes; North Atlantic Treaty Organization; Oil [23, 25-26]; Poland

NUCLEAR WEAPONS—*See* Atomic Energy [1-8]; Disarmament
NURSING HOMES—*See* Medicine & Health [3, 17]
NUTRITION—*See* Famine & Food; Obituaries [Davis]; Welfare & Poverty

OBIE AWARDS—*See* THEATER

OBITUARIES

William (Bud) Abott, 78, straight man of the Abott and Costello comedy team (1931-57); April 24 in Los Angeles.

Gen. Creighton W. Abrams, 59, Army chief of staff since 1972; commander of U.S. forces in Vietnam (1968-72), oversaw gradual U.S. withdrawal from the war; as chief of staff supported reduction of support forces eliminating seven Army headquarters; Sept. 4 in Washington.

Forrest (Phog) Allen, 88, National Collegiate Athletic Association (NCAA) coach mostly with the University of Kansas (1908-09, 1920-56); retired with most wins in NCAA basketball history (771 wins, subsequently broken); Sept. 16 in Lawrence, Kan.

Stewart Alsop, 60, well-known member of the Washington press corps, wrote syndicated column with his brother Joseph (1945-58) before joining *Saturday Evening Post* (1958-68) and finally *Newsweek*; coauthored books included *The Center* (1968) and *Sub Rosa* (1945), wrote *Stay of Execution* (1973) about his bout with leukemia from which he eventually died; May 26 in Washington.

Miguel Angel Asturias, 74, Guatemalan writer and diplomat; won Nobel Prize (1967) for his novels on the exploitation of Latin America's poor, the theme of his trilogy—*Strong Wind, The Green Pope* and *The Eyes of the Dead*; ambassador to France (1966-70); June 9 in Madrid.

Mohammad Ayub Khan, 67, ruler of Pakistan (1958-69), forced from power following street demonstrations demanding a less authoritarian rule; brought a degree of stability to a shaky economy; April 20 in Karachi. He was buried with full military honors April 22.

Jack Benny, 80, one of the most famous American comedians; *The Jack Benny Show* featured on radio (1932-55) and television (1950-65) portrayed him as a violin-playing miser and became a national institution to millions of Americans; Dec. 26 of cancer in Los Angeles.

Alexander M. Bickel, 49, professor of law at Yale and one of the nation's foremost constitutional scholars; participated in the successful defense of the *New York Times* in the controversial Pentagon Papers case (1971); Nov. 7 of cancer in New Haven, Conn.

Charles E. Bohlen, 69, U.S. ambassador to the U.S.S.R. (1953-57) and top expert on Russia for over 30 years; involved in every major U.S.-Soviet policy development from 1934 to his retirement in 1968; Jan. 2 in Washington.

Hal Boyle, 63, Pulitzer Prize winning (1945) correspondent and columnist for the Associated Press; discontinued daily column in February after 30 years of writing covering three wars; April 2 in New York.

Otto Braun, 73, appointed military advisor to the Chinese Communists (1933-39) by the Soviet-led Comintern (Communist International), planned the Long March in which the Communists moved their headquarters inland (1934-35); Aug. 15 in East Berlin.

Walter Brennan, 80, veteran actor who appeared in over 100 films, starred in the television series *The Real McCoys* and won three Academy Awards (1936, 1938, 1940); Sept. 21 in Oxnard, Calif.

Jacob Bronowski, 66, scientist, poet, humanist; resident fellow of the Salk Institute since 1964, during World War II studied the effects of bombing on industry and the economy and later researched the effects of the atomic bombings, had recently completed a 13-part television series for the British Broadcasting Corporation on the place of science in history, *The Ascent of Man*; Aug. 22 in East Hampton, N.Y.

Johnny Mack Brown, 70, All-American college football player with the University of Alabama team that won the 1926 Rose Bowl, star of hundreds of Western movies in the 1930s and 40s; named to the College Football Hall of Fame (1957); Nov. 14 in Woodland Hills, Calif.

Dr. Carl J. Burckhardt, 82, Swiss minister to France (1945-49), president of the International Red Cross (1944-48) and League of Nations commissioner for the Free City of Danzig (1937-39) when he tried and failed to talk Hitler out of invading Poland; March 3 in Geneva.

Dr. Vannevar Bush, 84, key figure in the mobilization of technology for the Allies in World War II; convinced Franklin D. Roosevelt of the need for coordination of scientific research and in 1940 founded the National Defense Research Committee; leading participant in many key wartime programs, among them the atomic bomb project; June 28 in Belmont, Mass.

Jefferson Caffery, 87, once dean of American diplomatic corps; ambassador to Cuba (1934-37), Brazil (1937), France (1944-49) and Egypt (1949-55); had major role in settling British-Egyptian disputes over Suez canal bases; April 13 in Lafayette, La.

Murray M. Chotiner, 64, political adviser to President Nixon since 1946; Jan. 30 in Washington of a pulmonary blood clot caused by a car accident Jan. 23.

Dr. Edward U. Condon, one of leading U.S. physicists; played a key role in development of atomic bomb and radar programs, and in creation of the Atomic Energy Commission; March 26 in Boulder, Colo.

Katharine Cornell, 81, foremost actress of the American theater, 1921-61; famous for her roles in *The Barretts of Wimpole Street, Romeo and Juliet,* and *Candida.*

Jean Cardinal Danielou, 69, leading Jesuit theologian and staunch defender of papal authority; leader of the Catholic left after World War II; May 20 in Paris.

Adelle Davis, 70, well-known authority on nutrition, coined the phase "you are what you eat"; contended disease could be avoided by a good daily diet; wrote *Let's Eat Right to Keep Fit* (1954); May 31 in Palos Verdes Estates, Calif. of bone cancer.

Dizzy Dean (Jay Hanna Dean), 63, formed with brother, Paul, a dynamic pitching duo for the St. Louis Cardinals' famed Gas House Gang in the 1930s; won 150 games, threw 27 shutouts; in 1934 he won 30 games and lost seven, won two games in the World Series and was the National League's Most Valuable Player; member Hall of Fame (1953); July 17 in Reno, Nev.

Alexander P. de Seversky, 80, proponent of strategic air power, well-known World War I aviator; flew over 50 combat missions in the Czarist air force; later designed the first automatic synchronous bombsight; Aug. 24 in New York.

Vittorio De Sica, 73, neo-realist movie director, called himself "an artist of the poor," used common laborers rather than professional actors and filmed in the streets and alley rather than studios; won five Oscars including one for *The Bicycle Thief* (1949) and another for *The Garden of the Finzi-Continis* (1972); Nov. 13 in Paris.

Billy DeWolfe, 67, comedian-actor whose best known role was his impersonation of Mrs. Murgatroyd, a middle-aged matron, in the movie *Blue Skies*; also appeared in *Dixie, Tea for Two, Lullaby of Broadway* and *Call Me Madam*; appeared in other films and television programs; March 5 of lung cancer in Los Angeles.

Marshal Eurico Gaspar Dutra, 89, president of Brazil (1945-51) who outlawed the Communist Party and broke off relations with the U.S.S.R.; June 11 in Rio De Janeiro.

Edward K. (Duke) Ellington, 75, jazz composer, arranger, pianist and band leader; wrote over 6,000 musical pieces of varying length and genres including, *Solitude, Sophisticated Lady, In a Sentimental Mood* and *I Let a Song Go Out of My Heart*; awarded Presidential Medal of Freedom (1969), the Legion of Honor (1973) and elected to the Royal Swedish Academy of Music (1971); May 24 of pneumonia, a complication of lung cancer, in New York.

Cass Elliot, 33, well-known American pop singer; became famous with the Mamas and the Papas group (1965-68); July 29 in London, after a heart attack brought on by being overweight (220 pounds).

Yekaterina A. Furtseva, 63, the only woman in Soviet history to become a member of the ruling inner circle of the Communist Party; minister of Culture since 1960; Oct. 25 in Moscow.

Fu Tso-yi, 79, Chinese Nationalist general, surrendered Peking to the Communists in January 1949 rather than risk the destruction of the ancient capital; later served as minister of water conservation in the new regime (1949-63); reported April 25 in Peking.

Hans Gisevius, 68, German anti-Nazi, leading prosecution witness at the Nuremberg war crime trials; involved with group which tried to overthrow Hitler, which he described in *To the Bitter End* (1947); March 26 in Geneva.

Duke of Gloucester, 74, last surviving son of King George V, uncle of Queen Elizabeth II and eighth in line to the British throne; personal aide-de-camp of King George VI (1936-52); June 10 in Northamptonshire, England.

Harry Gold, 60, convicted atomic spy, key witness in atomic espionage trial of Julius and Ethel Rosenberg; died in Philadelphia Aug. 28, 1972, kept secret until Feb. 14.

Samuel Goldwyn, 91, born in Warsaw, Poland; pioneer Hollywood producer who joined brother-in-law Jesse L. Lasky and a lawyer in 1913 to form Jesse L. Lasky Feature Play Co., whose first movie, *The Squaw Man,* was an instant success and the first feature-length movie; broke with partners in 1917 to form Goldwyn Pictures Corp.; sold his company in 1923 to another corporation that formed Metro-Goldwyn-Mayer, but was never part of MGM; movies included *Wuthering Heights, The Best Years of Our Lives, Guys and Dolls* and *Porgy and Bess*; Jan. 31 in Los Angeles.

Ernest Gruening, 87, diplomat and journalist; senator (1958-69) and governor (1939-53) from Alaska; foe of U.S. military involvement in Vietnam, voted against 1964 Gulf of Tonkin resolution which justified U.S. military action there; June 26 in Washington.

Alan F. Guttmacher, 75, international leader in family planning; president of Planned Parenthood Federation of America since 1962; March 18 in New York.

Harry Hershfield, 89, cartoonist, humorist and columnist who gained widespread recognition in the 1940s with his radio show "Can You Top This?"; Dec. 15 in New York.

Georgette Heyer, 71, wrote over 50 books, mainly on historical and detective themes including *The Black Moth* (1921), *The Corinthian* (1941) and *Charity Girl* (1970); July 4 in London.

Luther H. Hodges, 76, governor of North Carolina (1954-60), a leading moderate in a time of racial stress; secretary of commerce (1961-64) under President Kennedy; Oct. 6 in Chapel Hill, N.C.

Paul G. Hoffman, 83, first administrator of the Marshall Plan after World War II (1948-50) under President Truman for which he received the Medal of Freedom (1973); managing director of the United Nations Development Program (1959-72); Oct. 8 in New York.

Frank Hogan, 72, Manhattan district attorney (1941-73); successfully prosecuted a number of racketeers, gangsters and city officials as well as sports and television quiz show scandal figures; later prosecution of students, militants and minorities beginning in 1968 led to accusations of vindictiveness; April 2 in New York.

Harry Hooper, 87, outfielder with the Boston Red Sox (1909-1920) which won five World Series championships and the Chicago White Sox (1921-25); elected to the Hall of Fame (1971); Dec. 17 in Santa Cruz, Calif.

H. L. Hunt, 85, oil magnate whose total holdings were estimated at $1 billion-$2 billion, most of which were the result of speculation including one in what turned out to have been one of the greatest oil finds of the century in Libya; president and founder of the Hunt Oil Company (Dallas); ultraconservative who made his views known in editorials, books and interviews; Nov. 29 in Dallas.

Chet Huntley, 62, former television newscaster, member of NBC's *The Huntley-Brinkley Report* (1956-70); was preparing to dedicate the recreational complex Big Sky which he had organized; March 20 in Bozeman, Mont.

Sol Hurok, 85, whose efforts for 65 years as impresario brought world renowned artists such as Andres Segovia, Artur Rubinstein, Anna Pavlova and Rudolf Nureyev to the U.S.; born in Russia, came to the U.S. in 1906 and later brought many performing companies from his homeland in cultural exchanges, including the Bolshoi Ballet and the Moiseyev dance companes; March 5 following a visit with Segovia in New York.

Haj Amin el-Husseini, 80, Grand Mufti of Jerusalem and powerful leader in the Arab world in the 1940s and early 1950s; a fierce anti-Zionist, who fought the founding of Israel and worked as a Nazi collaborator during World War II; July 4 in Beirut.

B. Everett Jordan, 77, North Carolina Democratic senator (1958-72), led 1964 Senate investigation into the activities of Bobby Baker, Senate aide later convicted of income tax evasion, larceny and fraud; March 15 in Saxapahaw, N.C.

Anne Klein, 51, major figure in American design; opened Anne Klein & Co. in 1968; March 19 in New York.

William F. Knowland, 65, former senator from California (1945-58) who charged that U.S. neglect led to a Communist take-over in China; editor and publisher of the *Oakland Tribune*; Feb. 23 of self-inflicted gunshot wounds in Guerneville, Calif.

Josef Krips, 72, conductor of the Viennese school of conducting, career spanned 53 years with the Vienna Philharmonic, the Vienna State Opera and the London, Buffalo and San Francisco Symphonies; Oct. 12 in Geneva, Switzerland.

Arthur Krock, 87, reporter, Washington bureau chief and columnist for the *New York Times* (1927-67); won three Pulitzer prizes (1935, 1938, 1951) declining the third; wrote *In The Nation* (1966), *Memoirs: Sixty Years On the Firing Line* (1968), *The Consent of the Governed and Other Deceits* (1971); April 12 in Washington.

Par Lagerkvist, 83, Swedish author of novels, dramas, poems and short stories; won the Nobel Prize in 1951; works include *The Dwarf* (1945) and *Barabbas* (1951); July 11 in Stockholm.

Charles A. Lindbergh, 72, became one of the world's most celebrated heroes when he flew solo from New York to Paris in the Spirit of St. Louis in 1927; Lindbergh's infant son was kidnapped and later found murdered in 1932. The subsequent apprehension and conviction of Bruno Hauptmann were given unprecedented world press crime coverage; later, his opposition to U.S. entry into World War II led to his Air Corps resignation following U.S. entry into the war; became a strong proponent of conservation; Aug. 26 in Maui, Hawaii.

Walter Lippman, 85, political journalist whose columns influenced world opinion; President Ford called his death the loss of "a great American" and praised his role in "shaping a new standard of journalism"; awards included two Pulitzer Prizes (1958, 1962), the Presidential Medal of Freedom (1964) and Overseas Press Club awards for interpretation of foreign news (1953, '55, and '59); Dec. 14 in New York.

Frank McGee, 52, NBC-TV newscaster since 1957, host of *Today* show since 1971; April 17 of pneumonia resulting from treatment of cancer of the bone marrow since 1970, in New York.

V. K. Krishna Menon, 77, Indian diplomat; ambassador to Great Britain (1947-52); defense minister (1957-62); Oct. 6 in New Delhi.

Darius Milhaud, 81, influential and prolific French composer, one of the first classical musicians to work in the jazz idiom; composed some 15 operas, 19 ballets, 18 quartets, 20 sonatas, 12 symphonies and 34 concertos; June 24 in Geneva, Switzerland.

Capt. Edward H. Molyneux, 79, British fashion designer; opened a design house in Paris in 1919 following distinguished military career; designed for well-known personalities in theater and politics; March 22 in Monte Carlo, Monaco.

Agnes Moorehead, 67, stage, screen and television actress who appeared in almost 100 films; April 30 in Rochester, Minn.

Wayne L. Morse, 73, senator from Oregon who served as Republican (1945-52). Independent (1953-55) and Democrat (1956-68); at center of battles over environment, education and labor issues; was one of two senators who voted against 1964 Gulf of Tonkin resolution justifying the U.S. action in Vietnam; July 22 in Portland, Oregon. (Morse had won the Democratic nomination to one of Oregon's Senate seats May 28.)

Karl E. Mundt, 74, representative (1938-48) and senator (1948-73) (R., S. Dakota); staunch anti-Communist during the McCarthy period and, with Richard Nixon investigated the alleged Communist activities of Alger Hiss; suffered a stroke (1969) which left him unable to appear in Congress, refusal to resign led to a Senate decision (1972) which relieved him of his posts as a ranking Republican; Aug. 16 in Washington.

Tina Niarchos, 45, wife of Stavros Niarchos, Greek millionnaire shipowner, former wife of Aristotle Onassis (1946-61) also a Greek shipping magnate, and Marquess of Blandford of English royalty (1961-71); Oct. 10 of an accidental overdose of sleeping pills in Paris, according to a coroner.

David Oistrakh, 65, Soviet violinist and conductor; gave recitals in all the major cities and played with most of the leading orchestras of the world; became a lecturer (1934) and later a full professor (1937) at the Moscow Conservatory; was awarded the Stalin Prize (1942), the Soviet Union's highest honor; Oct. 24 in Amsterdam during a concert tour with the Amsterdam Philharmonic.

Margaret Leech Pulitzer, 80, historian, who won two Pulitzer prizes, one for *Reveille in Washington* (1942) and the second for *In the Days of McKinley* (1960); March 24 in New York.

Buford Pusser, 36, sheriff in Tennessee (1964-70) whose exploits as crime-buster led to the movie *Walking Tall*; was to star in sequel; Aug. 21 in an auto accident near Adamsville, Tenn.

Oliver Quayle 3rd, 52, public opinion poll specialist and board chairman of Quayle, Plesser & Co.; April 14 in Hanover, N.H.

Peter Revson, 35, considered top U.S. road-racing driver, won the pole position and finished second in the 1971 Indianapolis 500, won the British and Canadian Formula One Grand Prix in 1973; March 22 in a crash during a practice run for the South African Grand Prix in Johannesburg.

Cornelius Ryan, 54, novelist of war narratives, whose works included *The Longest Day* (1959) and *The Last Battle* (1965) which together sold over 10 million hard-cover copies, and *A Bridge Too Far* (1974); Nov. 23 of cancer.

Clay L. Shaw, New Orleans businessman acquitted of plotting to assassinate President Kennedy (1969); Aug. 15 in New Orleans.

David A. Siqueros, 77, Mexical muralist noted for his social consciousness; awarded Mexico's highest cultural prize, the National Prize for Art; Jan. 6 in Mexico City.

Gen. Carl A. Spaatz, 83, first Air Force chief of staff (1947-48) and commander of U.S. strategic bombing forces in Europe and the Pacific in World War II; July 14 in Washington.

Lewis L. Strauss, 77, member (1946-50) and chairman of the Atomic Energy Commission; key figure in shaping U.S. thermonuclear policy; embroiled in controversy over terminating security clearance of J. Robert Oppenheimer, father of the atomic bomb, and the controversial Dixon-Yates power contract; controversies contributed to Senate opposition to his appointment as secretary of commerce; Jan. 21 in Brandy Station, Va.

Ed Sullivan, 73, long-time Broadway columnist for the *New York Daily News* and master of ceremonies for one of the most successful television variety shows (1948-71) which was named after him; Oct. 13 in New York.

Jacqueline Susann, 53, novelist whose *Valley of the Dolls* (1966) was the world's best-selling novel with over 17 million copies sold and which, along with *The Love Machine* (1969) and *Once Is Not Enough* (1973) made her the first novelist to have three consecutive books atop the *New York Times'* best seller list; all three novels were made into movies; Sept. 21 of cancer in New York.

Dr. Earl W. Sutherland Jr., 58, researcher on the mechanisms that control organisms at the cellular level; won the 1971 Nobel Prize in physiology and medicine for his basic research on hormones; March 9 in Miami.

Dan Topping, 61, co-owner of the New York Yankees (1945-65) during which time team won 15 American League baseball pennants and 10 world championships; May 18 in Miami Beach.

Stepan Cardinal Trochta, 68, Czechoslovakia's only cardinal in 1947, sent to prison for "espionage for the Vatican" in 1954; conviction canceled and returned to office in 1968; April 6, in Vienna.

Amy Vanderbilt, 66, syndicated columnist on etiquette since 1954; wrote *Amy Vanderbilt's Complete Book of Etiquette* (1952); Dec. 28 of multiple fractures and internal injuries suffered in a fall from a second-story window in New York.

Earl Warren, 83, governor of California (1942-53), chief justice of the U.S. Supreme Court (1953-69); appointed to the court by President Eisenhower; advocate of school desegregation decisions first displayed in the landmark "Brown v. Board of Education of Topeka" case (1954); favored the broadening of criminal suspects' rights as well as the principle of one-man, one-vote; July 9 in Washington. A state funeral was held at the Supreme Court July 12 with 12 past and present justices serving as pallbearers. Burial took place at Arlington National Cemetery.

Arthur K. Watson, 55, executive for International Business Machines (IBM), who built the IBM World Trade Corporation into a world-enterprise; ambassador to France (1970-72); July 26 in Norwalk, Conn.

Del Webb, 75, part-owner of the New York Yankees (1945-1964), owned construction and hotel empire; July 4 in Rochester, Minn.

Hazel Wightman, 87, won 45 national tennis titles in 45 years; donated the Wightman Cup in women's tennis; named to the Tennis Hall of Fame; Dec. 5 in Chestnut Hill, Mass.

Marshal Georgi Konstantinovich Zhukov, 77, one of the Soviet Union's heroes of World War II; led the Red Army into Berlin, praised by military tacticians for his hard-driving leadership; dismissed and downgraded by Stalin after war and again by Nikita Khrushchev but rehabilitated in 1965; June 18 in Moscow.

See also AUSTRIA; AUTO RACING; BALLOONING; BURMA; CHINA, COMMUNIST; CYPRUS [2, 17]; ELECTIONS [9]; FRANCE [1]; GERMANY, WEST [8]; IRELAND, REPUBLIC OF; NEW ZEALAND

OBSCENITY & PORNOGRAPHY—Court narrows obscenity ruling's scope. The Supreme Court June 24 ruled that the movie *Carnal Knowledge* was not obscene under guidelines promulgated by the court in 1973. In a parallel decision, the court upheld the obscenity convictions of six men for mailing obscene matter—a brochure advertising the "illustrated presidential report on the commission on obscenity and pornography."

Carnal Knowledge, which depicted the contrasting sex lives and marriages of two friends from their college years to middle age, had been declared obscene by an Albany, Ga. jury. The Georgia Supreme Court, applying the high court's 1973 obscenity standards, upheld the Albany jury. "Our own view of the film," Justice William H. Rehnquist wrote for the unanimous court, "satisfies us that *Carnal Knowledge* could not be found under the [court's 1973] standards to depict sexual conduct in a patently offensive way." It was a "serious misreading" of the 1973 decision to conclude that juries had "unbridled discretion" to decide what was obscene, Rehnquist said.

The second decision affirmed by a 5-4 decision the obscenity convictions of six Los Angeles men for mailing material that showed sexual acts and behavior forbidden under the 1973 guidelines. According to the U.S. 9th Circuit Court of Appeals, which affirmed the convictions, the brochure had pictures of "heterosexual and homosexual intercourse, sodomy and a variety of deviate sexual acts." The original trial jury had been unable to decide whether the book itself was obscene.

See also EDUCATION; TELEVISION & RADIO

OCEANOGRAPHY—*See* NORWAY; SPACE [8]; TERRITORIAL WATERS
OFFICE OF ECONOMIC OPPORTUNITY—*See* WELFARE & POVERTY
OFFICE OF MANAGEMENT & BUDGET—*See* APPOINTMENTS & RESIGNATIONS; BUDGET; ENVIRONMENT & POLLUTION [2]; SCIENCE; VETERANS
OHIO—*See* CONGRESS; ELECTIONS [5, 7, 9-10]; ENERGY CRISIS [6]; GAMBLING; POPULATION; WEATHER

OIL—The Arab producing states continued using oil as a political and economic weapon in 1974 with the pricing policies of the Arab oil states drastically affecting an already-shaky world monetary structure and, in turn, national economies. [For detailed information on the monetary situation, see MONETARY DEVELOPMENTS. See also ENERGY CRISIS and specific countries.]

The Embargo

[2] U.S. warnings to the Arabs about the effects of a continuing oil embargo were voiced in separate statements Jan. 7-8 by Defense Secretary James R. Schlesinger and Vice President Gerald R. Ford. In a television interview, Schlesinger warned the American public might be provoked into the use of force in order to end the ban. Ford said the economic disorder caused by the cutoff might result in a reduction of U.S. food shipments to the Middle East and North Africa. The Arabs reacted to the threats by reporting plans to blow up their oil fields in the case of U.S. military intervention. Saudi Arabian Petroleum Minister Sheik Zaki al-Yamani warned major oil-consuming nations Jan. 12 that any counteraction they might take would result in a possible head-on "confrontation."

[3] Several consuming nations made unilateral agreements with oil-producing states during January. [See below] France confirmed Jan. 9 that it had signed an agreement with Saudi Arabia under which France would receive 27 million tons of crude oil over the next few years. Saudi Arabia had announced Jan. 7 it would get French warplanes and other military equipment in exchange. Great Britain concluded an agreement with Saudi Arabia Jan. 15 and with Iran Jan. 25. A *New York Times* report from Beirut Feb. 3 said Britain was to receive an immediate increase of 200,000 barrels a day from Sauid Arabia. The Iranian agreement involved an exchange of five million additional tons of crude oil for about $240 million worth of industrial goods. The price of the oil would be about $7 a barrel, less than Iran received from concessionary oil firms.

[4] Disagreement between Arab states over U.S.-sponsored troop disengagement plans with Israel surfaced during January when Libya and Iraq were reported opposed to efforts by Egyptian President Anwar Sadat to lift the oil embargo. A U.S. government official said Jan. 29 that Sadat's appeal to other Arab leaders to lift the embargo was in response to a pledge made to Secretary of State Henry A. Kissinger that he would urge such a move in appreciation for the secretary's efforts in helping achieve the Israeli-Egyptian troop disengagement agreement. Sadat's position was that Kissinger's mediation was a reflection of change in American policy in the Middle East which warranted a shift in Arab oil policy. Sadat's proposals were rejected by Libya, which did not feel there was enough of a change in U.S. actions to warrant lifting the ban; and by Iraq which rejected an invitation by President Nixon to attend a world energy conference in Washington, scheduled for Feb. 11. The two nations were joined in their objections by other Arab states. Kuwaiti Foreign Minister Sheikh Sabah al-Ahmad al-Jaber Jan. 21 said, "Lifting the oil measures is still linked to Israeli

withdrawal from occupied Arab territories and the restoration of the rights of the Palestinian people." Syrian Foreign Minister Abdel Halim Khaddam announced Feb. 3, "Syria will accept military disengagement on the Golan Heights front only if it is made part of a plan for a total Israeli withdrawal from Arab territories conquered in the 1973 and 1967 wars." Saudi Arabia and Kuwait assured Syria they would continue the oil stoppage against the U.S. until Israel and Syria agreed to disengagement on Syrian terms. The U.S. reacted to the hard-line Arab statements on Feb. 6 when Kissinger said continuation of the ban "must be construed as a form of blackmail." It was the first time Kissinger used the word blackmail to describe the embargo. Kissinger also said the U.S. had been led to expect an end to the embargo in view of recent American peace efforts and criticized bilateral oil deals saying "all nations have a common problem of how to insure their supply and how to relate their crisis to the structure of the world economy."

[5] The beginning of the end of the oil embargo came during a meeting in Tripoli, Libya March 13 of the petroleum ministers of nine Arab states: Abu Dhabi, Algeria, Bahrain, Egypt, Kuwait, Libya, Qatar, Saudi Arabia and Syria. (Of the nations belonging to the Organization of Arab Petroleum Exporting Countries (OAPEC) only Dubai and Iraq were absent.) The agreement to lift the embargo was revealed by an unidentified Libyan official. The decision was to be announced at a full meeting of the 13-member Organization of Petroleum Exporting Countries (OPEC) to be held in Vienna March 17. (Nations belonging to OPEC were Abu Dhabi, Algeria, Ecuador, Indonesia, Iran, Iraq, Kuwait, Libya, Nigeria, Qatar, Saudi Arabia, Venezuela, with Gabon holding an associate membership.)

[6] The OPEC meeting, convened on March 16 resulted two days later in a lifting of the embargo against the U.S. by seven of the Arab producing countries. Libya and Syria refused to join the majority, while Iraq boycotted the talks. One of the seven nations, Algeria, said it was removing the ban provisionally until June 1. The Vienna delegates had agreed, however, that oil prices would not be rolled back; nor would shipment be resumed to the Netherlands and Denmark because neither nation had "made clear their position on asking for a full [Israeli] withdrawal from occupied territories," according to a statement by Saudi Arabia. The formal statement on the results of the meeting explained that a shift in American policy away from Israel had promoted the producers to terminate the embargo. Although Algeria mentioned the "goodwill" of the U.S., Libya and Syria decided not to go along with the majority opinion in the belief the U.S. had not done enough to insure Israeli withdrawal.

[7] Oil shipments by Saudi Arabia to the U.S. were reported resumed March 27, although that nation had warned Western countries a week earlier that if no progress was made in resolving the Middle East dispute the Arabs might reimpose the embargo and also mobilize other developing nations to take similar action by withholding their natural resources. Libya charged that resumption of shipments were a result of an American "threat" which they did not explain.

[8] Although the Soviet Union had officially encouraged the Arab states in their embargo policies, the Associated Press reported April 1 that Russia had continued to export Soviet petroleum products throughout the period, using two Greek and two U.S. ships to transport gasoline products from the Black Sea port of Tuapse, the site of the major oil refineries. Other "leaks" were reported as well. *The Washington Post* said March 21 that, during January and February, Arab oil producers began to "look the other way" and let their crude oil be sold to U.S. overseas military forces by way of refineries in other non-embargoed countries. In April, the Federal Energy Office released secret reports showing that

there had been "leaks" from Libya in November-December 1973; from Saudi Arabia during the entire period with, however, a drastic reduction in January and February; and from Tunisia throughout. Major sources of oil for the U.S. were Canada, Venezuela, Nigeria, Iran and Indonesia, whose exports were increased during the embargo period. A total of 386,406,678 barrels of crude oil, valued at $2.3 billion were exported to the U.S. from 30 countries during November1973-February 1974. The FEO "leak" figures were disputed by a number of sources who cited transshipment delays as the reason for post-embargo deliveries.

[9] Deliveries to Holland by OAPEC nations were resumed as the result of a decision made during a Cairo meeting July 10. OAPEC lifted the embargo because it was now "convinced the Dutch government's attitude toward the Middle East had changed," Saudi Arabian Petroleum Minister Yamani said. Although the Dutch port of Rotterdam had lost about $9.4 million in port duties during the ban, oil reserves in that country had nevertheless increased 30%. The increase was attributed by the Dutch Economics Ministry to a drop in consumption as a result of mild weather, highway speed limits and gasoline price rises. (Unlimited shipments of oil to Denmark were quietly resumed later in the year.)

[10] Libya lifted its 14-month oil embargo against the U.S. without making an official announcement the *Times of London* reported Dec. 31. Foreign oil companies in Libya said that although they had not been officially informed of the government's action in ending the embargo, the decision would have little bearing on the resumption of shipments. They cited the high cost of Libyan oil, about $12.50 a barrel, $2.50 more than foreign companies had to pay for Persian Gulf oil. As a result, Libyan production had dropped to about 800,000 barrels a day in 1974 from an average of 2.2 million in 1973.

Price Developments

[11] In spite of an OPEC announcement Jan. 9 barring increased prices for crude oil until April 1, Algeria boosted its prices 75% on Jan. 17. The increase, retroactive to Jan. 1, raised the price per barrel from $9.25 to $16.21. At a Jan. 27 meeting in Tokyo between Algeria, Saudi Arabia and Japan, Algerian Industry and Energy Minister Belaid Abdelsalam opposed any cuts in oil prices, saying the current high rates were necessary in view of Algeria's balance of payments deficit and its heavy indebtedness to foreign countries. Saudi Arabian Petroleum Minister Yamani, said that although his nation regarded current prices as "fair and reasonable," it was concerned that the "present prices of oil will create some serious problems in the balance of payments of so many nations." Yamani said later that any cut in oil prices, however, must be taken jointly by all the oil producers. Algeria also sought a price renegotiation on a number of natural gas contracts to raise rates nearly 1,000% by 1979. Diplomatic sources described the demand as only an "extreme negotiating position" assumed as a starting point for new rounds of bargaining. The Algerian demand concerned new contracts between its state petroleum company, Sonatrach, and the U.S., France, West Germany and Great Britain. OPEC nations agreed June 17 to continue the posted price of oil at current levels for three months from July 1. They announced 2% increase in royalties levied against oil companies, however, citing the companies' "excessive profits." Saudi Arabia did not concur with the decision, fearing it might prejudice new negotiations with the Arabian American Oil Co.

[12] Saudi Arabia also did not approve the Sept. 13 decision made by OPEC to raise by 3.5% the taxes and royalties paid by foreign oil companies. The decision, taken at the end of a two-day meeting in Vienna, would raise the tax on a barrel

of oil by 33¢, effective Oct. 1. In imposing the increase, the OPEC countries argued that price increases in industrial countries for machinery and food required the boost. While Saudi Arabia did not oppose the increase, it felt that the action should be coupled with a reduction in the price of oil. (U.S. Federal Energy Administrator John C. Sawhill said Sept. 13 that some of the oil firms might absorb the rise, "but they won't absorb all of it.")

[13] Yamani told newsmen in Washington Oct. 2 that oil prices would decline if there were a political solution to the Arab-Israeli conflict. Yamani warned, however, that if the Israelis did not withdraw from occupied Arab territories, "this would produce a war" that would "have a very dangerous effect on prices, as well as on the supply of oil." "Any solution that will stop the fighting," he said, "is in the hands of the American government."

[14] Representatives of Kuwait and Egypt defended Arab oil policies before the U.N. General Assembly in late September and denied they had contributed to world inflation. Sheik Sabah al-Ahmad al-Jaber, Kuwait's foreign minister, said Sept. 30 that inflation had plagued the industrial nations since the end of World War II, and he attributed it to these nations' "inability to properly manage their domestic affairs." Sheik Sabah charged that the major oil companies had deliberately frozen oil prices for more than 25 years, while the prices of all basic commodities, manufactured products and services exported by advanced countries were rising. "Raising the price of oil was in essence the correction of an inequitable situation," he asserted. Egyptian Foreign Minister Ismail Fahmy asserted that the Arabs had used their oil only to secure their "legitimate rights" and had imposed the 1973 embargo only after "warning the countries which assist Israel" in maintaining control over Arab territory.

[15] Saudi Arabia, the United Arab Emirates and Qatar reduced their oil prices Nov. 10 but drastically raised taxes and foreign royalties paid by the foreign oil companies. The two moves left the government revenues and the cost of oil to consumers at about their current level. The three states said the purpose of their move was to reduce the companies' "excess profits" and to help the world's oil customers. The action was taken at the end of a two-day conference in Abu Dhabi that also was attended by representatives of Iran, Kuwait and Iraq, who refused to go along with the new price structure on the ground that such a decision should be taken by OPEC. Saudi Arabia, the United Arab Emirates and Qatar reduced the posted price for a barrel of oil from $11.65 to $11.25. The royalty rate on the posted price was increased from 16.67% to 20%, while the tax on the companies' net income was boosted from 67.5% to 85%. The new rates were retroactive to Nov. 1 and were to continue to July 1, 1975, according to the communique.

[16] The OPEC nations decided at a meeting in Vienna Dec. 13 to raise the price of oil and adopt a new uniform pricing system. Petroleum prices were to be increased about 38¢ a barrel, or almost 4%, Jan. 1, 1975 and were to continue at that level until Oct. 1, 1975. The decision to increase the government revenue per barrel for oil marketed through their foreign companies to a maximum of $10.12 from $9.74 followed a formula that had been adopted Nov. 10 by Saudi Arabia, United Arab Emirates and Qatar. An official communique indicated that OPEC's action was aimed at further reducing the profits of the major international oil companies. Under the new pricing system, OPEC for the first time based actual prices on government revenues instead of the posted price upon which tax and royalties were estimated. It was not clear from OPEC's action what the market price for crude oil, the price paid by an oil company or other middlemen, would be. Theoretically the new market price should be $10.46 a barrel. Jamshid Amouzegar of Iran said he believed the new market price would

be about $10.70 or $10.72. Abderrahamane Khene, outgoing OPEC secretary general, later gave an estimate of $10.65.

Latin American Developments

[17] Colombia raised its posted price for crude oil exports by 75%, to $14.20 a barrel, it was announced Jan. 25. The Venezuelan government Feb. 6 doubled to about $14 a barrel the price it charged petroleum companies for royalty oil. The increase, retroactive to Feb. 1, affected the one-sixth of each firm's output which accrued to the government either in cash or in kind. Increases in posted prices for Venezuelan oil through December 1973 had increased the nation's international monetary reserves to $2.418 billion. Venezuelan Mines Minister Hugo Perez La Salvia, reacting to the OPEC freeze announcement of Jan. 9, said it was an agreement only between six OPEC members from the Persian Gulf. The government, however, guaranteed preferential oil supplies to Central American nations to counter shortages they were suffering as a result of the Arab oil squeeze. The decision, announced Feb. 1, followed three days of talks between oil officials and representatives of Guatemala, El Salvador, Honduras, Costa Rica and Nicaragua.

Oil Prices & Developing Nations

[18] A summit meeting of 38 Moslem nations held in Lahore, Pakistan, Feb. 22-24, resulted in a "Declaration of Lahore" which established an eight-nation committee to study ways of easing the pressure of high oil prices on developing Moslem nations in Africa and Asia. However, the delegates rejected a proposal that would have provided a specific aid program by the Arab states to those nations. The committee members were Algeria, Egypt, Kuwait, Libya, Pakistan, Saudi Arabia, Senegal and the United Arab Emirates.

[19] The oil issue had been affecting Arab relations with other third-world countries. Petroleum prices had risen 30% and a promised grant of $200 million had not been received by the African Development Bank. The issue resulted in a report, printed in the *New York Times* March 3, that several black African nations were questioning the wisdom of siding with the Arabs on the Middle East conflict. Libya, Iran, Venezuela and Algeria strongly supported the principle of a special fund to assist developing countries during an OPEC meeting in Geneva April 7. No agreement was reached on the amount to be contributed to the fund, but an OPEC statement said it would come into effect when seven OPEC countries had ratified atricles governing its establishment and operation. Saudi Arabia, Kuwait and other Arab members avoided a firm commitment. The decision was implemented at an OAPEC meeting in June during which it was decided to provide 20-year interest-free loans to developing Arab nations. Another OAPEC meeting in Cairo July 11 resulted in the pledge of an $80 million fund to help compensate Arab oil-importing countries for the increase in prices. Beneficiaries would be Jordan, Lebanon, Mauritania, Morocco, Sudan, Somalia and both Yemens. At the meeting the conferees also agreed to the establishment of an Arab Energy Institute to search for new uses for oil, to conduct nuclear research and to study the possible use of solar energy.

[20] Nigeria announced July 31 it would sell oil to African countries at a cheaper rate than it offered to other nations. It also increased its annual subscription rate to the African Development Bank and announced it would no longer borrow from the bank, citing "other African countries who need its loans more urgently than Nigeria."

[21] Members of OPEC gave $8.6 billion in official economic assistance to developing nations during the first nine months of 1974, the International Monetary Fund (IMF) reported Nov. 18. The aid was in addition to the $3.1

billion made available to the IMF's oil facility for use by nations with balance of payments problems, and $1 billion loaned to the World Bank. Bilateral commitments made by OPEC nations over the nine-month period totaled $6.2 billion. Major donors were Iran ($2.8 billion) and Saudi Arabia ($2.4 billion). Multilateral aid totaled $2.4 billion, with the largest grant ($900 million) earmarked for the Islamic Development Bank.

Oil Consumer Actions

[22] Efforts by the consuming nations to meet the spreading crisis caused by Arab oil decisions centered on two areas: the need for conservation and development of new energy sources, and ways to meet the financial imbalance caused by the flow of world funds into Arab treasuries.

[23] Secretary of State Kissinger Jan. 10 called on oil-producing and oil-consuming nations to seek a long-term multinational agreement to deal with the energy shortage. His appeal followed a White House announcement Jan. 9 that President Nixon had asked foreign ministers of eight oil-consuming nations to a Washington conference Feb. 11 to discuss world energy problems. Those invited were Britain, Canada, France, Italy, Japan, the Netherlands, Norway and West Germany. Nixon had also sent messages to the OPEC nations inviting them to join in discussions at a later date. The Arab nations reacted to the upcoming conference by describing it as an effort to "internationalize oil resources by means of force." France, fearful that the conference would be seen as a consumers' cabal, was the last to accept the conference invitation, predicting a hostile Arab reaction. France's differences with the U.S. widened during the conference itself when French Foreign Minister Michel Jobert asserted the U.S. was using energy matters as "a pretext" to cover a "political" desire by the U.S. to dominate the relationships of Western Europe and Japan. The conference Feb. 13 adopted a 17-point proposal which included several key points to which France strenuously disagreed. Among the disputed points were proposals calling for joint measures to conserve energy, to allocate oil supplies in times of emergency and to speed research for new energy sources. France also objected to proposals for establishment of a coordinating group which would prepare for a consumer-producer conference and adoption of financial and monetary measures to avoid "competitive depreciation and the escalation of restrictions on trade and payments or disruptive actions in external borrowing." Jobert had also maintained that the conference should not take specific action, but should confine itself to merely an exchange of views.

[24] The final communique adopted was based largely on a seven-point program Kissinger had submitted in an address to the Feb. 11 session. Calling his plan "Project Interdependence," the secretary said the U.S. was prepared to share its technological expertise with others in the development of new energy sources and in arranging for improved cooperation between oil producers and consumers. The proposals set forth by Kissinger: (1) The U.S. would join other consumer nations in studying conservation methods to cut down on the use of energy. (2) In order to cushion the impact on major industrial nations, an international program would be set up to handle any interruption in, or manipulation of fuel supplies. (3) The U.S. would make "a major contribution" toward international research and development of new technology in energy programs. (4) The U.S. would be willing to share its energy with other consumers in times of shortages if those nations would offer to do the same. (5) International cooperation, including "new mechanisms," must be carried out to deal with distribution of capital from oil revenues. (6) New foreign aid programs were required to help less wealthy consumers that suffered even more from high

oil prices. (7) Consumers and producers should discuss what constituted a "just price" for oil and how to insure long-term investments.

[25] A series of meetings, growing out of the February conference, took place throughout the year. A formal agreement on an oil pool was adopted by the 12-nation group after a two-day meeting in Brussels Sept. 19-20. The pool would provide supplies to any member country when, as the result of an embargo, their oil imports dropped more than 7%. The plan was to be managed by a new agency within the Organization for Economic Cooperation and Development (OECD). The U.S. had released details of the plan after a preliminary meeting of the Energy Coordinating Group (ECG) in Brussels July 29-31. Other proposals included a reduction in consumption during a crisis by 7%-10% through the use of such measures as high gasoline excise taxes, rationing or government intervention in allocation of oil supplies. ECG oil producers (the U.S., Britain, Canada and Norway) would share their output with members in time of need. Norway was the only member who did not immediately approve the plan, saying it could not do so until its Parliament had debated the issue. Norway had begun to develop vast oil reserves in the North Sea and there was opposition in Oslo to any sharing arrangement that would conflict with sovereignty over its oil supply.

[26] The ECG was replaced by a 16-nation International Energy Agency formed in Paris Nov. 15, established within the OECD framework. Twenty-one OECD nations voted to set up the agency, but five of them, including France, Greece and Finland, refused to join. France argued that the consumer nations should be negotiating with the producer states rather than forming a bloc that would antagonize them. Norway, reluctant to give up control over its own oil, joined as an associate member, participating in the oil pool on a voluntary basis in return for a nonvoting seat on the governing board. Members of the new agency were: Austria, Belgium, Britain, Canada, Denmark, Ireland, Italy, Japan, Luxembourg, the Netherlands, Spain, Sweden, Switzerland, Turkey, the United States and West Germany.

[27] A U.S. official who had attended the IEA's meeting in Paris the previous week said Dec. 22 the agency's chairman, Viscount Etienne Davignon of Belgium, had been authorized to brief Jean-Pierre Brunet, the French Foreign Ministry's chief economic officer, after each agency meeting. Brunet in turn would submit proposals for the agency's consideration that France regarded as essential in preparing for the projected conference between oil-consumer and oil-producing nations in 1975. In another action aimed at closer French-IEA cooperation, President Valery Giscard d'Estaing permitted the agency to be established within the OECD, of which France was a member. He also allowed the Executive Commission of the European Economic Community (EEC) to have observer status with the IEA. France, along with other OECD and EEC members, had the veto power to block cooperative action with other international agencies.

U.S. Position

[28] U.S. officials declared in September that continued high prices set by the oil-producing nations imperiled the world's economy and could lead to "confrontation" and "a breakdown of world order and safety." The warnings were contained in speeches delivered by President Ford to the opening of the World Energy Conference in Detroit; by Secretary Kissinger to the United Nations General Assembly; and by Defense Secretary Schlesinger in response to newsmen's questions prompted by the Ford and Kissinger warnings. In speaking to the General Assembly Sept. 23, Kissinger noted that the U.S. had launched

programs with such oil producing nations as Saudi Arabia and Iran to help them diversify their economies. He implied that if such cooperation failed to ease oil prices, the U.S. might change its policy. In his address the same day, Ford asserted that the U.S. recognized the oil producers' need to develop their own economies, "but exorbitant prices can only distort the world economy, run the risk of a worldwide depression, and threaten the breakdown of world order and safety." The President noted that "throughout history, nations have gone to war over natural advantages, such as water, food or convenient passages on land or sea." But he pointed out that in this nuclear age "war brings unacceptable risks for all mankind." Schlesinger said Sept. 25 that the U.S. had no intention of seeking military action against oil-producing nations in the Middle East, but instead was seeking a solution to rising prices through "amicable discussions."

[29] Arab anger over the comments by President Ford and Kissinger was expressed Sept. 24 by political leaders, public figures and the press, who accused the U.S. of waging a war of nerves against the Arab countries. Kuwaiti Petroleum Minister Abdel Rahman al-Atiki said if the U.S. went ahead with plans to form a bloc of oil-consuming nations, a confrontation with the oil producers was inevitable. French Foreign Minister Jean Sauvagnargues said Sept. 24 that U.N. delegates and their governments seemed "apprehensive about the implicit threats" in the Kissinger and Ford statements. Shah Mohammed Reza Pahlevi of Iran reacted to Ford's address by rejecting the President's bid to cut oil prices. He called instead on industrial nations to reduce prices of their exports first.

Petrodollar Issue

[30] Sen. Henry M. Jackson (D. Wash.) Nov. 11 urged major oil-consuming nations to establish a special council of economic and finance ministers authorized to work for a reduction of oil prices and to protect the international banking system from an unmanageable flow of investments by oil producing nations. In a London speech before the Pilgrims Society, Jackson opposed the International Monetary Fund plan, favored by many European states, which would recycle petrodollars through oil-consuming states in the forms of loans and investments. Jackson also advocated that the industrial nations control their own financial infrastructures in order to prevent them being overwhelmed by the volume of OPEC investments.

[31] Secretary of State Kissinger offered a petrodollar recycling plan Nov. 14 in a speech at the University of Chicago in which he proposed a $25 billion international lending agency, financed by the consumer nations, to help industrial states cope with the high cost of oil. Kissinger also favored creation of a special trust fund to assist developing nations which had $20 billion in payments deficits. Kissinger's recycling plan was detailed by Treasury Secretary William E. Simon in a New York speech Nov. 18. Simon proposed that the oil facility be associated with the OECD rather than with the 130-member IMF, in which developing and oil-producing nations were heavily represented. Simon said the U.S. contribution to the loan facility would be financed through the Treasury Department's existing $5 billion Exchange Stabilization Fund, which engaged in international lending operations to stabilize the dollar. (In testimony before the Joint Economic Committee of Congress Nov. 25, Simon said a final decision had not been made about the amount of the U.S. contribution, but he said it was his "preliminary view" that the U.S. would furnish 25%-30%, or about $8 billion, of the total funds needed. Simon also told the committee that if necessary, the U.S. could meet its payments through the purchase of U.S. government securities by oil exporting nations. Operation of the oil facility

"would not require inflationary expansion of money and credit," Simon said, or "lead to an increase in the federal government debt.") U.S. participation would require Congressional authority. Simon repeatedly sought to assure committee members at the Nov. 25 hearing that the Administration would consult with Congress as negotiations to establish the fund were undertaken. Simon had been on record earlier as opposing efforts to institutionalize the recycling process through establishment of another international group, favoring instead increased use of the private credit and investment markets to channel oil revenues to oil consuming nations.

[32] It was reported Oct. 28 that major international banks had reached the saturation point for excess oil revenues and were not accepting new deposits from oil exporting nations. Because of the size of the petrodollars influx, currently estimated at about $65 billion, and because the money often was kept on very short-term deposit, bankers said they had been unable to lend the money efficiently and safely.

[33] The Bank for International Settlements (BIS) announced Nov. 29 that oil exporting nations had invested $27 billion in surplus oil revenues in U.S., Britain and Western Europe during the first nine months of 1974. Nearly half was believed invested in traditional reserve assets, such as government obligations. According to a BIS breakdown, $8 billion was invested in the U.S., $4 billion in Great Britain, $12 billion in Eurodollar investments in London and $3 billion in Eurodollar deposits elsewhere in Europe.

[34] According to the *New York Times* Dec. 23, France and other countries had established investment controls requiring prior notification of, and formal application for, major share acquisitions. Belgium and the Netherlands also had machinery to prevent foreign takeovers, the *Times* said. West Germany and Italy reportedly were hampered in efforts to control unwanted investments because they lacked disclosure laws requiring that the identity of investors be revealed. In the U.S., Kissinger announced Dec. 7 that a study had been launched to determine whether there were sufficient safeguards against the foreign takeover of critical defense industries.

Statistics

[35] According to figures compiled by the Venezuelan Mines Ministry for the first six months of 1974 and reported Oct. 7, the Soviet Union was the world's largest oil producer. Soviet production rose by 10% during the period to total 9,018,000 barrels a day, the ministry said. The U.S. was the second largest producer with 8,995,000 barrels a day, a .1% drop from the first half of 1973. The world's other major oil producers, as ranked by the Venezuelan ministry: Saudi Arabia—8,336,000 barrels a day; up 11.7%. Iran—6,131,000 barrels; up 5.4%. Venezuela—3,113,000 barrels; down 7.1%. Kuwait—2,846,000 barrels; down 6.1%. Nigeria—2,259,000 barrels; up 31.4%. Libya—1,887,000 barrels; down 17.7%. Canada—1,823,000 barrels; up 2.4%. Iraq—1,743,000 barrels; down 8%. According to figures released Oct. 23 by the Federal Energy Administration, the U.S. imported some 4 million barrels of crude oil daily. Canada supplied 24.7% of the total. Other major suppliers were: Nigeria (17.5%), Iran (15.5%), Venezuela (11.2%), Saudi Arabia (8.3%) and Indonesia (7.8%). The American Petroleum Institute announced Nov. 10 that U.S. consumption of petroleum products during the first 10 months of 1974 averaged 16.5 million barrels a day, down 3.7% from the same period of 1973. Domestic oil production during the same 10-month period also declined. Production at a rate of 8.5 million barrels a day was off 3.5% from the previous year.

See also ABU DHABI; AFRICA; ALGERIA; ARGENTINA [15]; AUSTRALIA [4, 22]; AUTOMOBILES [4, 12]; AVIATION [1, 3-4]; BELGIUM; CAMPAIGN FINANCING [21];

CANADA [21-27, 29]; COSTA RICA; DAHOMEY; ECONOMY, U.S. [7, 18, 23, 27]; ECUADOR; ENERGY CRISIS; EUROPEAN ECONOMIC COMMUNITY [6-11, 17]; FAMINE & FOOD; FRANCE [17-19]; GERMANY, WEST [16]; GREAT BRITAIN [6, 11, 18, 22-25]; INDIA; ITALY [6]; JAPAN [6-8]; KENYA; KUWAIT; LIBYA; MEXICO [1, 4-5]; MIDDLE EAST [17]; MONETARY DEVELOPMENTS [10, 13, 22-23]; MOROCCO; NETHERLANDS [1-4]; NICARAGUA; NIGERIA; NORWAY; PERU [13]; QATAR; SAUDI ARABIA; SHIPS & SHIPPING; STOCK MARKET [5]; SUGAR; SWEDEN; TARIFFS & TRADE; TAXES; TERRITORIAL WATERS; TRINIDAD & TOBAGO; UNION OF SOVIET SOCIALIST REPUBLICS [38-40]; UNITED NATIONS [3]; URUGUAY; VENEZUELA; VIETNAM, REPUBLIC OF [40]; ZAIRE; ZAMBIA

OIL TANKERS—*See* SHIPS & SHIPPING
OKLAHOMA—*See* CRIME [41]; WEATHER; WOMEN'S RIGHTS

OLYMPICS—Senate votes Amateur Sports Board. The Senate, by a 62-29 vote July 9, approved legislation creating a five-member federal Amateur Sports Board to oversee the administration of sports represented in the Olympic games. The bill also provided for speedy arbitration for athletes barred from competition because of jurisdictional disputes between athletic sanctioning organizations. Under the terms of the bill, a sports association would be limited to controlling competition in only one Olympic sport, although it might be allowed to control as many as three if all the sports would benefit from common administration. One probable effect of this section would be to break the control exercised by the Amateur Athletic Union (AAU) over the U.S. Olympic Committee (USOC). The House did not act on the measure.

USOC adopts athletes' bill of rights. The USOC announced Dec. 16 the adoption of a bill of rights for athletes. The action was part of a sweeping revision of the organization's constitution approved unanimously by the USOC at its biennial meeting in Orlando, Fla. The chief provision established compulsory arbitration by the American Arbitration Association of all disputes between athletes and the constituent sports organizations of the USOC. This would remove the USOC from controversies between the AAU and the National Collegiate Athletic Association (NCAA).

Moscow, Lake Placid get 1980 Olympics. The International Olympic Committee (IOC) Oct. 23 awarded the 1980 summer Olympic games to Moscow and the winter Olympics to Lake Placid, N.Y. The Soviets, who waged a multimillion dollar publicity campaign for two years, narrowly won over Los Angeles. Representatives of Lake Placid, the site of the 1932 winter Olympics, had no rivals in their bid for the 1980 games.

OMAN—*See* APPOINTMENTS & RESIGNATIONS; MONETARY DEVELOPMENTS [5]
OPIUM—*See* NARCOTICS & DANGEROUS DRUGS
OREGON—*See* CRIME [29]; ELECTIONS [5, 7]; ENERGY CRISIS [8]
ORGANIZATION OF AFRICAN UNITY (OAU)—*See* AFRICA; ETHIOPIA [13]; SEYCHELLE ISLANDS
ORGANIZATION OF AMERICAN STATES (OAS)—*See* CHILE [4]; CUBA; LATIN AMERICA
ORGANIZATION OF ARAB PETROLEUM EXPORTING COUNTRIES—*See* OIL [5, 9]
ORGANIZATION FOR ECONOMIC COOPERATION AND DEVELOPMENT (OECD)—*See* JAPAN [8]; MONETARY DEVELOPMENTS [2]; OIL [25-27, 31]; PORTUGAL [10]; TARIFFS & TRADE
ORGANIZATION OF PETROLEUM EXPORTING COUNTRIES (OPEC)—*See* AFRICA; ECUADOR; KUWAIT; MEXICO [5]; OIL [5-6, 11-13, 15-17, 19, 21, 30]; TARIFFS & TRADE; UNITED NATIONS [11]
OZONE LAYER—*See* ENVIRONMENT & POLLUTION

P

PAKISTAN

Relations with India & Bangla Desh

Pakistan moved closer to normalization of relations with India and Bangla Desh, which were still strained as a result of the 1971 Indian-Pakistani war that led to the creation of Bangla Desh from what had previously been East Pakistan. Prisoners were exchanged and some links with India restored. The situation remained tense, however, as the Pakistan government objected to India's explosion of a nuclear device and the annexation of the kingdom of Sikkim.

Pakistan had refused to recognize Bangla Desh, in spite of mounting pressure from such Moslem countries as Egypt, Indonesia and Saudi Arabia, who sought to heal the split in the Islamic world. A meeting of the foreign ministers of the 38 Islamic countries on Feb. 21 finally resulted in Bangla Desh agreeing to Pakistan's demands for the cancellation of trials for 195 Pakistanis being held on charges of atrocities allegedly committed during the war. Pakistan then agreed to recognize the new state, with Prime Minister Zulfikar Ali Bhutto announcing the decision at the opening of the Islamic summit conference Feb. 22. The agreement between India, Pakistan and Bangla Desh was formalized in New Delhi April 9. Provisions included: release of all Pakistani prisoners held by Bangla Desh; Pakistan's acceptance of an unspecified number of the Bihari minority seeking to emigrate from Bangla Desh; and agreement between India and Pakistan for an exchange of delegations to negotiate plans for resumption of postal and air services, travel between the two nations and trade, economic and cultural exchanges. Bangla Desh agreed to drop charges against the 195 Pakistanis "as an act of clemency," while Pakistan "condemned and deeply regretted any crimes that may have been committed" by its force during the conflict. The prisoner exchange ended April 30 when India returned 734 Pakistani prisoners, completing the repatriation of 93,000 Pakistanis held in India for more than two years. Among those freed was Lt. Gen. A. A. K. Niazi, who had led Pakistani troops in East Pakistan. A group of 206 Bengalis had been flown from Karachi to Dacca March 24, completing the repatriation of Bangla Desh nationals stranded in Pakistan since the war.

Further progress was halted June 1 when Pakistan postponed a June 10 meeting with India that was to take up restoration of postal, telecommunication and travel relations. Citing India's May 18 nuclear test, Pakistan said the talks should be put off until the situation was more favorable. Although both India and Pakistan accused each other in July of provocative troop movements along their mutual frontiers, the two nations finally signed the restoration agreement Sept. 14 in Islamabad. Complicating relations between the two countries still further was the status of Kashmir, which was claimed by both. Pakistani fears about the July troop movements were expressed by Bhutto in a *New York Times* interview July 8 during which he said India's military actions could be part of a "grand design" to intimidate Pakistan at a time when New Delhi was about to make "some unpleasant political decision" over the future of that state. On Sept. 25 Pakistan announced the merger of the ancient principality of Hunza with the Gilgit region of the Pakistani-controlled section of Kashmir, sending its officials to take over government of the region. India denounced the annexation of Hunza as "unilateral action" and accused Bhutto of "haste and arbitrariness." Pakistani nervousness over India's intentions also led Bhutto, in July and in September, to urge the U.S. to resume supplying arms to his nation. "We stand vindicated in our analysis" of India's policies as a result of its virtual annexation of Sikkim, Bhutto declared Sept. 10. "Half our country is gone, half of Kashmir is gone. They marched into Goa and took that. They have gone nuclear. And now they have swallowed Sikkim." Bhutto warned that if the U.S. refused to send arms, Pakistan would "have to consider" leaving the Central Treaty Organization (CENTO) to which it belonged with the U.S., Britain, Turkey and Iran. In its turn, India warned Oct. 16 that U.S. arms sales to Pakistan could result in "a serious setback" to Indian-U.S. relations. An Indian Foreign Ministry official, in an interview in the *New York Times,* said Pakistan had "more than made up all her losses" since the 1971 war, and had 14 infantry divisions, compared with the 12 it had in 1971. Pakistan, he contended, had purchased jet fighters from France and was receiving free weapons from China. Although there was no direct diplomatic U.S. reply to the request for aid, Secretary of State Henry Kissinger and Bhutto issued a joint communique following an Oct. 31 meeting in Pakistan which said that both nations agreed that renewed efforts should be made to prevent the spread of nuclear weapons." Kissinger, who was in Pakistan as part of an Asian tour, also conveyed a message from President Ford that stressed the U.S. commitment to Pakistan "would remain an important principle of American foreign policy."

India and Pakistan signed a protocol in New Delhi Nov. 30 restoring normal trade relations. The embargo was to be lifted in December. The agreement to end the trade ban, taken after four days of talks, fulfilled an aspect of the July 1972 peace treaty ending the December 1971 war. Details of the trade pact were to be worked out at a later date. Initially, trade would be on a government-to-government basis or through government-controlled trade corporations. Exchanges would be conducted on the basis of most-favored-nation treatment and freely convertible currency. Direct shipping services were to be restored. Indian-Pakistani telephone service, severed during the 1971 war, was restored Oct. 15.

The problem of the Bihari minority in Bangla Desh was still unresolved following a June 27-29 meeting in that nation between Bhutto and Bangla Desh Foreign Minister Kamal Hussein. By terms of the April 9 agreement, Pakistan had said it would accept more than the 140,000 (out of 500,000) Biharis it had intended to absorb. During the June conference, however, Pakistani officials said they had offered to appoint a committee to consider the emigration of the Biharis to Pakistan. Hussein expressed disappointment with the results of the talks which had also considered the transfer of assets claimed by Dacca but which had been held by Pakistan since the war. Pakistan said it would study this issue too.

Baluchistan Rebellion

The government June 25 conceded a resurgence of rebel activity in Baluchistan where tribesmen were in a military struggle against the central government. Opposition members in the National Assembly said 900 persons had been killed in recent government operations in the province, but the charges were officially denied.

During a tour of Baluchistan and the North-West Frontier Provinces, Bhutto spoke in Quetta Aug. 2, appealing to rebel tribesmen to put down their arms by Oct. 15 or face a concerted drive by Pakistan's military forces. The prime minister charged that Afghanistan was encouraging anti-government activity by the Baluchis. Bhutto also reiterated his July 28 proposal for a non-aggression treaty with Kabul, warning that if Afghanistan persisted in its territorial claims over the area, Pakistan might support tribal separatist movements in Afghanistan. The prime minister narrowly escaped assassination during his Quetta speech when a hand grenade meant for him detonated in the hand of the assailant and killed the man. The official Pakistan news agency reported Aug. 12 that 22 members of a student organization had been arrested in connection with the incident. The agency charged that three foreign-trained guerrillas had been sent by Afghanistan to kill Bhutto in an attempt to stir up trouble between rival Baluchi and Pathan tribesmen.

Bhutto extended the Oct. 15 amnesty deadline to Dec. 15 on the day it was due to end, saying that the rebellion "has come to an end." Afghanistan had warned Sept. 23 that Pakistan could precipitate a war between the two countries if it carried out its threats against the rebels. Afghan Deputy Foreign Minister Waheed Abdullah had expressed sympathy for the Baluchis, who had ethnic ties with the Afghans. According to a government White Paper on the rebellion released Oct. 20, 385 persons, including 144 Pakistani soldiers and 241 rebels, had been killed since May 1973 in the anti-insurgency operations. A total of 5,500 insurgents was said to have surrendered in that period.

Other Developments

Banks, industries nationalized. The government Jan. 1 nationalized shipping lines, oil-distribution companies and the country's 15 domestic banks. The eight foreign banks in Pakistan were not affected but were barred from opening new branches.

Fundamental rights restored. Prime Minister Bhutto announced Aug. 14 the restoration of the rights of citizens to apply to the courts for enforcement of fundamental constitutional rights, including safeguards from arrest and detention and for freedom of assembly and association. These rights had been rescinded in 1969 in the crisis following the forced resignation of President Mohammad Ayub Khan who had ruled as a military "strong man" for ten years. Bhutto said his government had decided to remove the curbs "despite the fact that we are not yet rid of our anxiety about the situation along our borders and the danger of internal subversion."

See also ATOMIC ENERGY [3]; EARTHQUAKES; FAMINE & FOOD; FORD, GERALD R.; MIDDLE EAST [28]; OBITUARIES [AYUB KHAN]; OIL [18]; UGANDA

PALESTINIANS—*See* AVIATION [14]; CIVIL RIGHTS [19]; DENMARK; EGYPT; ISRAEL; LEBANON; LIBYA; MIDDLE EAST [3, 8, 17-36, 40-43, 45]; NETHERLANDS [11]; OIL [4]; UNITED NATIONS [2, 4, 8-10]

PANAMA—Preliminary canal agreement. The U.S. and Panama agreed in principle for the first time to end U.S. jurisdiction over the Panama Canal and Zone, the *Washington Post* reported Jan. 10. The preliminary agreement, disclosed by U.S. government sources, was reached by Panamanian Foreign Minister Juan Antonio Tack and U.S. Ambassador at Large Ellsworth Bunker in talks in Panama City Jan. 6-7. The agreement was signed in Panama City Feb. 7 by Tack and by U.S. Secretary of State Henry Kissinger. The principles of the new pact included: an agreement to abrogate the 1903 treaty; elimination of the concept of perpetuity for any new treaty; termination of U.S. jurisdiction over Panamanian territory; the right of the U.S. to provide for the "operation, maintenance, protection and defense of the canal" which Panama would share; an "equitable share" of canal income for Panama, and equality in canal administration; and bilateral agreement on provisions to enlarge canal capacity. Article Six of the treaty also dealt with its termination, upon which the U.S. was granted "the rights necessary to regulate the transit of ships" and to "operate, maintain, protect and defend the canal." Kissinger said in the hour-long signing ceremony at Justo Arosemena Palace that the new canal treaty must "restore Panama's territorial sovereignty" over the Canal Zone, but must also preserve U.S. interests and participation in the waterway. "In the past," he declared, "our negotiation would have been determined by relative strength. Today we have come together in an act of reconciliation."

The signing of the preliminary agreement was met by opposition in the U.S. by Congressional supporters of continued American control, resulting in a March 29 resolution introduced by Sen. Strom Thurmond (R, S.C.), ranking Republican on the Armed Services Committee and Sen. John McClellan (D, Ark.), chairman of the Appropriations Committee. Thurmond denied the canal was in Panamanian territory, arguing that the U.S. obtained the Canal Zone through both treaty and purchase. Sen. Gale McGee (D, Wyo.), chairman of the Western Hemisphere Subcommittee of the Foreign Relations Committee, said April 1 that an armed confrontation with Panama was possible if a mutually acceptable new canal treaty was not negotiated. One opponent of the treaty, the American Federation of State, County and Municipal Employes, which represented 6,000 workers in the Canal Zone, reversed its stand Feb. 5, asking that any resulting changes in terms and conditions of employment be worked out through collective bargaining. Some of the opposition was based on fears about the stability of the Panamanian government. Rep. John M. Murphy (D, N.Y.), a senior member of the House Panama Canal Subcommittee, claimed he had recently received information "from a source of highest integrity" of plots to "overthrow the military government," headed by Gen. Omar Torrijos. Although Torrijos' regime was generally regarded as stable, the Panamanian government had recently taken a series of steps against various opposition groups.

The government had announced Jan. 25 that it had arrested five members of the National Civilista Front, which it described as an organization which was financed by Panamanian exiles in the U.S. and which "tried to change [Panama's] form of government" and subvert the public order. The attorney general's office said the alleged subversives—who included Jaime Jacome Diaz, secretary general of the outlawed Liberal Party, and Luis Enrique de Gracia, a former federal deputy, both arrested Jan. 16—were being questioned along with other suspects. The total number of detainees was not disclosed. The *Miami Herald* reported Feb. 2 that at least 11 persons had been arrested in the previous two weeks, including Edwin Lopez and Arnulfo Escalona, former Liberal deputies, and Mario Bernaschina and Bernardo Lemos, members of the National Civilista Front.

Sources close to the U.S.-Panamanian negotiations expected a new canal treaty to be ready for signature early in 1975, the *Washington Post* reported Dec. 23. The optimism reportedly followed a recent U.S. agreement to give Panama jurisdiction over the Canal Zone at the end of five years, in exchange for Panamanian consent to a continued U.S. military presence in the zone. The countries had not yet agreed on how long U.S. troops might remain or their numbers. Also undecided was an increase in canal rent to be paid by the U.S. The rental was currently $2.3 million per year, and a tentative figure of $35 million per year was being discussed, the *Post* reported.

See also APPOINTMENTS & RESIGNATIONS; CHILE [7]; CUBA; DOMINICAN REPUBLIC; LATIN AMERICA; PERU [12]; SUGAR

PANOV, VALERY—*See* UNION OF SOVIET SOCIALIST REPUBLICS [28]

PAPUA NEW GUINEA—Papua New Guinea Chief Minister Michael Somare announced March 12 that his country would seek full independence from Australia Dec. 1. Australian Prime Minister Gough Whitlam had promised, on March 1, an estimated $A500 million in economic aid over the next three years. On that same date, U.S. Deputy Secretary of State Kenneth Rush agreed the United States would provide educational grants enabling PNG citizens to study in the U.S., particularly at the post-graduate level. The funds also would finance visits by PNG officials to America for a period of up to 30 days to observe political and other aspects of U.S. life.

Radio Australia reported from Port Moresby Sept. 30 that it was unlikely that Papua New Guinea would gain its total independence from Australia by the Dec. 1 target date. Radio Australia's assessment that it would be 1975 before the territory achieved that status was based on approval by the PNG's House of Assembly Sept. 30 of a government proposal that unspecified laws associated with the Constitution must be adopted before independence. The measure required two separate House meetings before the legislation was adopted; the House had only one more meeting planned for 1974.

See also AUSTRALIA [13]

PARAGUAY—Students, peasants seized. Some 100 students and peasants were arrested and turned over to military tribunals after they demonstrated against the high cost of living and renewed their demands for the release of political prisoners, the London newsletter *Latin America* reported March 1. The government charged the students and peasants had formed a united front and engaged in subversive activities. However, the archbishop of Asuncion, Ismael Rolon, declared in a sermon that their demands were just and asserted that peasants had to work five days to pay for one day's food.

Stroessner asks 'dialogue.' President Alfredo Stroessner called Aug. 14 for a "great national dialogue" among political parties, hinting he would liberalize his regime in exchange for cooperation from opposition groups. Most groups appeared to welcome the call, with the exception of the Christian Democrats, who were split over it, according to *Latin America* Nov. 15. The Radical Liberal Party, the largest opposition force, said Sept. 13 that it was "ready to talk," but asked that the government first grant greater freedom of expression and political assembly.

See also BRAZIL [2, 10]; LATIN AMERICA; SUGAR

PARKINSON, KENNETH W.—*See* WATERGATE [87, 93, 103]

PATENTS—U.S. District Court Judge Barrington D. Parker Jan. 18 ruled that no federal agency could give away publicly financed inventions or patents to private business without first obtaining authorization from Congress. He cited as the basis for his decision Article IV, Section 3 of the Constitution, which says in part: "Congress shall have the power to dispose of and make all needful rules and regulations respecting... property belonging to the United States." The ruling involved patent licensing regulations promulgated by the General Services Administration (GSA), which became effective in May 1973 and which were challenged in a suit by 11 congressmen and Public Citizen Inc., a public interest group sponsored by consumer advocate Ralph Nader. The Defense Department was most directly affected by the decision, as it accounted for the bulk of federal spending on research and development.

See also ANTITRUST ACTIONS [4-5]; ENERGY CRISIS [40]; GERMANY, WEST [14]

PEACE CORPS, U.S.—*See* APPOINTMENTS & RESIGNATIONS; PERU [17]
PELL, SEN. CLAIBORNE—*See* CUBA; EDUCATION; ROCKEFELLER, NELSON
PENNSYLVANIA—*See* ELECTIONS [5]; ENERGY CRISIS [6]; ELECTIONS [7, 9]; GAMBLING; LABOR [13]

PENSIONS—Rail pension veto overridden. Congress enacted into law Oct. 16, by overriding a veto by President Ford for the first time, a bill revising the railroad retirement system and refinancing it with an annual infusion of $285 million through the year 2000. The system currently was in arrears by $4.5 billion, largely because of a decline in the number of workers paying into the retirement fund and a dual-benefit practice permitting rail workers to receive both railroad retirement and Social Security benefits. About 40% of the one million rail workers in the country had worked other jobs long enough to qualify for Social Security as well as railroad retirement. As cleared by Congress Sept. 30, after overwhelming votes of approval in both houses, the legislation would have phased out the dual-benefit system and replaced it with coverage for all working years, railroad and non-railroad, under Social Security and supplemental benefits for rail service, financed by the industry and managed by the federal government, to raise the benefits to the higher level of the railroad system.

President Ford vetoed the bill Oct, 12, objecting to funding the deficit with money from the Treasury. He preferred reduction of benefits or the industry financing the deficit, he said. But the bill, the focus of a strong lobbying effort by rail labor and management, had enough support in both houses to provide the two-thirds majority required for enactment by overriding. The House voted to override by a 360-12 vote Oct. 15. The Senate overrode the next day 72-1.

Pension reform bill. A bill establishing federal standards for private pension plans was cleared by Congress Aug. 22. Final passage in the Senate was voted that day 85-0. The House had approved it by a vote of 407-2 Aug. 20. President Ford signed the bill during a Labor Day ceremony Sept. 2 attended by several hundred labor and business leaders and members of Congress. While not requiring companies or unions to establish a pension plan, existing and future plans would have to conform to the bill's standards. Currently, there were more than 300,000 private pension plans with assets of more than $160 billion covering an estimated 23-35 million workers. Under the bill, called the Employe Benefit Security Act of 1974, standards were set for eligibility, vesting and funding of benefits. A federal reinsurance system was to be established to prevent loss of benefits from failure of a plan. Deadline for major provisions of the act was Jan. 1, 1976.

Eligibility was extended to all employes with at least one year of service and who were at least 25 years of age. For vesting, or entitlement to receive benefits, the bill provided a choice of three alternatives: (1) 100% of pension rights after 10 years of service; (2) 25% after five years, gradually increasing to 100% after 15 years; (3) 50% when a worker's age plus his years of service totaled

45, gradually increasing to 100% over five years. A worker would be eligible to receive his vested benefits if he left the company before retirement. Transferral of his vested portion to a new employer's plan would depend upon consent of the new employer. The standards for funding required regular payments by a company into a plan and payments commensurate with adequate coverage. To insure against loss of benefits if a plan were terminated or had insufficient funds, a Pension Benefit Guaranty Corporation was to be established within the Labor Department with funding from premiums by companies with pension plans.

Self-employed persons would be permitted a tax deduction for their retirement plans of 15% of earnings, or a maximum of $7,500. Persons not in private or government pension plans would be permitted a tax deduction of up to 15% of annual income, or not more than $1,500, to establish a retirement account.

See also LABOR [9, 19]; TELEVISION & RADIO; VETERANS

PENTAGON PAPERS CASE—*See* CAMPAIGN FINANCING [5]; DEFENSE [3]; WATERGATE [15, 21, 24, 26, 31, 59, 62, 78-86]

PERCY, SEN. CHARLES H.—*See* CONSUMER AFFAIRS [2]; POLITICS [1]

PERU

Government

[1] **Cabinet, military shuffles.** President Juan Velasco Alvarado made a number of changes in the Cabinet and the military leadership at the end of 1973, it was reported Jan. 4. Gen. Francisco Morales Bermudez was promoted to army chief of staff, and was replaced as economy and finance minister by Gen. Guillermo Marco del Pont. Morales Bermudez' new post placed him in direct line to succeed Gen. Edgardo Mercado Jarrin as defense minister and prime minister, and effectively made him Velasco Alvarado's chosen successor, according to the London newsletter *Latin America* Jan. 11. Velasco reportedly emphasized this by making a pointed public reference to Mercado's scheduled retirement in a year's time.

[2] **AP banned; leaders seized, deported.** The government May 31 banned Popular Action (AP), the party of ex-President Fernando Belaunde Terry, and announced the deportation of its secretary general, Javier Alva Orlandini, and its national secretary for political affairs, Javier Arias Stella. An official statement accused AP of mounting a "campaign full of innuendo and lies" against "the prestige of the revolutionary government and the unity of the armed forces." The party had expressed agreement with Vice Adm. Luis Vargas Caballero, who resigned as navy commander and navy minister May 30 after calling for greater freedom of speech. Fernando Belaunde Terry denounced the action against AP from his exile in Washington, D.C. June 1 and 3.

[3] **Belaunde barred.** Ex-President Belaunde was prevented from crossing the Peruvian border from Ecuador Aug. 30. He was deported from Ecuador the next day for making political statements. Belaunde had offered to go to jail in Peru if the military government would release several leaders of his banned movement. The arrested AP leaders were reported freed Sept. 27 after the Supreme Court ruled there was insufficient evidence against them.

[4] **Anti-torture campaign.** The government joined a campaign by newspapers and magazines to end alleged torture of political and common prisoners by police. The campaign was led by the pro-government magazine *Oiga*. President Velasco acknowledged the torture scandal and replaced the chief of the national investigations police, it was reported Sept. 11. The Interior Ministry simultaneously began legal action against four policemen accused of using torture during interrogations.

[5] **Law to aid Indians.** The government issued a law in June to aid Indians in the northeastern jungle, it was reported Sept. 16. The measure, called the Law of Native Communities and of Farming and Cattle Raising in the Jungle and the Highland Jungle Regions, was popularly known as the Jungle Law. It established the legal existence of tribal societies, guaranteed their territorial rights, protected common and collective property, recognized tribal justice and provided training and technical assistance, according to the *New York Times.*

Press Developments

[6] **News media curbed.** The military regime closed the nation's leading news magazine June 13 and expropriated the major newspapers July 27. The expropriation of the newspapers, added to the government's control over national radio and television, was supported by many workers in the news media but protested by hundreds of residents of Lima, by newspapers throughout Latin America, and by the Inter-American Press Association (IAPA). The government, which had become increasingly sensitive to criticism, had accused independent newspapers of resisting broad reforms and encouraging political apathy. The opposition news magazine *Caretas* was shut down June 13 after it published a refutation of President Velasco's charge that a May 17 meeting between editors of *Caretas* and two conservative newspapers was part of an antigovernment conspiracy. Co-publisher Enrique Zileri Gibson was ordered deported, but he went into hiding.

[7] Armed police occupied the Lima offices of the nation's six leading newspapers early July 27, and the government issued a series of decrees pledging to turn over the dailies to professional, workers' and peasants' organizations within a year. Luis Miro Quesada, publisher of Peru's oldest newspaper, the conservative *El Comercio,* was placed under house arrest. Under the decrees, newspaper owners would receive an immediate 10% cash settlement and the remaining compensation in annual installments over a 10-year period with 6% interest. *El Comercio* would be turned over to peasant organizations; *Correo,* to the professional sector; *La Prensa,* to workers' communities; *Ojo,* to writers, artists and intellectuals; *Ultima Hora,* to cooperative and other public services organizations; and *Expreso,* to educational organizations. In the meantime, the newspapers continued to publish under the direction of committees appointed by the government.

[8] **Caretas to reappear.** The government announced Aug. 8 that *Caretas* would be allowed to resume publication and that the deportation order against its co-publisher, Enrique Zileri Gibson, had been rescinded. International protests against the newspaper expropriation continued. IAPA adopted a resolution Aug. 5 accusing the Peruvian government of "an arrogant abuse of power based mainly on the persuasive use of guns." In a milder criticism of the newspaper expropriation Aug. 13, Mario Vargas Llosa, Peru's leading novelist, said the measure was "well-intentioned" but carried the danger of "reducing the possibility of criticizing the [Peruvian] revolutionary process."

[9] Zileri was fined $1,200 and sentenced to one year in prison Sept. 24 for allegedly "damaging the reputation of the revolutionary government." The charge stemmed from an article in the Aug. 28 issue of *Caretas* which said the government had dropped a $690 million excess profits claim against International Petroleum Corp., a subsidiary of Exxon Corp. of the U.S., which had been nationalized in 1968. Abandonment of the claim was part of a February settlement between Peru and the U.S. over compensation for expropriated firms, *Caretas* reported. *Caretas* reappeared Aug. 28 after being closed by the government for 75 days. In that issue, Zileri wrote that the magazine would print even more "discrepancy and

dissent" than before to compensate for the government's new "domination of the daily press."

[10] **Magazines closed, newsmen exiled.** The military government delivered a further blow to its critics Nov. 19 when it banned the magazines *Oiga* and *Opinion Libre,* ordered the expulsion of nine journalists and one opposition politician, and issued arrest warrants for five prominent lawyers. The moves followed the closing Nov. 14 of the English-language *Peruvian Times,* a financial weekly that had irritated the regime two months earlier by printing details of a $330 million oil pipeline contract between the state firm Petroperu and Japanese companies. *Oiga* editor Francisco Igartua and *Opinion Libre* editor Guido Chirinos were among the journalists ordered deported Nov. 19. Igartua flew to Mexico Nov. 22, where he charged that "dissent has become a crime in Peru." The closings reportedly left only one independent magazine in Peru, *Caretas.*

Economy

[11] **U.S. firms to be compensated.**The U.S. and Peruvian governments signed an agreement Feb. 19 under which Peru would pay $150 million to compensate 11 U.S. companies whose properties it had nationalized in recent years. The settlement provided for Peru to pay the U.S. government $76 million for eventual distribution to the 11 companies, under terms to be decided by the U.S. State Department. In addition, Peru would pay $74 million directly to five of the firms—Cerro Corp., W. R. Grace & Co., Star-Kist Foods Inc. (a subsidiary of H. J. Heinz Co.), Goldkist Inc. and Cargill Inc. The bulk of the money would go to Cerro for its expropriated copper subsidiary, Cerro de Pasco Corp.

[12] **Anchovy fishing resumes.** Anchovy fishing resumed off the Peruvian coast March 5, after the government rescinded a year-long ban and authorized a 500,000-ton catch, very small by old standards. Private and state-owned Peruvian fishmeal companies also were involved in surveying and trial fishing off the coasts of Panama and Mexico's Baja California in joint ventures with the Panamanian and Mexican governments, it was reported March 15.

[13] **Petroleum contracts modified.** The state oil firm Petroperu was drafting a series of substantial modifications in its standard petroleum production-sharing contracts to take advantage of higher international oil prices, according to the *Andean Times' Latin America Economic Report* March 22. The production split between private oil companies and Petroperu would be increased in new contracts to 60/40 in Petroperu's favor, compared with the current 50/50—56/44. The modifications would not affect the 18 production-sharing contracts signed with international companies and consortia in 1970-73, each covering one million hectares in Peru's largely unexplored eastern jungles. Forty-two international firms were directly involved in oil exploration under these pacts.

[14] **Social property law.** The government April 30 announced its long-awaited Social Property Law, which would establish decentralized, independent and profit-making enterprises controlled by their own workers. The new social property enterprises (EPS) would be owned by the workers, but most of their profits would be either reinvested or plowed back into the social property sector to create new enterprises. EPS workers would be under strict checks and obligations, losing their jobs, for instance, for not appearing for work. Though they would earn slightly more money if their firm was doing well, the main emphasis was on a type of merit system under which unpaid overtime work was rewarded by training opportunities, promotions to posts with higher pay, and better housing and family benefits.

[15] **Food supply scandal.** A major scandal was disclosed Oct. 16 when the

armed forces took control of EPSA, the state agricultural marketing agency, and the government opened criminal proceedings against 105 dismissed employes. According to officials, the former employes had cheated citizens out of $140 million worth of scarce food supplies. They had used foreign currency earmarked for food imports to smuggle luxury items into the country for sale at Lima boutiques and hotels. They had also smuggled out food for sale at high prices in neighboring Ecuador, Chile and Bolivia. Seventy-two dismissed employes were arrested, it was reported Oct. 25. EPSA's former executive director, Manuel Diaz Cano, was seized in Lima Nov. 6. Two Cabinet officials resigned because of the scandal. Trade Minister Luis Barandiaran Pagador, an air force general, quit Oct. 16 after accepting responsibility for the smuggling. He was replaced Oct. 18 by Luis Arias Grazziani, another air force general. Agriculture Minister Enrique Valdez, an army general, resigned Nov. 6. He was succeeded the next day by Gen. Enrique Gallegos.

[16] **Soviet military technicians visit.** U.S. government sources reported Feb. 25 that Soviet military technicians had arrived in Peru to train Peruvian soldiers in the use of Russian T55 medium tanks purchased in 1973. Peru was the first South American nation to receive Soviet military advisers. The development reportedly alarmed the Chilean military junta. In a related development reported March 9, a Chinese military delegation arrived in Peru for an eight-day visit. The delegation, invited by the Peruvian army, was headed by the Chinese army's deputy chief of staff.

[17] **Peace Corps ousted.** The military government asked the U.S. to withdraw its 137 Peace Corps workers from Peru within 90 days, a U.S. State Department spokesman announced Nov. 14. The government said Peruvians could do the Peace Corps' work, which was mostly in agricultural development projects. However, government-controlled newspapers charged Nov. 15 that the Peace Corps was linked to the U.S. Central Intelligence Agency.

See also BRAZIL [10]; CHILE [27]; COPPER; DOMINICAN REPUBLIC; LATIN AMERICA; MEXICO [21]; SUGAR; UNITED NATIONS [6, 15]; VENEZUELA; WATERGATE [40]; WEATHER

PESTICIDES & HERBICIDES—*See* CHEMICAL & BIOLOGICAL WEAPONS; ENVIRONMENT & POLLUTION [15, 18]; FAMINE & FOOD

PETERSON, HENRY E.—*See* APPOINTMENTS & RESIGNATIONS; ENERGY CRISIS [24]; WATERGATE [24, 82]

PETRODOLLARS—*See* MONETARY DEVELOPMENTS, INTERNATIONAL; OIL [30-34]

PHILIPPINES—In spite of a June offer of amnesty by President Ferdinand E. Marcos, the Moslem rebellion continued during 1974. The government also suffered attacks from the Communists' New Peoples Army (NPA) and was in conflict with some elements in the Roman Catholic Church.

The first outbreak in fighting between Moslem forces and government troops in 1974 occured in January on Mindanao Island, center of the rebel activity. A major battle followed Feb. 4, spreading to the city of Jolo in the Sulu Islands, off the southern tip of Mindanao where at least 32 civilians were killed in a rebel mortar attack on a refugee camp. More than 30,000 civilians were reported to have fled Jolo during the fighting, which resulted in government troops regaining control of the city Feb. 12 after a brief rebel occupation. The armed forces announced the surrender March 2 of Aminkadra Abubakar, the Moslem mayor of Jolo. Abubakar said most of his policemen had linked up with the insurgents. Officials said the mayor blamed the Feb. 7 burning of the city on Maoists.

The Moslems offered Marcos their own peace plan at a meeting of their leaders in Mindanao June 6. This plan included a demand that all government troops withdraw from the fighting zones. Marcos announced June 12 that he would form a joint commission of Christians and Moslems to conduct talks with those rebels willing to surrender. He also announced creation of an agency to settle land conflicts between Moslems in Mindanao and Christian settlers from the north.

Fighting broke out again June 20, with an estimated 19,000 persons fleeing their homes as a result. In an attempt to contain the rebellion, Marcos ordered civilian groups armed to assist regular army troops, it was reported Aug. 10. (The rebellion was reported to have spread to the island of Davao, as well as continuing in Cotabato Province where rebels were laying siege to the capital city.) Meanwhile, government troops Aug. 24 raided the Sacred Heart Novitiate in Quezon City outside Manila. Twenty-one persons were arrested, including the Rev. Jose Blanco, who was charged with rebellion. Blanco, an outspoken lecturer and youth organizer, was accused of being secretary general of an anti-government village organization plotting to overthrow the government. Blanco was released and placed in the custody of his religious superiors Aug. 27. Thirteen of his students also were freed. The action followed a meeting between Marcos and Roman Catholic leaders, who, on Sept. 1, released the text of a church petition which asked that "bold steps be taken to gradually lift martial law and thus pave the way for healing the wounds of the nation." (Marcos had assumed emergency powers in September 1972 to deal with the rebellion.)

Attacks by the rebels continued in August-September in Lanao del Sur Province, Sacol Island and South Catabato Province. Government sources reported Sept. 21 at least 26 clashes since Sept. 1 involving either Moslem or NPA rebels. At least 50 government soldiers were reported slain, along with 30 NPA soldiers, an undetermined number of Moslems and 35 civilians.

Marcos had received a plan to end the Moslem rebellion from Mohammed Hassan el-Tohamy, secretary general of the Islamic Conference, following a week's visit to Manila, it was reported Sept. 5. The proposal called for rebel recognition of the sovereignty of the Philippines in exchange for an autonomous Moslem state under Philippine jurisdiction. The Moslems dropped their previous demand for secession. Marcos reacted to the plan by inviting Tohamy back to Manila to pursue his mission.

The Supreme Court handed down a decision Sept. 17 upholding the constitutionality of Marcos' assumption of emergency powers in 1972. The decision rejected a challenge and an appeal for freedom brought by former Sen. Benigno S. Aquino and 30 other prominent persons arrested after imposition of martial law. Aquino was the only one among the 31 still detained.

Twenty-seven leaders of the outlawed Communist Party surrendered Oct. 11 and gave up their weapons. Marcos later ordered the Defense Department to grant safe-conduct passes to other Communist Party leaders so that more firearms could be collected.

On Dec. 12, Marcos announced plans to release 622 of the 5,234 persons jailed since the proclamation of martial law in 1972. Of those imprisoned, 1,165 had been classified as political detainees charged with crimes "against the security of the state." In issuing the partial amnesty, the president expressed regret that it was not possible to amnesty all the prisoners, but said the government "cannot be indifferent to those who rekindle rebellion." Marcos had also taken another step in order to meet criticism of his government when, on Oct. 26, he had eased press curbs by abolishing the Media Advisory Council and the Bureau for Mass Media. They were to be replaced by self-regulatory councils.

See also JAPAN [10]; WEATHER

POLAND—Migration accord set. Polish and West German negotiators agreed Jan. 30 on details of a plan to allow ethnic Germans living in Poland to emigrate to the West over a two-five year period. About 50,000 people would be repatriated in 1974 under the plan, which had to be approved by the two governments.

Vacationers jump ship. At least 81 passengers aboard a Polish cruise liner defected in Denmark, West Germany and Norway, it was reported Feb. 1-Feb. 7. West German authorities said the 64 who left the ship in Hamburg, most of them artisans, would be allowed to settle in West Germany without being granted political asylum status.

Vatican contacts set. The Vatican announced July 5 it had agreed to establish "permanent working contacts" with Poland as a step toward normalizing relations. The announcement followed two days of talks in Rome between Polish Deputy Foreign Minister Josef Czyrek and Archbishop Agostino Casaroli, the Pope's ranking foreign affairs aide who had conducted similar talks in Warsaw in February. Observers noted that establishment of direct channels of communication had circumvented the Polish episcopate, significantly reducing the influence of the country's bishops and their primate, Stefan Cardinal Wyszynski.

Government shifts. Franciszek Szlachcic, believed to have been Poland's second most powerful official, was removed as secretary of the Polish United Workers' Party (PUWP, the Polish Communist Party) Central Committee June 25. He retained his seat on the Politburo, the party's ruling body. Although no reasons for the actions were given, some news reports suggested that a link might have been uncovered connecting Szlachcic with the 1971 opposition movement against PUWP First Secretary Edward Gierek.

The Council of State released Deputy Premier Jan Mitrega from his post as minister of mining and power, Warsaw television announced Sept. 24. The following day five additional office changes within the ministry were announced. Observers believed the shakeup was a result of a mine disaster during the summer in which 32 persons were killed. (It was reported Oct. 12 that Poland's 350,000 coal miners were believed to have been given wage increases of up to 30% at the time of the ministry shakeup. The raises reportedly were not publicized lest they provoke wage demands from other sectors of the labor force.)

Stefan Jedrychowski, the last close associate of former leader Wladislaw Gomulka remaining in the Polish Cabinet, was replaced as finance minister Nov. 21 by Henryk Kisiel, deputy foreign trade minister.

Trade with West rising. Trade between Poland and the U.S. increased from a total of $250 million in 1972 to $330 million for the first half of 1974, according to a *Journal of Commerce* report Sept. 11. Agricultural commodities accounted for most of the trade, but industrial goods were gaining in importance. Six U.S. and Canadian banks signed an agreement with the Polish state mining agency to provide financing totaling $100 million to help develop a copper industry in Poland, the *Wall Street Journal* reported Oct. 7. (West Germany and Poland signed a 10-year economic, industrial and technological cooperation agreement in Bonn Nov. 1 after nearly two years of negotiations. The accord established a joint economic commission to meet every year and also specified that West Berlin was included under its terms.)

Gierek visits U.S., sees Ford. First Secretary Gierek met with President Ford in Washington Oct. 8 and 9. Gierek was the first Communist bloc leader to meet with Ford since he became President, and the foremost Polish official to visit the U.S. since World War II. The two men signed documents which, according to State Department officials, gave the U.S. more comprehensive ties with Poland than with any other Communist country except the Soviet Union. At the end of Gierek's Oct. 6-13 U.S. visit, it was announced that Ford accepted an invitation to visit Poland next year. Among the documents signed Oct. 8 and 9 were two declarations of "friendship" and "good political relations," regarded as unique in U.S. relations with Soviet bloc governments. The declarations envisioned a doubling of two-way trade volume to $2 billion annually by 1980.

See also ARGENTINA [18]; COMMUNISM, INTERNATIONAL; EUROPEAN SECURITY; GERMANY, WEST [13]; MIDDLE EAST [15]; SOCCER; SWEDEN

POLICE—*See* CIVIL RIGHTS [9, 11]; CRIME [2, 4, 31-37]; HEARST, PATRICIA; LABOR [2]; PRESS

POLITICS

1976 Presidential Elections

[1] **Ford.** White House Press Secretary J. F. terHorst said Aug. 21 that President Ford "is now of the opinion he probably will run in 1976." The President's position was restated Nov. 15 with a statement declaring a definite intention to run, issued by the new press secretary, Ron Nessen. (In an earlier press conference, Oct. 6, the President was asked if the illness of Mrs. Ford and "the surprisingly harsh reaction" to the Nixon pardon had changed his plans. In answer, Ford said he had "seen nothing to change that decision.") After Ford's August announcement, observers noted that his intentions would discourage opposition for the 1976 Republican nomination. One of those affected was Sen. Charles H. Percy (Ill.) who had said Feb. 8 he "would like to be a candidate." On Aug. 14, Percy said his own exploratory candidacy had been put "on the back burner and maybe into the deep freeze" by Ford's accession to the presidency.

[2] **Wallace.** Gov. George C. Wallace (D, Ala.) anounced his bid Feb. 22 for an unprecedented third term and implied his decision foreshadowed another presidential bid. "As governor of Alabama again," he said, "I will be in a position to see that those I represented in 1968 and 1972 will be represented... in 1976." Wallace's campaign fund organization, intact since 1968, raised more than $1 million in 1973.

[3] **McCarthy.** Former Sen. Eugene J. McCarthy, currently teaching at the New School for Social Research in New York, was named honorary chairman Aug. 25 of a new independent political group, The Committee for a Constitutional Presidency. At a news conference in Chicago, McCarthy said he would be a "deadly serious candidate for the White House in 1976" if the committee, whose present functions were primarily educative, decided "to have me do so."

[4] **Kennedy.** Sen. Edward M. Kennedy (D, Mass.) announced Sept. 23 he would not be a presidential candidate in 1976. Kennedy told a Boston press conference that his decision, based on personal family considerations, was "firm, final and unconditional. There is absolutely no circumstance or event that will alter the decision. I will not accept the nomination. I will not accept a draft. I will oppose any effort to place my name in nomination in any state or at the national convention, and I will oppose any effort to promote my candidacy in

any other way." He said he expected to be a candidate for re-election to the U.S. Senate in 1976. Kennedy, 42, was the acknowledged leading prospect for the Democratic presidential nomination in 1976 despite the liability of the tragic accident on Chappaquiddick Island in 1969 when a girl passenger was drowned in a car Kennedy was driving. Kennedy told reporters that the incident was not a major factor in his decision.

[5] **Udall.** Rep. Morris K. Udall (D, Ariz.) announced Nov. 23 that he was a candidate for the 1976 Democratic presidential nomination. The first Democrat to enter the race officially, Udall made the announcement in Bedford, N.H. Udall said he would enter New Hampshire's March 1976 primary, the nation's earliest. Known as a liberal and a conservationist, Udall, 52, a member of Congress since 1961, said the "three E's—environment, economy, energy"—would dominate his campaign.

[6] **Carter.** Gov. Jimmy Carter (Ga.), 50, announced his candidacy Dec. 12 for the Democratic presidential nomination. Carter, whose term was expiring, had already traveled extensively on political assignment for the Democrats to coordinate the 1974 Congressional and gubernatorial campaigns. Outlining his stands, he advocated the "most extreme rigidity" in enforcing desegregation. "The time for racial discrimination is over," he said.

Democratic Party

[7] **Democrats adopt charter.** The Democratic Party adopted a charter Dec. 7, the first such action by a major U.S. political party. The action was taken at the first non-presidential convention in U.S. politics. Some 1,900 delegates attended the mid-term "mini-convention" in Kansas City, Mo. Dec. 6-8. While the major business of the convention was the charter, an "economic recovery" program was espoused by the delegates Dec. 6 as an alternative to the "callous economic nonsense" of the Ford Administration. Although the charter was adopted by an overwhelming shout of approval, the hard won unanimity came only after a compromise had been reached to avert a walkout by blacks over enfranchisement for minority groups. The charter would go into effect for the 1980 national convention; rules for the 1976 convention were adopted in 1972.

[8] **Minority representation conflict.** The controversy at the convention, as it had all year, focused on the party's "affirmative action" plan for minority participation in its affairs. The new rules, approved by the Democratic National Committee March 1, were designed to avoid the problems of the 1972 convention over "quotas" for blacks, women and youth. Although mandatory quotas had been prohibited in the charter version, proportional representation was required at all levels of the delegate selection process with performance of the requirement to "be considered relevant evidence" in the case of challanges. However, composition of the delegations alone would "not constitute prima facie evidence of discrimination." If the state party "had adopted and implemented and approved affirmative action programs" which encouraged full participation by all Democrats, "the party shall not be subject to the challenge based solely on delegation composition or primary results." The blacks, backed in their efforts by a women's caucus and endorsed by Spanish-Americans, were adamantly against the clause, saying that under its provisions their representation had dropped from 19% in 1972 to 9% at the mini-convention. A compromise was worked out with the help of the Democratic governors, United Automobile Workers President Leonard Woodcock, and Chicago Mayor Richard J. Daley. The governors had considered the issue at their Nov. 18 meeting in Hilton Head, S.C. The compromise, as presented by Gov. Reubin Askew (Fla.) allowed delegate composition as "relevant evidence." However, "if a state party

has adopted and implemented an approved and monitored affirmative action program," delegate composition or primary results could not be the sole reason for challenge. The compromise brought objections from AFL-CIO President George Meany and some party regulars, especially conservative Southerners, who viewed it as a capitulation to one group.

[9] In other action Dec. 7, the delegates voted 1,006-823 to reject a requirement that the party hold a mandatory mid-term convention. A proposal to require one in 1978 failed 968-851.

Republican Party

[10] **Ruling on GOP delegate allotment.** U.S. District Court Judge William B. Jones Jan. 11 ruled against part of the selection process adopted for the 1976 Republican National Convention. The process, adopted at the 1972 convention, was held in part to be unconstitutional by denying equal treatment. The part held unconstitutional allotted 4½ additional delegates to any state returning a majority vote in 1972 for President Nixon, or additional bonus delegates to states electing a Republican governor, senator or majority House contingent. Such flat bonus awarding of delegates, the court held, would prove to be disproportionately advantageous to small states.

[11] **Woman selected to head GOP.** President Ford Sept. 4 named Mary Louise Smith, 59, of Iowa as chairman of the Republican National Committee. She replaced George Bush who had been named envoy to China. Richard D. Obenshain, Virginia state Republican chairman, was selected to succeed Smith as co-chairman. Their appointment by the Republican National Committee was ratified Sept. 16. Mrs. Smith was the first woman to head the party. (Jean Westwood of Utah headed the Democratic National Committee in 1972.)

[12] **GOP initiates reform rules.** The Republican Party Dec. 8 initiated reform procedure to open participation in its national convention and to maintain surveillance over fund raising and spending by its presidential candidates. Proposals on these matters were adopted by the Rule 29 Committee, which met for two days in Washington Dec. 7-8. The committee, headed by Rep. William A. Steiger (Wis.), had been established by the Republican National Convention in 1972 to review party rules and procedures. The committee's decisions were subject to approval by the Republican National Committee. The Rule 29 group Dec. 8 adopted by voice vote a rule calling upon state GOP organizations to "take positive action and endeavor to assure greater and more equitable participation of women, young people, minority and heritage groups and senior citizens in their political process and to increase their representation at the 1976 national convention." The state groups were urged to submit to the national committee examples of activities "designed to create the opportunity for participation in all party activities for all peoples regardless of race, creed, national origin, religion, sex or age." The national committee was to "review and comment" on the proposals. The rule was not binding on the state organizations, but a quota system for delegates was specifically ruled out by the Rule 29 Committee. The final form of the rule represented a compromise betwen reform forces led by Rep. Margaret M. Heckler (Mass.) and conservatives led by Mississippi GOP chairman Clarke Reed.

[13] The campaign fund rule called for a seven-member committee headed by the party chairman to receive periodic reports from the presidential candidate's campaign committee. A member of the national committee was to sit on the board of the campaign committee.

See also CAMPAIGN FINANCING; CIVIL RIGHTS [19]; EDUCATION; ELECTIONS; FORD, GERALD R.; HOUSING; KENNEDY, SEN. EDWARD M.; NIXON RICHARD M.;

OBITUARIES [CHOTINER, GRUENING, HODGES, HUNT, JORDAN, KNOWLAND, MORSE, MUNDT]; VOTING RIGHTS; WATERGATE AFFAIR

POLLUTION—*See* ENVIRONMENT & POLLUTION

POMPIDOU, GEORGES JEAN—*See* FRANCE [1, 8]; MONETARY DEVELOPMENTS [16]

POPE PAUL VI—*See* BIRTH CONTROL; BUTZ, EARL L.; HUNGARY; MEXICO [20]; RELIGION [12-18]

POPULATION—Statistics. The Census Bureau reported Jan. 1 that the U.S. population was 211.7 million, including armed forces and federal employes abroad and their dependents. The gain of 1.5 million over 1972 included 3.2 million births, 2 million deaths and 350,000 net immigration. The world's population increased by 76 million in one year to 3.782 billion, it was reported March 20. Asia had 2.154 billion people, Europe 469 million, North America 332 million and the Soviet Union 248 million.

The Census Bureau reported July 23 that population growth and migration patterns among states since the 1970 census were significantly different from previous trends, with some Southern states showing heavy net in-migration and the Northern states having moderately heavy out-migration. Reporting on data for the April 1970-July 1973 period, the bureau said there was a net migration of 1,428,000 persons into the South and 751,000 into the West, while the Northeast lost 150,000 to migration and the North-Central area lost 298,000. (All states showed net population gains during the period because of the excess of births over deaths.) Florida had the highest population increase, 888,000, with 782,000 attributable to migration. Of the states showing net migration losses, New York had the highest numerical loss (268,000), and Ohio showed the highest percentage loss (1.7%).

The bureau had reported May 30 that the basic indices of population growth had reached new lows in 1973. The crude birth rate—number of births per 1,000 population—was 14.9, compared with 18.2 in 1970 and 15.6 in 1972. The theoretical fertility rate was 1.9 children per couple, well below the replacement rate of 2.1. The rate in 1970 had been 2.5.

Growth curb trend reported. Despite questions of racial discrimination and other infringements on individual rights, the number of communities attempting to limit population growth was rapidly increasing, according to a report published by the *New York Times* July 28. According to the report, the Department of Housing and Urban Development had found that 226 communities had imposed temporary or long-term moratoriums on such growth essentials as water and sewer connections, building permits and land subdivisions. Other forms of growth limitation included restrictive zoning: large lot requirements and restrictions on multiple dwellings. Such practices had led to charges of bias against racial minorities and the poor.

Population plan adopted. The U.N. World Population Conference convened Aug. 19 in Bucharest, Rumania. It ended Aug. 30 with adoption of a vaguely worded Plan of Action to slow the pace of world population growth. The document was approved by acclamation after extensive revisions sought mainly by underdeveloped countries led by Communist and Latin American nations. It failed to set national or international population goals, or to focus on the possibility that overpopulation would soon overtax the world's supplies of food and other resources (Experts at the conference had warned that the world had food reserves for only 30 days and that an expected drop in the 1974 grain harvest threatened catastrophe.)

The plan subordinated population control to economic and social development, seeing the latter as the key to solving population problems. The plan recognized that "per capita use of world resources is much higher in the more developed than in developing countries," and urged industrial nations "to adopt appropriate policies in population, consumption and investment, bearing in mind the need for fundamental improvement in international equity." It affirmed the basic right of couples to freely decide the number and spacing of their children, and to have the information, education and means to do so. Nations were asked to make these means and information available to their citizens, but no target date was set for compliance. The plan also strongly recognized the right of women to contribute to economic development and to participate in all spheres of life on an equal basis with men.

Delegates from industrial nations and many population and food experts privately expressed disappointment that the conference did not emphasize the need for urgency in finding remedies for population growth and its attending problems, the *Washington Post* reported Sept. 1.

Discussions at the conference were marked by disagreements over solutions: one view advocated population control while the other stressed economic development and assistance by the rich nations to the poor. Chinese chief delegate Huang Shu-tse said Aug. 21 that the U.S. and the Soviet Union were "trying to shift the blame for global problems onto the Third World." U.S. expert Lester R. Brown, speaking Aug. 20 at the Population Tribune—a related, non-governmental conference—said development of high-yield food grains, known as the Green Revolution, had achieved all that could be expected, partly because fertilizers were now in such short supply and party because population growth had outpaced even the highest food production rates. A view moderating between the two solutions was presented at the Tribune Aug. 26 by John D. Rockefeller 3rd, chairman of the Rockefeller Foundation, who reversed his long-standing position on family planning. Calling on industrial nations to "assist in broadening the choices available to the poorer nations," Rockefeller endorsed a new approach which "recognizes that rapid population growth is only one among many problems facing most countries."

See also ABORTION; BIRTH CONTROL; FAMINE & FOOD; HUNGARY; WELFARE & POVERTY

PORNOGRAPHY—*See* OBSCENITY & PORNOGRAPHY

PORTUGAL

Coup Ousts Dictatorship

[1] **Armed forces seize power.** Rebel military officers, calling themselves the Armed Forces Movement, seized control of the government in a virtually bloodless coup April 25, ending more than 40 years of civilian dictatorship begun by the late Premier Antonio Salazar. The coup began early in the morning, when a raiding party seized a Lisbon radio station and broadcast an appeal to the Republican National Guard, the Lisbon police and other military units in the capital not to oppose the uprising and cause "unnecessary bloodshed." Rebel forces simultaneously ringed Lisbon, seized the airport and took control of government ministries. Military resistance collapsed quickly, although some Lisbon National Guard units reportedly continued to hold out April 26 and some resistance was reported from police in charge of the Caxias prison, where a large number of the government's political prisoners were being held. No military casualties were reported in Lisbon, but at least one civilian was reported killed and 20 were wounded. Other uprisings occurred simultaneously in Santarem (50 miles north of Lisbon), in Lamego (a base in north central Portugal) and in Tomar and Oporto.

[2] Premier Marcello Caetano and President Americo Thomaz were arrested by the rebels, and leadership was assumed by a seven-man "Junta of National Salvation" pledged to bring democracy to Portugal and peace to its African colonies. The junta apparently was dominated by Gen. Antonio de Spinola. After seizing power, the rebels issued a proclamation stating that the uprising had resulted from 13 years of continued colonial fighting, "the growing climate of total detachment of the Portuguese in relation to political responsibilities they owe as citizens" and the denial of rights. The proclamation also pledged that general elections for a constituent national assembly would be held "as soon as possible." Spinola April 26 appeared on radio and television with five of the six other members of the junta and pledged freedom of thought and speech, the creation of a civilian provisional government headed by a military man and free elections for both a national assembly and a new president.

[3] **Aftermath of coup.** Following the military coup, the country returned to relative normality with little bloodshed. A total of 10 deaths was reported April 28, with the casualties including policemen who resisted the coup and bystanders inadvertently shot by citizens celebrating the takeover. The junta, issuing warnings against violence by leftist demonstrators and attacks by citizens on members of the political police, sent tanks into Lisbon to discourage unrest. Shops, cafes and restaurants reopened April 26, but banks remained closed through April 30 to prevent a massive flight of capital. (Border guards and airport security officers searched persons leaving the country and stopped those carrying large quantities of money.) Political and labor organizing began immediately and accelerated April 28, when airports were reopened and land travel to and from Spain resumed, allowing the return of hundreds of political exiles. Among the first to return were Socialist Party leader Mario Soares April 28 and Communist party leader Alvaro Cunhal April 30. Both received tumultuous welcomes from thousands of followers and met after their arrival with Gen. Spinola. Both Soares and the Portuguese Democratic Movement (a coalition of Socialists, Communists and Christian Democrats) called for independence of the African colonies after meeting with Spinola. The statements marked the first open disagreement between the junta and opposition political forces.

[4] **Old regime dismantled.** The junta April 29 issued a series of decrees effectively dismantling the ousted civilian dictatorship. The measures officially deposed Caetano, Thomaz and all Cabinet members; dismissed the governors of Angola and Mozambique; replaced the three military chiefs of staff; dissolved the National Assembly, the Council of State and the only legal party under the old government. (Thomaz, Caetano, former Interior Minister Cesar Moreira Baptista and ex-Defense Minister Joaquim Silva Cunha were exiled April 26 to the Portuguese island of Madeira, where they were confined in a palace.) Other decrees proclaimed an amnesty for all political prisoners and dismissed the heads of Portugal's six universities. (An estimated 100 political prisoners had been released April 27 and their places in jail taken by members of the old regime's political police, which the junta abolished.) In further action, the junta: May 2 declared an amnesty for the thousands of men who had deserted the armed forces or evaded the draft to avoid fighting in the colonies if such men would report promptly for military service; May 6 offered a cease-fire to guerrillas in the colonies, on the condition that colonial liberation movements accept the "framework of the democratic program of the armed forces"; May 9 agreed to allow labor unions to form a confederation. Gen. Francisco da Costa Gomes, a junta member who was reappointed chief of the general staff, May 11 reiterated the junta's cease-fire offer to colonial guerrillas, but backed up a threat of intensified war (first voiced in Angola May 5 and in Lisbon May 6) by stating

that "a majority of parties will surely be of the opinion that the fight must go on." (The colonial rebels were seeking independence from Portugal, rather than the federative status offered by the junta.)

[5] **Provisional government formed.** Spinola was proclaimed provisional president May 15 and announced a 15-man cabinet the same day. Spinola, who said he would give up the presidency within a year after elections were held, was proclaimed president by Costa Gomes, who said Spinola would rule with the powers of the current authoritarian constitution. (Spinola had been dismissed as deputy chief of the general staff by the deposed government March 14 for writing *Portugal and the Future,* an instant best-seller which severely criticized government policies, particularly the colonial wars. The book argued that Portugal could not win a military victory over rebel movements in Portugal's African territories. A brief military uprising by Spinola's supporters had followed March 16, but had been quashed when other military units refused to join.) In his May proclamation, Costa Gomes also praised the young officers who apparently organized the military coup, asserting they had carried out the "most dignified revolution in contemporary history."

[6] The new left-center cabinet announced by Spinola May 15 included: Premier—Adelino da Palma Carlos, a liberal law professor whose moderate opposition under the ousted regime had caused him to be banned from teaching and public office for several years; foreign—Soares; minister without portfolio—Cunhal; justice—Socialist Francisco Salgado Zenha; social communications (information)—Socialist Raul Rego; labor—Communist Avelino Pacheco Goncalves; defense—Lt. Col. Mario Firmino Miguel, a member of the young officers' group; and interior—centrist Joaquin Magalhaes Motta. Twenty-two deputy ministers, representing a wide variety of political views and technical skills, also were named.

[7] **Actions against deposed government.** Leftist members of the provisional government advocated trials for Caetano and Thomaz for crimes laid to the secret police and other agencies during their dictatorship. However, the junta, apparently believing such a trial would deeply divide the country, on May 20 sent Caetano and Thomaz into exile in Brazil which received them on condition that they abstain from political activity. In an apparent move to appease critics of the deportation, officials announced May 24 that two former ministers, a vice admiral, an army general and colonel and a former National Assembly deputy would be tried for crimes committed under the dictatorship. The cabinet officials were former Interior Minister Moreira Baptista and ex-Defense Minister Silva Cunha who were transferred back to Lisbon from Madeira May 23.

[8] The new government also began inquiries directed at finding the participants in Portugal's most notorious political assassination, the murder of Gen. Huberto Delgado in 1965. The judicial police announced July 30 that ten members of the abolished secret police, including the force's leader, Fernando da Silva Pais, were charged in the case. Seven were under arrest and the other three, including Delgado's alleged assassin, Casimiro Montero, were still at large.

[9] **Labor developments.** A wave of strikes in May and June resulted in a series of restrictive government actions. The strikes began May 15 when more than 8,000 workers at the Lisnave shipyard in Lisbon, the nation's largest employer, struck for a 50% wage increase, profit-sharing and better working conditions. The strike ended May 23 after their demands were granted. The shipyard workers strike was followed by protests by bus and train conductors who refused to accept fares from passengers May 15-16. Other strikes were mounted by workers in the textile, auto and baking industries and by employees of the subway system who all sought wage increases.

[10] The Organization for Economic Cooperation and Development

announced May 20 that Portuguese inflation for the 12 months ending in March had reached 30%. Spinola warned May 29 that economic disruption played into the hands of "reactionaries and counterrevolutionaries." He asserted, "It is not by way of anarchy, economic chaos, disorder and unemployment that we build the Portugal of the future." Spinola also warned in a second speech May 31 that the country could not "distribute wealth before we produce it."

[11] In an effort to still criticism of its management of the economy and of its African policy, the government June 22 instituted severe restrictions on all news media. The press restrictions apparently had been demanded by Spinola, who reportedly told military leaders June 13 that he would resign unless he was given powers to stop the extreme left from subverting the program of the Armed Forces Movement. (The government June 7 had arrested Jose Luis Saldanha Sanches, the editor of the weekly newspaper *Luta Popular* and leader of the extreme leftist Movement to Reorganize the Portuguese Proletariat (MRPP). Sanches had written an article urging soldiers in Portugal and its colonies to "desert with their weapons." The Communist Party had approved the arrest.) In the first crackdown under the new laws, the Lisbon newspapers *A Capital* and *Republica* were fined July 3 for publishing news of a demonstration against the arrest of two officers who had refused to accept a plan to assume military control of Lisbon's strikebound post office. *A Capital, Republica* and another Lisbon paper, *Diario de Lisboa* were prohibited from publishing Aug. 2 after they had printed reports the day before of an MRPP rally where speakers had denounced the government's African policy. The suspension was lifted Aug. 3. In a move to ease tension with the press, the government announced Aug. 6 that a joint committee of newspaper management personnel and journalists would draw up the final version of the new press law.

[12] The government also published a law Aug. 28 establishing severe limits on the right to strike. At the same time it broke a stoppage by ground employes of TAP, the national airline, by placing the strikers under military orders. Although the new law allowed strikes for the first time in more than 40 years, it forbade stoppages for political and religious reasons, and for the purpose of upsetting the terms of a collective bargaining agreement. Strikes by policemen, firemen, military personnel and magistrates were illegal, as were strikes to show solidarity with striking workers in another profession.

[13] **Government changes.** Major disagreements between left and right-wing members of the government escalated in July, leading Spinola to resign as president Sept. 30. He was replaced by Costa Gomes.

[14] An internal cabinet struggle had led to the resignation July 9 of Premier Palma Carlos and four centrist ministers after the Council of State denied a request by Palma Carlos for additional powers. Palma Carlos had asked the Council to make ministers directly responsible to him, rather than to Spinola, and to grant him other powers he deemed necessary to effectively carry out his duties. Spinola, too, had been rebuffed by the Council which he had asked to approve a series of proposals, including one which would set the presidential election for Oct. 31, instead of the spring of 1975. (According to most press reports, an early election would have benefited Spinola.) When the Council rejected pleas from Palma Carlos and Spinola, the former resigned, leaving the cabinet dominated by Socialists, Communists and other leftists who opposed Spinola's attempts to increase his powers. Spinola dismissed the entire cabinet July 11 and named army Col. Vasco dos Santos Goncalves as the new premier July 13. Goncalves was considered a leftist and an architect of the Armed Forces Movement's program to end the wars in its African territories as quickly as possible. Goncalves named a new military-dominated cabinet July 17. The new

ministers were sworn in by Spinola the next day. At the ceremony, Goncalves recognized the right of African terrorists to self-determination.

[15] **Spinola quits.** Spinola resigned Sept. 30 following a week-long buildup of tension between rightists and leftists within and outside the government. The two groups had clashed Sept. 27 outside a Lisbon bullfight arena where hundreds of conservatives had massed to cheer Spinola and denounce Goncalves, both of whom were attending a charity bullfight inside. After the clashes, leftists began preparations to disrupt a pro-Spinola "silent majority" rally scheduled for the next day. The government had previously banned the extreme right-wing Portuguese National Party; while a new right-wing newspaper, *Bandarra,* violently attacked the Communist Party and other leftist groups.

[16] Resigning with Spinola were three other members of the seven-man junta, all of whom were conservatives and were linked by leftists to an alleged right-wing plot against the provisional government. The government charged the plot was conceived by organizers of the pro-Spinola rally. Spinola had cancelled the rally under pressure from Goncalves and other leftists who maintained it would provoke a major armed confrontation between left and right. Seventy-seven persons had been arrested and awaited trial in connection with the plot, according to the *Washington Post* Oct. 2. Spinola delivered an emotional farewell address on radio and television Sept. 30, denouncing what he called the betrayal both in Portugal and its African colonies of the program of the Armed Forces Movement.

[17] Goncalves made an impassioned public rebuttal of Spinola's speech Sept. 30 in which he asserted elections would be held as scheduled in March 1975, although he admitted that some unexpected occurrence could prevent them from taking place.

[8] **New junta named.** The Council of State appointed five members to the Junta of National Salvation Oct. 15. The new junta members from the army were Brig. Gen. Carlos Soares Fabiao, the last governor of Portuguese Guinea (now Guinea-Bissau), and Lt. Col. Fisher Lopes Pires, a prominent member of the Armed Forces Movement. The new air force members were Cols. Pinheiro Freire and Mendes Dias, and the new navy member was Capt. Silvano Pereira.

[19] Spinola was retired Nov. 17 under a new military policy designed to "rejuvenate ranks and create new posts." Top generals, admirals and rear admirals would henceforth retire at 62 (Spinola was 64), brigadier generals and commodores at 60, and colonels and navy captains at 57. The policy apparently was aimed at restricting the influence of certain prominent military leaders, according to the *London Times* Nov. 18. There also was a plan to completely restructure the army, the *Times* reported Nov. 19.

[20] **Political parties law.** The provisional government published a law Oct. 31 requiring political parties to register at least 5,000 members to earn the right to run candidates in elections. The law empowered courts to disband parties which "systematically use methods which are illicit and against public morality or order, or which disrupt the discipline of the armed forces." The centrist Progressive Democratic Party (PPD) withdrew from the Portuguese Democratic Movement Nov. 5 after the latter decided to register as a party and run in the scheduled 1975 elections. The PPD charged the movement was controlled by the Portuguese Communist Party. (The Communists held a national congress in Lisbon Oct. 20, attended by an estimated 4,000—6,000 persons. For the first time the party published the names of members of its Central Committee, which included two women.)

[21] **Sao Tome, Principe independence set.** Portugal signed an agreement Nov.

26 to grant independence in July 1975 to the West African islands of Sao Tome and Principe. The agreement was reached in Algiers by Antonio de Almeia Santos, Portugal's overseas territories minister, and Miguel Trouvoado, a leader of the islands' liberation movement. Until independence, the islands would have a provisional government under a Portuguese high commissioner. A constituent assembly would be elected five days before independence was proclaimed. Sao Tome and Principe lay 125 miles west of Gabon in the Gulf of Guinea. They had a combined population of some 61,000 persons.

The Economy

[22] Government plans to correct an economy whose inflation rate—30%—was the highest in Europe, were adversely affected when tourism, a major source of income, fell off partially as a result of cholera outbreaks in the nation during the height of the tourist season in July-August. (More than 1,000 cases and 20 deaths were reported by Aug. 24.) The economy also was affected by a rising unemployment rate due to West Germany's decision in 1973 to cut off immigration of foreign workers, many of whom were Portuguese.

[23] Economic help for Portugal was forthcoming when the First National City Bank of New York announced Sept. 16 that a five-year, $150 million standby credit had been arranged for that nation by a group of international banks. It was the largest Eurocredit ever organized for Portugal and the first international loan arranged for Lisbon since the civilian dictatorship was overthrown. The Soviet Union vowed Nov. 2 to give economic assistance to Portugal "with regard for available resources." Soviet President Nikolai Podgorny made the pledge at a meeting with members of a Portuguese delegation which visited Moscow Oct. 29-Nov. 3. The group was headed by Minister Without Portfolio Cunhal, head of the Portuguese Communist Party.

Foreign Relations

[24] **Ties with Communist nations.** Portugal agreed to exchange ambassadors wih Rumania June 1 and with the Soviet Union June 9. Portugal had not had normal diplomatic relations with Rumania for 25 years, or with Russia since 1917. The renewal of relations was facilitated by the Portuguese Communist Party's faithful adherence to the Moscow political line, according to most reports. Portuguese party leader Cunhal had lived in Moscow during part of his exile under the ousted civilian dictatorship. Portugal also established diplomatic relations with Yugoslavia and East Germany, it was reported June 20; and with Czechoslovakia June 27.

[25] **Mitterrand visits.** French Socialist leader Francois Mitterrand visited Portugal July 2-5. He spent most of his time at Socialist Party meetings, but he met July 3 with Palma Carlos, then premier, and with Provisional President Spinola. Mitterrand's visit reflected concern on the part of Portuguese Socialists about the growing popular support of the Communist Party, their principal rival on the left, the *New York Times* reported July 3. Shortly before Mitterrand's arrival, the Socialist Party issued a radical, anti-capitalist declaration in an apparent effort to draw more support from workers.

[26] **India ties set.** Portugal and India reestablished diplomatic relations Sept. 24, after Lisbon recognized India's full sovereignty over Goa, Damao and Din, the small, formerly Portuguese enclaves near Bombay. Relations between the two countries had been suspended in 1961 when Indian troops occupied Goa.

[27] **Costa Gomes in U.S.** Provisional President Costa Gomes visited the U.S. Oct. 16-20, addressing the United Nations General Assembly in New York and conferring with President Ford and Secretary of State Henry Kissinger in Washington. The purpose of the trip was to reaffirm Portuguese ties with the

U.S. and the North Atlantic Treaty Organization (NATO), and to secure U.S. and international aid for the troubled Portuguese economy, according to most press reports. Costa Gomes was accompanied by Foreign Minister Soares and by Vitor Constancio, secretary of state for economic planning.

[28] At the General Assembly Oct. 17, Costa Gomes asked financial aid for Portugal's "peaceful revolution" and urged the U.N. to lift the embargoes and restrictions it imposed on Lisbon under the ousted civilian dictatorship. Costa Gomes departed from his prepared text to ask African nations to believe in the "honesty and sincerity" of Portugal's vow to free its African colonies. After the address, Foreign Minister Soares conferred with African delegates and urged them to establish diplomatic relations with Lisbon as soon as possible. Costa Gomes met with Ford at the White House and with Kissinger at the State Department Oct. 18. Soares told the press after the meetings that Costa Gomes had requested U.S. economic aid in five areas—railways, highways, education, energy and geothermal power.

[29] On his return to Lisbon Oct. 20, Costa Gomes stressed Portuguese membership in NATO, asserting: "We have a geostrategic position that obliges us to make a choice." He said the government's continuing support for NATO corresponded with "the wishes of the Portuguese people."

See also AFRICA; ANGOLA; APPOINTMENTS & RESIGNATIONS; COMMUNISM, INTERNATIONAL; EUROPEAN SECURITY; GUINEA-BISSAU; MACAO; MOZAMBIQUE; PORTUGUESE TIMOR; SPAIN [1]; UNITED NATIONS [2]

PORTUGUESE TIMOR—Col. Fernando Aldeia, governor of Portuguese Timor, announced that a referendum would be held in 1975 to determine the status of the territory, it was reported June 3. Three political groups were reportedly vying for control—one seeking to maintain a Portuguese presence, one demanding total independence and one supporting integration with Indonesia. (Portuguese Timor was the eastern half of the Indonesian island of Timor.)

POSTAL SERVICE—Higher postal rates took effect March 2 and Postmaster General E. T. Klassen warned that further increases could be expected because of rising wage and fuel costs. Among the higher rates were a 2¢ boost for first class letters (to 10¢), airmail letters (to 13¢) and postcards (to 8¢).

The House passed 277-129 without change June 19 a Senate bill delaying a scheduled series of postal rate increases for magazines, newspapers and nonprofit organizations. President Nixon signed the bill into law June 30. Under the legislation, the full rate increase scheduled to go into effect in 1976 for newspapers, magazines and other mailers of regular second-class mail was delayed until 1979. Mailers of books, records and other fourth-class items would get the same delay.

See also AVIATION [2]; CANADA [37]; FRANCE [16]; OBSCENITY & PORNOGRAPHY

POVERTY—*See* WELFARE & POVERTY

PRESIDENCY—*See* FORD, GERALD R.; NIXON, RICHARD M.; POLITICS; WATERGATE AFFAIR

PRESS—Shield law developments. The American Bar Association (ABA) House of Delegates Feb. 4 went on record by 157-122 vote opposing bills before Congress that would grant reporters the right to refuse to reveal confidential sources of information to investigators, prosecutors or judges. Proponents of the shield law resolution told the delegates that newsmen needed such a law to expose corruption in government. Without it, they said, news sources could not talk without fear of public exposure. Opponents argued that newsmen's privilege would encourage grand jury secrecy violations, hamper the ability of victims of libel to protect themselves against irresponsible reporting and ultimately cause the public to demand regulation of the press.

California's shield law was tested in the state courts in proceedings growing out of the 1970-71 Charles Manson murder trial. The case involved chief prosecutor Vincent Bugliosi, defense lawyer David Shinn and former *Los Angeles Herald-Examiner* reporter William Farr. A Los Angeles grand jury had indicted Bugliosi and Shinn June 28 for perjury, saying they had lied when they denied violating a court rule prohibiting discussions of the case with the press. The indictment followed testimony by Farr who conceded that two of the six Manson trial attorneys had supplied him with a secret transcript of an interview with a prospective prosecution witness. However, Farr refused to name the attorneys. Farr, who had already served a 46-day contempt of court jail sentence for refusing to name sources, was sentenced by Manson trial Judge Charles H. Older, July 29, to five days in jail and fined $500 for his continued refusal to identify the lawyers. The original contempt citation against Farr had been overruled by Judge Raymond Choate July 2. Choate accepted arguments by Farr's attorneys that an amendment to the California press shield law protected a reporter from being forced to disclose news sources to a grand jury. But Choate noted that the law did not interfere with Judge Older's right to question Farr on his sources and to sentence him to jail for civil contempt if he did not respond.

Farr's continuing refusal to answer questions about the source of articles he wrote during the Manson trial resulted in dismissal of perjury charges Dec. 4 against Shinn, who was accused of lying to a grand jury after he denied being the source of stories. Los Angeles Superior Court Judge Earl Broady, who had dismissed charges against Bugliosi Oct. 4, ruled Dec. 4 that Farr was protected by California law from being forced to reveal confidential sources. Without the testimony of Farr, who was the only potential witness against Shinn, the perjury charges could not be substantiated, Brody said.

Florida press reply law voided. The Supreme Court June 25 unanimously declared unconstitutional a Florida law that required a newspaper to print a reply by a political candidate who had been criticized in the newspaper's columns. The law was an unconstitutional restriction of freedom of the press, the court said. In its ruling, the court reversed a Florida Supreme Court decision allowing Pat L. Tornillo Jr., a teacher's union official, to demand that the *Miami Herald* print his replied to two critical editorials that appeared in 1972 when he was running for the state House of Representatives. Writing for the court, Chief Justice Warren E. Burger, argued that telling an editor what he had to publish had the same effect as telling him what he could not print which would not be "consistent with 1st Amendment guarantees."

Telephone records issue. The Reporters Committee for Freedom of the Press said Feb. 11 it would seek a court order enjoining the American Telephone & Telegraph Co. (AT&T) from secretly providing law enforcement agencies with telephone records of newsmen. The suit, aimed at insuring newsmen of notice of service so they would be able to fight the subpoenas in court, followed disclosure by the *St. Louis Post-Dispatch* Feb. 1 that the Justice Department had issued secret subpoenas in 1971 for the telephone records of the *Post-Dispatch,* Knight Newspapers Inc. and Leslie H. Whitten, an associate of syndicated columnist Jack Anderson.

The Internal Revenue Service (IRS) Feb. 13 returned to the Chesapeake and Potomac Telephone Co. (C&P) telephone records of the Washington bureau of the *New York Times* that it had secretly subpoenaed Jan. 8. The IRS said it had subpoenaed the records as part of an investigation into a leak of information by an IRS employe. The records were procured by an "administrative summons," a legal instrument normally reserved for tax evasion cases and one not giving notice to the person or organization under scrutiny.

AT&T announced Feb. 15 that it would notify its customers when records of their long distance phone calls were subpoenaed by government investigators. The phone company also agreed to supply the records only in response to subpoenas, not simply to written requests as had been the policy in the past. However, AT&T qualified its announcement, saying subscribers would be notified in all cases except when "the agency requesting the records directs the company not to disclose, certifying that such a notification could impede its investigation and interfere with enforcement of the law." A spokesman for the Reporters Committee for Freedom of the Press said the exception potentially nullified AT&T's entire commitment to advance notification.

Press defense vs libel suits limited. The Supreme Court ruled by a 5-4 vote June 25 that the press did not enjoy the same protection against libel suits filed by private citizens that it did against suits by public figures. Private citizens could recover "actual damages" for "defamatory falsehoods" without having to prove "actual malice," a condition required of publc figures suing for libel. The court's ruling reversed lower court decisions that overruled a $50,000 libel award to Chicago attorney Elmer Gertz. Gertz had been retained in 1969 by the parents of a youth, who was fatally shot by a Chicago policeman the year before. In March 1969, *American Opinion*, the monthly publication of the John Birch Society, printed an article which portrayed Gertz, who was then representing the parents in a civil suit against the policeman, as a "Communist-fronter" and as a participant in a "Communist campaign against the police."

Writing for the majority, Justice Lewis F. Powell Jr. said private citizens should not have to prove as much as public officials. Public figures usually had access to the media to counteract false statements, and individuals seeking public prominence did so with the knowledge that they were inviting greater attention and the attendant risk of "defamatory falsehoods," Powell said.

Knight-Ridder merger. Ridder Publications, based in New York, and Knight Newspapers, headquartered in Miami, voted in separate meetings to approve a merger of the companies effective Nov. 30. The new company, to be known as Knight-Ridder Newspapers, would publish 35 daily newspapers in 16 states with a combined revenue of over $550 million in 1974. The combined company would have a total seven-day circulation of 26.9 million, the largest of any newspaper group. Knight newspapers were concentrated in the eastern third of the nation, Ridder Publications from the Midwest to the Far West.

See also APPOINTMENTS & RESIGNATIONS; ARGENTINA [2, 13]; AUSTRALIA [15]; BRAZIL [3, 5]; CANADA [2]; CHILE [11]; CRIME [21]; DEFENSE [2]; FORD, GERALD R.; FRANCE [7]; GAMBLING; GERMANY, WEST [2]; GUYANA; KOREA, REPUBLIC OF [14]; NIXON, RICHARD M.; OBITUARIES [ALSOP, BOYLE, KNOWLAND, KROCK, LIPPMANN]; PERU [6-10]; PHILIPPINES; PORTUGAL [11]; POSTAL SERVICE; PRIVACY [3]; PULITZER PRIZES; RUMANIA; SOUTH AFRICA [4-5]; SRI LANKA; TELEVISION & RADIO; UGANDA; VIETNAM, REPUBLIC OF [18-21, 34]

PRICE FIXING—*See* ANTITRUST ACTIONS; BOOKS; SUGAR
PRICES—*See* AGRICULTURE; AUTOMOBILES [1-9]; AVIATION [1-4, 7-9]; BANKS & BANKING; ECONOMY, U.S.; SUGAR; WELFARE & POVERTY
PRINCIPE ISLAND—*See* PORTUGAL [21]
PRISONERS OF WAR—*See* CYPRUS [21, 24]; LAOS; MIDDLE EAST [4, 8-9]; PAKISTAN; VIETNAM, REPUBLIC OF [31-33]
PRISONS—*See* CRIME [41-42]; NETHERLANDS [13]; ROCKEFELLER, NELSON [7, 23]; VOTING RIGHTS

PRIVACY & ELECTRONIC SURVEILLANCE—Kissinger wiretap controversy. Charges that Secretary of State Henry A. Kissinger had initiated wiretapping against 13 federal officials and four newsmen from 1969-71 led to the Secretary's threat to resign June 11. He was cleared of the charges by the Senate Foreign Relations Committee Aug. 6.

[2] Kissinger's threat to quit came during an emotional news conference in Salzburg, Austria, during President Nixon's stopover preparatory to his Mideast tour. It was prompted by reports from unidentified Congressional sources that Kissinger had a more extensive role in federal wiretapping efforts than he had led senators to believe at his confirmation hearing in 1973. (At the hearing, Kissinger said he had consented to the practice in 1969 on the advice of John Mitchell and J. Edgar Hoover because of his concern over leaks of sensitive material.) During the Salzburg press conference, Kissinger said, because of "egregious violations" of national security items, he had spoken to the President in 1969 and Nixon had ordered "the institution of a system of national security wiretaps." Kissinger said his office supplied the names of persons with access to the security data. Kissinger also told reporters he had sent a letter to the Senate Foreign Relations Committee requesting a new review of the charges, among them one stating that he had prior knowledge of formation of the White House investigation unit known as "the plumbers" in 1971. The controversy was further complicated by circulation, to members of the House Judiciary Committee, of unpublished White House transcripts which revealed a Feb. 28, 1973 remark by the President that Kissinger had asked the taps be instituted. Kissinger maintained the President's comments were "based on misapprehension."

[3] A resolution backing Kissinger was introduced in the Senate late June 12 with early sponsorship of 39 Republicans and Democrats. By June 13, 52 senators had signed the resolution, including Majority leader Mike Mansfield (D, Mont.) and Minority Leader Hugh Scott (R, Pa.). The resolution, submitted by Sen. James B. Allen (D, Ala.), said the Senate "holds in high regard Dr. Kissinger and regards him as an outstanding member of this Administration, as a patriotic American in whom it has complete confidence, and whose integrity and veracity are above reproach." Among those supporting Kissinger were Sen. Barry Goldwater who, on June 12, accused the *Washington Post* of committing an "act of treason" by publishing secret FBI documents that indicated Kissinger had initiated some of the wiretaps. The *Washington Post* called it "an outrageous charge." Reports on the FBI documents had been published June 12 by the *Post*, the *New York Times* and the *Boston Globe*, along with reports of Kissinger's Salzburg news conference. According to one document, entitled "Sensitive Coverage Placed at Request of White House" and dated May 12, 1973, specific requests for the wiretaps had come from either Kissinger, then national security adviser, or his aide, Gen. Alexander M. Haig Jr., currently White House chief of staff. The document was addressed to Leonard M. Walters, then assistant director of the FBI, now retired. Another document, dated May 13, 1973, said "it appears that the project of placing electronic surveillance at the request of the White House had its beginning in a telephone call to Mr. J. Edgar Hoover on May 9, 1969, from Dr. Henry A. Kissinger." The document also said a preliminary estimate of the wiretap operation was that there had been no evidence of federal illegality gleaned from the wiretaps nor any instance that data had been leaked to unauthorized persons.

[4] William D. Ruckelshaus, former acting director of the FBI, supported Kissinger June 16 in his account of his wiretapping role in 1969-71. Ruckelshaus, who first investigated the wiretapping effort and reported on it a

year earlier, said Kissinger's role was "pretty much as he's described it." Appearing on the CBS "Face the Nation" program, Ruckelshaus suggested an explanation for one of the questions involved: whether Kissinger did or did not initiate the wiretaps. "In the sense that he supplied the names, he initiated it," he said. "But his definition of initiation is that it wasn't his idea to tap; he simply complained about the leaks."

[5] The Senate Foreign Relations Committee Aug. 6 reaffirmed its support for Kissinger after probing his role in the wiretapping of 17 officials and newsmen from 1969 to 1971. In a report unanimously approved, the committee concluded that there were "no contradictions" between Kissinger's testimony at his confirmation hearings in 1973 "and the totality of the new information available."

[6] **Tax data privacy.** President Nixon revoked a 1973 executive order March 21 which had permitted the Agriculture Department to inspect farmers' individual income tax returns as part of its statistics-gathering operations. A White House spokesman said the revocation had been recommended by Vice President Gerald R. Ford, who had been named head of an Administration panel on privacy rights.

[7] Sen. Lowell P. Weicker Jr. (R, Conn.), a member of the Senate Watergate Committee, accused the Internal Revenue Service (IRS) April 8 of acting as a "public lending library" for White House efforts to aid political friends and harass political enemies. Appearing at a joint hearing of Senate Judiciary Subcommittees on Constitutional Rights and Administrative Practice and Procedure, and the Foreign Relations Subcommittee on Surveillance, Weicker disclosed a collection of documents, gathered by the Watergate Committee, showing politically motivated tax audits, undercover White House investigations and military spying on civilians. One 1969 IRS memo describing the creation of a special activists "study unit" advised that the unit's function of examining tax returns of "ideological, militant, subversive, radical or other" organizations must not become publicly known, since disclosure "might embarrass the Administration." The unit was abolished in August 1973 after, according to Weicker, assembling tax data on about 10,000 person. According to the documents, former presidential counsel John W. Dean 3rd and former White House and Treasury Department official John J. Caulfield—both involved in the Watergate coverup—were central characters in political use of the IRS.

[8] President Ford signed an executive order Sept. 20 restricting White House access to income tax returns. The order specified that only the President could direct disclosure of any tax return to a member of the White House staff. To do so, the President personally would request in writing the desired returns and personally designate in writing the person authorized to see the return on the President's behalf. The order was a companion piece to the Treasury Department proposal, submitted to Congress Sept. 11, which would limit access to income tax returns by government units other than the White House. The IRS would, however, be required to furnish information to the President if requested. White House employes could obtain access to such material with a signed personal request from the President.

[9] **IRS watched 'subversives.'** The National Council of Churches and the Urban League were on the list of potentially subversive organizations the IRS kept under tax surveillance in 1969-73, according to the Tax Reform Research Group Nov. 17. The group, a Washington-based affiliate of Ralph Nader's Public Citizen, obtained the list as part of IRS data released to it in a Freedom of Information Act case. According to the data, the IRS set up a special group, eventually named the Special Services Staff (SSS), July 2, 1969, one day after a

White House aide, Tom Charles Huston, informed the IRS that President Nixon wanted the agency "to move against leftist organizations." The SSS was to monitor tax records and keep watch over "ideological, militant, subversive, radical and similar type organizations," the documents revealed.

[10] Files were collected on 2,873 organizations and 8,585 individuals before the SSS was dismantled in August 1973. A final report said 78% of these were found to have "no apparent revenue significance or potential." The other 22% of the files were said to have been preserved. No serious tax cheating was reported discovered by the operation, which produced about $100,000 in additional tax revenues. The National Council of Churches and Urban League were on an early list of 99 targets. Others included the Unitarian Society, Americans for Democratic Action, the John Birch Society, Welfare Rights Organization, the Congress of Racial Equaliy and Church League of America.

[11] **Army curbs spying on civilians.** Secretary of the Army Howard H. Callaway issued an order, effective Oct. 1, that would curtail surveillance by Army intelligence of most U.S. citizens. Under the terms of the order, the Army would still be empowered to investigate U.S. civilians working for the Defense Department abroad. Surveillance of civilians not affiliated with the Defense Department would not be permitted unless there was "substantial evidence" of illegal activities that threatened Army troops, property or functions. In a related development, the Army's highest-ranking intelligence officer stationed in West Germany admitted in a sworn statement filed in Washington federal district court Oct. 28 that the Army, in the course of its "countersubversion" operations in West Berlin and West Germany, had penetrated civilian organizations, had civilian phones tapped and had intercepted mail, at least until September. The affidavit was filed in connection with a suit against the Army by a group of U.S. civilian and political organizations in West Germany. They charged the Army with illegally spying on their activities and tapping their telephones.

[12] **Supreme Court upholds anti-espionage taps.** The Supreme Court Oct. 15 declined to hear a challenge to the President's right to authorize warrantless wiretaps to gather foreign intelligence. The court's refusal to hear the case, which involved the 1964 espionage conviction of Soviet national Igor A. Ivanov, did not signify its approval or disapproval of wiretapping, but had the effect of permitting federal agents to continue the practice. In upholding Ivanov's conviction, the Court of Appeals for the 3rd Circuit had ruled that the evidence obtained from the wiretap was admissible in court if the surveillance had been found to be reasonably related to the exercise of presidential power in the area of foreign affairs.

[13] **Protection of privacy.** A bill to restrict federal collection and use of data on individuals was approved by the Senate Dec. 17 and House Dec. 18. The bill required public disclosure by agencies of any computer data bank operation by them or collection of data on individuals. The individuals would have the right to inspect such files and correct information. Exchange of the data between agencies was barred without the individual's permission except for "routine" exchanges, such as for paycheck information. There was an exemption in the bill for data on individuals kept by federal law enforcement agencies. The bill barred the sale or rental of mailing lists maintained by federal agencies and prohibited, beginning in 1975, state and local governments from requiring Social Security numbers as a condition for voting or registering a car or obtaining a driver's license. A special commission was to be established to study the problems of protection of individual privacy in this area.

See also CANADA [9]; CENTRAL INTELLIGENCE AGENCY; CRIME [3, 31]; EDUCATION; FORD, GERALD R.; NIXON, RICHARD M.; RADICALS; SAXBE, WILLIAM B.

PROTEST—*See* Indian Affairs; Kent State; Radicals
PROXMIRE, SEN. WILLIAM—*See* Defense [6, 11]; Energy Crisis [2]; Space [12]; Union of Soviet Socialist Republics [33]
PUBLISHING INDUSTRY—*See* Books; Copyright; Education; Labor [16]; Postal Service; Press; Pulitzer Prizes
PUERTO RICANS—*See* Civil Rights [6]

PUERTO RICO—Government shipping fleet. The Puerto Rican legislature had passed a bill creating a government-owned merchant fleet at an investment of $300 million, and the government had signed a memorandum of agreement to buy 12 container ships and 12,000 trailer vans from the three major container ship firms serving the island, it was reported June 18. The controversial plan had been set by Gov. Rafael Hernandez Colon in hopes of holding down ocean freight rates and making Puerto Rico more tempting to investors, according to the *New York Times*. The bill was passed in the legislature along party lines.

End to Culebra shelling set. The Defense Department and the Puerto Rican government announced June 27 that "unqualified decisions" had been made to stop naval practice shelling on Culebra Island, off Puerto Rico, by July 1, 1975. Firing on smaller islands in the area, the Culebra cays, would end as soon as possible after that but no later than Dec. 31, 1975.

ITT unit purchased. Ownership of the Puerto Rico Telephone Co., a subsidiary of International Telephone and Telegraph Corp. (ITT), was transferred to the government's Puerto Rico Telephone Authority, it was reported July 26. The ITT unit had been a source of dispute in recent years. Subscribers had complained repeatedly about its service, and there had been numerous proposals for a government takeover.

The authority would pay ITT about $165 million in cash, bonds and notes, of which $40 million represented taxes to be paid to the Commonwealth Treasury Dept. The authority would assume the phone company's long-term obligations. The purchase had been opposed by the major Puerto Rican opposition group, the New Progressive Party. Party leader Carlos Romero Barcelo called it a bad deal, according to a report June 20.

PULITZER PRIZES—The 58th annual Pulitzer Prizes in journalism, letters and music were presented in New York May 7. For the second consecutive year, prizes went to journalists who investigated the activities of President Nixon and irregularities in his re-election campaign. The national reporting awards, with two coequal winners of $1,000, went to James R. Polk of the *Washington Star-News* for his disclosure of alleged irregularities in the financing of the 1972 Nixon campaign, and Jack White of the *Providence* (R.I.) *Journal-Bulletin* for disclosure of the President's income tax returns. The decision to give White an award came amid dissent from the approval committee, some of whom considered the publication of the tax returns, normally confidential material, as "illegal" reporting. For the second time in the history of the award, there was no winner in either drama or fiction. The award for public-service went to *Newsday* (Long Island) for its investigation of illegal narcotics trafficking. It was the third such award for *Newsday*.

Among the other winners: **Letters:** General Nonfiction—Ernest Becker, *The Denial of Death*. Biography—Louis Sheaffer, *O'Neill, Son and Artist*. History—Daniel J. Boorstin, *The Americans: The Democratic Experience*, third volume in a series. Poetry—Robert Lowell, *The Dolphin*. Music—Donald Martino, *Notturno*. **Journalism:** General local reporting—Arthur M. Petacque and Hugh F. Hough of the *Chicago Sun-Times* for uncovering evidence that led to a reopening of Sen. Charles Percy's (R, Ill.) daughter's murder case. Special local reporting—William Sherman of the *New York Daily News* for exposing abuses in New York City's Medicaid program. International reporting—Hedrick Smith of the *New York Times* for coverage of relations between the Soviet Union and its Eastern European allies. Editorial writing—F. Gilman Spencer of the *Trenton* (N.J.) *Trentonian.* Spot news photography—Anthony K. Roberts, Associated Press. Feature photography—Sal Veder, Associated Press. Criticism—Emily Genauer, *Newsday* (Long Island). Commentary—Edwin A. Roberts Jr. of the *National Observer.* Editorial cartooning—Paul Szep of the *Boston Globe.*

QR

QADDAFI, MUAMMAR EL—*See* AFRICA; EGYPT; LIBYA; SUDAN

QATAR—Under an agreement signed in Doha Feb. 20, Qatar gained a 60% share in the operations of Shell Oil Co. of Qatar and the Qatar Petroleum Co. The new participation accord, effective from Jan. 1, replaced one negotiated in 1973 which had given the government an immediate 25% interest in the two foreign firms, increasing by stages to 51% in 1984.

See also APPOINTMENTS & RESIGNATIONS; OIL [5, 15]

QUOTA SYSTEMS—*See* CIVIL RIGHTS [7]; POLITICS [8-9]

RADICALS—Weatnermen indictments dropped. U.S. District Court Judge Julius J. Hoffman Jan. 3 dismissed the 1970 indictment of 12 Weathermen charged with conspiring to incite the "days of rage" riots in Chicago in October 1969. Dismissal had been requested by government attorneys, who said that Supreme Court restraints on wiretapping would have hampered prosecution of the case.

Wiretap disclosure ordered. U.S. District Court Judge Aubrey E. Robinson Jr. ruled in Washington Jan. 11 that the Justice Department must reveal the nature and extent of wiretaps and other surveillance of antiwar activists in 1968-69. The ruling came in a civil suit filed in 1969 under the Omnibus Crime Act of 1968 providing compensation for victims of illegal wiretapping. The suit had been delayed during criminal trials of some of the plaintiffs, including the "Chicago Seven." Other plaintiffs were the War Resisters League, the Catholic Priests Fellowship, the Southern Conference Education Fund and the Black Panther Party.

'Gainesville 8' sue U.S. Seven members of the Vietnam Veterans Against the War and one of their supporters filed a $1.2 million lawsuit in U.S. district court in Washington, May 28, charging that the government had illegally infiltrated the defense camp during their 1973 trial. The eight had been acquitted of conspiring to violently disrupt the 1972 Republican National Covention. The suit alleged that Emerson L. Poe, a paid informer for the Federal Bureau of Investigation, had reported regularly to the prosecutors on defense tactics during the trial, depriving the defendants of constitutional rights of due process.

Subversives list abolished. The attorney general's controversial list of subversive organizations—27 years old and not updated since 1955—was abolished by presidential order June 4. Attorney General William B. Saxbe said it was "now very apparent that it serves no useful purpose." According to the Justice Department, all but about 30 of the 300 organizations still on the list had been out of existence for five years or more.

Fugitive radical surrenders. Jane L. Alpert, who pleaded guilty in connection with a series of bombings in New York City in 1969, ended four years in hiding Nov. 14 when she surrendered to federal authorities. After pleading guilty in 1970, she jumped bail and disappeared before sentence was passed. In May, while in hiding, Alpert wrote an open letter from the underground denouncing Samuel Melville, her former boyfriend and leader of the militant group responsible for the bombings. (Melville was killed in the Attica [N.Y.] prison uprising of 1971.)

FBI anti-radical activities revealed. Attorney General Saxbe and Clarence M. Kelly, director of the FBI, Nov. 18 released some details of a Justice Department report on certain FBI counterintelligence operations conducted from 1956 to 1971 under the designation COINTELPRO. The Justice Department report revealed that COINTELPRO had been composed of seven different programs, with five directed at domestic organizations and individuals and two aimed at foreign intelligence services, foreign organizations and individuals connected with them. Among the domestic targets of COINTELPRO were two black civil right groups not considered radical by many observers: the Southern Christian Leadership Conference (SCLC) and the Congress of Racial Equality (CORE). All the programs were abruptly terminated in mid-1971 by J. Edgar Hoover, the late FBI director. The first COINTELPRO operation, which was against the U.S. Communist Party, was an outgrowth of the "Red Scare" of the mid-1950's, and was begun in 1956 on Hoover's orders.

Other COINTELPRO operations and their effective dates were: Socialist Workers Party (1961-1971), white hate groups (1964-1971), black extremists (1967-1971) and New Left (1968-1971). The other two COINTELPRO efforts were Espionage or Soviet Satellite Intelligence (1964-1971) and Special Operations (1967-1971). According to the report, which for national security reasons declined to provide any details, the overall objectives of the latter two programs were to encourage and stimulate counterintelligence efforts against hostile foreign intelligence sources and foreign communist organizations. In all, various FBI field offices submitted 3,247 proposals for domestic counterintelligence; 2,370 were approved and implemented. More than half the proposals concerned the U.S. Communist Party, the report said.

Saxbe and Kelley said the New Left groups targeted by the FBI were Students for a Democratic Society (SDS), the Progressive Labor Party, the Weathermen and the Young Socialist Alliance. Black groups subject to FBI operations were CORE, the SCLC, the Student Nonviolent Coordinating Committee (SNCC), the Black Panther Party, the Revolutionary Action Movement and the Nation of Islam. So-called White Hate groups that were objects of FBI counterintelligence efforts were various Ku Klux Klan organizations, the Minutemen, the American Nazi Party and the National States Rights Party.

FBI free to watch Socialist parley. Thurgood Marshall, associate justice of the Supreme Court, Dec. 27 refused to set aside an appellate court ruling allowing the FBI to send agents and informants to the convention of the Young Socialist Alliance, which opened in St. Louis Dec. 28. The 2nd U.S. Circuit Court of Appeals Dec. 24 had reversed an injunction issued Dec. 16 by U.S.

District Court Judge Thomas P. Griesa that prohibited the FBI from conducting surveillance of the Young Socialist Alliance, the youth affiliate of the Socialist Workers Party. Griesa had acted on a complaint that FBI surveillance of the leftward-leaning political group inhibited people from attending its meetings and exercising their freedom of speech.

See also AMNESTY & CLEMENCY; CENTRAL INTELLIGENCE AGENCY; INDIAN AFFAIRS; KENT STATE; PRIVACY [9-10]

RADIO—*See* TELEVISION & RADIO

RAILROADS—Penn Central controversy. The Penn Central Co. filed suit in the U.S. Court of Claims in Washington April 10 seeking $280 million, plus interest and costs, from the U.S. government, which was accused of "taking Penn Central property." The parent company charged that the government violated its rights under the Fifth Amendment when the railroad was ordered to continue operations despite the fact that "it was certain that such a continuation would result in substantial operating deficits." A $20 million deficit had been incurred each month since February 1973 when a Senate resolution was adopted by Congress and approved by President Nixon to maintain Penn Central operations in the public interest. Rail service was maintained under that provision until the 1973 Regional Rail Reorganization Act took effect in January 1974.

SEC files Penn Central fraud charges. The Securities and Exchange Commisson (SEC) May 2 accused the Penn Central Co., several of its subsidiaries including the bankrupt Penn Central railroad, 12 top officials of the firm, and its former auditor of directing a massive fraud scheme leading up to the railroad's collapse in 1970. The SEC complaint, filed in U.S. district court in Philadelphia, cited financial mismanagement and deceit that had allegedly occurred in the period between 1968, when the Pennsylvania Railroad merged with the New York Central Railroad to form the Penn Central Transportation Co., and 1970 when bankruptcy papers were filed for the reorganized railroad. The general aim of the scheme, the SEC alleged, was to defraud investors by providing or endorsing false earnings reports that presented an unduly optimistic analysis of the firm's financial health. The railroad's collapse was believed to have cost investors billions of dollars. Named in the complaint were Stuart T. Saunders, former chairman of the railroad and its parent company; David C. Bevan, former chief financial officer for both companies; and three former directors—Edward J. Hanley, Franklin J. Lunding and R. Stuart Rauch. Bevan and three other defendants were accused of diverting $4 million in corporate funds to a Liechtenstein bank account. The nation's largest accounting firm and Penn Central's former auditor, Peat, Marwick, Mitchell & Co., was accused of certifying false earnings statements which, the SEC declared, Peat Marwick "knew or should have known to be false and misleading." Bevan, Fidel Goetz, the Rosenbaums and former Penn Central Vice President William R. Gerstnecker were indicted by a federal grand jury Sept. 11.

Restructuring plan opposed. The Transportation Department's plan to restructure the Northeast and Middle West rail system operated by the Penn Central and other bankrupt carriers was opposed by the Interstate Commece Commission (ICC), labor and some of the lines involved. The ICC reported May 2 its "fundamental disagreement" with the plan, which called for abandonment of 15,575 of the 61,184 miles of railroad trackage in 17 states and the District of Columbia. Some of the proposed trackage to be eliminated, an estimated 5,000 miles, was owned by solvent lines linked into the Northeast area. Two of the seven lines involved in the reorganization—the Erie Lackawanna Railway and the Boston & Maine Corp.—opposed inclusion in the new system. And Norfolk & Western Railway President John P. Fishwick warned the ICC March 18 the plans for the new Northeast system could be a "step toward nationalization" if a new railroad were established to dominate service in the region. The Norfolk & Western was one of the solvent lines not included in the reorganization but with trackage to be eliminated under the department's plan.

Amtrak funding. A bill authorizing $200 million to cover operating deficits of Amtrak, the National Railroad Passenger Corporation, was adopted by the Senate Oct. 10 and House Oct. 15. It was signed by President Ford Oct. 28. Congress raised the ceiling on federally guaranteed loans to Amtrak from $500 million to $900 million. The bill directed Amtrak to repair its passenger equipment "to the maximum extent practicable" and connecting lines to maintain their equipment "as expeditiously as possible" pending takeover by Amtrak. Amtrak was barred from discontinuing, until July 1, 1975, service over routes operating on Jan. 1, 1973. Amtrak announced Oct. 26 that it was increasing fares on most of its routes by 10%, effective Nov. 15. The need for the increase was blamed on rising fuel, labor and materials costs. Inflation had also been cited as the need for an earlier nationwide fare increase of 5% that had taken effect in April.

Northeast rail reorganization upheld. The Supreme Court, by a 7-2 vote Dec. 16, upheld the constitutionality of the Regional Rail Reorganization Act of 1973. The court rejected arguments by creditors of the bankrupt Penn Central Railroad that the act failed to provide them with sufficient compensation. (Under the law, the Penn Central and several other bankrupt carriers in the Northeast would be reorganized into a single, self-sustaining system, the Consolidated Rail Corp., or Conrail.) The ruling reversed a decision by a special three-judge federal district court panel that the act ignored potential dissipation of creditors' assets resulting from the law's prohibition against abandoning or curtailing money-losing services of the affected carriers.

See also CIVIL RIGHTS [16]; LABOR [11]; PENSIONS; TRANSPORTATION

RAW MATERIALS—*See* TARIFFS & TRADE
RAY, DIXY LEE—*See* APPOINTMENTS & RESIGNATIONS; ATOMIC ENERGY [19]; ENERGY CRISIS [30]
REBOZO, CHARLES G.—*See* CAMPAIGN FINANCING [15-16]; WATERGATE [34, 93]
RECORDS—*See* COPYRIGHT; MUSIC
RED CROSS—*See* CYPRUS [21]; FAMINE & FOOD; MIDDLE EAST [4-5, 9]; OBITUARIES [BURCKHARDT]
REFUGEES—*See* CHILE [6-7]; CYPRUS [16, 20]; HAITI; HONG KONG
REINECKE, ED—*See* CAMPAIGN FINANCING [11]

RELIGION

General Developments

[1] **Worship habits.** The results of the Gallup Poll on religious service attendance, reported Jan. 13, showed that 40% of U.S. adults attended a church or synagogue during a typical week in 1973. Roman Catholic church attendance was reported at 55% in 1973, down from 71% 10 years earlier. Protestant attendance was 37% in 1973, down from 38% in 1964, and Jewish attendance was reported at 19% in 1973, up from 17% in 1964.

[2] **Evangelistic churches show gains.** According to statistics reported May 5 from the 1974 *Yearbook of American and Canadian Churches,* theologically conservative or evangelistic Protestant denominations were gaining membership. The Southern Baptist Convention, the nation's largest Protestant denomination, showed a 2% increase to 12,065,333; the Mormons (Church of Jesus Christ of Latter-Day Saints) were up 2.5% to 2,185,810; the Jehovah's Witnesses were up

3.9% to 431,179; the Seventh Day Adventists were up 3.5% to 449,188; and the Assemblies of God were up 2% to 1,099,606. Losses were reported by the American Baptist Churches in the U.S.A. (5%), the Episcopal Church (4.8%), the United Presbyterian Church in the U.S.A. (3.5%), and the United Methodist Church (1.7%). Estimates put the total number of Protestants at 71,648,000, Roman Catholics at 48,460,000, Jews at 6,115,000, and Eastern Orthodox at 3,739,000.

[3] **World evangelical fellowship formed.** Most of the 2,700 delegates from 150 countries attending a 10-day meeting of the International Congress on World Evangelization in Lausanne, Switzerland, July 24 approved creation of a 30-member continuation committee which would constitute a new fellowship of evangelical Protestants representing all continents.

[4] **Parents form anti-cult group.** A small group of parents whose children had joined religious cults met in Denver, and Aug. 31 announced the formation of the Citizens Freedom Foundation, a national organization to fight the influence of the cults. The parents, citing 5,000 cults in the U.S. registered as non-profit organizations, denied the cults were a fad and said they were "in control of thousands of children," 80% of whom needed psychiatric care after leaving the cult, the parents claimed. The group was organized by Ted Patrick who had specialized in taking wayward youths out of such cults by a method called "deprogramming." (Patrick had been found guilty of false imprisonment after he held two young women for deprogramming against their parents' wishes.)

[5] **Korean evangelist in New York.** The Rev. Sun Myung Moon, head of the Unification Church formed by Moon in Korea 20 years ago, preached to an overcrowded Madison Square Garden audience in New York, N.Y., Sept 18 about the second coming of the Messiah and the fall of Adam and Eve. Moon, considered controversial because of his views on the second coming, was heckled by fundamentalist groups. By the end of the sermon, half the audience had left the hall. Some of Moon's followers believed him to be the successor of Jesus Christ, but his detractors criticized his magnetic hold on the young. The sect claimed 10,000 adherents in the U.S. and 600,000 worldwide with representatives in 40 countries.

Episcopal Church

[6] In a ceremony at the Church of the Advocate in North Philadelphia July 29, four bishops of the Episcopal Church and 11 women deacons defied church law when the bishops ordained the women to the church's priesthood. Official reaction to the ordination came July 31 when two of the women were suspended by the bishops of their dioceses, and presiding Bishop John Maury Allin, national leader of the church, called an Aug. 14 meeting of the House of Bishops to consider disciplinary action.

[7] The House of Bishops met in emergency session in Chicago Aug. 14-15 and voted overwhelmingly that the "necessary conditions for valid ordination" to the priesthood of the 11 women had not been satisfied. The statement was advanced as an opinion but had the effect of demoting the 11 women to deacons. However, the bishops also urged the 1976 general convention to reconsider the question of female ordination, and asked restraint until then. Presiding Bishop Allin said such a change in the constitution had to be approved by two successive conventions and could keep women from the priesthood until 1979.

[8] Dr. Charles V. Willie, a black layman who had given the sermon at the women's ordination July 29, Aug. 18 resigned the vice presidency of the House of Deputies, the laity and lower clergy unit within the general convention of the Episcopal Church, and his seat on the executive council which governs between conventions, to protest the decision by the House of Bishops.

[9] Although the House of Bishops' original meeting on the ordination ended without formal sanctions against retired bishops Edward R. Welles II, Daniel Corrigan, and Robert L. DeWitt, and Bishop Jose Antonio Ramos of Costa Rica, who had all ordained the women, charges which could lead to an ecclesiastical trial were later filed by four bishops, it was reported Sept. 27. The charges alleged failure to secure proper recommendations from standing committees of the home dioceses of the women, and failure to secure permission from the Philadelphia church rector. The House of Bishops met Oct. 17 in Oaxtepec, Mexico, and voted 97-36 to reaffirm the right of women to ordination, but barred such ordination until 1976 when the Episcopal general convention would meet.

[10] The Rev. Alison Cheek, one of the 11 women, consecrated the elements of the eucharist at the Episcopal Church of St. Stephen and the Incarnation in Washington, D.C. Nov. 10. Congregants from many faiths crowded the church and applauded Cheek whose action marked the women's determination in the controversy over their right to be priests. Cheek had celebrated the eucharist on another occasion, Oct. 27, Reformation Day, at the interdenominational Riverside Church in New York City with the Rev. Jeanette R. Piccard and the Rev. Carter Heyward, also ordained in the Philadelphia ceremony.

[11] The Massachusetts Conference of the United Church of Christ ruled that it would accept the Episcopal women priests as ministers within its own ranks, it was reported Dec. 6. The Rev. Avery Post, president of the conference, said there was "a real groundswell of support" for the action. The standing committee of the Washington diocese voted 5-1 to approve ordination for qualified candidates "without regard to gender," and placed pressure on the diocesan bishop to ordain qualified women, it was reported Dec. 17.

Roman Catholic Church

[12] **Pope issues plea on Jerusalem.** Pope Paul VI urged Roman Catholics April 5 to increase pilgrimages to Jerusalem to strengthen the presence of the church there and in other parts of the Holy Land (Israel). In a specific reference to the status of the holy places in Jerusalem, the pope said that "the continuing existence of situations lacking a clear juridical basis that is internationally recognized and guaranteed" constituted a threat to peace. The statement stressed that the pope's appeal was "intended to have no other significance than a religious and charitable one." This was later confirmed by a Vatican aide, who denied at a news conference that the appeal had any political meaning.

[13] In a Feb. 5 interview with the Israeli newspaper *Haaretz*, Vatican spokesman Federico Alessandrini had said "Internationalism of Jerusalem which the church originally supported is not a realistic solution today." In a weekly general audience on April 10, however, the pope announced support for "an appropriate international juridical guardianship for the holy places" in the Middle East. A revised version of the statement issued later by the Vatican press officers raised the question whether the pope had hardened his position and was now advocating internationalization of the city, a move Israel had always rejected.

[14] **Lutheran-Catholic accord reached.** A joint commission of U.S. Roman Catholic and Lutheran theologians declared March 3 that the issue of papal primacy "need not be a barrier to reconciliation" of the two churches, divided since the 16th century. The 5,000 word statement, entitled "Ministry and the Church Universal: Differing Attitudes Toward Papal Primacy," was regarded as a major ecumenical breakthrough, although its conclusions were not binding on the churches. The controversial Catholic doctrine of papal infallibility was not

discussed but agreement was reached in other basic areas. (The commission, formed in 1965, also had produced past statements of consensus on the Nicene Creed, baptism, the ministry and the eucharist.)

[15] **Pope sees modern role for Mary.** In a major document urging increased devotion to Mary, released March 21, Pope Paul VI described her as a "new woman," who "while completely devoted to the will of God, was far from being a timidly submissive woman or one whose piety was repellent to others."

[16] **Jesuit dismissed on abortion issue.** The Rev. Eamon Taylor, provincial supervisor of New York, Sept. 6 announced the dismissal of the Rev. Joseph O'Rourke, a member of the West Side Community of the Society of Jesus, who Aug. 20 had baptized the 3-month-old son of a Massachusetts woman who publicly favored a woman's right to have an abortion.

[17] **Vatican sets up Judaism, Islam panels.** The Vatican announced Oct. 22 the formation of a commission for Judaism to be attached to the Secretariat for Christian Unity, presided over by Johannes Cardinal Willebrands. At the same time the Vatican created the Commission for Islam headed by Sergio Cardinal Pignedoli, head of the Secretariat for Non-Christians.

[18] **Six saints named.** Pope Paul VI announced Dec. 12 that he would proclaim six new saints during the 1975 Holy Year. They included Mother Elizabeth Ann Bayley Seton, the first to be born in the U.S. In completing the canonization procedure, the pope approved the legitimacy of a miracle attributed to Mother Seton in which a four-year-old girl was cured of acute lymphatic leukemia. Born in New York City in 1774, Seton started the first U.S. Catholic free school. She also organized the Sisters of Charity, the first religious order for women. She died in Baltimore in 1821. Mother Frances Xavier Cabrini, a naturalized U.S. citizen born in Italy, was canonized in 1946.

Lutheran Church

[19] **Controversy splits Lutheran seminary.** Concordia Seminary in St. Louis, the largest Lutheran theological school in the U.S., became the focal point of a long-standing theological dispute between conservatives and moderates in the Lutheran Church-Missouri Synod when the school's president, the Rev. Dr. John H. Tietjen, was suspended Jan. 20. Tietjen was accused of administrative malfeasance and advocating false doctrine. The controversy involved the entire 2.8 million member denomination (with congregations in all states) in a bitter disagreement over whether all of the Bible, except the Psalms and the Book of Revelation, was interpreted as the literal and historical truth. The dispute began with the election of the Rev. Jacob A. O. Preus as president in 1969 when conservatives and fundamentalists began to re-exert control over the church after 10 years of gains by a moderate faction. Nearly all of the school's 520 resident students launched a strike Jan. 21 to protest Tietjen's suspension. Forty-eight professors and members of the executive staff who had joined the boycott were dismissed Feb. 18 after ignoring an ultimatum to return to their teaching duties. Nearly 400 students announced Feb. 19 that they would continue their studies under the dismissed professors at a seminary in exile held at the Jesuit-run St. Louis University Divinity School and the Eden Theological Seminary, associated with the United Church of Christ. (Only 17 students and two professors remained on the Concordia campus, it was reported Feb. 2.)

Presbyterian Church

[20] **Presbyterian merger.** The General Assembly of the predominantly northern 2.8 million member United Presbyterian Church voted unanimously June 25 to study a plan to unite with the 900,000 member Presbyterian Church

in the United States (Southern Presbyterians). The Southerners, meeting a few blocks away in Louisville, Ky., had undertaken similar action the week before. The Presbyterian Church had splintered over the question of slavery in 1861. Conservatives had split off from the southern church in recent years.

See also ABORTION; AFRICA; BIRTH CONTROL; BRAZIL [4]; BUTZ, EARL L.; CAMBODIA; CHAD; CHILE [14]; CRIME [22]; ETHIOPIA [3]; IRELAND, NORTHERN; ISRAEL; ITALY [9]; KOREA, REPUBLIC OF [9, 13]; MIDDLE EAST [36]; PHILIPPINES; RHODESIA; SAXBE, WILLIAM B.; TAXES

REPUBLICAN PARTY—*See* CAMPAIGN FINANCING [7-10]; ELECTIONS; POLITICS
REVENUE SHARING—*See* BUDGET; CIVIL RIGHTS [11]
RHODES, REP. JOHN J.—*See* CONGRESS; ELECTIONS; WATERGATE [19]

RHODESIA—Rhodesian Prime Minister Ian Smith announced Dec. 11 that an immediate cease-fire had been agreed to by his white-minority government and black nationalists after prolonged fighting in the northern frontier. In a televised address, he said all detained black leaders and followers of the various nationalist movements would be released at once and that a constitutional conference would be held on the nation's political future to determine how the black majority would enter the government. (About 250,000 of Rhodesia's 5.7 million population were white.)

The Salisbury government Dec. 30 threatened to call off plans for the projected constitutional conference with black nationalists unless guerrillas ceased their operations. It had been announced Dec. 24 that guerrillas had killed four members of the South African police force serving in northeasern Rhodesia. The ANC issued an apology for the incident, blaming difficulties in communicating news of the cease-fire to the field. ANC leader Bishop Muzorewa had said Dec. 12 that the cease-fire was to take place immediately; however, Robert Mugabe, executive secretary of ZANU, asserted Dec. 15 that the cease-fire agreement had been an informal one. The Rhodesian government began releasing black political detainees Dec. 16, and by Dec. 24 had released 80 of the 300-500 reportedly imprisoned, according to the French newspaper *Le Monde* Dec. 26.

The government had previously tried to deal with the guerrilla activity by increasing military call-ups and offering financial incentives to encourage re-enlistment; by moving the black population into enclaves where they could be more strictly controlled by the government; and by using white settlers to inhabit the sparsely-populated northeast areas where the guerrillas were active. Clashes between the two forces were reported throughout the year. In one incident, 20 guerrillas were killed in a border clash near Mount Darwin May 19, among them several leaders of the Zimbabwe African National Union (ZANU). Government and rebels had both received support from other nations: South Africa had donated $10 million worth of aid for Rhodesia's security programs, while Baghdad Radio announced March 28 that Iraq had given $60,000 to the insurgents. Religious groups, including members of the Anglican, Roman Catholic and Methodist churches of Rhodesia circulated a report charging government security forces with acts of brutality to blacks, it was reported Aug. 22. Roman Catholic bishops had, on April 2, demanded an inquiry into allegations of brutality, but the government refused on the grounds that it would be "harmful to the morale" of the forces.

Previous attempts at settlement had broken down when members of the African National Council (ANC), the only legal black political organization in Rhodesia, rejected the government's June offer to increase black representation in Parliament from 16 to 22 seats. The ANC said the concession fell "far short of demands." The round of talks leading to a settlement, begun Dec. 4, had broken down Dec. 7 after Rhodesia rejected demands for immediate acceptance of the principle of majority rule before any constitutional conference was held. According to the subsequent agreement, the conference would take place "without any pre-condition."

Smith announced the cease-fire Dec. 11 after a series of meetings in Lusaka, Zambia, between representatives of the Rhodesian nationalist groups, government officials, and leaders of Zambia, Tanzania and Botswana. Two jailed black nationalist leaders, both in prison for the past 10 years, were released to attend. They were Joshua Nkomo of the Zimbabwe African People's Union (ZAPU) and the Rev. Ndabaningi Sithole of ZANU, the more militant of the two organizations and the one responsible for the guerrilla war. Also attending were Bishop Abel Muzorewa, ANC; Presidents Kenneth Kaunda, Zambia, and Julius Nyerere, Tanzania, and Sir Seretse Khama, Botswana. Also cooperating in effecting the cease-fire was South African Prime Minister John Vorster who had worked behind the scenes to bring an end to the hostilities. Vorster said Oct. 23 that both his nation and its black neighbors had to choose "between peace on the one hand or an escalation of strife on the other." Zambia's President Kaunda hailed Vorster's speech as "the voice of reason for which Africa and the rest of the world have been waiting."

Before the Dec. 11 cease-fire agreement was announced, Rhodesia's four black nationalist movements had signed an agreement, the Zimbabwe Declaration of Unity, in Lusaka Dec. 9 to unite into a single body and "struggle for the total liberation of Zimbabwe," the name by which they identified Rhodesia. The declaration, if implemented, would bring the ANC, ZANU, ZAPU and the Front for the Liberation of Zimbabwe (Frolizi) together, with the ANC acting as an umbrella organization within which the groups would "merge their respective organs and structures." The seven-point document stated that the movement's four leaders "recognized the inevitability of continued armed struggle until the total liberation of Zimbabwe" and pledged to hold a congress within four months to adopt a constitution, establish policy and choose a leadership for "the united people of Zimbabwe."

Other Developments

Ruling party wins elections. The Rhodesia Front (RF) party of Prime Minister Smith won an easy victory in the July 30 election, securing all 50 white seats in Parliament for the third successive time since 1962. The RF won more than 70% of the vote cast. The liberal opposition Rhodesia Party (RP) won 18% of the vote for the 38 seats which it had challenged. Challengers from the extreme right-wing Rhodesia National Party were also defeated. Blacks elected eight of their 16 representatives to Parliament. (The other eight were appointed posts.) Seven of the victors were supporters of the ANC. None of the government-supported black candidates of the African Progressive Party were elected.

See also AFRICA

RIBICOFF, SEN. ABRAHAM—*See* ENERGY CRISIS [2]; MEDICINE & HEALTH

ROCKEFELLER, MARGARETTA (HAPPY)

Margaretta (Happy) Rockefeller, 48, underwent surgery for the removal of her left breast, 32 adjacent lymph nodes and part of the underlying chest wall muscle Oct. 17 after doctors at a New York City hospital had confirmed that one large and two small nodules in her breast were malignant. A pathological examination of the removed lymph nodes indicated that cancer had not spread.

Mrs. Rockefeller's doctors gave her a 90% chance of full recovery. She was released from the hospital Oct. 24. Mrs. Rockefeller underwent a second mastectomy for removal of her right breast Nov. 25. After the operation, her doctors predicted a complete recovery.

See also MEDICINE & HEALTH [23-25]

ROCKEFELLER, NELSON A.—President Ford announced Aug. 20 that Nelson A. Rockefeller, 66, former governor of New York for 15 years, was his choice to be the 41st vice president of the U.S. The nomination was sent to Congress that day for confirmation which required a simple majority vote of each house. Rockefeller was sworn in Dec. 19. It was the first time in history that both a president and vice president who occupied those offices had not been elected to them. Rockefeller became the second vice president to be seated without being subjected to a general election; President Ford was the first.

[2] Rockefeller's assumption of the office of vice president had been delayed as the House and Senate probed the Rockefeller family financial interests; the nominee's tax payments and cash gifts to various government figures; and the funding of a derogatory biography of Arthur J. Goldberg financed during Rockefeller's campaign against Goldberg for governor of New York in 1970.

[3] The announcement of Rockefeller's nomination was made in a brief ceremony in the Oval Office at the White House attended by Congressional leaders of both parties and the Cabinet, who were informed of Ford's choice just prior to the announcement. (Other names reported on the selection list were Republican National Chairman George Bush; Sen. Howard H. Baker [R, Tenn.]; Gov. Daniel J. Evans [R, Wash.]; Elliot L. Richardson, who had held several Nixon Cabinet posts; Donald Rumsfeld, ambassador to NATO; and Melvin R. Laird, Nixon's first defense secretary.) During the announcement ceremony, broadcast on national radio and television, President Ford praised Rockefeller as "a good partner for me." In his speech, Rockefeller accepted the challenge as a "great honor" to serve the President and through him all of the people of the country.

[4] Although reaction to the nomination was generally favorable from both conservative and liberal, Republican and Democratic members in Congress, dissent was expressed by Sen. Barry Goldwater (R, Ariz.) who said Rockefeller had "ducked out on at least two presidential races," an apparent reference to 1964 when Goldwater was the unsuccessful nominee, and to Richard Nixon's 1968 campaign. Though Goldwater said he could support the nomination, he voiced doubt that Rockefeller would be acceptable to "rank-and-file Republicans" in 1976.

[5] Rockefeller's vast family fortune was the principal topic as the Senate Rules Committee held a series of public hearings on his nomination as vice president. Rockefeller expressed hope that the "myth" about the family financial empire would be "dissipated" by the hearings. Sen. Robert C. Byrd (D, W.Va.) led the challenge on the issue—whether the Rockefeller money posed a problem of undue power for a vice president. Byrd also aggressively interrogated Rockefeller on the pardon President Ford extended to former President Nixon, on the agreement concluded by the Administration at the same time with Nixon on disposition of his presidential papers and tapes and on the doctrine of executive privilege. However, Byrd said after the Sept. 24 session that he agreed with the committee chairman, Sen. Howard W. Cannon (D, Nev.), that there was nothing in sight that would endanger confirmation. Cannon had stated that view Sept. 11 in announcing the committee's vote to ask Rockefeller to make a full public disclosure of his worth in lieu of a requirement for divestiture of holdings or establishment of a blind trust.

[6] Testifying Sept. 23, Rockefeller read parts of a 72-page autobiographical statement submitted to the committee. It included summaries of his tax returns for the past 10 years. His own contribution to various philanthropic and charitable institutions totaled $33 million, he said, not counting the $20.5 million pledged in art and real estate. Among the personal financial data he disclosed: his total holdings amounted to $218 million, mostly in trusts; he was the life beneficiary of trusts totaling $116.5 million; his wife was the beneficiary of securities and trusts totaling $3.8 million and his six children held assets totaling $35.6 million; he had paid $69 million in taxes during his lifetime; his income over the past decade totaled $46.8 million, of which about $1 million a year in tax-free securities held by two trusts was not subject to taxation. Byrd sought a commitment from Rockefeller on the Nixon pardon issue. Cannon had asked, in light of Ford's statement at his vice presidential hearings that the country "wouldn't stand for" a prior pardon of a president, "What assurances do we have that your responses will be anything more than empty phrases given at the moment?" Rockefeller affirmed a "total inclination" against granting such a pardon, adding that at the same time he "would not amend the Constitution—and renounce the power that the Constitution gives to a president." Byrd said the committee was "wasting its time" without a firm commitment from Rockefeller. He asked him, "Do you, yes or no, consider the questions today to be hypothetical" and the answers "can be lightly put aside at some future date?" "The answer is no," Rockefeller said.

[7] Questioned Sept. 24 about the Attica, N.Y. prison revolt in 1971, Rockefeller called it "a great tragedy" and stated his position against "negotiating with people who are holding hostages on threat of death."

[8] Byrd Sept. 25 challenged Rockefeller for a commitment that he would not invoke executive privilege to keep any member of the executive branch from testifying to Congress on non-security matters. Rockefeller said he could think "of no cause at the present time in which I would invoke the doctrine" but said it would be "irresponsible to make a flat commitment."

[9] Cannon said Oct. 9 he would make public the response of Rockefeller to the panel's request for full details of financial gifts Rockefeller had made over the years to various associates. Recent disclosure of substantial gifts to such persons as Secretary of State Henry A. Kissinger, former New York State Republican Chairman L. Judson Morhouse and William J Ronan, chairman of the Port Authority of New York and New Jersey, put the nomination of Rockefeller as vice president into immediate controversy.

[10] The gift to Kissinger—$50,000 in early 1969 after Kissinger left the Rockefeller staff and before he joined the Nixon Administration—was disclosed by the Gannett newspaper chain. A Kissinger spokesman confirmed the report Oct. 4, saying Rockefeller had told Kissinger at the time he wanted to make him a gift "at the close of their some 15 years of association." Reports of the Morhouse gift surfaced at the same time. Morhouse, a former member of the New York State Thruway Authority, had been sentenced to two-three years imprisonment in 1966 on bribery and unlawful-fee charges stemming from a state liquor authority scandal in New York. The conviction was upheld by higher state courts but Rockefeller commuted his sentence in 1970.

[11] Rockefeller's press secretary Hugh Morrow confirmed Oct. 5 the Kissinger and Morhouse gifts and said Ronan also received a gift but did not specify the sum. Rockefeller had made "many gifts to institutions and individuals" over the years, Morrow said, and had paid the appropriate gift taxes. Any impropriety was denied. The Kissinger gift had been made out of gratitude for long-time service, Morrow said. The Morhouse gift—$86,000—was made to ease

"overwhelming financial problems," he said, and in Ronan's case, it was "friendship and the governor's desire to help keep a good man in government." According to Morrow, Rockefeller loaned Morhouse $100,000 in 1969, when Morhouse was GOP state chairman, then an unsalaried post. Because of Morhouse's illness and financial problems, Rockefeller canceled the outstanding balance of the loan—$86,000—in 1973 and paid federal and state gift taxes of about $48,000. The gift to Ronan was also in the form of a debt cancellation, Morrow said, and was made after Ronan resigned in April 1973 as chairman of the (New York State) Metropolitan Transportation Authority, carrying a $75,000 a year salary, and before he became chairman of the Port Authority, an unsalaried post. The size of the gift to Ronan was disclosed Oct. 7—$550,000. Ronan, who currently was a paid adviser to the Rockefeller family and a trustee of the New York State Power Authority ($12,500 annual salary), had borrowed that amount in a series of loans over the years, Morrow explained Oct. 8, and Rockefeller canceled the entire debt in the spring of 1973 as a gift that "could be related," Morrow said, "to the year-end bonus given to executives of large corporations." The gift tax paid by Rockefeller in this instance totaled $330,000.

[12] The gift controversy led Rockefeller Oct. 15 to request "immediate" Congressional hearings on his nomination because the issue was "being tried in the press . . . without my having the opportunity to present all the facts." Rockefeller also was linked Oct. 10 to a derogatory biography of Arthur J. Goldberg published during Rockefeller's campaign against Goldberg for governor of New York in 1970. The request for hearings was made to Cannon and the House Judiciary Committee Chairman, Peter W. Rodino Jr. (D, N.J.).

[13] In response to reports that the Congressional probers were looking into the book affair, Rockefeller had issued a statement Oct. 10 saying that he was unaware of it at the time but his brother Laurance had invested $60,000 in the book as a business venture. The book, *Arthur J. Goldberg, The Old and the New*, by Victor Lasky, was expected to "sell well," the statement said, but "was a total flop," and Laurance sustained a net loss of about $52,000 but did not take a tax deduction on the business loss. "Had he only told me about it at the time," Rockefeller said, "I would have been totally opposed to it and would have strongly advised against his participation in any form." He said he learned about Laurance's investment through the Federal Bureau of Investigation (FBI) during a background check because of the vice presidential nomination. Rockefeller said he told the FBI he had heard of the book at the time "but knew nothing about its preparation or financing." An aide had told him early in the 1970 campaign, Rockefeller said, that Lasky was working on a Goldberg biography but he "really didn't pay any attention because I never felt that such books coming out during campaigns cut much ice one way or another. I never heard any more about it until the book was out and someone showed me a copy, which I never even opened." [See below] The Rockefeller campaign organization in 1970, however, reportedly received 100,000 copies of the book.

[14] Later Oct. 10, Goldberg expressed shock that the Rockefellers "would participate in such a dirty campaign trick" and said they owed him an apology "for financing a scandalous and libelous book." Rockefeller apologized to Goldberg Oct. 12, by telephone, the text of which was released to the press. Citing the "derogatory" book, it said: "I take full responsibility for the whole regrettable episode."

[15] On the money gifts, Rockefeller made public Oct. 11 a list of 20 current and former public officials and staff aides to whom he had given about $2 million over the past 17 years. The list, prepared for the Congressional inquiries, was released because of leaks to the press, which Rockefeller deplored as "very

unfair in terms of the privacy of individuals and also unfair in the sense of giving an atmosphere of uncertainty and suspicion."

[16] The Senate Rules Committee opened the second phase of its confirmation hearings Nov. 13-14. Rockefeller was apologetic Nov. 13 about the Goldberg book, which he called a "hasty, ill-considered decision in the middle of a hectic campaign." "Let's face it, I made a mistake," he said in revising his earlier version of the affair. Rockefeller admitted that he, rather than his brother Laurance, initiated the financing venture. He stressed that his previous "incorrect" version of the financing came from faulty recollection and that he was "delinquent in not clearing this up sooner."

[17] Rockefeller also was questioned Nov. 13 about his substantial money gifts. Pressed by Sen. Claiborne Pell (D, R.I.) about whether he would continue the practice if he became vice president, Rockefeller said he was "hesitant" to renounce it solely on "humanitarian" grounds. "I would have to think that under certain circumstances I would want to help," he said. "There might be a case where I would feel in humanity that I ought to do something."

[18] There were several further financial disclosures Nov. 13: Rockefeller's net worth was estimated by the Congressional Joint Committee on Internal Revenue Taxation at $73 million, higher than Rockefeller's own latest estimate of $62 million; a total of $3,265,374 in political contributions was made by Rockefeller over the past 18 years, $1,031,637 of it to his own presidential campaigns. The Rockefeller family's political contributions exceeded $20 million.

[19] Rockefeller was questioned primarily Nov. 14 about his money gifts. He conceded that his generosity could be "misinterpreted" and offered to "cut it out." He volunteered to pledge in writing to forego gifts or loans to federal employes if confirmed except for "nominal" gifts, such as for birthdays or weddings, or "in the event of medical hardships of a compelling human character."

[20] The Rules Committee Nov. 22 voted 9-0 to recommend confirmation of Rockefeller as vice president. By the same vote, the committee refused to impose any formal requirement on Rockefeller to put his holdings in a blind trust or to refrain from making any further personal gifts of money to public officials.

[21] The committee had ended its hearings on the nomination Nov. 18. The House Judiciary Committee opened its hearings on the nomination Nov. 21.

[22] During Rockefeller's second day of testimony before the House Judiciary Committee Nov. 22, Democratic members expressed concern about the issue of a person of Rockefeller's great wealth being placed in such high political office. "I'm not sure you are fully sensitive to the depth of this feeling" among the public, Rep. Wayne Owens (D, Utah) said. Rockefeller replied that the hearings had been "tremendously instructive to me. I have gotten an insight into the reaction around the country. I'm grateful. I am sympathetic to what you say. I am weighing everything." Rockefeller promised another member, Rep. Edward Mezvinsky (D, Iowa), to discuss with his family Mezvinsky's request for disclosure to the committee of the financial holdings of the entire family.

[23] Closely questioned Nov. 22 by Rep. Charles Rangel (D, N.Y.) on the 1971 Attica, N.Y. prison riot, in which 43 persons were killed, Rockefeller admitted for the first time making a "serious mistake" in his handling of the situation by not ordering officials to retake the prison in the early part of the crisis before the pressure intensified further. He continued to defend his decision not to personally negotiate with the prisoners. Just before the move to retake the prison, Rockefeller said, he was asked to go to Attica by aides who felt unsure of what he could accomplish but hoped for a miracle. "Well, I'm no messiah," Rockefeller said. "I didn't see there was anything I could do. So there on

national television would be Nelson Rockefeller and he would be the man who failed. That's the way I read it."

[24] Confirmation of Rockefeller was opposed Nov. 25 by spokesmen for the Liberty Lobby, National Right to Life Committee, National Lawyers Guild and American Conservative Union. A variety of reasons was cited, including his wealth, Attica and his veto of a New York bill to repeal the state's pro-abortion law. Arthur O. Eve, a New York assemblyman who was chairman of the observer team at Attica in 1971, accused Rockefeller of "engineering the massacre."

[25] Spokesmen for Americans for Democratic Action (ADA) and the United States Labor Party testified against Rockefeller Nov. 26, and testimony was taken for and against him on the Attica issue. Committee Chairman Rodino was concerned about the question of whether Rockefeller "should be precluded from this opportunity to serve" because of his wealth alone, aside from other considerations. When ADA spokesman Joseph L. Rauh Jr. responded in the affirmative, Rodino said the conclusion "doesn't sit too well with me."

[26] University of California professors G. William Domhoff and Charles L. Schwartz testified Dec. 2 that Rockefeller family financial advisers were "actively involved" in directing a dozen major U.S. corporations and sat on the boards of directors of nearly 100 corporations over a number of years, the combined assets of the corporations currently amounting to some $70 billion. The Rockefeller family and the institutions established by the family "have been extremely influential," the professors reported, "in shaping this country's foreign policy, conservation and population policies, many aspects of the arts and sciences and perhaps still more."

[27] J. Richardson Dilworth, head of an investment team for 84 members of the Rockefeller family, testified Dec. 3 that the family owned securities or received lifetime income from trusts owning securities worth a total of $1,033,988,000. In addition, charitable institutions created by the Rockefellers but not benefitting them nor under their control, were valued at an additional $1 billion. "The family members are totally uninterested in controlling anything," Dilworth reported. They were "simply investors."

[28] The Senate confirmed Rockefeller's nomination by a 90-7 vote Dec. 10. The votes against confirmation were cast by Republicans Barry Goldwater (Ariz.), Jesse Helms (N.C.) and William Scott (Va.) and Democrats James Abourezk (S.D.), Birch Bayh (Ind.), Howard Metzenbaum (Ohio) and Gaylord Nelson (Wis.).

[29] The House Judiciary Committee recommended confirmation by a 26-12 vote Dec. 12. The opposition votes were cast by 12 Democrats; nine Democrats joined all 17 committee Republicans on the affirmative side. The opposition included six of the eight Democrats who voted in 1973 against the nomination of Gerald Ford as vice president. The House Judiciary Committee report on its investigation, issued Dec. 19, recommended confirmation of Rockefeller as a "fit and qualified" nominee.

[30] The House vote Dec. 19 to approve the nomination was 287-128 (153 R & 134 D vs 99 D & 29 R). The vote was taken after a six-hour debate featuring an unusual opposition coalition of liberal Democrats and conservative Republicans. The Democrats expressed concern over the merging of great economic power—Rockefeller's wealth—with great political power in the nation's second-highest public office. The conservatives considered Rockefeller a liberal and "big-spender."

[31] The oath of office was administered later Dec. 19 by Chief Justice Warren E. Burger in a ceremony in the Senate chamber following the House's vote. President Ford attended the ceremony, which was televised, the first time an

event had been televised in the Senate chamber. In a brief speech, Rockefeller expressed "a great sense of gratitude for the privilege of serving the country I love" and asserted that "there is nothing wrong with America that Americans cannot right." He pledged to cooperate with the President and Congress in coping with "the grave new problems we confront as a nation and as a people."
[32] Rockefeller's role in the Ford Administration was the topic of a meeting with Ford at the White House Dec. 21. White House Press Secretary Ron Nessen said afterward Rockefeller would serve as vice chairman of the Domestic Council, of which Ford was ex-officio chairman. Rockefeller would have a major role in "explaining" the President's domestic and foreign programs "throughout the country," Nessen said. Rockefeller, at his own request, would have a "special interest in handling the Domestic Council role in coordinating activities with governors and mayors," Nessen said. Rockefeller also would be vice chairman of the National Security Council and a member of a special commission overseeing foreign policy for implementation and improvement. Other assignments were to help plan for the nation's bicentennial in 1976 and to help recruit "top people" for the Administration. Rockefeller was to make a special study for Ford of the White House mode of obtaining scientific advice.

See also KISSINGER, HENRY A.

RODINO JR., PETER W.—*See* ROCKEFELLER, NELSON [12, 25]; WATERGATE [7-35, 50]

ROMAN CATHOLIC CHURCH—*See* ABORTION; BIRTH CONTROL; BRAZIL [4-5, 7]; BUTZ, EARL L.; CHILE [14]; HOMOSEXUALS; HUNGARY; IRELAND, NORTHERN; ITALY [9]; KOREA, REPUBLIC OF [9, 13]; MEXICO [20]; MIDDLE EAST [36]; NICARAGUA; OBITUARIES [DANIELOU, TROCHTA]; PHILIPPINES; POLAND; RELIGION [1-2, 12-18]; RHODESIA; SPAIN [2, 9-10, 12-13]; TAXES; VIETNAM, REPUBLIC OF [19-20, 25]

ROWING—*See* BOATING

RUMANIA—Ceausescu's powers increased. Nicolae Ceausescu, Rumania's head of state and Communist Party leader, was sworn into the newly-created post of president of the republic March 28. Under his new title, Ceausescu also became commander in chief of the armed forces. In a broader government reorganization which took place at a March 25-26 meeting of the party's Central Committee, the ruling Presidium was abolished. In its place, a "permanent bureau" was established to function as a super-governmental body to coordinate activities between party and state. Ceausescu supporters were appointed to bureau posts in a further reinforcement of the leader's powers. At the plenary meeting March 26, the resignation, for reasons of "health and age" of Premier Ion Maurer was announced. Maurer, who had been ill since a 1970 car accident, was replaced by Deputy Premier Manea Manescu.

Censorship eased. Under a new press law published March 30, editors would be responsible for censoring their own publications. Previously, the Preventive Press Control in the Committee of Press and Printing screened all articles before they were published. While it guaranteed freedom of the press, the new law stipulated that each journalist must "serve with devotion the cause of communism and struggle for application of the domestic and international policies of state and party."

Soviet relations remain cool. The attendance of Soviet Premier Alexei N. Kosygin at Rumania's Aug. 22 observance of its 30th anniversary of Communist rule apparently did not generate improved relations between the two countries. Despite gestures by Bucharest to appease the U.S.S.R., Kosygin returned to Moscow Aug. 24 without holding substantive talks with Rumanian leader Ceausescu. Kosygin spurned invitations to extend his visit. The publication

Sept. 15 of basic policy theses prepared for the 11th Congress of the Rumanian Communist Party, to be held in November, again rejected rapprochement on Soviet terms with the declaration that "under the conditions of growing and diversifying activity of the Communist and workers' parties, the existence of a center aiming at coordinating them is no longer possible."

11th Communist Party Congress. The 2,450 delegates to the 11th Rumanian Communist Party Congress in Bucharest Nov. 25-28 reelected President Ceausescu to a new five-year term as general secretary of the party. In a gesture considered an attempt to dispel rumors of a "personality cult," Ceausescu had rejected Nov. 26 a congress proposal that he be confirmed party leader for life; he retained, however, nearly absolute control over the country. [See above] Soviet Politburo member Andrei Kirilenko attended the conference, indicating some improvement in relations between the two countries.

See also COMMUNISM, INTERNATIONAL; EUROPEAN SECURITY; POPULATION; PORTUGAL [24]; UNION OF SOVIET SOCIALIST REPUBLICS [5, 12]

RUMSFELD, DONALD—*See* APPOINTMENTS & RESIGNATIONS; FORD, GERALD R.; ROCKEFELLER, NELSON [3]

RUSH, KENNETH—*See* APPOINTMENTS & RESIGNATIONS; ECONOMY, U.S. [3]

SAN MARINO—In general elections held Sept. 9 for the 60-seat legislative Grand and General Council, the Christian Democratic Party lost two seats to the Communists and Socialists, but with 25 seats still remained the leading political party. The Communists won 15 seats, a gain of one since the 1969 elections; the Socialists, a partner in the outgoing Cabinet led by Christian Democrats, obtained eight seats, up one from 1969; the Social Democrats won nine seats, a loss of two; and three minor parties picked up the other three seats.

See also Communism, International; European Security

SAUDI ARABIA—Saudis to get Aramco control. Saudi Arabia was to increase its 25% share of the concessions and assets of the Arabian American Oil (Aramco) to 60% under an interim agreement announced June 10. The accord was reached in discussions that had started in Geneva June 4 between Aramco officials and Saudi Petroleum Minister Sheik Ahmed Zaki al-Yamani. (No other details of the agreement were announced.) The pact was to be retroactive to Jan. 1. Saudi government sources said June 12 that the agreement was part of a plan to lower the price of crude oil. The accord would have the immediate effect of increasing Saudi Arabian oil production available to the government for direct sales to customers. [See below]

Oil production cut. Oil production was sharply cut in August, the Saudi government and Aramco confirmed Aug. 26. Aramco said the drop in output from the August target of 8.5 million barrels a day to less than 8 million was the result of bad weather disrupting freighter loadings at the company's terminal at Ras Tanura, Saudi Arabia. Other sources, however, attributed the production cut to the fact that Aramco's customers were purchasing less oil because of a world surplus and many of the firm's storage tanks in Europe and elsewhere were filled to capacity.

Saudi-Aramco talks recessed. Negotiations opened in London Dec. 9 for total nationalization of Aramco by Saudi Arabia. The discussions were recessed Dec. 10; no plans for a resumption were announced. The Saudis were seeking control of the remaining 40% of the firm. Participating in the talks were Oil Minister Yamani and officials of the four U.S. oil companies in the Aramco consortium—Exxon Corp., Mobil Oil Corp., Texaco, Inc., and Standard Oil Company of California.

France sells arms to Saudis. Saudi Arabia had purchased $800 million worth of weapons from France under an agreement signed in Riyadh, Defense Minister Prince Sultan ibn Abdel Aziz announced Dec. 3. Aziz said the shipments would include anti-aircraft missiles and anti-tank weapons. The deal also was said to involve 200 AMX-30 tanks, 250 armored cars and machine-gun carriers and 38 Mirage III planes. The defense minister said the arms would be purchased with cash over a period of four years.

See also AUSTRALIA [20]; ENERGY CRISIS [2-3]; ETHIOPIA [15]; FAMINE & FOOD; GREAT BRITAIN [21]; MIDDLE EAST [7, 10, 38, 41]; MONETARY DEVELOPMENTS [5, 23]; NIXON, RICHARD M.; OIL [2-5, 8-9, 11-13, 15, 18-19, 28, 35]; PAKISTAN

SAWHILL, JOHN C.—*See* APPOINTMENTS & RESIGNATIONS; ENERGY CRISIS [4, 8, 19, 24, 29-30, 39]; OIL [12]

SAXBE, WILLIAM B.—Saxbe becomes attorney general. William B. Saxbe was sworn in Jan. 4 as attorney general. In remarks at the Justice Department ceremony, Saxbe called himself a "law and order man" predicated on his belief in "a society operated in a manner to give each individual the opportunity to express himself without the fear of Big Brother taking over [or] interfering in his personal life . . . in the name of protection or in the name of defense." On the special federal Watergate prosecution being conducted by Leon Jaworski, Saxbe affirmed the probe's independence. "He has his operation and I have mine," Saxbe said. "I don't know of any place I'd get involved unless he wants me to." Saxbe, who had announced he would not seek re-election in 1974, resigned from the Senate Jan. 3.

Anti-semitism controversy. Saxbe was strongly criticized April 3 by Benjamin R. Epstein of the Anti-Defamation League (ADL) of the B'nai B'rith for his remarks that day linking McCarthy-era Communism to "Jewish intellectuals." Epstein called Saxbe's statement "incredible" and said "Mr. Saxbe's comment confirms the ADL's newest findings about the insensitivity of otherwise responsible Americans to the harmful impact of false anti-Jewish stereotyping." Jacob Sheinkman, president of the American Jewish Congress, questioned Saxbe's fitness for office. He said Saxbe's "aspersions of the loyalty of American Jews is incompatible with his responsibilities as head of the Justice Department." Saxbe, an Episcopalian, issued a clarification April 4, saying he had "long felt that there was a great deal of anti-Semitism in the Communist witch-hunts of the late 1940s and 1950s." "Much of it was directed at some highly visible Jewish intellectuals who were considered sympathetic to Russia." "Because of the Soviet posture toward issues of importance to Jews, this is no longer the case today and I believe this change can best be seen by the totally different type of individual involved in terrorist groups now operating." Saxbe's clarification did not satisfy Howard M. Squadron of the American Jewish Congress who April 4 demanded that Saxbe resign or that President Nixon dismiss him.

See also AMNESTY & CLEMENCY; ANTITRUST ACTIONS [11]; APPOINTMENTS & RESIGNATIONS; CONGRESS; CRIME [36]; GAMBLING; RADICALS; UNION OF SOVIET SOCIALIST REPUBLICS [6]; WATERGATE [71]

SCHLESINGER, JAMES R.—*See* AMNESTY & CLEMENCY; CENTRAL INTELLIGENCE AGENCY; DEFENSE [1]; MIDDLE EAST [39-40]; NARCOTICS & DANGEROUS DRUGS; NORTH ATLANTIC TREATY ORGANIZATION; OIL [2, 28]; VETERANS

SCHMIDT, HELMUT—*See* GERMANY, WEST [2-5, 13]; ITALY [6]; NORTH ATLANTIC TREATY ORGANIZATION

SCHOOL BUSING ISSUE—*See* CIVIL RIGHTS [1-8]

SCIENCE—White House science panel urged. A blue-ribbon committee appointed by the National Academy of Sciences urged President Nixon and Congress June 26 to re-establish in the White House a panel of scientists to advise the Administration on matters of science and technology. The proposal recommended Congressional creation of a Council for Science and Technology that would work with other White House agencies on a co-equal basis. Such a scientific council would aid the White House Office of Management and Budget in the allocation of resources for the government's scientific and technological programs, the report suggested. Since the dismantling of the White House scientific advisory apparatus in 1973, the academy's report noted, there had been no provision at the top level of government and analysis of such problems as the food crisis or development of programs in the energy field or transportation.

See also ARCHEOLOGY; BOOKS; ENERGY CRISIS [25]; INTELLIGENCE; NOBEL PRIZES; OBITUARIES [BRONOWSKI, BUSH, CONDON]; SPACE; TERRITORIAL WATERS; UNION OF SOVIET SOCIALIST REPUBLICS [25-27]; UNITED NATIONS [16-19]; VIETNAM, REPUBLIC OF [39]

SCOTT, SEN. HUGH—*See* PRIVACY [3]; WATERGATE [11, 19, 68]

SECRET SERVICE, U.S.—*See* AGNEW, SPIRO T.; FORD, GERALD R.; WATERGATE [12, 69-70, 98]

SECURITIES & EXCHANGE COMMISSION (SEC)—*See* APPOINTMENTS & RESIGNATIONS; BANKS & BANKING; CIVIL RIGHTS [21]; RAILROADS; STOCK MARKET [6-7]; WATERGATE [74-76]

SEGRETTI, DONALD H.—*See* WATERGATE AFFAIR [26, 77]

SELECTIVE SERVICE SYSTEM—*See* AMNESTY & CLEMENCY; DEFENSE [10]

SENATE—*See* CONGRESS

SENEGAL—New cooperation accords with France. Senegal and France signed 44 agreements March 29, constituting total renegotiation of the accords reached upon Senegal's independence in June 1960. Under the new accords, the French military base at Dakar was transferred to Senegal, but France was permitted to retain use of the facilities. Other terms provided for a partial withdrawal of French troops, from the 2,250 presently stationed there to 1,300 in 1975.

Frontier incidents with Gambia. Senegalese forces invaded Gambian territory July 10-24, taking 20 prisoners and wounding several persons, government sources in the Gambian capital of Banjul said Aug. 7. A protest note was delivered to the Senegalese ambassador who, according to the August issue of *Africa Research Bulletin*, apologized for the incident on instructions from Dakar.

Opposition party formed. A legal opposition party, the Senegalese

Democratic Party, was formed in Dakar in September, the *Washington Post* reported Nov. 19. Led by lawyer and economist Abdoulaye Wade, the party favored increased nationalization of foreign-owned industries and greater independence from France and Western influences.

See also AFRICA; CHINA, COMMUNIST; FAMINE & FOOD; OIL [18]

SEYCHELLES ISLANDS—The ruling Seychelles Democratic Party (SDP) headed by Chief Minister James Mancham won 52.4% of the vote in elections held for the Legislative Assembly April 25. The opposition Seychelles Peoples United Party (SPUP) received 47.6%. The SDP was given 13 Assembly seats and the SPUP two. SPUP followers staged violent demonstrations April 26 in the capital city of Victoria on the main island of Mahe, protesting the party's under-representation in the Assembly.

Appearing before the United Nations Committee on Colonialism in New York May 17, Mancham explained that he was seeking independence for his country because neither the British Labor Party nor the Conservatives was interested in closer links between Britain and the Seychelles. In a London statement on March 29, Mancham said the Islands would become independent one year after April elections were held in the British-owned Indian Ocean archipelago. The SDP had previously advocated continued British sovereignty. In his London declaration, however, Mancham said independence was sought because the opposition SPUP was receiving financial and moral support from the Organization of African Unity (OAU) to campaign for full independence.

SHAH PAHLEVI, MOHAMMED RIZA—*See* AUSTRALIA [21]; INDIA; OIL [29]
SHIELD LAWS—*See* PRESS

SHIPS & SHIPPING—Queen Elizabeth 2. All 1,648 passengers from the ocean liner *Queen Elizabeth 2* were transferred to *Sea Venture*, a Norwegian cruise ship, following two days adrift April 2-3 after a breakdown of the main boiler system, 820 miles east of Florida. The rescue ship headed for Bermuda where the passengers were flown back to New York. Cunard Lines, operators of the ship, estimated losses at $1.2 million which included full refunds. Experts reported that a failure of the ship's alarm system prevented early detection of an apparent oil leak which caused the boiler shutdown.

Monitor wreck reported found. The *U.S.S. Monitor*, the Union vessel involved in the first clash between ironclads (with the South's *Merrimack*) March 9, 1862, during the Civil War, was located on the floor of the Atlantic off Cape Hatteras, N.C., an oceanographic researcher at Duke University reported March 7. The *Monitor* had sunk in a gale Dec. 31, 1862.

Oil tanker bill vetoed. President Ford withheld his signature and pocket vetoed a bill Dec. 30 that would have required at least 20% of oil imported into the U.S. be carried on U.S. tankers. The requirement would have risen to 25% in mid-1975 and to 30% in mid-1977. The President would have had emergency authority to waive the requirement in the national interest. Currently, 6% of the country's imported oil was carried by U.S. flag ships. Ford said in his veto statement the bill "would have an adverse impact" on the country's economy and its foreign relations. "It would create serious inflationary pressures" by increasing the price of oil, he said, and "it would further stimulate inflation in the ship construction industry." He also objected that the bill "would serve as a precedent for other countries to increase protection of their industries," which was contrary to the trade bill and to "a large number of our treaties of friendship, commerce and navigation."

See also CAMPAIGN FINANCING [23]; FRANCE [19]; GREAT BRITAIN [11-18]; INDIA; LABOR [14-15]; MIDDLE EAST [28]; PUERTO RICO; SPACE [13]; TERRITORIAL WATERS

SHULTZ, GEORGE P.—*See* APPOINTMENTS & RESIGNATIONS; ECONOMY, U.S. [2]; LATIN AMERICA; TARIFFS & TRADE
SIERRA LEONE—*See* ALUMINUM & BAUXITE

SIKKIM—King signs new Constitution. Chogyal (King) Palden Thondup Namgyal signed a bill July 4 that formally gave Sikkim a new Constitution, ending 332 years of monarchial rule and making the king a virtually powerless figurehead. The chogyal's agreement to the new charter followed a warning by the National Assembly that if he did not give his approval "there would be no role for him to play in Sikkim." (In elections held in April, a party opposed to the chogyal had won all but one of the 32 Assembly seats.)

The Assembly had approved a new Indian-drafted Constitution that provided for Sikkimese representation in the Indian Parliament, control of Sikkim's economic development by India's Planning Commission and extension of Indian economic institutions to Sikkim. Executive powers were vested in a chief executive, an Indian to be appointed by New Delhi. The chogyal had visited New Delhi June 25-29 in an unsuccessful attempt to persuade Indian officials to permit the protectorate to keep its separate identity. (Riots and strikes in support of the chogyal had broken out in the capital city of Gangtok on June 22. Indian police fired tear gas and used clubs to break up the demonstrations. The Indian army was placed on alert as all Sikkimese government employes except the police were on strike.)

Though still objecting to the loss of Sikkim's separate identity and political status, the chogyal signed the new charter because "it is my incumbent duty as a constitutional head to give assent if the people's representatives return the bill to me." A new five-member cabinet was sworn in July 24, headed by Chief Minister Kazi Lhendup Dorji, who had organized a popular movement against the chogyal in 1973.

See also PAKISTAN

SIMON, WILLIAM E.—*See* AGRICULTURE; APPOINTMENTS & RESIGNATIONS; CANADA [22]; ECONOMY, U.S. [6]; ENERGY CRISIS [8-9, 12]; LABOR [12]; MONETARY DEVELOPMENTS [24]; OIL [31]; SUGAR; UNION OF SOVIET SOCIALIST REPUBLICS [14-15]
SINGAPORE—*See* JAPAN [10]
SINO—SOVIET DISPUTE—*See* COMMUNISM, INTERNATIONAL
SIRICA, JOHN J.—*See* WATERGATE AFFAIR [9, 36, 43, 47, 52, 56-58, 87-100]
SMOKING—*See* MEDICINE & HEALTH [26]
SOARES, MARIO—*See* ANGOLA; GUINEA-BISSAU; MOZAMBIQUE [3]; PORTUGAL [3, 6, 27-28]

SOCCER—Stampede kills 49. Thousands of Egyptian soccer fans, unable to gain entrance to a full stadium in Cairo broke through restraining barriers and caused an onrush which left 49 trampled to death Feb. 17.

West Germany wins World Cup. West Germany defeated the Netherlands 2-1 in the final match of the 10th World Cup soccer competition in Munich July 7. Poland had topped Brazil (the 1970 cup holder) 1-0 for third place July 6.

SOCIAL SECURITY SYSTEM—*See* BUDGET; MEDICINE & HEALTH [8]; PENSIONS; PRIVACY [13]
SOLAR ENERGY—*See* ENERGY CRISIS [24]; OIL [19]

SOLZHENITSYN, ALEXANDER—A worldwide controversy broke out with the late December 1973 publication in the West of excerpts from *The Gulag Archipelago,* the newest work of dissident Soviet author Alexander Solzhenitsyn. The book provided a firsthand account of the pervasive secret police system, the executions and prison camp deaths in the years between the Bolshevik Revolution and the death of Joseph Stalin. It also reported Stalin's police network had not been dismantled, although mass arrests and atrocities had diminished since de-Stalinization by Nikita Khrushchev in the mid-1950s. (Solzhenitsyn had spent 11 years in prison and internal exile between 1945-1956 for having privately criticized Stalin. He had been completely exonerated of all charges, he said, in a 1956 court decision which cited him for "personal heroism" at the front.) Solzhenitsyn said he had decided to publish *Gulag* because the secret police had uncovered a copy, and not to aid reactionary propaganda in the West, as the authorities had claimed. The storm over the book caused Solzhenitsyn's forcible exile Feb. 13. He was also deprived of his Soviet citizenship.

The Soviet public was informed about the book for the first time Jan. 4, when a nationwide television broadcast, while not revealing the book's subject matter, accused the writer of "malicious slander." Solzhenitsyn had charged that the number of arrests, executions and prison terms under the Soviet regime ranged from 10 to 1,000 times greater than under the Czarist government; and wrote of Russians who fought against their country during World War II in what he called an unprecedented display of disaffection with their government.

(In a Jan. 8 broadcast, China claimed that one million prisoners were being held in over a thousand Soviet labor camps, and that the Soviet government was using methods ranging from psychiatric drugs to "tanks and paratroopers" to suppress dissent. Although the broadcast was part of the continuing war of polemics between the two nations, the figures were confirmed in a *New York Times* report Jan. 11 which cited U.S. Central Intelligence Agency estimates based on satellite photographs. The photographs indicated that 2.4 million-2.5 million people were in Soviet prisons. Others contended the figure was one million, approximately 10,000 of whom were political prisoners. The prison population in the U.S., the highest in the West, was 425,000.)

The regime's campaign against Solzhenitsyn included attacks on him from prominent and ordinary citizens printed in magazines and newspapers, a special half-hour broadcast devoted to "viewers' questions about bourgeois propaganda," and the display of an unusual eight-foot poster portraying him as a traitor, displayed in a major Moscow thoroughfare. The author was backed in public statements or letters by some well-known dissidents, among them physicist Andrei Sakharov; poet Yevgeny Yevtushenko, who charged that Soviet youth had been kept almost totally unaware of Stalinist crimes; and historian Roy Medvedev, a Marxist, who had disagreed with Solzhenitsyn and other dissenters in the past. Sakharov said in a Jan. 20 interview that a shift in power to the hardliners had apparently occurred within the Soviet leadership.

Worldwide reaction to the Soviet attacks on Solzhenitsyn resulted in his arrest Feb. 12 at his wife's Moscow apartment and his deportation to West Germany the following day. (In a Dec. 10 Stockholm speech accepting the Nobel Prize he had been awarded in 1970, the writer attributed his safety to the attention given him by the West. Solzhenitsyn had not personally accepted the award in 1970 for fear that he would not be allowed to return to Russia if he left.) He was believed to be the first Soviet citizen to be forcibly expelled from the country since Leon Trotsky was exiled in 1929.

Upon arrival in West Germany on a Soviet airliner, the writer was taken to the home of fellow Nobel laureate author Heinrich Boll. He traveled to Switzerland on Feb. 15, where he was joined March 29 by his wife and family. Offers of asylum or immigrant status were made by a number of Western governments. U.S. Secretary of State Henry A. Kissinger said Feb. 13 that Solzhenitsyn would be welcome to reside in the U.S. but said the only problem for U.S.-Soviet relations posed by the author's case was "the extent to which our human, moral and critical concern" for him and other Soviet dissidents "should affect the day-to-day conduct of our foreign policy."

Solzhenitsyn kept up his criticism of the Soviet Union from exile. An essay dated Feb. 12 and circulated Feb. 17 titled "Live Not By Lies" asked Soviet citizens to refuse to repeat or endorse officially promoted falsehoods. Western newspapers March 3 published details of a letter Solzhenitsyn had written in September, 1973, addressed "to the rulers of the Soviet Union," in which he had appealed to the Kremlin to abandon Communism, disband the member republics of the Union, unwind industrialization and adopt an agriculturally-oriented posture. The published work reportedly had toned down its original attacks which were strongly critical of Western democracy. The document was criticized by Medvedev and Sakharov, who called some of its proposals "potentially dangerous," while Sakharov joined Solzhenitsyn in calling on the Soviet leadership to renounce Marxism and to relinquish the nation's non-Russian republics. The Swiss government announced March 12 that Solzhenitsyn and his family would reside in Switzerland.

See also UNION OF SOVIET SOCIALIST REPUBLICS [19]

SOMALIA—Soviet President Nikolai V. Podgorny made an official visit to Mogadishu July 9-13 and signed a treaty of cooperation with Somali President Mohamed Siad Barre. Podgorny was accompanied by Gen. Sergei Sokolov, first deputy minister of defense. According to a July 8 broadcast from Addis Ababa, sources in Kenya reported that the U.S.S.R. had recently given Somalia a squadron of seven MiG-21 fighter bombers. In a June 19 press conference, Barre had denied reports that the Soviet Union had naval or military bases in Somalia and said that his government would "never allow" such actions.

(An Israeli newsletter, the *Middle East Intelligence Survey*, said the Soviet Union and Somalia had recently signed a secret agreement allowing Moscow to build a new port north of Barbera for use by the Soviet Indian Ocean fleet, it was reported Nov. 20. The text of the cooperation treaty signed in July between Moscow and Mogadishu, printed in the Soviet Communist Party newspaper *Pravda* Oct. 30, included plans for increasing military assistance to Somalia.)

Somali high schools closed at the end of July for a year so that the nation's 30,000 students could perform as the principal workers in a literacy campaign and help to conduct Somalia's first nationwide census, the *New York Times* reported June 16.

See also AFRICA; DEFENSE [14]; OIL [19]

SOUTH AFRICA

Apartheid Developments

[1] **Black-white ties sought.** Kwazulu Chief Gatsha Buthelezi and United Party Transvaal Province leader Harry Schwarz signed a five-point declaration of principle, published Jan. 6, calling for a peaceful evolution of South Africa toward a black-white federation. The white opposition United Party, which won about one-third the vote in the most recent election, had supported a modified form of apartheid, or racial segregation.

[2] In a continuation of a trend begun three years ago, several restrictions

against blacks and other non-whites in labor and public accommodations were eased by the national and local governments in January, prompted largely by labor shortages. Natal Province decided to accept black nurses to care for whites in private hospitals, it was reported Jan. 25. Also reported that day were a new industrial agreement to allow blacks to become motor mechanics, a decision to eliminate token safety checks by whites when black gold miners prepared dynamite charges, and the hiring of black traffic policemen by Bloemfontein, a conservative Afrikaner city. The Johannesburg City Council announced a series of measures Jan. 30 to eliminate "petty apartheid" in areas under its jurisdiction. Nonwhites would be able to use at all times facilities open to them only on certain days in the past, including parks, museums, libraries, art galleries and the city zoo. Separate services for whites and blacks in some municipal departments would be eliminated, and race designation signs would be removed from park benches and bus shelters. The council said it would ask the federal government to change the law barring blacks from purchasing homes in the black townships. Private office buildings would be encouraged to eliminate separate elevators, and restaurants and theaters would be asked to offer better service to blacks. The move was opposed by National Party members of the council, which was controlled by the United Party. Similar action had been taken in Pietermaritzburg, and Durban and Cape Town had said they would follow suit.

[3] Maj. Gen. J. R. Dutton, acting chief of the army, said Dec. 9 that the South African army was opening its ranks to black soldiers. Dutton said the soldiers, who would form an all-black corps, would be paid the same as white soldiers and would be allowed to carry arms; however, there were no plans to train black officers.

[4] **Restrictive bill approved.** The Affected Organizations Bill, extending the government's power to suppress anti-apartheid groups, was rushed through Parliament's final pre-election sitting Feb. 26. The bill, proposed Feb. 19, gave the nation's president power to bar organizations engaging in politics from receiving any funds from foreign countries, at the risk of $30,000 fines and 10-year jail sentences. Politics was not defined in the bill. The government would have sweeping powers to investigate suspected organizations, with heavy penalties for obstruction of the investigation. The government had also asked for revision of the Riotous Assemblies Act giving magistrates authority to ban any meeting of any size, and giving police wide powers to enforce the ban. Anyone in the news media disseminating the speech of anyone banned from a meeting could be jailed for a year.

[5] **Editor, militant leaders arrested.** As many as 50 people were arrested in police raids conducted Sept. 25-30 in Durban, Johannesburg, Germiston, Kokstad and Kingwilliamstown as South African authorities began a roundup of militant black leaders. The arrests came after police broke up a rally in Durban Sept. 25 of some 1,000 supporters of the Front for the Liberation of Mozambique (FRELIMO). (The demonstration had been banned under the Riotous Assemblies Act.) It was reported Sept. 30 that all leaves for the security police had been canceled. Among those arrested Sept. 25 was John O'Malley, the white editor of the *Durban Daily News*. He was charged under the Riotous Assemblies Act with having provided illegal advertising of the rally by reporting that the organization planned to go ahead with it despite the ban. The editors of 14 English language newspapers issued a statement Sept. 27 criticizing O'Malley's arrest.

Bantustan Independence

[6] **Vorster meets with black leaders.** Prime Minister John Vorster held discussions with seven of the nine African tribal homeland (Bantustan) leaders

March 6, in the first official meeting convened between blacks and whites in South Africa. The meeting came about as a result of the Umtata summit conference of Bantustan leaders in November 1973. (Under the Bantustan program, black Africans, who represented 83% of the nation's population, were allotted 14% of the land.) The talks, described by one black leader as "brutally frank," centered on the government's plan for separate development of the black Bantustans, culminating in their independence from white South Africa.

[7] The ruling political party of the Transkei Bantustan voted unanimously March 12 to request independence from South Africa within the next five years, with the provisos that it received all the land promised it by then and that its claims to other areas should not be prejudiced.

[8] Eight of South Africa's nine Bantustans declared Nov. 16 that, contrary to the government's projected goal, they would not seek independence at present lest they forfeit their right to a full share of the nation's wealth. The eight leaders said they would not accept independence until their fragmented territories were consolidated and provided with a viable economic infrastructure. The only Bantustan to maintain a commitment to independence was the Transkei. Divided in two parts, the Transkei was considered the only Bantustan with a significant chance for economic viability; the eight other Bantustans were split into more than 50 fragments. In a political speech Nov. 5, Vorster had reiterated his government's goal of majority-ruled independent Bantustans.

Labor Unrest

[9] **Unionists banned.** The government banned and placed under house arrest three white trade union leaders in Durban Feb. 1, for helping organize black workers. Two of the three had helped organize the Durban textile workers strike Jan. 18-22, while all three had participated in talks between black unionists and British trade union representatives in 1973. The textile workers, most of whom were Zulus, won wage increases Jan. 22. The five-year banning orders would effectively curtail union activities for the three.

[10] **46 die in gold mine riots.** Two African miners were killed and five seriously injured when police tried to quell a riot that broke out after a pay dispute at the Loraine gold mine in the Orange Free State May 29. Four miners were killed and 14 others, including seven policmen, were injured following rioting at the Harmony gold mine near Welkom June 9. One miner was killed in a disturbance June 11 at the Merrispruit mine near Welkom. Fresh outbreaks of fighting between Xhosa and Basuto tribesmen working in the Welkom and Carletonville gold mines had resulted in the deaths of 32 miners since March, it was reported April 17.

[11] **Minimum wage for black miners raised.** Pretoria announced that minimum wages for 400,000 black miners would rise 33% to a monthly income equivalent to $106, it was reported Oct. 22. This compared with a $572 monthly minimum income for the 4,000 white miners. A shortage of mine workers had spurred the government to intensify gold mine mechanization efforts, it was reported Nov. 4. The government had also initiated a program to recruit urban blacks to work in the mines, according to a Nov. 20 report. (About three-quarters of the gold mining industry's 375,000 black workers were migrant laborers from the neighboring black African countries of Malawi, Mozambique, Lesotho and Botswana.)

Other Developments

[12] **Elections widen Vorster margin.** In general elections April 24, Prime Minister Vorster's National Party (NP) gained four seats in the South African House of Assembly, giving the NP 122 of 169 seats and a majority of 75. The

next day Vorster hailed the elections, held a year before the expiration of his five-year term, as "a clear indication that the people had once again chosen the policy of separate development" (leading to the ultimate independence of the now semi-autonomous Bantustans). The Progressive Party (PP), South Africa's most liberal official political party which advocated a qualified franchise for all South Africans in a multiracial state, increased its representation from one to six seats. (A by-election at Pinelands June 3 gave the PP an additional seat.) (The country's 18 million black, colored and Asian peoples, who had their own legislatures, were not franchised to vote in the national elections. Only 1.6 million of a white electorate of 2.2 million cast votes because 43 candidates were unopposed.) The elections constituted a clear defeat for the official opposition, the United Party (UP) which lost five seats for a total of 41. The UP had been split in pre-election disputes between reformist and conservative factions.

[13] **U.S. defense cooperation reported.** According to a *Washington Post* report Oct. 20, sources in the South African Department of Defense said Western defense cooperation had been assured, with the U.S. reportedly in agreement with Pretoria on the need to protect the Cape of Good Hope sea route. (British and French cooperation was also noted: Great Britain's navy had sent a flotilla of nine warships to Cape Town to participate in exercises with the South African fleet Aug. 28 and an 11-ship contingent arrived Oct. 14 for a second series of joint operations. A French flotilla had reportedly departed from Brest for the Cape Oct. 14.) In a further development, a secret report, known as National Security Study Memorandum 39, prepared by the U.S. National Security Council in 1969, provided the basis for a policy "tilt" toward the white-ruled nations of southern Africa, acording to a report by columnist Jack Anderson Oct. 11. The policy option reportedly endorsed by presidential order in early 1970 was that of "selective relaxation of our stance toward the white states," an option which included proposals advocating an easing of the official U.S. embargo on arms shipments to the southern African nations by allowing "more liberal treatment" of "dual purpose equipment" that could serve either military or civilian purposes. According to the *Washington Post* Oct. 13, State Department officials had conceded that constraints on Export-Import Bank loan facilities for South Africa had been "slightly loosened," as per the memorandum's recommendation. The report stressed South Africa's strategic location on the Cape of Good Hope sea route and growing Soviet activity in the Indian Ocean; noted that U.S. direct investment in South Africa totaled $700 million and "yields a highly profitable return;" and pointed out that South Africa was an important supplier of uranium.

[14] **Simonstown naval base expansion.** South Africa announced a five-year plan to treble the size of the Simonstown naval base, it was reported Nov. 7. Defense Minister P. W. Botha had offered Nov. 4 the facilities of the base to "every country in the free world which is friendly toward us." The statement followed the veto in the United Nations Security Council by the U.S., France and Great Britain of a resolution to expel South Africa from the U.N.

See also AFRICA; AUTO RACING; JORDAN; MEDICINE & HEALTH [29]; MONETARY DEVELOPMENTS [4]; MOZAMBIQUE [17]; NOBEL PRIZES; RHODESIA; SOUTH WEST AFRICA; TENNIS; UNITED NATIONS [4-6, 8-10]

SOUTH CAROLINA—*See* ELECIONS [7]; ENERGY CRISIS [9]; WOMEN'S RIGHTS
SOUTH DAKOTA—*See* ARICULTURE; ELECTIONS [1, 5]
SOUTH KOREA—*See* KOREA, REPUBLIC OF
SOUTH VIETNAM—*See* VIETNAM, REPUBLIC OF

SOUTH-WEST AFRICA (NAMIBIA)—South-West Africa talks proposed. South Africa informed the U.N. Sept. 26 that it would participate in interracial talks to determine the "future pattern of constitutional development" in South-West Africa (Namibia), the territory it had administered since World War I. The proposed talks were rejected that day by the South-West Africa People's Organization (SWAPO), the territory's major black political group, which demanded "nothing less than . . . self-determination" and also insisted that all Namibians be allowed to return to the territory "unconditionally." In a New York interview reported Oct. 12, South African Foreign Minister Hilgard Muller said "all options are open" for the disputed territory, including independence "should the people of South-West Africa so decide in the exercise of their right to self-determination." Muller conferred in Washington with State Department officials and members of Congress Oct. 11. (The U.N. Educational, Scientific and Cultural Organization [UNESCO] Oct. 21 granted associate membership to South-West Africa.)

Namibia freedom demanded. The Security Council demanded Dec. 17 that South Africa make a "solemn declaration" to grant independence to Namibia, which it ruled in defiance of U.N. directives. The Council unanimously passed a compromise resolution condemning Pretoria's "illegal occupation" of Namibia and its introduction of "racially discriminatory and repressive laws and practices" there. The measure advised South Africa to take several steps toward freeing Namibia by May 30, 1975. If Pretoria did not comply, the Council would consider "appropriate measures to be taken under the [U.N.] Charter."

See also Nobel Prizes

SOUTH YEMEN—*See* Defense [14]

SPACE—Skylab 3 mission ends. Three astronauts—Marine Lt. Col. Gerald P. Carr, civilian scientist Dr. Edward G. Gibson and Air Force Lt. Col. William R. Pogue—Feb. 8 safely completed the record-setting Skylab 3 space mission, splashing down in the Pacific at 11:18 EDT. The crew members, who never had flown in space before the Nov. 16, 1973 launching that took them to Skylab, were the world's most experienced space flyers by the time of splashdown. They had remained in orbit a record 84 days, one hour and 17 minutes, had circled the earth a record 1,214 times and had traveled a record 34.5 million miles in orbit. The Skylab 3 flight and the $2.6 billion three-mission Skylab program produced the greatest volume of scientific and medical data ever accumulated in a manned spaceflight mission or series—accumulating miles of tape-recorded medical and scientific data, more than 40,000 photos of the earth and more than 182,000 photos of the sun. Skylab 3 was the last scheduled U.S. manned flight until the joint U.S.-Soviet mission planned for July, 1975. It was the U.S.' 30th manned flight.

[2] The three astronauts suffered initial vertigo upon their return to earth, but were found to be in better shape than the crews of Skylab 1 and Skylab 2 had been in after shorter stays in space. Although the Skylab 3 astronauts had apparently suffered some deterioration in their cardiovascular systems during the early weeks of the mission, an improvement had started in after about six weeks. Their muscular condition showed little or no deterioration, partially because they had followed a much heavier program of exercise than had earlier crews.

[3] Prior to leaving Skylab, Carr and Gibson performed the mission's fourth and final extra-vehicular activity (EVA) Feb. 3, moving outside the Skylab to retrieve six film cassettes from the solar telescopes, check on particles in space and the effects of solar rays and micrometeorites and to photograph the earth's upper atmosphere. The return to earth began early Feb. 8, after the astronauts had loaded their Apollo command vehicle with their films, tapes, notes, equipment and other mementoes. Upon splashdown in the Pacific, the Apollo spacecraft capsized, but on-board balloons quickly righted it for recovery by the

aircraft carrier *New Orleans*. The splashdown was the first conclusion of a U.S. manned space flight not covered by live television. Such coverage was omitted because of a considerable lessening of public interest in space flight.

[4] **Mariner 10 passes Venus, Mercury.** The U.S. space probe Mariner 10, launched in November 1973, sent back data during February and March on Venus and Mercury. A pass-by on Sept. 21 resulted in photographs of Mercury's sunlit, southern face. The probe suffered some problems during its early flight—notably an inexplicable failure of its prime power pack Jan. 8 (necessitating a switch to the Mariner's back-up system) and a faulty gyroscope Jan. 29 which caused a waste of 25% of the probe's control fuel. It still was able, however, to make close observations of the two planets. It flew to within 3,585 miles of Venus on Feb. 5, sending back to the Jet Propulsion Laboratory (JPL) in Pasadena, Cal. measurements and photographs suggesting that Venus probably was not closely related to earth and that previous theories of the planet's development were erroneous. The Mariner's measurements implied that hydrogen in the upper atmosphere of Venus had come from the solar wind (gases blown from the sun), rather than from water on the planet itself; and that the solar wind was not deflected from Venus because there was no strong magnetic field around the planet.

[5] Mariner 10 passed within 466 miles of Mercury March 29. It sent back to the JPL more than 800 close-up photographs confirming earlier radar studies that the planet, like the moon, consisted of undulating hills and dales pockmarked with craters. Other data was less expected. According to preliminary analysis, the probe revealed the unexpected presence of an atmosphere, one hundred-billionth as dense as that of earth and composed of helium, with lesser amounts of argon and neon. Conspicuously absent, except in minute quantities, was atmospheric hydrogen. (Soviet astronomer Nikolai Z. Kozyrev Feb. 7 had reported an "extensive" presence of hydrogen on Mercury.) Also unexpected was the probe's indication of an enveloping magnetic field one-thousandth as strong as that surrounding earth. According to measurements by the Mariner, temperatures on Mercury varied between a daytime temperature of 800°F and a twilight temperature of -280°F. For several days after the fly-by, JPL astronomers thought they had found a small moon in orbit around Mercury, but computer analysis showed the suspected object to be a very hot star in the constellation Corvus about 100 light years distant.

[6] **Pioneer 10 returns data on Jupiter.** Radio signals transmitted by the U.S. interplanetary space probe Pioneer 10 revealed that temperatures in the upper atmosphere of Jupiter reached 800°F, it was reported by the JPL April 13. Earth-based measurements had not been higher than -220°F. Arvydas Kliore of the JPL, while admitting that he had no explanation of the higher temperatures around Jupiter, hypothesized that a layer of dust in the upper atmosphere trapped energy from the sun, creating a greenhouse effect. Analysis of other Pioneer data showed periodic bursts of highly charged particles as far as 100 million miles from Jupiter and indicated that Pioneer 10 had passed in and out of the magnetic field of Jupiter no fewer than 17 times as it left the vicinity of the planet. National Aeronautics and Space Administration (NASA) scientists said Sept. 10 that analysis of data from Pioneer 10 indicated that Jupiter was a mass of intensely hot, compressed hydrogen with winds reaching speeds of 300 to 400 miles an hour. If the planet had a solid center, they said, it was a rocky core squeezed by liquid metallic hydrogen at temperatures over 50,000°F and pressures of more than 3 million earth atmospheres. The Great Red Spot, they said, appeared to be a towering Jovian hurricane, whose vortex was 25,000 miles deep.

[7] **Pioneer 11 completes Jupiter mission.** The U.S. interplanetary space probe Pioneer 11 passed within 26,600 miles of Jupiter Dec. 2 and then sped into outer space for a rendezvous with Saturn in 1979. Despite instrumentation problems caused by the planet's intense radiation, the fly-by was a success, NASA scientists at the Ames Research Center in Mountain View, Calif. said. Pioneer 11 passed beneath the planet's south pole where Jupiter's powerful gravitational forces captured the spacecraft, swinging it behind the planet and off into space. (NASA scientists noted that it was the slingshot effect caused by Jupiter's gravity that enabled Pioneer 11 to rush by the planet before it could accumulate lethal doses of radiation.) Initial data from Pioneer 11 confirmed that the regular stripes girdling Jupiter's equatorial regions were not present in the polar latitudes. Instead, the deep indigo polar areas were pockmarked with seething, red convection cells, which apparently served as vents for rising gases. Pioneer 11 also produced the best photographs yet of Callisto, the second largest of Jupiter's 13 moons.

[8] **Communications, weather satellites launched.** Other satellites launched through the year included Westar I and II, communications satellites owned by Western Union Corp. Westar I, launched into orbit aboard a NASA Delta Rocket April 13, and Westar II, sent into space Oct. 11, would increase the company's capacity for commercial and personal communications, teletype, telephone and television data transmission. On May 13 NASA launched the first satellite powerful enough to broadcast directly to individual television receivers. The $180 million Applications Technology Satellite (ATS-F) No. 6 was sent into a 22,300-mile-high orbit from Cape Canaveral, Fla. It was expected to remain aloft six years and perform the primary function of broadcasting educational and public health programs into remote areas of the U.S. and, after a year, to India. The U.S. also launched, May 17, a new type of weather satellite capable of transmitting a steady stream of weather photographs. The first of a series of three satellites, the 630-pound Synchronous Meteorological Satellite (SMS), would, among other things: monitor eruptions on the sun that might endanger astronauts or passengers in supersonic transports; relay premonitory signs of earthquakes or tidal waves; obtain data on mid-ocean sea conditions; and transmit weather data to remote stations.

[9] **Soviet probes reach Mars.** Efforts by the Soviet Union to explore Mars suffered a reversal March 14 when one of its space probes, Mars 7, shot past the planet at a distance of 800 miles and Mars 6 lost contact before it touched down on the Martian surface. The Soviet news agency Tass attributed the orbital miss by Mars 7 to the "failure of the onboard systems." Western observers suggested that Mars 6 might have been caught in a fierce Martian wind storm and dashed to pieces against the planet's landscape. Before Mars 6 ceased to transmit, it relayed signals indicating that the Martian atmosphere contained "tens of per cent" argon, an inert gas. The finding strengthened the view that Mars once could have supported life and might do so again. Prior to the Mars 6 and 7 shots, Tass had reported Feb. 13 that Mars 5 had successfully orbited Mars and was transmitting photos of the planet's surface. Tass also reported that Mars 4 had failed to orbit Mars, missing the planet by 1,300 miles because of a "breakdown in one of the onboard systems."

[10] **Soviet craft attempted link-ups.** Two Soviet cosmonauts returned safely to earth July 19 after completing a 15-day mission during which their Soyuz 14 space vehicle successfully docked with an orbiting Salyut 3 space station. However, a successor craft, Soyuz 15, abruptly ended its mission after only two days in orbit Aug. 28, apparently having failed to achieve a link-up with Salyut 3. Preparation for the link-ups had begun with the launching of the Salyut 3

space laboratory June 25. The cosmonauts aboard the Soyuz 14 were rocketed into space July 3 from the Soviet space center at Baikonur in Kazakhstan. During their 17th orbit in the Soyuz 14, the cosmonauts, Air Force Col. Pavel Popovich and Air Force Lt. Col. Yury Artyukhin, completed their link-up with Salyut 3. It was the first Soviet docking since June 1971, when the three-man crew of the Soyuz 11 spent 22 days aboard Salyut 1. The Soyuz 11 cosmonauts perished during re-entry because of a leak in the spacecraft.

[11] The follow-up mission by Soyuz 15 ended Aug. 28, two days after it had begun. Other than a brief announcement that cosmonauts Gennadi Sarafanov and Lev Demin had returned safely to earth after making an unusual night landing, the official Soviet press agency Tass gave no further details. Western observers suggested, however, that either the cosmonauts had failed to achieve a link-up and were running low on oxygen or that the condition of the Salyut 3 station had seriously deteriorated.

[12] **Soyuz 16 hailed as successful rehearsal.** The two-man crew of the Soviet Union's Soyuz 16 spacecraft returned to earth safely Dec. 8 after completing a six-day mission that was hailed by Soviet space officials as a successful rehearsal for the U.S.-Soviet orbital link-up planned for July 1975. After completing 96 orbits of the earth, the craft, which carried cosmonauts Anatoly V. Filipchenko, an Air Force colonel, and Nikolai N. Rukavishnikov, a civilian engineer, parachuted onto the steppes of Kazakhstan 190 miles north of the town of Jezkazgan, the Soviet press agency Tass reported. While news of technical aspects of the mission was scant, the Soviet government provided intensive media coverage of the mission, including broadcasts of tapes of the blastoff at the Baikonur Space Center and a televised visit to the mission control center set to function during the joint mission. Observers attributed the unusual openness to official Russian pique over U.S. criticism of the Soyuz program. U.S. Sen. William Proxmire (D, Wis.) Sept. 5 urged a serious re-examination of the Soyuz-Apollo program in light of the failure of Soyuz 15 to accomplish its goal of rendezvousing and docking with an orbiting Salyut spacecraft. Proxmire also said the "safety record of the Soviet spacecraft is dismal and shows no evidence of getting any better."

[13] **Soviet satellites track ships.** The *Washington Post* reported April 26 that the Soviet Union had launched into orbit during the last four years 8-10 satellites that used radar to monitor surface ship traffic around the world. Intelligence sources, the *Post* said, believed that the radar satellites were still experimental, operating for six weeks at a time over the Indian Ocean or the Baltic Sea. These sources suggested that the aim of the Soviet program was to be able to track U.S. submarines as they made their way under water. Using infrared radar, the satellites might be able to detect heat dissipated into the oceans by the submarines, the sources said.

See also Budget; Union of Soviet Socialist Republics [4]

SPAIN

Government

[1] The three-way conflict between left, right and moderate factions in Spain's government, which had been intensifying since the December 1973 assassination of right-wing Premier Adm. Luis Carrero Blanco, escalated still further following the military coup in Portugal. The resignation under pressure by the leftists of Portugal's conservative junta leader, Gen. Antonio de Spinola, led to fears by Spain's rightists that the Spanish Communist Party might bcome as powerful as its Portuguese counterpart after Generalissimo Francisco Franco's death or retirement.

[2] Carrero was replaced by Premier Carlos Arias Navarro Jan. 2. Arias, who had built a reputation as a law-and-order prosecutor, pledged both firmness and liberalization in his Jan. 4 policy speech, saying his new Cabinet would "give great importance to the development of political participation." (Earlier statements by Franco and Carrero promising new structures for political participation had not yet been implemented.) In appointing his new Cabinet Jan. 3, Arias had excluded all members of the Roman Catholic lay movement, *Opus Dei,* which played a major role in the development of a more modern Spanish economy and in attempts to improve relations with both Western Europe and the Communist countries. Arias also dropped two right-wing cabinet members who had been advocated for the premiership until Franco and moderate military leaders intervened on Arias' behalf.

[3] **Arias pledges reforms.** Arias promised Feb. 12 in an 80-minute speech to the Cortes, Spain's parliament, to provide institutional means for "34 million Spaniards" to participate in political and economic life, and he set deadlines for submission to the Cortes of certain specific reforms. Arias said a bill would be submitted by May 31 providing for election of mayors and presidents of the provincial assemblies, who had been appointed by the national or provincial governments in the past. Another bill, to bar government officials from holding seats in the Cortes, would be introduced by June 30. A long-promised bill to allow for national political associations, or political parties, was again promised, but without any submission date. Labor and management could form separate organizations within the official syndicates under another proposed bill, and different trades would also be allowed to organize to "defend their peculiar interests."

[4] **Conflict within the military.** Lt. Gen. Manuel Diez Alegria, chairman of Spain's defense staff, was retired by Franco June 14 amid an apparent struggle between moderate and conservative officers for control of the armed forces. Following Carrero's assassination, Diez Alegria had helped organize a crisis management group which temporarily seized control of the country and curbed rightists who demanded a show of force and widespread arrests of leftists. Diez Alegria and other moderate senior officers also felt that Spain must revive political parties if it wished to avoid chaos on Franco's death. (Spain had only one legal party, the National Movement.) Diez Alegria, who also advocated reducing the military's political power, was replaced June 15 by Lt. Gen. Carlos Fernandez Vallespin. Fernandez was considered a moderate, but his elevation was seen as a victory for rightist generals who opposed his predecessor's ideas, according to press reports.

[5] **Franco ill; delegates power to prince.** Franco, ill with phlebitis complicated by internal bleeding, delegated his authority as chief of state July 19 to his designated successor, Prince Juan Carlos de Borbon. The transfer of power was provisional, allowing Franco to reassume his office if and when he wished. To prevent any possible outbreak of violence, the army, the paramilitary civil guard and the secret service were placed on alert, and police and civil guard leaves were canceled, it was reported July 20. However, the country remained calm. While Franco lay ill, the council of the National Movement, the only legal political organization, met July 22 to discuss liberalizing the political system. The council approved a document recommending the establishment of "political associations" under the movement's direct control. The proposal would be submitted to the government for action.

[6] Franco resumed his duties Sept. 2, one day after doctors declared him "clinically cured." His resumption of power ended, at least temporarily, the most intense campaign for political liberalization in Spain since 1939, the

Washington Post reported Sept. 3. Juan Carlos was reported in favor of the policy. Moderate military officers had made it clear to the Prince and to their civilian associates that while they favored a democratic monarchy, they would not move to change the political system while Franco was alive. Meanwhile, Juan Carlos was reluctant to exercise his authority lest it be interpreted as a move to permanently exclude Franco from power.

[7] **Rightists boost pressure; Cabanillas fired.** Information Minister Pio Cabanillas was dismissed Oct. 29 as rightists increased pressure on the government to abandon its political liberalization plans. Finance Minister Antonio Barrera de Irimo resigned in protest Oct. 30 and other government officials followed suit in subsequent days. Cabanillas and Barrera were considered two of the most progressive Cabinet ministers. Cabanillas had allowed a relative measure of press freedom, unprecedented since the Spanish Civil War in the 1930s. Hard-liners had demanded his ouster for months. (Cabanillas was replaced Oct. 30 by Leon Herrera Esteban, deputy interior minister, and Barrera was succeeded by Rafael Cabello de Alba, an automobile manufacturing executive.)

[8] **Opposition coalitions formed.** The Democratic Junta of Spain, a coalition of Communists, Socialists, liberal monarchists, moderates, businessmen and former government officials, had announced its formation in Paris July 30 and called for the restoration of democracy in Spain. A Junta manifesto was handed to newsmen by Santiago Carrillo, secretary general of the Spanish Communist Party, and Rafael Calvo Serer, a former newspaper publisher and member of *Opus Dei.* The manifesto called for a provisional government to replace the Franco regime; total amnesty for political prisoners; legalization of all political parties; separation of Church and State; freedom of the press, of the judiciary and of labor union organization; free elections; and other measures. The Carlist Party, a monarchist group, announced Sept. 20 it would join the Junta. Another opposition coalition, the Spanish Social Democratic Union, announced its formation in Madrid Oct. 17. Led by prominent professional men, it pledged to follow a program parallel to that of "other European Social Democratic Parties."

Basque Developments

[9] **Basque bishop detained.** Divisions between the government and the Roman Catholic Church deepened Feb. 27 when the bishop of Bilbao, Antonio Anoveros Ataun, was placed under house arrest in retaliation for issuing a strongly worded homily calling for "just freedom" and autonomy for the Basque people.

[10] The government dropped its attempt to exile Anoveros after the Permanent Commission of the Spanish Episcopal Conference issued a statement supporting the bishop and defying the regime to try him under the provisions of Spain's 1953 concordat with the Vatican. The decision, which eased the worst church-state crisis since the end of the Spanish Civil War, was considered a defeat for Arias, who had promoted a confrontation with the Vatican on the issue, according to the *Washington Post* March 13. The church commission issued its statement March 9 after two days of meetings called by the archbishop of Madrid, Vicente Cardinal Enrique y Tarancon. It denied that Anoveros' recent call for "just freedom" for the Basque people had been intended as an "attack on national unity." The denial was not the official apology the government had sought, but was still considered "conciliatory." However, the conflict was not fully resolved, according to press reports. The Vatican sent a special envoy, Msgr. Agnello Acerbi, to Madrid March 11 to meet with leaders of the Spanish

church hierarchy and Foreign Minister Pedro Cortina, in anticipation of a decision by Spain to unilaterally renounce the Church-State concordat.

[11] **More Basques blamed in Carrero murder.** A government order published April 6 added four more alleged Basque terrorists to the list of persons wanted in connection with Carrero's assassination. (The Basque movement, ETA, had claimed credit for the deaths Dec. 20, 1973, saying it had been done to avenge the killing of nine Basque militants and to fight repression in Spain. The Spanish Interior Ministry had named seven persons wanted in connection with the assassination. However, four hooded figures claiming to be ETA members told French newsmen Dec. 28, 1973, that they had conducted the assassination and that those named were innocent.) The Madrid newspaper *Informaciones* reported April 6 that two of the four suspects recently named were in Belgium. The government had requested their extradition but Belgium had refused, the paper said. The government news agency Cifra had said March 21 that France had been asked to extradite the six Basques originally sought in Carrero's killing, but France had refused.

Terrorist Activities

[12] **Anarchist executed.** Anarchist Salvador Puig Antich, 26, who had been sentenced to death Jan. 9 for killing a policeman who had tried to arrest him in September 1973, was garroted in the Barcelona city jail March 2. Franco had ignored pleas for clemency from European governments, the Vatican, the Spanish Roman Catholic hierarchy, and numerous individuals and organizations inside and outside Spain. Puig Antich had been apprehended by the policeman in connection with a bank robbery. Two teen-aged accomplices, who along with Puig Antich were charged with membership in the Iberian Liberation Movement, a leftist splinter group, were sentenced to five and 30 years, respectively, for the robbery. It was the first execution with political overtones and the first by garroting since two Catalan anarchists were garroted in August 1963. The garrote was a centuries-old Spanish torture and death device consisting of an iron collar tightened around a victim's neck until he died of either strangulation or a broken spine. University students clashed with police in Madrid and Barcelona March 4 after demonstrating against Puig Antich's execution. Demonstrations continued the next day in the two cities and spread to Bilbao and San Sebastian.

[13] Protests against the garroting continued in Spain and abroad March 6-15. Hundreds of persons demonstrated in two working class districts of Barcelona March 7, shouting slogans for Puig Antich and against Franco, who approved the execution. On March 10 police surrounded a Barcelona church in which some 2,000 persons gathered for a memorial service for Puig Antich. Several thousand persons demonstrated against the garroting in Paris March 10. Also in France, unknown persons had thrown Molotov cocktails at the Spanish tourist office and a Spanish bank in Marseilles March 6, and at a branch of the Bank of Bilbao in Hendaye March 8. All three incidents apparently protested the garroting. The Hendaye bank was virtually destroyed. The European Parliament passed a resolution the night of March 14-15 condemning the execution of Puig Atich and asserting that "the repeated violations of the fundamental rights of many of the Spanish regime . . . preclude the entrance of Spain into the European Community."

[14] **Communists, anarchists seized.** Police reported arresting 67 Communists, anarchists and Catalan separatists in Madrid, Barcelona and Alicante April 8-29, accusing many of them of planning May Day terrorist attacks. The arrest of three Communists, including two alleged members of the Central Committee of

the outlawed Communist Party, was announced in Madrid April 8. The most important was said to be Francisco Romero Marin, who commanded a Republican brigade during the Spanish Civil War.

See also APPOINTMENTS & RESIGNATIONS; AUTO RACING; CHILE [24]; COMMUNISM, INTERNATIONAL; EUROPEAN SECURITY; GUATEMALA; MONETARY DEVELOPMENTS [4]; OIL [26]; PORTUGAL [3]; SPANISH SAHARA; SWITZERLAND

SPANISH SAHARA—Several Spaniards were killed Jan. 26 in fighting between rebels and government forces, the Moroccan trade union daily *Maghreb-Informations* reported March 20. Five insurgents were arrested Jan. 27 in a continuation of the clash.

Morocco renewed its campaign to regain the Spanish Sahara in a series of statements and actions initiated May 25 with the government's announcement that King Hassan II "and all of his loyal subjects are firmly dedicated to recover" the territory. Hassan began mounting his campaign on the diplomatic front, deciding to send, according to the French newspaper *Le Monde* July 18, political as well as government envoys to various capitals to argue the Moroccan cause. Spain July 2-3 had informed the ambassadors of Morocco, Mauritania and Algeria that it was determined to administer the territory until such time as the colony's future would be decided "by the free will of the Saharan people." In a July 6 communication, Hassan warned Generalissimo Francisco Franco against unilateral action in the Sahara territory and said July 8 that "we will under no circumstances permit a puppet state to exist in the southern part of our country." In remarks reported July 10, Hassan said Morocco was ready to undertake "the decisive battle" and announced that 1975 would be "a year of mobilization" to recover the "usurped area of the fatherland."

Hassan shifted the tone of his campaign to regain the Spanish Sahara by military force and asked Sept. 17 that the question be placed before the World Court in The Hague. Hassan asked the court to decide whether the territory was, as Spain alleged, a legal no man's land which had been under no nation's jurisdiction before Spain assumed authority or whether, as the king maintained, the territory had been ruled by Morocco before Spain acquired administrative control. Hassan said he would present legal documents to support his contention. (Spain had informed the United Nations Aug. 20 that it would hold a referendum on the political future of the Spanish Sahara during the first half of 1975.)

The U.N. General Assembly Dec. 13 adopted a resolution to place the question of sovereignty over the Spanish Sahara before the World Court.

SPINOLA, ANTONIO DE—*See* ANGOLA; GUINEA-BISSAU; MOZAMBIQUE [3, 13]; PORTUGAL [3, 5-11, 13-19, 25]

SPORTS—*See* specific sport; OBITUARIES [ALLEN, BROWN]; OLYMPICS; WOMEN'S RIGHTS

SRI LANKA—Prime Minister Sirimavo Bandaranaike issued an order April 20 closing down the Sun Group, which published about 16 newspapers in Sri Lanka, following increasing press criticism of the government for food shortages and economic difficulties. The regime had previously seized the Associated Newspapers of Ceylon, Ltd., which published five dailies, books and weekly journals.

Bandaranaike had told a May Day rally in Colombo May 1 that the opposition United National Party (UNP) was attempting to overthrow the government. UNP leader Junius Richard Jayawardene charged at a rival gathering that the government's April emergency law restricting public rallies was a violation of the Constitution. The UNP had planned to stage 150 public meetings and demonstrations throughout the country April 21 to draw attention to food shortages and high prices, but was prevented by the police.

Emergency regulations enacted by the government Dec. 21 provided for the outlawing and confiscation of assets of political parties that participated in paramilitary activities or challenged by illegal means the validity of the Constitution. The new law was particularly directed at the Trotskyite Lanka Sama Samaja Party, which had publicly announced it had organized "armies" at places of work.

See also AVIATION [14]; FAMINE & FOOD

STANS, MAURICE—*See* WATERGATE [74-76]

STATE DEPARTMENT, U.S.—*See* specific country; APPOINTMENTS & RESIGNATIONS; CAMPAIGN FINANCING [12]; CENTRAL INTELLIGENCE AGENCY; CHILE [6]; CYPRUS [17, 23]; DOMINICAN REPUBLIC; KISSINGER, HENRY A.; MEXICO [9]; NARCOTICS & DANGEROUS DRUGS; PERU [11, 17]; VIETNAM, REPUBLIC OF [34-36]

STATE OF THE UNION MESSAGE—*See* NIXON, RICHARD M.; WATERGATE [4]

STEEL INDUSTRY—*See* ANTITRUST ACTIONS [8]; AUTOMOBILES [3]; CIVIL RIGHTS [13]; ECONOMY, U.S. [7, 9]; ENVIRONMENT & POLLUTION [13]; FRANCE [19]; LABOR [11, 17-20]; VENEZUELA

STEINBRENNER, GEORGE M.—*See* CAMPAIGN FINANCING [23]

STERILIZATION—*See* WELFARE & POVERTY

STOCK MARKET

Market Developments

[1] **Dow Jones falls.**The Dow Jones industrial average closed at 616.24 points on Dec. 31, 1974, on the New York stock exchange, up 12.99 for the day and ending the year with a mild recovery. The market had registered steady losses throughout the year, falling steadily from its peak of 1,051.7 on Jan. 11, 1973. The average one year later, Jan. 11, 1974, was 841.41, reflecting investors' dual fears about inflation and recession, both closely tied to the oil situation and record interest rates. The market dropped below 800 for the first time May 29, when the average registered 795.37. It rose again, however, on June 3 to 821.26 on news of a drop in prime lending rates. An increase in the rates later in the month brought the average below 800 again, to 790.68 on July 2; followed by a plunge to 770.57 on July 8 when 1,441 stocks dropped in price. More than 600 stocks hit new 1974 lows that day while only 137 advanced. The average marked a four-year low. The market rallied, however, July 12, climbing to 787.23 on news that the rise in demand for business loans at major New York banks in the week ending July 10 had dropped from the previous week's high level. Although the average dipped again, sharp advances were made Aug. 5-7 on rumors that President Nixon would resign. The Dow was 797.56 at the closing of trading Aug. 7. Investor pessimism, however, caused a break below the 600-level Oct. 1, closing on Oct. 4 at 584.56. (It was the lowest closing since Oct. 26, 1962, during the height of the Cuban missile crisis, when the index was at 569.02) The market then rallied during the week of Oct. 7-11, gaining 73.61 points, its largest weekly advance in the history of the exchange, to close at 658.17. A decline in the prime rate and other evidence that money and credit would be easier to obtain spurred the market rally. However, the recovery was uneven. Announcement of a 6.5% unemployment rate during November and reports of mounting layoffs triggered a 12-year low of 577.6 on Dec. 6, a loss of 41.06 points for the week.

[2] **Reaction to prices.** The malaise affecting Wall Street was reflected in the sale of a seat on the New York Stock Exchange for $70,000 July 9. It was the lowest price paid since February 1958. The securities industry itself faced

mounting losses. Member firms of the New York Stock Exchange posted their fifth consecutive monthly loss in August when the aggregate monthly deficit totaled $27 million, according to reports Oct. 7. A July deficit of $17.5 million had been reported reported Sept. 17. Combined losses for the first eight months of 1974 totaled $102 million, compared with the $217.2 million deficit registered during the first eight months of 1973. To offset these continuing losses, the exchange voted to extend the trading day by half an hour (10 a.m.-4 p.m. EST) in an effort to increase the volume of trading. The longer trading day took effect in New York and other cities Oct. 1. (The American Stock Exchange also voted to lengthen its trading day.) The average daily volume of trading on the New York Stock Exchange during the first nine months of the year had been an estimated 13.4 million shares, compared with 15.1 million during the same period of 1973.

[3] Soaring interest rates on the short-term money market continued to draw investors from the long-term equity market. New York City was forced to withdraw a $438 million bond issue July 9 citing "crushing" costs because the only bid received for it carried an interest charge of 7.92%. The rate was 1.75% higher than the charge on a similar bond issue offered by the city in April, according to the city comptroller, and would have resulted in total interest costs of $254 million over the seven year, four month average life of the bonds. Bell Telephone Co. of Pennsylvania, which had one of the highest corporate credit ratings in the nation, July 15 paid a record 9.73% interest to borrow $175 million on 40 year debentures.

[4] **Stock cash payment reduced.** The Federal Reserve Board Jan. 2 lowered its margin requirements for purchasing or carrying stock on credit from 65% to 50%. The required deposit on short sales also was reduced from 65% to 50%. Investors had not been required to put up as little as 50% of the purchase price since November 1963, when the margin was raised to 55%. The Federal Reserve "noted the sharp reduction that has occurred in stock market credit since" the margin was raised to 65% in November 1972.

[5] **Commodity trading commission.** A bill to strengthen federal regulation of commodity futures trading was signed into law Oct. 23. It had been passed by the House Oct. 9 and the Senate Oct. 10. An independent commission was to be established to regulate the exchanges. It would be empowered to seek injunctions to halt abuses and to intervene directly in markets to curb threatened or actual manipulation, or major imbalance arising from a government activity, domestic or foreign. (The New York Cotton Exchange had instituted futures trading for crude oil contracts Sept. 10, marking the first time that buy and sell orders for future deliveries of crude oil were accepted in a commodities market.)

Criminal Actions

[6] **National Student Marketing case.**A federal grand jury in New York Jan. 17 indicted seven persons, including a partner in the nation's largest accounting firm, Peat, Marwick, Mitchell & Co., for making false and misleading statements in the National Student Marketing Corp.'s (NSM) proxy material during 1968-69. (NSM's collapse as a glamor stock in 1970 was believed to have cost Peat, Marwick investors more than $100 million, according to the Wall Street Journal Jan. 18.) In February 1972, the SEC had charged Peat and Marwick and several persons (NSM officials) named in the grand jury indictment, and two prominent law firms with fraud in the NSM affair.

[7] Cortes W. Randell, founder of the NSM Corp., who pleaded guilty to stock fraud charges Aug. 20, was sentenced to 18 months in prison and fined $40,000 in New York City federal court Dec. 27. In addition, a partner and a former employee of Peat, Marwick, Mitchell & Co. were sentenced for making false and

misleading statements involving National Student Marketing in a proxy statement filed with the SEC in 1969. The accounting firm's partner, Anthony M. Natelli, was sentenced to 60 days in jail and fined $10,000; Joseph A. Scansaroli, who worked for Peat, Marwick in 1968 and 1969, was sentenced to 10 days in jail and fined $2,500. Both men were found guilty in a November trial on charges they had falsely portrayed National Student Marketing as a company with extremely large sales and earnings. Two former sales executives of National Student Marketing, Dennis M. Kelly and Robert C. Bushnell, who had also pleaded guilty to stock fraud charges, were sentenced. Kelly was given a 10-month prison term and a fine of $10,000, Bushnell was fined $4,000 with a suspended six-month prison sentence.

[8] **Securities law violations charged.**The SEC accused Seaboard Corp., 12 other firms and 16 persons with fraud in a suit filed March 5 in U.S. district court in Los Angeles. According to the agency, investors in the Los Angeles-based mutual funds management firm were defrauded of more than $9 million through mutual fund manipulations and mismanagement of company funds by officials of the firm attempting to manipulate the price of Seaboard's own stock. The SEC asked the court to require three top officials in the firm to give up $800,000 in "illegal profits" gained by the alleged misappropriations and fictitious stock sales during 1970-73.

[9] **Home-Stake swindle investigated.** About 120 investors in Home-Stake Production Co., an Oklahoma-based oil drilling venture, claimed that they lost $8.8 million, or 81% of the money they invested in the tax shelter, from 1964-1972, according to the *Wall Street Journal* July 3. The firm was under criminal investigation by the SEC for allegedly swindling $100 million from its investors, many of whom were well known businessmen and entertainers, in a "Ponzi" scheme in which quarterly income payments were made to investors from their own and new investors' funds rather than from company operations. (The pyramid type swindle took its name from Charles Ponzi, a Boston confidence man of the 1920s). A federal grand jury in Los Angeles Dec. 12 indicted 13 former Home-Stake officials and associates on 39 counts of stock and tax fraud.

[10] **Equity Funding ex-chief pleads guilty.** Stanley Goldblum, former chairman and president of the bankrupt Equity Funding Corp., pleaded guilty Oct. 8 to five felony counts of conspiracy and fraud related to the Equity stock swindle. The guilty plea was entered in U.S. district court in Los Angeles after Goldblum had been on trial for five days. He had been named in 45 counts of a 105-count indictment returned against him and 21 other persons; 18 of them had already pleaded guilty to various counts. A separate trial had been ordered Sept. 23 for the three remaining defendants—Julian Weiner, Solomon Block and Marvin Lichtig, all former accountants with Equity's auditing firm. Criminal charges were still pending against Goldblum and other former Equity officials in Illinois and New Jersey, where Equity subsidiaries had operated. Scores of civil suits also had been filed against Goldblum and some of his co-defendants in the criminal proceedings.

[11] Robert M. Loeffler, the trustee appointed by the court to salvage the life insurance and mutual funds conglomerate, filed a reorganization report with the court Nov. 1 after 18 months of investigations. Loeffler concluded that the Equity fraud, which succeeded in raising the value of its stock by inflating stated assets and minimizing its liabilities, could have been detected at an early stage if the firm's independent auditors had made more careful checks of dubious corporate practices.

See also ANTITRUST ACTIONS [1-3]; **BANKS & BANKING; CONSUMER AFFAIRS** [1]; **HUGHES, HOWARD; RAILROADS; VESCO, ROBERT L.; WATERGATE** [74-76]; **WELFARE & POVERTY**

SUDAN—A number of Sudanese officers were arrested in the Sudan in connection with a Libyan-inspired plot to overthrow the government of President Gaafar el-Nimeiry, the Lebanese newspaper *An Nahar* reported May 22. Among those arrested was Col. Saad Bahr, former commander of the western region and a Nimeiry supporter in quashing the 1971 coup attempt against the government. In a May 11 interview, Nimeiry had laid blame for the recently exposed plot on Libyan leader Col. Muammar el-Qaddafi whom he accused of interfering in Sudan's internal affairs. (According to an April 19 report, Sharif al-Hindi, leader of the Sudanese opposition movement, the National Front, was in Libya receiving financial aid from the Tripoli government.

President Nimeiry June 25 freed eight Palestinian guerrillas after they had been convicted the previous day of killing two U.S. diplomats and a Belgian envoy in a siege at the Saudi Arabian embassy in Khartoum March 2, 1973. The U.S. recalled its ambassador in protest June 25. The eight men were turned over to the Palestine Liberation Organization (PLO) June 25 and were flown to Cairo. They had been convicted of murder and sentenced in a Khartoum court June 24 to life imprisonment following a trial that had begun June 1. Nimeiry immediately commuted the sentences to seven years, and announced his decision to turn the guerrillas, members of the Black September group, over to the PLO. Egypt imprisoned the guerrillas when they arrived in Cairo.

President Nimeiry announced July 22 that clemency would be extended to those who had been implicated in the 1971 coup attempt and to students involved in the 1973 university disruptions. The announcement followed the release from prison of other opposition leaders in March, among them seven long-term political prisoners including former Premier Sadik al-Mahdi and former head of the Sudanese Journalists Union, Bachir Muhammad Said. Former German mercenary Rolf Steiner, who had been sentenced in 1971 to life imprisonment for his part in the southern Sudanese rebellion, was released from jail and left Khartoum for West Germany March 31.

Eight non-commissioned army officers found guilty of planning a coup d'etat were sentenced Dec. 2 to prison terms of up to six years. The fates of 18 other officers placed on trial with them Nov. 15 remained to be decided. The charges related to a conspiracy President Nimeiry had announced as thwarted in October.

See also AFRICA; AUSTRALIA [20]; OIL [19]

SUGAR—House kills Sugar Act. The House of Representatives rejected a bill June 5 to extend the Sugar Act for five years. The program set domestic and foreign sugar quotas and provided subsidies for domestic producers. Its current authorization would expire Dec. 31. The surprise defeat came on a 209-175 vote (121 R & 88 D vs. 128 D & 47 R). Opponents of the bill, supported by consumer groups, cited current sugar prices, the highest since 1920, and the large subsidy payments to the industry. Supporters of the extension, backed by domestic farm and sugar-grower associations, contended that the program stabilized prices and assured adequate supplies.

Sugar processor's profits soar. The nation's largest beet sugar processor, Great Western United, reported Oct. 23 that its third quarter profits were more than 1,200% higher than the previous year's level. Net income was $20.9 million for the period ending Sept. 30, compared with $1.6 million in 1973. Sales were up 97% over the previous year. Operating profits in the firm's sugar division rose more than 1,000% to $44.6 million, compared with $4 million the previous year. The price of raw cane sugar on the nation's commodities market had increased as estimated 300% during the past year.

Sugar Act extended. The White House announced Nov. 18 that President Ford had set a sugar import quota of seven million tons for 1975 and extended the existing tariff schedule beyond Dec. 31, when the current Sugar Act was due to expire. Both moves were aimed at reducing the domestic price of sugar. According to the Administration, the sugar quota was intentionally set at a high level to permit all the sugar sold by foreign exporters to enter the country. The current quota on sugar imports was 6.7 million tons, but during 1974 the U.S. was expected to import only 6 million tons, half of all the sugar consumed in the country. (The existing quotas also applied on a country by country basis, in contrast to the new executive action which was nonrestrictive.)

Speculation fuels price hikes. Speculation on the world sugar market reportedly contributed to dramatic sugar price increases. It was reported Nov. 11 that Arab oil producers were investing surplus revenues in sugar. Since January, their purchases were estimated at 3 million-4 million tons, about 20% of all the sugar traded on the world market. Another major factor in the price rises, according to an unidentified United Nations official Nov. 10, was a series of major sugar beet crop failures in the Soviet Union. Sugar prices hit record levels Nov. 19 on the New York Coffee and Sugar Exchange. Future contracts for March delivery climbed the 2¢ a pound limit to 63.2¢. The spot price, the actual cost for immediate delivery after sale, was also up to the maximum 63.5¢. The two major U.S. refiners Nov. 15 announced their sixth major price increase since Oct. 9, bringing the estimated retail price to about 63¢-65¢ a pound. On Jan. 1, consumers had paid about 18¢ a pound. Both firms said the rising cost of raw sugar necessitated the increase. As retail prices soared, the refiners' profits were also reaching record highs. Amstar Corp., the largest refiner which marketed under the Domino brand, had a 250% increase in net income and a 59% rise in sales for the fiscal quarter ending in September, the *New York Times* reported Nov. 1. Sucrest Corp. announced Nov. 15 that sales had increased 139% in the September fiscal quarter over the comparable period of 1973.

Hearings probe sugar price rise. The Council on Wage and Price Stability held hearings Nov. 25-26 to investigate the recent sharp rise in sugar prices. Treasury Secretary William E. Simon, President Ford's chief economic spokesman, opened the meeting to restate the Administration's flat opposition to price controls on any commodity, including sugar. The council heard conflicting testimony on the causes of inflated sugar prices. Consumer groups accused refiners of profiteering and monopolistic practices and said a "gross" miscalculation by the Agriculture Department of expected sugar consumption in the U.S. during 1974 also contributed to the price spiral; refiners blamed the increase on speculation on the world markets; economists noted that world sugar consumption had outpaced sugar production since the 1970-71 crop year, exerting upward pressure on prices; a spokesman for the chief sugar exchange market in the U.S. denied that speculators had forced up prices. According to a report prepared by the wage-price council staff, "all sectors of the U.S. sugar industry have in varying degrees reaped large windfall gains" or inventory profits, but the growers had been the chief beneficiaries of high retail prices. Wage-price council figures showed that the price of raw sugar had increased 413% on the world market in the one-year period since November 1973, rising from 9.95¢ a pound to 51¢ a pound.

Three of the nation's largest sugar refiners—Amstar, Sucrest and CPC International—Dec. 2 announced a 7% cut in sugar prices (about 5¢ a pound). It was the first price reduction in 20 months and followed announcements of seven price increases over a five-week period. The last increase, totaling about 12%, was announced Nov. 22 by Amstar, Sucrest and the National Sugar Refining Co. Prices also were dropping on the world market. By Dec. 3, sugar futures had declined the daily permissible limit of 2¢ a pound for seven consecutive sessions.

Latin sugar cartel formed. Twenty nations in Latin America and the Caribbean formed a sugar producers' union to protect world sugar prices, currently at record levels. Formation of the cartel, called the Group of Latin-American and Caribbean Sugar Exporting Countries, was announced Nov. 28 by Francisco Cano Escalante, president of the Mexican National Sugar Commission, following a meeting of representatives of the member nations Nov. 25-27 on the island of Cozumel, off Mexico's Caribbean coast. Cano said the union, which accounted for 60% of world sugar production, would hold its first formal policy session in April 1975 in the Dominican Republic. The union members included Mexico, the Dominican Republic, Argentina, Barbados, Brazil, Colombia, Costa Rica, Cuba, Ecuador, El Salvador, Guatemala, Guyana, Honduras, Jamaica, Nicaragua, Panama, Paraguay, Peru, Trinidad & Tobago and Venezuela.

Six sugar firms indicted. Six U.S. sugar firms were indicted Dec. 19 by a federal grand jury in San Francisco on charges of fixing prices in 23 West and Midwest states. Two criminal indictments and two companion civil suits, filed by the Justice Department, accused the defendants of engaging in separate price fixing conspiracies in two regional markets on the West Coast and in the Midwest. Named as defendants were Great Western Sugar Co.; American Crystal Sugar Co.; Holly Sugar Corp.; California and Hawaiian Sugar Co.; Amalgamated Sugar Co.; and Consolidated Foods Corp. A third civil suit, filed against Utah-Idaho Sugar Co. and the National Sugar Beet Growers Federation, alleged a similar conspiracy in Western and Mountain states. Justice Department spokesmen said the charges grew out of an 18-month investigation into pre-1973 pricing practices of the $2.5 billion U.S. sugar market, and were not related to the current high price of sugar. However, the spokesman added that the "current pricing patterns of the sugar industry are still under investigation."

See also AGRICULTURE

SUMMIT MEETINGS—*See* DISARMAMENT

SUPREME COURT—According to a *New York Times* report July 1, the four justices appointed by President Nixon—Chief Justice Warren E. Burger, Harry A. Blackmun, Lewis F. Powell Jr. and William H. Rehnquist—voted together on 75% of the cases decided by the court during its 1973-74 term. In all but one of the 103 times they cast votes together, the Nixon justices formed the nucleus of a court majority. A second bloc was formed by Justices William O. Douglas, William J. Brennan Jr. and Thurgood Marshall, who voted together 74% of the time. Justice Byron R. White agreed with the Nixon justices on 85% of their joint votes, while Justice Potter Stewart voted with them 82% of the time.Douglas was the court's most prolific writer of opinions with 60, Burger the least with 16 opinions. Burger had asserted in 1973 that the court was overworked and its caseload should be narrowed by some sort of screening process. (Decisions of the court will be found under the related category; e.g., CRIME, etc.)

See also BANKS & BANKING; CIVIL RIGHTS [3, 6-7, 18]; CRIME [1-6, 40]; DEFENSE [9]; JUDICIARY; KENT STATE; OBITUARIES [WARREN]; OBSCENITY & PORNOGRAPHY; PRESS; PRIVACY [12]; RAILROADS; TAXES; TELEVISION & RADIO; VOTING RIGHTS; WATERGATE [36, 52-53]; WOMEN'S RIGHTS

SURINAM & NETHERLANDS ANTILLES—Surinam would gain independence by the end of 1975, while the Netherlands Antilles would wait at least until 1980, according to an agreement reached in talks in The Hague May 18-21. The conference participants were Dutch Premier Joop den Uyl, Surinam leader Henk Arron and Netherlands Antilles leader Juancho Evertz. Both autonomous territories, Surinam was located in northeast South America and the Netherlands Antilles were islands in the West Indies. Evertz maintained that the Dutch government should restore the full strength of the marine garrison on Curacao. He opposed the Dutch proposal that defense of the islands should be jointly guaranteed by a military alliance with Venezuela, the U.S., and the Netherlands.

Dutch Premier den Uyl had supported Surinamese Premier Arron's appeal for the 90,000 Surinamese residing in the Netherlands to return home, the London newsletter *Latin America* reported Aug. 30. The two leaders said Surinam's economy would be damaged if the present wave of emigration—running at more than 1,000 a week— did not end. Most of the new emigrants were East Indians who feared discrimination after independence of the autonomous territory, planned for 1975.

See also ALUMINUM & BAUXITE.

SURVEILLANCE—*See* PRIVACY & ELECTRONIC SURVEILLANCE

SWEDEN—Economic compromise reached. A 4-billion kronor ($866 million) compromise program aimed at stimulating the economy was reached Feb. 25 between the government and right-wing and centrist opposition parties. Subsequently approved by the Riksdag (Parliament), the plan provided for a 5½-month reduction of 3% in the value-added tax (a levy applied to each stage of the production and distribution of goods) from its current level of 17.6%, effective April 1; payment of special child allowances and old age pensions in April; and substantial subsidies on basic foods. The Social Democrats had opposed the reduction of the value-added tax, while the opposition wanted it lowered by 5%. The temporary value-added tax (VAT) reductions expired Sept. 15. However, to prevent increases in the prices of basic foodstuffs as a result of the reversion to the standard VAT rate, the government lowered the price ceilings on meat and milk; farmers would receive compensation for the price drop in addition to existing farm price supports. The Riksdag Dec. 4 approved income tax reductions for 1975 totaling 2 billion kronor ($470 million) annually, primarily benefiting low- and medium-income groups. Employers would bear most of the financial burden of the measures by paying higher payroll taxes and taking over the employes' share of health insurance contributions.

Final approval for new Constitution. The Riksdag, by a 321—19 vote Feb. 27, gave final approval to a new Constitution that removed most of the monarch's residual authority and formally acknowledged the conversion in 1971 of the Riksdag into a single-chamber legislature. The Constitution, to enter into force Jan. 1, 1975, provided for a reduction in Riksdag seats from 350 to 349 after the next general election in order to prevent a recurrence of the current even split between the government and opposition. Among other provisions, it authorized the speaker of the Riksdag, rather than the king, to appoint a new premier; codified the existing parliamentary system for the first time; and included a bill of rights, until now embodied in various statutes.

Rift with U.S. ended. The 15-month diplomatic rift between the U.S. and Sweden ended March 21 when each nation named an ambassador to the other. In response to Premier Olof Palme's public criticism of U.S. bombing in Indochina in 1972, the U.S. had recalled its ambassador to Stockholm and told the Swedish government not to send a new envoy to Washington. Robert Strausz-Hupe, 71, currently U.S. ambassador to Belgium, was named envoy to Sweden. At the same time Sweden named Count Wilhelm Wachtmeister, 50, a career diplomat, as ambassador to the U.S.

Polish economic pact signed. During a visit by Palme to Poland April 1-4, a 10-year program of industrial, technical and scientific cooperation between Sweden and Poland was signed. The agreement, signed on Sweden's behalf by Industry Minister Rune Johansson, was followed by commercial agreements between the Polish government and Swedish companies, involving industrial construction and tractor and truck production. The 10-year accord would pave the way for joint oil prospecting in the Baltic Sea and the joint building of offshore oil rigs; it also provided for Swedish participation in the expansion of Polish coal and copper mining.

Atomic power plan backed. A committee of experts endorsed government plans to locate combined nuclear power and district heating plants near Sweden's three major population centers, Stockholm, Gothenburg, and Malmoe, it was reported Aug. 13. In a 300-page report published after a five-year study, the committee proposed that nuclear plants should be located outside a 20-kilometer (12½ mile) radius of city centers, with unpopulated areas in a 2-3 kilometer radius around the plants. The 2 kilometer limit already applied to Swedish reactors. The committee calculated statistically that a major accident to a reactor resulting in heavy radioactive releases would occur only from 1-10 times in a million years or once in 1,000 years on a world scale, if the number of reactors planned worldwide were taken into consideration.

See also APPOINTMENTS & RESIGNATIONS; CHILE [3, 6-7, 24]; COMMUNISM, INTERNATIONAL; EUROPEAN SECURITY; FAMINE & FOOD; HOCKEY; MONETARY DEVELOPMENTS [4, 11, 15, 17]; NOBEL PRIZES; OBITUARIES [LAGERKVIST]; OIL [26]; UNITED NATIONS [15]

SWIMMING—The U.S. swimming team defeated East Germany 198-145 in a two-day dual meet in Concord, Calif. ending Sept. 1. The heavily favored East German women's team, which included six world record holders, outscored the U.S. women's team 84-79, but the East German men did not win any of their 15 events. The East German women had become involved in controversy Aug. 21, when the team doctor of Sweden's national swimming team suggested that the women might partly owe their swimming ability to injections of male sex hormones. Bengt Eriksson offered his observation during the European swimming championships in Vienna Aug. 18-25, in which the East German women shattered 14 world marks.

SWITZERLAND—Jura canton creation voted. By a 2,745 majority, the predominantly French-speaking electorate of the Jura region, which formed part of the 565-square-mile German-speaking canton of Bern, voted June 23 to establish a separate canton, Switzerland's 23rd. Only three of the seven Jura districts voted for the new canton; the remaining four could hold a second plebiscite within six months to decide whether to remain part of Bern. Authority to amend the Constitution would have to be approved in a national referendum. The Jura had been attached to the canton of Bern by the Congress of Vienna in 1815. French-speaking separatists had waged a long campaign for their own canton.

Foreign workers' entry curbed. The government July 9 decided to tighten restrictions on the entry of foreign employes into Switzerland, effective Aug. 1. Entry restrictions would be extended to public health, teaching and agricultural sectors, previously exempt from the regulations. The number of new year-round entry permits to be granted to foreign workers in 1974 was set at a maximum of 25,000.

Bid to oust foreigners rejected. In a national referendum Oct. 20, the Swiss electorate rejected a proposal to deport half the nation's 1.1 million foreigners, including 300,000 immigrant workers, by the end of 1977. The proposal, rejected by 66% of the voters, was defeated in all 25 cantons. Leaders of all sectors—government, church, nearly all political parties, union and industry—had opposed the plan drawn up by Valentin Oehen, a member of Parliament and leader of a right-wing splinter party, the National Action against Foreign Domination of People and Homeland. Foreigners comprised nearly one-sixth of the nation's 6.4 million inhabitants, but about one-third of its work force, with immigrants mainly filling the menial jobs. Some 52% of the foreigners were Italians; Spaniards and West Germans each comprised 11%.

Banking actions. In an effort to stem the sharp influx of foreign funds into Switzerland, the government Nov. 20 imposed a 3% quarterly tax on new foreign-held Swiss franc bank deposits and abolished interest payments on such accounts, retroactive to Oct. 31. The move rescinded the government's authorization Oct. 16 to resume, as of Oct. 31, interest payments on foreign-held accounts. Such payments had first been banned in 1971; and a negative interest tax on non-resident deposits imposed in 1972 had since been repealed gradually. Fritz Leutwiler, president of the Swiss National Bank, said Nov. 20 that the government had acted because of the influx into Switzerland of dollars held by oil-exporting countries. Switzerland, he said, would not allow the Swiss franc to become a refuge for foreign funds. Between Oct. 16 and Nov. 18, the franc had appreciated by more than 10% against the dollar, according to one report. With an estimated 40% rise in the value of the Swiss franc against the dollar during the past two years, Switzerland's export and tourist industries had suffered.

The lower house of Parliament voted 98-0 Dec. 12 to ratify a treaty with the U.S. that would permit disclosure of information on secret Swiss bank accounts in U.S. criminal cases. The measure was aimed primarily at U.S. organized crime. The treaty still required ratification by the Swiss upper house and by the U.S. Senate.

See also BANKS & BANKING; CHILE [24]; COMMUNISM, INTERNATIONAL; EUROPEAN SECURITY; GREAT BRITAIN [27]; ITALY [7]; MONETARY DEVELOPMENTS [19, 23]; OIL [26]; RELIGION [3]; SOLZHENITSYN, ALEXANDER; UNION OF SOVIET SOCIALIST REPUBLICS [19]; UNITED NATIONS [18]

SYMBIONESE LIBERATION ARMY—*See* HEARST, PATRICIA
SYMINGTON JR., J. FIFE—*See* CAMPAIGN FINANCING [12]

SYRIA—Syrian President Hafez al-Assad issued a series of decrees Aug. 12 shuffling the military command. Maj. Gen. Hikmat Khalil al-Shihabi was appointed chief of staff, replacing Maj. Gen. Youssef Chakkour, who was named a deputy defense minister. Maj. Gen. Naji Jamil also was appointed a deputy defense minister and retained his post as air force commander.

Under an agreement signed in Damascus Nov. 20, the U.S. was to provide Syria with 75,000 tons of wheat and 25,000 tons of rice at a cost of about $22 million. Syria was to pay for the shipments in dollars over 20 years, at 3% annual interest.

See also APPOINTMENTS & RESIGNATIONS; GERMANY, WEST [14]; GREECE [10]; IRAQ; ISRAEL; LIBYA; MIDDLE EAST [1-10, 22, 33, 36, 38, 41, 46]; NETHERLANDS [11]; OIL [4-6]

TANKERS—*See* Ships & Shipping

TANZANIA—President Julius K. Nyerere ended an official visit to China March 31, having met March 25 with Chairman Mao Tsetung, the third such meeting since 1965. Tanzanian Foreign Minister John Malecela announced an agreement April 1 under which China would provide Tanzania with an interest-free loan of about $75 million over five years to develop coal and iron ore mines in the South and link them with a railway.

President Nyerere warned Tanzanians April 4 not to waste or hoard food in the wake of spreading drought which had resulted in failure of most of the country's maize, rice and wheat crops. He said maize and wheat would be imported and noted that considerable foreign exchange would be lost because of the failure of cash crops normally sold abroad.

Tanzanian authorities announced the release of 29 political detainees from mainland jails April 28. Most had been arrested in connection with the 1964 Zanzibar revolution or the 1972 assassination of that island's leader. Among those freed were three former members of the Zanzibar Cabinet overthrown in the 1964 coup. (A Zanzibar court had convicted 44 persons and acquitted 17 others of treason at the end of a year-long trial stemming from the 1972 assassination, it was reported May 16.)

See also Famine & Food; Mozambique [7, 16]; Rhodesia; Uganda; United Nations [15]

TARIFFS & TRADE—Trade pact with U.S.S.R. Among the key developments in the U.S. word trade picture was the passage of a trade reform bill containing provisions linking trade concessions for the Soviet Union to Soviet emigration policy. Also included were anti-cartel provisions. [See below] The bill was passed Dec. 20 in the Senate by a 72-4 vote, and in the House by 323-36. [For a full description of the controversies and compromises leading to final passage, see the Union of Soviet Socialist Republics (U.S.S.R.).]

U.S. lead-import ruling. The U.S. Tariff Commission rejected April 3 a March 29 request from Treasury Secretary George Shultz to reverse its Jan. 10 decision ordering the imposition of special dumping duties on lead imports. The Tariff Commission had ruled that low-priced primary lead metal imports from Canada and Australia were harming U.S. industry. The duties had not yet been imposed. The U.S. imported about 13% of its primary imports from Canada and 7% from Australia, the two countries against which the tariff decision had been rendered. Shultz sought the reversal on the grounds that the tariff was not "consistent" with the government's anti-inflation effort.

The Treasury Department ordered the penalty duties imposed April 16. Describing the imposition of duties as "a ministerial act over which I have no discretion," Treasury Secretary Shultz reiterated his reluctance to issue the order and said the extra levies would "provoke an increase in U.S. lead prices while doing nothing to alleviate the current shortage of a product which is basic to our economy."

Wheat import quota suspended. President Nixon Jan. 25 lifted the import quota on wheat for five months to provide a "stabilizing effect" on domestic wheat prices, which were at record levels. Nongovernmental analysts predicted, however, that the Administration's use of higher priced foreign wheat, principally from Canada, to stabilize domestic prices would cause further increases in the cost of wheat for U.S. consumers. (New Agricultural Department figures released Jan. 30 showed that 714 million bushels of wheat were exported during the last six months of 1973. Their record value was $2.62 billion, more than triple the value of exports during the same period of 1972. China was the largest single purchaser within the six-month period, buying 95 million bushels worth $272.4 million.) The U.S. had set wheat import levels at 800,000 bushels annually but the quota had not been met since 1965 when the U.S. support price was higher than the world price. Since July 1, 1973, less than 100,000 bushels had been imported.

Raw materials parley ends. The U.N. General Assembly's special session on raw materials and world development ended May 2 following approval the night before of two documents largely drafted by underdeveloped nations—an action program and a declaration of principles for a "new international economic order." The documents, approved without a vote, were considered weak, but they signaled a change in relations between the world's rich and poor countries, according to many delegates. British Ambassador Ivor Richardson said May 2: "This Assembly will, in later years, be seen as a turning point . . . . Things will never be the same again."

The meeting, which had begun April 9, had been preceeded March 19-22 in Algiers with a conference of the 75 members of the nonaligned nations. Keynote of that conference was an opening day speech by Algerian Minister of Foreign Affairs Abdelaziz Bouteflika who, citing the "joint action" of the oil-producing states, called for a similar response by Third World nations with regard to their raw materials. In a final, 17-page communique issued March 22, the conference warned the industrial powers that the nonaligned nations would, if necessary, work unilaterally to obtain what they considered a fair price for their raw materials. (The raw materials threat was linked to a Mideast solution March 20 when Saudi Oil Minister Sheik Ahmed Zaki al-Yamani warned that failure to solve the problem might result in "very serious increases in raw material prices.") The General Assembly session had been sought by Algeria who, it was reported, sought to deflect mounting criticism of Arab oil producers for oil policies which had hurt poor as well as prosperous nations.

Algerian President Houari Boumedienne addressed the session April 10. Boumedienne minimized the damage done by rising oil prices, asserting: "The impact of oil in overall cost makeup has always been ridiculously small." He said current inflation was caused by "over-consumption and gadgetization," and waste that was "rampant throughout the developed countries." U.S. Secretary of State Henry Kissinger appeared before the session April 15. He pledged a major effort by the U.S. to help developing countries, but warned against use of "the politics of pressure and threats." Kissinger warned commodity producers against jointly raising prices as had members of the Organization of Petroleum Exporting Countries. "Large price increases coupled with production restrictions involve potential disaster: global inflation followed by global recession from which no nation could escape," he asserted.

The action program, as finally approved, included establishment of an emergency operation to help the world's poorest countries maintain essential imports over the next 12 months (with a call on industrialized nations and other potential contributors to announce their aid by June 15); and establishment of a special fund under U.N. auspices, with voluntary contributions from industrialized countries and others, to provide emergency relief and development assistance beginning Jan. 1, 1975. The action program also proposed improved trade and commodity arrangements and more favorable financial terms for poor countries. The declaration of principles included provisions upholding the right of countries to nationalize their industries (without any reference to prompt and adequate compensation); a demand that developing nations be compensated for past exploitation by colonialists and others; a call for development of cartel-like associations of poor nations; and link of any rise in the price of manufactured goods to the price of the raw materials produced by the poorer countries.

Earlier, in his second annual international economic report to Congress Feb. 7, President Nixon had warned that the U.S. "has moved from an era of near self-sufficiency to one of rising dependence on foreign resources with a concomitant need to earn more foreign exchange to pay for these imports." But, Nixon added, it was unlikely that nations producing these vital raw materials could exploit their advantageous trade position by forming a cartel or "monopoly" similar to the Arab's control of the petroleum market.

Nixon cited four obstacles to the formation of such a cartel: (1) Extractive (or producing) nations would experience significant unemployment if any attempt were made to cut back production and hence control supply while forcing up prices. Arab countries, successful in this strategy, were unaffected by unemployment troubles during the period of production cutback. (2) Arab countries were able to absorb the losses caused by a reduction in sales volume during this production slowdown period (and during the later embago) because they had ample supplies of foreign reserves to cushion the drop in revenues. Extractive states, which in most cases were also the poorer, developing nations, lacked the foreign reserves to carry them through this tight period of curtailed production. (3) While the demand for oil has continued to rise, the demand for certain other raw materials has been more closely associated with worldwide economic trends and in the course of an international slowdown, demand could decline. (4) In a period of reduced demand, producing countries lacked a strong bargaining position. It was possible that the situation could be reversed as extractive nations competed for markets.

OECD pledges to bar trade curbs. The governments of 24 non-Communist industrial nations belonging to the Organization for Economic Cooperation and Development (OECD) agreed May 30 not to impose unilateral trade restrictions for one year while efforts were made to resolve trade problems resulting from inflation and the quadrupling of imported oil prices. (New Zealand joined the organization May 29, 1973.) A code of good conduct, barring protectionist trade actions such as unilateral restrictions on imports and incentives to stimulate exports, was adopted at the conclusion of the OECD's two-day conference in Paris. Member nations also agreed to abstain from "destructive competition in official support of export credits," but no sanctions were voted against nations violating the good conduct pledge.

Court voids 1971 Nixon import surcharge. The U.S. Customs Court in New

York City ruled July 8 that President Nixon had exceeded his constitutional authority in 1971 when he imposed a 10% import tax surcharge. In its unanimous decision, the three-judge panel ordered the Treasury Department to refund the $481 million it had collected during the last four months of 1971 when the tax was in effect. Designed to reverse the U.S.'s deteriorating international balance of payments position, the surcharge was imposed Aug. 15, 1971, the same date that Nixon announced a 90-day wage-price freeze. In a strongly worded opinion, Chief Judge Nils A. Boe concluded that Nixon's action "exceeded authority delegated to the President." Only Congress had the power to levy and collect taxes, duties, imposts and excises and to regulate foreign commerce, Boe said.

Court approves voluntary trade curb. The U.S. Circuit Court of Appeals for the District of Columbia Oct. 15 affirmed by a 2-1 vote a lower court ruling that the President could arrange "voluntary" trade restraints with foreign steel producers. The decision concerned a 1969 agreement between the State Department and steel makers in Japan and the European Coal and Steel Community, under which the manufacturers consented to limit exports to the U.S. The State Department also agreed not to seek import restrictions through duty increases, quotas or other actions.

See also AGRICULTURE; ALUMINUM; ARGENTINA [15, 18]; AUSTRALIA [12, 20-22]; AVIATION [2, 5-6]; BANGLA DESH; BANKS & BANKING; BRAZIL [11-12]; BULGARIA; CANADA [22, 26-34]; CHILE [23-26]; CHINA, COMMUNIST; COFFEE; COPPER; CUBA; CZECHOSLOVAKIA; DAHOMEY; ECONOMY, U.S. [27]; ECUADOR; EGYPT; ENERGY CRISIS [26-27, 29]; EUROPEAN ECONOMIC COMMUNITY; FINLAND; GERMANY, WEST [16]; INDIA; IRAN; JAPAN [14]; LATIN AMERICA; MEXICO [4-5, 21]; MONETARY DEVELOPMENTS [12]; NIXON, RICHARD M.; OIL; PAKISTAN; POLAND; RUMANIA; SHIPS & SHIPPING; SUGAR; SWEDEN; SYRIA; UNION OF SOVIET SOCIALIST REPUBLICS [3, 5-15]; URUGUAY; YUGOSLAVIA [9]

TAXES—California tax credit voided. A three-judge federal panel in San Francisco ruled unconstitutional Feb. 1 a 1972 California law allowing up to $125 in personal income tax credits for each child attending private school. Citing a 1973 U.S. Supreme Court decision involving New York, the panel said the California law had a similarly improper result—"state sponsorship of religious activity." The court noted that the law would benefit only those taxpayers sending their children to sectarian schools, a "substantial majority" of which were Catholic schools with religious instruction as part of the curriculum.

A California superior court judge ruled in Los Angeles April 10 that the district-by-district property tax system of school financing violated equality guarantees of the state constitution, and ordered that alternative methods be found. The ruling, which allowed the current system to remain in effect until a comprehensive new plan could be devised, came in a six-year-old suit which had been sent back to the lower court for trial.

Suits to halt tax status changes barred. The Supreme Court ruled May 15 that non-profit organizations that lost their tax-exempt status could not sue to enjoin the Internal Revenue Service (IRS) from collecting taxes while their lawsuits seeking to restore their exemptions were being contested in court. An organization originally denied an exemption or one that lost its exemption would have to pay its taxes when they were due and then test the IRS's action in a suit seeking a refund, the court said.

House delays tax bill. The House Ways and Means Committee Nov. 21 approved a tax bill that would phase out the oil depletion allowance, raise the industry's taxes by about $3 billion and lower taxes by about $2 billion for low- and middle-income taxpayers. The oil depletion allowance permitted a producer to exempt the first 22% of income from taxation, a tax savings for the industry estimated at $2 billion a year. The committee's bill would reduce the exemption to 15% in 1974, eliminate it for about three-fourths of all U.S. oil in 1975 and for the remainder in 1979. A "windfall profits tax" would also be imposed on the industry to raise about $1 billion in 1975. The income tax changes for individuals would increase the standard deduction from 15% to 16%, the maximum standard deduction from $2,000 to $2,300 and the income level for exemption from taxation, e.g., from $4,300 to $4,900 for a family of four. A tax change for utilities also was provided to permit them the 7% tax write-off on modernization and expansion permitted other corporations.

In a separate piece of legislation, the committee approved Nov. 21 an income tax exemption, designed to aid the housing industry, on the first $500 of interest earned on savings accounts.

President Ford expressed support for the tax bill at his news conference Dec. 2. It provided "needed tax relief for low-income citizens while taxing windfall profits of certain oil companies," he said. "I don't support every provision in this committee bill but on balance it is a good bill and badly needed at this time."

The bill was defeated Dec. 12 when the House Rules Committee refused on a 9-5 vote to permit the House to consider it. Opponents argued it was too late in the session to consider a major tax bill and some preferred to have the more liberal incoming Congress consider tax revision.

Henderson convicted on tax charges. Conductor Skitch Henderson was convicted by a federal court jury in New York City Dec. 12 on charges that he filed false federal income tax returns in 1969 and 1970 by reporting that a music library he donated to a university was worth $350,000. He was found not guilty on two other charges of tax evasion in 1970 and obstruction of a 1971 tax audit. He was accused of attempting to evade a 1969 tax law change by backdating the gift of his music library of several hundred compositions to the University of Wisconsin.

10 firms paid no '73 federal taxes. Ten major U.S. corporations, including four banking firms, paid no federal income taxes in 1973, despite combined profits of $976.3 million, according to Rep. Charles Vanik (D, Ohio). Another 20 firms, with profits totaling $5.3 billion, paid an effective federal income tax rate of 1%-10%, he charged Dec. 18. Vanik, a member of the House Ways and Means Committee, said the study, conducted by his staff and the Congressional Joint Committee on Internal Revenue Taxation, proved the need for tax reform because, in failing to pay federal taxes, the corporations violated no laws. They merely took advantage of existing tax subsidies and other advantages, Vanik said. The survey examined data on 143 major companies. According to the report, they paid an effective federal income tax rate of 23.6% less than half the statutory corporate tax rate of 48%. The 10 companies paying no federal taxes: Freeport Minerals Co.; Texas Gulf Inc.; United Air Lines; Trans World Airlines; Consolidated Edison Co. of New York; American Electric Power Co.; Western Bancorp.; Chemical New York Corp.; Bankers Trust New York Corp.; and Continental Illinois Corp. Twelve oil firms surveyed paid an effective income tax rate of 9.6% in 1973, up from 7.9% in the previous year.

TELEPHONES & TELEGRAPHS—*See* ANTITRUST ACTIONS [7]; PRESS; PUERTO RICO; SPACE [8]

TELEVISION & RADIO—Ford Foundation to end public TV aid. The Ford Foundation, one of the major supporters of public, noncommercial television, decided to end its financial aid, it was reported Jan. 24. A foundation spokesman said an "orderly withdrawal" over the next four or five years had been decided upon because public television was becoming increasingly able to stand on its own as government appropriations and viewer donations grew.

Eased cable TV rules urged. A White House report, released Jan. 16 by the Office of Telecommunications Policy, called for division of the cable television industry into cable system operators and independent programming organizations, and eventual removal of most government regulation. The report, prepared by a Cabinet committee, recommended that cable TV be given the same freedom-of-the-press status as the print media: subject to the strictures of copyright, antitrust, libel and obscenity laws, but exempt from the fairness and equal time rules applied to broadcast media. The report also recommended that TV networks, local broadcasters and newspapers be permitted to enter the cable industry either as system owners or programmers. (Current Federal Communications Commission [FCC] regulations prevented network ownership of cable operations and ownership by local stations of cable systems within their broadcast area.) "Pay-TV," involving a charge per program on top of subscription fees, the report said, should be unregulated except for a current FCC rule preventing cable TV from taking live sports events from broadcasters and transmitting them on Pay-TV.

Cable TV wins copyright ruling. The Supreme Court ruled 6-3 March 4 that cable television systems were not subject to U.S. copyright laws when they imported distant TV signals and broadcast them to paid subscribers. In 1968, the court had exempted cable TV from payment of royalties for copyrighted programs originating locally.

TV Emmy Awards. The 26th Annual Emmy Awards were announced in Los Angeles May 28 by the National Academy of Television Arts and Sciences. "The Autobiography of Miss Jane Pittman," (CBS) the fictional story of a 110-year-old former slave, played by Cicely Tyson, was named best drama special with Miss Tyson winning the actress of the year award for a special. Other winners: **Comedy series**—*M*A*S*H* (CBS). **Variety series (musical category)**—*The Carol Burnett Show* (CBS). **Actor (comedy series)**—Alan Alda in *M*A*S*H*. **Actress (comedy series)**—Mary Tyler Moore in *The Mary Tyler Moore Show* (CBS). **Actor (drama)**—Hal Holbrook in *Pueblo* (ABC). **Drama (series)**—*Upstairs, Downstairs* (PBS). **Sports award program**—ABC's *Wide World of Sports* and Jim McKay, host. **Children's special**—Marlo Thomas, *Free to Be You and Me* (ABC). **Comedy, variety or music special**—*Lily* (CBS). **Limited series**—*Columbo* (NBC). **Director (series)**—Robert Butler for *The Blue Knight,* Part III (NBC). **Director (special program)**—Dwight Hemion, for *Barbra Streisand and Other Musical Instruments* (CBS). **Writer (series)**—Treva Silverman, *The Lou and Edie Story* of *The Mary Tyler Moore Show* series. **Writer (special)**—Fay Kanin for *Tell Me Where It Hurts* (CBS). **Supporting actress (comedy)**—Cloris Leachman, *The Mary Tyler Moore Show.* **Supporting actor (comedy)**—Rob Reiner, *All in the Family* (CBS). **Supporting actress in a special (drama)**—Joanna Miles, *The Glass Menagerie* (ABC). **Supporting actor in a special (drama)**—Michael Moriarty, *The Glass Menagerie.* **Supporting actress (comedy, variety)**—Brenda Vaccaro, *The Shape of Things.* **Supporting actor (comedy, variety)**—Harvey Korman, *The Carol Burnett Show.*

FCC 'fairness' ruling voided. A three-judge federal appeals panel in Washington Sept. 27 overturned a 1973 decision by the FCC that NBC had violated the agency's fairness doctrine in a broadcast of a documentary program critical of pension plans. By a 2-1 vote, the court reversed the FCC order requiring NBC to televise additional material favorable to pension systems to counteract the weight of the original program ("Pensions: the Broken Promise" in 1972). The court said the fairness doctrine was still valid but cautioned the FCC that "editorial judgments of the licensee mustn't be disturbed if reasonable and in good faith." The court said that especially in regard to investigative journalism, the broadcaster's judgment was not to be overturned unless the FCC could make a clear showing that "the licensee has been unreasonable and that there has been an abuse of journalistic discretion rather than an exercise of that discretion."

Networks win suit dismissal. Judge Robert J. Kelleher of U.S. District Court in Los Angeles dismissed an antitrust suit brought against the three major television networks by former Attorney General John Mitchell in 1972, it was disclosed Nov. 15. The suit charged that the networks had monopolized prime time programming by broadcasting only those shows which they produced or in which they had substantial interests. The government had asked that the networks be prohibited from obtaining financial interests in programs from independent producers. Lawyers for the networks argued that the suit had been filed by the Nixon Administration to harass the networks because they had broadcast news that the Administration did not like. The suit was dismissed "without prejudice," permitting the Justice Department to refile separate civil antitrust suits against each of the three networks Dec. 10.

See also BOXING; CANADA [2]; COPYRIGHT; GAMBLING; OBITUARIES [BENNY, BRENNAN, HUNTLEY, MCGEE, SULLIVAN]; PRESS; SPACE [3, 8]; UNION OF SOVIET SOCIALIST REPUBLICS [18]

TENNESSEE—*See* ELECTIONS [5, 7]; WEATHER; WOMEN'S RIGHTS

TENNIS—WCT severs USLTA relations. World Championship Tennis (WCT) announced Jan. 24 it would no longer recognize the authority of the U.S. Lawn Tennis Association (USLTA), the ruling body for U.S. amateur tennis. Lamar Hunt, WCT president, said WCT would arrange its own schedule of events and cease to pay sanctioning fees of $20,000 a year to the USLTA. Hunt said the "WCT has come to question whether there is justification for an amateur body to assert nationwide control of professional tennis." However, Hunt added that the WCT tour would not compete with the USLTA-sponsored U.S. Open (Forest Hills) or the national championships in England (Wimbledon), France and Italy, all sanctioned by bodies federated with the USLTA.

Europeans bar WTT players. The French Tennis Federation, protesting an agreement between the International Lawn Tennis Federation (ILTF) and the nascent World Team Tennis (WTT) organization, walked out of an ILTF meeting in Paris Feb. 15 and announced that the French championships, both indoor and outdoor, would not be open to players signing WTT contracts. The French were quickly joined by sanctioning bodies from eight other European nations, all of which announced similar decisions. The ILTF and WTT Feb. 14 had reached an agreement whereby WTT would play the ILTF $48,000 a year for recognition and arrange its schedules so as not to conflict with the Davis Cup, the U.S. Open and other national competitions. As part of the pact, special provisions were to be made for the French and Italian Opens: certain WTT players were to be assured places in these tournaments and their earnings were to be guaranteed. Offered this and other complicated options, the French walked out of the meeting. Meanwhile, WTT began its first season of play May 6, with 16 teams in the U.S. and Canada.

South Africa wins Davis Cup. South Africa won the Davis cup by default Oct. 4 when India refused to play in the cup's finals competition because of South Africa's policy of apartheid. South Africa had advanced to the final round with a victory over Italy, and India had defeated the Soviet Union. (The Soviets had also indicated they would not play the South Africans in the cup finals). The U.S. team had been eliminated Jan. 13 by Colombia. Australia, the defending champion, had been defeated by the Indian team May 14. It was the first time since 1937 that the Davis cup had been won by a country other than the U.S. or Australia.

Newcombe captures WCT title. John Newcombe of Australia won the WCT title May 12, defeating Bjorn Borg of Sweden 4-6, 6-3, 6-3, 6-2. The WCT finals, held in Dallas, culminated a nine-week 28 event tour worth $1.5 million in prize money. The tour was divided into three groups—Red, White and Blue—of 28 players each, with the top two players from each group and two other players from any group with the most accumulated points qualifying for the finals. Newcombe, who won $50,000, had defeated Stan Smith, 1973 WCT champion, to reach the finals, and Borg had dispatched Jan Kodes.

Connors wins U.S., Wimbledon titles. Jimmy Connors, 22, crushed veteran Australian tennis professional, Ken Rosewall, 6-1, 6-0, 6-1, to capture the men's singles title of the U.S. Open at Forest Hills, N.Y. Sept. 9. Connors had also faced Rosewall, 39, in the finals of the All England Championship at Wimbledon July 6, defeating him 6-1, 6-1, 6-4. Connors needed only 78 minutes to win at Forest Hills and 90 minutes at Wimbledon. Connors received $22,500 for his victory in the U.S. Open; at Wimbledon he earned $25,000.

Connors, winner of the Australian Open Jan. 1, was denied a chance to complete a grand slam by the French Tennis Federation, which prohibited his participation in the French Open championships, the second leg of tennis' grand slam. The French had barred all players involved in the new U.S. WTT League. Connors and Evonne Goolagong, winner of the women's singles title in the Australian Open, filed suit in Paris May 30 to challenge the ban but failed to receive a favorable ruling. (Connors played for the Baltimore entry of the WTT and Goolagong for the Pittsburgh team.) Despite not appearing in the French Open, Connors received an additional $35,000 Sept. 9 for the best record in grand slam competition.

In the women's singles finals at Forest Hills Sept. 9, Goolagong lost to Billie Jean King 3-6, 6-3, 7-5. King, who won the singles title for the fourth time, received $22,500. In the semifinals the day before, Goolagong had defeated Chris Evert, ending a victory streak by Evert of 56 straight matches and 10 straight tournaments. Evert had beated Russia's Olga Morozova 6-0, 6-4 for the All England women's singles title July 5. In Paris June 16, Evert had defeated Morozova 6-1, 6-2 for the singles title of the French Open.

Denver wins first WTT title. The Denver Racquets edged the Philadelphia Freedoms 28-24 to win the first WTT championship Aug. 26. That victory, combined with a 27-21 win by Denver Aug. 25, gave the Racquets a 2-0 triumph in the best of three series. In semifinal play, Denver had eliminated Minnesota and Philadelphia had defeated Pittsburgh.

Vilas wins Grand Prix title. Guillermo Vilas of Argentina, who began the year as an obscure pro, clinched the $96,000 Commercial Union Grand Prix award with a first-round victory in the Argentine tournament in Buenos Aires Nov. 19. The win gave him an unsurmountable lead in the Grand Prix circuit point standings over U.S. pro Jimmy Connors. Including his triumph in the Masters Grand Prix tournament in Melbourne, Australia Dec. 15, Vilas won seven Grand Prix events. His 1974 earnings exceeded $225,000.

USLTA ranks Connors, Evert No. 1. The USLTA announced Dec. 10 that it had ranked Jimmy Connors, winner of the U.S. and Australian Opens and at Wimbledon, as the No. 1 men's singles player in the U.S. for 1974. Following Connors in the men's rankings were Stan Smith, Marty Reissen, Roscoe Tanner and Arthur Ashe. The USLTA said Dec. 12 that it had ranked Chris Evert, winner of 15 tournaments during the year, as the top U.S. women's singles player for 1974. Evert was followed in the rankings by Billie Jean King, Rosemary Casals, Nancy Gunter and Julie Heldman.

See also OBITUARIES [WIGHTMAN]

terHORST, J. F.—*See* APPOINTMENTS & RESIGNATIONS; ELECTIONS [13]; FORD, GERALD R.; POLITICS [1]; WATERGATE [64-65]

TERRITORIAL WATERS—Aegean Sea conflict. Turkish and Greek officials made "representations" to one another's governments in a dispute over sovereignty in the Aegean Sea, it was reported Feb. 25, following the Greek announcement of oil and natural gas finds off the island of Thassos. Turkey had awarded two U.S. companies exploration rights in the eastern Aegean, in areas it considered international waters. In their claims, the two governments presented conflicting interpretations of the doctrine of the continental shelf, the criterion adopted by the 1958 Geneva convention for determining territorial waters. Turkey, which signed but did not ratify the document, held that continental shelf jurisdiction did not extend to the Greek islands; Greece insisted that its more than 350 Aegean islands had a legitimate continental shelf. Turkey sent a naval research vessel, accompanied by minesweepers, submarines and a cruiser, to the disputed Aegean waters in search of oil May 29. Unconfirmed reports from Athens May 29 said that Greek troops had been placed on alert, that leaves had been canceled and that additional aircraft had been moved into Salonika. Following an April 16 announcement by the state-owned Turkish Petroleum Company that it would soon begin prospecting for oil, Greek Premier Adamantios Androutsopoulos warned May 8 that any attempt by Ankara to explore for oil in what Greece considered its territorial waters would be regarded as a belligerent act.

A discussion June 27 between Greek Premier Androutsopoulos and Turkish Premier Bulent Ecevit on contested Aegean Sea rights ended in a deadlock, according to Athens and Ankara sources. The meeting was held in Brussels during the North Atlantic Treaty Organization (NATO) summit which the two leaders were attending. A Greek proposal May 25 that discussions be conducted on the basis of the 1958 Geneva convention on territorial limits had been rejected June 5 by Ankara which claimed that negotiations must be conducted "without preconditions." Greece had announced that it planned to extend its territorial waters from six to 12 miles, it was reported June 9. The Turkish foreign minister said Ankara would not accept such an action. It was reported June 16 that a Turkish research ship had been sent on a second survey mission into the Aegean to search for oil; in response, Greece had placed its forces on partial alert. The Turkish government announced that it would grant four more licenses for oil exploration in the Aegean, according to a July 8 report. Turkey announced July 18 that it had extended its territorial waters in the Aegean Sea. A map published in the official gazette indicated that Ankara had unilaterally expanded its jurisdiction to cover an additional 3,900 square miles toward the median line dividing the Turkish mainland and the Greek coast.

World Court rules on 'cod war.' The International Court of Justice at The Hague July 25 ruled 10-4 that Iceland's unilateral decision in 1972 to extend its fishing limits from 12 to 50 nautical miles could not apply to Britain or West Germany. In separate decisions the court said British and West German fishing vessels could not be excluded by unilateral action from the disputed area. Iceland, which had maintained the court had no jurisdiction and refused to plead its case, rejected the ruling. The sometimes violent dispute with Britain had ended in 1973 with a two-year agreement limiting Britain's annual catch in the disputed zone.

Sea law parley inconclusive. The 3rd U.N. Conference on the Law of the Sea, which had opened June 20, adjourned in Caracas, Venezuela Aug. 29, after more than 5,000 delegates and observers from 148 nations failed to agree on any of the more than 100 issues they discussed. The conference was reportedly the largest international meeting in history. The delegates voted Aug. 26 to hold a follow-up session in Geneva March 17-May 3, 1975, to draft a treaty to replace the 17th century code governing use of the world's oceans.

The conference was deadlocked on four major issues on which industrialized nations, led by the U.S. and U.S.S.R., opposed underdeveloped countries, backed by China. The issues were:

National sovereignty—Virtually all nations supported extension of territorial waters from three to 12 miles, and establishment of a further 188-mile "economic zone" in which coastal states would have the right to exploit natural resources. However, many developing nations also wanted control over fishing, navigation, scientific research and antipollution measures in the economic zone, which the rich nations opposed.

Deep sea mining—Developing nations sought creation of a strong international seabed authority to exercise tight control over mineral exploitation licenses in the area outside national jurisdiction.

Straits passage—The 12-mile territorial limit would place more than 100 straits within the jurisdiction of individual countries. The U.S., Great Britain and the Soviet Union insisted there be unimpeded passage through straits for all ships including warships. Many developing countries, in whose waters the straits would fall, demanded for coastal states the right to control the passage of military shipping, insisting on prior notice of such traffic and the right to refuse passage under certain circumstances.

Pollution control—The developing nations sought mild controls for themselves and strict ones for the industrialized nations. The industrialized countries wanted uniform international standards.

See also NORWAY

TERRORISM—*See* ARGENTINA [5-14]; ATOMIC ENERGY [13]; AVIATION [14]; CANADA [7]; DOMINICAN REPUBLIC; FRANCE [9]; GERMANY, WEST [8]; HEARST, PATRICIA; IRELAND, NORTHERN [8-15]; IRELAND, REPUBLIC OF; ITALY [10-12]; LIBYA; MEXICO [6-16]; MIDDLE EAST [18-33, 35-36]; NETHERLANDS [11-13]; NICARAGUA; SPAIN [12-14]; SUDAN; URUGUAY; WEST INDIES ASSOCIATED STATES

TEXAS—*See* ELECTIONS [7]; WEATHER

TEXTILE INDUSTRY—*See* ANTITRUST ACTIONS [10]

THAILAND—U.S. withdraws forces. The U.S. troop withdrawal, begun in September 1973, continued during 1974. According to a Defense Department spokesman, the reduction of forces was made possible because "the situation had stabilized" in Indochina in recent months. Nearly 600 Americans began leaving Jan. 2; about 10,000 members of the Air Force and one-third of the B-52s and fighter-bombers were to be withdrawn in the months following negotiation of a new agreement in March. (In January the U.S. had removed 25 EB-66 electronic warfare planes.) The Thai Supreme Command announced June 28 that agreement had been reached on the U.S. withdrawal from two of its six remaining air bases by the end of 1974. Air America, funded by the U.S. Central Intelligence Agency, ceased flying from Thailand June 30.

CIA controversy. Thailand formally complained to the U.S. Jan. 17 over a note a CIA agent had sent to the government which purported to be from a Thai rebel leader seeking peace with Bangkok. The U.S. embassy acknowledged the note after three Bangkok newspapers reported on the matter. The CIA letter was said to have been sent by a U.S. agent to Premier Sanya Dharmasaki from the provincial capital of Sakon Nakhon, in an area where 1,600-2,000 rebels were believed to be operating. The message, signed on behalf of the Communist Party of Thailand in the northeast, proposed a cease-fire in exchange for local autonomy in "liberated areas" near the Laotian border. The agent was said to have sent the letter in the belief that it would increase defections of the rebels to the government side. A Foreign Ministry statement said U.S. Ambassador William N. Kintner had met with Premier Sanya and was told of "the dissatisfaction of the students and people" with the CIA's "interference in the internal affairs of Thailand." Kintner apologized and assured Sanya that the agent responsible for the letter had been returned to the U.S. U.S. officials in Washington announced Jan. 18 plans to reduce the 150-man CIA force in Thailand and to limit its operations in the country. Most of the CIA agents were involved in counter-insurgency and the rest in combatting drug smuggling from Burma.

Premier withdraws resignation. Sanya resigned as premier of Thailand May 21, but later withdrew his resignation following public and political appeals that he remain at his post. Sanya was named to succeed himself in a royal decree issued May 27. A military alert had been delared throughout the country after Sanya's announcement.

New Constitution approved. Thailand's new Constitution was approved by the National Assembly by a 280-6 vote Oct. 5. The charter, providing for a popularly elected 240-300 member House of Representatives and a 100-member Senate chosen by a king, was promulgated by King Phumiphol Aduldet Oct. 7. Students had been demanding the abolition of the proposed Senate and a clause requiring parliamentary approval of the stationing of foreign troops in Thailand. This would apply to U.S. air bases that were sanctioned by the previous government.

Thanom returns; expelled. Exiled former Premier Thanom Kittikachorn was placed under house arrest after secretly returning to Thailand from the U.S. Dec. 27. He was expelled from the country Dec. 29. Thanom had left Thailand for the U.S. after a student uprising in October 1973 forced him to resign.

See also BURMA; JAPAN [10]; LAOS; VIETNAM, REPUBLIC OF [32]

THEATER—Tony awards. The 28th annual Antoinette Perry (Tony) awards for distinguished achievement in the Broadway theater during the 1973-74 season were presented April 21 by the League of New York Theaters under the auspices of the American Theater Wing in New York. *The River Niger,* a drama of a black family whose son had returned from the service, was cited as the best Broadway play. *Candide* won five Tony awards. Other winners. **Musical—** *Raisin.* **Dramatic actor**—Michael Moriarty, *Find Your Way Home.* **Dramatic actress**—Colleen Dewhurst, *A Moon for the Misbegotten.* **Musical actor**—Christopher Plummer, *Cyrano.* **Musical actress**—Virginia Capers, *Raisin.* **Dramatic supporting actor**—Ed Flanders, *A Moon for the Misbegotten.* **Dramatic supporting actress**—Frances Sternhagen, *The Good Doctor.* **Musical supporting actor**—Tommy Tune, *Seesaw.* **Musical supporting actress**—Janie Sell, *Over Here.* **Dramatic director**—Jose Quintero, *A Moon for the Misbegotten.* **Musical Director**—Harold Prince, *Candide.*

Scenic design—Franne and Eugene Lee, *Candide.* **Book**—Hugh Wheeler, *Candide.* **Costume design**—Franne Lee, *Candide.* **Lighting design**—Jules Fisher, *Ulysses in Nighttown.* **Choreography**—Michael Bennett, *Seesaw.* **Musical score—**

Frederick Loewe, Alan Lerner, *Gigi.* **Special awards**—Dramatic revival of an American play, *A Moon For The Misbegotten.* Artistic development of the musical theater, *Candide.* Contribution to the theater of comedy, Peter Cook and Dudley Moore, *Good Evening.* Concert entertainment—Bette Midler and Liza Minnelli.

Off-Broadway 'Obies.' The 19th annual Obie Awards for achievement in off-Broadway and off-off-Broadway theater were presented in New York June 2. *The Village Voice,* a weekly newspaper, was the sponsor. The winners: **Best play**—*Short Eyes* by Miguel Pinero. **Distinguished plays**—*Bad Habits* by Terrence McNally, *When You Comin' Back, Red Ryder?* by Mark Medoff and *The Great MacDaddy* by Paul C. Harrison. **Best foreign play**—*The Contractor* by David Storey. **Distinguished direction**—Marvin F. Camillo, *Short Eyes,* Robert Drivas, *Bad Habits,* David Licht, *Hard to Be a Jew,* John Pasquin, *Moonchildren* and Harold Prince, *Candide.* **Distinguished performances**—Barbara Barrie, *The Killdeer,* Joseph Buloff, *Hard to Be a Jew,* Conchata Ferrell, *The Sea Horse,* Loretta Greene, *The Sirens,* Barbara Montgomery, *My Sister, My Sister,* Zipora Spaizman, *Stepenyu,* Elizabeth Sturges and Kevin Conway, *When You Comin' Back, Red Ryder?* **Music**—Bill Elliott, *C.O.R.F.A.X.* **Costumes**—Theoni Aldredge, The Public Theater. **Set Design**—Holmes Easley, The Roundabout Theater, and Christopher Thomas, *The Lady from the Sea.* **Special citations**—The Bread & Puppet Theater; The Brooklyn Academy of Music for British Theater Season; CSC Repertory Company and Robert Wilson for *The Life and Times of Joseph Stalin.*

See also OBITUARIES [CORNELL, MOOREHEAD]

TOGO—President Etienne Eyadema charged that the French Compagnie Togolaise des Mines du Benin had tried to kill him by causing the crash of an airplane in which he was flying Jan. 24, it was reported Feb. 2. Two Togolese and French technical assistance officers were killed in the crash. Eyadema had announced Jan. 10 an increase from 35% to 51% in the government share of the company, but raised this to 100% after the crash, it was reported Feb. 2.

Eyadema announced May 8 that he had dropped his "imported Christian first name" and would henceforth use the African first name of Gnassingbe. He said he was remaining a Christian and did not mean for his countrymen to follow his example.

TORNADOES—*See* WEATHER

TRACK & FIELD—Neil Cusack, an East Tennessee State University student from Ireland, won the 78th running of the Boston Marathon April 15. He completed the 26-mile, 385-yard course ahead of the other 1,704 starters in the time of 2:13:39. In the 98th annual Intercollegiate Association of Amateur Athletics of America (IC4-A) outdoor track and field competition in Pittsburgh May 25, the Penn State University team was victorious. New world records were set during 1974 for the following important events: *1,500 meter run* (3:32.2) Feb. 2 by Filbert Bayi of Tanzania in Christchurch, New Zealand; *100 yard dash* (9.0) May 11 by Ivory Crockett of the U.S. in Knoxville, Tenn.; *Women's 200 meter dash* (22.0) June 13 by Irena Szewinska of Poland in Berlin; *Women's 400 meter run* (49.9) June 22 by Szewinska in Warsaw; *Women's high jump* (6'4.75") Sept. 8 by Rosemarie Witschas of East Germany in Rome; *Women's shot put* (70'8.25") Sept. 21 by Helena Fibingerova of Czechoslovakia in Gottwaldov, Czechoslovakia.

TRADE—*See* TARIFFS & TRADE

TRANSPORTATION—**Congress votes funds.** The fiscal 1975 appropriations for the Transportation Department and related agencies was passed in final form by the House Aug. 13 and Senate Aug. 15 and was signed by the President Aug.

28. The appropriations total of $3,237,625,000 was $239,354,552 less than the budget request and $339,178,994 more than the fiscal 1974 amount. Among the major items: Federal Aviation Administration—$1,693,439,000; Federal Railroad Administration—$199,002,000, of which $130,275,000 was for grants to Amtrak (National Railroad Passenger Corporation); Federal Highway Administration—$47,989,000, including $5,915,000 for motor carrier safety, $8,685,000 for highway safety research and development and $965,000 for highway beautification; National Highway Traffic Safety Administration—$70,874,000; Urban Mass Transportation Administration—$49,340,000; Coast Guard—$879,415,000; Civil Aeronautics Board—$84,878,000.

Transit grants reported. Several federal grants for urban mass transit were reported by the *Wall Street Journal* July 3-9. The awards by the Transportation Department were to cover 80% of project costs, with the remainder to come from local and state funds. Chicago received $70 million for modernization of bus and rail systems, including new buses, new rapid transit stations and track replacement. New York City received separate grants of $51.1 million and $33 million for bus purchases and subway improvement. The latter grant had previously been earmarked for highway construction. Separate grants totaling $95.9 million went to the Philadelphia area for subway, streetcar and commuter-line improvements, construction of a downtown-airport rail link and a downtown bus-pedestrian mall. Maryland received $60 million for a planned subway system in Baltimore and for new buses. The San Francisco area received $13 million to cover cost increases in previously-financed bus and ferryboat improvements and to purchase additional buses and other equipment.

Long-term mass transit aid enacted. A six-year, $11.8 billion mass transit program was cleared by Congress Nov. 21 and sent to President Ford who signed it into law Nov. 26. The President had urged passage of the bill during the concluding House debate Nov. 21. A large part of the bill's funds—$7.8 billion—was allotted to capital improvements, such as purchase of new buses and subway cars. The remainder was to be distributed according to local choice, either for additional capital improvements or for operating expenses. The long-term $11.8 billion version had been devised in a House-Senate conference committee with the strong support of President Ford and big-city mayors. New York Mayor Abraham Beame, whose city was expected to get $170 million from the bill in the current fiscal year, or possibly enough to keep the 35¢ subway fare from rising, was credited with proposing a key provision in the final version of the bill—an option for the cities to use up to 50% of their capital fund allotment for operating expenses provided that the funds were restored the following year.

See also APPOINTMENTS & RESIGNATIONS; AUTOMOBILES; AVIATION; BUDGET; ENERGY CRISIS [6]; HIGHWAYS; NIXON, RICHARD M.; RAILROADS; SCIENCE; SHIPS & SHIPPING

TREASURY, U.S. DEPARTMENT OF—*See* AGNEW, SPIRO T.; APPOINTMENTS & RESIGNATIONS; BANKS & BANKING; CIVIL RIGHTS [11]

TRINIDAD & TOBAGO—Prime Minister Eric Williams announced Jan. 17 that Texaco Trinidad Inc., a subsidiary of the U.S. firm Texaco Inc., had agreed in principle to sell participation in its local oil refinery to the government. Williams added that the government would build a new refinery in a joint venture with a Middle East nation. The nation was believed to be Iran, which had continued to ship oil to Trinidad's refineries despite the Arab oil embargo.

See also ALUMINUM & BAUXITE; LATIN AMERICA; SUGAR

TRUDEAU, PIERRE ELLIOT—*See* AUSTRALIA [23]; CANADA [3-8, 10-11, 13, 16, 24, 27, 32, 34]; JAPAN [11]

TUNISIA—40 students jailed in university unrest. The police and Public Order Brigade broke up demonstrations at the University of Tunis April 19, arresting 24 students who were sentenced the following day to a year's imprisonment and three who were given six-month sentences. The demonstrators were protesting sentences of four to six months given April 17 to 13 arrested students charged with "acts of violence." The major student demand had been for the free election of representatives to the national student union. Two hundred university professors issued a statement April 25 supporting the call for a representative student union and denouncing the April 19 police intervention on university grounds. Classes reportedly resumed three weeks later.

Bourguiba offers clemency. President Habib Bourguiba issued a clemency decree July 24, the day before the 16th anniversary of the republic, under which two opponents of his regime were released from prison. Ahmed Ben Salah, who had been sentenced to three additional years in June 1973 following his escape from prison, and an accomplice convicted with him in 1970 of high treason were both freed from a Tunis prison. Bourguiba July 23 pardoned some 40 youths jailed in April for participating in University of Tunis disturbances.

175 Marxists sentenced. The Tunisian High Court Aug. 24 sentenced 175 students, workers and intellectuals found guilty of "plotting, maintenance of an unauthorized association, offense against the chief of state and propagation of false information" to prison terms of six months to 10 years. Many of those convicted were members of the Socialist Study and Action Group of Tunisia, a Marxist organization headquartered in Paris. The defendants had admitted being Communists, (the Communist Party had been banned in Tunisia since 1963) but had denied plotting to overthrow the government.

Party congress enhances Bourguiba role. The ninth National Congress of the Destourian Socialist Party met in Monastir Sept. 12-15 and unanimously proclaimed Bourguiba president of the party for life, a step leading to his proclamation as president of the republic for life under forthcoming constitutional changes. Bourguiba had previously rejected the titles and had been re-elected by popular vote every five years since the republic's first elections in 1959. Running unopposed in general elections Nov. 3, Bourguiba was re-elected to a fourth consecutive five-year term as president.

Libyan merger delayed. Tunisia and Libya announced an agreement Jan. 12 to merge their two countries into a single nation to be known as the Islamic Arab Republic. Plans to implement the unification, however, were delayed following strong opposition from Algeria and Morocco and a Tunisian announcement that the proposed union required further consultations with Libya. Tunisia invited Algeria, Morocco and Mauritania to join the union.

See also AFRICA; ALGERIA; MIDDLE EAST [34]; OIL [8]

TURKEY—Government crisis. Acting Premier Naim Talu, who had been trying to form a government since December, 1973, tendered his resignation Jan. 10 after failing to assemble a national coalition or a coalition of right-wing parties. On Jan. 13 the Republican People's Party (RPP) and the National Salvation Party (NSP) announced they had agreed to form a coalition government. President Fahri Koruturk approved the arrangement Jan. 15 and formally asked RPP leader Bulent Ecevit to form a Cabinet. The coalition would give a dominant position to the moderate leftist RPP. The NSP would be the first avowedly Islamic party to enter a Turkish government since the republic was established in 1923. The coalition cabinet was formally approved Jan. 26. It included 17 RPP members and eight from the NSP. Ecevit assumed the post of premier; deputy premier was Necmettin Erbakan of the NSP.

Ecevit said, it was reported Jan. 17, that amnesty legislation planned by his party would exclude those held for violent political crimes, in deference to fears among armed forces leaders. The amnesty would include common crimes and crimes of conscience. However, when the amnesty bill was presented under Ecevit's auspices its provisions would have extended to approximately 4,000 political prisoners, in addition to freeing or reducing the sentences of about 50,000 others. Parliament eliminated the former provision in the bill and passed it May 15, causing the RPP to announce four days later it was withdrawing from the coalition, a move which would bring down the government. The RPP decision was rescinded May 20 after a meeting between Ecevit and Erbakan. The problem of political amnesty was resolved July 2 when the Constitutional Court ruled, by a 10-5 vote, to annul that section of the May law which had denied amnesty to political prisoners. Prisoner releases began July 12 when hundreds of Turkish intellectuals were freed. Also benefiting from the amnesty were three Americans, jailed on drug charges in 1972, who had their life sentences reduced to 24 years; and seven American servicemen also jailed on drug charges who were released. Two Lithuanians who had hijacked a Soviet airliner in 1970 and sought asylum in Turkey also were freed. The amnesty law also affected Turkey's political parties since many of the leaders of the banned Turkish Workers' Party (TWP) were released. A number of former TWP members participated in the formation of a new political party, the Turkish Socialist Workers' Party (TSWP) which was announced in Ankara June 22. The TSWP became the first legal left-wing organization to appear in Turkey since the 1971 ban on the TWP. President of the new party was Ahmet Kacmaz.

Government resigns. The shaky coalition between the RPP and the rightist NSP finally collapsed Sept. 18 as major differences arose over the issue of Cyprus. The RPP favored a negotiated settlement which would provide for an independent Cyprus with federated Greek and Turkish regions, while the NSP called for partition of the island and annexation of the Turkish section. Ecevit's resignation, however, was seen as an attempt to convert the popularity he had gained as a result of Turkey's actions on Cyprus into political support which would return him to power with a stronger and more cohesive government. Although President Fahri Koruturk on Sept. 20 asked Ecevit to form a new government, the premier was unable to do so. President Koruturk asked Justice Party leader Suleyman Demirel to try to form a government, but Demirel also failed in his attempt, he informed Koruturk Oct. 4. Ecevit, who had remained as caretaker premier, resigned for a second time Nov. 7, but agreed to remain in office "for a reasonable amount of time" during which, he said, either a new government must be formed or elections held.

Student violence hits Ankara. More than 70 persons were injured in violent student disturbances that erupted in Ankara Nov. 8 between left- and right-wing political groups. Army troops were called in to quell the armed battles.

New government formed. The government crisis ended briefly with the appointment Nov. 13 of an independent premier, Sadi Irmak, to head an interim government. Irmak, who was a senator and a professor of medicine, resigned Nov. 29 after losing a vote of confidence in the Grand National Assembly. President Koruturk asked Irmak to stay on in a caretaker capacity until a new government could be formed.

See also Aviation [10, 14]; Communism, International; Cyprus; European Security; Greece [1, 12]; Iraq; Narcotics & Dangerous Drugs; North Atlantic Treaty Organization; Oil [26]; Pakistan; Territorial Waters

TYPHOONS—*See* Weather

UGANDA—Military uprising quelled. President Idi Amin emerged in control of the country after defeating an apparent military coup attempt in Kampala March 24. Within 24 hours of re-establishing order, the military government had begun systematic killings of army officers believed involved in the abortive uprising, Ugandan sources said March 25. Most of those being executed were members of the Lugbara tribe and Christians; Amin was a Kakwa Moslem. (The 12,000-man army included 2,000 Lugbaras.) According to Ugandan sources quoted in Associated Press reports March 25, Amin might have provoked the outbreak among dissident troops to eliminate them. Tribal and religious conflicts had been brewing in the military for months, they said, and as many as 90,000 potential opponents of Amin had been massacred since 1971.

More than 300 Lugbara tribesmen had reportedly fled Uganda by March 31 to seek refuge in Zaire and the Sudan following the unsuccessful coup attempt March 24. The French newspaper *Le Monde* reported March 29 that 400 people had been executed in Kampala alone within six hours after President Amin reasserted control. Most of those killed were Christian Lugbaras believed involved in the abortive uprising.

Asian recruitment program. Having expelled some 50,000 Asians from Uganda in 1972-73, President Amin nonetheless dispatched a high-level delegation to Islamabad, Pakistan, April 19, to recruit skilled Pakistanis for employment in Uganda. The delegation interviewed doctors, engineers, teachers, technicians and accountants.

'Reign of terror' charged. The Geneva-based International Commission of Jurists released a 63-page report June 4 in which Amin was accused of creating a state in which there was "a total breakdown in the rule of law." The report charged that "the effect of . . . massive and continuing violations of human rights has been to create a reign of terror from which thousands of people, Africans as well as Asians, have sought refuge in voluntary exile. Those remaining are in a constant state of insecurity."

British, Kenyan papers banned. The Ministry of Information announced June 8 that, effective immediately, "all imperialist newspapers" would be banned from Uganda. Cited in the ban were four British papers, including the *London Times,* and all Kenyan newspapers. The ban followed accusations leveled by President Amin June 5 that Britain was disseminating "unfounded propaganda" about Uganda. The charge apparently arose from British reports of the highly critical International Commission of Jurists' study on Uganda released June 4. Amin warned that all Britons would be expelled from Uganda within two days if the reports did not cease. He said June 7 he would give Britain "one more chance."

Military alert at Tanzania border. President Amin Aug. 2 lifted a military alert he had imposed Aug. 1 in the face of an alleged threat from Tanzania. Kampala massed several thousand troops at the border and warned that it would invade Tanzania to establish a new, more defensible border along the Kagera River. (This would have involved the annexation of some 500 square miles of Tanzanian territory.) Dar es Salaam denied that an invasion of Uganda was planned but called an alert of Tanzanian troops and increased deployment along the border. The two nations' armies were of approximately equal strength, according to an Aug. 1 report.

British envoys expelled. Uganda announced Nov. 5 that Britain had to reduce its 50-member staff of its high commission in Kampala to five by Nov. 10. The staff would not be allowed to travel outside the capital without permission from the Ugandan Foreign Ministry. In an unusually swift retaliatory action Nov. 6, Britain ordered Uganda to cut its London diplomatic staff from 12 to five. President Amin had threatened Nov. 3 to expel all 1,500 British nationals from Uganda after renewing charges that the British press was defaming him and his country.

Foreign minister dismissed. President Amin Nov. 28 fired his foreign minister, Elizabeth Bagaya, "for the good of the country and the security of Uganda." In a Uganda radio announcement he charged that she had "made love to an unknown European in a toilet" at Paris' Orly airport and had contacts with British and American intelligence agents. She was placed under house arrest in Kampala Dec. 2 and released Dec. 6. Bagaya was defended by United Nations and French officials who expressed disbelief at the charges Nov. 29-30. Amin himself assumed the direction of the Foreign Ministry, according to a Dec. 1 report.

ULSTER—*See* Ireland, Northern

UNEMPLOYMENT—*See* Automobiles [1-9]; Economy, U.S. [1, 6, 10-13, 15, 18-20, 22, 27-28]; Labor [5-8]; Stock Market [1]

UNION OF SOVIET SOCIALIST REPUBLICS (U.S.S.R.)

Soviet-U.S. Relations

[1] The spirit of detente between the U.S. and the U.S.S.R. continued in 1974. There were two summit meetings during the year. President Nixon traveled to Moscow on June 27; President Ford to Vladivostock on Nov. 23. Chief purpose of both meetings was an agreement on nuclear arms limitation. A number of limited accords were signed by President Nixon July 3 with a fuller agreement reached during President Ford's trip. (Details of the negotiations and their results will be found under Disarmament.)

[2] **Kissinger confers in Moscow.** After three days of talks with Communist Party General Secretary Leonid Brezhnev, Foreign Minister Andrei Gromyko and other Soviet officials, U.S. Secretary of State Henry Kissinger returned to Washington March 28 without achieving the "concrete progress" he had predicted upon his arrival March 24. No specific agreements emerged from the meetings, particularly with regard to the second round of the strategic arms limitation talks (SALT II) which Kissinger had established as the topic of highest priority for the meetings. However, some compromise was reported on

other issues: The U.S. reportedly agreed with the Soviet Union on the value of a 35-nation summit meeting to ratify the final document to be issued from the European security conference being held in Geneva. Previously, the West had demanded Soviet concessions on human rights in exchange for such a meeting. Kissinger was said to have been given some "clarifications" on Soviet emigration policy, in hopes of improving Congress' disposition toward granting better trade terms to the U.S.S.R.

[3] **Moscow summit.** In a gesture that broke protocol, Soviet leader Brezhnev met with President Nixon at Moscow's Vnukovo Airport upon his arrival for their third summit meeting June 27. In 1972, the Soviet leader had remained at the Kremlin. The leaders began their formal talks the next day, with three agreements emerging, none of which were of major significance. The agreements dealt with cooperation in the housing and construction fields; in development programs for non-nuclear forms of energy, the environment and conservation; and a medical accord on heart research. A 10-year economic agreement was signed June 29, calling on both nations to facilitate trade and working conditions for trade representatives. Like the other accords, these augmented already-existing 1972 agreements.

[4] The discussions continued in Yalta, the Crimean Black Sea resort, June 29-30, after which Nixon made a one-day trip on July 1 to Minsk, where he visited two World War II memorials. The talks reconvened in Moscow July 2. The next day a number of limited documents on nuclear relations were signed, none of which constituted a hoped-for breakthrough toward permanent agreements on limiting offensive nuclear weapons. A communique issued in Moscow July 3 before the President's departure took note of other areas in which agreements had been made: environmental protection, space ventures, transportation innovations, cultural exchanges and the establishment of new consulates. With respect to international problems, the two sides: called for implementation of U.N. Security Council Resolution 338 to establish "a just and lasting peace settlement" in the Middle East, taking into account "the legitimate interests of all peoples, including the Palestinian people"; noted "certain further improvements" in the situation in Indochina; expressed continued support for the United Nations; and urged an early conclusion for the Conference on Security and Cooperation in Europe with results that would permit a final summit meeting of the heads of state involved. The President returned to the U.S. July 3.

[5] **Eximbank loans.** The U.S. Export-Import Bank suspended March 11, for an indefinite period, the consideration of all export credits to the Soviet Union, Poland, Rumania and Yugoslavia. The action followed a General Accounting Office (GAO) determination, reported March 9, that such Eximbank loans could not be granted without the approval of the President on each individual project. The Justice Department was expected to rule on the matter. The GAO's finding was based on a 1945 Congressional act, amended in 1968, prohibiting the extension of credits to any Communist country unless the President decided that such credits were in the national interest and so notified Congress. Eximbank contended that it had based its Soviet actions on a single blanket authorization by President Nixon Oct. 18, 1972, that it was in the national interest for the bank to extend credit for the sale or lease "of any product or service" to the U.S.S.R. (National interest determinations had been made for Yugoslavia in 1967 and for Poland and Rumania in 1971.) At issue was the financing of energy explorations which critics charged could then be used as a political weapon against the U.S.

[6] The Export-Import Bank announced March 22 that it would resume its program of credits to the Soviet Union, Poland, Rumania and Yugoslavia.

However, energy-related loans would remain stalled. Attorney General William Saxbe notified President Nixon March 21 that the procedures followed by the bank in the past were legal and could be resumed.

[7] The Export-Import Bank announced May 21 it had approved a $180 million bank credit, at 6% interest, to help finance a $2 billion Soviet natural gas and fertilizer complex. The largest single such loan to date, it brought Eximbank credits to the Soviet Union to nearly $470 million. A consortium of private banks, headed by the Bank of America, would provide a matching loan at a "blended" interest rate of 7.8%. Worked out by Armand Hammer, chairman of the Occidental Petroleum Corp., the project called for the import by the U.S. of Soviet fertilizers in exchange for superphosphoric acid from the U.S.

[8] A bill putting restrictions on U.S. government credit to the Soviet Union was cleared by Congress Dec. 19 for the President. The bill would extend the lending authority of the Export-Import Bank for four years at a $25 billion level. It set a $300 million ceiling on credit to the Soviet Union, which the President could raise if he found it in the national interest, subject to Congressional approval. The bill also barred any Eximbank credit for production, transport or distribution of energy from the Soviet Union. A $40 million ceiling was set on loans or guarantees for exploration of energy in the Soviet Union. Both the Soviet Union and the U.S. State Department expressed displeasure at the adoption of the restrictions. State Department officials said Soviet Ambassador Anatoly Dobrynin had told Kissinger Dec. 18 that Moscow regarded the credit limitation as a failure of the U.S. to live up to its side of detente.

[9] **Trade pacts.** Efforts by a group of Congressmen, among them Sen. Henry M. Jackson (D, Wash.), led to a trade bill offering the Soviet Union most-favored-nation status in return for easing restrictions on Jewish emigration. There was opposition to linking trade with emigration from the Administration. At a Naval Academy commencement speech June 5, President Nixon said, "We cannot gear our foreign policy to the transformation of other societies."

[10] A key official in the Ford Administration reported Sept. 7 that Moscow and Washington had reached agreement on the emigration issue, with the U.S.S.R. agreeing to permit at least 60,000 Jews and other Soviet citizens to emigrate each year, a 70% increase over 1973's record emigration figures. President Ford and Soviet Foreign Minister Gromyko held talks in Washington Sept. 20-21. Ford had met with Sen. Jackson Sept. 20 before seeing Gromyko. Jackson later told reporters that "the Russians have come 180 degrees" with respect to concessions on the issue. He noted that the disagreement over the Administration's trade bill was no longer between Moscow and the U.S. Congress, but, rather, between the Administration and Congress with the difficulty centering on the legislative form and language provisions for U.S. review. A formal compromise between the nations' positions was detailed in an exchange of letters Oct. 18 between Kissinger and Jackson. Although there was no specific guarantee in the number of emigrants to be allowed, a White House statement Oct. 21 said, "It will be our assumption that... the rate of emigration... would begin to rise promptly from the 1973 level." In his letter to Jackson, Kissinger listed the "criteria and practices [which] will henceforth govern emigration from the U.S.S.R.," according to Soviet assurances. They barred punitive actions against would-be emigrants such as job dismissal or demotion, emigration taxes and "unreasonable or unlawful impediments" to emigration.

[11] Although Jackson and some U.S. Jewish sources had suggested that the backlog of Soviet Jewish emigration applications totaled as many as 130,000, Jewish activists in Moscow estimated the backlog at about 80,000. Jewish sources were divided on whether applications to emigrate would mount in view of the

apparent Soviet concessions. Emigration of ethnic Germans was expected to reach roughly 6,000 in 1974 and by some estimates could rise to 20,000 in 1975, according to the Oct. 20 report. Other Soviet ethnic minorities had also shown interest in emigrating. (The emigration of Soviet Jews to Israel dropped by almost 50% in 1974, according to official figures released Dec. 20 by the Intergovernmental Committee on European Migration. The committee said 16,537 Soviet Jews had migrated to Israel since Jan. 1; the total for 1973 was 32,500.)

[12] A comprehensive foreign trade bill was passed by the U.S. Congress Dec. 20, despite strong Soviet denials that the Kremlin had pledged freer emigration of Jews as a condition for trade benefits. [See below] The Senate passed the bill by a 72-4 vote; the House passed it by a 323-36 vote. In its final version, the bill gave the President the authority to eliminate tariffs of 5% or lower, and to reduce by three-fifths tariffs above 5%. The President could negotiate elimination of non-tariff barriers, on an industry-by-industry basis, subject to Congressional approval. Tariffs could be eliminated on goods from developing nations, with exceptions for Communist countries (but not Rumania and Yugoslavia), any country restricting supplies to the U.S. in a cartel-like operation and countries discriminating against the U.S. on trade or refusing compensation for confiscations. Exemptions also were provided for certain goods, such as shoes, electronics and watches. The bill called for relief to industries hurt by imports unless the President found it not in the national interest, but Congress could overrule him. A major provision of the bill would grant trade concessions to the Soviet Union if Soviet emigration curbs were eased, especially against Jews. Congress left the Soviet provision intact despite Soviet disavowal Dec. 18 of any commitment on its part on the issue.

[13] The Soviet Union Dec. 18 disavowed the compromise agreement on the extension of U.S. trade benefits in exchange for freer Soviet emigration which had been set forward in a series of letters revealed by Jackson Oct. 18. The denial, revealed prior to agreement on the bill by a House-Senate conference committee that night, was brushed aside by congressmen as a "face-saving" gesture. The statement distributed by the official Soviet press agency Tass asserted that "leading circles" in the U.S.S.R. "flatly reject as unacceptable" any attempts to attach conditions to the extension of trade benefits or to otherwise "interfere in the internal affairs" of the Soviet Union. Accompanying the statement, Tass also circulated a letter, dated Oct. 26, from Foreign Minister Gromyko to Kissinger, in which Gromyko rejected the content of the letter exchange documented by Jackson as presenting "a distorted picture of our position."

[14] **Soviet grain purchases.** Officials of two major U.S. grain exporting firms agreed Oct. 5 to cancel Soviet orders for corn and wheat valued at $500 million after meeting at the White House with President Ford, Treasury Secretary William E. Simon and Agriculture Secretary Earl L. Butz. In a statement issued later that day, the White House said that at the meeting with representatives of Continental Grain Co. and Cook Industries Inc., Ford had "expressed his strong concern about the potential domestic impact that such sales could have at a time when the U.S. is experiencing a disappointing harvest of feed grains." The Senate Permanent Investigations Subcommittee had issued a final report July 28 of its study of the controversial sale of massive supplies of U.S. grain to the Soviet Union in 1972. Butz and two former assistant secretaries, Clarence Palmby and Carroll Brunthaver, were singled out for responsibility for what the subcommittee termed a "$300 million error in judgment" that had resulted in depleted U.S. grain reserves, farm product shortages, higher food prices and the current crisis in the livestock industry. The panel, which was chaired by Sen. Jackson, was critical of the Administration's handling of the grain sale. "The Russians

and the large [U.S.] grain [exporting] companies reaped the major benefits," Jackson said. Subsidies costing $300 million were paid to the six exporting firms serving as middlemen in the deal. These payments were "unjustified," according to the committee, which added that the government's Commodity Exchange Authority was "derelict in its oversight responsibility" when it mishandled an investigation into possible market manipulation by the exporting companies. The Genral Accounting Office had concluded Feb. 13 that there was no evidence that the exporting firms had reaped excessive profits from the Soviet deal or profited from inside information. Three of the companies lost money on the sale, according to the GAO. However, the exporting companies eventually profited from the sale, the GAO said, because the Soviet transaction pushed up domestic grain prices and subsequently, federal subsidies paid to exporters.

[15] Simon announced Oct. 19 that the Soviet Union would be allowed to purchase up to 1.2 million metric tons of U.S. wheat and 1 million tons of corn, valued at an estimated $380 million, through June 30, 1975. The Soviets had agreed not to make any "further purchases in the U.S. market crop this year," Simon added. According to arrangements for the new grain sale negotiated by Simon during an Oct 13-16 visit to Moscow, the Soviet Union also agreed that shipments would be made in phased intervals to further minimize the disruptive effects of the purchase on the U.S. market.

Dissidents

[16] **Andrei Sakharov.** In excerpts from the introduction to a forthcoming collection of Andrei Sakharov's writings, published by the *New York Times* March 5, the nuclear physicist called on "all international organizations concerned... to abandon their policy of non-intervention in the internal affairs of the socialist countries as regards defending human rights and to manifest the utmost persistence." He specifically cited 1.7 million Soviet prisoners suffering under "malnutrition, pitiless formalism, and repressions."

[17] During the year Sakharov and other protestors appealed to prominent figures on behalf of a number of imprisoned dissidents, among whom was biologist Vladimir Bukovsky, who was reported in fragile health in the punishment cells of a labor camp where he was serving five years of a 12-year sentence for anti-Soviet activities. It was reported June 14 that Bukovsky had been moved from the camp to a prison near Moscow. Sakharov began a hunger strike June 29 to protest "the illegal and brutal repression of political prisoners," specifically citing the Bukovsky case. Sakharov said he was taking the step to reinforce his appeal, made in a letter earlier in the week, to President Nixon and Soviet leader Brezhnev, to deal with the issue of human rights. Sakharov said July 4 he had abandoned the hunger strike for medical reasons. Sakharov, his wife and four other persons signed an appeal to the West on behalf of mathematician Leonid Plyushch, who was reported near death after being incarcerated for over a year, it had been reported Feb. 9. Sakharov charged drugs were used on Plyushch which had removed his ability to read, write or exercise. Over 500 French mathematicians signed an appeal Feb. 7 for Plyushch and fellow mathematician Yuri Shikhanovich, also being held in a mental hospital. Shikhanovich was reported released July 18.

[18] Moscow cut off the TV broadcasts of three major U.S. networks July 2 as American correspondents, in the Soviet Union for Nixon's visit, tried to send filmed reports on Soviet dissident activities. Two of the broadcasts included interviews with Sakharov. Despite several attempts to broadcast explanations of the interruptions as well as the reports themselves, the networks were each time blacked out within seconds.

[19] **Other dissidents.** Viktor Nekrasov, 62, awarded the Stalin prize in 1947 for

his novel *In the Trenches of Stalingrad*, was expelled from Moscow to his home city of Kiev March 22, ostensibly for violating residence regulations. He had denounced official controls on writers and literature March 11, refusing to join a Soviet campaign against exiled novelist Alexander Solzhenitsyn and Sakharov. Nekrasov was given an exit visa to go to Switzerland for two years, private sources in Moscow disclosed Aug. 4. He arrived in Zurich Sept. 12. (Nekrasov had been a Communist Party member for 30 years until his expulsion in 1972.)

[20] Pavel Litvinov, grandson of Stalinist-era Foreign Minister Maxim Litvinov, left the Soviet Union with his family March 18 and applied in Vienna for a U.S. visa, which was granted March 19. The Soviet Union had issued the dissident physicist a visa for Israel.

[21] Soviet ballet dancer Mikhail Baryshnikov defected to the West June 29 while on tour as a guest artist with the Bolshoi Ballet in Toronto, Canada. He had been the leading male dancer with Leningrad's Kirov Ballet. In an interview with the *Toronto Globe and Mail* July 4, Baryshnikov asserted that his decision to defect was for personal and artistic, not for political, reasons.

[22] Silva Y. Zalmanson, who was given a 10-year sentence in 1970 for the attempted hijacking of a Soviet aircraft, was released from jail Aug. 23 and ordered expelled to Israel. She flew to Vienna Sept. 10 after meeting with her husband, Eduard S. Kuznetsov, who remained imprisoned for the same hijacking offense.

[23] Simas Kudirka, the Lithuanian seaman who sought unsuccessfully to defect in 1970 by jumping from a Soviet vessel to a U.S. Coast Guard cutter off Massachusetts, arrived in New York Nov. 5 with his American-born mother, Marija Sulsiene, his wife and two children. Kudirka had been released from a Soviet prison camp in August, shortly after being granted U.S. citizenship on the basis of his mother's birth. His release and emigration were seen as a Soviet gesture to Washington on the emigration controversy.

[24] **Authorities yield on art exhibit.** Swift condemnation in the West of the disruption of an unofficial art showing staged Sept. 15 apparently contributed to a policy reversal by Soviet authorities who subsequently gave permission for such an exhibit to be mounted in a Moscow park Sept. 29, the first public display of art works not pre-submitted to the state for approval in approximately 50 years. Bulldozers, dump trucks and water-spraying trucks overran the Sept. 15 exhibit as it was being set up in an empty lot in a Moscow suburb by 27 underground Soviet artists not recognized by the official Artists' Union. The broad condemnation in the Western press was believed responsible for light treatment of the arrested artists and the decision by Soviet authorities to permit a re-staging of the exhibit without interference.Permission for the Sept. 29 show in Ismailovo Park was officially authorized by the Moscow City Council Sept. 24. An estimated 10,000 people flocked to the showing, which was given no publicity through any official channels. Some 60 artists, including four from the official Artists' Union, participated in the exhibit.

Jewish Emigration

[25] **Scientists' protest.** The government announced May 17 that a planned scientific conference organized by Jewish scientists in the Soviet Union was deemed a "provocative action" and warned that participation would be severely curtailed, if not wholly prohibited. According to its organizers, the primary objective of the conference was to "maintain the scientific competence of Jews excluded from scientific work because they had applied to emigrate to Israel." More than 70 scientists from the Soviet Union, the U.S., Great Britain and Israel were expected to participate in the meeting, scheduled for July 1-5. (Statistics

published in the April issue of *Vestnik Statistiki,* a government journal, showed that Jews accounted for 14% of the Soviet Union's scientists and doctoral degrees, although they represented only 1% of the population.)

[26] More than 50 Jews were arrested in Moscow, Leningrad, Odessa and Kishinev June 21-24 in an apparent effort to forestall the scientific meeting and possible demonstrations during President Nixon's visit to the Soviet Union. Among those arrested June 21 were Drs. Viktor Brailovsky, Mark Azbel and Alexander Voronel, prominent scientists who were organizers of the scientific meeting. Jewish sources in Moscow charged that Nixon's June 5 speech disavowing U.S. interference in U.S.S.R. internal affairs had given Moscow a "free hand" in going ahead with the arrests, it was reported June 22.

[27] Soviet security agents (KGB) July 1 blockaded the Moscow apartment building in which the scientific meeting was to be held. A number of participants who arrived for the conference were prevented from entering the building and were taken away by agents.

[28] **Panovs, others allowed to leave.** The Soviet Union allowed a number of individuals to emigrate or leave the country in the early weeks of June, in a possible gesture to generate goodwill before President Nixon's forthcoming Moscow summit meeting. Jewish ballet dancer Valery Panov and his wife, Galina, also a ballet dancer, arrived in Tel Aviv June 15 after being granted permission June 7 to emigrate to Israel. The couple had struggled for two years in their efforts to leave. British Prime Minister Harold Wilson had appealed personally to Soviet Premier Alexei Kosygin June 6 on behalf of the Panovs. Many British groups had earlier promised protest demonstrations and boycotts of a six-week tour of Britain by the Bolshoi Ballet, which began June 12.

[29] **Jewish activists appeal on exit curbs.** A number of Soviet Jewish activists had addressed letters to President Ford and other U.S. officials Oct. 22-Nov. 21 charging that Soviet authorities were intimidating prospective emigrants from taking advantage of the compromise agreement to permit freer emigration from the U.S.S.R. in return for U.S. trade benefits. The *Washington Post* reported Nov. 5 that 100 Jews from nine Soviet cities had addressed an open letter to Sen. Henry Jackson (D, Wash.) charging that the military draft was being used to punish Jewish youths who sought permission to emigrate.

[30] **Polsky, Voronel emigrate to Israel.** Jewish physicist Victor Polsky, 44, left Moscow for Israel Dec. 22, having received permission to emigrate Nov. 15. He had lost his job at the Moscow Institute nearly four years earlier when he first applied to leave the Soviet Union. He had been repeatedly denied a visa on security grounds. Polsky was fined 100 rubles (about $140) after having been found guilty Oct. 18 of felonious reckless driving, a charge placed against him in March when his car struck the daughter of an Interior Ministry official in Moscow. At the trial, the defense contended the girl had been attempting suicide; hospital records to that effect had been suppressed, Jewish groups alleged. (Western reporters, two U.S. lawyers and several prominent dissidents had been allowed to attend the trial.)

[31] Jewish physicist Alexander Voronel, 43, arrived in Israel Dec. 29. He had been given permission to leave Dec. 11. Voronel, who had left his job at the Institute of Physical-Technical and Radio-Technical Measurements when he first applied to emigrate in April 1972, had in recent months been arrested and otherwise harassed for organizing unauthorized seminars for unemployed Jewish scholars.

Government Actions

[32] **Supreme Soviet elections.** The Soviet press reported June 19 that 99.79% of the electorate had voted June 16 for the 1,517 candidates who ran unopposed for

the 767 seats in the Soviet of the Union and 750 seats in the Soviet of Nationalities which together comprised the Soviet legislature. Another .19% of the electorate either obliterated the candidate's name or wrote in another. The election revealed two notable developments: the fall from favor of Culture Minister Yekaterina A. Furtseva and the retirement of veteran Communist leader Anastas I. Mikoyan, whose career had been in eclipse since he was removed from the Politburo in 1966. Furtseva, 64, the only woman on the nation's Council of Ministers, had been closely associated with former Soviet Premier Nikita Khrushchev, under whom she served from 1957-61 on the Communist Party Politburo (then known as the Praesidium). Rumors of her imminent dismissal had long circulated in Moscow. The immediate catalyst in her fall from favor, however, was her alleged abuse of her office: she had had an ostentatious $170,000 dacha built in her daughter's name outside of Mosow. Furtseva, though dropped from the Supreme Soviet, retained her ministerial post. She died Oct. 25 and was replaced Nov. 14 by Pyotr Nilovich Demichev, 56. Demichev, Central Committee secretary for cultural and ideological matters and an alternate member of the Politburo, was considered a proponent of strict control over cultural policy.

[33] **CIA: Soviet arms spending exceeds U.S.** A U.S. Central Intelligence Agency (CIA) analysis showed that the Soviet Union's military budget had increased in recent years to the point where Moscow had spent more on military expenditures in dollar terms in 1973 than had the U.S. Details of the comparative analysis were released July 19 by Sen. William Proxmire (D, Wisc.) in a declassified version of secret testimony April 24 by CIA Director William E. Colby before the Joint Congressional Economic Committee, of which Proxmire was chairman. The U.S.S.R.'s defense effort to be the equivalent of $80 billion in 1973; U.S. defense spending for that year totaled $76 billion. The Soviet defense program, the report estimated, absorbed 6%-10% of the Soviet gross nationl product, which was figured to be the equivalent of $660 billion annually. As a share of the U.S. GNP, American defense spending had declined from 9.4% in 1968 to about 6% in the last two years. The U.S. GNP equalled $1.1 trillion in 1973. Colby also said there was an "across the board" technological lag in the Soviet Union, notably in computers and in the complexity and accuracy of missiles.

[34] The Supreme Soviet adopted Dec. 20 a proposed 1975 budget which set government expenditures at 208.5 billion rubles ($285.3 billion), 200 million rubles less than planned income. Delivered by Finance Minister Vasily Garbuzov, the budget included 17.4 billion rubles ($24 billion) for defense, a decrease of more than 1% from the 1974 budget. However, the Soviet military budget did not reflect total defense spending, which was actually distributed under various categories within the entire budget.

[35] **Crops, consumer goods miss '74 targets.** The annual report on the Soviet economy's performance, presented to the Supreme Soviet Dec. 18, revealed that the rate of overall economic growth in 1974 was 5%, missing the 6.5% growth target chiefly because of a sharp downturn in agricultural production and, secondarily, a failure to achieve consumer industries output goals, despite major industrial gains. The report disclosed that the 1974 grain harvest would total 195.5 million tons, 10 million tons below the scheduled goal, but still ranking as the second largest harvest in Soviet history.

[36] (Communist Party General Secretary Brezhnev had announced March 15 that the party's Central Committee had approved a $45 billion agricultural project for the 1976-1980 five-year plan. The program, reminiscent of the late Nikita Khrushchev's once-denounced virgin lands project, accounted for more than 33% of the plan's total agricultural allotment. Details of the project were

given April 3. To be implemented over 15 years, the project called for development of the Soviet Union's non-black soil zone, comprising 125 million acres of marginal land extending across European Russia from the Baltic Sea into Siberia. In keeping with Moscow's aim of improving the livestock sector of the economy in order to enrich the Soviet diet, the project was intended primarily to foster the growth of cattle farming.)

[37] **New internal passport system.** The Soviet Unio announced Dec. 25 it would expand and simplify its internal passport system and relax certain restrictions on domestic travel. The Ministry of Internal Affairs said Dec. 26 that collective farmers and state-farm workers would be entitled to the new passports which would no longer designate social status. The measure affected about 46 million farm workers previously denied domestic travel passports in order to forestall their migration to urban areas. The new passport system would be implemented in 1976-1981, it was reported.

Energy Developments

[38] **Oil target increased.** Soviet Oil Minister Valentin D. Shashin announced an increased target for Soviet oil production in 1974 of 450 million tons, eight million more than the goal set in January, it was reported April 11. The increased production, he said, would help the Soviet Union maintain its oil supplies to socialist bloc countries which accounted for 54% of the total exported. Shashin said May 27 that the Soviet Union had ruled out construction of an oil pipeline from Irkutsk in central Siberia to Kakhodka on the Sea of Japan. Instead, he said, a railway would be constructed linking with the existing Trans-Siberian network at Komsomolsk on the Amur River. Explaining the shift, Shashin stressed that "anything you want" could be shipped by rail, while a pipeline could transport only oil. He noted that the rail line would open the region to industrial development. Shashin enunciated what was essentially a more nationalistic oil policy for the U.S.S.R., also precluding foreign participation in oil resource development. He admitted only two possible forms of foreign participation in the Soviet oil business—in the exchange of technical information and in the sale of oil equipment—but he emphasized that the U.S.S.R. was fully capable of carrying out any oil projects on its own.

[39] **Coal, not oil, for Japan.** Tokyo and Moscow signed an agreement June 3 under which Japan would grant the U.S.S.R. the equivalent of $450 million in credits in exchange for 104.4 million tons of Soviet coal from 1979 to 1980. It was their largest accord to date and followed on the heels of the Soviet Union's announced abandonment of the oil pipeline project, a planned Soviet-Japan deal which Tokyo had considered vital to the maintenance of its fuel supplies.

[40] **Iran natural gas pact signed.** The U.S.S.R. and Iran signed an agreement which raised the price of natural gas exported to the Soviet Union by 85%, from 30.7¢ to 57¢ per 1,000 cubic feet, retroactive to Jan. 1, it was reported Aug. 19. Negotiations had opened in Tehran Aug. 6 after earlier talks, held June 24-26 in Moscow, had broken off, reportedly with the Soviets' rejection of Iran's proposed doubling of the gas price. Iran supplied the Soviet Union with 10 billion cubic meters of natural gas annually and Moscow sold a comparable amount to Europe. Following Tehran's unilateral decision to double the gas price July 2, Iranian government sources stressed that the price increase was actually modest and represented a gesture of goodwill since the real market value of natural gas would have allowed quadrupling the price to $1.20 per 1,000 cubic feet. The Tehran sources also noted that the Soviet Union sold gas to West Germany, France and Austria at 57¢ per 1,000 cubic feet.

See also ALBANIA; ARCHEOLOGY; ARGENTINA [18]; ATOMIC ENERGY [8, 10];

UNITED NATIONS (U.N.)—135 members. At the beginning of 1974, the 135 U.N. member states were:

Afghanistan
Albania
Algeria
Argentina
Australia
Austria
Bahamas
Bahrain
Barbados
Belgium
Bhutan
Bolivia
Botswana
Brazil
Bulgaria
Burma
Burundi
Byelorussia
Cameroon
Canada
Central African Rep.
Chad
Chile
China
Colombia
Congo Republic
Costa Rica
Cuba
Cyprus
Czechoslovakia
Dahomey
Democratic Yemen
Denmark
Dominican Republic
Ecuador
Egypt
El Salvador
Equatorial Guinea
Ethiopia
Fiji
Finland
France
Gabon
Gambia
German Democratic Rep.
Germany, Federal Rep. of
Ghana
Greece
Guatemala
Guinea
Guyana
Haiti
Honduras
Hungary
Iceland
India
Indonesia
Iran
Iraq
Ireland
Israel
Italy
Ivory Coast
Jamaica
Japan
Jordan
Kenya
Khmer Republic
(formerly Cambodia)
Kuwait
Laos
Lebanon
Lesotho
Liberia
Libya
Luxembourg
Madagascar
Malawi
Malaysia
Maldive Islands
Mali
Malta
Mauritania
Mauritius
Mexico
Mongolia
Morocco
Nepal
Netherlands
New Zealand
Nicaragua
Niger
Nigeria
Norway
Oman
Pakistan
Panama
Paraguay
Peru
Philippines
Poland
Portugal
Qatar
Rumania
Rwanda
Saudi Arabia
Senegal
Sierra Leone
Singapore
Somalia
South Africa
Soviet Union
Spain
Sri Lanka (Ceylon)
Sudan
Swaziland
Sweden
Syria
Tanzania
Thailand
Togo
Trinidad and Tobago
Tunisia
Turkey
Uganda
Ukraine
United Arab Emirates
United Kingdom
United States
Upper Volta
Uruguay
Venezuela
Yemen Arab Rep.
Yugoslavia
Zaire
Zambia

29th General Assembly

[2] The 29th General Assembly opened at U.N. headquarters in New York Sept. 17 with an unusually strident address by its president, Algerian Foreign Minister Abdelaziz Bouteflika. The Assembly admitted three new member states, raising its total membership to 138. The nations were Bangla Desh, formerly part of Pakistan; Guinea-Bissau, a former Portuguese colony in West Africa; and Grenada, a former British colony in the Caribbean. Bouteflika, unanimously elected president as the 13-week Assembly session began, said he accepted the office as a representative of "generations of freedom fighters who contributed to making a better world with weapons in their hands." He asserted these fighters had shown that "revolutionary violence is the only way for peoples to liberate themselves." Bouteflika defended the right of Palestinians "to freely exercise their right to self-determination," and warned that the international community would not accept a "Middle East bargain" in which "the conquered territories [were not] returned." Bouteflika praised Portugal for beginning to free its African colonies, and asserted that the people of Indochina had defeated the "aggressors," presumably the U.S. Delegates and other observers appeared surprised by the harshness of Bouteflika's remarks, according to the *New York Times* Sept. 18. Bouteflika himself admitted at the end of his address that it "certainly is not customary" for the General Assembly president to be so outspoken.

[3] President Ford addressed the General Assembly Sept. 18, pledging increased U.S. food assistance to needy countries and challenging oil-producing nations to stop using petroleum as a political and economic weapon. Ford urged all countries to join in a "global strategy for food and energy" and warned that "failure to cooperate on oil and food and inflation could spell disaster for every nation represented in this room." Ford told the General Assembly that the U.S. "recognizes the special responsibilities we bear as the world's largest producer of food," but he said "it has not been our policy to use food as a political weapon despite the oil embargo and recent oil price and production decisions." He emphasized that "energy is required to produce food, and food to produce energy."

[4] **Palestinian debate set.** The Assembly Sept. 22 approved an agenda with a record number of items including Korea, the Cyprus conflict, South Africa's membership in the U.N. and, for the first time, debate on the Palestinian issue as an item separate from the Middle East conflict. Inclusion of the Palestinian issue in the agenda was proposed by all 20 Arab delegations and by representatives of 23 other countries, most of them African or Communist. It was vigorously opposed by Israel, whose chief delegate, Yosef Tekoah, denounced the Palestine Liberation Organization Sept. 21 as a group of "murderers." (For details of the debate, see MIDDLE EAST.)

[5] **Assembly suspends South Africa.** Bouteflika suspended South Africa from participating in the remainder of the Assembly session Nov. 12. The Assembly upheld his action by a vote of 91-22, with 19 abstentions. In an unprecedented ruling, Bouteflika held that the Assembly's rejection of the South African delegation's credentials in September expressed the body's "will" to suspend South Africa. Delegates from the U.S. and other countries argued unsuccessfully that Bouteflika had violated the U.N. Charter, which required a recommendation of expulsion from the Security Council. The Assembly action barred South Africa from appearing, speaking, making proposals or voting in the session, which was scheduled to close Dec. 17. It did not suspend South Africa from any other U.N. body. South Africa recalled its U.N. ambassador

Nov. 13 and froze its $1 million annual contribution to the world organization. Bouteflika ruled after negotiating for hours with delegates from black African nations, according to press reports. One Western diplomat said the Africans had threatened to dilute their support for the Arab countries in the Assembly's Palestine debate if they were not backed on the South Africa issue, the *New York Times* reported Nov. 13.

[6] A resolution to expel South Africa from the U.N. had been vetoed in the Security Council Oct. 30 by the U.S., Great Britain and France. Ten Council members voted for expulsion (assuring passage of the resolution if there were no veto) and two, Austria and Costa Rica, abstained. The expulsion votes were cast by Cameroon, Kenya and Mauritania—which jointly introduced the resolution Oct. 25—and the Soviet Union, China, Byelorussia, Australia, Indonesia, Iraq and Peru. The vote followed the failure of negotiations among a number of Council members to avert a veto. The U.S., Great Britain and France proposed as a compromise that the Council condemn South Africa and establish subsidiary bodies to pressure it to change its policies, but the African nations refused to go along, according to the *Washington Post* Oct. 31. U.S. Ambassador John Scali warned before the vote that expulsion of South Africa would set a "shattering precedent which could gravely damage the U.N. structure." He called racial discrimination in South Africa "evil" and "ugly," but asserted Pretoria could not be pressured to change its policies if it were not in the U.N.

[7] **Cambodian regime keeps Assembly seat.** The General Assembly Nov. 27 defeated an attempt to transfer Cambodia's seat from the Lon Nol government in Pnompenh to the government in exile of Prince Norodom Sihanouk in Peking. Delegates narrowly approved a resolution introduced by 23 states which called for conciliation between Lon Nol and Sihanouk, and urged U.N. Secretary General Kurt Waldheim to consult with both parties and report to the 1975 Assembly session. The Assembly would not "press for any further action" until it examined Waldheim's report, the resolution stated. The measure was approved 56-54, with 24 abstentions. Diplomats attributed the result to a distrust of China by other Asian nations, vigorous U.S. lobbying on behalf of the Lon Nol government, and Soviet reluctance to lobby on behalf of Sihanouk, according to the *New York Times* Nov. 29.

[8] **Assembly 'tyranny' alleged.** The U.S. and other Western nations unexpectedly denounced the General Assembly's Third World majority Dec. 6, touching off a debate with developing countries on the purpose of the United Nations organization. U.S. Ambassador Scali charged during the Assembly's debate on strengthening the U.N. that a number of recent Assembly resolutions were passed by a numerical majority of nations which in fact represented only a fraction of the world's population. This "tyranny of the majority," he alleged, has offended the nations most capable of supporting the U.N. and implementing its resolutions, particularly the U.S. "Many Americans are questioning their belief in the United Nations," Scali said. "They are deeply disturbed." Scali said the new Assembly majority tended to pass "one-sided, unrealistic resolutions that cannot be implemented" and that disregarded the U.N. Charter. He reminded delegates that the Assembly was not a legislature and that its resolutions were only advisory; its true function, he said, was to reconcile opposing views. Scali cited the Assembly debates on the Middle East and South Africa as examples of "self-centered actions" which endangered the U.N.'s future. The Assembly had granted observer status to the Palestine Liberation Organization, and it had limited Israel to one speech during the debate on the Palestine issue. The debate had also resulted in a resolution which stated that the Palestinians had an

inalienable right "to return to their homes and property from which they have been displaced..." No mention was made of Israel.

[9] Other Western delegates made speeches supporting Scali's position. French Ambassador Louis de Guiringaud, representing the European Community, said "a private cult seems to be emerging, monopolizing certain areas" of U.N. debate and decision-making. Israeli Ambassador Tekoah said Scali had "succeeded to unmask the sad truth about the abysmal decline of the United Nations and its domination by forces inimical to the spirit and purposes of the charter."

[10] Developing nations were unprepared to reply to the Western charges. Algerian Ambassador Abdellatif Rahal, complaining that the Western minority had unexpectedly engaged in a "premeditated festival of statements that were unjust, exaggerated and inelegant," obtained a recess in the debate to enable the Third World nations to prepare an answer. When debate resumed Dec. 11, Rahal rejected Scali's assertion that the U.N. had disillusioned the U.S. Congress and citizenry. Rahal noted that when the U.S. had commanded a majority in the Assembly, it had pushed through resolutions in its own interest, such as the one providing for partition of Palestine in 1947. The U.S. and its allies had "the additional advantage of having taken part in drafting the charter and the rules of procedure of our organization and have thus been able to insure that their own views would prevail."

[11] **Economic charter adopted.** The General Assembly Dec. 12 approved a broad and controversial economic charter proposed by Mexican President Luis Echeverria Alvarez. The non-binding declaration, called the Charter of Economic Rights and Duties of States, was adopted 120-6, with the U.S., Great Britain, West Germany, Denmark, Belgium and Luxembourg voting against it. Ten nations, including Japan, France and Canada, abstained. Under the charter, every nation had full sovereignty over all its wealth, resources and economic activities, and possessed the right to regulate foreign investments in accordance with its laws and to supervise transnational corporations with its jurisdiction. One provision gave nations the right to expropriate foreign properties without guaranteeing equitable compensation. The charter also upheld the right of nations to organize commodity cartels such as the Organization of Petroleum Exporting Countries. Opponents of the declaration said it did not take into account the concerns of the industrialized as well as the developing countries, but they reportedly tempered their objections in deference to President Echeverria.

[12] **Assembly recessed.** The Assembly recessed Dec. 18, leaving itself the option of reconvening to debate the Middle East situation before the next session began in September 1975. Assembly President Bouteflika called the session historic and possibly revolutionary. Bouteflika defended his South African and PLO rulings at a farewell press conference Dec. 20, asserting that he could not be coerced and he had at all times carried out the will of the Assembly's majority.

[13] The U.S. continued to oppose decisions by the Assembly's Third World majority on the last day of the session. Delegate Clarence Ferguson announced the U.S. would boycott the United Nations Emergency Operation, a special fund established in June to aid the nations worst hit by the increase in prices of food, oil and other commodities. The U.S. had argued earlier that bilateral arrangements and existing agencies such as the World Bank were adequate to channel aid to poor nations. However, observers noted the U.N. fund would be controlled by developing countries—unlike the World Bank, which was

dominated by the U.S.—and many interpreted the boycott as retaliation against the Assembly majority.

[14] The Assembly Dec. 14 had ratified by consensus a legal definition of aggression on which the U.N. had worked since 1945. The term was defined as "the use of armed force by a state against the sovereignty, territorial integrity or political independence of another state, or in any other manner inconsistent with the Charter of the United Naions." The text said the definition must not prejudge "the right to self-determination, freedom and independence" of people forcibly deprived of that right, "particularly peoples under colonialist or racist regimes or other forms of alien domination, nor the right of these peoples to struggle to that end and to seek and receive support." Among acts defined as constituting aggression were "the blockade of the ports or coasts of a state by the armed forces of another state"; "the action of a state in allowing its territory . . . to be used by [another] state for perpetrating an act of aggression against a third state"; and "the sending by or on behalf of a state of armed bands, groups, irregulars or mercenaries, which carry out acts of armed force against any other state . . ."

[15] **Security Council members elected.** The General Assembly Oct. 11 elected five countries to serve two-year terms on the Security Council beginning Jan. 1, 1975. The nations were Sweden, Italy, Guyana, Japan and Tanzania. They would replace Austria, Australia, Indonesia, Kenya and Peru, whose terms on the Council would expire at the end of 1974.

[16] **UNESCO session held.** Magda Joboru, a Hungarian professor, was elected president of the 18th session of the General Conference of the U.N. Educational, Scientific and Cultural Organization (UNESCO) Oct. 18. She was the first woman to preside over the conference since 1945. The conference voted Oct. 25 to grant observer status to the Palestine Liberation Organization. The vote was 80-2 with 17 abstentions. The U.S. and Israel voted against and the nine members of the European Community abstained. UNESCO adopted a resolution in Paris Nov. 20 to withhold $26,000 a year in UNESCO aid from Israel because of its "persistence in altering the historical features" of Jerusalem "by undertaking [archeological] excavations which constitute a danger to its monuments." The vote was 64-27, with 26 abstentions. The U.S. and most Western European countries, including France, voted against the resolution. The Arab nations, the Communist bloc and a number of third-world countries approved. UNESCO Nov. 21 approved a resolution to exclude Israel from its European regional group by a 48-33 vote, with 31 abstentions, including France. As in the previous day's balloting, the latest resolution was approved by the Arab, Communist and third-world delegations. The U.S., Canada, 14 Western and 12 Latin American countries were among those voting against. UNESCO Nov. 22 voted 75 to 14, with 16 abstentions, to supply funds to the PLO and to African liberation movements.

[17] The Israeli government issued a statement Nov. 24 declaring it would continue the archaeological excavations in Jerusalem despite the UNESCO vote. Israel's chief delegate to UNESCO, Nathan Bar Yaakov had denounced the organization Nov. 22 for withholding financial assistance from his country and ousting it from its regional groups. Before leaving Paris for home, Bar Yakkov charged that the Arab and Communist countries that now dominated UNESCO had transformed it from a "technical and professional operations" to "the scene of political warfare." A French junior Cabinet minister, Francoise Giroud, secretary of state for the condition of women, Nov. 25 rejected an invitation to address UNESCO because of its "shocking" decisions taken against Israel. Mrs.

Giroud's action followed publication of a manifesto protest against UNESCO signed by 31 French intellectuals, including Jean-Paul Sartre.

[18] The conference's votes against Israel had moved the Swiss Senate to vote Dec. 3 to cut 10% from Switzerland's annual contribution to the UNESCO budget. Sales of greeting cards by the U.N. Children's Fund (UNICEF) had fallen off because of negative reactions by supporters of Israel who confused UNICEF with UNESCO, according to press reports Dec. 3. The U.S. Senate voted to withhold U.S. financial support from the agency—which amounted to a quarter of its $170 million biennial budget.

[19] Several hundred intellectuals and artists including 19 Nobel laureates, declared in a letter in the French Newspaper *Le Monde* Dec. 14 that they would not participate in UNESCO programs until the agency reversed its recent resolutions against Israel. The signatories inclued Saul Bellow and Mary McCarthy, U.S. authors; Francois Truffaut, French film director; and Dr. Kenneth Arrow, an economist at Harvard University who won the 1972 Nobel Memorial Prize in Economics. Arrow and two other Nobel laureates—Drs. Julius Axelrod, a neurobiologist, and Hans Bethe, a physicist—had met with U.N. Secretary General Waldheim Dec. 13 to protest what they called the "corruption" of UNESCO by the recent actions against Israel.

See also AUSTRALIA [23]; BIRTH CONTROL; BULGARIA; BURMA; BUTZ, EARL L.; CAMBODIA; CHEMICAL & BIOLOGICAL WEAPONS; CHILE [1]; CHINA, COMMUNIST; CYPRUS [6-7, 9-10, 13, 16, 18-22]; DENMARK; ETHIOPIA [12-13]; EUROPEAN ECONOMIC COMMUNITY [17]; FAMINE & FOOD; GUINEA-BISSAU; IRAN; IRELAND, REPUBLIC OF; ISRAEL; KOREA, PEOPLE'S REPUBLIC OF; KOREA, REPUBLIC OF [17]; MEXICO [18]; MIDDLE EAST [6, 8-15, 23-24, 27, 30]; NARCOTICS & DANGEROUS DRUGS; NOBEL PRIZES; OBITUARIES [HOFFMAN]; OIL [14, 28-29]; POPULATION; PORTUGAL [27-29]; SOUTH AFRICA [14]; SOUTH WEST AFRICA; SPANISH SAHARA; SUGAR; TARIFFS & TRADE; TERRITORIAL WATERS; UGANDA; UNION OF SOVIET SOCIALIST REPUBLICS [4]; URUGUAY; VIETNAM, PEOPLE'S REPUBLIC OF; WEATHER

UNITED NATIONS CHILDREN'S FUND (UNICEF)—*See* UNITED NATIONS [18]; VIETNAM, PEOPLE'S REPUBLIC OF

UNITED NATIONS EDUCATION, SCIENTIFIC & CULTURAL ORGANIZATION (UNESCO)—*See* SOUTH WEST AFRICA; UNITED NATIONS [16-19]

UPPER VOLTA—The 1,750-man army, led by President Sangoule Lamizana, himself a general, deposed the government of Premier Gerard Kango Ouedraogo, suspended the Constitution and dissolved the National Assembly Feb. 8. Lamizana said in a radio broadcast that day that political factionalism had been threatening a "catastrophic situation."

See also AFRICA; FAMINE & FOOD

URBAN AFFAIRS— *See* HOUSING; TRANSPORTATION

URANIUM—*See* AUSTRALIA [22]; GABON

URUGUAY

Government

Vice President Jorge Sapelli, who had refused to sit on the military-backed Council of State, had been dismissed in December 1973 in a further violation of the Constitution by Pres. Juan Maria Bordaberry, it was reported Jan. 4. (The Council of State had been created in June 1973 when, under pressure from the military, Bordaberry dissolved Congress giving all congressional functions to the Council. Most prominent politicians had refused to sit on the Council, among them Sapelli who had demanded an early return to constitutional rule. Major decisions, however, were expected to remain in the hands of the military-dominated National Security Council.) Further changes occurred when Interior Minister Col. Nestor Bolentini resigned without explanation Feb. 11; and Finance Minister Manuel Raul Pazos left the government, also without explanation, Jan. 31. Bolentini had been a close ally of Bordaberry, according to a Feb. 15 report in the London newsletter *Latin America.* His departure signaled a change in the president's relations with the military. Military pressure also brought the resignation of Agriculture Minister Benito Medero June 11.

Bordaberry said Sept. 4 that the ban on political activities would continue indefinitely, and that opponents of the measure could "lose all hope" of ever returning to the "prostituted" system of government which he and his military backers allegedly ended. He declared that the elections scheduled for November 1976 would not take place under "the political and institutional system which died on 27 June 1973" (the day Bordaberry assumed dictatorial powers), and that the new Constitution being drafted would be for "the nation and not the political parties."

Bordaberry had named the commanders of the three military branches to the new Economic and Social Council, an executive body under his leadership which would make or review all of the government's social and economic decisions. The council, installed Aug. 1, also included the defense and economy ministers and the director of the Office of Planning and the Budget. Military officers also had taken over the major state owned enterprises, including the power and petroleum companies and the Central Bank, under a decree issued June 27. This move, an apparent attempt to revitalize the economy and streamline the bureaucracy, had been promised for more than a year.

Opposition to Government

Press developments. The government Feb. 9 closed down the left-wing weekly *Marcha* and arrested its director, assistant director and editor. Two days later Uruguay's leading writer, novelist Juan Carlos Onetti, also was arrested. *Marcha,* the only remaining publication openly opposing the military-dominated regime, was ostensibly closed for printing in its Feb. 8 edition a short story which the government considered "pornographic." The story, titled "The Bodyguard," by Winston Nelson Marra, was awarded a prize by a *Marcha* literary jury. It treated the execution of a police inspector by Tupamaro guerrillas four years ago, and contained a number of violent, sexual scenes. Onetti's arrest was protested by European and Latin American writers and by Amnesty International, the London-based organization working for release of political prisoners. Onetti was released from jail May 14 along with the director and three editors of *Marcha. Marcha* was allowed to resume publication, but it was closed again after two issues. A presidential decree, reported June 8, banned the magazine for five months, a period which a *Marcha* spokesman said might force the publication to close permanently. *Marcha* reappeared Nov. 8. However, it was banned again Nov. 26, apparently permanently, for continuing to employ "subversive" writers accused of "attacking the sovereignty of the state."

The Interior Ministry March 13 ordered foreign news agencies operaing in Uruguay to send it copies of all news dispatches they sent abroad. The order enforced a decree of October 1973. Interior Undersecretary Luis Vargas Garmendia said the measure did not constitute censorship, but reflected "the desire of the government to know what type of information is being sent abroad. If a discrepancy exists between the story and reality, a representive of the agency will be called in to clarify the error."

Torture charges renewed. Charges that Uruguayan political prisoners were tortured by police and military authorities were revived at the United Nations June 16 by representatives of the International Commission of Jurists (ICJ) and Amnesty International, two private grups with U.N. consultative status. "Torture and other forms of mistreatment are a regular practice—of that I have no doubt whatever," said Niall MacDermot, ICJ secretary general. At least 50% of Uruguay's political prisoners were tortured, he said.

Military aide killed. Col. Ramon Trabal, military attache to the Uruguayan embassies in Paris and London, was assassinated by unknown persons in Paris Dec. 19. A telephone caller told the French news agency AFP Dec. 19 that Trabal was killed by the "Raul Sendic International Brigade," a leftist group, for his role in pursuing and allegedly torturing Tupamaro guerrillas in Uruguay, including Tupamaro founder Raul Sendic.

Economy

Beef stocks pile up. Slaughterhouses were ordered to stop work because of difficulties in exporting beef to Uruguay's traditional market, the European Economic Community, caused by high tariffs imposed by France and Italy, according to the *Andean Times' Latin America Economic Report* April 12. Uruguay derived 80% of its export earnings from beef and wool. Wool too had become difficult to sell, since Japan and other purchasing countries were now spending their money on oil, *Latin America* reported. Without its expected beef and wool earnings, Uruguay would find it difficult to buy oil, expected to cost $140 million in 1974, according to the *Andean Times* Feb. 22.

Cost of living soars. Uruguay's cost of living rose by 100% in 1974, *Latin America* reported Dec. 20. It was the third such rise in as many years. The economy had continued to deteriorate late in the year despite the efforts of Economy Minister Alejandro Vegh Villegas, who floated the peso, freed imports from controls, and gradually abandoned price controls, according to *Latin America* Dec. 6. The peso was devalued by 7.95% Nov. 13. It was the 11th devaluation of 1974.

See also ARGENTINA [2, 5]; BRAZIL [10]; LATIN AMERICA

U THANT—*See* BURMA

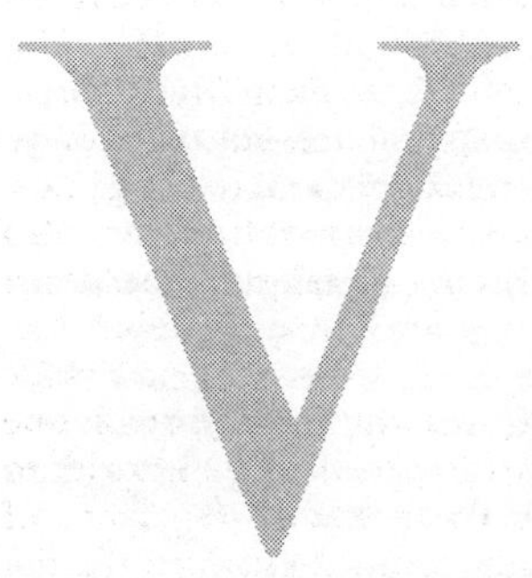

VATICAN—*See* EUROPEAN SECURITY; HUNGARY; MEXICO [20]; MIDDLE EAST [36]; NICARAGUA; POLAND; RELIGION [12-18]; SPAIN [9-10, 12-13]

VENEZUELA—Nationalization policies. Venezuela took steps to nationalize its oil, iron and steel industries in 1974, following a policy outlined Jan. 1 by outgoing President Rafael Caldera. In his nationwide New Year's message, Caldera cited the oil industry as "fundamental to our economy" and said its activity "must pass into the hands of the national public sector." Caldera also said other key industries such as milk, electrical energy and television should also revert to state ownership.

The March 12 inaugural address of incoming President Carlos Andres Perez also stressed nationalization. In an apparent bid for a Venezuelan leadership role in Latin America, Perez said, "We must take up the defense of Latin American rights, trampled by the economic totalitarianism of the developed countries. Venezuela now has the opportunity to offer Latin America, with the backing of oil, efficient cooperation to carry out the common struggle for independent development, decent prices for other raw materials and a just and balanced participation in world trade." To help other Latin countries, Venezuela would establish a trust fund within the Inter-American Development Bank (IDB) "without humiliating vetoes," Perez declared. The reference apparently was to the U.S.' vetoes in recent years of projected IDB loans to Chile and Peru.

U.S. oil firms operating in Venezuela March 12 reacted to Perez' statements on oil with what the *Wall Street Journal* called "stoical acceptance." The companies, which had preferred Perez among the 12 candidates in the December 1973 election, reportedly felt they would receive "fair" compensation for their Venezuelan properties. Perez had told foreign newsmen March 11 that it was "logical and suitable" for the U.S. firms to have a continuing role in Venezuelan oil marketing and technology. However, he had added that Venezuela would maintain its current high oil prices even if other countries reduced theirs.

Perez announced May 16 that the government would nationalize the oil industry "immediately," paying "just compensation" to foreign companies. He did not, however, set a timetable for the takeover and indicated, on June 9, that the government would move cautiously. Perez also moved closer to nationalizing the iron ore industry, the nation's most important economic sector after oil, by appointing a policy-making National Iron and Steel Council May 21. The government was negotiating with U.S. Steel Corp. and Bethlehem Steel Corp., which controlled the industry, in an effort to form mixed companies dominated by Venezuelan capital. (Perez had, on April 29, announced a sweeping new economic policy which, in addition to the iron and steel nationalizations, also would require other foreign firms to sell 80% of their capital to Venezuelan nationals within three years. Among the firms affected was Sears Roebuck Co. which owned 14 stores of varying sizes in Venezuela. To enact the economic reforms, Perez had asked for extraordinary powers over the economy for one year, which Congress granted him May 30. Congress also gave Perez authority to increase wages by 5%-25%, an action which resulted in layoffs of thousands of workers before the government issued a one-month prohibition against the firings.)

The government presented a draft law for nationalization Aug. 20, and a revision on Oct. 17. The October version gave the government total control of foreign marketing of Venezuelan crude oil and petroleum derivatives; barred mixed companies in the nationalized industry, but allowed state firms to make contracts to carry out their activities. It also asked immediate occupation of the petroleum industry if no agreement were reached on compensation for foreign corporations; and established job stability for oil workers. Regarding compensation, the draft bill said the government would offer the foreign firms a sum, and if the firms rejected it, the matter would be referred to three experts—one chosen by the attorney general, one by the oil companies and one by the Supreme Court. After hearing from the experts, the court would set the compensation figure.

Meanwhile, the government continued negotiations with U.S. Steel Corp. and Bethlehem Steel Corp. Argenis Gamboa, a Venezuelan representative in the talks, said Oct. 24 that compensation to the companies would not exceed $200 million. Perez said the nationalization would be decreed in the first days of December, but Venezuela would respect all commitments it had to the steel firms, it was reported Nov. 26.

Other oil developments. The government Feb. 6 doubled to about $14 a barrel the price it charged petroleum companies for royalty oil. (Increases in posted prices for Venezuelan oil through December 1973 had increased the nation's international monetary reserves to $2.418 billion, according to International Monetary Fund statistics reported Feb. 2.) A production cutback of 5% was ordered, effective April 15, to conserve large volumes of natural gas which were produced jointly with oil but were burned off at the oilfields because of insufficient gas processing facilities. More than half of the nation's 3.3 million barrel per day production was delivered to the U.S.; however, officials said the cutback would not affect U.S. or other traditional markets. Prices were raised again June 30 to $14.43 a barrel, with foreign companies also paying an additional 21¢ a barrel in taxes. The government Oct. 1 raised the income tax paid by the foreign companies by 3.5%, to 63.5% of the posted price per barrel. The measure, retroactive to Jan. 1, would increase the companies' 1974 tax bill to $40 million and boost the government's 1974 oil earnings to over $10 billion, according to press reports.

Other economic developments. The government announced July 4 that foreign investment in Venezuela would be channeled into new areas, such as agricultural and heavy machinery production in accordance with a decision made by the Andean Group which also limited foreign ownership of local firms to 20% and remittance of profits abroad to 14%. (The Andean Group was composed of Bolivia, Chile, Colombia, Ecuador, Peru and Venezuela.)

A study released by the U.S. Agriculture Department Jan. 19 had said that Venezuela was suffering from a food shortage caused by a decrease in national food production due to droughts and increased world food prices. On May 3 the Venezuelan government reported it would have to import $350 million worth of maize, beans, soya beans, sorghum and wheat to cover the 1974 food deficit. The government planned to spend more than $1 billion over the next five years to improve irrigation systems, it was reported June 7.

Due partly to the influx of oil dollars, Venezuela's inflation rate had at least doubled during the past year, according to reports. Venezuelan inflation, which usually ran at an annual rate of 3%, had risen to 6.18% during the first half of 1974, according to government statistics reported Oct. 12. To control inflation, the government announced a new system of price controls Nov. 5, allowing increases in only two staple foods, eggs and edible oils. To prevent its increased oil income from contributing to price rises, the administration earmarked billions of dollars for domestic development programs and loans to foreign countries and international organizations. Among domestic investments, the government set aside $185 million-$230 million to purchase oil tankers for a national fleet Oct. 14; established a multimillion dollar urban development fund Nov. 15; and earmarked more than $700 million to improve housing, medical services, education and employment in the eastern Guayana region Nov. 17.

See also AVIATION [14]; BOXING; CHILE [5, 7, 17, 27]; COFFEE; CUBA; DOMINICAN REPUBLIC; LATIN AMERICA; MEXICO [1, 21]; MONETARY DEVELOPMENTS [5]; NETHERLANDS [1]; OIL [5, 8, 17, 19, 35]; SUGAR; SURINAM; TERRITORIAL WATERS

VESCO, ROBERT L.—Costa Rican President Jose Figueres signed into law a controversial extradition bill which, critics charged, was specifically designed to protect fugitive U.S. financier Robert Vesco, it was reported March 29. It said a foreigner could not be extradited on a simple request from abroad. Vesco, a friend of Figueres, was sought by the U.S. on fraud charges and was implicated in the Watergate scandal. [See WATERGATE AFFAIR 74-76] He had a home and investments valued at $25 million in Costa Rica. The law was opposed by student groups, newspapers, opposition legislators, ex-President Mario Echandi and even President-elect Daniel Oduber, due to take office May 8.

Two Vesco business associates were cited for failing to appear before a federal grand jury investigating possible criminal fraud charges against Vesco, the *Wall Street Journal* reported April 9. Milton F. Meissner, former president of Vesco's Investors Overseas Services Ltd. (IOS), and Gilbert R. J. Straub were named in the contempt citation. Richard Clay had also been found in civil contempt for failing to testify before the grand jury. Vesco, Clay, Meissner, Straub and others were defendants in the SEC's suit charging them with "looting" $224 million from IOS and other Vesco-controlled companies. Straub was reported to be in Costa Rica with Vesco, a fugitive from several U.S. warrants for his arrest. Meissner, released on bail in March after spending nearly a year in a Luxembourg jail on charges of fraud related to the IOS affair, was believed to be in the Bahamas with Clay.

A jet aircraft used by Vesco was seized by U.S. customs officials Aug. 21 in San Antonio, in connection with Vesco's alleged involvement in gun running. It was also reported that the plane was used to ferry prostitutes between Los Angeles and Costa Rica. It was the third Vesco jet confiscated by authorities. Alwyn Eisenhauer, Vesco's personal pilot, flew Vesco's personal plane, a Boeing

707, out of Panama May 10, acting under an impoundment order signed by a New Jersey Supreme Court justice. Eisenhauer said he spirited the plane away in an effort to recoup more than $50,000 owed him by Vesco.

See also WATERGATE [74-76]

VETERANS—Benefits increase. Congress Oct. 10 approved legislation increasing education benefits for veterans. The bill was aimed at post-Korean War and Vietnam era veterans. Among the provisions of the bill: monthly educational benefits were increased 22.7%, raising the allowance for a single veteran with no dependents from $220 to $270 a month; monthly allowances for veterans receiving on-the-job training or vocational rehabilitation for the disabled were increased 18.2%; the period during which a veteran would be entitled to educational assistance was lengthened from 36 to 45 months (the additional time was for undergraduate work only); the Veterans Administration was authorized to lend up to $600 annually to cover educational costs of eligible veterans.

The new bill became law Dec. 3 when Congress voted to override a veto by President Ford. The vote in the House was 394-10. The Senate vote was 90-1, with only assistant Senate Republican Leader Robert Griffin (Mich.) voting to uphold the veto. Ford had vetoed the measure on the ground that the increase beyond the 18.2% boost projected in the federal budget was inflationary. After the override, White House Press Secretary Ron Nessen said the President would send Congress a request for an $814 million supplemental appropriation to cover the budgetary excess in the current fiscal year.

Pentagon abolishes discharge codes. Secretary of Defense James R. Schlesinger March 22 announced discontinuation of the use of numerical codes on military discharge papers. Under the system abolished by Schlesinger, one of about 500 code numbers was affixed by a commanding officer to the discharge papers of a serviceman to indicate conditions under which he left. Some of the numbers were prejudicial, indicating the serviceman was financially irresponsible, a bet wetter, a drug user, or in some other way unsuitable for military service. Although the meaning of the numbers was supposed to be known only to the Pentagon, private employers were able to obtain information on their meaning and used them to deny men employment even though the men had not undergone judicial action. Schlesinger said that all veterans honorably discharged during the last two decades would be permitted new discharge papers minus the code numbers. All discharge papers issued in the future would contain no indication as to why a veteran left the service.

VA chief leaves post. Veterans Administrator Donald E. Johnson April 22 announced his intention to resign. Johnson, whose ouster had been sought by Congressional critics and veterans organizations, would be eligible for a government pension June 19 after five years as head of the Veterans Administration (VA). The controversy surrounding Johnson was heightened April 23 by Sen. Alan Cranston (D, Calif.), who charged Johnson with violating the Hatch Act, which prohibited federal employes from soliciting campaign money or engaging in a partisan political campaign. According to Cranston, a key aide to Johnson—with Johnson's knowledge—urged VA employes to buy $100 chances to attend a $1,000-a-plate campaign dinner held for Nixon in the spring of 1972. This information, Cranston said, had been turned over to the office of the Watergate special prosecutor and to the Civil Service Commission. Johnson denied any knowledge of political fund-raising within the VA.

Earlier criticism of Johnson had focused on his alleged failure to fight for interests of veterans, that he succumbed to the wishes of the Office of Management and Budget and that he had deliberately "bungled" the bureaucracy. Not only had Johnson forced competent high level officials out of the VA, Cranston charged, but he replaced them with "incompetents, former campaign officials, ex-creeps [Committee to Re-elect the President] and inexperienced, under-qualified administrators...."

Ford announced his appointment of former Rep. Richard L. Roudebush (R, Ind. 1961-71), 56, a past Veterans of Foreign Wars (VFW) commander (1957), as administrator of the Veterans Administration at a Chicago VFW convention Aug. 19. Roudebush had been the VA's deputy administrator since January.

Report criticizes VA hospitals. According to a VA study made public Oct. 26, critical staff and space shortages had compromised the ability of VA hospitals to provide emergency care. The former serviceman who sought emergency care was "taking a chance," the hospital survey warned. The report, ordered by President Nixon in March after widespread reports of inadequate care in the 171-VA hospital system, urged Congress to immediately increase the current VA budget by $190 million and to add another $235 million for the following year. The increases, the report said, should all go toward attracting and retaining competent medical personnel.

Veterans home loans. A bill making veterans eligible for a second guaranteed home loan was passed by the Senate Dec. 13 and House Dec. 17. The President signed the bill Dec. 31. Applying to veterans who served since the start of World War II, the previous limit of one loan per veteran would be lifted if a previous loan were paid off. The guarantee would be raised to $17,500 (was $15,000) and would be extended to loans for condominiums. The amount of loan guarantee for mobile homes would be increased. The measure would also provide a 22% increase (formerly 18.5%) in benefits for disabled veterans attending college or vocational rehabilitation programs.

Ford signed legislation Dec. 23 to provide a 12% cost-of-living increase for veterans or survivors receiving pension benefits. The bill had been passed by the House Dec. 7 and Senate Dec. 10.

See also AMNESTY & CLEMENCY; APPOINTMENTS & RESIGNATIONS; BUDGET; HOUSING

VICE-PRESIDENT, U.S.—Legislation designating an official residence for the vice president received final approval of the Senate June 26 and House June 28 and was signed by President Nixon July 12. The residence was on the grounds of the U.S. Naval Observatory in Washington, and was currently occupied by the Chief of Naval Operations. The changeover to the vice president would be effective upon termination of service of the incumbent chief.

[For details of the nomination, confirmation investigations and swearing-in of Nelson A. Rockefeller as vice-president of the U.S., see ROCKEFELLER, NELSON A.]

See also AGNEW, SPIRO T.

VIETNAM, PEOPLE'S REPUBLIC OF (NORTH VIETNAM)—North Vietnam expressed interest in setting up diplomatic relations with the U.S., but only under certain conditions, according to a white paper published by the Foreign Ministry Jan. 17. The document, issued to mark the first anniversary of the signing of the Paris peace agreements, said "normalization" of ties between Washington and Hanoi depended on complete U.S. disengagement from South Vietnam, fulfillment of the U.S. pledge to reconstruct North Vietnam and respect for the "fundamental national rights of the Laotian and Cambodian peoples."

The U.N. Childrens Fund (UNICEF) April 16 announced plans for aid to North Vietnam and to areas held by the Viet Cong in the South. UNICEF Director Henry Labouisse said the three-year program called for $18 million to be spent rebuilding schools in the North and $4.5 million to be spent in the South. He said he had asked the UNICEF board for $8 million for the program; the balance would come from special contributions by governments. (European countries, Japan, Australia, New Zealand and Algeria had already contributed more than $12 million.)

See also AUSTRALIA [2]; CAMBODIA; LAOS; VIETNAM, REPUBLIC OF [1-8, 11-13, 26-33]

VIETNAM, REPUBLIC OF (SOUTH VIETNAM)

War Developments

[1] In spite of the 1973 cease-fire, the war continued unabated. By Dec. 31 the South Vietnamese command reported that more than 80,000 persons had been killed in fighting throughout the country in 1974: 61,019 North Vietnamese and Viet Cong troops, 15,241 South Vietnamese soldiers and 3,454 civilians. This was the highest fatality total for any year of the war, except for 1972 when nearly 150,000 soldiers had been reported killed. The government said since the start of the January 1973 cease-fire agreement, government losses had totaled 27,355 soldiers killed, 110,777 wounded and 15,084 missing. According to command estimates, Communist deaths were 104,670 during that period.

[2] The *New York Times* reported Jan. 6 the North Vietnamese were making progress in constructing infiltration routes in the Central Highlands along a north-south road network known as Corridor 613. They were also reported to have developed west-east systems which jutted into disputed and government-held areas, raising the danger of cutting South Vietnam in half. Two days earlier, claiming the "war had restarted" Prseident Nguyen Van Thieu declared, "We should not allow the Communists a situation in which their security is guaranteed now in their own zone so that they can launch harassing attacks against us.... We should carry out these activities not only in our zone but also in the area where their army is now stationed."

[3] With heavy fighting taking place between government and Communist troops South Vietnamese Information Minister Hoang Duc Nha warned March 30 that North Vietnam was preparing a general offensive aimed at conquering South Vietnam. His charge was coupled with an intelligence report that North Vietnam was sending civilians into Viet Cong-controlled areas in the South to establish farms and populate the areas. The move, Nha said, was based on Hanoi's fear that the Viet Cong "would probably be willing to get into a political settlement" on their own with Saigon. Fighting escalated in the Central Highlands in March in a series of clashes near half a dozen government outposts. They were described as the bloodiest since the 1973 cease-fire agreement. The battle, described by Saigon as the start of a Communist offensive in that area, had been precipitated—according to government claims—by a North Vietnamese artillery, rocket and mortar barrage March 16 against government positions along a road 10 miles north of Kontum city. South Vietnamese soldiers suffered heavy casualties April 2 in heavy fighting eight miles northeast of the city.

[4] North Vietnamese troops April 12 captured the South Vietnamese ranger base at Tong Le Chan, 55 miles northwest of Saigon, ending a 13-month siege of the strongpoint near the Cambodian border. Another government camp was captured April 16 as ranger troops withdrew from Base 711 on a provincial road just south of Pleiku city in the Central Highlands.

[5] Thousands of South Vietnamese troops carried out two separate thrusts into Cambodia April 29 and 30, the first since the January 1973 cease-fire agreement. The incursions were an effort to relieve a government outpost under siege in

South Vietnam and to recapture another base in Communist hands. The fighting that raged between North and South Vietnamese troops several miles inside the country through May 2 was in violation of Article 20 of the truce accord that barred either side from "using the territory of Cambodia or Laos to encroach on the sovereignty and security of one another." In the first thrust, government troops April 29 crossed the frontier into Cambodia in the Go Dau Hau area, 35 miles northwest of Saigon, in an operation aimed at lifting the month-long Communist siege of the Duc Hue base to the south. The second government incursion April 30 was carried out from Moc Hoa, 20 miles southwest, and was designed to encircle a North Vietnamese force that had captured the Vietnamese base at Long Khot April 29. A force of about 60 armored personnel carriers and 3,000 troops were engaged in a pincer action aimed at closing in on the North Vietnamese from the east in Cambodia and from the west in South Vietnam.

[6] Major action shifted to the Saigon area when North Vietnamese forces May 16 launched a strong drive toward strategic Ben Cat, 25 miles from the capital. Ben Cat was in the heart of the Iron Triangle along the Saigon River corridor leading from Cambodia to Saigon. Thousands of government troops moved into the village May 18 after the Communists advanced that day to within a half mile of the town, capturing three nearby government outposts and seizing a village. Government troops launched a major counterattack May 20, meeting fierce resistance from the Communists. Heavy fighting continued around Ben Cat into June. On June 3 the rebel troops had shelled the Bien Hoa area, 15 miles northeast of Saigon, killing 43 persons and wounding 83, most of them civilians. One of the targets struck was the Tan Hiep prison, housing Viet Cong and other political prisoners. Most of the dead were women political prisoners and their children, police said. A *New York Times* report July 27 on the May-June fighting in the Ben Cat area north of Saigon said South Vietnam had committed most of a 12,000-man division in a futile effort to recapture all the territory lost to the Communists. Government forces were said to have suffered about 2,600 casualties, including at least 500 killed.

[7] Fighting erupted in the vicinity of Danang July 18 and continued through July 30. Communist forces launched the attacks July 18 and surrounded Duc Duc, 25 miles southwest of the city. They shelled the Danang air base July 19 and 29, causing mostly civilian casualties. On July 29 they captured seven government outposts south of Danang around the district capital of Thuong Duc. The next day government forces recaptured one of the seven outposts, while North Vietnamese troops seized the district capital of Nang Buk in the Central Highlands.

[8] Continued attacks by North Vietnamese and Viet Cong troops around Danang and reports by U.S. officials Aug. 7-8 that North Vietnam had alerted its troops in South Vietnam and six home-based divisions raised speculation that the Communist forces were preparing for a major offensive in the south. According to U.S. analysts, there had been a sharp increase recently in Communist supply movements in the South. North Vietnam's forces in the South were also said to be stronger than at any previous time—more than 200,000 combat soldiers, with another 100,000-150,000 support troops and guerrillas. The North's forces within its own borders were estimated at 300,000-350,000.

[9] Communist forces attacked South Vietnamese troops Aug. 15-17 about 15-20 miles from Saigon in the closest thrust to the capital in more than two years. A Saigon communique said two separate Communist attacks, 15 and 20 miles north of the capital, were repulsed Aug. 15. After launching a tank assault Aug.

17, Communist forces drove south of Ben Cat to within 18 miles of the center of Saigon. The Bien Hoa air base, 20 miles northeast of Saigon, came under Communist shelling Aug. 10-14. In fighting in the north-central provinces, several South Vietnamese outposts were captured as the Communists continued the drive they had launched in that area July 17.

[10] A *Washington Post* report from Saigon Aug. 25 said South Vietnam, in a major policy shift, had decided to abandon military outposts it no longer had resources to defend. It was believed the change was being forced by diminishing U.S. military assistance, marking the first time that Saigon was following a general policy of drawing its forces back to stronger defense lines in the interior, the newspaper said. A government official was quoted as saying that "remote outposts were being closed down to save the large amounts of fuel and ammunition that it takes to keep them going."

[11] Communist forces were said by South Vietnamese military sources Oct. 4 to have apparently captured Chuong Nghia, one of the government's last bases between the Central Highlands city of Kontum and the coast, opening an important supply corridor to Viet Cong and North Vietnamese troops. Another government base on Route 5, Gia Vuc, had been seized by the North Vietnamese Sept. 20, according to a government report.

[12] Major fighting broke out in the southern part of South Vietnam Dec. 6. Nearly 3,000 government and Viet Cong and North Vietnamese troops suffered casualties through Dec. 10. The fighting was linked to rivalry for the winter rice crop and was centered in the Mekong Delta's Chuong Thien Province and the provinces surrounding Saigon, including Tay Ninh, Hau Nghia and Kien Tuong, bordering Cambodia. Fighting also began, later in the month, for control of Phuoc Long Province, near Saigon. South Vietnamese forces Nov. 20 had recaptured the last of three outposts in the Iron Triangle, 25 miles north of Saigon. The government had fought a bloody six-month campaign for the positions that had been overrun by the Communists in May.

[13] The Saigon command characterized the fighting as "clearly the beginning of the long predicted 1975 dry season offensive" by the Communists. The U.S. expressed hope Dec. 9 that the North Vietnamese "will recognize the futility of broadening their attacks and will end actions which are in violation of the Paris truce agreements." The South Vietnamese military intelligence was reported Dec. 3 to have obtained documents indicating that the Communists were planning a sharp increase in fighting in the forthcoming dry season.

[14] South Vietnamese government defenses deteriorated further as Communist forces captured more district towns in continued fighting in the southern part of the country Dec. 22-26. The Saigon command reported the Communist seizure Dec. 22 of Bu Doc, a district capital of Phuoc Long Province. The stronghold, 70 miles north of Saigon, was overrun after heavy shelling and ground attacks. Half the 300 defenders had retreated to the provincial capital of Phuoc Binh, it was reported. The district capital of Tanh Linh in Binh Tuy Province, 70 miles northeast of Saigon, came under Viet Cong siege Dec. 23 and was captured Dec. 25. Another district capital in Phuoc Long Province, Don Luan, was captured by Communists Dec. 26, giving them control of all the major towns in the province except its beleaguered capital. The town, 50 miles notrh of Saigon, was the fifth such outpost to be captured since the start of the Communist offensive Dec. 6. It had been defended by about 100 militiamen.

Government Developments

[15] On Jan. 19, the National Assembly approved by a 153-52 vote a constitutional amendment that would permit President Thieu to run for a third term

when his current four-year term expired in 1975. The amendment also extended the presidential term to five years, but limited tenure to two terms. About 40 opposition legislators had staged a protest against passage earlier in the day, calling the law "dictatorial."

[16] Thieu made major Cabinet changes Feb. 16 after asking all but two of the 24 ministers to resign. A government announcement two days later said the change was designed to improve the efficiency of the administration. In May, Thieu dismissed his assistant for political affairs, Nguyen Van Ngan who had been one of the president's most trusted political advisers. An official report attributed the dismissal to budgetary reasons, but other reports charged Ngan with being a Communist spy. A third possible cause was the internal power struggle in the government between two factions, one headed by Ngan and the other by Information Minister Hoang Duc Nha, who was related to Thieu.

[17] On June 19 Thieu announced a drive against corruption and a ban on political activities in the armed forces and the civil service. A military court was reported June 5 to have sentenced 19 officers to prison terms of 1-8 years for accepting bribes from soldiers who were listed as present for duty when actually they were out of the army working at lucrative civilian jobs. In an austerity measure aimed at the military, generals were ordered to sharply reduce their personal staffs, it was reported June 5. The move was believed tied to Saigon's fears that the U.S. Congress would slash aid to South Vietnam. U.S. funds were believed to pay for about 40% of South Vietnam's military salaries.

[18] The government began an anti-press drive in August, after various newspapers had printed articles on military and governmental corruption. Police confiscated issues objectionable to Thieu. On Sept. 8, the newly-formed Committee Struggling for the Right to Freedom of the Press and of Publication issued a statement denouncing the government for "oppressing and terrorizing the press, newspapermen, writers and artists." The group was composed of publishers, journalists and opposition politicians.

[19] More than 5,000 Catholics in Hue staged a protest Sept. 15 against alleged government corruption and the behavior of police who had used tear gas to break up a similar Catholic rally in the city Sept. 8. Several hundred persons staged a demonstration in Saigon Sept. 20 to protest a government order to seize that day's issues of three city dailies that had published the full text of a statement accusing Thieu of six instances of corruption. The statement, made the previous day by the Rev. Tran Huu Tranh, accused Thieu of amassing illegal houses and properties, implication in a fertilizer scandal, engineering the heroin traffic and turning the profitable central Vietnam rice distribution over to an aunt. The Ministry of Information said Sept. 20 that the three newspapers had published libelous attacks "without supporting evidence."

[20] Thieu answered the attacks on him in a broadcast Oct. 1, saying that charges he had made money on various illegal land and housing deals "were either exaggerated or simply groundless." He offered to resign if "the entire people and army have no confidence in me." Conceding there was corruption in the army and government, Thieu pledged to reduce it "within three months." A demand for Thieu's resignation to pave the way for an end to the war and repressive government had been the theme of a demonstration staged in Saigon Sept. 29 by a broad opposition front, including Catholic priests, Buddhists and opposition politicians. Copies of a "corruption indictment" were distributed at the meeting. Two American newsmen employed by CBS News and the Associated Press were beaten by 10 men believed to be plainclothesmen as they covered the Saigon demonstration.

[21] The unrest continued when, on Oct. 20, a group of stone-throwing

protesters attacked the National Assembly building in Saigon, again denouncing governmental handling of the military situation and calling for resignation of the president. (A group of 22 National Assembly deputies, most of whom normally cooperated with the government, had marched to the presidential palace in Saigon Oct. 14 to voice their grievances against Thieu. Their action had followed a dispute earlier in the day in which some members charged government interference in the election of Assembly officers.) Two opposition leaders said Oct. 22 that police had arrested 14 students on charges of organizing the anti-government demonstrations. The arrests were regarded as the first sign of a tougher position being taken by the government in the face of the growing dissent. In another move to diffuse the opposition, two days later Thieu forced the resignation of four Cabinet ministers and announced the planned ouster of 377 army officers for "corruption and dishonest activities." Among those Cabinet members removed was Information Minister Hoang Duc Nha, a relative of Thieu's, whose responsibilities included press censorship. An alliance of newspaper publishers and press associations had called for his resignation the day before. Opposition forces remained dissatisfied with the actions.

[22] Thieu made other moves at the end of the month when he announced the transfer of three powerful military commanders to lesser positions. The action was denounced again by the opposition as insufficient and was followed by an Oct. 31 demonstration in Saigon which was the most violent since the protests began. At least 90 persons were injured in the clash between police and protesters, including two opposition deputies. (Organized labor, which had supported Thieu, joined the growing opposition to the president Oct. 29 when Tran Quoc Buu, president of the 300,000-member Confederation of Vietnamese Trade Unions, called for elimination of corruption, implementation of the Paris truce agreements and establishment of democratic liberties.)

[23] A revolt of Montagnard tribesmen had also erupted in the Central Highlands in July over a series of grievances ranging from theft of tribal lands by private individuals and government officials, to inadequacies of public services, particularly health and education. The government had crushed two previous uprisings in 1964 and 1965. A rebel document reported that from July-September 160 Montagnards had been "lost, killed and massacred," by South Vietnamese police. About 50 people, mostly Vietnamese civilians, were said to have been killed by the rebels in August in highway ambushes and holdups in the province.

[24] Thieu appointed seven new Cabinet ministers Nov. 28 as street demonstrations against his government continued. An opposition leader assailed Thieu's ministerial changes, saying his group would not accept them. The new Cabinet appointees were: Nguyen Van Hao, deputy premier for economic development; Ho Van Cham, acting information minister, who also was to retain his position of minister of veterans affairs; Le Quang Truong, finance, replacing Chau Kim Nhan, who had resigned in October; Nguyen Van Diep, head of the newly formed Ministry of Trade and Supply, replacing Nguyen Duc Cuong, who had been minister of trade and industries; Nguyen Tien Hung, minister of planning; Doan Minh Quan, agriculture, and Nguyen Huu Tan, vice minister of industry.

[25] Hundreds of police Nov. 28 blocked attempts by anti-government Roman Catholic demonstrators to march from outlying sections of Saigon to the center of the city. Scattered violence erupted in some sections of the city, however, as stonethrowing Catholic youths fought with police. The Catholics had sought to march to support three opposition newspapers whose managements were to go on trial Nov. 28 on charges of printing a defamatory accusation against

President Thieu by the Rev. Tran Huu Thanh, head of the Catholic anticorruption movement. (The National Assembly Nov. 14 had voted 76-0 to approve a slight relaxation of the press law but retained Thieu's right to confiscate issues of newspapers. Approval by the Senate and signature by Thieu were assured.)

Peace & Political Proposals

[26] The Viet Cong March 22 proposed a new plan aimed at resolving the political and military impasse in South Vietnam. An accompanying statement denounced the U.S. and South Vietnam for continued violation of the Paris truce accords. It called for an end to U.S. military and internal involvement in South Vietnam. South Vietnam, though calling the plan a "propaganda trick," did not reject it outright. The embassy in Paris March 23 suggested that the Viet Cong delegates join Saigon in setting up working groups for detailed negotiations on four of the Communist points: restoration of democratic liberties; establishment of a National Council of National Reconciliation and Concord (provided for in the 1973 Paris peace agreements); national elections, organized by the Council; and resolving the problems of the armed forces of both sides. The North Vietnamese had also called for an immediate end to the fighting and return of all captured and detained Vietnamese civilians and military personnel.

[27] Peace talks were suspended by Saigon April 16 because of what the South Vietnamese called the increasing number of truce violations committed by Communist forces. Foreign Minister Vuong Van Bac deplored the Viet Cong's rejection of "the very concrete and constructive" proposals submitted by his government during the Paris talks.

[28] The Viet Cong's Provisional Revolutionary Government (PRG) broke off military and political contacts with South Vietnam May 10 and 13. The PRG's delegation to the Two-Party Joint Military Commission walked out of a meeting with South Vietnamese representatives in Saigon May 10 after announcing it would not attend future sessions until Saigon restored its diplomatic privileges and immunities. This was in reference to the severance by the government April 30 of the Viet Cong delegation's telephone service and liaison flights between Saigon and its headquarters at Loc Ninh, and the termination of its weekly news briefings. (The action had been taken because, according to spokesmen, the Viet Cong was spreading "false news and distorting arguments, prejudicing the host country and misleading world opinion.") The PRG delegation to the political talks in Paris announced May 13 an indefinite suspension of its meetings with the South Vietnamese delegation.

[29] The PRG and South Vietnam resumed meetings in Saigon June 11 with discussions on restoration of the Communist delegation's diplomatic status. The PRG had agreed to the talks June 8 following a unilateral action June 7 by Saigon which restored the Viet Cong's telephone lines to Saigon, permitted resumption of their weekly news conferences and resumed weekly liaison flights to the Viet Cong administrative center at Loc Ninh. The Viet Cong and North Vietnamese, however, quit the talks June 22, withdrawing as well from the Four-Party Joint Military Team (JMT) which was charged with the search for men missing in action. A statement issued by the PRG and supported by the North Vietnamese demanded written guarantees of the "privileges and immunities" of the Communist delegations in Saigon, adoption of a "serious" negotiation stance by South Vietnam and a response to the Communists' "sensible" six-point peace plan of March 22. South Vietnam June 12 had proposed a new six-point cease-fire agreement, calling for an immediate halt to the fighting, the return of Communist soldiers to pre-cease-fire lines, withdrawal of North Vietnamese troops and their equipment from the South, release of military and

civilian prisoners, respect for the International Commission of Control and Supervision (ICCS), and serious political negotiations.

[30] The ICCS was saved from financial collapse when South Vietnam contributed $2.8 million and the U.S. $4.1 million to the organization Sept. 23 and 25, permitting it to continue operations for at least another two months. The commission, with a $5 million debt, had been on the verge of withdrawing its truce observers from the South Vietnam countryside because of its inability to pay its contracting bill. North Vietnam and the PRG refused to provide funds to the ICCS. A PRG spokesman said Sept. 21 that his side would not pay "until the United States stops its military engagement and interference in South Vietnam."

POWs & MIAs

[31] South Vietnam and the Viet Cong March 8 completed the release of the last prisoners of war officially listed as captured before the January 1973 cease-fire. The agreement on the prisoner release, following a seven-month suspension, had been announced by negotiators for both sides Feb. 5. A previous agreement had been reached Jan. 4 but the accord broke down. Since the signing of the Paris agreement, South Vietnam had freed 26,880 Communist soldiers and 5,081 civilians. According to government figures, 248 civilians had decided to remain on the government side. The Viet Cong had repatriated 606 government soldiers and 5,336 civilians. Both sides continued to hold an undetermined number of military and civilian prisoners captured since the cease-fire.

[32] North Vietnam released the remains of the last of the U.S. servicemen known to have died in captivity in North Vietnam. Twelve of the bodies were flown from Hanoi March 6 in a U.S. Air Force transport plane to the American base at U Thapao, Thailand for definitive identification. An additional 11 bodies were flown to the base March 13. The North Vietnamese still held the body of a B-52 crewman who had died when his plane was shot down.

[33] The U.S. called on the Viet Cong and North Vietnam Dec. 20 to immediately release information on 87 American servicemen missing in action, whose fate, the Defense Department claimed, was known by the Communists. The Communists rejected the U.S. request Dec. 24. Since April 1973 the U.S. had privately passed on to the North Vietnamese and Viet Cong information of the 87 men, 35 of whom were missing in South Vietnam and the 52 others in North Vietnam. A North Vietnamese Foreign Ministry statement Dec. 24 said Hanoi would refuse to meet the U.S. request until all aspects of the Paris truce agreement were implemented, including Washington's pledge to provide North Vietnam with economic assistance. U.S.-North Vietnamese aid talks had been suspended in July 1973 after the U.S. accused North Vietnam of truce violations.

U.S. Relations

[34] A dispute over the extent and purpose of U.S. aid to South Vietnam broke out Feb. 25 with publication in the *New York Times* of reports that U.S. "aid directly supports South Vietnamese violations and so breaks the spirit" of the truce accords. In an 18-page cablegram to the State Department in Washington, U.S. Ambassador Graham A. Martin said the article, written by David K. Shipler of the *Times* Saigon bureau, "contains numerous inaccuracies and half-truths." Martin added Shipler's article "deliberately omits or skeptically treats the flagrant Communist violations of the Paris accords."

[35] On March 13, Sen. Edward M. Kennedy (D, Mass.) called on Secretary of State Henry A. Kissinger to clarify the U.S. policy of continued economic and military assistance to Indochaina. Kissinger replied to Kennedy in a letter dated March 25 that while "the U.S. has no bilateral written commitment" to South Vietnam, the Nixon Administration's aim "continues to be to help strengthen the

conditions which made possible" the January 1973 Paris agreement on ceasefire and U.S. troop withdrawal. As a signatory to that accord, the U.S. was committed to fullfill its obligations to Saigon by supporting self-determination for its people and by providing the country with "the means necessary for its self-defense and for its economic viability," Kissinger said. Kissinger's letter was followed by a State Department statement April 1 denying Kennedy's allegations that the Nixon Administration had made "new commitments" to South Vietnam. In releasing Kissinger's letter, Kennedy April 1 called the secretary's reply "a welcome but disturbing clarification." He said it appeared that Kissinger was propounding a "new rationalization for our continued heavy involvement in Indochina," that the Administration was apparently now interpreting the Paris agreement "as creating new American commitments to South Vietnam."

[36] Ambassador Martin and the U.S. embassy in Saigon were criticized "for selective reporting" on military activities in that country, according to a staff report issued Aug. 5 by the Senate Foreign Relations Committee. The document accused the officials of the U.S. embassy of doctoring their reports to Washington to minimize cease-fire violations committed by South Vietnamese forces and to obscure South Vietnam's shaky security situation. The embassy's policy "closely followed the public line of the South Vietnamese government in justifying South Vietnamese measures which precipitated the temporary breakdown in May 1974 of the talks in Paris and Saigon" between the South Vietnamese and the Viet Cong, the report said. The report also questioned Ambassador Martin's prediction that the Administration's request for $750 million in economic assistance for the current fiscal year would benefit South Vietnam. The statement said the funds would merely represent "a continuation of the past aid strategy of supporting the Vietnamese economy..., in order to fill fiscal and trade deficits."

[37] The U.S. House of Representatives April 4 had rejected,177-154, a Nixon Administration-sponsored request to increase military aid to South Vietnam. As a result, the House action, which was described by observers as unexpected, left the Defense Department without the authorization necessary to spend beyond the $1.126 billion limit set by Congress when it approved the fiscal 1974 defense appropriations bill.

[38] The Pentagon told the Senate Armed Services Committee that it had found an extra $266 million for military aid to South Vietnam, it was reported April 16. The announcement meant that South Vietnam would receive supplemental military aid for the rest of fiscal 1974 (ending June 30) although Congress had refused to raise spending ceilings as requested by the Nixon Administration. The Pentagon said it had found money left over from fiscal 1972 and 1973, which could be used for aid to South Vietnam, if Congress did not object. Subsequently, the Senate committee voted to allow the Pentagon to use the $266 million. The House Armed Services Committee was also reported to have agreed to this solution. But the full Senate rejected the procedure by a 43-38 vote May 6.

Other Developments

[38] A study by the National Academy of Sciences, reported Feb. 22, concluded that U.S. use of chemical herbicides in the Vietnam War did damage to the ecology of South Vietnam that might last as long as a century. The study, ordered by Congress and commissioned by the Pentagon, was made by 17 scientists from the U.S., Sweden, Great Britain and South Vietnam.

[40] The Saigon government announced Aug. 28 that oil deposits had been found Aug. 25 in the China Sea, 190 miles south of the South Vietnamese town of Vung Tau. The discovery was made by Pecten Vietnam, a U.S. oil company.

Company officials said several months of further drilling and testing were necessary before it could be determined whether the oil reserves had commercial value.

[41] All 70 persons aboard an Air Vietnam Boeing 727 airliner were killed Sept. 15 when a would-be hijacker exploded two hand grenades. The plane, en route from Danang to Saigon, crash landed at an airfield at Phan Rang, 175 miles northeast of the capital. According to airline officials, the pilot had radioed five minutes before the explosion that a man dressed in army uniform had forced his way into the cockpit and demanded to be flown to Hanoi.

See also CALLEY, WILLIAM L.; CAMBODIA; CHINA, NATIONALIST; DEFENSE [5]; ENVIRONMENT & POLLUTION [15]; FORD, GERALD R,; FOREIGN AID; THAILAND; VIETNAM, PEOPLE'S REPUBLIC OF

VIETNAM WAR—*See* AMNESTY & CLEMENCY; CHEMICAL & BIOLOGICAL WEAPONS; DEFENSE [9]; FOREIGN AID; RADICALS; VETERANS

VINYL CHLORIDE—*See* ENVIRONMENT & POLLUTION [18]

VIRGINIA—*See* AVIATION [11]; ELECTIONS [5]; ENERGY CRISIS [8]; LABOR [13]; WEATHER

VLADIVOSTOCK SUMMIT MEETING—*See* DISARMAMENT; MIDDLE EAST [42]; UNION OF SOVIET SOCIALIST REPUBLICS [1]

VOTING RIGHTS—In an action announced Jan. 16, the Supreme Court held 7-2 that states could not deny the right to vote to prison inmates, who were otherwise eligible to vote. (Only a felony conviction caused the loss of suffrage in New York State.) The case involved 72 inmates in the Monroe County, N.Y. jail, who were serving misdemeanor sentences or awaiting trial and who had not been permitted to vote.

The House refused May 8 to consider a bill to permit voters to register for federal elections by postcard. The vote was 204-197 (160 R & 44 D vs. 177 D & 20 R). A conservative coalition against the bill was composed of Republicans wary of being outregistered by Democrats under the procedure and Southern Democrats with the same concern about blacks. The bill had been approved by the Senate in 1973.

See also INDIAN AFFAIRS

WATERGATE AFFAIR—During 1974 the Administration scandals came to a climax with the resignation and subsequent pardon of President Nixon. Although they included a wide range of abuses and illegalities, these scandals were generally referred to as the "Watergate affair," since they had emerged as a consequence of the discovery of the 1972 break-in at the Democratic National Committee's offices in the Watergate office building in Washington. In the first section under this topic, *Impeachment & Resignation*, the editors trace the specific impeachment proceedings and pressures that culminated in Nixon's resignation after the House Judiciary Committee voted articles of impeachment. The second section, entitled *The Struggle for the Presidential Papers & Tapes*, covers the conflict between the White House and Special Prosecutor Leon Jaworski over the evidence contained in Nixon's tapes of conversations with his aides. The Supreme Court's resolution of the struggle in Jaworski's favor finally forced Nixon to make public recordings that made impeachment or resignation inevitable. The third section consists of excerpts from the key tapes. The fourth section covers President Ford's pardon of Nixon. The fifth and final section reports on the trials in the [Robert L.] Vesco case, the [Lewis J.] Fielding break-in and the Watergate cover-up.

[2] The Watergate affair raised fundamental questions about the traditional ways candidates of both major parties financed their campaigns. This issue is covered in the topic CAMPAIGN FINANCING & ABUSES.

Impeachment & Resignation

[3] Succeeding revelations of wrongdoing in the executive branch, first revealed by the arrest of the Watergate burglars in 1972, culminated in

extraordinary pressures leading to the first presidential resignation in American history. On Aug. 8, 1974 President Richard M. Nixon turned over his office to Vice President Gerald R. Ford. The constitutional responsibility for impeachment investigation proceedings rests with the House of Representatives. This section of the Watergate story, therefore, deals mainly with the actions of that body. A key issue in the House proceedings was the definition of an impeachable offense. The wording in the Constitution gives, as the basis for such an action, commission of "treason, bribery or other high crimes and misdemeanors." The House Judiciary Committee held that a violation of criminal law need not occur. The Association of the Bar of the City of New York concluded the phrase referred to "acts which, like treason and bribery, undermine the integrity of the government." The White House, on the other hand, defined the phrase more narrowly, saying "a president may only be impeached for indictable crimes."

[4] **Nixon's State of the Union Message.** President Nixon delivered his State of the Union Message in person before a joint session of Congress Jan. 30. At the conclusion of his nationally televised prime-time address, Nixon added "a personal word" on "the so-called Watergate affair." Nixon said, "As you know, I have provided to the special prosecutor voluntarily a great deal of material. I believe that I have provided all the material that he needs to conclude his investigations and to proceed to prosecute the guilty and to clear the innocent. I believe the time has come to bring that investigation and the other investigations of this matter to an end. One year of Watergate is enough. I recognize that the House Judiciary Committee has a special responsibility in this area.... I will cooperate so that it can conclude its investigation, make its decision and I will cooperate in any way that I consider consistent with my responsibilities for the office of the Presidency of the United States. There is only one limitation: I will follow the precedent that has been followed by and defended by every President from George Washington to Lyndon B. Johnson of never doing anything that weakens the office of the President of the United States or impairs the ability of the President of the future to make the great decisions that are so essential to this nation and the world."

[5] **House backs committee powers.** By a vote of 410-4 Feb. 6, the House approved a resolution ratifying the Judiciary Committee's impeachment investigation and granting the panel broad subpoena power to compel testimony or production of documents from any source, including the President. In the final House vote, the four members voting against the resoultion—all Republicans—were Ben B. Blackburn (Ga.), Earl F. Landgrebe (Ind.), Carlos J. Moorhead (Calif.) and David C. Treen (La.).

[6] **Aides say House need not allege crime.** In a study on the nature of presidential impeachment, counsel for the House Judiciary Committee concluded that violation of criminal law need not be a requisite for impeachment. The study, released by the committee Feb. 21, was prepared by the panel's special counsel John M. Doar and its Republican counsel Albert E. Jenner. The committee's ranking Republican, Rep. Edward Hutchinson (Mich.), disagreed. "There should be criminality involved," he said. The study found that the standard for presidential impeachment could include commission of "constitutional wrongs that subvert the structure of the government, or undermine the integrity of the office and even the Constitution itself." It found that a president's "entire course of conduct in office" could be considered as, "in particular situations, it may be a course of conduct more than individual acts that has a tendency to subvert constitutional government." It found that, flowing from the constitutional requirement that a President

faithfully execute the laws, he was responsible "for the overall conduct of the executive branch." President Nixon asserted at a televised news conference Feb. 25 that he did not expect to be impeached. He said his interpretation of the Constitution required commission of a criminal offense by a President for impeachment.

[7] **Panel asks Nixon for data.** The Judiciary Committee sent a request to the White House Feb. 25 for specific information for its impeachment inquiry. The committee had received from special Watergate prosecutor Jaworski Feb. 21 a list of 700 pages of documents and 17 tapes that his office had received from the White House for its grand jury investigations. The committee's request to the White House for specific items reportedly was based on this list. Jaworski had turned the list, not the items themselves, over to the Judiciary panel after assurance the committee was intent upon rules to protect the confidentiality of its sensitive material. In a March 7 letter to Chairman Peter Rodino (D, N.J.) in response to the committee's request, presidential counsel James D. St. Clair said President Nixon would provide the committee with the same materials already given to Jaworski, but would not comply with requests for further materials as those already released were "more than sufficient to afford the Judiciary Committee with the entire Watergate story." (The St. Clair letter reflected the view given by Nixon in his March 6 news conference, during which the President also said that he would respond to written questions under oath or meet with members of the committee at the White House "to answer any further questions under oath that they may have.") In response to St. Clair's letter, committee counsel Doar said that if subpoenas for the materials were issued and the President were to defy or ignore them, his actions could lead to a contempt of Congress citation, itself possibly an impeachable offense.

[8] The confrontation over the tapes and materials began to build when, on March 12, White House Press Secretary Ronald L. Zeigler said the committee's request for data threatened the separation of powers principles of the Constitution. Zeigler said the committee should define what it considered an impeachable offense before the probe went any further. At a joint news conference March 13, Rodino and Hutchinson stood firm about the request for data from the White House. Both opposed the White House suggestion that the committee define impeachable behavior. Each congressman must make his own decision, they said.

[9] **Sirica directs report to House panel.** U.S. District Court Judge John J. Sirica ruled March 18 that a secret grand jury report and compilation of evidence dealing with President Nixon's role in the Watergate case should be released to the House Judiciary Committee for its impeachment investigation. The grand jury had submitted the material to Sirica March 1 with its indictment of seven former White House and campaign aides in connection with the Watergate cover-up. The U.S. Court of Appeals upheld the decision March 21.

[10] **Buckley urges resignation.** Nixon's cause was dealt a severe blow March 19 when one of his chief supporters, Sen. James L. Buckley (Conservative-Republican, N.Y.), urged the President to resign because he had lost his 1972 election mandate to carry out his proclaimed goals. In a public statement, Buckley proposed "an extraordinary act of statesmanship," the act of "Richard Nixon's own voluntary resignation." The "trauma" of Watergate had stripped Nixon of the ability to fulfill his mandate, Buckley said, and there was a "spreading cynicism" about the political process and "a perception of corruption that has effectively destroyed the President's ability to speak from a position of moral leadership." Resignation was the only way to resolve the crisis, Buckley said, impeachment could not. A Senate trial would be a "Roman

circus" and either verdict—to convict or not to convict—would leave an "embittered" segment of the electorate. One would think "that the media had hounded" Nixon out of office, the other that "Congress had placed political expediency above its duty." Nixon said at a news conference later March 19 that Buckley's plea "does not cause me to reassess my position." Buckley's call for Nixon's resignation did not generate a positive response from conservatives in Congress, but the impact of his announcement was clear. (The only other Republican senator to call for Nixon's resignation was Edward W. Brooke [Mass.], a liberal.)

[11] **White House stiffens stance.** The White House continued to assert its refusal to release further data requested by the House Judiciary Committee for its inquiry. The stand evoked a warning from Senate Republican Leader Hugh Scott (Pa.) that a continued confrontation on the issue would lead to impeachment. Strong statements on the issue also came from Democratic leaders. The White House stand was emphasized in a series of statements by Ziegler. The first statement came March 23 in response to two articles in that day's *Los Angeles Times*. One quoted unidentified Congressional sources as saying the White House was prepared to give the Judiciary Committee the additional tapes it was seeking because of Scott's warning. The other reported that a key tape of the March 21, 1973 meeting between Nixon and his former counsel John W. Dean 3rd was not ambiguous about the President's involvement in the Watergate cover-up. According to the *Times*, the tape corroborated Dean's earlier statements and contained other "surprises" showing that Nixon had not given orders to stop the cover-up. Ziegler denied both stories and accused the House Judiciary Committee of being responsible for divulging confidential materials. As for the story of the March 21, 1973 Dean tape, Ziegler said there were "interpretations far different" from "the one-sided, partial, out-of-context" account in the Los Angeles newspaper.

[12] **Federal aid to homes put at $17 million.** According to a House subcommittee report, sent to the House Government Operations Committee by a 6-4 party-line vote March 21 and approved by the committee by a 36-0 vote May 14, federal spending at President Nixon's private estates in California and Florida and at the Bahamas home of Nixon friend Robert H. Abplanalp totaled $17.1 million. The figure was higher than the $10 million reported by federal agencies in 1973 because of the addition of $7.1 million in personnel costs—largely pay and maintenance costs for permanently assigned personnel at the three sites. The subcommittee report, originally disclosed in a statement by subcommittee chairman Jack Brooks (D, Tex.), dealt with "the loose arrangements" for U.S. payment of items "not requested by the Secret Service," submission of "after-the-fact requests, procurement of items far in excess of security needs, the obligation of federal funds by nongovernmental personnel and other such practices...."

[13] **Back taxes assessed by IRS, congressional panel.** The White House announced April 3 that President Nixon would pay $432,787.13 in back taxes plus interest (for a total of about $465,000) on the basis of an April 2 report from the Internal Revenue Service (IRS) that he owed that amount. The Nixon announcement followed by about four hours release of a staff report of the Congressional Joint Committee on Internal Revenue Taxation that found Nixon's income tax delinquency totaled $476,431 during his first term as President. Nixon had asked the committee in December 1973 to re-evaluate two controversial items—a deduction for his gift to the National Archives of his vice presidential papers and his failure to pay capital gains tax for the sale of some California property—that substantially reduced his federal income tax

obligations. (The committee had decided not to limit its investigation to those two items.) In the White House statement April 3, Nixon disclaimed responsibility for preparation of his 1969-72 tax returns, but—since he had stated he would abide by the judgment of the committee—said he would pay the back taxes. Noting that the Congressional staff report indicated that the proper amount to be paid must be determined by the IRS, he said that he was using the amount calculated by the IRS in its unreleased report. The IRS specified, in closing its investigation, that it would not seek a civil fraud penalty against the President for the years involved. However, IRS Commissioner Donald Alexander April 7 declined to reveal whether a 5% negligence penalty was included in the IRS assessment. The White House April 4 announced that the assessment "almost virtually wiped out" Nixon's personal savings (estimated at $432,000 in cash and $988,000 including real estate) and that the President would "have to borrow a substantial amount in order to meet this obligation." The Congressional staff report—which was "a report only" and "not a demand for back taxes"—was released prior to formal assessment by the committee. It stressed that no attempt had been made "to draw any conclusions whether there was, or was not, fraud or negligence involved," on the part of the President or his representatives. In summary, the staff disallowed the $482,018 deduction for the gift of Nixon's vice presidential papers, since the deed of the gift allegedly was not completely signed until April 10, 1970 (following the July 25, 1969 effective date on the elimination of such deductions); had been signed by presidential aide Edward Morgan rather than by the President; and entailed a gift "so restricted" that it was an undeductible "gift of a future interest in tangible personal property." The report also held that a capital gain of $117,835 should have been reported in 1970 on the sale of excess San Clemente acreage; that a capital gain of $151,848 rather than $142,912 should have been declared in 1969 on the sale of Nixon's New York City apartment because of "the depreciation and amortization allowable" resulting from use of the apartment "in a trade or business by Mr. Nixon"; and "that depreciation on the San Clemente house and on certain furniture purchased by the President, business expense deductions taken on the San Clemente property, as well as certain expenditures from the White House 'guest fund' [all totaling $91,452] are not proper business expenses and are not allowable deductions." The report also stated that the President should have declared as income $27,015 for flights in government planes by Nixon's family and friends "when there was no business purpose for the furnishing of the transportation" and that Nixon should declare as income $92,298 in improvements made to his Key Biscayne and San Clemente estates, since the improvements were "undertaken primarily for the President's personal benefit." (The California Franchise Tax Board ruled April 12 that President and Mrs. Nixon owed the state $4,263.72 in back taxes, about $1,000 in interest on the delayed settlement and a penalty of $39.17 for failing to file a 1970 return. The President's attorneys agreed to pay the back taxes promptly. The ruling was based on Nixon being a nonresident with income generated from within the state. Part of Nixon's salary as President was prorated by the state as California income on the basis of time he was at San Clemente on "working vacations.")

[14] **House tapes deadline.** The White House's continued refusal to release further data resulted, April 4, in the Judiciary Committee unanimously issuing an April 9 deadline for surrender of the tapes. After that, Chairman Rodino said, "we will subpoena them if we must." The White House declined comment on the deadline other than to repeat that the tapes issue was the subject of meetings between counsel for the President and the committee. The deadline was transmitted in a letter from Doar to St. Clair. Responding to the deadline in a

letter to Doar, St. Clair, April 9, said President Nixon had ordered a review of the material in question and would furnish by April 22 "additional materials" that would "permit the committee to complete its inquiry promptly." The letter did not indicate which tapes or material would be turned over to the committee. The Judiciary Committee April 11 rejected the offer contained in St. Clair's letter and voted to issue a subpoena ordering the President to turn over, by April 25, "all tapes, dictabelts or other electronic recordings, transcripts, memoranda, notes or other writings or things" related to 42 presidential conversations the committee deemed relevant to its inquiry. (The deadline was later extended to April 30.)

[15] President announces tape transcript release. President Nixon, in a televised address April 29, said that he would turn over to the Judiciary Committee the next day, and make public, 1,200 pages of edited transcripts of his conversations with key aides concerning Watergate. Nixon stated that the transcripts included "all the relevant portions of all the subpoenaed conversations that were recorded and related to Watergate or the cover-up" and asserted that he had "nothing to hide." He also said that the transcripts covered other conversations, not subpoenaed by the committee, "but which have a significant bearing on the question of presidential action with regard to Watergate." In order for the committee to verify the transcripts, the President invited Rodino and Hutchinson "to come to the White House and listen to the actual full tapes of these conversations.... If there should be any disagreement over whether omitted material is relevant, I shall meet with them personally in an effort to settle the matter." He said that he personally had decided the questions of relevancy in constructing the transcripts. In announcing his decision to release the transcripts, Nixon reasserted his duty to defend the principle of executive privilege, but said he believed it now was vital "to restore the principle itself by clearing the air of the central questions" involved and to provide the evidence "which will allow this matter to be brought to a prompt conclusion." The President said that he expected the transcripts to become "grist for many sensational stories in the press." The tapes "will embarrass me and those with whom I have talked" and would "become the subject to speculation and even ridicule," and parts "will be seized upon by political and journalistic opponents." In essence, the transcripts would show, Nixon said, "that what I have stated from the beginning to be the truth has been the truth, that I personally had no knowledge of the break-in before it occurred, that I had no knowledge of the cover-up" until March 21, 1973, that he never offered clemency and that, after March 21, "my actions were directed toward finding the facts and seeing that justice was done." Nixon specifically cited several conversations with Dean. The transcripts "show clearly" he said, that, contrary to Dean's charge, he was fully aware of the cover-up in September 1972, "I first learned of it" from Dean on March 21, 1973, some six months later. In his March 21 talk, he said, he kept returning to Watergate break-in defendant E. Howard Hunt's blackmail threat, "which to me was not a Watergate problem but one which I regarded, rightly or wrongly, as a potential national security problem of very serious proportions." (Nixon was apparently referring to Hunt's threat to reveal the Ellsberg case break-in) "I considered long and hard," Nixon said, "whether it might in fact be better to let the payment go forward, at least temporarily." In the course of this consideration "and of just thinking out loud," he suggested several times that meeting Hunt's demands "might be necessary." Nixon also quoted from the transcripts that "in the end we are going to be bled to death" and "it is all going to come out anyway and then you get the worst of both worlds" and in effect it would "look like a cover-up. So that we cannot do."

[16] The transcripts, released with a White House legal brief April 30, did not cover 11 of the 42 conversations subpoenaed by the committee. According to White House Counsel J. Fred Buzhardt, four of the conversations, occurring April 15, 1973, were not recorded because the machine ran out of tape; five occurred on telephones that were not connected to a recorder; and tapes of two others were not found, the implication being that the conversations did not occur. The transcripts themselves were liberally sprinkled with deletions marked "unintelligible," "expletive deleted" or "inaudible." The brief attached to the transcripts said the expletives had been removed, except where necessary to maintain relevancy, in the interest of good taste. Other deletions, the brief stated, were removed to eliminate characterization of third persons and material not relating to the President's conduct. Despite the deletions, much of the conversation in the transcripts was profane, as was the tone of much of the material. The brief accompanying the transcripts asserted President Nixon's innocence in the Watergate affair and attacked in particular Dean's credibility. It indicated that Dean repeatedly had perjured himself in sworn testimony, and accused him of trying to blackmail the President in an effort to gain immunity from prosecution. [For the contents of the crucial conversations, see the section under the centered heading *Excerpts from Key Tapes.*]

[17] **Non-compliance motion voted.** The House Judiciary Committee voted 20-18 May 1 to inform President Nixon by letter that he had "failed to comply with the committee's subpoena" requesting the White House tapes and documents. In addition to the absence of 11 of the 42 subpoenaed conversations, the President's response to the subpoena did not cover notes or memorandums or Dictabelts requested under the subpoena. Doar also informed the panel the White House transcripts were "not accurate." After comparison with some overlapping material obtained previously, some of it from the special prosecutor, the staff's own tape experts, Doar said, had been able to "pick up parts of conversations" that were marked "unintelligible" in some of the White House transcripts. Doar also said there were sections of the White House transcripts where words had been omitted without any notation that the deletion had been made.

[18] In rules of procedure for the hearings adopted unanimously May 2, the committee approved television and radio coverage of open sessions and of participation within limits, for presidential counsel St. Clair. St. Clair would be permitted to attend all the sessions, open or closed; to call witnesses for the President, although he would be required to tell the committee in advance "precisely" what the testimony was expected to be; to make objections relating to examinations of witnesses or admissibility of testimony, subject to the chair's rulings; to question any witness, subject to the chair's decisions on length and scope of the questioning.

[19] **Reaction to transcripts.** Release of the transcripts was followed by harsh criticism from a number of sources, among them many Republicans, including Senate Leader Scott (Pa.) who called the White House activities "immoral"; House Leader John Rhodes (Ariz.) who said the transcripts were "devastating" and resignation a "possible option"; and Interior Secretary Rogers C. B. Morton who said, "We have seen a breakdown in our ethics of government which I deplore and which I am having a very difficult time living with." Vice President Ford mixed his reaction to the transcript material, which he deplored, with renewed support for the President. He was "a little disappointed" by the transcripts, he said in Myrtle Beach, S.C. May 3.

[20] **Judiciary committee begins hearings.** The Judiciary Committee May 9 opened its hearings to determine whether to recommend the impeachment of President Nixon. The committee's leaders pledged in an 18-minute public ceremony to conduct a fair and nonpartisan inquiry. Then, after a brief

procedural debate, the committee went into a closed three-hour session to hear a presentation of the events leading up to the June 1972 Watergate burglary.

[21] The committee held 18 closed evidentiary hearings between May 9-June 21, hearing witnesses—also in closed session—July 3-11. Confidentiality became an issue following several leaks of evidence. On May 16 St. Clair, in a letter to Rodino, asked that all proceedings be made public because the "selective" leaking of information was "prejudicing the basic right of the President to an impartial inquiry on the evidence." Rodino rejected the request, contending the best way for the public to be fully informed would be for Nixon to release all the material the panel had requested. Among the areas explored at the hearings: the date on which the President first learned of the Watergate cover-up; Administration dealings with ITT and the dairy industry; the Administration's secret domestic surveillance activities and its use of the IRS for political benefit; involvement of the Administration in the 1971 burglary of the office of Daniel Ellsberg's psychiatrist; Nixon's personal income tax situation; and the bombing of Cambodia in 1969. Witnesses called were: Paul O'Brien, a lawyer for the Nixon re-election committee; Frederick C. LaRue, former official of the Nixon re-election campaign; William O. Bittman, Hunt's former lawyer; former Attorney General John N. Mitchell; Dean; Herbert W. Kalmbach, Nixon's personal attorney; Charles W. Colson, former special counsel to the President; and Assistant Attorney General Henry E. Petersen.

[22] During the hearings, the struggle over presidential materials continued. Among other materials, subpoenas were issued for the June 23, 1972 tape, when moves allegedly were made to involve the CIA in curbing the Watergate probe by the FBI [See 34-36 below]; additional material on the ITT and milk fund controversies; tapes involving discussions of the White House special investigations unit, efforts to use the IRS for political purposes and those potentially related to knowledge of false testimony by presidential subordinates. By the end of the hearings the Committee had subpoenaed a total of 147 tapes. Citing release of the transcripts and other documents as sufficient, the White House repeatedly rejected the subpoenas, leading the panel to formally notify the President May 30 that his refusal to comply "might constitute a ground for impeachment." Earlier, on May 30, Committee counsels Doar and Jenner said the transcripts could not be accepted as a substitute as they were "inadequate and unsatisfactory," a view supported by Rodino who also cited "misstatements," "omissions" and "misattributions." In rejecting Nixon's offer to have Rodino and Hutchinson listen to the withheld tapes, Doar said it was constitutionally required that every member of the committee and the House make a personal judgment and the responsibility could not be delegated. In a letter to the committee June 10, Nixon asserted the doctrine of executive privilege took precedence even over an impeachment inquiry on the principle of separation of powers.

[23] **Committee transcripts released.** The Judiciary Committee released its own transcripts of some Watergate conversations involving the President that varied from the White House transcripts of the same talks released April 30. The committee's transcripts of eight White House conversations, occurring between Sept. 15, 1972-April 16, 1973, contained indications that the President was more involved in the cover-up than portrayed in the White House version. In nearly all cases where substantial discrepancies existed, the White House version put the President in a better light. The committee's transcripts were prepared by its staff from tape recordings and transcripts received from the White House and the Watergate grand jury. The committee version of the tapes was condemned by St. Clair who, on July 9, said there were no "significant differences" between the two. Vice President Ford told a news conference July 18 that because he was concerned about discrepancies between White House and House Judiciary

Committee transcripts of presidential tapes, he had requested and received permission to listen to portions of two tapes. Ford said he now understood how there "could be a different interpretation of the words that were spoken." Asked which version was more accurate, he replied, "I think you could read it either way."

[24] **Committee issues Watergate evidence.** The House Judiciary Committee released July 11 an eight-volume, 4,133-page record of the evidence assembled by its staff dealing with the Watergate break-in and its aftermath. Seven volumes consisted of the material presented by the staff to the committee members in closed sessions in May and June. The eighth volume was President Nixon's rebuttal presented to the committee by St. Clair. The staff material consisted of statements of information and supporting material; there was no attempt to present findings. The St. Clair material—242 pages—did contain conclusions and was much narrower in scope than the staff record. It focused primarily on the controversial payment of $75,000 to Hunt. St. Clair re-stated the President's position that he first learned of the Watergate cover-up on March 21, 1973, then launched an inquiry and took action to bring the facts to the proper authorities. The bulk of the evidence released was already on the public record, but there were some new disclosures. Among them, contained in secret grand jury testimony released as supportive material, was Hunt's admission that his demand for the money was accompanied by a threat to reveal not only his Watergate knowledge, but also facts relating to the burglary of the office of Ellsberg's psychiatrist.

[25] The committee continued its release of evidence July 16 with issuance of findings detailing repeated White House attempts, some of which were successful, to gain confidential tax information on individuals from the IRS and to use tax-return audits to hurt political enemies and protect friends of the President. Among the evidence was testimony by Randolph W. Thrower, who resigned as commissioner in January 1971 after trying, without success, to warn the President of the damage such interference could cause. Thrower's successor, Johnnie Walters, also reported pressure on him from Dean and Ehrlichman, the latter repeatedly pressing for action to create a tax problem for Lawrence F. O'Brien, then Democratic national chairman. The White House had more success in obtaining IRS data on the taxes of Gerald Wallace, brother of Gov. George C. Wallace (D, Ala.); and in getting favorable tax rulings for Nixon supporters such as evangelist Billy Graham and actor John Wayne.

[26] The Judiciary Committee July 18 released a four-volume 2,090-page record of the evidence accumulated by its staff concerning clandestine activities sponsored by the White House. A 225-page rebuttal by St. Clair accompanied the publication of the evidence. The evidence, much of which was already public, specifically dealt with the operations of the "plumbers" investigative unit, wiretaps on 13 government officials and four newsmen, the White House-financed activities of political trickster Donald H. Segretti, activities of John J. Caulfield and Anthony T. Ulasewicz, who made secret inquiries for the White House, and the stillborn domestic surveillance plan of 1970, which called for the lifting of restraints against certain illegal activities. (The plan died because of opposition by FBI Director J. Edgar Hoover.) The mass of evidence suggested that clandestine White House activities originated because of national security concerns but later became overtly political operations. In 1971, White House efforts against news leaks took the form of 17 wiretaps against government officials and newsmen, as well as the creation of the "plumbers." As for the "plumbers," one previously unreleased document showed that Nixon was

warned by Ehrlichman March 21, 1973 of the possible illegality of the "plumbers" 1971 break-in at the office of Ellsberg's psychiatrist. St. Clair's defense of the President consisted of White House memorandums, including a hitherto unpublished 1973 affidavit by Henry A. Kissinger, demonstrating Administration anxiety over leaks of classified information from 1969 through 1971.

[27] On July 19 the House Judiciary Committee released two volumes each of evidence on the Administration's handling of antitrust suits against ITT, and on charges that the President had raised the federal price supports for milk in return for dairy industry campaign pledges. Also included were St. Clair's rebuttal arguments. [For further information on these controversies see the topic CAMPAIGN FINANCING ABUSES.]

[28] **St. Clair defends the President.** St. Clair's defense of Nixon took the form of oral arguments before a closed session of the Judiciary Committee July 18 and a 151-page written brief made public July 20. His written brief contended that there was no "conclusive evidence" of presidential actions that would warrant impeachment. According to committee members, St. Clair's oral arguments were consistent with his strategy of focusing on the payment of "hush money" to Hunt which, the President's special counsel argued, was the only charge that could potentially constitute an impeachable offense. In his final arguments, St. Clair surprised the committee by introducing the edited transcript of part of a taped conversation that the President had refused to turn over to the committee despite a subpoena. The transcript was of part of a March 22, 1973 conversation between Nixon and Haldeman and it concerned aid to the Watergate defendants. St. Clair later told newsmen that the gist of Nixon's remarks to Haldeman was that he was unaware of and disapproved of blackmail payments to Hunt.

[29] **Impeachment articles voted.** The House Judiciary Committee recessed July 30 after approving three articles of impeachment charging President Nixon with obstruction of justice in connection with the Watergate scandal, abuse of presidential powers, and attempting to impede the impeachment process by defying committee subpoenas for evidence. The committee rejected two other proposed articles, one charging that Nixon had usurped the powers of Congress by ordering the secret bombing of Cambodia in 1969, the other concerning income tax fraud and the unconstitutional use of government funds to make improvements on his properties in California and Florida. The committee's final deliberations, which were nationally televised, began July 24 with a motion by Rep. Harold D. Donohue (Mass.), second ranking Democrat on the panel. "I move that the committee report to the House a resolution, together with articles, impeaching the President of the United States, Richard M. Nixon." Following Donohue's motion, Rodino opened 10 hours of general debate, after which the committee concerned itself with amending and voting on each proposed article.

[30] The first article was adopted July 27 by a 27-11 vote. Six Republicans joined the panel's 21 Democrats in voting for impeachment. The article had been attacked by the anti-impeachment bloc of Republicans for its lack of specificity. Pro-impeachment committee members responded that general charges were preferable because they allowed later introduction of evidence currently not on hand. They also said that the evidence compiled, while circumstantial, was overwhelming. The article charged the President with "a course of conduct . . . designed to delay, impede and obstruct the investigation" of the Watergate break-in; and with attempts "to cover up, conceal and protect those responsible; and to conceal the existence and scope of other unlawful covert activities." It listed nine ways in which this was done: (1) "Making or

causing to be made false or misleading statements. . . ." (2) "Withholding relevant and material evidence or information. . . ." (3) "Approving, condoning, . . . and counseling witnesses with respect to the giving of false or misleading statements. . . ." (4) "Interfering or endeavoring to interfere with the conduct of investigations. . . ." (5) "Approving . . . and acquiescing in the surreptitious payment of substantial sums of money to obtain silence. . . ." (7) "Disseminating information" from the Justice Department to the subjects of investigations "for the purpose of aiding and assisting such subjects in their attempts to avoid criminal liability." (8) Deceiving the people of the United States "into believing that a thorough and complete investigation had been conducted . . . and that there was no involvement [of executive branch personnel] in such misconduct. . . ." (9) Causing "prospective defendants, and individuals duly tried and convicted, to expect favored treatment . . . or rewarding individuals for their silence of false testimony."

[31] The second article was approved July 29 by a 28-10 vote. Rep. Robert McClory (Ill.), second ranking Republican on the committee who opposed Article I, joined six Republican colleagues and 21 Democrats in recommending Nixon's impeachment for abuse of power. This omnibus charge against Nixon, which McClory called the "crux" of the matter, specifically focused on the following allegations: Personally and through his subordinates and agents, Nixon attempted to use the IRS to initiate tax audits or obtain confidential tax data for political purposes. He initiated a series of secret wiretaps under the guise of "national security" and misused the results of the taps. He authorized and permitted to be maintained in the White House a secret, privately financed investigative unit which engaged in "covert and unlawful activities," including the 1971 burglary of the office of the psychiatrist of Pentagon Papers trial defendant Daniel Ellsberg. He failed to act on the knowledge that "close subordinates" endeavored to impede the Watergate investigation and related matters. He "knowingly misused the executive power by interfering" with the lawful activities of the FBI, the CIA, the Justice Department, and the Watergate special prosecutor's office.

[32] The third article in the bill of impeachment, approved July 30, charged that the President had sought to impede the impeachment process by refusing to comply with eight committee subpoenas for 147 recorded White House conversations and other evidence. Although the article was introduced by McClory, it failed to gain broad bipartisan backing and passed by the narrow margin of 21-17. Rep. Lawrence J. Hogan (R, Md.) joined McClory and 19 Democrats to insure passage. Democrats Walter Flowers (Ala.) and James R. Mann (S.C.) voted to oppose the article. (Hogan, on July 23, had become the first Republican member of the committee to announce he would vote for impeachment.) Rep. Ray Thornton (D, Ark.) offered an amendment, adopted 24-14, designed to make clear that presidential defiance of a Congressional subpoena was an impeachable offense only in an impeachment inquiry and not in response to a committee drafting legislation.

[33] The fourth article, proposed by Rep. John J. Conyers Jr. (D, Mich.), charged that Nixon had usurped Congress' power to declare war by approving and then concealing from Congress the secret bombing of Cambodia in 1969. After limited debate July 30, the committee rejected the article 26-12. Nine Democrats joined the committee's 17 Republicans in opposing it. The fifth article to be considered by the impeachment panel concerned the President's personal finances. This article, sponsored by Rep. Edward Mezvinsky (D, Iowa), failed by a vote of 26-12 July 30. Nine Democrats and 17 Republicans voted to oppose.

Roll Call Votes on Articles

	I	II	III	IV	V
Democrats					
Rodino (NJ)	Yes	Yes	Yes	No	Yes
Donohue (Mass)	Yes	Yes	Yes	No	No
Brooks (Tex)	Yes	Yes	Yes	Yes	Yes
Kastenmeier (Wis)	Yes	Yes	Yes	Yes	Yes
Edwards (Cal)	Yes	Yes	Yes	Yes	Yes
Hungate (Mo)	Yes	Yes	Yes	Yes	No
Conyers (Mich)	Yes	Yes	Yes	Yes	Yes
Eilberg (Pa)	Yes	Yes	Yes	No	Yes
Waldie (Cal)	Yes	Yes	Yes	Yes	No
Flowers (Ala)	Yes	Yes	No	No	No
Mann (SC)	Yes	Yes	No	No	No
Sarbanes (Md)	Yes	Yes	Yes	No	No
Seiberling (Ohio)	Yes	Yes	Yes	No	Yes
Danielson (Cal)	Yes	Yes	Yes	No	Yes
Drinan (Mass)	Yes	Yes	Yes	Yes	No
Rangel (NY)	Yes	Yes	Yes	Yes	Yes
Jordan (Tex)	Yes	Yes	Yes	Yes	Yes
Thornton (Ark)	Yes	Yes	Yes	No	No
Holtzman (NY)	Yes	Yes	Yes	Yes	Yes
Owens (Utah)	Yes	Yes	Yes	Yes	No
Mezvinsky (Iowa)	Yes	Yes	Yes	Yes	Yes
Republicans					
Hutchinson (Mich)	No	No	No	No	No
McClory (Ill)	No	Yes	Yes	No	No
Smith (NY)	No	No	No	No	No
Sandman (NJ)	No	No	No	No	No
Railsback (Ill)	Yes	Yes	No	No	No
Wiggins (Cal)	No	No	No	No	No
Dennis (Ind)	No	No	No	No	No
Fish (NY)	Yes	Yes	No	No	No
Mayne (Iowa)	No	No	No	No	No
Hogan (Md)	Yes	Yes	Yes	No	No
Butler (Va)	Yes	Yes	No	No	No
Cohen (Me)	Yes	Yes	No	No	No
Lott (Miss)	No	No	No	No	No
Froelich (Wis)	Yes	Yes	No	No	No
Moorhead (Cal)	No	No	No	No	No
Maraziti (NJ)	No	No	No	No	No
Latta (Ohio)	No	No	No	No	No

[34] **Steps to resignation.** The vote in the Judiciary Committee combined with the Supreme Court's July 24 decision that Nixon must give up the tapes subpoenaed by the special Watergate prosecutor [See 53-56] forced the President to reconsider his stand against resignation. On Aug. 3, the President retired to the presidential retreat, Camp David, in the Catoctin Mountains with Mrs. Nixon, his daughters and sons-in-law, David and Julie Eisenhower and Edward and Tricia Cox, and his friend, Charles G. Rebozo. The next day, he summoned St. Clair, White House Chief of Staff Alexander M. Haig Jr., Ziegler and his speech writers, Patrick J. Buchanan and Raymond K. Price Jr. They remained at Camp David for about five hours. The decision was made to issue a statement of early complicity in the Watergate cover-up, and the supporting tapes, which was done Aug. 5.

[35] The presidential statement and tape transcripts effectively constituted a confession to obstruction of justice—the charge contained in the first article of impeachment voted by the Judiciary Committee. The transcripts covered three meetings with Haldeman on June 23, 1972, six days after the Watergate break-in. Informed that the FBI's probe of the break-in was pointing to officials in his re-election campaign, Nixon instructed Haldeman to tell the FBI, "Don't go any further in this case period!" While Nixon's earlier statements on the Watergate case attributed his concern over the FBI's investigations to national security problems and possible conflicts with the CIA, the latest transcripts—and Nixon's own statement about them—finally indicated thai political considerations had played a major role. According to the transcripts, Nixon told Haldeman to base

the curtailment of FBI activities on possible reopening of questions about the CIA's role in the abortive 1961 "Bay of Pigs" invasion of Cuba (some of the Watergate burglary conspirators had been involved in the CIA operation). Haldeman assured Nixon that the CIA ploy would give L. Patrick Gray, then acting FBI director, sufficient justification to drop the investigation of the "laundering" (through a Mexican lawyer and bank) of the campaign funds used to finance the Watergate operation. In the written statements announcing release of the transcripts, Nixon said his "preliminary review" of some of the materials in May had resulted in his recognition that the tapes "presented potential problems," but he had informed neither his staff, his counsel or the Judiciary Committee of his findings. "This was a serious act of omission for which I take full responsibility and which I deeply regret." Nixon also admitted that the June 23, 1973 tapes showed he had discussed the "political aspects" of the FBI's Watergate investigation and that he was "aware of the advantages" of using the CIA to block the FBI probe on the grounds of "sensitive national security matters." Acknowledging that a House vote of impeachment was "virtually a foregone conclusion," Nixon also urged that "the evidence be looked at in its entirety, and the events be looked at in perspective." Nixon concluded that the full record "does not justify the extreme step of impeachment and removal of a President."

[36] Nixon's statement said the three key transcripts had been made public partly as a result of the process of compliance with the Supreme Court's July 24 order. [For a summary of the tapes, see heading *Excerpts from Key Tapes*] In setting procedures for compliance with the order, U.S. District Court Judge Sirica, who was to screen the tapes before transmitting them to the Watergate prosecution, had suggested that St. Clair personally review the tapes, along with Nixon. (St. Clair had told the Supreme Court that he had not listened to any of the tapes.) According to news reports Aug. 5-6, St. Clair had first become aware of the incriminating material involving Nixon and the cover-up during this review and—threatening resignation—had insisted that the transcripts be made public and that Nixon let it be known that he had withheld evidence from his counsel. St. Clair, Haig and Rep. Charles E. Wiggins (R, Calif.), a spokesman for the Nixon defense in the House, reportedly convinced Nixon to resign after learning the contents of the secret June 23 tapes.

[37] President Nixon's statement and release of new tapes Aug. 5 had a devastating effect upon his support in Congress. That support had been perceptibly slipping away since the House Judiciary Committee's televised hearings and decision to bring impeachment articles to the House. By Aug. 6, the collapse of Nixon support appeared almost total. Only two of the 435 House members took public stands against impeachment—Rep. Otto E. Passman (D, La.) and Rep. Earl Landgrebe (R, Ind.). The remaining 10 members of the Judiciary Committee who opposed the impeachment articles in that panel's hearings, reversed their stands Aug. 6. "I feel that I have been deceived," one of them, ranking GOP member Hutchinson commented. A conservative Southern Republican, Rep. Joel Broyhill (Va.), a longtime Nixon supporter, said simply, "He's gone."

[38] **Nixon resigns.** Before noon on Aug. 8, Nixon met in the Oval Office with Ford and informed him, as he reportedly had Kissinger the evening before, that he was resigning. Ziegler appeared in the press room to announce, in stricken tones, that the President would address the nation that evening. The news of resignation was disseminated that afternoon. Shortly before 7:30 p.m., Nixon met briefly with his family and then with Congressional leaders. Half an hour later, Nixon returned to the White House and went to the Cabinet Room, where about 40 of his staunchest supporters in the Congress had assembled. The parting was tearful on both sides. The President then went to the Oval Office for his resignation speech.

[39] Nixon's 16-minute speech of resignation was delivered at 9 p.m. EDT and was seen by a national television audience estimated at 110-130 million people. "Throughout the long and difficult period of Watergate, I have felt it was my duty to persevere; to make every possible effort to complete the term of office to which you elected me," Nixon said. But, the President continued, it had become "evident" in the last few days that he no longer had a "strong enough political base in the Congress to justify continuing that effort." "... With the disappearance of that base, I now believe that the constitutional purpose has been served, and there is no longer a need for the process to be prolonged," he said. The President said he had never been a "quitter." Nonetheless, he was resigning to spare the country a fight for his personal vindication that would absorb the attention of Congress and the President in the months ahead, when both branches needed to place their "entire focus" on the problems of world peace and domestic inflation. Nixon said he "deeply regretted" any injuries that came in the course of the events that led to his decision to resign. "I would only say that if some of my judgments were wrong—and some were wrong—they were made in what I believed at the time to be the best interests of the nation." He thanked those who had supported him and said he held "no bitterness" toward those who had not.

[40] **Reaction to resignation.** World leaders greeted Nixon's resignation with a mixture of regret and relief. In commentary in the Soviet Union, Nixon was portrayed as a victim of an inter-party struggle and of attacks by the media, but there was emphasis that relations between the U.S. and the Soviet Union would not be affected by a change in presidents. A Dutch official asserted the resignation culminated a "process of democratic purification," and Danish Premier Poul Hartling declared Aug. 9 that "only in a society with a free press and a strong sense of justice is it possible to experience a political development as the one the world has now witnessed." Former Israeli Premier Golda Meir asserted that Israelis would not forget that Nixon "has been a faithful friend and had done great things to strengthen" Israel. The official Chinese news agency Hsinhua reported the resignation without commentary. Indian Foreign Minister Swaran Singh said that Nixon had resigned "in the best tradition of democracy," bowing to "the preponderant public opinion in his country." Peruvian President Juan Velasco Alvarado, whose relations with the U.S. had improved recently after years of strain, commented that the resignation was "a shame, because Nixon gave himself for his country."

[41] **Jaworski: no agreement made.** There was widespread speculation both before and after Nixon's resignation as to what legal action, if any, might be taken against him as a private citizen. A key element in the issue was the fact that Nixon had been named as an undicted co-conspirator in the cover-up case, even without the latest damaging transcripts. The grand jury had reportedly wanted to indict Nixon but had been dissuaded by Watergate special prosecutor Jaworski. In a statement released after the resignation announcement Aug. 8, Jaworski said that bargaining regarding possible immunity from prosecution had not played a part in Nixon's decision to leave office. Congressional opinion on possible prosecution was divided: the *New York Times* reported Aug. 9 that many members felt Nixon should be subject to the same liability to prosecution as any ordinary citizen, but some members followed the general line of argument that the disgrace of resignation was sufficient punishment.

The Struggle for the Presidential Papers & Tapes

[42] The conflict between the Administration, the courts and the Congress over access to presidential papers and tape recordings was a crucial element in the 1974 Watergate proceedings. The tapes, especially, could provide uncontestable evidence sorting out the conflicting and contradictory testimony of the Watergate participants. Access to the tapes and other materials was sought by: (1) the special prosecutor's office, headed by Leon Jaworski; (2) the Senate select committee investigating Watergate; (3) the House Judiciary Committee, charged with investigation of grounds for impeachment of the President. (Events concerned with access to the tapes by the special prosecutor and the Senate committee will be found in this section. Because of their relevance to the final promulgation of the impeachment articles, however, the House Judiciary Committee's actions with regard to this question will be found in the previous section: *Impeachment & Resignation*. For information on specific recordings, see heading: *Excerpts from Key Tapes*.)

[43] **Senate committee tape proceedings.** President Nixon Jan. 4 informed the Senate Watergate Committee that he would not comply with its wide-ranging subpoenas for tapes and other material. In a letter to committee Chairman Sam J. Ervin Jr. (D, N.C.), Nixon called the subpoenas "an unconstitutional usurpation of power" which would destroy presidential confidentiality. In an answer released later that day Ervin replied that the committee wished access only to evidence relating to political activities by Nixon, his aides and re-election committees, and "information in the possession of the President of criminal violations on the part of his aides." Vice President Ford supported Nixon's position during an appearance on the National Broadcasting Co.'s "Meet the Press" program Jan. 6, calling the requests "a fishing expedition." The Senate committee petitioned the federal district court Jan. 7 to enforce its original subpoena for presidential tapes and documents, a request which earlier had been dismissed for lack of jurisdiction by Judge Sirica. The U.S. Court of Appeals had returned the case to Sirica for a ruling under a new law on jurisdiction. Sirica, as chief judge, reassigned the case to Judge Gerhard A. Gesell.

[44] Meanwhile, on Jan. 4, Boston lawyer James D. St. Clair was named special presidential counsel in charge of Watergate matters, replacing J. Fred Buzhardt Jr., who was named counsel to the President. Although Buzhardt's new position was technically a promotion, his replacement by St. Clair was widely seen as a reflection of Nixon's dissatisfaction with Buzhardt's handling of the tapes issue.

[45] Answering the Senate committee's request on Jan. 17 the President's attorneys urged Judge Gesell to reject the attempt to gain access to five tapes subpoenaed in 1973, arguing that the issue was political, not judicial, in nature. Citing the President's "power to withhold information from Congress" in the public interest, the White House said Nixon had responded to the committee's "political decision" with a "political determination" that compliance would not be in the public interest. On Jan. 25 Gesell requested that President Nixon file a personal statement explaining why he was withholding the tapes. Gesell said if Nixon wished to invoke executive privilege, he should submit to the court "the factual ground or grounds for his determination that disclosure to the select committee would not be in the public interest." Responding to Gesell's request on Feb. 6, President Nixon contended the Senate committee "has made known its intention to make these materials public," which would "seriously infringe upon the principle of confidentiality." Nixon also cited the "possible adverse effects upon ongoing and forthcoming criminal proceedings" if public release should follow. The Senate committee's reply, filed the following day, said the

President's claims were still too vague to upset the subpoena. Gesell, however, accepted part of Nixon's claims the following day when he dismissed the committee's suit on grounds that publicity surrounding the panel's hearings might be harmful to criminal prosecutions. Gesell said the committee had not demonstrated a "pressing need" for the tapes; but he also rejected the President's contention "that public interest is best served by a blanket, unreviewable claim of confidentiality over all presidential communications." Gesell said that other Congressional demands for tapes "in furtherance of the more juridical constitutional process of impeachment would present wholly different considerations."

[46] The committee filed an appeal Feb. 25, arguing that the court could not impose a judicial need to avoid pretrial publicity above the legislature's requirement for relevant evidence. In its brief the committee said it would keep the tapes secret while criminal actions were proceeding. The judicial argument, however, prevailed when, on May 23, the U.S. Court of Appeals for the District of Columbia ruled 7-0 that the Senate Watergate Committee had not shown a need compelling enough to require enforcement of its subpoena.

[47] **Tape gaps and re-recording issues.** On Nov. 21, 1973 Sirica had announced formation of an advisory panel of technical experts to "study the authenticity and integrity" of the Watergate tapes surrendered to the court the previous month. The advisory panel had been created after discovery of an 18½-minute gap in the tape of a June 20, 1972 conversation between Nixon and H. R. Haldeman. According to Haldeman's notes already in evidence, the conversation had dealt with the Watergate break-in. The President's personal secretary, Rose Mary Woods, had testified in November 1973 that she had accidentally caused the erasures. After hearing a preliminary report, Jan. 15, indicating the possibility of deliberate tampering, Sirica recommended that a grand jury investigate "the possibility of unlawful destruction of evidence and any related offenses." During the hearings on the panel's preliminary report, Woods' attorney, Charles S. Rhyne, argued that White House lawyers had, in effect, "pleaded her guilty" for the gap. He referred to the transcript of a Nov. 21, 1973 meeting between White House lawyers and Sirica during which presidential counsel Buzhardt had said there was no innocent explanation.

[48] While legal maneuvers over possession of the tapes continued, the matter of tape erasures and possible re-recording became a battle of conflicting technical opinions. Citing White House and prosecution sources, the *Washington Post* reported Feb. 17 that the court-appointed panel of technical experts had found "technical indications" that two of the tapes might be re-recordings rather than originals as claimed by the White House. In reply the same day, St. Clair said an independent, White House-sponsored "technical investigation" did not "indicate a re-recording was made." St. Clair also maintained that the disputed 18½-minute gap "could well have been and probably (was) caused by the admittedly defective recording machine" used by Miss Woods. This opinion was also offered the following day by Allan D. Bell Jr., president of Dektor Counter-intelligence and Security Inc. of Springfield, Va. Bell, who said he had volunteered his services to Woods' attorney, maintained his firm had found that a defective part in the recorder (which also had been found by the court-appointed panel), or any variations in the recorder's electric power, could have caused the machine's erase and record heads to make the reported marks on the tape. Conflicting technical opinions were again given June 4 with the release of the final report by the court-appointed panel which confirmed its earlier findings that the gap and buzzing sounds had been put on the tape during a process of manual erasing and re-recording. The panel said it drew "no inferences about such questions as whether the erasure and buzz were made accidentally or

intentionally, or when, or by what person or persons." Although conceding that the gap and buzz might have been caused by a machine malfunction, the report concluded that only its explanation "accounts for the data in their entirety and the patterns they form." St. Clair also released a report June 4 prepared by Michael Hecker of the Stanford Research Institute (SRI) which had been retained by the White House. Hecker said SRI was in "general agreement" with the court's panel, but was "uncomfortable with the degree of certainty" in the rejection of machine malfunction as a possible explanation for the gap.

[49] **CIA destroyed its Watergate tapes.** The CIA destroyed tape recordings related to the Watergate break-in one day after it had acknowledged receipt of a letter from Senate Majority Leader Mike Mansfield (D, Mont.) asking the CIA to save any Watergate evidence it might have, National Broadcasting Co. (NBC) News reported Jan. 31. William E. Colby, director of the CIA, Jan. 29 had admitted the destruction of all but one of its tapes from the Watergate period. All other tapes had been destroyed periodically "when the storage space got too full," Colby added.

[50] **Special prosecutor's office.** The conflict over access to the tapes was further complicated by questions of jurisdiction over the material they contained. On Jan. 12 special prosecutor Leon Jaworski said that unless the courts ruled otherwise, he would resist sharing with the House impeachment inquiry any materials furnished him by the White House. Jaworski contended that there were legal restrictions which confined access to the grand jury probes. House Judiciary Committee Chairman Rodino warned Jan. 22 that if his committee had no access to the data and had to duplicate it by its own effort, the committee's inquiry would be delayed by a year beyond the April target date.

[51] Jaworski said Feb. 14 that he and the White House had reached an impasse on release of presidential tapes and documents and that it was "clear that evidence I deem material to our investigations will not be forthcoming." In a letter to Senate Judiciary Committee Chairman James O. Eastland (D, Miss.)—to whom Jaworski had promised to report on the progress of his dealings with the White House—the prosecutor said he had been informed Feb. 13 by St. Clair that release of the material would be "inconsistent with the public interest and the constitutional integrity of the Presidency." The outstanding requests concerning the break-in and cover-up included 27 recordings of conversations Jaworski said he had requested in January, telling the White House that "each of the conversations is material to a particular facet of our investigation." In a written statement Feb. 15, St. Clair said Nixon had "fully cooperated" with the prosecutor "to the extent consistent with the constitutional responsibilities" of the Presidency. As for the additional requests, St. Clair said compliance "would have the necessary result of further delaying grand jury deliberations many months." A "careful review" of the request had led to the conclusion that this new material "was at best only corroborative of, or cumulative to, evidence already before the grand jury and therefore not essential to its deliberations." Under these circumstances, St. Clair said, Nixon had decided that "continued and seemingly unending incursions into the confidentiality of presidential communications was unwarranted."

[52] Judge Sirica April 18 ordered a subpoena issued on the White House for tapes, transcripts and other documents relating to 64 presidential conversations. Sirica acted at Jaworski's request of April 16. In papers filed with the court, Jaworski said the materials would be needed for the trial of the seven cover-up defendants, scheduled for Sept. 9. The 64 conversations listed by Jaworski were between Nixon and former key aides Haldeman, John D. Ehrlichman and Charles W. Colson, all cover-up defendants, and former counsel John W. Dean

3rd. The dates ranged from June 20, 1972, three days after the Watergate break-in, to June 4, 1973, the date said by Nixon to have included his personal review of some tapes. The April 18 subpoena was followed by a bid to quash it based on claims of executive privilege by Nixon's lawyers on May 1. On May 20 Sirica ordered Nixon to comply with a subpoena for evidence, and Jaworski charged that the White House had attempted to "undercut" his role as an independent prosecutor. In a situation similar to that which led to the 1973 dismissal of Archibald Cox, the first special prosecutor, the White House said Sirica's order would be appealed. Sirica's ruling was a point-by-point rejection of arguments advanced by St. Clair in an effort to have the subpoena quashed. Sirica's ruling supporting access to the evidence by both the court and the prosecutor came a week after a closed hearing, during which—according to the decision—St. Clair had argued that the subpoena did not conform with evidentiary rules of relevance and necessity, and that the dispute between Nixon and Jaworski was an "intra-branch" affair in which the courts should have no role. Sirica rejected the White House contention that Jaworski's role could be limited by presidential order, noting that the prosecutor was "vested with the powers and authority conferred upon his predecessor pursuant to regulations which have the force of law." Sirica said Jaworski had full authority to determine whether to contest a presidential assertion of executive privilege, and added that the prosecutor's independence had been "affirmed and reaffirmed by the President and his representatives." He ordered that the material be submitted to the court for his private examination, along with "particularized" claims of privilege, a procedure which had been followed in dealing with tapes in late 1973. Sirica ordered the material turned over by May 31, but stayed execution of the order pending completion of appeals.

[53] **Supreme Court enters case.** Four days after Sirica's ruling, St. Clair filed notice with the U.S. Circuit Court of Appeals in order to have the ruling overturned. Within hours, Jaworski countered with a direct petition to the Supreme Court, sidestepping normal appellate processes, because of "imperative public importance." Jaworski argued that if the Supreme Court did not enter the case until after all other remedies had been exhausted, the cover-up trial scheduled for Sept. 9 might have to be postponed until the spring of 1975. A White House brief was filed May 30, opposing "any attempt to shortcut the usual judicial process" because of the weight of the issues involved. (At a news conference later that day St. Clair declined to predict whether Nixon would comply with a Supreme Court decision, calling it a "hypothetical situation.") The court accepted Jaworski's petition May 31. The court June 15 widened its consideration of the Presidential tapes case to include the issue of whether the Watergate grand jury had the right to name Nixon as an unindicted co-conspirator in the Watergate cover-up. [See centered heading: *Trials*] Consideration of the grand jury's citation against the President had been sought by St. Clair.

[54] The court July 8 heard oral arguments in the historic cases captioned "The United States vs. Richard M. Nixon" and "Richard M. Nixon vs. the United States." In three hours of oral presentation, punctuated with questions from the eight justices considering the case, (Justice William H. Rehnquist had withdrawn) the two sides re-emphasized positions they had taken in lower court proceedings, Jaworski insisting that there was no constitutional basis for a sweeping claim of privilege—especially when a criminal conspiracy was involved, and St. Clair maintaining that compliance with Jaworski's subpoena for tapes of 64 White House conversations would irrevocably weaken the presidency. Speaking first, Jaworski said constitutional government would be in

"serious jeopardy if the President—any President—is to say that the Constitution means what he says it does, and that there is no one, not even the Supreme Court, to tell him otherwise." Responding to questions, Jaworski said the question of executive privilege was "a very narrow one... whether the President, in a pending prosecution, can withhold material evidence from the court, merely on his assertion that the evidence involves confidential communications." St. Clair argued that because of the impeachment inquiry and its "realistic fusion" with the special prosecutor's criminal proceedings, the subpoena issue had already influenced and would continue to have an effect on the restricted legislative function of impeachment. St. Clair suggested that confidentiality of presidential conversations should be absolute in order to insure proper functioning of the office, adding that in the case of wrongdoing "very few things are forever hidden." Addressing the grand jury citation, St. Clair said the President "was not above the law by any means. But law as to the President has to be applied in a constitutional way which is different from anyone else." Given this, St. Clair added, the citation was an "intrusion" on a function "that is solely legislative and not judicial."

[55] **Court rules against Nixon.** The Supreme Court ruled 8-0 July 24 that President Nixon must provide "forthwith" the tapes and documents relating to 64 White House conversations subpoenaed by Jaworski. The decision did not mention the impeachment inquiry in the House, and it defined the limits on presidential privilege on the relatively narrow grounds of the evidentiary needs imposed by Watergate criminal cases. In an opinion written by Chief Justice Warren E. Burger, a Nixon appointee, the court said that a generalized claim of executive privilege, while not explicitly provided by the Constitution, was "constitutionally based." But in the current case, Burger continued, such an assertion of privilege "must yield to the demonstrated, specific need for evidence in a pending criminal trial." In a statement issued later the same day from San Clemente, Calif., Nixon said he had instructed St. Clair to "take whatever measures are necessary" to comply with the decision "in all respects." Addressing a secondary issue in a footnote to the opinion, the court left standing a grand jury citation of Nixon as an unindicted co-conspirator in the cover-up case. Calling this issue "unnecessary" to resolution of the privilege question, Burger said the court had "improvidently" granted a White House petition for review of Sirica's refusal to expunge the citation. The court also denied a White House request that the court examine the grand jury's evidence to determine if the citation was justified.

[56] Burger rejected White House contentions that the tape dispute was an internal issue within the executive branch and should not be considered by the court. A "mere assertion of a claim of 'intra-branch' dispute," Burger wrote, was insufficient. The court noted that regulations establishing the independence of Jaworski's office had the force of law and had not been revoked by the attorney general. Burger also ruled that Jaworski had made sufficient preliminary showing that the potential evidence in the tapes and documents was both relevant and necessary to a criminal proceeding. Turning to the White House argument that the separation of powers doctrine should preclude judicial review of a claim of presidential privilege, Burger wrote, "it is emphatically the province and duty of the Judicial department to say what the law is." Burger conceded that a President's need for candor and objectivity from advisers deserved "great deference from the courts." But without a claim of need to protect "military, diplomatic or sensitive national security secrets," the court said, the confidentiality of presidential communications would not be "diminished" by submission of the material to Judge Sirica for private

inspection under strict security precautions. On the other hand, the court said, the impediment imposed upon the administration of justice by such a claim of absolute privilege would "upset the constitutional balance" of government and "gravely impair the role of the courts."

[57] **Tapes released, gaps revealed.** The White House turned over to Sirica July 30 the tapes of 20 Watergate-related conversations, beginning the process of compliance with the previous week's Supreme Court decision. St. Clair said in submitting the tapes that he knew of no gaps or "abnormalities," but in a statement outlining claims of privilege submitted the next day, St. Clair noted that five minutes and 12 seconds of an April 17, 1973 meeting had not been recorded. St. Clair attributed the missing segment to a delay in replacing a reel of spent tape with a fresh one. In the July 31 statement outlining claims of privilege, the White House contended that 23 segments totaling about 48 minutes were unrelated to Watergate and should not be transmitted to Jaworski.

[58] The White House disclosed to Sirica Aug. 9 that 17 minutes of a subpoenaed 31-minute telephone conversation between Nixon and Colson on March 21, 1973 was not recorded because the White House recording equipment "ran out" of tape. The latest submission brought to 55 the number of conversations turned over to Sirica. Of the missing nine, St. Clair had said that six were phone calls made from phones not connected to the recording system, two took place in locations excluded from the system and that one could not be found.

Excerpts from Key Tapes

[59] In terms of their role in the events leading to President Nixon's resignation, the most important recordings were those of June 23, 1972, Sept. 15, 1972 and March 21, 1973. The first, not released by Nixon until shortly before his resignation, details the plan to have the CIA intervene in the FBI investigation into the Watergate break-in. The March 21 transcript reveals Nixon's complicity in a plan to buy the silence of Hunt and the President's awareness of Hunt's threats to reveal the 1971 Fielding break-in. (Nixon had contended the Fielding affair was a legal operation having to do with matters of national security.)

[60] **The June 23, 1972 (10:04-11:39 a.m.) Transcript.** The President and Haldeman in the Oval Office, joined briefly by Press Secretary Ziegler. Haldeman turned quickly to the ominous implications of the FBI's investigation of the Watergate break-in:

Haldeman: Now, on the investigation, you know the Democratic break-in thing, we're back in the problem area because the FBI is not under control, because Gray doesn't exactly know how to control it and they have—their investigation is now leading into some productive areas—because they've been able to trace the money—not through the money itself—but through the bank sources—the banker. And, and it goes in some directions we don't want it to go.... The way to handle this now is for us to have Walters call Pat Gray and just say, "stay to hell out of this—this is ah, business here we don't want you to go any further on it." That's not an unusual development, and ah, that would take care of it.

President: What about Pat Gray—you mean Pat Gray doesn't want to?

Haldeman: Pat does want to. He doesn't know how to, and he doesn't have, he doesn't have any basis for doing it. Given this, he will then have the basis....

Haldeman: ... We're relying on more and more people all the time. That's the problem and they'll stop if we could take this other route.

President: All right.

Haldeman: And you seem to think the thing to do is get them to stop?

President: Right, fine....

Haldeman: The FBI interviewed Colson yesterday.... And after their interrogation of Colson yesterday, they concluded it was not the White House, but are now convinced it is a CIA thing, so the CIA turnoff would—

President: ... You call them in.

Haldeman: Good deal.

President: Play it tough. That's the way they play it and that's the way we are going to play it.

After discussion of unrelated subjects, Nixon returned to the FBI-CIA problem, instructing Haldeman: "When you get in (unintelligible) people, say, 'Look, the problem is that this will open the whole, the whole Bay of Pigs thing, and the President just feels that ah, without going into the details—don't, don't lie to them to the extent to say no involvement, but just say this is a comedy of errors, without getting into it, the President believes that it is going to open the whole Bay of Pigs thing up again. And, ah, because these people are plugging for (unintelligible) and that they should call the FBI in and (unintelligible) don't go any further into this case period!"

[61] The Sept. 15, 1972 (5:27-6:17 p.m.) Transcript. The President, Haldeman and Dean in the Oval Office. The meeting was held on the same day the original Watergate indictments were returned and, according to Dean's testimony before the Senate Watergate Committee, signaled Nixon's early awareness that efforts were being made to keep various investigations contained. At one point during the conversation, Nixon commended Dean on his handling of the potentially harmful effects of the break-in by saying, ". . . the way you have handled all this seems to me has been very skillful putting your fingers in the leaks that have sprung here and sprung there." Later in the meeting, after discussion of the various investigations, Nixon concluded ". . . you just try to button it up as well as you can and hope for the best, and remember basically the damn business is unfortunately trying to cut our losses." Dean replied that at least there had been "no effect" on Nixon, and Haldeman interjected that aside from minor "lower level" connections and references to Colson, the affair had been kept "away from the White House."

Also discussed were potential retaliatory measures to be taken against those whom Dean characterized "as less than our friends because this will be over some day and we shouldn't forget the way some of them have treated us." The President agreed: ". . . they are asking for it and they are going to get it. We have not used the power in this first four years as you know. We have never used it. We have not used the Bureau and we have not used the Justice Department but things are going to change now. And they are either going to do it right or go." Dean comments: "What an exciting prospect."

[62] The March 21 1973 (10:12-11:55 a.m.) Transcript. The President and Dean in the White House Oval Office, later joined by Haldeman. Dean begins: "The reason that I thought we ought to talk this morning is because in our conversations I have the impression that you don't know everything I know and it makes it very difficult for you to make judgments that only you can make on some of these things. . . . I think that there is no doubt about the seriousness of the problem we've got. We have a cancer within, close to the Presidency, that is growing. It is growing daily. It's compounded, growing geometrically now, because it compounds itself. That will be clear if I, you know, explain some of the details of why it is. Basically, it is because (1) we are being blackmailed; (2) people are going to start perjuring themselves very quickly that have not had to perjure themselves to protect other people in the line. And there is no assurance—"The President interrupts, "That that won't bust?" Dean responds: "That that won't bust. . . ." Dean told Nixon that Watergate began as an innocent request by the White House for campaign intelligence against the Democrats. However, Liddy became involved and the final result was the bugging of the Democratic National Committee at its Watergate headquarters. When the burglars were arrested, they demanded money to see them through the November elections, as well as attorney's fees. After Dean says "I talked with Mitchell about that last night—" The President interrupts: "Either that or it blows right now?" Dean: "That's the question . . ."

Shortly afterwards, Dean outlines his worries about "this growing situation" involving blackmail and potential perjury. "If this thing ever blows, then we are in a cover-up situation" and suggests a meeting between him, Haldeman, Ehrlichman and Mitchell in which they can "figure out . . . how this can be carved away from you so that it does not damage you or the Presidency. . . ." The President and Dean discuss various reactions "if we can't hold this," among them complete disclosure. This brings up another problem when Dean says, "Well, I have been a conduit for information on taking care of people out there who are guilty of crimes." The President responds: ". . . I wonder if that doesn't have to be continued? Let me put it this way: let us suppose you get the million bucks, and you get the proper way to handle it. You could hold that side?" Dean: "Uh, huh." The problem of clemency again comes up, with Dean informing Nixon that Hunt is "now demanding clemency or he is going to blow." The two men agree that such a course of action would be politically impossible as it might involve the President. Dean says, "in a way you should not be. . . ." Dean says he has no "plan on how to solve it right now," but suggests they begin to think "in terms of how to cut the losses. . . ."

Dean also tells Nixon that Mitchell had initiated the arrangements for the money. Cash was raised by Kalmbach, laundered through "a Cuban committee" and "some of it was given to Hunt's lawyer, who in turn passed it out." Dean also tells the President that "that is an obstruction of justice" in which he, Haldeman, Ehrlichman and Mitchell are involved. He also brings up the point that "this is going to be a continual blackmail operation by Hunt and Liddy and the Cubans" and that "Hunt has now made a direct threat against Ehrlichman" in which he had said "'I have done enough seamy things for he and Krogh, they'll never survive it.'" The President asks, "Was he talking about Ellsberg?" Dean: "Ellsberg, and apparently some other things. I don't know the full extent of it." Dean then goes on to outline the problem of the continued blackmail demands which will "compound the obstruction of justice situation." Nixon and Dean discuss the amount of money required, with Dean saying the cost would be "a million over the next two years." The President: "We could get that. . . . You could get a million dollars. You could get it in cash. I know where it could be gotten. It is not easy, but it could be done." The two men then discuss who might handle the problem, both agreeing on Mitchell. Shortly after the President asks "Don't you think you have to handle Hunt's financial situation damn soon?" Later Nixon, speaking to Dean, says: "Would you agree that that's a buy-time thing, you better damn well get that done, but fast?"

Haldeman joins the meeting and the three men then discuss the possibilities of asking for another grand jury proceeding before which, the President suggests, "we will have the White House appear. . . . And that gives you a reason not to have to go before the Ervin and Baker committee." Dean suggests: "You can take the 5th Amendment." Haldeman: "And the Ervin Committee is a hell of a lot worse to deal with." Dean suggests a drawback to this course of action in that the U.S. Attorney's office will grant immunity to "all those criminal defendants." Haldeman: "It's Hunt's opportunity." Nixon: "That's why for your immediate things you have no choice but to come up with the $120,000, or whatever it is. . . ."

[63] The March 22, 1973 (1:57-3:43 p.m.) Transcript. The Judiciary Committee's transcript of a conversation between Nixon, Mitchell and others contained a 16-page dialogue between Nixon and Mitchell that was not included in the White House version. In it, Nixon was critical of President Eisenhower for ousting his aide Sherman Adams over a gift scandal. Referring to Eisenhower, Nixon said: "He only cared about—Christ, 'Be sure he was clean.' Both in the fund thing and the Adams thing. But I don't look at it this way. And

I just—that's the thing I am really concerned with. We're going to protect our people, if we can." In the same context, Nixon remarked: "And, uh, for that reason, I am perfectly willing to—I don't give a shit what happens. I want you all to stonewall it, let them plead the Fifth Amendment, cover-up or anything else, if it'll save it—save the plan. That's the whole point." Nixon later remarked, "...You know, up to this point, the whole theory has been containment, as you know, John."

Nixon Pardoned by Ford

[64] **Former president issues statement.** President Ford granted former President Nixon a full pardon Sept. 8 for all federal crimes he "committed or may have committed or taken part in" during his term in office. Nixon issued a statement accepting the pardon and expressing regret that he had been "wrong in not acting more decisively and more forthrightly in dealing with Watergate." The White House also announced Sept. 8 that the Ford Administration had concluded an agreement with Nixon giving him title to his presidential papers and tape recordings but guaranteeing they would be kept intact and available for court use for at least three years. The pardon for Nixon was unexpected. Ford made his announcement from the Oval Office on Sunday morning after attending church. After reading a brief statement on his decision before a small pool of reporters and photographers—the event was filmed for broadcast later—Ford signed a proclamation granting Nixon the pardon. Nixon had not been formally charged with any federal crime. The announcement drew wide protest and some support. Generally, it was split along partisan lines. One protester was White House Press Secretary J. F. terHorst, the first appointee of the Ford Administration, who resigned Sept. 8 as a matter of "conscience."

[65] In his statement, Ford said Nixon and "his loved ones have suffered enough, and will continue to suffer no matter what I do." "Theirs is an American tragedy in which we all have played a part," he said. "It can go on and on, or someone must write 'The End' to it. I have concluded that only I can do that. And if I can, I must." There were no historic or legal precedents on the matter, Ford said, "but it is common knowledge that serious allegations and accusations hang like a sword over our former President's head and threaten his health as he tries to reshape his life." He cited the "years of bitter controversy and divisive national debate" and the prospect of "many months and perhaps more years" before Nixon "could hope to obtain a fair trial by jury in any jurisdiction" of the country. Ford continued: "During this long period of delay and potential litigation, ugly passions would again be aroused, our people would again be polarized in their opinions, and the credibility of our free institutions of government would again be challenged at home and abroad."

[66] In accepting the pardon Sept. 8, Nixon said he hoped that this "compassionate act will contribute to lifting the burden of Watergate from our country." He spoke of "the depths of my regret and pain at the anguish my mistakes over Watergate have caused the nation and the Presidency." He knew, he said, "that many fair-minded people believe that my motivation and actions in the Watergate affair were intentionally self-serving and illegal. I now understand how my own mistakes and misjudgments have contributed to that belief and seemed to support it. This burden is the heaviest one of all to bear. That the way I tried to deal with Watergate was the wrong way is a burden I shall bear for every day of the life that is left to me."

[67] White House counsel Philip W. Buchen said Sept. 8 that the pardon for Nixon had been granted without any demands being made upon Nixon, that no effort had been made to obtain acknowledgment of wrongdoing. He also said the

advice of the Watergate special prosecutor, Leon Jaworski, had not been sought. Buchen said Sept. 10 that Ford "did not make a deal" with Nixon on the pardon before Nixon left office. He made the point, in another press briefing, that the granting of a pardon "can imply guilt—there is no other reason for granting a pardon." The fact that someone accepted a pardon, he said, "means that it was necessary for him to have the pardon."

[68] There was immediate protest from Congress against the pardon to Nixon. The White House was flooded with telephone calls and telegrams from the public. According to a Sept. 10 *New York Times* poll, public support for Ford had dropped sharply; 32% believed he was doing a good job, 33% a fair job, 25% a poor job and 10% had no opinion. The Democratic Congressional leadership was outspoken in criticism Sept. 8. Senate Majority Leader Mansfield, responding that "all men are equal under the law," said "that includes Presidents and plumbers." However, Senate Republican Leader Scott (Pa.) said Ford acted "with great humanity to bring an end to an American tragedy."

[69] Expense developments. The Ford Administration's request for $850,000 for pension and expenses for former President Nixon was itemized at the opening of Congressional hearings Sept. 11. Arthur F. Sampson, administrator of the General Services Administration (GSA), gave a new accounting on several items to the Senate Appropriations subcommittee headed by Sen. Joseph M. Montoya (D, N.M.). A former $100,000 item for "miscellaneous" expenses was reduced to $26,000, and a new item of $110,000 was included for construction, equipment and security of a vault to hold Nixon's papers and documents. Montoya noted that 13 persons receiving total annual salary of $340,000 were currently on the White House payroll and assigned full time to Nixon. They included Ronald L. Ziegler, press secretary, $42,500; Raymond K. Price Jr., speechwriter, $40,000; Rose Mary Woods, secretary, $36,000; Franklin Gannon, $35,300; Stephen B. Bull, $34,000; Michael Sterlacci, $28,263; Kenneth L. Khachigan, $27,500; Marjorie P. Acker, $23,000; Dianne Sawyer, $21,000; Anne Grier, $14,026; Nora Vandersommen, $14,457; Jeanne F. Quinlan, $13,003, and Jo Ellen Walker, $9,967. The Nixon fund request included $202,000 for payroll for aides, and Sampson said this would not cover the above persons unless President Ford separated them from the White House payroll. Nor did the $850,000 include the $622,000 annual payroll for Secret Service protection for Nixon. Sampson Sept. 13 revised the number of federal employes on loan to Nixon to a total of 21, including a valet and maid on the payroll of the National Park Service.

[70] The House Oct. 2 approved a $200,000 funding for pension and other allowances and transition expenses for Nixon. A transition fund of $100,000 was voted 342-47, and a $100,000 fund for pension and allowances was approved 321-62. The pension allotment was $55,000, the share from August through June 1975 of the $60,000 annual pension to which a former President was entitled by law. The House attached a proscription against use of the funds to build storage facilities for Nixon's presidential tapes and documents. An amendment to bar use of the money to transport the papers and tapes from Washington to Nixon in California without consent of Congress was approved by voice vote. The Senate passed an appropriations bill Nov. 20 containing $200,000 for Nixon's pension and transition expenses. Sen. Montoya, releasing data provided by the White House, Oct. 8 had said 64 government employes were assigned to Nixon's San Clemente, Calif. estate. Secret Service protection there was costing $622,000 a year and federal costs for personnel at Nixon's Key Biscayne, Fla. home were costing more than $500,000 a year. The bill also contained a provision to bar transfer of Nixon tapes and papers to his San Clemente home.

[71] Jaworski announces resignation. Leon Jaworski announced Oct. 12 his resignation as Watergate special prosecutor. The resignation, to be effective Oct. 25, was submitted to Attorney General William B. Saxbe. It was accepted by President Ford. Jaworski explicitly denied there was any connection between his resignation and the pardon or the suggestions that Nixon be indicted to test the pardon. In an interview published Oct. 16, Jaworski conceded that the pardon of Nixon had prevented an indictment and trial but he said the pardon itself, and evidence that was or would become public would show Nixon guilty of obstruction of justice. Henry S. Ruth Jr. was named Oct. 23 by Saxbe as Jaworski's replacement.

[72] **Ford on Nixon pardon: 'no deal.'** President Ford, in an historic appearance before a House subcommittee Oct. 17, defended his pardon of former President Nixon. (A presidential appearance before a Congressional committee was a rarity, historians citing only one such instance in U.S. history—Abraham Lincoln's visit to the House Judiciary Committee in 1862 to explain how a newspaper was able to publish his State of the Union Message before the speech was delivered.) Ford was not put under oath for his testimony, in which he reiterated he had made "no deal" with Nixon on the pardon, but had acted "out of my concern to serve the best interests of my country." The hearing which was televised, was before the House Criminal Justice Subcommittee of the Judiciary Committee. Its members were allotted five minutes each to question the President after his 5,000-word opening statement. The toughest questioning was by Rep. Elizabeth Holtzman (D, N.Y.), but, protesting the time limit, she did not wait for answers except to one query, whether Ford would be willing to turn over to the panel all tape recordings of his conversations with Nixon. Ford responded that the Nixon tapes were safe, "in our control," and being held for the Watergate special prosecutor. They "will not be delivered to anybody until a satisfactory agreement is reached with the special prosecutor's office," Ford said. The subcommittee voted 6-3 Nov. 22 to drop the probe of the pardon issue.

[73] **Ownership of presidential materials.** President Ford signed into law Dec. 19 a bill giving the federal government custody of the official tapes and papers of former President Nixon. The bill had been passed by both houses of Congress Dec. 9. It did not, however, designate ownership of the material, which was to be put in the permanent custody of the GSA. Nixon would have access to the material, which also was to be made available in judicial proceedings. Also written into the bill was establishment of a commission to prepare a report on legislation to cover handling of documents of public officials. The new law nullified an agreement, signed Sept. 6, by Nixon and GSA Administrator Sampson giving the former President control of the material. Nixon had stated in the agreement his intention to donate "a substantial portion" of his papers to the nation. All tapes were to be destroyed on Sept. 1, 1984 or at Nixon's death, if it occurred prior to that date.

Trials

[74] **Mitchell, Stans acquitted.** Former Attorney General Mitchell and former Commerce Secretary Maurice H. Stans, directors of Nixon's 1972 re-election campaign, were acquitted April 28 by a federal district court jury in New York City of all charges stemming from a secret $200,000 cash campaign contribution from Robert L. Vesco, a financier whose mutual funds dealings were under investigation by the Securities and Exchange Commission (SEC). The government had accused Mitchell and Stans of conspiracy, obstruction of justice and perjury for attempting to block the SEC investigation in return for the contribution; and for subsequently lying to a grand jury about their roles. The verdict was widely seen as a significant boost to Nixon's campaign against

impeachment, partly because the Vesco issue effectively would be removed from consideration by the House Judiciary Committee, but also because Dean's credibility was brought into question. (Dean had been a principal witness against Mitchell and Stans and was one of the President's chief accusers.) Interviewed after the verdict, jurors on a panel of nine men and three women said the basic issue in their 26 hours of deliberation had been the credibility of government witnesses versus that of the defendants. Among the factors operating in their decision, according to jury members, were: Dean's previous guilty plea to other Watergate charges, giving him a possible impetus to cooperate with the government in order to obtain leniency in sentencing; a feeling that Mitchell and Stans did not have "the need" to lie; doubts over the credibility of prosecution witness and former SEC Chairman G. Bradford Cook in light of his confession March 29 in cross examination that he had committed perjury in testimony before congressional committees and before the grand jury which indicted Mitchell and Stans; and the failure of the prosecution to present Vesco himself for testimony. (The U.S. had failed to extradite Vesco from Costa Rica.)

[75] The Mitchell-Stans trial had begun Feb. 19 after three postponements. The case had gone to the jury April 25 after 42 days of testimony from 59 witnesses and frequent moves for mistrial by the defense. Prosecution witnesses, several of them reluctant, testified March 5-April 3; and defense witnesses testified April 5-19. Testimony ended April 22 with the appearance of prosecution rebuttal witnesses. The prosecution attempted to prove that Mitchell and Stans had repeatedly interfered directly and indirectly with the SEC investigation of Vesco and had attempted to modify or delay the SEC complaint against Vesco in order to conceal information about the secret Vesco contribution, which Vesco reportedly threatened to reveal unless SEC "harassment" of him was stopped. Among the key witnesses at the trial were: Harry Sears, former Republican majority leader in the New Jersey State Senate, who had headed President Nixon's re-election campaign in that state; William J. Casey, former chairman of the SEC; Cook, who had resigned as SEC chairman because of his involvement in the case; and Dean. Dean was on the stand March 25-27. Among the key points in his testimony was Dean's statement that Mitchell had called him about the case at least 19 times. In October 1972—before the election and before filing of the SEC suit—Mitchell asked him to seek a postponement from the SEC until after the election. Dean testified he phoned Casey and then later reported to Mitchell that Casey had said, "'It's going to be very hard to do anything about this.'" In subsequent meetings with Stans and Mitchell they agreed to return the money. Cook testified March 27-29, saying that Stans asked him on four occasions to limit the SEC's investigation of Vesco's contribution (which had been revealed Feb. 28, 1973) or to conceal circumstances surrounding the giving of the cash.

[76] Mitchell and Stans took the stand in their own defense April 10-16 and April 17-19, respectively. Mitchell denied that he had ever attempted to "fix or quash" the SEC probe of Vesco and that he involved himself in the investigation only once, when he had called Casey to discuss Vesco's claims of harassment by the SEC staff. The impact of Mitchell's testimony was somewhat lessened, however, by his lapses of memory on crucial points of testimony given by Sears, Dean and other government witnesses. Stans, in often emotional testimony, swore that he "never did anything to help Robert Vesco" and sought to explain his alleged false statements to a grand jury as unintentional and attributable to a faulty memory caused by distress over his wife's serious illness.

[77] **Chapin trial.** Dwight L. Chapin, former appointments secretary to President Nixon, was sentenced to a prison term of 10-30 months May 15 for

lying to a grand jury about his involvement in political sabotage operations during the 1972 presidential campaign. Chapin had been convicted on two perjury counts April 5 in connection with grand jury testimony on his dealings with Donald H. Segretti, the "dirty trickster" of the 1971-72 presidential campaign. After 11½ hours of deliberation, the jury found that Chapin had lied when he denied in testimony before the Watergate grand jury any knowledge of Segretti's distribution of fake Democratic campaign literature. Segretti, who had been released March 25 after serving 4½ months of a six-month sentence for his political sabotage, appeared April 2 as the first prosecution witness. Segretti testified that Chapin had recruited him in the summer of 1971 for a job which he said Chapin had referred to as "pulling pranks." During the following year, Segretti said, he met with Chapin personally at least seven times to report on his activities. On one occasion, Chapin told him he should "concentrate" on Sen. Edmund S. Muskie (D, Me.), then the front-runner in the Democratic primary campaigns. One of the techniques used against Muskie, Segretti said, was to distribute scurrilous—and false—material about other Democrats on Muskie stationery. Testifying in his own defense April 3, Chapin portrayed himself as too concerned with important White House affairs to pay much attention to Segretti's political pranks.

[78] Fielding break-in trial. John D. Ehrlichman was found guilty July 12 by a federal jury in Washington of conspiring to violate the civil rights of Dr. Lewis J. Fielding, the psychiatrist of Pentagon Papers defendant Daniel Ellsberg. Three other defendants in the trial—G. Gordon Liddy, Bernard L. Barker and Eugenio Martinez—were convicted of the same charge. Ehrlichman was also found guilty of three of four counts of making false statements. The defendants had been indicted by a second Watergate grand jury March 7. Also indicted at that time were former presidential counsel Charles W. Colson and burglar Felipe De Diego. (Ehrlichman and Colson had been indicted in the Watergate cover-up [see below]; Liddy, Barker and Martinez had been convicted in the Watergate break-in; and De Diego had been named as an unindicted co-conspirator in a California state case relating to the Fielding burglary.) Also named in the March 7 indictment as unindicted co-conspirators were Egil Krogh, E. Howard Hunt and David R. Young. [See [80] below]

[79] Krogh had been sentenced Jan. 24 to six months in prison on the civil rights violation charge. All other federal and state charges against him were dropped in return for the guilty plea he had made Nov. 30, 1973. Krogh had said he would cooperate with regard to the other prosecutions, but had deferred giving information until after sentencing. Krogh denied having received "specific instruction or authority" from the President regarding the break-in. In a statement released after his sentencing, Krogh said that the "Fielding incident" took place in the context of an intense "national security concern expressed by the President," but that instructions to gather data on Ellsberg must have been "relayed" by Ehrlichman. Krogh was released from prison June 21. Charges against De Diego were dismissed by Judge Gerhard Gesell May 21 because De Diego had been given immunity by the prosecutors in return for his testimony. Colson had pleaded guilty in Washington federal court June 3 to a felony charge that he "unlawfully...did...endeavor to influence, obstruct and impede the Ellsberg trial." In return for the plea, all other charges pending against him were dropped. As part of the understanding, Colson consented to give sworn testimony and to provide relevant documents in his possession regarding the Fielding matter and in other Watergate-related cases. Colson was sentenced to one-three years in prison and fined $5,000 by Gesell June 21. Before sentencing, Colson read to the court a statement which also, like Krogh's, cited the "threat to national security" as the reason for his actions. While admitting he had not questioned the rightness or propriety of what he had done, Colson said he had acted on urgings from the President who "believed he was acting in the national interest." Colson added, "During the time I served in the White House, I rarely questioned a presidential order." As a result of his guilty plea, Colson was disbarred June 25 from the practice of law by the U.S. District Court for the District of Columbia. He entered the Maxwell (Ala.) Air Force Base federal prison Sept. 17.

[80] In a list of 19 "overt acts," the March 7 indictment charged the conspiracy began July 27, 1971, with a memorandum from Krogh and Young (then co-directors of the plumbers) to Ehrlichman dealing with a request for a psychiatric study of Ellsberg. Between that date and July 30, when Ehrlichman was informed that the request had been turned over to the CIA, Hunt sent Colson a memo proposing that Ellsberg's files be obtained from Fielding's office. Krogh and Young later informed Colson they would "look into" Hunt's suggestion. Ehrlichman Aug. 11 approved a "covert operation," provided he was given "assurance [which he received from Krogh and Young Aug. 30] it is not traceable." Meanwhile, Colson, Young and Krogh began discussing raising covert funds to pay the actual burglars; and Young and Colson also concentrated on how to "get the information out" on Ellsberg. Ehrlichman instructed Colson to prepare a "game plan" on possible use of the materials taken from Fielding's office. Near the first of September, Colson arranged to obtain $5,000 in cash, which was repaid by a transfer from the Trust for Agricultural Political Education, a dairy industry group (See Campaign Financing & Abuses). Krogh delivered the money to Liddy Sept. 1; and Liddy and Hunt immediately went to Los Angeles to meet with Barker, De Diego and Martinez. The latter three broke into Fielding's office Sept. 3. The final act of conspiracy covered by the indictment came March 27, 1973, when Ehrlichman "caused the removal of certain memoranda" on the burglary "from files maintained at the White House."

[81] (Los Angeles Superior Court Judge Gordon Ringer March 13 dropped California state charges against Ehrlichman, Young and Liddy in connection with the Fielding burglary. Despite the dismissal, however, a perjury charge against Ehrlichman for allegedly lying to a Los Angeles grand jury was allowed to stand. In dismissing the charges, Judge Ringer also vacated a subpoena served on President Nixon by the defendants. The subpoena, announced by Ringer Jan. 29, required President Nixon to testify before the California court Feb. 25 for a pretrial hearing and April 15 for the trial.)

[82] The question of national security as a defense was raised by both Colson and Ehrlichman. In an affidavit submitted to the U.S. district court in Washington April 30, Ehrlichman said the President had twice "indicated his after-the-fact approval" of the Fielding break-in, and that Nixon had ordered Assistant Attorney General Henry E. Petersen to keep the Watergate investigators away from the break-in because national security matters were involved. Gesell ruled May 24 that the defendants could not cite national security as legal justification and that the President was without the constitutional right to authorize such actions without a warrant even when national security was involved. Conceding that "warrantless invasion" of a premise had been approved by the Supreme Court "under carefully delineated emergency circumstances," Gesell asserted no such circumstances obtained in the Fielding case and that the search "of Dr. Fielding's office was therefore clearly illegal under the unambiguous mandate of the 4th Amendment."

[83] Among those testifying at the trial were Young, Krogh, Ehrlichman,

Martinez, Barker and Secretary of State Henry Kissinger. Nixon testified in the form of a sworn written reply to six questions submitted by the defense. Essentially, Krogh and Young provided evidence supporting the indictment, although both men conceded that Ehrlichman had never used the term "break-in." In addition, discussing the Aug. 11 memo, Young told of meetings with Ehrlichman during one of which "Ehrlichman replied that there was no question about what had actually happened, but that he had taken those memos out [of the files] and thought he should keep them because they were a little too sensitive and showed too much foresight." Young said he did not tell Ehrlichman he had made his own copies. Krogh testified that after he had received the Aug. 11 memo with Ehrlichman's initials and the "not traceable" notation, "It was clear to me that an entry operation would have to be undertaken to examine those files." Young, the first witness to take the stand, had been given a grant of immunity from prosecution. Krogh appeared July 2. Ehrlichman testified in his own defense July 9. The essential points made in his appearance were: (1) that he considered a covert operation to be "a private investigation, where the people don't identify themselves, as from the FBI"; (2) that he had not learned of the break-in until after it occurred; and (3) that he had been too busy to look at the files and had returned them to Young. Kissinger, in a 108-second appearance July 10, denied knowledge of or authorization for any attempt by the CIA or others to obtain Ellsberg's psychological profile. Earlier, on July 9, Martinez and Barker testified that they had been led to believe "matters of national security" were involved, necessitating the Fielding break-in.

[84] The questions to Nixon were delivered to the Whie House July 9. In a letter accompanying the replies, the President said he had decided to respond "as a matter of discretion and in the interest of justice." (Judge Gesell said the submission of written interrogatories was "not an order, merely a request" to which the President had acceded.) In his replies, Nixon said he had "authorized the special investigations unit to prevent and halt leaks of vital security information and to prepare an accurate history of certain critical national security matters which occurred under prior Administrations." The President said Ehrlichman was given "general supervisory control" over the unit and that he had emphasized to Ehrlichman "that this was a highly classified matter which could be discussed with others only on an absolutely 'need to know' basis." The President said he was first informed of the break-in on March 17, 1973 and that he had never given authorization for a warrantless search of Fielding's files.

[85] Instructing the jury on the conspiracy charge July 12, Gesell said that it need not find Ehrlichman had known in advance of plans for a "covert entry" into Fielding's office files to obtain Ellsberg's psychiatric records. Moreover, Gesell told the jurors, the law had been broken if the government attempted to acquire private information without a search warrant, he said. Gesell's instructions struck at the heart of Ehrlichman's defense that he had not authorized an illegal break-in but merely a legal "covert operation."

[86] Ehrlichman was sentenced to 20 months to five years in prison July 31. He received the same sentence for each of two other perjury charges on which he was convicted. The sentences, a minimum of 20 months, were to run concurrently. Liddy received a sentence of one to three years in prison, to be served concurrently with his present sentence of six years, eight months to 20 years. Barker and Martinez were placed on probation for three years by Gesell. Gesell said they had been "duped" by high government officials and had been punished enough.

[87] **Four convicted of cover-up.** Four key aides to former President Nixon were found guilty by a federal court jury in Washington Jan. 1, 1975 of

conspiracy to obstruct justice in connection with the June 17, 1972 break-in at the Watergate headquarters of the Democratic National Committee. A fifth defendant was found not guilty. The nine-woman, three-man jury was given final instructions by presiding Judge Sirica Dec. 30, 1974 and deliberated about 15 hours before returning its verdict. The verdicts: H. R. Haldeman, former chief of staff at the Nixon White House, was convicted of one count of conspiracy, one count of obstruction of justice and three counts of perjury with regard to his Senate Watergate Committee testimony concerning his and Nixon's knowledge of the cover-up. John Mitchell, former attorney general and director of the Committee to Re-elect the President, was found guilty of one count of conspiracy, one count of obstruction of justice, two counts of making false declarations to the grand jury regarding covert intelligence-gathering operations against the Democrats and one count of perjury for having denied in testimony before the Senate Watergate Committee that he discussed destruction of documents at a meeting two days after the break-in. John Ehrlichman, former domestic affairs adviser to Nixon, was found guilty of one count of conspiracy, one count of obstruction of justice and two counts of making false declarations to the grand jury when he denied being able to remember various facts about the break-in and the cover-up. Robert Mardian, a former assistant attorney general and attorney for the Nixon re-relection committee, was found guilty of one count of conspiracy. Kenneth W. Parkinson, a re-election committee attorney hired after the break-in to deal with Watergate-related litigation, was found not guilty of one count of conspiracy and one count of obstruction of justice.

[88] The conspiracy charge against the defendants involved payment of $429,500 in hush money to the seven original Watergate break-in defendants, destruction of documents, offers of presidential clemency and schemes to obstruct investigations and other functions of government agencies. Charles Colson, special counsel to Nixon, and Gordon Strachan, an aide of Haldeman's, were also named in the original cover-up indictment. Cover-up charges were dropped against Colson, however, when he pleaded guilty in connection with the Ellsberg burglary. [See above] Strachan's case was severed from the main trial to allow determination of whether the indictment against him was based on testimony he gave under immunity from prosecution.

[89] The judicial process had begun March 1, 1974 in a 15-minute session in the courtroom of Judge Sirica when the judge accepted the indictments and a sealed report naming Nixon as an unindicted co-conspirator from grand jury foreman Vladimir N. Pregelj. At a brief arraignment hearing March 9, the seven pleaded not guilty to all charges.

[90] Sirica July 9 denied a series of motions by the defendants for separate trials, dismissal, delaying the start of the trial, and moving the trial out of Washington. Sirica rejected as premature the defense contentions that inflamatory publicity had made a fair trial impossible. He added, however, that his decision not to move the trial would be reconsidered if a jury could not be selected in Washington. The first legal action against former President Nixon as a private citizen was taken Aug. 15 in the form of a subpoena to appear as a witness for Ehrlichman in the pending cover-up trial. Acting at the suggestion of the U.S. Court of Appeals, Sirica Aug. 22 postponed the beginning of the Watergate cover-up trial to Sept. 30, later changed to Oct. 1. In papers filed with the appeals court Aug. 21, Ehrlichman said Philip W. Buchen, counsel to President Ford, had, at least temporarily, denied him access to his files still in the White House. A White House spokesman said later in the day that Nixon had apparently stopped allowing defendants access to their files shortly before his resignation, and that Buchen was reviewing current policy. The White House announced Aug. 23 that access would be reinstated, but defendants would not be allowed to make copies or take notes. Buchen's office said the decision had been cleared with Nixon.

[91] Nixon Sept. 19 received a second subpoena to appear as a witness at the Watergate cover-up trial, scheduled to begin Oct. 1. The second summons came from Jaworski. Jaworski's office declined to comment on the reason for the subpoena, but defense sources said he had been forced to take the action to officially establish the authenticity—and admissibility—of Nixon's Watergate tape recordings, which were expected to be a principal source of evidence for the prosecution. The issue put the trial in jeopardy because of the controversy over Nixon's health and the possibility that Nixon would use illness as grounds for avoiding compliance with the subpoena.

[92] Jury selection in the trial of the five defendants began Oct. 1. A separate, later trial had been ordered the previous day for Strachan, the sixth defendant. Sirica said complications involving Strachan's indictment and his contention that he had given information under a grant of immunity should be resolved in a pretrial hearing. Sirica said that rather than delay the trial further he would consider Strachan's case separately. Attorneys for Nixon requested Oct. 3 that he be excused from appearing as a witness. Sirica did not reveal the grounds cited and said the motions would remain sealed until a jury was sequestered. (Dr. John C. Lungren, Nixon's personal physician, said in Long Beach, Calif. Sept. 30 that his patient, who was suffering from a serious case of phlebitis, would not be fit to travel to Washington for 1-3 months. Lungren added that Nixon might be able to give a written deposition in California in two or three weeks. Lungren said the next day that the clot had begun to clear up and that the latest tests showed no signs of any new clots.) Selection of a 12-person jury and six alternates, which took two weeks, was completed Oct. 11, and the jurors were sequestered for the remainder of the trial.

[93] Richard Ben-Veniste, assistant special Watergate prosecutor, opened the trial, outlining Oct. 14 charges against the five defendants, as well as the evidence and theory of events he said would establish their guilt. While much of what Ben-Veniste outlined had been disclosed before the Senate Watergate committee in 1973 and the House Judiciary Committee during its impeachment proceedings, the assistant prosecutor charged for the first time that some of the more than $400,000 paid as hush money to the original Watergate defendants had come from a fund controlled by Charles G. Rebozo, Nixon's personal friend. [See CAMPAIGN FINANCING & ABUSES] William Frates followed Oct. 15 with an opening statement charging that his client, Ehrlichman, had been lied to and used by Nixon, who was seeking to hide his own complicity in Watergate. Lawyers for Mardian and Parkinson asserted that their clients' involvement in the cover-up was at most peripheral and not a cause for indictment. Counsel for Haldeman and Mitchell reserved their opening arguments until completion of the prosecution's case.

[94] John Dean, who had been sentenced to one-four years in prison for his role in the cover-up Aug. 2, took the witness stand Oct. 16 and 17 as the government's first witness. Nearly all of what he said had already been revealed in nationally televised hearings before the Senate Watergate committee. His testimony frequently matched verbatim his testimony before the Senate panel. During Dean's second day of testimony Oct. 17, all those present in the courtroom donned earphones connected to a central system playing the White House tape recordings. It was the first public playing of the tapes. Dean's testimony, which mirrored the chronology of the events, was given in conjunction with the recordings. Among the tapes was the recording of the Sept. 15, 1972 meeting of Nixon, Dean and Haldeman. It coincided with the

indictment that day of the seven original Watergate conspirators. In that meeting, Nixon congratulated Dean for handling the Watergate matter very skillfully. [See centered heading: *Excerpts from Key Tapes*] Dean Oct. 22 completed his chronological account of the alleged cover-up, and then was cross-examined by the attorneys for the defendants, who sought to discredit his character, the accuracy of his memory and his motives for testifying.

[95] Convicted Watergate break-in conspirator E. Howard Hunt testified Oct. 28-29 that he had withheld the "entire truth" about Watergate until his appearance at this trial. He had begun to have a change of heart about his testimony, Hunt said, when the White House tape transcripts were released April 30 and he realized "that these men were not worthy of my continued loyalty." He had been silent because of promises of a light prison sentence or clemency made to him by Colson. Hunt conceded that he had threatened to tell the "seamy things" he had done for Ehrlichman, but denied this was blackmail, saying it was only an attempt to get a long overdue debt paid. He confirmed, however, that his lawyer had received $75,000 for him the night of March 21, 1973. Hunt also said that G. Gordon Liddy had received approval for intelligence-gathering against the Democrats from Mitchell, but conceded on cross-examination that he had received this information from Liddy and had never met or talked with Mitchell about any of the plans.

[96] Jeb Stuart Magruder, who had been sentenced May 21 to 10 months to four years for his role in the affair, testified Oct. 31 that he, Mitchell and Mardian had agreed the morning after the arrest of the Watergate burglars that one possible way to divert investigators from the Nixon campaign organization would be to give the appearance that the CIA was involved in the break-in. Magruder had testified Oct. 30 that on March 28, 1973, when the Watergate cover-up was coming apart, he went to Mitchell with a "laundry list" of things he would need if he went to jail. The list, which included money, clemency and help in later finding a job, contained about a dozen items, Magruder said. Mitchell approved each item and asked him not to break his silence about Watergate, Magruder said.

[97] The prosecution disclosed Nov. 4 the existence of what it called a "bombshell document," which disputed the contention by Nixon that money was paid to the original Watergate break-in defendants only for "humanitarian" reasons. The document, a two-year-old memorandum presumed lost, had been prepared by Hunt, who asserted in testimony Oct. 29 that he had given it to his attorney with the instructions that it be passed on to those supplying funds. The memorandum, dated Nov. 14, 1972, complained that the Administration had been "deficient in living up to its commitments." The memorandum added that the defendants would soon meet to determine a joint response "to evidence of continued indifference on the part of those in whose behalf we suffered the loss of our employment, our futures and our reputations as honorable men." The document ended, "The foregoing should not be interpreted as a threat. It is among other things a reminder that loyalty has always been a two-way street." A section titled "Items for Consideration" included the statement that the "Watergate bugging is only one of a number of highly illegal conspiracies engaged in by one or more of the defendants at the behest of senior White House officials. These as yet undisclosed crimes can be proved."

[98] Testimony of witnesses regarding the cover-up was frequently interrupted by arguments on the authenticity of the tapes. After hearing about installation and operation of the system from two Secret Service agents as well as from former presidential aide Alexander P. Butterfield, Sirica ruled the tapes admissable as evidence Nov. 7.

[99] Vernon A. Walters, deputy director of the CIA, and L. Patrick Gray 3rd, former acting director of the FBI, appeared as witnesses Nov. 11. Both testified in conjunction with the playing of the key June 23, 1972 tape which had led to Nixon's resignation. The tape revealed Nixon's agreement with Haldeman's plan to have Walters call Gray, telling him the break-in was a CIA matter in which the FBI should not interfere. Walters said that in a meeting later that morning between him, CIA Director Richard Helms, Haldeman and Ehrlichman, Helms had said the CIA had nothing to do with the break-in, a fact of which he had already informed Gray. Haldeman, however, insisted on the plan, saying it was "the President's wish..." Walters said he then met with Gray, citing the presidential authority. Gray told the court that he held up the FBI investigation for two weeks following Walters' request, but finally concluded he needed a formal, written request from the CIA. However, Walters refused to do this at a July 6 meeting, then admitted there was no CIA connection to Watergate. Herbert W. Kalmbach, former personal attorney to President Nixon, appeared as a witness Nov. 12. During the three months following the arrest of the Watergate burglars, Kalmbach testified, he helped raise and distribute about $220,000 to the burglars and their families.

[100] Sirica appointed a panel of doctors Nov. 13 to determine whether Nixon was physically able to give testimony in the trial. The panel, approved by both sides, was led by Dr. Charles Anthony Hufnagel, a heart surgeon with Georgetown University Hospital in Washington, D.C. The panel informed Sirica Nov. 29 that Nixon's poor health would not permit a Washington court appearance until at least Feb. 16, 1975. Nor would the former President be able to give a sworn deposition until Jan. 6, 1975. Sirica ruled Dec. 5 that the cover-up trial would be concluded without the testimony of Nixon. Sirica said the court would not take a deposition of Nixon "while it appears that he is so ill... that [it] could jeopardize his health." Sirica also indicated he doubted the value of Nixon's testimony.

[101] Opening the defense Nov. 25, William G. Hundley, Mitchell's chief counsel, asserted that his client had not approved plans for the Watergate break-in and had not been involved in subsequent payments to the break-in defendants. Authorization for the plans that led to the break-in, Hundley contended, had come from Magruder, who was being pressed by the White House for political intelligence about the Democrats. Mitchell had in fact rejected three proposals for political espionage, Hundley said. Mitchell took the witness stand Nov. 26, 27, and 29. He recalled being approached by Liddy on three separate occasions about plans for political intelligence against the Democrats. Each time, Mitchell testified, he had rejected Liddy's schemes. Authorization for the plan that eventually led to the break-in came from Magruder. Moreover, Mitchell said, he had not learned of Liddy's involvement in the break-in until after it had occurred. Mitchell was questioned by James Neal, the chief prosecutor, about his meeting in early July 1972 with two FBI agents who sought to learn what he knew about the break-in. By the time of the FBI interview, Mitchell conceded, he had learned of Liddy's involvement and that Magruder had been pressured into approving Liddy's plans for political espionage. Nonetheless, Mitchell testified, he had not volunteered his information to the FBI agents, to the grand jury or anyone else because his paramount concern was not to damage the re-election chances of Nixon.

[102] Haldeman testified in his own defense Nov. 29 and Dec. 2-5. Throughout his testimony, Haldeman insisted that much of what was said on the White House tape recordings was subject to differing interpretation. Haldeman maintained that he had not known what was meant when he was told at a March 22, 1972, White House meeting that Hunt had been "taken care of."

Perhaps Hunt had been taken care of in a way that was not financial, Haldeman suggested.
[103] Ehrlichman appeared in his own defense Dec. 9-12. During his four days on the witness stand, Ehrlichman made no effort to deny that a cover-up had occurred. Rather, he sought to show that he had known "pitifully little about Watergate" until nine months after the break-in had taken place and that he had been deceived and manipulated by Nixon. Mardian, who testified on his own behalf Dec. 13, 16 and 17, asserted that his involvement in the Watergate affair had been the result of his job as the re-election committee's lawyer for Watergate-related matters. He denied having relayed, the day of the break-in, a message to then Attorney General Richard Kleindienst seeking the release from jail of the five men arrested at the Watergate complex. He also insisted that he had not helped devise a cover story about Watergate and that he had not been involved in the payment of hush money to the original Watergate burglars. In testimony Dec. 17 and 18, Parkinson said he had not knowingly played a role in the cover-up. Moreover, Parkinson contended that during the period following the break-in, he had confined his interests to the civil suit arising from the incident. While he admitted he had learned isolated details about the break-in and its aftermath, Parkinson maintained that he had not pursued any of that information.

See also APPOINTMENTS & RESIGNATIONS; CAMPAIGN FINANCING; ELECTIONS [11-12]; FORD, GERALD R.; MONETARY DEVELOPMENTS [18-19]; NIXON, RICHARD M.; PRIVACY [1-5]; PULITZER PRIZES; RADICALS; ROCKEFELLER, NELSON [6, 16]; SAXBE, WILLIAM B.; VESCO, ROBERT L.; VETERANS

WEATHER—At least 60 persons died and over 100,000 were left homeless in three northwestern provinces in Argentina following severe flooding, it was reported Feb. 17. Floods in Brazil killed an estimated 2,000-5,000 persons in March. The rains, which ended March 29, followed months of drought and caused over $400 million in damage which left more than 300,000 homeless. The worst hit area was Tubarao, an agricultural community in southern Santa Catarina, with a population of 70,000. As many as 1,000 persons were reported dead. Waters of the Tubarao River reportedly rose over 36 feet within hours. Severe flooding also occurred in the north where whole towns were evacuated and many cattle drowned. There were reports of malaria, yellow fever, and typhoid.

The worst tornadoes in 49 years ripped across a corridor extending from Georgia to Ontario Province April 3-4, killing an estimated 350 persons and leaving 1,200 injured and thousands homeless. Damage was estimated at $1 billion. Six states were declared disaster areas, becoming eligible for massive federal aid. They included: Kentucky, the most devastated state (Brandenburg, population 1,600, was almost completely leveled) with 71 deaths reported; Alabama with 72 dead; Tennessee with 46 dead; Indiana, 39 dead; Georgia, 16 dead; and Ohio, 37 dead. (Xenia, Ohio, population 25,000, reported 35 killed and half the town destroyed.) Ontario Province reported eight deaths. Other states reporting deaths: North Carolina 5, Michigan 3, Illinois 2, Virginia 1 and West Virginia 1. A moderate earthquake struck areas of the Midwest about the same time but there were no reports of injuries. Tornadoes and flash floods whipped across the Midwest June 8-10, killing 30 persons. Arkansas, Kansas and Oklahoma were declared disaster areas. The National Weather Service said the storm system was nearly as powerful as the one that struck April 3.

At least 250 people were killed and 500 more were missing and believed dead after landslips, believed triggered by torrential rains, wiped out three villages in the Peruvian Andes April 25. Some 10,000 families were evacuated from villages threatened by a huge lake formed by the landslips. Rescue squads returning from some of the more remote districts of the disaster area reported there were no signs of life "just an even carpet of mud and rock." At least 200 persons were killed by flooding and landslides in Brazil, it was reported May 1.

Typhoon Gilda swept through virtually all of Japan and part of South Korea killing at least 108 persons and causing $334 million in damages, it was reported July 11.

An estimated 260 persons were reported dead in India as incessant rains during a six-week period ending Aug. 11 caused swollen rivers to rush down the Himalayan mountains. Seven northeast states were flooded leaving millions homeless. There was a crushing effect on crops, and four million persons were reported on the brink of starvation. A cyclone had also struck the northeast region Aug. 15, killing at least 20 persons. At least 2,500 persons were killed following monsoon rains which had left 20,000 of Bangla Desh's 55,000 square miles under water. Property and crop damage was estimated at $2 billion. It was reported Aug. 12 that the floods were subsiding following two months of rainfall. Aircraft were dropping $2.5 million worth in food and 20 tons of medical supplies, including cholera vaccine, allocated by the United Nations, to those marooned. Cholera was reported widespread, with the problem in the cities aggravated by masses of people crowding in from flooded areas.

Week-long monsoon rains, sweeping across the main island of Luzon in the Philippines, left 78 dead and nearly a million homeless from flooding, it was reported Aug. 21. Emergency aid was being airlifted in a joint effort of Philippine and U.S. aircraft. According to Aug. 19 reports, President Ferdinand Marcos said "the worst appears to be over." Some 70 persons had been killed on Luzon June 11 when tropical storm Dinah ripped across the island. Another 52 persons were killed during typhoons that swept acoss the Philippines in October.

Hurricane Carmen struck southwest Louisiana but rapidly weakened and was reduced to tropical storm status Sept. 8. No deaths were reported but officials estimated damage to the state's sugar-cane crop at $50 million. Twelve persons were reportedly drowned after cloudbursts produced flash flooding throughout central Texas Nov. 24. All of the victims were in cars that were swept away by flood waters.

Nearly 19 inches of snow fell in Detroit Dec. 1-2, the city's worst snowstorm in 88 years. Eighteen persons reportedly died after heart attacks suffered while attempting to shovel snow.

See also AGRICULTURE; ARGENTINA [17]; AUSTRALIA [17]; CHAD; ETHIOPIA [10]; FAMINE & FOOD; HONDURAS; INDIA; MOUNTAIN CLIMBING; NIGERIA; SPACE [8]

WELFARE & POVERTY—Sterilization program curbed. U.S. District Court Judge Gerhard A. Gesell ruled in Washington March 15 that regulations proposed by the Department of Health, Education and Welfare (HEW) to cover federally-financed sterilizations of poor persons were "arbitrary and unreasonable" and failed to give sufficient protection to minors and mentally incompetent persons. HEW had been attempting to draw up regulations because of disclosures of sterilization of retarded minors in federally-aided clinics and, as Gesell noted in his decision, evidence that welfare recipients had been threatened with loss of benefits if they refused sterilization. Noting that in recent years 100,000-150,000 low-income persons had been sterilized annually in federal programs, Gesell said the matter was of major national significance. Government, including Congress, he said, should "move cautiously" to set regulations in "one of the most drastic methods of population control" which could irreversibly deprive unwilling or immature persons of their rights.

House OKs OEO abolition, Senate extends program. By a vote of 331-53 May 29, the House approved and sent to the Senate a bill abolishing the Office of Economic Opportunity (OEO)—a long-term goal of the Nixon Administration—but extending the remaining OEO programs and transferring them to other Cabinet-level agencies. The bill would authorize $3.76 billion for the programs for fiscal 1975-77, including $1 billion for community action (local groups administering employment and education aid for the poor). The program would be run by a new Community Action Administration in HEW. The OEO's role in the Head Start program for pre-school children was also transferred to HEW and funded at $1.58 billion for the three years. Community economic development programs would be transferred to the Commerce Department; migrant labor and work training programs would be transferred to the Labor Department; and OEO's role in aiding minority business would be taken over by the Small Business Administration.

The Senate voted Dec. 13 for legislation to extend the OEO and sent the bill to a House-Senate conference committee. The bill reported by the committee was cleared by both houses Dec. 19. It extended OEO programs through fiscal 1977. The agency itself would continue to exist at least until June 15, 1975. Under the bill, President Ford had the option of proposing a reorganization plan after March 15, 1975 to transfer community action programs to HEW. Congress could reject the plan by a joint resolution, but the President could veto it. Earlier, House-Senate conferees had accepted, with some minor modifications, the provisions in the House bill requiring a gradual decline in the federal share of the community action programs costs. President Ford signed the bill Dec. 20.

Hunger, poverty found worsening. The Senate Select Committee on Nutrition and Human Needs was told during hearings June 19-21 that the nation's needy were getting hungrier and poorer and that government programs dealing with hunger were ineffective. A report prepared for the committee by a panel of outside experts cited steeply rising food costs and inequities in federal food programs, particularly food stamps, as the major problems. The panel noted that between December 1970 and March 1974, food stamp benefits for a family of four had increased 34% while the cost of foods in the Agriculture Department's "economy" food plan—the basis for food stamp allocations—had increased 42%. With the cheapest foods undergoing the sharpest price increases during that period (124% for rice, 256% for dried beans), the poor did not have the "spending down" option available to higher-income groups. The report said only about 15 million of an estimated 37-50 million eligible persons were buying food stamps, and that many were not even aware of their eligibility.

Poverty legal aid approved. By a vote of 77-19 July 18, the Senate gave final approval to a bill establishing an independent legal services corporation for the poor. The House had cleared the compromise measure July 16 by a vote of 265-136, and President Nixon signed it into law July 25. Establishment of the independent corporation removed legal services functions from the moribund OEO. The bill authorized funding of $90 million for fiscal 1975, $100 million for 1976 and open-ended funding for 1977. Subsequent appropriations would be limited to two-year periods.

Poverty area unemployment reported. A report released by the Labor Department Aug. 29 showed that in 1973 the unemployment rate in metropolitan center poverty areas was almost twice that in non-metropolitan poverty areas: 9% vs. 4.7%. A "poverty area" was defined as a census tract in which at least one-fifth of the residents had incomes at or below the poverty level ($4,540 a year for a non-farm family of four).

Social services meeting. Representatives of the poor, the aged, the handicapped, the young, minority groups, and consumers met in Washington

Sept. 19-20 with Administration officials and Congressional leaders to discuss ways to curb inflation in the fields of social welfare, health, and education. Controversy quickly dominated the proceedings. Delegates to the conference charged Sept. 19 that the Administration planned to implement one of its principal anti-inflation policies—fiscal restraint—by making major budgetary cutbacks in HEW's social services programs. Asked why the poor should be expected to make the greatest sacrifices in the fight against inflation, Alan Greenspan, chairman of the Council of Economic Advisers, remarked, "Everybody is hurt by inflation. If you really want to examine percentage-wise who was hurt most in their income, it was Wall Street brokers." Catcalls drowned out the rest of his remarks. Greenspan denied charges that Administration policies were aimed at aiding big business.

See also BUDGET; EDUCATION; HOUSING; LABOR [5-8]; MEDICINE & HEALTH [5]; NIXON, RICHARD M.

WEST INDIES ASSOCIATED STATES—Nevis seeks separate government. The local governing council of the island of Nevis, citing the example of Anguilla, asked the British government to detach the island from the administrative structure with neighboring St. Kitts, it was reported June 2. (Anguilla had seceded from the West Indies associated state of St. Kitts-Nevis-Anguilla in 1967, protesting domination by the larger St. Kitts. Britain had taken control of the island in 1969 after landing a miniature "invasion" force, and in 1971 had assumed direct administration of the island, promising to review the situation in three years.)

Dominica enacts anti-terrorist bill. The legislature of the West Indies self-governing associated state of Dominica approved two emergency bills Dec. 6 strengthening the government's powers to combat Black Power terrorists accused of attacking whites. The measures empowered judges to order the destruction of literature used to further the aims of outlawed groups and authorized suspension without pay of civil servants who aided members of a banned group. The Caribbean island's 130-man police force and 30-man army had launched an offensive against a black terrorist movement called Dread Dec. 4, arresting several members who wore their hair in braids used to identify the group. (Patrick Roland John, 37, had been sworn in as premier July 28, one day after Edward Leblanc had resigned the post. Leblanc, head of the island's government since 1962, had said two weeks earlier that he was tired of politics. John had been deputy premier under Leblanc.)

St. Vincent, St. Lucia elections. The Labor Party of St. Vincent gained power in general elections held Dec. 9, winning 10 of the 13 House of Assembly seats. The People's Progressive Party, in power since 1972, won only two seats. In elections held May 8 in the associated state of St. Lucia, Premier John Compton's United Workers' Party (UWP) returned to power, winning 10 of the newly enlarged Assembly's 17 seats. The UWP had previously held six seats, and the Labor Party four. The UWP had previously asked the government to seek independence for St. Lucia.

WEST VIRGINIA—*See* EDUCATION; ENERGY CRISIS [6]; LABOR [13]; WEATHER
WHITE HOUSE—*See* CRIME [20]; FORD, GERALD R.; NIXON, RICHARD M.
WILSON, HAROLD—*See* CYPRUS [5]; EUROPEAN ECONOMIC COMMUNITY [13]; GREAT BRITAIN [3-6, 15]; IRELAND, NORTHERN [5-6]; UNION OF SOVIET SOCIALIST REPUBLICS [28]
WIRETAPPING—*See* CANADA [9]; CENTRAL INTELLIGENCE AGENCY; CRIME [3]; PRIVACY; RADICALS; WATERGATE [31]
WISCONSIN—*See* AGRICULTURE; ELECTIONS [5]; ENVIRONMENT & POLLUTION [12]

WOMENS' RIGHTS—ERA developments. Ohio became the 33rd state to ratify the Equal Rights Amendment Feb. 7. Legislatures in Montana and Maine had ratified Jan. 21 and Jan. 18, respectively. Ratification attempts had failed in all three states in 1973. The amendment failed in the Georgia House of Representatives Jan. 28 after a debate in which a male legislator said the measure was "stinking of communism" and would "lower our ladies down to the level of men."

An attempt by Nebraska, one of the ratifying states, to rescind its approval was still to be tested in court. The Tennessee legislature April 23 became the second to attempt to rescind its approval of the Equal Rights Amendment to the U.S. Constitution. The state had approved the measure in 1972.

Representatives of 26 national organizations supporting the equal rights amendment announced Dec. 10 they would concentrate their campaign in 10 states in an effort to achieve final ratification in 1975. The states, cited in a plan devised by a political consultant firm, were Illinois, Missouri, North Carolina and North Dakota—all listed as almost certain of prompt favorable action; Arizona and Oklahoma—regarded as good but not certain of favorable; Florida—deemed good for later ratification; and Indiana, Nevada and South Carolina.

Maternity decisions. The Supreme Court ruled 7-2 Jan. 21 that a public school system could not force a pregnant teacher to take a maternity leave until a few weeks before she was due to bear a child. The case involved the school systems of Cleveland, Ohio and Chesterfield County, Va., a Richmond suburb, which required pregnant teachers to begin maternity leaves during their fifth month of pregnancy. In so ruling, the court majority rejected arguments of the school systems that early maternity leave insured continuity of instruction and protected the health of the teacher and her unborn child.

U.S. District Court Judge Robert R. Merhige of Richmond, Va. ruled April 14 that the General Electric Co. (GE) had practiced sexual discrimination in denying disability benefits to pregnant employes. Merhige rejected company arguments that denial of benefits was justified because pregnancy was a "voluntary" disability, noting that similar standards were not applied to male employes incurring disabilities which might also be deemed voluntary.

The Supreme Court ruled June 17 that a California job disability insurance program did not unconstitutionally discriminate against women because it did not include benefits for normal pregnancies. The California program, which excluded "any injury or illness caused by or arising in connection with pregnancy and for a period of 28 days thereafter," was contested by four women no longer able to work because of pregnancy. Financed by deductions from the wages of its participants, the California program was mandatory for all employes not covered by private disability programs certified by the state. In its 6-3 decision, written by Justice Potter Stewart, the court reasoned that in excluding benefits for normal pregnancies, California was not discriminating against anyone eligible for insurance protection, but that it had decided against insuring all employment disability risks.

Educational discrimination. The Department of Health, Education and Welfare (HEW) June 18 proposed regulations against sex discrimination in educational institutions receiving federal aid. The rules, designed to implement legislation passed in 1972, would affect institutions from pre-elementary through graduate levels, but allow numerous exemptions, particularly in the area of admissions. A prohibition against discrimination in recruiting and admissions would apply to high school-level vocational schools, co-educational public colleges and all graduate and professional schools. Pre-elementary,

elementary, non-vocational secondary schools, private undergraduate colleges and the few traditionally one-sex public colleges would be exempt from the prohibition. In an explanatory statement issued with the regulations, HEW said institutions whose admissions were exempt from coverage would be required to treat all students nondiscriminatorily once members of both sexes had been admitted. (The 1972 law had exempted from all coverage military institutions at the secondary and higher education levels, and church-related institutions to the extent that compliance would violate religious tenets.)

Regarding treatment of students, the regulations would ban sex discrimination in such benefits as insurance, employment assistance and counseling, as well as in scholarships and other financial aid. Sex-segregated classes would be prohibited in all subjects except hygiene and sex-education classes, if parents objected to integrated classes on sex. In the controversial area of athletics, the rules would permit, but not require, teams of mixed sexes. If a school chose to establish separate teams, "comparable" types and levels of competition would have to be provided for women, and discrimination in the provision of equipment and supplies would be banned. The regulations would permit single-sex housing, but would require that facilities be comparable and ban discrimination on availability, curfews, fees and rules regarding off-campus housing.

U.S. District Court Judge Oliver Gasch ruled in Washington June 19 that since law and custom forbade women's participation in combat roles, a "legitimate government interest" was served by the refusal of the Air Force and Naval Academies to admit women. Gasch noted that military officials had described the primary purpose of the service academies as preparation of combat officers.

Equal pay, promotion rulings. The Supreme Court ruled 5-3 June 3 that an employer's retention of some traditional night shift pay differentials favoring male employes over women was a violation of the Equal Pay Act. The ruling involved two Corning Glass Works plants, in Corning, N.Y. and Wellsboro, Pa., in which male night shift inspectors had been paid more than female day shift inspectors doing the same work. This policy was changed in 1966 when Corning opened night shift jobs to women and again in 1969, when the company decided to pay all subsequently hired workers at the same base rate, regardless of sex or shift worked. Employes hired before 1969 continued to receive a higher night differential. Finding that the company's pre-1966 employment practices violated the Equal Pay Act, the court decided that Corning failed to "cure" its violation, despite opening the night shift to women. Moreover, the 1969 company decision to abolish shift differentials still did not end the violation because those hired previously continued to receive the higher night shift rates. Corning had not proved, the court said, that the pre-1966 night shift pay differential was added compensation for night work. There was substantial evidence that it reflected the fact that men would not work for the low wages paid day shift women workers, the court said.

The U.S. district court in San Francisco gave final approval July 24 to a settlement of class action sex discrimination suits brought against the Bank of America, the world's largest private bank. Rather than the back-pay provisions that had become the norm in settlements involving other companies, the agreement provided that the bank would pay $3.75 million over five years into trust funds which would give incentives for female employes to undertake management training, educational and other "self-development" programs leading to management-level promotions. The agreement set hiring and promotion goals under which the proportion of women officers would be increased from the current 31% to 40% by December 1978, with the sharpest percentage increases to occur in the higher management levels. (About 73% of the bank's 54,000 employes were women.)

Bias in credit. President Ford Oct. 29 signed into law a Federal Deposit Insurance Corp. bill that included an amendment to outlaw credit discrimination based on sex or marital status. The bill had been approved by the House Oct. 9 and the Senate Oct. 10.

Little League admits girls. A spokesman for Little League Baseball, Inc. announced June 12 in Williamsport, Pa. that the organization would "defer to the changing social climate" and allow girls to play on its teams. Little League sanctioned play by 2.5 million boys between ages 8 and 12 in the U.S. and 31 foreign countries. The action followed a New Jersey state appellate court ruling March 29 that since Little League used public facilities for recruiting and for games, it constituted a "public accommodation" and, as such, had to be open to girls. President Ford signed into law Dec. 26 legislation that would allow girls to play Little League baseball. The bill, approved by voice vote in both houses of Congress Dec. 16, changed the wording of the federal charter of Little League Baseball Inc., striking the word "boy" each time it appeared and replacing it with the term "young people."

See also ABORTION; APPOINTMENTS & RESIGNATIONS; AUSTRALIA [8]; CIVIL RIGHTS [8-10, 13, 15]; CRIME [26, 34]; ELECTIONS [2]; FRANCE [6]; MEDICINE & HEALTH [23-25, 34]; MOUNTAIN CLIMBING; POLITICS [8-9, 11-12]; RADICALS; RELIGION [6-11]

WOODS, ROSE MARY—*See* CAMPAIGN FINANCING [16]; WATERGATE [47, 69]
WORLD BANK—*See* IRAN; MONETARY DEVELOPMENTS [7-9]; NICARAGUA; OIL [21]; UNITED NATIONS [13]
WOUNDED KNEE—*See* INDIAN AFFAIRS

YZ

YEMEN—The army, led by Col. Ibrahim al-Hamidi, deputy commander in chief, ousted the government of the Yemen Arab Republic in a bloodless coup d'etat June 13 and established a ruling junta. The dissidents called on Premier Hassan Makki and his 22-member Cabinet to continue in office. (Makki had been appointed premier earlier in the year by President Abdul Rahman al-Iriani following the Feb. 11 dismissal of Abdullah al Hagri.) The coup followed the resignation on June 12 of President Iriani, two other members of the executive Republican Council, and the speaker of the Consultative Council, Sheik Abdullah Ahmar. Iriani and ousted chief of staff Col. Hussein al-Massiri, were out of the country at the time. The junta, calling itself the Command Council, June 14 suspended the Constitution, abrogated the legislative Consultative Council and dissolved the country's only political organization, but pledged to re-establish civilian rule as soon as possible. A Command Council statement said the army was forced to act because of the "collapse in the internal political situation, administrative slackness and corruption in bureaucracy." Also removed from his post by the army action was Foreign Minister Mohammed Ahmed Noman. He was shot to death June 28 in Beirut by an unknown assailant.

See also APPOINTMENTS & RESIGNATIONS; OIL [19]

YUGOSLAVIA

Government

[1] **New charter proclaimed.** Yugoslavia proclaimed a new Constitution Feb. 21 that strengthened the powers of the central government and Communist Party, while providing for greater economic and political control by workers through factory councils. The fourth Constitution since President Tito consolidated power after World War II mandated that national and regional legislatures be composed of workers and other non-professional politicians, who

would retain their jobs while serving as deputies. The delegates would be selected from individual factories and other economic units, rather than from geographic constituencies, by a complicated procedure. A collective presidency of nine rotating members would take over after the death of Tito, who would remain president for life. The system was designed to counteract regional nationalism.

[2] Yugoslavia's new Federal Assembly convened May 15 and elected Tito president for life May 16. The Assembly also elected eight of Tito's trusted wartime associates, one from each of Yugoslavia's six republics and two autonomous regions, to the new collective presidency. The most significant development in the selection process was the naming of Edvard Kardelj, a Slovene, to the group. Kardelj had been in political eclipse following the economic reforms introduced in the late 1960s, but had emerged as Tito's heir apparent.

[3] **Tito's policies reaffirmed.** The 10th Congress of the League of Communists met in Belgrade May 27-30, reaffirming the domestic and foreign policies of President and Party First Secretary Tito. In an opening address May 27, Tito expounded on Yugoslavia's status as a nonaligned nation and stressed that economic decentralization must be accompanied by political centralization, advancing national efforts to identify party and government more closely with the working class. (The Soviet Union was represented at the congress by an official delegation, rather than by mere observers, for only the second time since World War II. Moscow had declined to send any representative to the 1969 congress.)

Dissidents

[4] **Cominformist plot.** President Tito announced Sept. 12 that an organized group of Cominformists had been uncovered in Yugoslavia and suggested that foreign interests had been involved. The trials in Pec and Titograd (in the Kosovo-Metohija Autonomous Oblast and Montenegro Republic, respectively) of 32 alleged members of the group which, it was charged, "was working against the socialist self-managing constitutional order and the independence of Yugoslavia," ended with the announcement Sept. 20 that sentences ranging from one to 14 years of "severe imprisonment" had been passed against all 32. In a Sept. 12 address in Jesenice, in the Slovene Republic, Tito said the Cominformists had tried to organize "some kind of Stalinist party" and had succeeded in holding a congress. He noted that the group had a large amount of material which was printed abroad and had elected a leadership whose director lived outside of Yugoslavia. (Sept. 13 reports said the group's leaders were Mileta Perovic, who operated out of Kiev, capital of the Soviet Union's Ukrainian Republic, and Vlado Dapcevic, who operated out of Brussels. Both had escaped from Yugoslavia in 1958, having been jailed in 1948 for their support of the Soviet Communist Party after Tito broke with Stalin.)

[5] Although little information about the Cominformist plot was disseminated through official channels (other than Tito's speech and the sentencing announcement), high Yugoslavian Communist Party sources had said, according to Sept. 18 and 28 reports, that the Soviet Union was directly implicated in the plot.

[6] **Mihajlov arrested again.** Prominent writer Mihajlo Mihajlov was arrested at his home in Novi Sad Oct. 7 and charged with disseminating hostile propaganda and association with foreign emigre organizations. Some of his essays recently written for Western publications had reportedly been reprinted in two Russian emigre journals.

[7] **Former Chetniks jailed.** Djura Djurovic, a wartime opponent of Tito, was sentenced Oct. 23 to five years in prison on charges that he wrote anti-Tito articles for foreign publications five years ago. Zagorka Stojanovic-Kojic was sentenced to three years as an accomplice. The 74-year-old Djurovic had been arrested on the charges Nov. 22, 1973; he had previously served 17 years of a 20-year sentence for his Chetnik activities and was released in 1962. (The Chetniks were wartime supporters of Yugoslavia's exiled royal government and fought against Tito's Communist partisans.)

[8] **Croatian separatists killed.** Two armed terrorists, alleged to be members of the Ustashi, the Croatian separatist group, were "uncovered and liquidated" by Croatian security forces in the republic's mountainous Velebit region Oct. 29, the Croatian Secretariat for Internal Affairs announced Nov. 1. A militia officer was also killed in the fighting. The two terrorists were identified and linked to 1972 separatist activities. In another incident related to indications of growing nationalistic sentiment in the republic, 16 Croatians were charged with trying to set up an illegal organization which advocated separatism and which was connected with Croatian exiles in the West (the Ustashi), according to official sources in Zadar Oct. 19.

Foreign Relations

[9] **Yugoslav-Italian tensions mount.** Belgrade and Rome exchanged heated notes during March in the revived issue of contested sovereignty in the Trieste "Zone B" border area. A March 11 note from the Italian government, protesting Yugoslavia's placement of border markers in the Yugoslav zone, rekindled the 22-year-old border dispute between the two countries. (Placement of the border markers had been prescribed by Yugoslav's new Constitution. On March 30 Belgrade reiterated several earlier pronouncements and noted that "the Italian bearing leads to the further threatening of the foundations of mutual relations and constitutes a blow to stability in this part of Europe." Reports from Italy tended to stress Rome's non-combative posture in the border dispute. However, it was reported March 28 that Italy, Yugoslavia's most important trading partner, had banned imports of Yugoslavian meat and abrogated, without notice, a bilateral banking agreement.

[10] Naval maneuvers by Italian and U.S. North Atlantic Treaty Organization forces in the north Adriatic Sea were denounced by Yugoslavia April 2 as "deliberate and organized anti-Yugoslav activity." "We cannot and must not see the intention of the Italian armed forces and the American 6th Fleet as separate from the present action of the Italian irredentism and government aimed at laying claim to and separating parts of our territory from our homeland." The Yugoslav Council for National Defense was convened April 2 to examine "problems of security and defense." Rome subsequently informed Belgrade of the exercise's termination, it was reported April 10, at the same time noting "uncustomary Yugoslav troop movements in the frontier region."

[11] **Yugoslavia-Austria Slovene dispute.** Yugoslavia and Austria exchanged notes beginning in October in a resumption of a dispute over the status and rights of the Slovene and Croat minorities in Austria's Carinthia and Burgenland Provinces. Yugoslavia Oct. 29 accused Austria of mistreating its ethnic Slav minorities by denying them cultural and linguistic rights guaranteed in the quadripartite treaty of 1955 which restored Austria's sovereignty. Belgrade's note repeatedly cited Austrian "neo-Nazi tendencies." Vienna, in its response, Dec. 2, presented a note expressing "surprise" at the accusations. Rejecting the charges, Austria cited the existence of Slavic minority organization and schools and demanded that Belgrade prove its charges.

See also ALBANIA; ALUMINUM; CHILE [6]; COMMUNISM, INTERNATIONAL; EUROPEAN SECURITY; MEXICO [19]; PORTUGAL [24]; UNION OF SOVIET SOCIALIST REPUBLICS [5, 12]

ZAIRE—The U.S. Export-Import Bank announced Jan. 15 it would make a $102 million loan for a 1,000-mile extra-high voltage transmission line to serve the Zaire copper industry. First National City Bank of New York would supply another $102 million, guaranteed by the Export-Import Bank. The $326 million project would involve about $250 million of purchases of U.S. equipment. The Export-Import Bank approved a $56.3 million loan at 8% interest to help finance a copper mining and processing project in Zaire. It guaranteed a comparable loan at a higher interest rate from a group of private U.S. banks, it was reported Oct. 3.

The government created a state-owned company to take over all petroleum product distribution, it was reported Jan. 16. The companies affected were the Royal Dutch-Shell Group, Texaco, Mobil Oil Corp., British Petroleum Co. and Petrofina of Belgium. The Gulf Oil Corp. offshore wells, and the exploration activities of Texaco and Royal Dutch-Shell were apparently unaffected.

Greek President Phaidon Gizikis made a personal appeal to Zaire President Mobutu Sese Seko for the welfare of Greek nationals in Zaire, all of whose property had been seized without immediate compensation in the past few months. According to a Feb. 11 report, the Greeks were forced into refugee camps and barred from leaving the country. Most of the Greeks had been shopkeepers, although some owned plantations and other large businesses.

President Mobutu "in self defense" May 10 broke the treaty of friendship signed with Belgium in June 1970. Brussels had declined March 26 to ban a book which criticized Mobutu's career. Written by a Belgian lawyer, *The Rise of Sergeant Mobutu to President Sese Seko* had been banned in France where it was published. The book accused the African leader of having acquired his power by eliminating all his rivals, beginning with Patrice Lumumba.

See also AFRICA; ANGOLA; APPOINTMENTS & RESIGNATIONS; BOXING; COPPER; MOZAMBIQUE; [7]; UGANDA

ZAMBIA—Gasoline prices were raised in Zambia by as much as 40%, it was reported June 16. The price rise followed a February ban by the Labor Ministry on pay increases, due to last for a one-year period.

Zambia and the Anglo-American Corp. announced an agreement in principle Aug. 15 for the government to assume management of Nchanga Consolidated Copper Mines, which produced 420,000 tons of copper annually and accounted for 12% of world copper exports. The agreement, retroactive to Aug. 1, terminated contracts which still had 5½ years to run. Compensation was set but was not disclosed; sources in Lusaka said Anglo-American would receive the equivalent of $52 million.

See also COPPER; MOZAMBIQUE [7, 12]; RHODESIA

ZIEGLER, RONALD L.—*See* FORD, GERALD R.; MIDDLE EAST [38]; NIXON, RICHARD M.; WATERGATE [8, 11, 34, 38, 60, 69]

ZIMBABWE—*See* RHODESIA

ZINC—*See* AUTOMOBILES [3]

ZONING—*See* POPULATION